THE SCIENCE OF EMOTIONAL INTELLIGENCE

Knowns and Unknowns

Edited by
Gerald Matthews, Moshe Zeidner,
and Richard D. Roberts

OXFORD
UNIVERSITY PRESS
2007

OXFORD

UNIVERSITY PRESS

Oxford University Press, Inc., publishes works that further
Oxford University's objective of excellence
in research, scholarship, and education.

Oxford   New York
Auckland   Cape Town   Dar es Salaam   Hong Kong   Karachi
Kuala Lumpur   Madrid   Melbourne   Mexico City   Nairobi
New Delhi   Shanghai   Taipei   Toronto

With offices in
Argentina   Austria   Brazil   Chile   Czech Republic   France   Greece
Guatemala   Hungary   Italy   Japan   Poland   Portugal   Singapore
South Korea   Switzerland   Thailand   Turkey   Ukraine   Vietnam

Published by Oxford University Press, Inc.
198 Madison Avenue, New York, New York 10016

www.oup.com

Oxford is a registered trademark of Oxford University Press

Library of Congress Cataloging-in-Publication Data
The science of emotional intelligence : knowns and unknowns /
edited by Gerald Matthews, Moshe Zeidner, and Richard D. Roberts.
    p. cm. — (Series in affective science)
Includes bibliographical references and index.
ISBN: 978-0-19-518189-0 (cloth)
1. Emotional intelligence.   I. Matthews, Gerald.   II. Zeidner, Moshe.   III. Roberts, Richard D.
BF576.S35 2007
152.4—dc22   2006101516

9 8 7 6 5 4 3 2 1

Printed in the United States of America
on acid-free paper

THE SCIENCE OF EMOTIONAL INTELLIGENCE

SERIES IN AFFECTIVE SCIENCE

Series Editors
Richard J. Davidson
Klaus Scherer

The Nature of Emotion: Fundamental Questions
Edited by Paul Ekman and Richard J. Davidson

Boo! Culture, Experience, and the Startle Reflex
By Ronald Simons

Emotions in Psychopathology: Theory and Research
Edited by William F. Flack Jr. and James D. Laird

What the Face Reveals: Basic and Applied Studies of Spontaneous Expression Using the Facial Action Coding System (FACS)
Edited by Paul Ekman and Erika Rosenberg

Shame: Interpersonal Behavior, Psychopathology, and Culture
Edited by Paul Gilbert and Bernice Andrews

Affective Neuroscience: The Foundations of Human and Animal Emotions
By Jaak Panksepp

Extreme Fear, Shyness, and Social Phobia: Origins, Biological Mechanisms, and Clinical Outcomes
Edited by Louis A. Schmidt and Jay Schulkin

Cognitive Neuroscience of Emotion
Edited by Richard D. Lane and Lynn Nadel

The Neuropsychology of Emotion
Edited by Joan C. Borod

Anxiety, Depression, and Emotion
Edited by Richard J. Davidson

Persons, Situations, and Emotions: An Ecological Approach
Edited by Hermann Brandstätter and Andrzej Eliasz

Emotion, Social Relationships, and Health
Edited by Carol D. Ryff and Burton Singer

Appraisal Processes in Emotion: Theory, Methods, Research
Edited by Klaus R. Scherer, Angela Schorr, and Tom Johnstone

Music and Emotion: Theory and Research
Edited by Patrik N. Juslin and John A. Sloboda

Handbook of Affective Sciences
Edited by Richard J. Davidson, Klaus R. Scherer, and H. Hill Goldsmith

Nonverbal Behavior in Clinical Settings
Edited by Pierre Philippot, Robert S. Feldman, and Erik J. Coats

Memory and Emotion
Edited by Daniel Reisberg and Paula Hertel

Psychology of Gratitude
Edited by Robert A. Emmons and Michael E. McCullough

Thinking about Feeling: Contemporary Philosophers on Emotions
Edited by Robert C. Solomon

Bodily Sensibility: Intelligent Action
By Jay Schulkin

Who Needs Emotions? The Brain Meets the Robot
Edited by Jean-Marc Fellous and Michael A. Arbib

What the Face Reveals: Basic and Applied Studies of Spontaneous Expression Using the Facial Action Coding System (FACS)
(2nd edition)
Edited by Paul Ekman and Erika L. Rosenberg

The Development of Social Engagement: Neurobiological Perspectives
Edited by Peter J. Marshall and Nathan A. Fox

Feelings: The Perception of Self
By James D. Laird

The Handbook of Emotion Elicitation and Assessment
Edited by James A. Coan and John J. B. Allen

The Science of Emotional Intelligence: Knowns and Unknowns
Edited by Gerald Matthews, Moshe Zeidner, and Richard D. Roberts

Foreword

When emotional intelligence was introduced to the reading public, interest was quick and intense. Everyone knew that whereas some people are friendly or charismatic, others are cranky or boring; so perhaps such striking differences might derive from this kind of intelligence. It was said, moreover, that EQ might be more fundamental than IQ and predict success in life. Better still, unlike IQ, it could perhaps be learned, or at least improved. With such an introduction, there was considerable enthusiasm in psychology to see what this newly discovered object really was. Gerald Matthews, Moshe Zeidner, and Richard Roberts have been in the forefront of substituting evidence for intuition and hyperbole. Their 2002 book, *Emotional Intelligence: Science and Myth*, became the principal resource for those who wondered how to understand emotional intelligence. Now, in this volume, they have gathered some of the most prominent researchers in the area to offer expert views on important aspects of this topic.

In *The Science of Emotional Intelligence: Knowns and Unknowns,* Matthews, Zeidner, and Roberts have provided a structure in which they have asked their contributors to answer specific questions. After their own introduction, they have invited, in the first section, some of the most prominent researchers in the field of research on emotions to provide essential background for the conceptualization of emotions and emotional intelligence. The second section concerns measurement, which remains a key issue. There is not yet clear agreement on how best to measure emotional intelligence, but agreement may be approached by being clear. In the third section, the editors have invited researchers to present the all-important evidence on the success of clinical, organizational, and educational applications. They have also included a contribution about the role emotions may play in the development of intelligent computers that have become integral to our lives. They conclude by summarizing what has been established, and what remains to be known.

Emotions came back onto the agenda in psychology in the 1950s, having been made seemingly irrelevant by the behaviorists. Their marginalization was one of the few matters in which the cognitive scientists of the 1960s seemed at first to agree with the behaviorists. In the new century, our world faces renewed perils of a strongly emotional kind. We have the impression that if we humans really could learn to become more emotionally intelligent, we could do better than we have done, and better than we are doing now. Perhaps we could exchange the emotionally appealing but short-term individual reinforcements (about which we learned from the behaviorists) with longer-term care for our planet. Perhaps we could replace self-righteous grudges, cognitive strategizing, and international violence with empathy for our fellow beings. Whether we could is among the unknowns.

Keith Oatley
Director, Cognitive Science Program
University of Toronto, Canada

Preface

The main purpose of this edited volume is to provide an up-to-the-date account of the scientific status and taxonomic models of emotional intelligence, to explore the state of the art in assessment and applications of the construct, and to provide recommendations for future research. Indeed, there may be various abilities, skills, and personality dispositions that could loosely be described as "emotionally intelligent." One aim of the present book is to discriminate different aspects or domains of emotional competence (which may or may not be aligned under a general factor). A clearer conceptualization will support advances in psychological assessment. For example, self-report methods may be appropriate for some facets of emotional competence but not others, whereas there is also clearly a need to develop a range of objective assessments.

Another important aim is to locate different components of emotional intelligence in relation to existing structural models of ability and intelligence so as to progress toward a more comprehensive differential psychology. A multidimensional approach to emotional intelligence may also clarify theoretical issues. Clearly different levels of explanation may be appropriate for different facets of competence, ranging from neural bases for recognizing and regulating emotion to high-level metacognitive routines for making sense of emotional experience. Most important, the book aims to translate this sharp theoretical focus into practical recommendations in occupational, educational, clinical and other contexts, to improve the utility of future assessment approaches, and to inform intervention efforts.

The book departs from typical edited volumes in requesting a panel of internationally acclaimed scholars to address specific questions that must be answered for the field to progress. Invited contributors were allocated to one of three sections concerning the conceptualization, assessment, and practical utility of emotional intelligence. In addition to presenting their own perspectives, each contributor addressed a set of questions linked to the focal issue covered by the section. With an introduction written by the editors that set the stage, and a conclusion that attempted to synthesize these various perspectives, the book consists of five sections in total.

In Section I, Gerald Matthews, Moshe Zeidner, and Richard D. Roberts (Chapter 1) review current research investigating emotional intelligence, identifying key difficulties in current conceptualization, assessment, and application. This chapter highlights the principal controversies in the field at present that differentiate some of the main perspectives on this construct. The chapter also introduces the key questions posed to each of the contributors.

Section II of this volume addresses the nature of emotional intelligence and, in particular, how the construct should be defined and conceptualized. It aims, in particular, to draw upon contemporary human emotion theory, an approach that has remained relatively neglected in contemporary accounts of emotional intelligence. Contributors to this section include noted emotions theorists James R. Averill (Chapter 2), Edmund T. Rolls (Chapter 3), Klaus R. Scherer (Chapter 4), and Carroll Izard, Christopher Trentacosta, Kristen King, Judith Morgan, and Michelle Diaz (Chapter 5), as well as expert differential psychologists K. V. Petrides, Adrian Furnham, and Stella Mavroveli (Chapter 6), and Nicholas R. Burns, Veneta A. Bastian, and Ted Nettelbeck (Chapter 7).

These expert contributors were each encouraged to differentiate emotional intelligence from related constructs and suggest counterarguments to the criticism leveled at emotional intelligence that it is simply an old wine in a new bottle. Experts were each invited to outline their own perspectives on the nature of emotional intelligence, and to address the following questions:

1. How should emotional intelligence be conceptualized? Should it be a competence, a skill, an adaptive outcome, a set of cultural beliefs, or some other construct?
2. Is the concept of emotional intelligence compatible with the existing theories of emotion and of cognitive intelligence?
3. What are the key components, facets, or branches of emotional intelligence?
4. How is emotional intelligence distinct from existing personality and ability constructs? Could a multistratum psychometric model integrate a dimension or dimensions of emotional intelligence with existing personality and ability constructs?
5. How does emotional intelligence change over the life span, quantitatively and qualitatively?
6. How might emotional intelligence contribute to adaptation to real-world social environments?

Section III concerns approaches to the measurement of emotional intelligence and related constructs. Presently, there appear some problems with several of approaches currently used to assess emotional intelligence; we wished not only to document shortcomings but provide suggestions for bringing the field forward. Contributors to this section included a clutch of experts who have published most widely in the domain of ability assessment (Ralf Schulze, Oliver Wilhelm, & Patrick C. Kyllonen, Chapter 8); those who have specific expertise in developing and validating measures of emotional (Susan E. Rivers, Marc A. Brackett, Peter Salovey, & John D. Mayer, Chapter 9) and social (Maureen O'Sullivan, Chapter 10) intelligence; and/or are acclaimed emotion (Andrew Ortony, William Revelle, & Richard Zinbarg, Chapter 11) or cognitive (Grit Herzmann, Vanessa Danthiir, Oliver Wilhelm, Werner Sommer, & Annekathrin Schacht, Chapter 12) theorists. Each contributor was asked to discuss how measurement problems may be circumvented. Experts in this section were also asked to consider the potential of new techniques going beyond traditional methods of assessment. Specific questions posed to each contributor were the following:

1. What are the strengths and weaknesses of current measures of emotional intelligence?
2. What is the optimal approach to the assessment of emotional intelligence?
3. Can self-reports and questionnaires ever provide assessments of intelligence and competence?
4. What are the most prevalent scoring procedures for emotional intelligence measures, and are they valid for ability measures?
5. What are the prospects for assessment of emotional intelligence using psychophysiological, developmental, and neurological measures?
6. What are the prospects for assessment of emotional intelligence using information-processing tasks?
7. What are the prospects or new techniques, such as the situational judgment test (SJT) methodology and applications of advanced psychometrics, leading to improved assessment?

A major impetus of emotional intelligence is tied to its potential applications in many fields. The practical utility of the construct is examined with regard to a number of such domains in Section IV. Experts in clinical (David D. Vachon & R. Michael Bagby, Chapter 13), occupational (Peter J. Jordan, Neal M. Ashkanasy, & Kaylene W. Ascough, Chapter 14), and educational (Joseph E. Zins, John W. Payton, Roger P. Weissberg, & Mary Utne O'Brien, Chapter 15) applications agreed to contribute their expertise for this book. Notably there is a good deal of research already coming out of these fields: The issues are whether tests for emotional intelligence should be used for selection, clinical intervention, and whether emotional intelligence can be improved through training. A relatively new frontier for application was also included: emotional intelligence in machines and information technology (Rosalind W. Picard, Chapter 16). In addition to covering advances in their respective fields, the invited contributors were asked to address the following set of questions:

1. What theoretical advances are necessary to support practical applications?
2. What are the cultural, social, and economic factors that may constrain or facilitate applications based on emotional intelligence?
3. Is there any practical advantage to focusing on emotional intelligence, rather than on specific contextualized skills?
4. In which real-world domains will emotional intelligence be most and least useful?
5. Can emotional intelligence be trained and, if so, how?

In the final section of the book, Section V, Richard D. Roberts, Moshe Zeidner, and Gerald Matthews (Chapter 17) distill and synthesize the main points made by the contributors in setting out a research agenda for emotional intelligence, balancing critical comments with an assessment of the prospects for genuine progress in building a science of emotional competence in the future. The concluding section identifies areas in which there is an emerging consensus on answers to these questions and highlights the main points of dissension, as well as key empirical studies necessary to resolve disagreements and further scientific understanding.

Acknowledgments

The idea for this edited volume grew out of a workshop that we organized that was sponsored by the Army Research Institute, Human Research Resources Organization, and the Educational Testing Service during September 2003 in Princeton, New Jersey. At that conference, it became obvious to us, as well as the many participants who attended this event, that there was a need to follow on from our previous book (*Emotional Intelligence: Science and Myth*). Our charge appeared not only to present a more contemporary account of emotional intelligence (many important advances have occurred in rapid time), but to offer a more diverse amalgam of theory, measures, and applications than have been offered up until the present time. We are grateful to the three participating organizations for their sponsorship of what became the catalyst for this edited volume.

Indeed, at this workshop we had the distinct privilege of meeting with Professors Klaus Scherer and Paul Ekman, who encouraged us to prepare this edited volume for the Oxford University Press special series in affective science. We are indebted to both of these internationally acclaimed scholars for providing the opportunity to create, compile, and finally channel this book to you, the reader. Special thanks also to Professor Keith Oatley, a recognized authority on emotions theory and research, who graciously agreed to write the foreword to this edited volume.

During the writing of our respective chapters and the editing of this book, The University of Cincinnati, University of Haifa, and Educational Testing Service (ETS) provided the facilities and resources necessary to undertake and complete this work. In addition, we would like to acknowledge the following senior staff and management from these institutions who supported the project from its inception: Professor Aaron Ben-Ze'ev (distinguished philosopher of emotions and President of the University of Haifa), Dr. Drew H. Gitomer (Distinguished Presidential Appointee, former ETS Senior Vice-President of Research and Development), and Dr. Ida M. Lawrence (ETS Senior Vice-President of Research and Development). While working on this book, one of the editors—Moshe Zeidner—took a sabbatical year at the Department of Experimental Psychology, Oxford University. We would like to thank Professor Edmund T. Rolls, Moshe's sponsor at Oxford, for providing him with a congenial academic atmosphere during this period.

Edited volumes can be difficult to produce, as anyone who has set out on this onerous task will testify. We are indebted to Kathy Howell, Jennifer Minsky, and Teresa Jackson from ETS for their work pulling together the important preproduction pieces.

Warm sentiments to the production team at Oxford University Press for making the final leg of this process (almost) enjoyable.

We are grateful to many people across the globe for other forms of support throughout this extended project. First and foremost, we would be remiss not to acknowledge our respective partners—Diana Ciupka, Eti Zeidner, and Cristina Aicher—each of whom have variously lost us for days as we grappled with logistical issues, stole time away from home to write a word here, a paragraph there, or reviewed one of the contributions by our distinguished panel. To each of you, many thanks for being the epitome of emotional geniuses. And to the following friends, family, students, and/or colleagues, hats off to you for being sounding boards, folks we can vent our frustrations on (and at), awesome motivators, or for just plain being there: Camilla Aicher, John R. Aicher, Anthony Betancourt, Iris Cohen, Daniel Eignor, T. J. Elliott, Walter Emmerich, Amanda Emo, Angela Fellner, Gregory Funke, Eugene Gonzales, Dafna Hadar, Almira Kustubayeva, Patrick Kyllonen, Zia McCabe, Carolyn MacCann, Katie Melua, Catherine Millett, Jennifer Minsky, Bill Monaghan, Dorit Olnik-Shemesh, Don Powers, Matthew D. Roberts, John Sabatini, Ralf Schulze, Inbal Shani-Zisovitch, Ayalla Shriki, Jonathan Steinberg, Namrata Tognatta, Michaela Turss, Cris Valkyria, Matthew Ventura, and Cathy Wendler.

Finally, an edited book would be nothing but for its contributions from the acclaimed scholars who we asked to give of their time, expertise, and knowledge to address pointed questions we felt needed answers. We are indebted to each of you (given next in the list of contributors) for the various chapters appearing in this volume. We appreciate your critical contributions, willingness to cope with a challenging, and often difficult, task and to respond to suggestions we raised so that the volume might cohere and be something special. Because of such efforts, we believe the volume is rather different from what has preceded it in the domain of scholarly accounts of emotional intelligence.

Soon after completing his chapter, one of our contributors, Joe Zins, passed away. We are very saddened by the loss of this dear friend and colleague. Joe was an outstanding scholar and a wonderful collaborator. He was internationally respected for his expertise in the areas of social and emotional learning (SEL), prevention, and individual and organizational consultation. Joe worked tirelessly throughout his career to use science to improve the lives of children. One of his final major projects was serving as senior editor of the extremely well reviewed book, *Building Academic Success on Social and Emotional Learning: What Does the Research Say?* The findings reported in that volume substantially advanced SEL research and school-based practice. Joe was a loving husband and father, and a caring friend who brought great joy to all who knew him. He will live forever in our hearts as a friend, pioneer, and leader in SEL.

We hope this volume will give readers a deeper understanding and appreciation of the current state of the art of emotional intelligence research and help in guiding future theory, research, and applications in this growing domain. Happy emotional, intelligent, and emotionally intelligent reading!

Gerald Matthews
Moshe Zeidner
Richard D. Roberts

Contents

Contributors

KAYLENE W. ASCOUGH, UQ Business School, University of Queensland, Brisbane, Queensland 4072, Australia

NEAL M. ASHKANASY, UQ Business School, University of Queensland, Brisbane, Queensland 4072, Australia

JAMES R. AVERILL, Department of Psychology, University of Massachusetts, Amherst, MA 01003, USA

R. MICHAEL BAGBY, Department of Psychiatry, 250 College Street, Toronto, ON M5T 1R8, Canada

VENETA A. BASTIAN, Department of Psychology, University of Adelaide, South Australia 5005, Australia

MARC A. BRACKETT, Department of Psychology, Yale University, PO Box 208205, New Haven, CT 06520-8205, USA

NICHOLAS R. BURNS, Department of Psychology, University of Adelaide, South Australia 5005, Australia

VANESSA DANTHIIR, Department of Psychology, Humboldt-University at Berlin, Unterden Linden 6, 10099 Berlin, Germany

MICHELLE DIAZ, Department of Psychology, University of Delaware, Newark, DE 19716, USA

ADRIAN FURNHAM, Department of Psychology, University College of London, Gower Street, London WC1E 6BT, England, UK

GRIT HERZMANN, Department of Psychology, Humboldt-University at Berlin, Unterden Linden 6, 10099 Berlin, Germany

CAROL IZARD, Department of Psychology, University of Delaware, Newark, DE 19716, USA

PETER J. JORDAN, Department of Management, Nathan Campus, Griffith University, 170 Kessels Rd, Nathan, Queensland 4111, Australia

KRISTEN KING, Department of Psychology, University of Delaware, Newark, DE 19716, USA

PATRICK C. KYLLONEN, Center for New Constructs, Educational Testing Service, Rosedale Rd, MS-16R, Princeton, NJ 08541, USA

GERALD MATTHEWS, Professor of Psychology, Department of Psychology, University of Cincinnati, Cincinnati, OH 45221, USA

STELLA MAVROELI, School of Psychology and Human Development, Institute of Education, University of London, 25 Woburn Square, London WC1H 0AA, England, UK

JOHN D. MAYER, Department of Psychology, University of New Hampshire, Conant Hall, 10 Library Way, Durham, NH 03824, USA

JUDITH MORGAN, Department of Psychology, University of Delaware, Newark, DE 19716, USA

TED NETTELBECK, Department of Psychology, University of Adelaide, South Australia 5005, Australia

KEITH OATLEY, Cognitive Science Program, University College, 15 Kings College Circle, University of Toronto, Toronto M5S 3H7, Canada

MARY UTNE O'BRIEN, Department of Psychology, University of Illinois at Chicago, 1007 West Harrison Street, Chicago, IL 60607-7137, USA

ANDREW ORTONY, Department of Psychology, Northwestern University, 110 Annenberg Hall, 2120 North Campus Drive, Evanston, IL 60208-2610, USA

MAUREEN O'SULLIVAN, Human Interaction Laboratory, University of California, 401 Pamassus Avenue, San Francisco, CA 94143, USA

JOHN W. PAYTON, Collaborative for Academic, Social, and Emotional Learning (CASEL), University of Illinois-Chicago, 1009 BSM MC 285, 1007 W. Harrison Street, Chicago, IL 60607-7137, USA

K. V. PETRIDES, School of Psychology and Human Development, Institute of Education, University of London, 25 Woburn Square, London WC1H 0AA, England, UK

ROSALIND W. PICARD, Media Laboratory, MIT, E15-020g, 20 Ames Street, Cambridge, MA 02139, USA

WILLIAM REVELLE, Dept. of Psychology, Northwestern University, 315 Swift Hall, Evanston, IL 60208, USA

SUSAN E. RIVERS, Dept. of Psychology, Yale University, PO Box 208205, New Haven, CT 06520-8205, USA

RICHARD D. ROBERTS, Educational Testing Service, Rosedale Rd., Mail Stop 16R, Princeton, NJ 08541, USA

EDMUND T. ROLLS, Department of Experimental Psychology, University of Oxford, South Parks Road, Oxford, OX1 3UD, England, UK

PETER SALOVEY, Dean of Yale College, Dept. of Psychology, Yale University, PO Box 208205, New Haven, CT 06520-8205, USA

ANNEKATHRIN SCHACHT, Department of Psychology, Humboldt-University at Berlin, Unterden Linden 6, 10099 Berlin, Germany

KLAUS R. SCHERER, Dept. of Psychology, University of Geneva, 7, rue des Battors, Geneva, CH-1205, Switzerland

RALF SCHULZE, Psychologisches Institut IV, University of Muenster, Fliednerstrasse 21, Muenster, NRW 48149, Germany

WERNER SOMMER, Department of Psychology, Humboldt-University at Berlin, Unterden Linden 6, 10099 Berlin, Germany

CHRISTOPHER TRENTACOSTA, Department of Psychology, University of Delaware, 109 McKinly Hall, Newark, DE 19716, USA

DAVID D. VACHON, Department of Psychiatry, University of Toronto, 250 College Street, Toronto, ON M5T 1R8, Canada

ROGER P. WEISSBERG, Department of Psychology (MC 285), University of Illinois at Chicago, 1007 West Harrison Street, Chicago, IL 60607-7137, USA

OLIVER WILHELM, Fakultat II Institut für Psychology, Humboldt-Universität zu Berlin, Rudower Chaussee 18, Berlin, D-10099, Germany

MOSHE ZEIDNER, Center for Interdisciplinary Research of Emotions, University of Haifa, Mt. Carmel, Haifa 31905, Israel

RICHARD ZINBARG, Department of Psychology, Northwestern University, 315 Swift Hall, Evanston, IL 60208, USA

JOSEPH E. ZINS (deceased), Department of Psychology, University of Cincinnati, 2600 Clifton Avenue, Cincinnati, OH 45221, USA

PART I

GENERAL BACKGROUND

I

Emotional Intelligence: Consensus, Controversies, and Questions

GERALD MATTHEWS, MOSHE ZEIDNER, AND
RICHARD D. ROBERTS

For many years, researchers have wondered what lies beyond academic intelligence. Of special interest was whether there exist abilities that predict real-world success over and above conventional cognitive measures. Recently, the construct of emotional intelligence (EI) has emerged as one of the most high profile constructs of this kind (Goleman, 1998; Matthews, Zeidner, & Roberts, 2002). Broadly defined, EI represents a set of core competencies for identifying, processing, and managing emotion. Research into EI has prospered, in part, due to the increasing importance of intelligence for people in modern society, with EI commonly claimed to predict clinical, educational, and occupational criteria above and beyond that predicted by general intelligence. However, despite a high level of public and scientific interest, the science of EI is in its early years, and many key questions remain unanswered.

As the field matures, it has become increasingly commonplace for academic psychologists to reject early, overstated claims made in popular works about the importance of emotional intelligence. Goleman's (1995) view, which states that EI may be as important as IQ in determining life success, set the scene for a multitude of tributes to this newly minted construct (see, e.g., Cooper & Sawaf, 1997). Such claims have turned out to be sitting ducks for the snipers of academia. They have conclusively been disconfirmed by a decade of rigorous empirical research that has followed. Decisively, Van Rooy and Viswesvaran's (2004) meta-analysis showed that even after correcting for statistical artifacts, the average correlation between EI and work performance was modest (i.e., around 0.24).

There is a danger that EI may be no more than a fad of the type common in business and education (Murphy & Sideman, 2006). The explosive growth of EI matches the

Author note: The views expressed here are those of the authors and do not reflect on the Educational Testing Service.

three defining characteristics of such fads identified by these authors: (1) a fast growth trajectory, (2) promise of a great deal more than can be delivered, and (3) provocation of intense reactions, both positive and negative. Such fads, Murphy and Sideman (2006) go on to argue, generally follow a natural life cycle. Interest tends to plateau, followed by a precipitous decline, although the fad may reemerge years or decades later. Although proponents may believe EI is here to stay, the skeptic may believe that EI will burn out before too long.

Notwithstanding, research on EI goes back to entirely respectable and sober research on social abilities and competencies pursued by a line of distinguished intelligence researchers (see Landy, 2006). Contemporary researchers have also made a persuasive case that EI measures add something new to conventional understanding of human individual differences (e.g., Mayer, Salovey, & Caruso, 2000a, 2000b). There are now several hundred peer-reviewed journal articles that deal with key issues including test development, personality and cognitive ability correlates of EI, and validation of tests of EI against measures of social functioning and adaptation. Although work on EI is open to various criticisms (e.g., Matthews et al., 2002), the field may still possess a sufficient groundswell of scientific support to constitute a legitimate branch of psychological science.

However, there are several difficulties in trying to evaluate the overall scientific contribution of EI research (Matthews et al., 2002). First, there is no agreed upon definition. It is unclear whether EI is cognitive or noncognitive, whether it refers to explicit or implicit knowledge of emotion, and whether it refers to a basic aptitude or to some adaptation to a specific social and cultural milieu (Zeidner, Matthews, & Roberts, 2001). Second, it is uncertain how EI may be best measured, with various tests of the construct failing to converge. Third, the practical utility of tests of EI is limited by these conceptual and psychometric deficiencies. Thus, available tests generally have questionable validity evidence for the tests to be used with confidence in making real-world decisions (Zeidner, Matthews, & Roberts, 2004). Moreover, intervention programs targeted to enhance EI sometimes lack clearly articulated theoretical and methodological rationales (Zeidner, Roberts, & Matthews, 2002).

The purpose of this book is to answer some of the key questions leading to arbitration of the value of EI for both practitioners and researchers alike. Where answers are not so readily forthcoming, we also hope to indicate appropriate priorities, not only for further empirical investigation, but also for testing a variety of likely applications. In this first chapter, we aim to present the state of the art in EI research and to justify the choice of key questions put to the contributors of this volume. Broadly, conceptualization, assessment, and application of research on EI appear paramount, and it appears natural to use these as demarcating topics both for this introduction and the edited volume that follows.

Conceptualization of Emotional Intelligence

EI is an elusive construct. Currently, there appears little consensus over how EI should be defined and conceptualized (Matthews, Roberts, & Zeidner, 2004; Matthews et al.,

2002; Roberts, Schulze, Zeidner, & Matthews, 2005). Most researchers would probably agree that popular definitions are too overinclusive to be useful. Defining EI as a laundry list of virtually every positive quality of character *except* for cognitive intelligence accomplishes nothing (cf. Goleman, 1995). Although research definitions are not immune to overinclusiveness, the majority of attempts to operationalize EI have tried to start from some conceptual analysis of the construct. The four-branch model of Mayer, Salovey et al. (2000a, 2000b), which will be covered often in this edited volume, is the best known and most influential conceptualization of this kind. It has inspired not just the ability tests for which Mayer, Caruso, and Salovey (2000) are renowned, but also questionnaire measures (see, e.g., Schutte et al., 1998). However, Mayer, Salovey et al.'s (2000b) division of ability models from more broadly defined mixed models recognizes that alternative conceptualizations are possible. Indeed, the concept of "trait EI," which embeds EI within the personality domain, appears to separate EI rather sharply from abilities as normally defined.

In the passages that follow, we set out to distinguish what is known from what is unknown in relation to conceptual issues. We start by discussing assertions that may be made with some degree of confidence; what are essentially sources of consensus concerning theories, models, and definitions of emotional intelligence. We move then to discuss sources of controversy; those things for which there is less agreement regarding the theoretical status, conceptual underpinnings, and models of emotional intelligence. We conclude this opening section with the key questions that we posed for contributors asked to tackle theoretical issues and why exactly we saw these as important topics to cover.

Sources of Consensus

EI Is Multifaceted

A variety of different conceptions, and definitions, of EI have been proposed, each spawning different operational measures of the construct. The various psychometrically adequate scales for EI appear to be measuring several different constructs. This assertion is supported most clearly by the weakness of correlations between objective tests and questionnaires based on self-report (Brackett & Mayer; 2003; Warwick & Nettelbeck, 2004), but other instances may be found. For example, Austin (2005) studied chronometric (i.e., time-based) measures that, by analogy with IQ research, should correlate with scores on EI tests. In fact, although she identified a distinct emotional–information processing factor, it failed to correlate significantly with EI scores from two leading assessments.

There is probably a consensus that trait EI may be studied separately from ability-based EI (e.g., Petrides & Furnham, 2003). However, it remains unclear if there is a single overarching general trait EI dimension, or if the various questionnaires may be picking up multiple, largely independent traits. Some questionnaires do exhibit a strong general factor (e.g., Bar-On, 2004; Petrides & Furnham, 2003), whereas others do not. Tett, Fox, and Wang (2005) extracted three independent factors from their questionnaire that they labeled as self orientation, other orientation, and emotional sharing.

As they point out, the first two factors correspond to Gardner's (1983) intra- and inter-personal intelligences, conceived as separate personal intelligences. By contrast, the Mayer, Caruso et al. (2000) model does not sharply separate emotion regulation in self and others. Thus, although it is agreed that EI may encompass multiple domains (e.g., Austin & Saklofske, 2005), it remains unclear how many separate domains should be discriminated, and whether general factors may be identified within each domain.

EI Overlaps With Other Constructs

A major issue is how EI should be aligned with other dimensions of ability and personality. The degree of overlap of EI with other constructs appears to be measure dependent, with multiple EI constructs appearing to relate differently to other factors. For example, objective measures of EI such as the Multifactor Emotional Intelligence Scale (MEIS) and Mayer-Salovey-Caruso Emotional Intelligence Test (MSCEIT), in keeping with an "ability model," correlate between 0.3 and 0.4 with general intelligence, and rather less with personality traits (e.g., Roberts, Zeidner, & Matthews, 2001). Perhaps one might envisage including an ability EI factor inside the multistratum model for ability advanced by Carroll (1993).

By contrast, questionnaire measures for EI overlap with standard personality traits to a degree that is often excessive. The most egregious example is Bar-On's (2004) Emotional Quotient Inventory (EQ-i), which correlates around 0.8 with low trait anxiety and general psychopathology (e.g., Bar-On, 1997; Newsome, Day, & Catano, 2000). Most of its reliable variance may be attributed to the five-factor model of personality (Dawda & Hart, 2000; Matthews et al., 2002). Other questionnaires appear to possess more unique variance but still show substantial intercorrelation with personality (see Matthews et al., 2002, 2004), raising the thus far unanswered question of how personality and EI traits should be interrelated within a common structural model. These conceptual issues relate to construct validity evidence for EI measures, a topic that we shall return to later in this chapter.

Individual EI Constructs Relate Meaningfully
to External Criteria

There is a growing body of evidence showing that various scales for EI correlate robustly with a variety of outcomes that plausibly signal social-emotional success (Day, 2004). Both MSCEIT subscales and various questionnaires purportedly assessing EI correlate with measures of well-being and social engagement (e.g., Lopes, Salovey, & Straus, 2003; Saklofske, Austin, & Minski, 2003). Validity coefficients tend to be higher for questionnaires, but, in this case, they are amplified by confounding with personality traits linked to social adjustment, such as extraversion. Given the overlap with personality and ability already noted, a critical issue is whether tests for EI show incremental predictive validity with key factors, including g and the Big Five personality factors, statistically controlled. Evidence for incremental validity is, however, clearly mixed. Several studies fail to show that scales for EI predict important criteria (e.g., academic success) with other traits controlled (Barchard, 2003; Brackett & Mayer, 2003), whereas still other studies demonstrate the obverse (e.g., Ciarrochi, Chan, & Caputi, 2000; Saklofske et al., 2003).

The skeptic may find several grounds for challenging the significance of extant criterion validity evidence. As Day (2004) points out, the additional contribution of EI to prediction over and above personality and ability is typically limited. The majority of studies have used criteria that are based on self-report; objective behavioral criteria are regrettably neglected. A concern with the occupational studies reviewed by Van Rooy and Viswesvaran (2004) is that many use supervisor ratings that may be influenced by the likability of the employee, rather than their job competence. At the same time, there seems to be growing confidence among organizational psychologists that tests for EI predict job performance to an extent that is practically useful (Daus & Ashkanasy, 2005). Our view is that the scope and importance of the validity coefficients for EI remains open for debate, but the proponents of EI have made progress in demonstrating that the scales have sufficient criterion validity to be taken seriously.

EI Relates to Exceptionality

A common tactic for gathering validity evidence for ability and personality measures is to show that they discriminate groups that are exceptional in terms of, for example, their intellectual capabilities, pathology, or social maladjustment. Support for the validity of EI may be found from similar sources. Case studies of emotionally gifted individuals provide some informal but persuasive evidence (Oatley, 2004). Quantitative differences in EI scores have been shown for groups such as therapists, psychiatric patients, and prisoners (e.g., Bar-On, 2004; Schutte et al., 1998), although these studies have typically neglected the possible confounding influences of personality and ability. The association between EI and (lack of) alexithymia has been important in establishing the clinical relevance of the construct (Parker, Taylor, & Bagby, 2001). Again, findings may vary with the measure of EI employed. Zeidner, Shani-Zinovich, Matthews, and Roberts (2005) showed that intellectually gifted children obtained elevated scores on the MSCEIT, but were lower in self-reported EI, demonstrating a failure of convergence.

EI Has a Well-Defined Developmental Trajectory

There is an extensive literature on social-emotional development in children that predates work on EI (e.g., Denham, 1998). There appears to be a fairly well defined sequence of markers of emotional development, beginning with the simple expressive and regulatory behaviors of the infant and culminating in active, insightful self-regulation sensitive to the social and cultural environment (Saarni, 2000). We have proposed that emotional competencies may be attached to three separate aspects of the developmental sequence: (1) basic temperaments shaped by innate biological attributes, (2) social learning of rule-based adaptive behaviors (e.g., emotion display rules), and (3) the development of self-reflective insight (Zeidner, Matthews, Roberts, & MacCann, 2003). There are empirical literatures focusing on such key issues as the nature of temperament (Rothbart & Bates, 1998), the shaping of emotional competencies by parent-child interaction (Eisenberg, Fabes, & Loyosa, 1997), and the role of language in shaping emotional awareness in older children (Shipman & Zeman, 1999). Studies of temperament, in particular, identify key individual difference factors such as negative emotionality, extraversion, and effortful control (Rothbart & Bates, 1998). In keeping with personality research, however, there is no suggestion of a single, overarching emotional competence factor.

The work of Izard (e.g., 2001) on emotional adaptiveness provides the clearest link between the developmental literature and emotional intelligence. He describes various competencies related to emotion knowledge and emotion perception, and he has developed and validated tasks such as identifying facial emotion from photographs, and asking children to say how characters in vignettes would feel. These measures are quite substantially correlated with verbal ability, but they show incremental validity in longitudinal studies as predictors of social maladjustment and emotional pathology (Fine, Izard, Mostow, Trentacosta, & Ackerman, 2003). We have questioned Izard's (2001) sharp conceptual separation of emotion and cognition elsewhere (Zeidner et al., 2003), but his work demonstrates how constructs related to EI may be effectively operationalized in children (see, e.g., Izard, Trentacosta, & King, 2005).

Sources of Controversy

We may contrast these emerging areas of theoretical consensus with several issues on which researchers are divided, sometimes sharply:

Is Research on the Right Track?

Some commentators (e.g., Brody, 2004; Landy, 2005) have questioned the value of the whole research enterprise as it is currently focused on resolving the conceptual status of EI. Brody challenges the psychometric status and predictive validity of ability tests of EI, whereas Landy (2005) claims that much of the applied work fails to meet elementary scientific standards, such as availability of data to other researchers. Even if it is accepted that the empirical studies are rigorous, the suspicion may be that the phenomena observed (e.g., rating one's response to contrived vignettes of no personal relevance) are laboratory bound, and of little relevance to real-life emotional functioning. The issue is one of scale and proportion. Does the person's EI mould the most important features of their existence, or is EI a marginal characteristic that plays second fiddle to more significant attributes such as *g* and the Big Five personality factors? The skeptic might claim that EI simply does not exist, except as a collection of minor additions to extant psychometric constructs. Alternatively, another skeptic might claim that EI does exist, but that current measurement strategies are misdirected. Promising conceptualizations are neglected because they are hard to assess (e.g., EI as contextualized knowledge or as unconscious, implicit competencies; Matthews et al., 2004, Matthews, Emo, Roberts, & Zeidner, 2006). Proponents of EI can respond by arguing on the basis of the accumulating research literature that tests for EI assess important human characteristics that differ from cognitive abilities and standard personality traits (e.g., Mayer, Salovey, & Caruso, 2004). Oatley (2004) has suggested overemphasis on measurement issues has led to neglect of the psychology of EI. The initial question, of course, calls for a Kuhnian answer; only time will tell whether the evidence is sufficient to persuade the research community that a paradigm shift is required.

Multiple "Intelligences": Is There Any Common Element?

We have already indicated that there seems to be little overlap between ability-based performance measures of EI and self-report measures. However, even if we transfer questionnaire measures to the personality domain, as "trait EI," significant difficulties remain. As we have pointed out in previous critiques (e.g., Matthews et al., 2002, 2004; Roberts et al., 2005), there are a variety of distinct ways of conceptualizing EI as a construct open to objective measurement. These include components of information-processing measured chronometrically (Austin, 2005), as explicit emotional knowledge (as featured in the MSCEIT), as implicit emotional knowledge and procedural skills, as an "ecological" construct related to person-environment fit in specific social contexts, and other perspectives (see Table 1.1). It is unknown whether constructs measured within each domain would correlate positively with one another. A possible basis for EI in implicit knowledge or processing has been especially neglected, despite recent interest in implicit features of personality and unconscious priming processes.

There are additional reasons from emotion theory to question whether an overarching EI construct is expected to generalize across different domains and measurement methods. One feature of many emotion theories (e.g., Oatley & Johnson-Laird, 1996; Panksepp, 1998; Scherer, 2003) is that there are multiple basic emotions supported by distinct neurological and cognitive systems. It is not self-evident that individual differences in the functioning of, say, the fear system, which is mainly localized in the amygdala, will relate to individual differences in other systems, such as happiness and disgust. It could reasonably be argued that EI relates not to individual emotions but to a superordinate emotion-regulation system located anatomically in the frontal lobes (cf. Rolls, 1999). However, in our view, EI researchers have done too little to separate emotion from meta-emotional regulation. Also surprising is the paucity of research evaluating whether individual differences in regulation generalize across the basic emotions.

Another unresolved issue is the mapping of *functions* onto *processes* (Matthews et al., 2004). Mayer, Caruso et al.'s (2000) four-branch theory, for example, is expressed in terms of functions; that is, what people can do with emotional information (perception, assimilation etc.). However, emotion theory typically describes multiple processes, at different levels of abstraction from the neural substrate, which may contribute to the overall functionality of emotions as integrated systems (Matthews & Zeidner, 2004). Emotion perception, for instance, depends on hardwired circuits for facial processing in the amygdala, as well as the use of high-level contextual information. For example, if a friend is wearing a sad face, we use our knowledge of his personality, social motives, and recent activities in evaluating whether what he is actually feeling, and whether he

TABLE 1.1. Some alternative conceptualizations of emotional intelligence.

Conceptualization	Examples of High EI Qualities	Possible Assessment Techniques
Temperament	A basic tendency to be positive, optimistic, and agreeable	Personality questionnaires
Character	Self-control, motivation, integrity, and morality	Personality questionnaires? Assessment of moral values may be problematic
Basic aptitudes for processing emotions	Fast and accurate perception, memory-retrieval, and reasoning processes	Objective performance on information-processing task (e.g., emotion Stroop)
Adaptiveness	Successful coping with life challenges and demands that elicit emotion	Questionnaire or observation-based assessment of coping resources
Acquired implicit skills observation	Accurate unconscious processing of culture-specific events nonverbal behaviors that support social interaction	Uncertain—two possibilities are (1) measurement of relevant behaviors, and (2) use of unconscious priming techniques
Acquired explicit skills	Knowledge of other people's beliefs about emotion, availability of consciously accessible strategies for emotion regulation	Standardized tests assessing specific beliefs
Insightful self-awareness	Consciously accessible self-beliefs and metacognitions that support personalized emotion regulation	Uncertain—some beliefs may be assessed by questionnaires; others may require "clinical" interview
Good emotional person-environment fit	Congruence of personal knowledge of emotion with the beliefs of the surrounding culture	Uncertain—cultural environment must be assessed independently from personal attributes

needs support. To say that EI relates to the perception function tells us nothing about whether EI is driven by low-level subcortical processing or high-level symbolic processing of contextual information, or some integration of multiple processes.

What Are the Criteria for EI?

Another fundamental difficulty is deciding what independent criteria for social-emotional competence should be predicted by EI measures (Matthews et al., 2002). Exacerbating this problem, most research uses self-report scales to assess both the predictors and criteria, with criterion contamination often coming into play. Thus, questionnaires for EI include items that refer to positive mood, optimism, and confidence; the very same criteria that many researchers wish to predict. Indeed, too little research has used objective behavioral criteria, though in the few isolated instances in which this information has been collected, evidence tends to be mixed. For example, the MSCEIT fails to predict attentional and working memory performance under stress (Matthews, Emo, Funke et al., 2006). EI questionnaires also fail to predict learning to use emotional information in a multicue discrimination task (Fellner et al., 2006). By contrast, studies have linked questionnaire measures to cortisol secretion (Salovey et al., 2002) and speed of facial processing (Petrides & Furnham, 2003).

Beyond these straightforward issues, there are more difficult conceptual issues that relate to what we mean by the term *intelligence*. It may be desirable to experience the emotions of others through empathy, or to stay calm in a crisis, but do these responses reflect a true ability? Indeed, can we ever say that a subjective feeling state—as opposed to cognitively based understanding—is "intelligent"? Some would say this is a category error. The counterargument might be that feelings signal adaptive predispositions (Lazarus, 1999) that may or may not be appropriate for the situation. Human intelligence, of course, is notoriously hard to define independently from its operationalizations, but generally some insight and explicit understanding is assumed. For example, in the emotional realm, we may not want to attribute intelligence to someone whose brain is wired to produce high levels of endorphins or whose neural networks automatically direct attention away from threat stimuli.

Another issue is the extent to which EI should be differentiated from character and ethical behavior, and from conformity to social norms. The selfish, Machiavellian individual may possess EI in the sense of perceiving and manipulating the weaknesses of others. At the extreme, individuals with antisocial personality disorder may possess social skills that allow them to exploit others (Harpur, Hart, & Hare, 2002), despite deficiencies in other areas of emotional functioning. There is also a tension between EI in the sense of fitting in with the social expectations of others and consensus norms, and EI in the sense of making insightful autonomous decisions about the value of social norms. Some Germans opposed the Nazis and were executed as a consequence. Certainly, these people were ethical and even heroic; but were they emotionally intelligent?

What Are the Dynamics of EI?

It is perhaps ironic that much EI research revisits one of the less attractive aspects of intelligence research: its tendency to present ability as a static set of constructs while ignoring the processes that support intelligent interaction with the external environment (c.f. Corno et al., 2002). Describing EI as a laundry list of desirable qualities unrelated to any independent theory is the most obvious example of this problem. More subtly, research on EI frequently ignores the person-situation interaction that has become fundamental to personality research (Magnusson, 1976). The basic point is that the expression of EI may vary—perhaps radically—depending upon the surrounding environment. Individual differences in EI may be more apparent in some contexts than in others, and EI may be adaptive in some settings but harmful in others (Ciarrochi, Deane, & Anderson, 2002). Borrowing from Caspi and Bem's (1990) account of person-situation interaction, we can identify at least three forms of interaction that remain almost entirely unexplored. How do high EI persons filter and interpret the social world around them (reactive interaction)? What kinds of behaviors does the high EI person provoke in others (evocative interaction)? Perhaps (consciously or unconsciously), the high EI person elicits more cooperation and support from other people, whereas the low EI person rubs them the wrong way. How does EI relate to choosing and shaping social environments (proactive interaction)? For example, low EI may be associated not just with a liking for harmful drugs (Trinidad, Unger, Chou, Azen, & Johnson, 2004), but also for picking friends that are a bad influence.

Is EI Adaptive?

Calling EI an ability signals that it refers to individual differences in adaptation; that the high EI person is, in some sense, better adapted to social-emotional functioning than the person of lower EI. This assumption needs empirical support, especially as self-reports of competence are sometimes viewed as circumspect (see Dunning, Heath, & Suls, 2004). The vision of the pioneers of tests for EI appears to have been that high EI is unequivocally adaptive (e.g., Mayer, Caruso, & Salovey, 1999). To enjoy high EI is to enjoy a variety of benefits, including life satisfaction, emotional connections with others, and occupational success. As we have previously mentioned, researchers differ sharply in their assessments of whether these predictions have been confirmed (e.g., Brody, 2004; Day, 2004; Mayer et al., 2004).

Obtaining evidence for criterion validity is an important first step here, but insufficient in itself to provide an adequate adaptive account of EI. Two important missing links are: (1) the lack of a dynamic, process-based account of how the psychological processes that support EI confer real-life benefits, and (2) an account of person-situation interaction that specifies the environmental challenges and demands for which high EI is necessary (see above). Research on these issues is lacking, so we will not labor the point further. It is worth noting, however, that some constructs allied to EI are thought to have a "dark side." For example, the dark side of high self-esteem appears as narcissism, denial of problems, and excessive self-enhancement (Baumeister, Campbell, Krueger, & Vohs, 2003).

The issue then is the environments or situations in which an inflated ego may be adaptive. Studies of the related construct of self-enhancement suggest that it confers both benefits and costs; for example, making a good impression on others in the short term, vs. longer term interpersonal difficulties (Robins & Paulhus, 2001). This brings such constructs into the realm of personality psychology, within which traits typically confer both advantages and vulnerabilities, whose expression depends on the situation (Matthews & Zeidner, 2004). Of course, researchers following an ability model for EI are more likely to argue that the interactive effect of EI and situational factors is ordinal rather than disordinal; in other words, that situational moderators of the effects of EI on outcomes influence the magnitude of the relationship rather than its direction. Contrary to such a view, Ciarrochi et al. (2002) found that superior objective emotion perception was related to greater stress response to daily hassles; there may be advantages to emotional insensitivity in some circumstances.

Key Questions

Thus far we have argued that there is some broad consensus on several issues: that EI is multifaceted, that there is overlap between EI and conventional personality and ability, that there is some evidence for criterion validity for specific tests of EI, that exceptional groups may be distinguished by high or low EI, and that there is a clear developmental path for social-emotional competencies in childhood. Conversely, researchers differ, sometimes sharply, on issues including the overall worth of the whole enterprise, whether there is any common element to the multifarious constructs labeled as EI, what the key outcome criteria should be in validation studies, how the "person-situation" dynamics of EI operate, and whether high EI is unequivocally adaptive. These agreements and disagreements inspire the following questions that have been put to the contributors to this volume.

1. *How should EI be conceptualized? Should it be a competence, a skill, an adaptive outcome, a set of cultural beliefs, or some other construct?* Researchers agree that there are multiple perspectives on EI. However, there are few systematic attempts to map the complete domain or to show that there is some interrelationship and coherence between different perspectives. Also lacking are criteria for deciding which constructs and definitions truly belong to the world of EI, and which are better treated as facets of conventional intelligence, personality, or other domains.

2. *Is the concept of EI compatible with the existing theories of emotion and of cognitive intelligence?* Research on EI has varied in the extent to which it refers to an explicit theory of emotion and/or cognition. Studies of cognitive intelligence support the notion of stable individual differences in aptitude and competence, and provide an account of the underlying neurological and information-processing characteristics of the highly intelligent person. It is unclear whether similar processes exist that support EI. By contrast, emotion theory (e.g., Lazarus, 1999) typically sees emotions as being neither unequivocally adaptive nor maladaptive. The challenge here is to determine how the multileveled processing that supports emotions (Matthews, Derryberry, & Siegle, 2000) can *support* global individual differences in competence.

3. *What are the key components, facets, or branches of EI?* Resolving uncertainties over the conceptualization and theory of EI requires better structural models. Various accounts of the key components of EI exist, but these models are in need of systematic comparison and integration. We also see a need for weeding out those constructs that are not well supported by research.

4. *How is EI distinct from existing personality and ability constructs? Could a multistratum psychometric model integrate a dimension or dimensions of EI with existing personality and ability constructs?* As also explored in the second section of this book, building better conceptual models of EI also requires better psychometric models that specify both the overlaps and the uniqueness of EI constructs in relation to personality and ability. At this point, we inquire about the prospects for better conceptualization of the relevant similarities and dissimilarities.

5. *How does EI change over the life span, quantitatively and qualitatively?* Different phases of the life span pose differing challenges. In childhood, the issue is how to relate existing studies of emotional development to individual differences in emotional

competencies, separating what is unique to EI from the temperamental factors that loom large in the emotional lives of children. Changes in emotional functioning in adulthood are evidently more subtle; beyond a general sense that emotional wisdom tends to increase with age, the changing nature of EI in the older adult years remains to be explored.

6. *How might EI contribute to adaptation to real-world social environments?* We have noted different views on EI and adaptation that correspond loosely to the differing perspectives of ability and personality researchers. Answering this question, in our view, requires greater engagement with the role of EI as a moderator of dynamic person-situation interaction, as well as stronger evidence for the predictive validity of tests for EI in relation to real-life outcomes.

Assessment of Emotional Intelligence

The case that reliable and valid assessment of EI is central to building a science of EI is straightforward to make (Matthews et al., 2002), and is generally accepted by researchers (cf. however, Oatley, 2004). As noted above, approaches to measurement of the EI construct have generally been understood within Mayer, Salovey et al.'s (2000b) influential distinction between ability models (suggesting objective tests) and mixed models (suggesting self-report measures) of the construct. Reviews of the various measures of EI (e.g., MacCann, Matthews, Zeidner, & Roberts, 2003) have generally been structured around this distinction, and we return to the issue in this section. However, several developments suggest that it may be time to move on from the Mayer, Salovey et al. (2000a, 2000b) dichotomy, at least in some respects. First, some questionnaire researchers, notably Petrides and Furnham (2003) claim that self-report inventories belong to the domain of personality ("trait EI") and do not measure abilities. Second, questions remain about whether Mayer, Salovey et al.'s (e.g., 2000) tests measure abilities akin to those assessed by conventional intelligence tests (Brody, 2004; Matthews et al., 2002). Some fresh thinking on how to measure social-emotional abilities or competencies may be required. Third, conceptual analyses of the kind discussed in the previous section imply that the current range of tests for EI may not adequately sample the full range of constructs that may be labeled as "EI"; again, new assessment methods may be needed. Thus, a review of assessment methods needs not only to evaluate extant tests against standard psychometric criteria, but to examine the fundamental principles being used to sample the domain of emotional competence as a basis for test development.

In this section, we review sources of consensus and controversy in assessment, leading to key questions put to the contributors to this volume.

Sources of Consensus

The discipline of psychometrics provides *relatively* uncontroversial principles for determining what constitutes sound assessment practices. Indeed, almost all major organizations concerned with educational and psychological testing have endorsed a set of standards for determining the efficacy of a given measure (AERA/APA/NCME Test Standards; American Educational Research Association, 1999). These standards address many different components. For example, they lay out a framework for interpreting reliability and validity; in essence, how the corpus of research should confirm the status of the instrument. Distilling the major components contained in the AERA/APA/NCME Test Standards, the following represent guidelines that appear requisite for all EI assessments:

1. Provide evidence for the reliability of the measure in question and information on the standard error of measurement.
2. Demonstrate that a meaningful relationship exists between the test's content and the construct that it is intended to measure (analogous to the previous standard's concern with content validity).
3. Provide theoretical and empirical analyses supporting (or disconfirming) relationships between the construct and the responses provided by the test taker (e.g., ensure that a response to a test supposedly measuring EI is not an artifact of extraneous factors such as social conformity, response bias, faking, or some other self-deception bias).
4. Demonstrate that the internal structure of the construct is as suggested by the underlying theoretical framework (unidimensional, composed of independent components, hierarchical in structure, etc.).
5. Localize the construct within the nomological net; in other words, the sphere of other individual differences variables that the assessment relates to. This includes establishing both convergent and discriminant evidence, test-criterion relationships, and documenting how validity generalizes across samples and situations.

Issues of consequential validity (i.e., demonstrating that the construct assessed by the test has meaningful societal consequences), fairness (i.e., showing that items are not biased against a particular subpopulation for inappropriate reasons), and how to appropriately document test development are also critical components of developing an EI measure (Matthews, Emo et al., 2006). All of these various processes are ongoing and should feed back to guide theoretical refinements, test development, and future cycles of research. Each piece of evidence is also equally important to establish.

Conceivably, with these standards firmly in place, there should be a good deal of consensus regarding how best to evaluate the scientific standing of EI assessments. To some extent this is the case, because testing the psychometric properties of various EI measures is one of the major undertakings in the literature. However, as we shall see shortly, although these test standards exist, those working in the field of EI are not always finding available measures to be robust and replicable. Nor are all of the test standards necessarily being given equal consideration when making judgments about an assessment's veracity. With these anomalies in mind, it is perhaps appropriate to first discuss those standards that EI researchers seem to have agreed are important for advancing the field, though we shall return later to discuss those that seem to have been neglected.

EI Assessments Need to Be Reliable

It seems to be fairly much agreed, whether one advocates either the self-report or a performance-based approach to the assessment of EI, that the attendant measures need to be reliable. The vast majority of research on self-reports has concentrated in particular on establishing internal consistency reliability via Cronbach's alpha (e.g., Bar-On, 1995; Schutte et al., 1998; Tett et al., 2005), whereas those subscribing to performance-based measures most generally calculate split-half (odd-even) reliability (e.g., Palmer, Gignac, Manocha, & Stough, 2005). Mayer et al. (2004) provide a rationale for the latter approach when using performance-based assessments administered in the fashion that they describe, though not all researchers evaluating tests like the MSCEIT seem to have appreciated this point (e.g., Yousefi, 2006). Of note, we are unaware of studies that report the standard error of the measurement of any EI test.

It is nonincidental that many of the subscales have marginal (i.e., less than 0.6) reliabilities both for self-report and performance-based measures, though superordinate constructs such as experiential EI, general EI, and the like have high reliability coefficients (i.e., in excess of 0.9). Strategies for improving the reliability of subscales, such as increasing the number of test items, have curiously been neglected. By way of illustration, the MSCEIT actually has fewer items than its predecessor the MEIS for several common subscales; and their reliabilities were marginal. There are also relatively few studies of the test-retest reliability of any measure. Moreover, although those that have been conducted are suggestive, they generally come from studies with fairly small sample sizes (e.g., Brackett & Mayer, 2003; Tett et al., 2005). In sum, although the concern for reliability is a mutual point of consensus among EI researchers, echoing a common theme throughout these passages, empirical findings are often equivocal. Indeed, the jury is still out on whether many existing tests have high enough reliability coefficients for use in applied settings.

EI Assessments Need a Variety of Validity Evidence

The AERA/APA/NCME Test Standards (1999) acknowledge construct validity as an all-encompassing, unifying concept overarching all types of validity evidence. Within this perspective, all forms of validity evidence listed earlier are merely supporting players in the cumulative, never-ending quest for construct validation. Extending this notion to the special case of EI, it may justifiably be claimed that the construct is too new to dismiss any of its measures out of hand. Equally, however, preliminary evidence for construct validity would appear requisite to push EI further along a scientific trajectory. It is important to keep in mind that construct validity requires that EI is based on a sound conceptual base, which, as discussed in the first part of this chapter, is not yet the case.

As mentioned earlier, not all forms of validity evidence have been the subject of extant empirical research on EI, and this is worth reiterating here. In the quest for construct validity evidence, research has tended instead to focus on interpretable group differences (encapsulated by Criterion 3 above), factor structure (Criterion 4 above), convergent and discriminant validity evidence (Criterion 5 above), and test-criterion relationships (also Criterion 5 above). In the passages that follow we discuss these validation strategies further and what we have learned thus far from the available research.

THEORETICALLY INTERPRETABLE GROUP DIFFERENCES   As is customary when attempting to acquire validity evidence, a major concern of EI researchers has been the identification of meaningful group differences, a topic we touched on briefly when discussing theoretical issues. The core driver of this form of validity evidence has been its successful application in individual differences research and its related applications in clinical, educational, and industrial/organizational psychology. Interpretable age differences, in particular, are tied to theoretical models of development and maturation in both intelligence and personality models, and have been touted also by some commentators as important validity criteria for EI assessments (Mayer, Salovey, & Caruso, 1999). Empirical evidence on this issue, however, is surprisingly scant. In addition, it should not be assumed that all of the factors comprising EI will necessarily show incremental gains over the life span (more especially if precedent is a driver of this validity argument). In the study of intelligence, for example, fluid intelligence has been shown to be subject to decline in the adult years (Horn & Hofer, 1992); similarly, certain personality factors rise and fall as a function of age (e.g., Costa & McCrae, 1994; McCrae et al., 1999).

Of note, age is but one variable that constitutes a group difference approach to acquiring validity evidence. Other variables include gender, socioeconomic status, ethnicity, and whether a member of a clinical group or not (see section "EI Relates to Exceptionality"). Of these, gender in particular has been the subject of serious empirical investigation by EI researchers (e.g., Harrod & Scheer, 2005; Lyons & Schneider, 2005; Petrides & Furnham, 2000a, 2006). Here it is often hypothesized that females will score higher on EI scales than males. However, the rationale for expecting this group difference often seems more rooted in folk psychology than a set of cogent, logical arguments. Indeed, it is entirely possible to construct EI scales in which such effects are minimized or reduced using, for example, differential item functioning analyses, though seldom, as we argue shortly, are these more sophisticated contemporary psychometric analyses performed by those working in the EI field.

Although we do not wish to make much of the issue, because to conduct carefully controlled studies with appropriate sensitivity is a challenging exercise, there is a rather glaring lack of validity evidence concerning ethnic or socioeconomic differences in EI. Indeed, we have traced a possible reason for the construct's pervasive appeal in wider society to its timely retort to the messages contained in Herrnstein and Murray's (1994) *The Bell Curve* (Matthews et al., 2002). The claim is simple: EI is available to all, in near equal measure; a claim constantly reiterated in Goleman (1995). If true, there should be demonstration that differences in EI according to ethnicity or SES are weak to nonexistent. One study that did tackle this issue found notably conflicting results. Using consensus scores, minority groups outperformed their majority counterparts on a general EI score obtained from a performance measure (the MEIS; Roberts et al., 2001). However, when expert scoring rubrics were used the result was reversed; though it may not be co-incidence that all experts belonged to the majority group. Because it really does represent a way of addressing adverse impact for minority groups, more studies of this kind are needed, but only if the data are reported in a sensitive manner.

FACTOR STRUCTURE   The issue of establishing the structural validity of a given EI assessment represents an empirical attempt to resolve the multidimensionality of the construct, a point we alluded to earlier in discussion of conceptual issues. Put another way, the issue here concerns the development of a taxonomic model for placing the subconstructs comprising each EI assessment, and showing that is relatively invariant across subpopulations, time, test administrators, and so forth. The importance of facto-rial stability should not be underestimated, especially if the subconstructs comprising a given measure are imbued with scientific meaning and/or are used to make personnel, educational, or clinical decisions (see, e.g., Horn & McArdle, 1992). There are a growing number of research papers, assessing both self-report and performance-based measures, where factorial stability is a chief concern (e.g., Austin, Saklofske, & Huang, & McKenney, 2004; Chapman & Hayslip, 2006; Gignac, Palmer, Manocha, & Stough, 2005; Palmer, Manocha, Gignac, & Stough, 2003; Roberts et al., 2001).

Although it is undoubtedly the case that there is consensus on the importance of this undertaking, the data attesting to the factorial validity of virtually every single extant measure of EI are equivocal. Consider the following. Schutte et al. (1998) postulated a single, general factor for the self-report inventory that they developed. However, Pe-trides and Furnham (2000) provide evidence instead for a four factor solution, whereas still other commentators (e.g., Saklofske et al., 2003) have not been entirely successful in replicating this, or other, factor solutions for this measure (see, e.g., Gignac et al., 2005, who lamentably consider their study the first to address this issue). Similarly, Matthews et al. (2002) reanalyzed data from Bar-On's (1995) EQ-i technical manual to reveal a number of inconsistencies in the hypothetical structure purportedly underlying this instrument (see also Livingstone & Day, 2005; Palmer et al., 2003). Performance-based measures fare no better. For example, although there are several studies that allege the MSCEIT has four recoverable factors (Mayer, Salovey, Caruso, & Sitarenios, 2001), virtually no published study has been able to find evidence for an independent emotional facilitation (i.e., using emotions to facilitate thought) construct (see, e.g., Palmer et al., 2005; Roberts et al., 2006). Problems in factor structure also hold true for the MSCEIT's predecessor, the MEIS (Roberts et al., 2001; Zeidner et al., 2001). Furthermore, re-search is sorely needed to test for factorial invariance of current measures of EI across different sociocultural groups.

CONVERGENT VALIDITY EVIDENCE   Based on available conceptualizations, it would seem that a consensus might be reached on the appropriate variables with which to demonstrate convergent validity evidence for EI assessments. In particular, moderate relations should exist between EI and independent measures of cognitive abilities (e.g., general intelligence, fluid abilities, crystallized abilities, and so forth), and indeed a good deal of the research with performance-based measures of EI have used this as a validation strategy. In sum, it appears that performance-based tests correlate differentially with different aspects of intelligence; positively relating to verbal, knowledge-based tests (i.e., crystallized intelligence), particularly for Understanding Emotion (Branch 3), at the same time being relatively weakly related to tests of reasoning ability (fluid intelligence; see Ciarrochi et al., 2000; Mayer, Salovey et al., 2000a; Roberts et al., 2001, 2006). Generally, the evidence suggests that ability-based EI measures index emotional knowledge, which is related to crystallized intelligence. Such a relationship supports claims that EI is malleable, rather than innate (Goleman, 1998).

There is a growing body of evidence that self-report assessments of EI, by contrast, assess dispositional traits rather than a form of intelligence. For example, Dawda and Hart (2000) reported large correlations between the EQ-i and Big Five factors as evidence for the high convergent validity of the model, assuming EI to be dispositional. Petrides and Furnham (2001) found similar results, indicating that trait EI is largely a composite of low neuroticism and high extraversion. Not all researchers make this claim however, and we will need to address therefore the relation between self-report EI and personality again in the section on discriminant validity evidence. Surprisingly perhaps, self-report measures of EI have thus far shown low (near zero) correlations with traditional forms of intelligence (see, e.g., Davies, Stankov, & Roberts, 1998; Derksen, Kramer, & Katzko, 2002; Sala, 2002; Zeidner et al., 2005). These findings indicate poor convergent validity evidence insofar that for self-report EI to legitimately constitute a form of intelligence these correlations should be moderate at least (Bowman, Markham, & Roberts, 2002).

It has been argued that if the meanings of the words *emotion* and *intelligence* are to be preserved, the term *emotional intelligence* should combine them in an effective manner (Mayer & Salovey, 1997). In particular, it should combine the ideas that emotions can make thinking more intelligent and that one can think intelligently about emotions. If correct, this suggests that an equally important source of convergent validity evidence is a demonstration that EI assessments relate to standard measures from the emotion literature. However, to date, there has been a paucity of research linking EI to other emotion constructs. Indeed, to present knowledge only one such published study has been conducted (Roberts et al., 2006), and here standard measures of emotion perception were virtually unrelated to MSCEIT emotion perception measures. Bar-On (2001) reports an even more alarming *positive* relation between the EQ-i and a measure of the Emotional Stroop; exactly the opposite effect might be expected according to available theories that would link EI to more effective attentional focusing when processing emotional stimuli.

A final piece of convergent validity evidence is the relations between available EI assessments. This is a tried and true validation strategy in both intelligence and personality assessment, and not surprisingly has been the source of several studies and a meta-analysis in the EI field (Van Rooy, Viswesvaran, & Pluta, 2005). The results again are not especially compelling. Three generalizations may be made. First, self-report assessments of EI tend to correlate highly with other self-reports. Second, because there are so few performance-based measures of EI, these are yet to be investigated; though as we have pointed out, the failure to at least consider relations between the MEIS and MSCEIT is a major oversight in the literature (Matthews et al., 2002). Finally, the correlation between performance-based and self-report assessments is surprisingly low, ranging somewhere between 0.2 and 0.3 across a slew of studies. More problematic, we have shown that opposite conclusions can be reached on the basis of these two different assessment approaches when one looks also at external variables like intelligence or at group differences (Zeidner et al., 2005).

DISCRIMINANT VALIDITY EVIDENCE   One of the major criticisms of self-report assessments is that they appear to measure a conglomeration of established personality traits, rather than a separate trait of EI (e.g., Davies et al., 1998; Mayer, Salovey et al., 2000a, 2000b; McCrae, 2000). A strong version of this argument notes that reconstituting personality factors, as EI, is pseudoscientific. There would appear no need to spend considerable research resources examining a purportedly new construct that in reality has well-established social, biological, and psychological correlates. The possibility that self-report assessments of EI simply repackage personality should not be dismissed lightly, and it has lead to a good deal of research in which self-report assessments are correlated with personality variables. Put more succinctly, demonstration that EI is differentiable from personality is also agreed to be an important validation strategy.

Unfortunately, the magnitude of correlation between the vast majority of self-report assessments of EI and (a lack of) neuroticism (particularly, anxiety) is strong, with moderate to high correlations also evident between the self-report assessments and agreeableness, conscientiousness, and extraversion, for a good deal of the available scales (see MacCann et al., 2003; Matthews et al., 2002). Given correlations with several personality variables it seems possible that once the variance associated with personality is partialed out, EI-related variance would be minimal.

Unlike self-report measures of EI, ability scales show discriminant validity evidence with respect to five-factor personality traits; a finding that has now been consistently replicated across a series of studies (e.g., Brackett & Mayer, 2003; Palmer et al., 2003; Roberts et al., 2001). All correlations are less than .30, and the MSCEIT shows a very weak negative correlation with neuroticism, whereas the MEIS shows a slightly stronger relation to neuroticism and a relation to agreeableness for all branches. In addition, understanding and management branches (of the MEIS) relate to openness and conscientiousness (but not strongly enough to be simply replicating tests of the five-factor model, as self-report assessments appear to do).

TEST-CRITERION RELATIONSHIPS   Given a major concern with using EI assessments in a variety of applications, arguably the major research endeavor on which there is consensus is that EI assessments need to demonstrate test-criterion relationships (i.e., exhibit predictive validity). There is an ever growing body of literature addressing this topic for both self-report and performance-based measures, which we covered quite extensively in our discussion of theoretical issues (see, especially, sections entitled "Individual EI Constructs Relate Meaningfully to External Criteria" and "What Are the Criteria for EI?"). If there is any take-home message for validity evidence from this previous review, as implied by these contrasting subtitles, it is this: Once again a seemingly consensual topic on validity has led to a great deal of controversy.

EI ASSESSMENTS NEED TO BE PREMISED ON JUSTIFIABLE SCORING RUBRICS   There is little doubt that simply by virtue of the method's widespread use across psychology, investigating self-reported EI can be justified as a research tactic. However, by contrast, compared to more traditional intelligence tests (e.g., Vocabulary, Matrices) the scoring of performance-based EI tests is difficult, as there is no algorithm for determining the correct answer (MacCann, Roberts, Matthews, & Zeidner, 2004; Roberts et al., 2001; Zeidner et al., 2001). Objectivity, or "the problem of the correct answer" (Mayer, Salovey et al., 2000a, 2000b), has proven hugely problematic in investigations of social intelligence, and has thus far proven an equally difficult issue to traverse in emotional intelligence research (see Kihlstrom & Cantor, 2000, for a review of measurement issues in social intelligence). The MSCEIT (and the earlier MEIS) deal with this problem in one of three ways: (1) assuming emotion experts know the answer (expert scoring), (2) assuming that the stimulus creators know the answer (target scoring), or (3) assuming that the correct answer is what people generally agree is correct (consensus scoring).

The use of expert panels to determine correctness refocuses the question from determining the correct answer to determining who is emotionally intelligent, which might not be any easier. Mayer and Geher (1996) suggested that psychologists are experts in EI, which assumes that knowledge of theories of emotion translates into emotional intelligence. This appears a more reasonable assumption for knowledge-based competencies (e.g., emotional understanding) than for more purely perceptual or cognitive measures (e.g., emotion perception). In short, the less the skill is based on explicit knowledge, the more error prone might be the experts' response. Indeed, the literature on cognitive task analysis (Chipman, Shraagen, & Shalin, 2000) shows that experts often lack understanding of the bases for skills, and their naïve psychological theories may not stand up to empirical scrutiny. Empirical findings on the MEIS reflect this expectation, with the lowest correlation between expert and consensus scores found for the emotion perception branch. Expert scoring of the MEIS was conducted by two of the test authors (both psychologists), whereas expert judgment of the MSCEIT was done by 21 members of the International Society of Research on Emotions.

Target scoring must also make some assumptions: for example, that targets themselves are able to express the emotion that they are feeling accurately. It is likely too that targets may report only pleasant or prosocial emotions, when they are in fact feeling something else. Mayer and Geher (1996) provide some empirical support for the latter view. At present, the test authors encourage consensus scoring, claiming that this method is the most psychoactive (Mayer, Salovey, & Caruso, 2002, p. 7).

Consensus scoring awards an item score equal to the proportion of people choosing a particular option or rating scale category (e.g., if 47% of people choose option [b], the score awarded to [b] is .47). Because the interpretation and use of emotion is largely a social phenomenon (e.g., Mayer & Beltz, 1998), equating correctness with agreement appears reasonable. Problems arise with using correctness-as-agreement to score tests, as roughly the same majority of people will get the answer correct on each item if the test is reliable. Consensually scored tests have very high levels of kurtosis and negative skew, and thus statistical analysis assuming multivariate normality cannot be validly applied to them (see MacCann, Roberts, Matthews, & Zeidner, 2004). Perhaps more important, selection at the top end of the scale becomes quite difficult, as the majority cluster close together at the high end.

MSCEIT consensus scores are strongly related to MSCEIT expert scores ($r = .93$ to $r = .99$; Mayer et al., 2002), indicating that both scoring methods index the same construct. However, this is not true of the earlier MEIS, particularly for emotion perception scores. Roberts et al. (2001) reported a *negative* correlation ($r = -.22$) between expert scores and consensus scores for MEIS Faces. Expert and consensus scores correlated at $r = .44$ across all tests, and $r = .07$ over the four emotion perception tests sampled in this study. This outcome is likely due to larger error variance in expert ratings for competencies that are perceptual rather than knowledge based, as well as the smaller expert panel used in scoring the MEIS.

Sources of Controversy

As seen from the preceding, in the consensually agreed upon quest for developing reliable, fair, and valid assessment of EI, there are a good deal of controversies evident in the actual detail; in this case hard, empirical findings. Mayer, Caruso et al.'s (2000) influential discrimination of ability and mixed models of EI signaled the biggest controversy of them all. Which of the two common measurement approaches—self-report or performance-based—is the appropriate method to use as an assessment vehicle? The evidence reviewed, and especially the lack of convergence between the two approaches, suggests that they may, in fact, herald two largely separate constructs, each of which may be evaluated independently. Our initial review of conceptual issues indicates other sources of controversy, notably whether the two methods are the only viable ones. Some viable conceptualizations that potentially support performance assessments may not be well operationalized by the MSCEIT (see Table 1.1). These include EI as a set of implicit skills, as basic information-processing routines, and as an adaptation to specific sociocultural standards for emotion. Arguably, the "tasks" performed in completing the MSCEIT may not be optimal for differentiating participants' competencies. There are a variety of largely unexplored techniques for performance-based assessment of EI, including assessments of contextual skills and competencies, chronometric methods (Austin, 2005), and implicit performance tasks (e.g., Schmukle & Egloff, 2005). As Table 1.1 indicates, it is far from clear that such tasks would index a single construct. Within the ability domain, "EI" may have a complex dimensional structure that may or may not prove to support an overarching general factor.

The current trend toward relating self-reports of EI to the personality domain (Petrides & Furnham, 2003) leaves the earlier mixed models of EI (e.g., Bar-On, 2000) in limbo. Should we abandon Bar-On's idea that questionnaires may be used to assess abilities, or does the notion still have credence? Again, it may be useful to explore differentiation of constructs within the self-report domain. Thus, although the split between performance and questionnaire tests looms large in the present context, other uncertainties over the optimal choice of assessment methods are appearing as the field develops. It is to be hoped that the current edited volume will contribute to resolving this controversy, because it is likely that uncertainties over assessment will constrain advances in the field.

The cliché "out of sight, out of mind," is not a dictum that any scientist would endorse, and is perhaps antithetical to any form of scientific progress. For this reason we contend that the following issues are also a source of controversy within contemporary approaches to EI assessment. Our intention here is to raise five missing elements, which may be gleaned by extrapolating research and methods covering emotions, personality, and intelligence to the field of EI. These also serve as an advanced warning of the various commentators' position on such matters; each touch upon these topics either directly or indirectly.

Is There a Need for Additional Validity Evidence?

Curiously, as mentioned earlier, there are some forms of validity evidence that are seldom, if ever, considered by EI researchers. In particular, there has been no published account supporting the content validity of any EI assessment, though this clearly appears as an important aspect of the current test standards. There is, of course, a problem in that vagueness of conceptualization makes it difficult to specify what the content of tests should be. Indeed, the face validity of both self-report and performance-based measures has been questioned (Matthews et al., 2003). Consequential validity is another form of validity evidence that has received short shrift. This form of validity evidence "requires evaluation of the intended and unintended social consequences of test interpretation and use" (Messick, 1988, p. 39). Consequential validity evidence is a relatively new addition to the test standards and is somewhat controversial in its own right. It is important to evaluate, however, because of the frequent misuse of test scores, an issue that actually may be more of a problem than any proponent of EI has thus far seriously entertained (see, however, Matthews et al., 2002). For example, Goleman (1995, 1998) paints a rosy, egalitarian world, providing all follow various suggestions made in his emotional intelligence trade-text. However, it remains to be seen whether assessment of EI might not result in similar, unintended social consequences as has sometimes occurred with various forms of cognitive testing. The issue is certainly one that should not simply be ignored. We will return to the issue in reviewing applications of research on EI.

Have Feedback and Diagnostics Been Given
Due Consideration?

Tied to the concept of validity is the absence of expert feedback for many EI assessments. For example, although numeric information is often supplied with tests like the MSCEIT and EQ-i, the feedback to the test taker is scant compared to analogous assessment instruments of intelligence, in particular. Nor is it entirely clear the form that this feedback might take given the paucity of carefully designed experimental and intervention studies of EI. Note too that the nature of feedback is an important criterion covered in the AERA/APA/NCME Test Standards (1999). In addition, cutoff points for identifying high versus low EI individuals, or for diagnosing problems of a clinical nature, are lacking in current measures.

Are the Stakes at Which Assessment
Is Targeted Defensible?

Basic research aside, psychological testing is generally conducted for some practical purpose, with varying implications. In general, practitioners and policy makers talk of the tests falling into one of three categories, corresponding to the consequences associated with the instrument in question for decision-making purposes. These are (1) high stakes (e.g., determining whether an individual can enter the college of their choice after taking an assessment); (2) medium stakes (e.g., ascertaining whether an individual may move into a higher position on the corporate ladder on the basis of a test score); or (3) low stakes (e.g., a test designed to give the individual a certain level of self-insight). Currently, there is considerable push to bring EI measures into the high-stakes testing arena. Clearly, however, in the absence of more carefully documented validity evidence, such usage is contentious.

Is It Not Time for More Advanced
Psychometric Analyses?

As alluded to at several points, thus far a good deal of EI research has been conducted without particularly advanced psychometrics. We are aware, for example, of no study using item response theory (Embertson & Reise, 2000; van der Linden, 1996), differential item functioning (Holland & Wainer, 1993), equating (Kolen & Brennan, 2004), or Bayes Net models (Glymour, 2001), to name but a few of the statistical procedures commonly employed in cognitive assessment today. Although each of these methodologies address very different features of test development and are relevant therefore to diverse aspects of the validation process, their absence in available studies of EI is perhaps noteworthy. These procedures are especially important for high-stakes assessment and feed in to a previous concern that we had for keeping the stakes that contemporary EI assessments are used at a justifiable level. Moreover, even when more widely employed statistical procedures such as confirmatory factor analyses are used, seldom is this done with any great level of psychometric sophistication (for an excellent overview of contemporary approaches using these methods, see Schulze, 2005). Moreover, without naming names, there are several instances in the published literature on EI in which we would suggest the reader be cautious of the implications drawn because an improper statistical procedure had been followed.

Key Questions

Thus far we have argued that there is less consensus regarding appropriate vehicles and methods for assessing EI than there appears to be for even the rather underdeveloped conceptual models that saturate the field. Arguably, this is an unsatisfactory state of affairs, one that may be conceived as inhibitory to the development of a systematic framework for conducting EI research. Certain points of consensus are virtually dictated by the scientific community, most especially with respect to standards set for psychological and educational measurement. For example, perforce, instruments designed to measure EI need to meet minimal standards for reliability, fairness, and validity. As we suggested earlier, some of this can be achieved simply by well-known techniques (e.g., lengthening a test often increases its internal consistency), whereas the jury is still out on whether or not more critical properties, such as construct validity evidence, has even partially been demonstrated for any given measure of emotional intelligence.

The two different approaches taken by researchers to the assessment of EI has led to two separate scientific literatures emerging on the topic. Often the findings coming out of these two emerging research traditions do not converge. Thus, it is perhaps an important undertaking of the current edited volume to provide a synthesis of these approaches, should this be possible. Conversely, synthesis may not really be possible; perhaps it is best to adopt one approach over another according to a cogent set of arguments. There is precedent for the latter, certainly in differential psychology. In particular, choice reaction time was seen as a viable approach to assessing intelligence (see, e.g., Galton, 1883) until Binet and Simon (1916/1983) adopted a richer set of assessment principles (see, however, Jensen, 1998, on whether this was totally justified or advantageous). Indeed, it is not clear that any of the current approaches to the assessment of EI are entirely appropriate, perhaps even more so given that over a century of research on emotions is seldom consulted by researchers trying to understand emotional intelligence.

Clearly, given the various issues that we raised earlier in discussion of the sources of both consensus and controversies in EI assessment, we might raise any number of questions for the present commentators to tackle. Indeed, conceivably, an entire book might be devoted to this topic alone. The end list that we settled on, however, was designed with the specific purpose of moving the field further along, should this be possible (rather than simply reiterating some of the shortcomings of the domain). In particular, we chose to address some of more tractable problems within EI research, giving the contributors high-level questions that would allow them certain degrees of freedom. Below, we pose these questions and make some preliminary comments justifying their inclusion in the current volume. Notably, the first four questions have at their core the complex interplay between validity and psychological assessment, whereas the last three questions have our experts consider possible alternative approaches that might conceivably represent the future of EI assessment.

1. *What are the strength and weaknesses of current measures of EI?* It is necessary to obtain a variety of expert opinion concerning this issue. The commentators that we have assembled to address this question include those with some vested interest, who have contributed to the literature with a specific operationalization of emotional intelligence. However, we have also invited contributors who are experts in the fields of emotion, intelligence, social intelligence, artificial intelligence, education, business, and clinical psychology. These proponents seem well placed to offer historical, new, and/or multidisciplinary perspectives that might enrich available approaches. By attempting to get a balance of such experts, we hope to tackle this highly emotive issue with a good deal of objectivity.

2. *What is the optimal approach to the assessment of EI?* Historical precedent is again apposite here. In the field of personality, self-report assessments have tended to dominate and inform the scientific literature. With respect to cognitive assessment, the optimal approach is clearly that grounded in veridical standards; answers that may judged on a continuum of correctness, according to criteria identified by experts in a given domain (Carroll, 1993; Guttman & Levy, 1991). In emotion research, however, both approaches are sometimes used (e.g., self-reports in mood research, see, for example, Watson, Clark, & Tellegen, 1988; whereas emotion perception measures use objectively correct standards, see Ekman, 1972; Matsumoto et al., 2000). Nor does the existence of an optimal approach preclude the development of alternative procedures. For example, in personality assessment, James (e.g., 1998) has developed the conditional reasoning paradigm, which attempts to provide a more objective measure of personality factors. Similarly, those working with the implicit attitudes test (IAT) have begun using this technique to assess a variety of noncognitive factors (e.g., Greenwald, McGhee, & Schwartz, 1998; Greenwald, Nosek, & Banaji, 2003).

3. *Can self-reports and questionnaires ever provide assessments of intelligence and competence?* We are not aware of any operational measure of intelligence that is based solely on self-report (largely because veridical standards exist for assessing the construct of interest in a compelling fashion). For example, assessing one's geographic knowledge by asking a question such as "What is the capital city of Bermuda?" seems more cost effective and valid than asking a person to "Rate how good you are in geography on a 7-point scale from awful to brilliant" (the answer to which might suddenly change if you were offered a decent sum of money). Given the choice to assess intelligence with a question that is factually verifiable or a subjective rating, even the staunchest advocate of the latter approach is forced to concede this is a no-brainer. Besides having a good deal more face and ecological validity, veridical items are less impervious to faking, coaching, or self-deception biases. Notwithstanding, self-estimates of intelligence (or related constructs, stressing in particular cognitive engagement) have been used in research settings to generate a variety of interesting findings (e.g., Ackerman & Goff,

1994; Furnham & Rawles, 1999; Rammstedt & Rammasayer, 2000), and it is perhaps important to not dismiss self-report approaches of EI out of hand.

4. *What are the most prevalent scoring procedures for EI measures, and are they valid for ability measures?* This issue was covered in some depth in our discussion of current consensus surrounding various forms of EI assessment. Thus, for self-report measures of EI, there is a tried and true set of scoring procedures common to this well-established scientific method. In the case of performance-based EI, there exist three options: consensus, expert, and target scoring. None of these approaches to scoring are instituted in other domains of individual differences (i.e., personality or intelligence research), and having our expert panel provide insights on the promises and pitfalls of these approaches may prove invaluable.

5. *What are the prospects for assessment of EI using psychophysiological, developmental, and neurological measures?* Clearly, given some of the limitations highlighted throughout for existent measures, it would appear incumbent on the present editors to pose this rather challenging, high-level question: Are there procedures out there that might readily be used to improve the measurement of emotional intelligence? Both this question and the two that follow are designed to challenge our expert panel, and in certain instances channel their expertise to consider the possibility of assessment spaces unconstrained by either self-report or performance-based methodologies. The three domains listed herein—psychophysiology, development, and neurology—represent areas that have been profitably explored both with respect to models of intelligence (see an integrative review of these findings in Neisser et al., 1996) and emotions (see, e.g., Cacioppo, Klein, Berntson, & Hatfield, 1993; Izard, 1991; and LeDoux, 2000; for each of the domains, respectively). Conceivably, there are three major ways assessments from these domains might be used to improve assessment of EI: (1) as assessment devices in and of themselves (though, pragmatically cost may limit this direct application); (2) as important means of obtaining validity evidence; and (3) as a means of providing explanatory models that might underlie the assessment frameworks of a particular operationalization of emotional intelligence.

6. *What are the prospects for assessment of EI using information-processing tasks?* Related to the final point above, in both personality (see, e.g., Matthews, Deary, & Whiteman, 2003) and cognitive assessment (see, e.g., Danthiir, Wilhelm, Schulze, & Roberts, 2005; Roberts & Stankov, 1999), information-processing tasks have been used in attempt to provide more explanatory models of psychological functions. Indeed, in his influential tome on human cognitive abilities, Carroll (1993) makes much of the fact that information processing tasks and models have done much to advance understanding of the processes underlying a variety of cognitive ability constructs. It seems fitting to ask the various contributors to the current volume to consider whether similar advances are possible using information processing tasks that might be specially redesigned to assess EI. Indeed, there is some preliminary evidence that this may be the case for certain classes of information tasks, like the inspection time paradigm (e.g., Austin, 2005), but

not others (see Roberts et al., 2006, who found problems getting meaningful individual differences in the Emotional Stroop task in a normal population). Of considerable import, information-processing tasks get around measurement problems outlined earlier for many EI assessments because responses may be aligned along a ratio scale, and they are less susceptible, in principle, to faking and coaching effects.

7. *What are the prospects for new techniques, such as the situational judgment test (SJT) methodology and applications of advanced psychometrics, leading to improved assessment?* As we have mentioned elsewhere (Roberts et al., 2005), the SJT methodology seems particularly well suited as a methodology for constructing tests of EI. The technique presents an individual with a description of a problematic or critical situation, followed by a number of possible problem-solving responses to this situation. Respondents must either identify an appropriate response from a list of alternatives or indicate their level of agreement with statements concerning appropriate behaviors (McDaniel, Morgeson, Finnegan, Campion, & Braverman, 2001). SJTs have been used for both selection and training, and they cover both cognitive and socioaffective dimensions (McDaniel, Hartman, & Grubb, 2003; McDaniel & Nguyen, 2001). Because the situations generated for SJTs come from critical incidents, provided by task specialists, they have high face and content validity. Notably, this question was framed so that still further alternative assessments could be discussed by the contributors, who, as a talented bunch, are likely engaged in testing new techniques and methods. Because researchers interested in SJTs are also involved in solving complex psychometric problems (see, e.g., Ployhart & Weekley, 2006), this also seemed an opportune section to consider the impact of using advanced psychometric models, mentioned earlier in discussion of certain controversies in the field.

Applications of Emotional Intelligence

As alluded to in the introduction, a major driving force fueling the growing public and scientific interest in EI, and cognate emotional and social competencies, is their potential applications to improving personal and societal well-being. Thus, EI has been claimed to play a pivotal role in such diverse domains as job performance, interpersonal relationships, educational achievements, clinical disorders, and even the design and performance of autonomous intelligent agents (computers, robots, etc.). This final section will address applications of EI to these various broad domains of human endeavor.

Cronbach and Gleser (1965) assert that the expected utility of a measure in organizational settings is a linear function of its predictive validity. Plausibly, EI may contribute to the increased value and utility of assessment batteries provided that these assessments have meaningful incremental predictive validity. However, as already demonstrated, empirical research has not always supported many of the validity claims surrounding this concept. Nevertheless, there is sufficient evidence for incremental validity of the better EI measures to suggest that a focus on EI may be relevant to enhancing personal, social, and organizational functioning and adaptation (Mayer, Salovey et al., 2000a, 2000b). There are also well-validated intervention programs that are designed to improve emotional functioning, especially in education (Zins, Weissberg, Wang, & Walberg, 2004). Such programs lend weight to the idea that elevating EI may be a valuable practical strategy in many real-life settings. Thus, in the passages that follow, we review sources of consensus and controversy in applications of EI to real-life contexts.

Sources of Consensus

Many scholars now working in the area agree that there has been an initial, irrational exuberance regarding the practical value of EI in applied settings (see, e.g., Landy, 2006). Barrett, Gross, Christensen, and Benvenuto's (2001) review suggests that much of the existing evidence bearing on the role of EI in occupational success is anecdotal, impressionistic, or collected by consulting companies and not published in the peer-reviewed literature. Further, Landy (2005) claims that much of the applied work fails to meet elementary scientific standards, such as availability of data to other researchers. Similarly, Zeidner et al. (2002) have pointed out that despite popular claims, most of the programs touted as effective EI programs lack clear conceptual frameworks, implementation analyses and checks, and sound evaluation designs. At present, there are few EI training programs that have been systematically constructed, implemented, and assessed. For example, some EI programs are being implemented in school settings without sufficient theoretical grounding, intervention hypotheses, or rigorous evaluation studies. Nevertheless, the failings of current applied work and training programs do not negate the possibility that more modest practical gains may be attainable.

EI Appears Related (Albeit Weakly) to
Performance Outcomes in Applied Settings

Overall, research suggests that EI modestly predicts outcomes in a variety of real-life settings, with evidence available mainly for occupational (Daus & Ashkanasy, 2005) and educational (Zins et al., 2004) contexts. In occupational settings, EI has been claimed to be directly predictive of work performance and job satisfaction, organizational citizenship, truancy at work, and prosocial behavior. A review by Daus and Ashkanasy (2005) suggests that for jobs that would appear logically to require a high level of EI (e.g., police officers), relationships between EI and job performance and satisfaction may be higher than those in which emotional demands are less obvious. There are, however, specific problems for the use of EI in occupational settings (Zeidner et al., 2004). These include the following: (a) failure to provide an adequate theoretical rationale for their use in a particular occupational setting, (b) lack of occupational specificity, (c) absence of normative data for different occupational groups, and (d) failure to provide evidence for predictive and discriminate validity (both within and among occupational clusters). Thus, the applied psychologist must fall back on clinical or professional judgment to gauge the role of EI in many contexts, lacking a proper evidence-based analysis.

In education, EI appears a rather weak predictor of academic success per se. Thus, based on a limited number of studies, the best estimate of the true validity coefficient for the relationship between EI and academic success (i.e., grades) is small (around 0.10). In fact, of all the performance domains, academic success may be the one in which EI has the least potential. Furthermore, the EI performance relationship appears to be both measure dependent (higher for self-report than ability measures), as well as criteria dependent (Van Rooy, Dilchert, Viswesvaran, & Ones, 2006). A more compelling argument, though, may be that EI indirectly mediates success by protecting students from barriers to learning such as mental distress, substance abuse, delinquency, teen pregnancy, and violence (Hawkins, Smith, & Catalano, 2004). Equally, the criterion space for studying academic success has so far been narrow; there is more to academic success than grades. Thus, retention, citizenship, and psychological well-being all appear important outcome variables to consider in the educational sector, each of which has so far received short shrift (Roberts et al., 2005).

It has also been claimed that EI has merit and practical utility in predicting a broad set of outcomes in the social domain, such as quality of social relationships, marital success, prosocial behaviors, and delinquent behaviors. Compared to academic performance and occupational criteria, these outcomes have often been difficult to measure and operationalize (Van Rooy et al., 2006). Clearly, as we suggested earlier, the theoretical rationale for why EI should be predictive of criteria in the social realm needs to be more fully delineated. Thus, a broadside approach should not be adopted whenever EI is used to try to predict any possible outcome without specifying how and why.

The Use of EI in Applied Settings
Needs to Be Cost-Effective

Current intervention programs should provide substantial measurable benefits in dollar returns in focal or target populations (e.g., students, employees, supervisors, clients), on a range of behaviors (e.g., prosocial behaviors, decreased interpersonal violence, study habits, job performance, psychological well-being). Conducting a cost-benefit analysis prior to implementing an EI intervention would thus appear highly advisable. Indeed, the payoffs for psychological screening to rule out emotional or social deficit may vary according to the nature of the target group, context, and applied setting.

Systematic Approaches Are Required to Match
EI Components to Applications

In the special contexts of organization and industry, there is currently no empirically validated taxonomy of job types corresponding to separate components of EI. Thus, we cannot ascertain what facets of EI are requisite for any given job cluster. Generally, the level of EI apparently critical for occupational success should be a function of how central EI may be to work activities. Thus, EI may be more important in service organizations than others. Furthermore, EI may be more important for those occupying lower positions in the hierarchy relative to those much higher up in the organizational chain (Daus, 2006). Thus, a more systematic approach to matching emotional competencies to career components is needed. For example, a fine-grained analysis of the emotional demands imposed on police officers might support development of a measure of emotional regulation that could be used to assess and select police officers. This measure, in turn, could be validated against job-specific behavioral criteria, such as frequency of angry verbal behaviors during encounters with the public. Just as traditional job analysis is increasingly being supplemented by cognitive task analysis, so, too, there appears a need for "emotional task analysis" to ascertain the affective requirements of different occupations. At present, practitioners may need to rely on a relatively superficial dissection of emotional requirements. However, as theories of emotional competence become more fully articulated, more theory-driven analysis of emotional tasks at work may become possible.

This approach might also be readily applied to academic and clinical settings. Indeed, to some extent, this has already occurred because most EI interventions inculcated in school environments, for example, tend to do so through the humanities, rather than science or mathematics (e.g., Goetz, Frenzel, Pekrun, & Hall, 2005). Similarly, EI interventions may work for a set of clinical symptoms (e.g., people suffering from mild depression, posttraumatic stress disorder), but not others (e.g., personality disorders). Moreover, measures of EI might be used to match clients to appropriate therapeutic interventions (Parker, 2005).

Sources of Controversy

Are Current Research Designs Adequate?

Studies assessing the predictive validity of EI have failed to employ measures of EI that predict career success or other important educational and social criteria. The most basic task for validation research is to show that EI measures reliably differentiate between low- and high-performing groups on particular criteria. In the occupational domain, such studies should focus on predicting success both across jobs and within jobs, identifying the occupations for which EI is more and less important (e.g., social workers vs. financial analysts). The use of EI component subtests also needs to be validated using large-scale, trait-performance validation designs. It is highly plausible that effective performance in different occupations involves different patterns of emotional (or social) characteristics. The criteria against which EI predictors in occupational selection and placement are validated should be valid, reliable, and uncontaminated. The same holds for educational, clinical, and social criteria.

Questionnaire measures, in particular, may be subject to criterion contamination, as we have noted throughout this chapter. Furthermore, social desirability factors may account for part of the common variance in the predictor-outcome relationship. The impetus of proponents of EI in applied settings should be on testing the validity of EI in predicting a wide array of meaningful criteria. As a first step, it would seem important to look for the variance explained by EI with regard to conventional criteria (e.g., in the workplace: supervisor's ratings of performance, objective criteria such as absenteeism) and whether EI remains predictive with general intelligence and personality factors statistically controlled.

To What Extent Is the Predictive Validity of EI
Moderated by the Nature of the Setting?

Before employing EI measures in a particular setting, it is essential to precisely identify the specific contexts, needs, and purposes for which that EI test is being used. Without sounding trite, different jobs call for varying levels of social and emotional involvement and activity. Disparate occupations also require different types of interpersonal interaction. In some jobs (e.g., social work), one interacts emotionally with others during most of the time on the job. Inside such professions, there is a real need to have frequent interchanges with clients at an emotional level. Incumbents within these jobs need to not only talk with others face to face and exhibit positive, prosocial behavior (e.g., receptionist), but also assess the reactions of others and attempt to influence others' emotions and motives (e.g., insurance agent). Some jobs require matching one's own behavior to the needs of others (e.g., psychotherapist), creatively influencing others by engaging their emotions, and transforming one's own emotions and also those of others. In other jobs (e.g., mathematician), one interacts with people a smaller percentage of time, such that the need to be able to recognize and manipulate others' feelings is relatively unimportant, but one may need to manage personal frustrations. By the same token, EI may be effective in predicting educational outcomes in some domains (e.g., social sciences) yet not be predictive of outcomes in others (e.g., math and physical sciences).

How Do We Best Employ EI Measures in
Practical Situations?

Should EI measures be used together with other variables in the predictor stock in a multiple regression prediction equation of relevant job or educational performance criteria, or used in a noncompensatory "multiple-hurdle" framework? In this case, a sequential model is adopted for integration of multiple measures used in any test battery that assesses, in turn, job or educational-relevant abilities, performance-relevant issues, and appropriate measures of EI. Although time consuming, this process will most likely result in more accurate assessment.

To What Degree Can We Develop and Train EI?

Programs for helping managers and would-be leaders, as well as students, to become more emotionally intelligent have mushroomed in recent years. Although many of these programs are promising, few have been modeled upon EI theory or designed in a way that is likely to lead to long-term change. Furthermore, intervention programs that seek to raise EI sometimes lack a clear theoretical and methodological rationale, and employ a miscellany of techniques, whose psychological bases are not always clear (Zeidner et al., 2002).

Emotional intelligence, and the competencies linked to it, are based on temperament, learning experiences, and reflective, goal-oriented experiences. One-day seminars or workshops can be valuable in educating people and raising awareness, but they may not by themselves lead to the kind of reprogramming that is required for significant improvement (Cherniss & Adler, 2000).

Which Components of EI Are Most Malleable?

At present, it remains uncertain which of the components of EI are most malleable and responsive to training; what the threshold level of EI is for training; or what age level are EI components most responsive to instruction and training. Equally, little is known of the following key facets of training: specific goals; specific EI components most responsive to training; most effective interventions to use for low versus average EI clients; and the minimal level of EI that a client needs to benefit from therapy. There is also a need for developing standards for program implementation, as well as employing cost-benefit analysis for assessing the return for costs associated with delivering EI programs.

Key Questions

Thus far we have argued that there is some broad consensus on several issues: emergence of more guarded opinion regarding the value of EI in practical settings; modest relationships between EI and outcomes; the need for systematic approaches to match EI components to applications; and the need for proven cost-effectiveness of EI programs in applied contexts. Conversely, applied researchers differ, sometimes sharply, on issues including the following: the degree to which predictive validity of current EI measures is mediated by ability and personality measures; whether current research designs are adequate; to what extent the predictive validity of EI is moderated by nature of the setting; how we best employ EI measures in practical situations; to what degree we can develop and cultivate EI; and which components of EI are most malleable. Overall, as for both theory and measurement, there appears more controversy than consensus concerning applications.

In this volume, expert opinion informs us "what is what" and "what is not" in the applied psychology of EI. Four applied areas are addressed: work, education, mental health, and information technology; areas in which EI has evidenced its greatest surges of popularity. Contributors were asked to consider a number of core issues and relate to them in their individual chapters. Next, we address these issues, largely inspired by the literature briefly reviewed in the preceding passages.

1. *What theoretical advances are necessary to support practical applications?* A precondition for any large-scale applications of EI in applied settings is the development of well-defined theoretical frameworks and assessment tools. Arguably, one of the primary initial tasks in any scientific endeavor is the systematic mapping out of the major components and facets in the universe of discourse under consideration (Kerlinger, 1973). However, as we have seen already, it is difficult to obtain a satisfactory justification or definitional framework for the construct of EI (Zeidner et al., 2001). Clearly, in order for EI to be useful in applied settings, the theoretical foundations of

EI need to be secured first; otherwise it will remain a fuzzy and slippery construct, with little practical value. It is critical that we settle the definitional issue before proceeding to operationalize and apply the construct in real-life settings. Thus, contributors were asked to detail the theoretical advances needed before applications are designed and implemented in real-life settings.

In addition to conceptual coherence, it is important in applied, as well as basic, research that measures of EI meet the standards discussed in the assessment section of this chapter. Notably, EI need not only predict variance above and beyond ability. Thus, EI may (a) predict different criterion behaviors than those predicted by cognitive ability, or (b) reduce the negative impact of selection based on ability measures alone for specific social groups (i.e., ethnic, social class, gender). In other words, we might find that (a) it is necessary to broaden the criterion space, or (b) conduct systematic research demonstrating that EI is a less-biased measure than IQ (Matthews et al., 2002). Such issues aside, EI is only one factor, along with abilities, interests, motivation, and personality traits that encompass sets of individual difference variables that are part of a person's psychological makeup (Lowman, 1991).

2. *What are the cultural, social, and economic factors that may constrain or facilitate applications based on EI?* How EI is affected by culture remains poorly understood. A working assumption when applying EI is that intervention programs need to be congruent with the values and beliefs of the target population and setting. Mayer, Caruso et al.'s (2000) view that EI relates to population consensus provides a possible avenue for investigating cultural factors. Perhaps surprisingly, however, little systematic research appears to have investigated the cross-cultural stability of consensus weights. Indeed, we presently have little information about cultural determinants of EI test performance or about the degree of fairness of current measures for different cultural groups.

It would also seem appropriate to adopt programs to meet local organizational contexts and needs, which perforce are culturally dependent. Applications also need to be informed by cultural, social, and ethical guidelines, as well as by scientific inquiry, particularly because the work is invasive in organizational, educational, and clinical contexts. Emotion theorists (e.g., Scherer & Wallbott, 1994) have pointed out that the appraisals that govern emotional response are strongly influenced by sociocultural differences in value and belief systems. Conversely, given that basic emotions are universally expressed and recognized, facets of EI including emotion perception may be partially independent from cultural, social, and economic factors.

3. *Is there any practical advantage to focusing on EI, rather than on specific contextualized skills?* As noted, applications of EI pose both challenges and unique affordances for improving the quality of human life in the information age. However, one unsettled issue in using EI measures in applied domains is whether practitioners should use omnibus measures of EI in applications or, instead, rely on specific contextualized traits and affective skills (e.g., optimism, assertiveness, impulse control, stress management). Research has yet to demonstrate the added value of using EI measures in applied settings relative to narrower measures of individual differences.

4. *In which real-world domains will EI be most and least useful?* At present, as should be self-evident from the preceding passages, the domains that have received the most attention by EI researchers are occupational and educational settings. Increasingly, however, consideration is also being given to social and clinical applications. We asked the contributors from each domain to answer a particularly evocative question: How does knowledge of their area of specialization stack up against what is known of other domains in which EI is being applied? In the passages that follow we provide a brief introduction to the specific fields that we thought especially worth considering.

In occupational contexts, EI is viewed as being a valuable potential resource by contributing to the improved prediction of organizational outcomes, particularly when there is a clear emotional skill required for successful performance. In fact, EI has been claimed to be predictive of individual task performance, especially in settings requiring leadership, teamwork or effective communication, and contextual or tacit performance (e.g., Abraham, 2005; Daus & Ashkanasy, 2005). EI may also relate to citizenship behavior, integrity, and effective personal relationships in organizational settings.

In education, EI skills and competencies, cultivated and trained in social and emotional learning programs, are commonly believed to be able to help motivate students to reach higher levels of achievement, become more socially and emotionally competent, and to become more responsible and productive members of society. Indeed, the long-term goal of implementing EI-based programs in the schools is to help develop student populations who are emotionally intelligent, and who will eventually become responsible members of society. It is thought that elevating EI will impact both overt academic goals, such as better grades, and the student's broader personal development (Zins et al., 2004). Reviews of the evidence on programs for social-emotional learning, including those using meta-analysis to demonstrate real change in outcome criteria, support their efficacy in improving mental health, academic performance, and remediation of various behavior problems (Greenberg, Weissberg, O'Brien, & Zins, 2003).

EI may also have considerable potential for clinical applications. Assuming EI is related to disordered affect and dysfunctional affect regulation (which, in turn, is related to psychopathology), it might play an important role in clinical diagnosis and treatment (Parker, 2005). Research on alexithymia highlights how difficulties in understanding and communicating emotion may be important in affective disorders (Taylor & Bagby, 2004). However, although many mental disorders are related to emotional dysfunctions and expressions of negative affect, the diversity of these disorders may mitigate against an unambiguous relationship with low EI (Matthews et al., 2002). Among the many practical concerns in the clinical domain are developing clinically sensitive diagnostic instruments; matching clients with appropriate therapeutic interventions; monitoring clients throughout the therapeutic process; and establishing relationships between emotional competencies, on one hand, and psychopathology and treatment effectiveness, on the other hand. However, given the paucity of EI research in the clinical domain, the question arises: Is there solid research in support of a systematic relationship between low EI and distinct clinical syndromes? Furthermore, is there any solid empirical basis for the assumption that treating EI may be therapeutically effective?

EI may also have considerable potential in the area of information technology, particularly given the strong likelihood that human emotions impact on the human-computer interface. The current state of the art suggests that these artificial intelligent agents are actually reasonably poor at accurately perceiving users' emotions or at providing emotionally appropriate feedback (Picard, 1997). Yet, given major developments in artificial intelligence, it stands to reason that future technology will soon allow machines various capabilities. These include sensing and recognizing various emotions; processing possible causes and effects of these emotions; regulating consumer emotions; and displaying emotions to facilitate the human-computer interface. Thus, EI may have considerable merit for advancing information technology approaches, particularly in programming emotionally sensitive agents. Ultimately, these agents might be able to sense and interpret human emotions more reliably via different input channels (facial, voice, postural); respond empathically to human feedback (particularly negative emotions of the user that are likely to escalate); and demonstrate skills that can be used to help people develop and assess abilities that contribute to EI (e.g., Matthews, 2005; Picard & Klein, 2002). Conceivably, too, such agents might be able to provide enhancement aids for education, the workplace, and even clinical applications (see, e.g., Picard et al., 2004).

5. *Can EI be trained and, if so, how?* Past evaluations of social and emotional learning (SEL) programs (Zins et al., 2004) consistently show that these programs achieve their goals of improving peer relations, helping students make good decisions, promoting healthy student development, reducing risks for dysfunctional behavior, and improving student achievement and attachment to school (provided the programs are well designed and executed). Aside from the SEL skills, safe and nurturing environments, along with opportunities for application, are essential to support the skills taught. Also, recent research in the occupational domain suggests that EI can contribute to positive organizational and interpersonal outcomes. Thus, training in EI competencies can lead to increased organizational citizenship behavior (Murray, Jordan, & Ashkanasy, 2004). There is also evidence that low EI teams can be trained to reach the same level of outcomes as high EI teams (Jordan, Ashkanasy, Hartel, & Hooper, 2002).

A common assumption in the literature is that EI can be trained in differing real-life contexts, given that one has a minimal amount of intelligence and EI on which to base the training. Clearly, program goals and content need to be tailored to the specific context and target populations. For example, in the educational or occupational context, the goal might be to train key emotional and social competencies to support academic learning or job performance. By contrast, in some clinical populations (e.g., those with alexithymia Asperger syndrome), the goal might be to train patients with emotional dysfunction how to manage their emotive problems, rather than to make them more emotionally intelligent per se.

Despite these successes, some questions remain. Regrettably, some practitioners have been so enthusiastic about the prospects of immediately modifying EI among target populations that they have put the cart before the horse, implementing programs without securing the necessary theoretical, measurement, and methodological groundwork (Zeidner et al., 2002). Returning to our previous remarks about grain size, it is also far from clear that successful programs operate by targeting some global intelligence, as opposed to highly specific skills tied to a particular context. The lack of theoretical grounding of programs makes it difficult to judge exactly how positive results are achieved, an understanding that would help to transfer successful interventions to other contexts and problems.

Concluding Comments

We trust that the issues raised throughout this introductory chapter serve as a providing a context for the reader to appreciate the many knowns and unknowns of EI that our expert contributors were asked to grapple with. Clearly, our perspective on some of these issues may contrast with some of these experts'; resolving such discrepancies represents an important aspect of scientific discourse and advancement. In the chapters that follow, each contributor will attempt to tackle the issues posed from his or her particular perspective, armed with his or her specialized expertise in a given domain. The core areas covered, as the present chapter suggests, are theory, assessment, and applications, with approximately an equal number of experts addressing these questions in three separate sections of this edited volume. Reflecting the complex interplay between each domain, doubtless we will find some contributors crossing over and addressing key questions in another topic area, but the demarcation is nonetheless important for tackling targeted issues that we felt required answers, if ever a fully fledged science of EI was to emerge. Ensuing commentaries by the contributors will likely invite still further discussion of broad issues, which we will attempt to synthesize in a concluding chapter.

References

Abraham, R. (2005). Emotional intelligence in the workplace: A review and synthesis. In R. Schulze & R. D. Roberts (Eds.), *International handbook of emotional intelligence* (pp. 255–270). Cambridge, MA: Hogrefe & Huber.

Ackerman, P. L., & Goff, M. (1994). Typical intellectual engagement and personality: Reply to Rocklin. *Journal of Educational Psychology, 86,* 150–153.

American Educational Research Association, American Psychological Association, and National Council on Measurement in Education (1999). *Standards for educational and psychological testing.* Washington, DC: American Educational Research Association.

Austin, E. J. (2005). Emotional intelligence and emotional information processing. *Personality and Individual Differences, 39,* 403–414.

Austin, E. J., & Saklofske, D. H. (2005). Far too many intelligences? On the communalities and differences between social, practical, and emotional intelligences. In R. Schulze & R. D. Roberts (Eds.), *International handbook of emotional intelligence* (pp. 107–128). Cambridge, MA: Hogrefe & Huber.

Austin, E. J., Saklofske, D. H., Huang, S. H. S., & McKenney, D. (2004). Measurement of trait emotional intelligence: Testing and cross-validating a modified version of Schutte et al. (1998) measure. *Personality and Individual Differences, 36*, 555–562.

Barchard, K. (2003). Does emotional intelligence assist in the prediction of academic success? *Educational and Psychological Measurement, 63*, 840–858.

Bar-On, R. (1995). *EQ-i: The emotional quotient inventory manual. A test of emotional intelligence.* New York: Multi-Health Systems.

Bar-On, R. (1997). *The Emotional Intelligence Inventory (EQ-i): Technical manual.* Toronto, Canada: Multi-Health Systems.

Bar-On, R. (2000). Emotional and social intelligence: Insights from the Emotional Quotient Inventory. In R. Bar-On & J. D. A. Parker (Eds.), *The handbook of emotional intelligence* (pp. 363–388). San Francisco: Jossey-Bass.

Bar-On, R. (2001). Emotional intelligence and self-actualization. In J. Ciarrochi, J. Forgas, & J. D. Mayer (Eds.), *Emotional intelligence in everyday life: A scientific inquiry* (pp. 82–97). Philadelphia, PA: Psychology Press.

Bar-On, R. (2004). The Bar-On Emotional Quotient Inventory (EQ-i): Rationale, description and summary of psychometric properties. In G. Geher (Ed.), *Measuring emotional intelligence: Common ground and controversy* (pp. 111–142). Hauppauge, NY: Nova Science.

Barrett, L. F., Gross, J., Christensen, T. C., & Benvenuto, M. (2001). Knowing what you're feeling and knowing what to do about it: Mapping the relation between emotion differentiation and emotion regulation. *Cognition & Emotion, 15*, 713–724.

Baumeister, R. F., Campbell, J. D., Krueger, J., & Vohs, K. D. (2003). Does high self-esteem cause better performance, interpersonal success, happiness, or healthier lifestyles? *Psychological Science in the Public Interest, 4*, 1–44.

Binet, A., & Simon, T. (1983). *The development of intelligence in children.* Baltimore, MD: Williams & Wilkens. (Original work published 1916)

Bowman, D. B., Markham, P. M., & Roberts, R. D. (2002). Expanding the frontier of human cognitive abilities: So much more than (plain) *g*! *Learning and Individual Differences, 13*, 127–158.

Brackett, M. A., & Mayer, J. D. (2003). Convergent, discriminate, and incremental validity of competing measures of emotional intelligence. *Personality and Social Psychology Bulletin, 29*, 1147–1158.

Brackett, M. A., Mayer, J. D., & Warner, R. M. (2004). Emotional intelligence and its relation to everyday behaviour. *Personality and Individual Differences, 36*, 1387–1402.

Brody, N. (2004). What cognitive intelligence is and what emotional intelligence is not. *Psychological Inquiry, 15*, 234–238.

Cacioppo, J. T., Klein, D. J., Berntson, G. G., & Hatfield, E. (1993). The psychophysiology of emotion. In M. Lewis & J. M. Haviland (Eds.), *Handbook of emotions* (pp. 119–142). New York: Guilford.

Carroll, J. B. (1993). *Human cognitive abilities: A survey of factor-analytic studies.* New York: Cambridge University Press.

Caspi, A., & Bem, D. (1990). Personality continuity and change across the life course. In L. A. Pervin (Ed.), *Handbook of personality theory and research* (pp. 549–575). New York: Guilford.

Chapman, B. P., & Hayslip, B., Jr. (2006). Emotional intelligence in young and middle adulthood: Cross-sectional analysis of latent structure and means. *Psychology and Aging, 21*, 411–418.

Cherniss, C., & Adler, M. (2000). *Promoting emotional intelligence in organizations*. Alexandria, VA: American Society for Training and Development.

Chipman, S. F., Schraagen, J. M., & Shalin, V. L. (2000). Introduction to cognitive task analysis. In J. M. Schraagen, V. L. Shalin, & S. F. Chipman (Eds.), *Cognitive task analysis* (pp. 3–23). Mahwah, NJ: Erlbaum.

Ciarrochi, J., Chan, A., & Caputi, P. (2000). A critical evaluation of the emotional intelligence construct. *Personality and Individual Differences, 28*, 539–561.

Ciarrochi, J., Deane, F. P., & Anderson, S. (2002). Emotional intelligence moderates the relationship between stress and mental health. *Personality and Individual Differences, 32*, 197–209.

Cooper, R. K., & Sawaf, A. (1997). *Executive EQ: Emotional intelligence in leaders and organizations*. New York: Grosset/Putnam.

Corno, L., Cronbach, L. J., Kupermintz, H., Lohman, D., Mandinach, E. B., Porteus, A. W., et al. (2002). *Remaking the concept of aptitude: Extending the legacy of R. E. Snow*. Mahwah, NJ: Erlbaum.

Costa, P. T., Jr., & McCrae, R. R. (1994). Set like plaster: Evidence for the stability of adult personality. In T. F. Heatherton, J. L. Weinberger, et al. (Eds.), *Can personality change?* (pp. 21–40). Washington, DC: American Psychological Association.

Cronbach, L. J., & Gleser, G. (1965). *Psychological tests and personnel decisions*. Urbana: University of Illinois Press.

Danthiir, V., Wilhelm, O., Schulze, R., & Roberts, R. D. (2005). Factor structure and validity of paper-and-pencil measures of mental speed: Evidence for a higher-order model? *Intelligence, 33*, 491–514.

Daus, C. S. (2006). The case for an ability-based model of emotional intelligence. In K. R. Murphy (Ed.), *A critique of emotional intelligence: What are the problems and how can they be fixed?* (pp. 301–324). Mahwah, NJ: Erlbaum.

Daus, C. S., & Ashkanasy, N. M. (2005). The case for the ability-based model of emotional intelligence in organizational behavior. *Journal of Organizational Behavior, 26*, 453–466.

Davies, M., Stankov, L., & Roberts, R. D. (1998). Emotional intelligence: In search of an elusive construct. *Journal of Personality and Social Psychology, 75*, 989–1015.

Dawda, D., & Hart, S. D. (2000). Assessing emotional intelligence: Reliability and validity of the Bar-On Emotional Quotient Inventory (EQ-i) in university students. *Personality & Individual Differences, 28*, 797–812.

Day, A. (2004). The measurement of emotional intelligence: The good, the bad and the ugly. In G. Geher (Ed.), *Measuring emotional intelligence: Common ground and controversy* (pp. 245–270). New York: Nova Science.

Denham, S. A. (1998). *Emotional development in young children*. New York: Guilford Press.

Derksen, J., Kramer, I., & Katzko, M. (2002). Does a self-report measure for emotional intelligence assess something different than general intelligence? *Personality and Individual Differences, 32*, 37–48.

Dunning, D., Heath, C., & Suls, J. (2004). Flawed self-assessment: Implications for health, education, and the workplace. *Psychological Science in the Public Interest, 69*, 106.

Eisenberg, N., Fabes, R. A., & Losoya, S. (1997). Emotional responding: Regulation, social correlates, and socialization. In P. Salovey & D. J. Sluyter (Eds.), *Emotional development and emotional intelligence: Educational implications* (pp. 129–167). New York: Basic Books.

Ekman, P. (1972). Universals and cultural differences in facial expressions of emotion. In J. Cole (Ed.), *Nebraska symposium on motivation*, (pp. 207–282). Lincoln: University of Nebraska Press.

Embretson, S., & Reise, S. (2000). *Item response theory for psychologists*. Mahwah, NJ: Erlbaum.

Fellner, A. N., Matthews, G., Warm, J. S., Zeidner, M., & Roberts, R. D. (2006). Learning to discriminate terrorists: The effects of emotional intelligence and emotive cues. In *Proceedings of the Human Factors and Ergonomics Society 50th Annual Meeting* (pp. 1249–1253). Santa Monica, CA: Human Factors and Ergonomics Society.

Fine, S., Izard, C. E., Mostow, A., Trentacosta, C. J., & Ackerman, B. P. (2003). First grade emotion knowledge as a predictor of fifth grade self-reported internalizing behaviors in children from economically disadvantaged families. *Development and Psychopathology, 15*, 331–342.

Furnham, A., & Rawles, R. (1999). Correlations between self-estimated and psychometrically measured IQ. *Journal of Social Psychology, 139*, 405–410.

Galton, F. (1883). *Inquiries into human faculty*. London: Dent.

Gardner, H. (1983). *Frames of mind: The theory of multiple intelligences*. New York: Basic Books.

Gignac, G. E., Palmer, B. R., Manocha, R., & Stough, C. (2005). An examination of the factor structure of the Schutte self-report emotional intelligence (SSREI) scale via confirmatory factor analysis. *Personality and Individual Differences, 39*, 1029–1042.

Glymour, B. (2001). Selection, indeterminism, and evolutionary theory. *Philosophy of Science, 68*, 518–535.

Goetz, T., & Frenzel, A. C., Pekrun, R., & Hall, N. (2005). Emotional intelligence in the context of learning and achievement. In R. Schulze & R. D. Roberts (Eds.), *International handbook of emotional intelligence* (pp. 233–254). Cambridge, MA: Hogrefe & Huber.

Goleman, D. (1995). *Emotional intelligence*. New York: Bantam Books.

Goleman, D. (1998). *Working with emotional intelligence*. New York: Bantam Books.

Greenberg, M. T., Weissberg, R. P., O'Brien, M. U., & Zins, J. E. (2003). Enhancing school based prevention and youth development through coordinated social, emotional, and academic learning. *American Psychologist, 58*, 466–474.

Greenwald, A. G., McGhee, D. E., & Schwartz, J. L. K. (1998). Measuring individual differences in implicit cognition: The implicit association test. *Journal of Personality and Social Psychology, 74*, 1464–1480.

Greenwald, A. G, Nosek, B. A., & Banaji, M. R. (2003). Understanding and using the Implicit Association Test: I. An improved scoring algorithm. *Journal of Personality and Social Psychology, 85*, 197–216.

Guttman, L., & Levy, S. (1991). Two structural laws for intelligence tests. *Intelligence, 15*, 79–103.

Harpur, T. J., Hart, S. D., & Hare, R. D. (2002). Personality of the psychopath. In P. T. Costa, Jr., & T. A. Widiger (Eds.), *Personality disorders and the five-factor model of personality* (2nd ed., pp. 299–324). Washington, DC: American Psychological Association.

Harrod, N. R., & Scheer, S. D. (2005). An exploration of adolescent emotional intelligence in relation to demographic characteristics. *Adolescence, 40*, 503–512.

Hawkins, J. D., Smith, B. H., & Catalano, R. F. (2004). Social development and social and emotional learning. In J. E. Zins, R. P. Weissberg, M. C. Wang, & H. J. Walberg (Eds.),

Building academic success on social and emotional learning: What does the research say? (pp. 135–150). New York: Teachers College Press.

Herrnstein, R. J., & Murray, C. (1994). *The bell curve: Intelligence and class structure in American life.* New York: Free Press.

Holland, P. W., & Wainer, H. (Eds.) (1993). *Differential item functioning.* Hillsdale, NJ: Lawrence Erlbaum.

Horn, J. L., & Hofer, S. M. (1992). Major abilities and development in the adult period. In R. J. Sternberg & C. Berg (Eds.), *Intellectual development.* New York: Cambridge University Press.

Horn, J. L., & McArdle, J. J. (1992). A practical and theoretical guide to measurement invariance in aging research. *Experimental Aging Research, 18,* 117–144.

Izard, C. E. (1991). *The psychology of emotions.* New York: Plenum Press.

Izard, C. E. (2001). Emotional intelligence or adaptive emotions? *Emotion, 1,* 249–257.

Izard, C. E., Trentacosta, C. J., & King, K. A. (2005). Brain, emotions, and emotion-cognition relations. *Behavioral and Brain Sciences, 28,* 208–209.

James, L. R. (1998). Measurement of personality via conditional reasoning. *Organizational Research Methods, 1,* 131–163.

Jensen, A. R. (1998). *The g factor: The science of mental ability.* Westport, CT: Praeger.

Jordan, P. J., Ashkanasy, N. M., Hartel, C. E. J., & Hooper, G. S. (2002). Workgroup emotional intelligence: Scale development and relationship to team process effectiveness and goal focus. *Human Resource Management Review, 12,* 195–214.

Kerlinger, F. N. (1973). *Foundations of behavioral research* (2nd ed.). New York: Holt, Rinehart, and Winston.

Kihlstrom, J. F., & Cantor, N. (2000). Social intelligence. In R. J. Sternberg (Ed.), *Handbook of intelligence* (pp. 380–395). Cambridge, UK: Cambridge University Press.

Kolen, M. J., & Brennan, R. L. (2004). *Test equating: Methods and practices* (2nd ed.). New York: Springer-Verlag.

Landy, F. J. (2005). Some historical and scientific issues related to research on emotional intelligence. *Journal of Organizational Behavior, 26,* 411–424.

Landy, F. J. (2006). The long, frustrating and fruitless search for social intelligence: A cautionary tale. In K. R. Murphy (Ed.), *The emotional intelligence bandwagon: The struggle between science and marketing for the soul of EI* (pp. 81–123). Mahwah, NJ: Erlbaum.

Lazarus, R. S. (1999). *Stress and emotions: A new synthesis.* New York: Springer.

LeDoux, J. E. (2000). Emotion circuits in the brain. *Annual Review of Neuroscience, 23,* 155–184.

Livingstone, H. A., & Day, A. L. (2005). Comparing the construct and criterion-related validity of ability-based and mixed-model measures of emotional intelligence. *Educational and Psychological Measurement, 65,* 757–779.

Lopes, P. N., Salovey, P., & Straus, R. (2003). Emotional intelligence, personality, and the perceived quality of social relationships. *Personality and Individual Differences, 35,* 641–658.

Lowman, R. L. (1991). *The clinical practice of career assessment.* Washington, DC: American Psychological Association.

Lyons, J. B., & Schneider, T. R. (2005). The influence of emotional intelligence on performance. *Personality and Individual Differences, 39,* 693–703.

MacCann, C., Matthews, G., Zeidner, M, & Roberts, R. D. (2003). Psychological assessment of emotional intelligence: A review of self-report and performance-based testing. *The International Journal of Organizational Analysis, 11,* 247–274.

MacCann, C., Matthews, G., Zeidner, M., & Roberts, R. D. (2004). The assessment of emotional intelligence: On frameworks, fissures, and the future. In G. Geher (Ed.), *Measuring emotional intelligence: Common ground and controversy* (pp. 21–52). Hauppauge, NY: Nova Science.

MacCann, C., Roberts, R. D., Matthews, G., & Zeidner, M. (2004). Consensus scoring and empirical option weighting of performance-based emotional intelligence (EI) tests. *Personality and Individual Differences, 36,* 645–662.

Magnusson, D. (1976). The person and the situation in an interactional model of behavior. *Scandinavian Journal of Psychology, 17,* 253–271.

Matsumoto, D., LeRoux, J., Wilson-Cohn, C., Raroque, J., Kooken, K., Ekman, P., et al. (2000). A new test to measure emotion recognition ability: Matsumoto and Ekman's Japanese and Caucasian Brief Affect Recognition Test (JACBART). *Journal of Nonverbal Behavior, 24,* 179–209.

Matthews, G. (2005). The design of emotionally intelligent machines. *American Journal of Psychology, 118,* 287–322.

Matthews, G., Deary, I. J., & Whiteman, M. C. (2003). *Personality traits* (2nd ed.). Cambridge, UK: Cambridge University Press.

Matthews, G., Derryberry, D., & Siegle, G. J. (2000). Personality and emotion: Cognitive science perspectives. In S. E. Hampson (Ed.), *Advances in personality psychology* (Vol. 1, pp. 199–237). Philadelphia, PA: Psychology Press / Taylor & Francis.

Matthews, G., Emo, A. K., Funke, G., Zeidner, M., Roberts, R. D., Costa, P. T., Jr., & Schulze, R. (2006). Emotional intelligence, personality, and task-induced stress. *Journal of Experimental Psychology Applied, 12,* 96–107.

Matthews, G., Emo, A., Roberts, R. D., & Zeidner, M. (2006). What is this thing called emotional intelligence? In K. R. Murphy (Ed.), *A critique of emotional intelligence: What are the problems and how can they be fixed?* (pp. 3–6). Mahwah, NJ: Erlbaum.

Matthews, G., Roberts, R. D., & Zeidner, M. (2003). Development of emotional intelligence: A skeptical—but not dismissive—perspective. *Human Development, 46,* 109–114.

Matthews, G., Roberts, R. D., & Zeidner, M. (2004). Seven myths about emotional intelligence. *Psychological Inquiry, 15,* 179–196.

Matthews, G., & Zeidner, M. (2003). Negative appraisals of positive psychology: A mixed-valence endorsement of Lazarus. *Psychological Inquiry, 14,* 137–143.

Matthews, G., & Zeidner, M. (2004). Traits, states, and the trilogy of mind: An adaptive perspective on intellectual functioning. In D. Y. Dai & R. J. Sternberg (Eds.), *Motivation, emotion, and cognition: Integrative perspectives on intellectual functioning and development. The educational psychology series* (pp. 143–174). Mahwah, NJ: Erlbaum.

Matthews, G., Zeidner, M., & Roberts, R. D. (2002). *Emotional intelligence: Science and myth.* Cambridge: MIT Press.

Matthews, G., Zeidner, M., & Roberts, R. D. (2005). Emotional intelligence: An elusive ability. In O. Wilhelm & R. W. Engle (Eds.), *Handbook of understanding and measuring intelligence* (pp. 79–99). Thousand Oaks, CA: Sage.

Mayer, J. D., & Beltz, C. M. (1998). Socialization, society's "emotional contract," and emotional intelligence. *Psychological Inquiry, 9,* 300–303.

Mayer, J. D., Caruso, D. R., & Salovey, P. (1999). Emotional intelligence meets traditional standards for an intelligence. *Intelligence, 27,* 267–298.

Mayer, J. D., Caruso, D., & Salovey, P. (2000). Selecting a measure of emotional intelligence: The case for ability scales. In R. Bar-On & J. D. A. Parker (Eds.), *The handbook of emotional intelligence* (pp. 320–342). New York: Jossey-Bass.

Mayer, J. D., & Geher, G. (1996). Emotional intelligence and the identification of emotion. *Intelligence, 22*, 89–114.

Mayer, J. D., & Salovey, P. (1997). What is emotional intelligence? In P. Salovey & D. J. Sluyter (Eds.), *Emotional development and emotional intelligence: Educational implications.* New York: Basic Books.

Mayer, J. D., Salovey, P., & Caruso, D. R. (1999). *Instruction Manual for the MSCEIT: Mayer Salovey Caruso Emotional Intelligence Test.* Toronto: Multi-Health Systems.

Mayer, J. D., Salovey, P., & Caruso, D. R. (2000a). Emotional intelligence as *Zeitgeist,* as personality, and as a mental ability. In R. Bar-On & J. D. A. Parker (Eds.), *The handbook of emotional intelligence* (pp. 92–117). San Francisco: Jossey-Bass.

Mayer, J. D., Salovey, P., & Caruso, D. R. (2000b). Competing models of emotional intelligence. In R. J. Sternberg (Ed.), *Handbook of human intelligence* (2nd ed., pp. 396–422). New York: Cambridge University Press.

Mayer, J. D., Salovey, P., & Caruso, D. R. (2002). *Mayer–Salovey–Caruso emotional intelligence test: Manual.* Toronto, Ontario: Multi-Health Systems.

Mayer, J. D., Salovey, P., & Caruso, D. R. (2004). Emotional intelligence: Theory, findings, and implications. *Psychological Inquiry, 15*, 197–215.

Mayer, J. D., Salovey, P., Caruso, D. R., & Sitarenios, G. (2001). Emotional intelligence as a standard intelligence. *Emotion, 1*, 232–242.

McCrae, R. R. (2000). Emotional intelligence from the perspective of the five-factor model of personality. In R. Bar-On & J. D.A. Parker (Eds.), *The handbook of emotional intelligence.* (pp. 263–276). New York: Jossey-Bass.

McCrae, R. R., Costa, P. T., Pedroso de Lima, M., Simoes, A., Ostendorf, F., Angleitner, A., et al. (1999). Age differences in personality across the adult life span: Parallels in five cultures. *Developmental Psychology, 35,* 466–477.

McDaniel, M. A., Hartman, N. S., & Grubb III, W. L. (2003, April). *Situational judgment tests, knowledge, behavioral tendency, and validity: A meta-analysis.* Paper presented at the 18th Annual Conference of the Society for Industrial and Organizational Psychology, Orlando.

McDaniel, M. A., Morgeson, F. P., Finnegan, E. B., Campion, M. A., & Braverman, E. P. (2001). Use of situational judgment tests to predict job performance: A clarification of the literature. *Journal of Applied Psychology, 86,* 730–740.

McDaniel, M. A., & Nguyen, N. T. (2001). Situational judgment tests: A review of practice and constructs assessed. *International Journal of Selection and Assessment, 9,* 103–113.

Messick, S. (1988). The once and future issues of validity: Assessing the meaning and consequences of measurement. In H. Wainer & H. Braun (Eds.), *Test validity* (pp. 33–45). Hillsdale, NJ: Erlbaum.

Murphy, K. R., & Sideman, L. (2006). The fadification of emotional intelligence. In K. R. Murphy (Ed.), *A critique of emotional intelligence: What are the problems and how can they be fixed?* (pp. 283–299). Mahwah, NJ: Erlbaum.

Murray, J. P., Jordan, P. J., & Ashkanasy, N. M. (2004). *Emotional intelligence, work skills, and training.* Paper presented at the Academy of Management Meetings, New Orleans.

Neisser, U., Boodoo, G., Bouchard, T. J., Jr., Boykin, A. W., Brody, N., Ceci, S. J., Halpern, D., Loehlin, J. C., Perloff, R., Sternberg, R. J., & Urbina, S. (1996). Intelligence: Knowns and unknowns. *American Psychologist, 51*, 77–101.

Newsome, S., Day, A. L., & Catano, V. M. (2000). Assessing the predictive validity of emotional intelligence. *Personality & Individual Differences, 29*, 1005–1016.

Oatley, K. (2004). Emotional intelligence and the intelligence of emotions. *Psychological Inquiry, 15*, 216–238.

Oatley, K., & Johnson-Laird, P. N. (1996). The communicative theory of emotions: Empirical tests, mental models, and implications for social interaction. In L. L. Martin & A. Tesser (Eds.), *Striving and feeling: Interactions among goals, affect, and self-regulation* (pp. 363–393). Mahwah, NJ: Erlbaum.

Palmer, B. R., Gignac, G., Manocha, R., & Stough, C. (2005). A psychometric evaluation of the Mayer-Salovey-Caruso Emotional Intelligence Test Version 2.0. *Intelligence, 33*, 285–305.

Palmer, B. R., Manocha, R., Gignac, G., & Stough, C. (2003). Examining the factor structure of the Bar-On Emotional Quotient Inventory with an Australian general population sample. *Personality and Individual Differences, 35*, 1191–1210.

Panksepp, J. (1998). *Affective neuroscience: The foundations of human and animal emotions.* New York: Oxford University Press.

Parker, J. D. A. (2005). The relevance of emotional intelligence for clinical psychology. In R. Schulze & R. D. Roberts (Eds.), *International handbook of emotional intelligence* (pp. 271–288). Cambridge, MA: Hogrefe & Huber.

Parker, J. D. A., Taylor, R., & Bagby, M. (2001). The relationship between emotional intelligence and alexithymia. *Personality and Individual Differences, 30*, 107–115.

Petrides, K. V., & Furnham, A. (2000). Gender differences in measured and self-estimated trait emotional intelligence. *Sex Roles, 42*, 449–461.

Petrides, K. V., & Furnham, A. (2001). Trait emotional intelligence: Psychometric investigation with reference to established trait taxonomies. *European Journal of Personality, 15*, 425–448.

Petrides, K. V., & Furnham, A. (2003). Trait emotional intelligence: Behavioural validation in two studies of emotion recognition and reactivity to mood induction. *European Journal of Personality, 17*, 39–57.

Petrides, K. V., & Furnham, A. (2006). The role of trait emotional intelligence in a gender-specific model of organizational variables. *Journal of Applied Social Psychology, 36*, 552–569.

Picard, R. W. (1997). Affective computing. Cambridge, MA: MIT Press.

Picard, R. W., & Klein, J., (2002). Computers that recognize and respond to user emotion: Theoretical and practical implications. *Interacting With Computers, 14*, 141–169.

Picard, R. W., Papert, S., Bender, W., Blumberg, B., Breazel, C., Cavollo, D., et al. (2004). Affective learning: A manifesto. *BT Technology Journal, 22*, 253–269.

Ployhart, R. E., & Weekley, J. A. (2006). Situational judgment: Some suggestions for future science and practice. In J. A. Weekley & R. E. Ployhart (Eds.), *Situational judgment tests: Theory, measurement, and application.* (pp. 345–350). Mahwah, NJ: Erlbaum.

Rammstedt, B., & Rammsayer, T. (2000). Sex differences in self-estimates of different aspects of intelligence. *Personality and Individual Difference, 20*, 869–880.

Roberts, R. D., Schulze, R., Zeidner, M., & Matthews, G. (2005). Understanding, measuring, and applying emotional intelligence: What have we learned? What have we missed? In R. Schulze

& R. D. Roberts (Eds.), *International handbook of emotional intelligence* (pp. 311–341). Cambridge, MA: Hogrefe & Huber.

Roberts, R. D., Schulze, R., O'Brien, K., MacCann, C., Reid, J., & Maul, A. (2006). Exploring the validity of the Mayer-Salovey-Caruso Emotional Intelligence Test (MSCEIT) with established emotions measures. *Emotion, 6*, 663–669.

Roberts, R. D., & Stankov, L. (1999). Individual differences in speed of mental processing and human cognitive abilities: Toward a taxonomic model. *Learning and Individual Differences, 11*, 1–120.

Roberts, R. D., Zeidner, M., & Matthews, G. (2001). Does emotional intelligence meet traditional standards for an "intelligence"? Some new data and conclusions. *Emotion, 1*, 196–231.

Robins, R. W., & Paulhus, D. L. (2001). The character of self-enhancers: Implications for organizations. In B. W. Roberts & R. Hogan (Eds.), *Personality psychology in the workplace* (pp. 193–222). Washington, DC: American Psychological Association.

Rolls, E. T. (1999). *The brain and emotion.* New York: Oxford University Press.

Rothbart, M., & Bates, J. (1998). Temperament. In W. Damon (Ed.), *Handbook of child psychology: Vol. 3. Social, emotional, and personality development* (5th ed., pp. 105–176). New York: Wiley.

Saarni, C. (2000). The social context of emotional development. In M. Lewis & J. Haviland (Eds.), *The handbook of emotion* (2nd ed., pp. 306–322). New York: Guilford.

Saklofske, D. H., Austin, E. J., & Minski, P. S. (2003). Factor structure and validity of a trait emotional intelligence measure. *Personality and Individual Differences, 34*, 707–721.

Sala, F. (2002). Emotional Competence Inventory (ECI): Technical manual. Boston: Hay/Mcber Group.

Salovey, P., Stroud, L. R., Woolery, A., & Epel, E. S. (2002). Perceived emotional intelligence, stress reactivity, and symptom reports: Further explorations using the trait meta-mood scale. *Psychology and Health, 17*, 611–627.

Scherer, K. R. (2003). Cognitive components of emotion. In R. J. Davidson, K. R. Scherer, & H. H. Goldsmith (Eds.). *Handbook of affective sciences.* New York: Oxford.

Scherer, K. R., Schorr, A., & Johnstone, T. (2001). *Appraisal processes in emotion.* New York: Oxford University Press.

Scherer, K. R., & Wallbott, H. G. (1994). Evidence for universality and cultural variation of differential emotion response patterning. *Journal of Personality and Social Psychology, 66*, 310–328.

Schmukle, S. C., & Egloff, R. (2005). A latent state-trait analysis of implicit and explicit personality measures. *European Journal of Psychological Assessment, 21*, 100–107.

Schulze, R. (2005). Modeling structures of intelligence. In O. Wilhelm & R. W. Engle (Eds.), *Handbook of understanding and measuring intelligence* (pp. 241–263). Thousand Oaks, CA: Sage.

Schutte, N. S., Malouff, J. M, Hall, L. E., Haggerty, D. J., Cooper, J. T., Golden, C. J., et al. (1998). Development and validation of a measure of emotional intelligence. *Personality and Individual Differences, 25*, 167–177.

Shipman, K., & Zeman, K. (1999). Emotion understanding: A comparison of physically maltreating and nonmaltreating mother-child dyads. *Journal of Clinical Child Psychology, 28*, 407–417.

Taylor, G. J., & Bagby, R. M. (2004). New trends in alexithymia research. *Psychotherapy and Psychosomatics, 63*, 68–77.

Tett, R. P., Fox, K. E., & Wang, A. (2005). Development and validation of a self-report measure of emotional intelligence as a multidimensional trait domain. *Personality and Social Psychology Bulletin, 31,* 859–888.

Trinidad, D. R., Unger, J. B., Chou, C., Azen, S. P., & Johnson, C. A. (2004). Emotional intelligence and smoking risk factors in adolescents: Interactions on smoking intentions. *Journal of Adolescent Health, 34,* 46–55.

Van der Linden, W. J. (1996). Assembling tests for the measurement of multiple traits. *Applied Psychological Measurement, 20,* 373–388.

Van Rooy, D. L., Dilchert, S., Viswesvaran, C., & Ones, D. S. (2006). Multiplying intelligences: Are general, emotional, and practical intelligence equal? In K. R. Murphy (Ed.), *The case against emotional intelligence: What are the problems and how can they be fixed?* (pp. 235–262). Mahwah, NJ: Erlbaum.

Van Rooy, D. L., & Viswesvaran, C. (2004). Emotional intelligence: A meta-analytic investigation of predictive validity and nomological net. *Journal of Vocational Behavior, 65,* 71–95.

Van Rooy, D. L., Viswesvaran, C., & Pluta, P. (2005). An evaluation of construct validity: What is this thing called emotional intelligence? *Human Performance, 18,* 445–462.

Warwick, J., & Nettelbeck, T. (2004). Emotional intelligence is...? *Personality and Individual Differences, 37,* 1091–1100.

Watson, D., Clark, L. A., & Tellegen, A. (1988). Development and validation of brief measures of positive and negative affect: The PANAS scales. *Journal of Personality and Social Psychology, 54,* 1063–1070.

Yousefi, F. (2006). Reliability and validity of a measure of emotional intelligence in an Iranian sample. *Psychological Reports, 98,* 541–548.

Zeidner, M., Matthews, G., & Roberts, R. D. (2001). Slow down you move too fast: Emotional intelligence remains an "elusive" intelligence. *Emotions, 1,* 265–275.

Zeidner, M., Matthews G., & Roberts, R. D. (2004). Emotional intelligence in the workplace: A critical review. *Applied Psychology: An International Review, 53,* 371–399.

Zeidner, M., Matthews, G., Roberts, R. D., & MacCann, C. (2003). Development of emotional intelligence: Towards a multi-level investment model. *Human Development, 46,* 69–96.

Zeidner, M., Roberts, R. D., & Matthews, G. (2002). Can emotional intelligence be schooled? A critical review. *Educational Psychologist, 37,* 215–231.

Zeidner, M., Roberts, R. D., & Matthews, G. (2004). The emotional intelligence bandwagon: Too fast to live, too young to die? *Psychological Inquiry, 15,* 239–248.

Zeidner, M., Shani-Zinovich, I., Matthews, G., & Roberts, R. D. (2005). Assessing emotional intelligence in gifted and non-gifted high school students: Outcomes depend on the measure. *Intelligence, 33,* 369–391.

Zins, J. E., Weissberg, R. P., Wang, M. C., & Walberg, H. J. (2004). *Building academic success on social and emotional learning: What does the research say?* New York: Teachers College Press.

PART II

EMOTIONAL INTELLIGENCE

Conceptual Frameworks

2

Together Again: Emotion and Intelligence Reconciled

JAMES R. AVERILL

The split between emotion and intelligence is ancient. Throughout the ages, attempts at reconciliation have been made, but with mixed success (Averill & Sundararajan, 2006). Like lovers who are incomplete when apart, and yet in frequent conflict when together, emotions and intelligence strike many theorists as fundamentally incompatible. One attempt at reconciliation, common during the Middle Ages (e.g., Augustine, Aquinas), was to distinguish between two kinds of emotions, *affections* and *passions*. Affections referred to emotions occurring at the intellectual level of the soul, and hence were considered to be uniquely human; passions referred to emotions occurring at the sensory level, and hence were to be found in animals as well as humans. As the term *emotion* gained currency around the middle of the eighteenth century, the distinction between affections and passions became blurred, and the emotions (now identified primarily with passions) were once again divorced from the intellect (Dixon, 2003). But now they are together again, this time under the rubric of emotional intelligence (EI). One purpose of this chapter is to explore whether they have enough in common to make this latest reconciliation work.

To be more specific, I address five questions posed by the editors: (1) How should EI be conceptualized? (2) Is the concept of EI compatible with the existing theories of emotion and of cognitive intelligence? (3) What are the key components, facets, or branches of EI? (4) How is EI distinct from existing personality and ability constructs? and (5) How might EI contribute to adaptation to real-world social environments? These and other questions posed by the editors raise difficult issues. The answers to some (e.g., questions involving the meaning of *intelligence* and *emotion*) presume psychological theories that are yet to be developed. The answers to other questions (e.g., the adaptive value of EI in real-world settings) presume empirical data that are yet to be collected. These difficulties, however, also provide an opportunity: They are a license to go beyond the known, to speculate, and even to be a bit contrary with respect to accepted wisdom.

In the discussions that follow, I contrast *emotional* intelligence with *cognitive* intelligence. This contrast risks perpetuating what I believe to be a false division between emotion and cognition, but it is helpful for expository purposes. By cognitive, I mean the capacity to reason abstractly and symbolically. The qualifications—abstract and symbolic—are needed in order to distinguish cognitive intelligence from the highly specialized abilities (cognitive in a broader sense) which allow a bird, say, to migrate over great distances. Psychometrically, cognitive intelligence is represented by g, the latent variable presumed to account for the covariance among different measures of IQ.

With regard to emotional intelligence, I draw primarily on the formulations of Salovey, Mayer, and their colleagues (e.g., Mayer, Salovey, Caruso, & Sitarenios, 2001; Salovey, Mayer, & Caruso, 2002). This is for the sake of brevity and uniformity; it is not meant to slight the significant contributions of others (e.g., Bar-On, 2000). I also assume as background the work of Matthews, Zeidner, and Roberts (2002), whose constructive critiques have done much to further research and sharpen debate in this area.

How Should EI Be Conceptualized: As a Competence, a Skill, an Adaptive Outcome, a Set of Cultural Beliefs, or Some Other Construct?

The short answer to this question is "any of the above." That is also the long answer. To illustrate what I mean, let me begin at the beginning, literally. Aristotle (*de Anima*, 412a 10, in McKeon, 1941, p. 555) made a distinction between two modes of being, potentiality and actuality. Potentiality becomes one thing or another when it is actualized. Actuality may, in turn, be divided into two grades. The first grade of actuality is the ability to function in a particular manner; the second grade is the expression of that ability. For example, all normal humans have the capacity (potential) to acquire language; a person growing up in France acquires the ability (first grade of actuality) to speak French; and a Frenchman engaged in conversation is expressing that ability (second grade of actuality). As this example illustrates, for a potential to be actualized, a set of cultural beliefs and rules are required (e.g., the grammatical rules that help distinguish French from English). To express oneself clearly and effectively in conversation may require additional skills, beyond the mere ability to speak.

In psychological theory, Aristotle's threefold distinction finds expression in a variety of ways; pursuing the example of language, it corresponds roughly to the distinction between deep structure (potential), surface structure (first grade of actuality), and verbal behavior (second grade of actuality). In personality theory, an analogous distinction is commonly made between source traits (potential), surface traits (first grade of actuality), and performance (second grade of actuality). I will follow the latter terminology here.

Performance variables are of ultimate importance, for unless a trait is manifested in behavior, it can have little adaptive value. Performance is also necessary for assessment. For simplicity in this discussion, however, I will not be concerned with performance; rather,

I will focus on the distinction between source and surface traits. This distinction is central to several questions raised by the editors, for example, whether emotional intelligence is distinct from existing personality and ability constructs, and possible changes in emotional intelligence across the life span. It is therefore important to examine the distinction carefully. As we shall see, one theorist's source trait can be, without contradiction, another theorist's surface trait.

Source and Surface Traits

Advocates of emotional intelligence assume it to be a source trait, an assumption questioned by many critics. No one doubts that there are emotional klutzes in this world, people whose emotional responses always seem inept and ill-suited to the situation; and, contrariwise, there are emotional virtuosos, people who could charm the skin off a potato. The question is whether such virtuosity is a potential, the product of good genes and a favorable early environment, that some people posses more than others, or whether it is a more surface characteristic, like the ability to speak French or play tennis, that can be acquired by most anyone through training.

Three criteria help distinguish a source from a surface trait: First, like basic concepts (e.g., stool, chair, furniture), source traits are *information rich*; they are neither too specific nor too *general* (Rosch, 1978). Most theorists would agree that cognitive intelligence as measured by IQ tests meets this requirement. Although cognitive intelligence can be broken down into facets, such as verbal and spatial capacities, these are too specific to be of maximum predictive value. At the other extreme, cognitive intelligence is only one kind of talent (athletic, musical, interpersonal, etc., being others). However, to say that a person is talented is like saying that a house is furnished; for many purposes, it is too broad to be informative.

Second, source traits are relatively homogeneous or *unitary*; that is, they tend to remain relatively stable over time and place, or, if they vary, it is in a uniform and predictable fashion. Cognitive intelligence also meets this criterion: For example, a person who is intelligent at 20 should—barring accident or disease—be intelligent at 60, relative to others of a comparable age; similarly, a person who is intelligent in one situation should be intelligent in other, comparable situations. Whether emotional intelligence demonstrates such invariance is yet to be determined.

Third, a source trait should be *independent* of other source traits. Put differently, one source trait should not be replaceable by some combination of other source traits, defined at the same level of analysis. This is another point of controversy regarding emotional intelligence, that is, whether it is distinct from existing personality and ability constructs.

The above three criteria, it is important to note, are not absolute. With regard to the first, the extent to which a trait is informative depends, in part, on the purpose of the inquiry and on already available knowledge. Similarly, with regard to the second, whether a trait is treated as unitary depends, in part, on what is taken as the proper unit of analysis within a hierarchical system of traits; and, with regard to the third, all traits involve simpler cognitive and physiological processes, and in that sense are "replaceable."

Cognition and Emotion

The distinction between source and surface traits can be crossed with another hoary distinction, namely, between cognitive and noncognitive processes. To avoid confusion, I should emphasize that I am here using *cognitive* in its traditional sense, which refers to processes that lead to knowledge. Like most conditions defined by negation, *noncognitive* is a heterogeneous category, identified more by what it is not than by what it is. But whatever else it entails, *noncognitive* has traditionally been used to include motivational and emotional processes (as in the tripartite division of the mind into cognition, conation, and emotion).

Etymologically, *cognition* is related to *noble*. Both words stem from the same root, *(g)nō* meaning "to know" (see, also, *ignorance*, the antithesis of knowledge, and *ignoble*, the antithesis of noble). The implication of this etymology is that cognition involves "higher," more esteemed thought processes, those involving rationality. Noncognitive processes, by contrast, help mediate the "lower" or more primitive aspects of human nature, the emotions included. (Confusion can arise because today in psychology, *cognition* is used broadly in reference to "information processing," whether related to knowledge or not; in this extended sense, emotions are also "cognitive.")

Table 2.1 depicts the cross between cognitive and noncognitive processes, on the one hand, and source and surface traits, on the other. Consider the upper left cell in the body of Table 2.1. *Cognitive intelligence* is a source trait that IQ tests are designed to measure. The symbol *g* is typically used to designate the common factor that accounts for covariance among various measures of cognitive processes. It might be suggested that the *g* factor best represents the source trait of cognitive intelligence, and that IQ tests are more like surface traits. However, as will be discussed shortly, these suggestions are not without difficulties. For the moment, suffice it to say that with appropriate encouragement and training, cognitive intelligence may be actualized in a surface trait of the kind assessed by the more knowledge-based Scholastic Achievement Tests (SATs) (upper right cell of Table 2.1). Similar considerations apply to noncognitive processes, the bottom row of Table 2.1, examples of which might include psychomotor coordination as a source trait, and athletic achievement as a surface trait.

Many talents, as for music, art, and leadership, stand in an ambiguous relation to the cells of Table 2.1. Emotional intelligence is similarly ambiguous. As noted earlier, *emotion* traditionally has been contrasted with *cognition*, as "lower" with "higher" thought processes. This traditional conception would place emotional intelligence in the bottom row of Table 2.1. Moreover, the popularity of workshops and training sessions designed to increase emotional intelligence suggest that it is more like a surface than a source trait. For reasons such as these, emotional intelligence might be expected to fall in the bottom right cell of Table 2.1.

That, however, is not the way its advocates conceive of emotional intelligence. They intend the *intelligence* in emotional intelligence to be understood as a source trait distinct from, but comparable to, the cognitive capacities currently assessed by IQ tests. On this conception, emotional intelligence would fall in the upper left rather than the

TABLE 2.1. Examples of four types of abilities formed by the intersection of cognitive and noncognitive processes with source and surface traits.

	Source Traits	Surface Traits
Cognitive processes (abstract, symbolic)	Cognitive intelligence (g)	Scholastic achievement
Noncognitive processes (concrete, stimulus bound)	Psychomotor coordination	Athletic achievement

bottom right cell of Table 2.1. Such a placement makes the concept of emotional intelligence seem paradoxical, even oxymoronic. In large part, however, the paradox is a legacy of our traditional contrast between cognition and emotion, as well as ambiguities inherent in the distinction between source and surface traits.

Further Observations on Source and Surface Traits

I introduced this discussion with the threefold distinction dating back to Aristotle between the potential to engage in some behavior (a source trait), the actualization of that potential in the form of a specific ability (surface trait), and the expression of that ability (performance). As Aristotle made clear, these distinctions are relative: What has been actualized in one context may provide the potential for further development in another context. To return to an earlier example, knowing a language such as French may be considered a surface trait in relation to the potential (deep structure) to acquire any language; however, knowing French can be considered a source trait in relation to the ability to write poetry in that language, because writing poetry requires further actualization. Put differently, we might say that source traits, surface traits, and performance are three points along a continuum. How we divide that continuum, where we place those three points, depends to a certain extent on prior theoretical and pragmatic considerations. Thus, although we can state in general terms the criteria for distinguishing a source from a surface trait, there always remains sufficient indeterminacy for one person's source trait to be another person's surface trait.

We could also recognize more than three points along the continuum; indeed, we often do, both in ordinary language and psychological theory. For example, *skill* falls somewhere between a surface trait and performance; *adaptive outcome* extends the continuum even beyond the point of performance; and *competence* might be the term of choice when we want to be inclusive, taking into account more than one point along the continuum (cf. Saarni, 2000).

How, then, should emotional intelligence be located along the continuum: Is it a source trait, a surface trait, a skill, a kind of performance, an adaptive outcome, or a competence? I began this discussion by saying "any of the above"; I now conclude by adding "it all depends." It depends, of course, on yet-to-be-collected data that would situate emotional intelligence among other variables; as important, it depends on the purposes to which tests of emotional intelligence are to be put. From a practical standpoint, an easily administered measure of emotional intelligence, such as the Mayer-Salovey-Caruso Emotional Intelligence Test (MSCEIT; Mayer, Salovey, Caruso, & Sitarenios, 2003), might be highly useful in a variety of applied contexts, regardless of whether it is conceived as a source or surface trait, or as some other variable. If that proves to be the case, theoreticians could—and surely will—argue about what it all means. That is the way science advances.

Is the Concept of EI Compatible With the Existing Theories of Emotion and of Cognitive Intelligence?

Consider for a moment the Neanderthals (*Homo neanderthalensis*), who inhabited much of Europe and Western Asia for about 200,000 years, until becoming extinct around 30,000 years ago. By most standards, Neanderthals were highly intelligent. In absolute size, their brain (about 1450 cc on average) was slightly larger than that of modern humans (*Homo sapiens*), albeit smaller in proportion to their more robust morphology. As well as can be conjectured, Neanderthals lived in small family groups in which communication was relatively direct (Finlayson, 2004). They most likely had some form of language, but whether for biological or cultural reasons, they have left little record of symbolic activity in the form, say, of art or similar artifacts. If Neanderthals were to take an IQ test, they most likely would do poorly.[1] How, then, might we characterize their ability to survive in a harsh and demanding environment for several hundred thousand years?

Epstein (1998) distinguishes between a rational cognitive system and an experiential cognitive system. The Neanderthals presumably were amply endowed with the latter, whereas modern humans operate at both the rational and experiential levels. It is the rational system that IQ tests largely assess. Epstein further postulates that *constructive thinking*—a type of thinking mediated by the experiential system—provides the basis for emotional intelligence.

The distinction made by Epstein (1998) is intuitively plausible, and it is backed by laboratory research in which, under certain conditions, subjects may act one way (e.g., make wrong but intuitively appealing probability estimates) even while admitting that a different decision would be more rational. But why stop with two cognitive systems? There are many ways to divide the intellectual pie. Guilford (1950) introduced one particularly influential dichotomy, convergent versus divergent thinking. Convergent thinking emphasizes factual knowledge and the application of existing skills to problems that have clearly defined answers; by contrast, divergent thinking branches out in multiple directions, exposing different and often novel possibilities. Standard IQ tests, Guilford suggested, are geared toward convergent thinking; divergent thinking, on the other hand, is related to creativity.

Examples such as the above, in which thinking is dichotomized into types (rational vs. experiential, convergent vs. divergent) could easily be multiplied. For example, in social psychology it is currently fashionable to distinguish between controlled versus automatic cognitive processes, and in phenomenological psychology, between reflexive and prereflexive experience. If we made 10 such dichotomies, and they were independent, we would have 2^{10}, or 1,024, cognitive systems or ways of thinking. But clearly, all such divisions are not independent, which brings us to the notion of general intelligence and to g, the latent variable presumed to account for the covariance among different cognitive processes.

An interesting thing has happened to IQ scores over the past few decades—in industrialized countries they have increased substantially, roughly 9 points per generation (Flynn, 1987). The reasons for these increases are not understood, but they clearly are not due to any change in genetic potential. The gains are particularly marked in tests that presumably have high loadings for g, such as the Raven Progressive Matrices. This does not necessarily mean, however, that g itself has changed, that is, that people have become increasingly intelligent. All IQ tests assess elements in addition to g, and it may be those elements that have undergone change over the generations.

Sternberg (2004) suggests that scores on standard IQ tests are as much a reflection of general education, as found in most modern industrial societies, as they are a reflection of a general intellectual capacity. For example, in a study of school-age children in Kenya, Sternberg and his colleagues constructed a test of tacit knowledge of the herbal medicines used by villagers to treat common diseases. Such knowledge involves the type of abstract reasoning indicative of cognitive intelligence. Nevertheless, when children's scores on the test of folk-medical knowledge were compared with their scores on standard intelligence tests (e.g., the Raven Coloured Progressive Matrices Test), the correlation was *negative*. Sternberg's (2004) explanation for this surprising result is that "children who spend their time learning the indigenous practical knowledge of the community may not always invest heavily in doing well in school, whereas children who do well in school generally may invest themselves less heavily in learning the indigenous knowledge" (p. 330).

Findings such as those by Flynn (1987) and Sternberg (2004) suggest that intelligence as measured by IQ tests is a surface trait that changes with time and training. Intelligence as a source trait might then be defined in terms of the g factor. But the latter conception also presents difficulties.

According to Demetriou (2002), considerable agreement exists that g reflects three general functions: (1) information processing efficiency and capacity, as in working memory; (2) the management of processing resources, as in selective attention; and (3) the ordering of goals and subgoals for optimal information processing. Suppose that these functions, or others like them, do in fact account for the g factor. Would we call them "intelligence" in any ordinary sense of the term? I suspect not. To explain, let me again draw an analogy with language. The potential to acquire language depends on a set of cognitive processes (deep structure), which do not, in and of themselves, constitute a language, such as English, French, or Chinese. Similarly, the cognitive processes represented by g may facilitate intelligent behavior, but they do not, in and of themselves, constitute an intelligence.

Put differently, g processes might contribute to a variety of intelligences, depending on other talents an individual might possess and the environment in which he or she is raised. Can g processes combine with emotional processes under favorable conditions to produce an emotional intelligence? Before addressing this question, we must examine the nature of emotion.

Essentialism Rejected

In contrast to the plethora of research and debate on the nature of intelligence, the emotions were relatively neglected as objects of study during most of the twentieth century. When they did receive attention, it was either in the form of emotional "disorders" or as stripped down motivational (drive) variables. Against this backdrop, the term *emotional intelligence* accrues a surprising, even ironic connotation. During the past decade, however, psychologists have rediscovered the emotions as phenomena of interest in their own right. The result has been a plethora of books and journals devoted to emotional topics. And, on a very general level, some consensus is beginning to emerge. I will trace briefly the broad outlines of that consensus. But first, let me say a few words about the older, "standard" view of emotion.

Unnatural Emotions is the title that Catherine Lutz (1988) chose for her book on the emotional life of the Ifaluk, a people of Micronesia. According to Lutz, the emotions of the Ifaluk are fundamentally different from those typically experienced in the West. But why call them "unnatural"? The title is, of course, ironic. Within the Western tradition, it is commonly assumed that emotions are a fundamental part of human nature, and hence the same everywhere; another, even more problematic assumption is that emotions considered basic in the West are representative of emotions everywhere. On these assumptions, emotions that differ radically from Western prototypes must be, in some fashion, "unnatural."

Ethnocentrism aside, what does it mean to say that some emotions are "natural," and hence invariant across time and culture? There is both a logical and a biological answer to this question. Within logic, a *natural kind* is an object or event definable in terms of necessary and sufficient conditions. Mathematical objects are good examples of natural kinds in this sense. For a number to be classified as even, it is necessary and sufficient that the number be divisible by 2. In classical terminology, "divisible by 2" is the *essence* of even numbers—all even numbers have it, and no odd number has it. Another important feature of natural kinds is that they are everywhere the same; for example, an even number will never evolve into an odd number, no matter where.

No one is likely to confuse emotions with even numbers. Nevertheless, emotions have commonly been viewed as natural kinds, universal and unchanging, definable in terms of necessary and sufficient conditions. And what might those necessary and sufficient conditions be? In addressing this question, the logical meaning of natural kinds easily shades into a biological assumption; that is, the essence of emotion is some biologically based attribute. Exactly what that attribute might be has, of course, been a matter of dispute—a peculiar feeling or *quale*, a pattern of physiological arousal, an expressive reaction, or an affect program in the brain are a few of the suggestions that have been made. I believe all such suggestions are based on a mistaken assumption, namely, essentialism.

Both reason (e.g., Griffiths, 1997) and empirical evidence (e.g., Fehr & Russell, 1984) suggest a different conception of emotions, namely, as *syndromes* of loosely related components (thoughts, feelings, actions), no one component of which is necessary or sufficient for the whole. Such a *componential approach* to emotion is becoming common (cf. Mayne & Bonanno, 2001; Parkinson, 1995; Scherer, 2004); its implications for a construct such as emotional intelligence are, I believe, far reaching. But before getting to that, I need to explain more fully the meaning of *emotion* or, more accurately, the various meanings of emotion, for like a set of Chinese boxes, when you lift the lid on one meaning, another is found inside.

Meanings of Emotion: Syndromes, Prototypes,
Schemas, and Episodes

By definition, an emotional syndrome is an organized pattern of responses (feelings, thoughts, and actions). To say that the responses are organized implies principles of organization. For some simple emotions, such as sudden fright, the primary organizing principles may be hardwired into the nervous system. For most emotions, however, the organizing principles are mainly (but seldom exclusively) social. That is, culturally specific beliefs (implicit folk theories) provide the blueprint or *prototype* according to which otherwise disparate components are integrated into coherent wholes.

Two types of beliefs about emotions can be distinguished—existential beliefs and values. As the name implies, existential beliefs are about what exists, what *is*. An existential belief need not be true; indeed, some may be based more on myth rather than on fact. For example, when people are in love they want to be together. That is a fact. That love lasts forever, and that there is only one true love, are also commonly held existential beliefs; they are, however, based more on myth than on fact. Needless to say, myths can lend meaning and significance to experience, sometimes even more than true beliefs.

Unlike formal scientific theories, our folk theories of emotion are prescriptive as well as descriptive; that is, they concern what *should be* as well as what *is*, whether in fact or myth. Prescriptive beliefs are based on values and lead to *rules* of emotion.

It is widely recognized that emotions are regulated by rules, for example, that you should not be too exuberant in public displays of affection. However, in addition to whatever regulatory functions they might have, many rules also have constitutive (enabling) functions. This is most easily illustrated with a nonemotional example: Grammatical rules not only regulate how a person speaks a language; they help constitute the language that is spoken. Without an English grammar, for example, there would be no English language. Something similar can be said about the rules of emotion. Without the rules of anger, say, there would be no anger, but some other emotional syndrome, or, in the absence of rules entirely, only inarticulate expressions of rage or frustration. (For a detailed analysis of the rules of anger, see Averill, 1982, 1993.)

Existential beliefs and social rules provide the prototypes after which the emotions commonly recognized within a culture are patterned. When the relevant beliefs and rules are internalized during socialization, we may speak of emotional *schemas*. Given appropriate eliciting conditions (an adequate provocation in the case of anger, say, or the loss of a loved one in the case of grief) relevant schemas will be activated; the result is an emotional *state*, that is, an episodic disposition to respond in a manner consistent with the cultural prototype.

Socialization never proceeds with complete fidelity; hence, each person's emotional schemas may differ somewhat from the cultural prototype. This means that no two people will experience an emotion in exactly the same way. Your anger will not be the same as my anger, although both may conform closely enough to the cultural prototype to be called by the same name.

The above picture, although complex, is still incomplete. It is too static: Emotional episodes unfold over time, sometimes enduring for hours, days, or even months or years (as in the case of grief or love). For all but the briefest intervals, the emotional episode is constructed "online," drawing on the person's unique talents, past experiences, and current concerns, as well as on the exigencies of the situation (Parkinson, 1995). In the process, a great deal of improvisation is possible.

I have called the above picture an "emerging consensus" view of emotion. By that, I do not mean to imply that everyone would agree with it in all detail. Mayer, Salovey, and Caruso (2004), for example, would not. Nevertheless, I do not believe there is anything in this view that is incompatible with the notion of emotional intelligence.

Emotion and Intelligence: Toward a Reconciliation

Hebb (in Hebb & Thompson, 1954) observed that humans are the most emotional as well as the most intelligent of beings. This cross-species covariation between intelligence and emotion is often overlooked or even denied, in part because of our long cultural tradition of treating the emotions as "brutish," "gut" reactions that interfere with "higher" (i.e., intelligent) thought processes (Averill, 1974). But I would go even further than Hebb did: Within the human species, more intelligent people are also more prone to be emotional—at least in terms of variety and subtlety, if not intensity.

Samuel Johnson observed: "A peasant and a philosopher may be equally *satisfied*, but not equally *happy*. Happiness consists in the multiplicity of agreeable consciousness. A peasant has not capacity of having equal happiness with a philosopher" (recorded by Boswell, 1791/1906, p. 315). I don't know whether philosophers are any happier than peasants, but that is not the point. There are many ways to be happy, and to appreciate those ways requires intelligence and discernment.

Happiness is not unique in this respect. Take anger, which is on everyone's list of "basic" emotions. The prototype of anger involves retribution for a deliberate (or negligent) offense; the retribution—which may involve aggression, but often does not—should be appropriate to the offense, and its purpose should be to correct the wrong or restore equity, not simply to inflict harm (Averill, 1982). *Retribution, offense, deliberate*, and *equity* are abstract concepts that presume an implicit theory of justice. Whatever else it entails, anger is a way of holding a person responsible for a misdeed, and, when appropriately expressed, of repairing a tear in the fabric of interpersonal relations.

It might be objected that most emotions occur too rapidly ("instinctively") to be intelligent. But many intelligent responses, even the kind of sudden insights that garner Nobel Prizes, occur suddenly to the individual who is sufficiently prepared. Beyond childhood, most emotions are overlearned responses. On those rare occasions when, as an adult, an emotion is experienced for the first time (falling in love, say, or grief on the death of a parent), the person may wonder whether his feelings are "real" or "true."

In short, I do not believe that current conceptions of intelligence and emotion are incompatible. Emotions require the appraisal of potential benefits or harms, and the coordination of appropriate responses, often under conditions of stress. The g factor processes that contribute to cognitive intelligence may thus also contribute to emotional intelligence. This is a different conception of the relation between emotion and intelligence than that advanced by Mayer et al. (2004). In their view, emotions are independent objects or sources of information on which intelligence operates. According to the present view, emotional and intellectual processes are in major respects (but not in every aspect) one and the same. Or, perhaps it would be more accurate to say that concepts such as emotion and intelligence refer to molar behavior interpreted within a social context. Such molar distinctions do not necessarily imply differences in underlying processes.

What Are the Key Components, Facets, or Branches of EI?

Mayer et al. (e.g., 2001) conceive of emotional intelligence as comprising four branches, namely, the ability (1) to "perceive" or experience emotions accurately, (2) to use emotional information to facilitate thought and action, (3) to understand the meaning and significance of emotions, and (4) to manage emotions in one's self and others. These four facets make logical sense, but only empirical research will tell whether they are the best way to divide up emotional intelligence. I will limit my remarks to the relation between emotional intelligence and emotional creativity, which might be regarded as another facet of emotional intelligence, or perhaps as a separate ability with facets of its own.

The possibility for emotional creativity follows from a componential approach to emotion. It thus stems from a different theoretical tradition than does Mayer et al.'s concept of emotional intelligence (for a comparison of these two approaches, see Averill, 2004). To recapitulate briefly what I said earlier with respect to current theories of emotion, emotional syndromes consist of semi-independent components, none of which is necessary and sufficient for the whole. In addition to any biological (genetic) predispositions, emotional syndromes gain coherence through beliefs (implicit theories) about what is and what should be. But beliefs change, and rules vary, and when they do, so, too, do the corresponding emotional syndromes.

Emotionally intelligent persons presumably understand the beliefs and rules that make an emotion meaningful, and they are able to appraise a situation accurately and express their feelings adroitly. If the response conforms to the prototype, it is liable to be effective and hence "intelligent." Emotional intelligence in this sense is *convergent*; that is, the episode converges onto the cultural prototype. Two other outcomes are possible: An emotional episode can *diverge* from its prototype in ways that are either harmful or beneficial. If the response is harmful, the episode might be labeled *neurotic*; if, on the other hand, the response proves beneficial for the individual or group, even though it deviates from the norm, it might be regarded as *creative*.

Individual Differences in Emotional Creativity

Not all people are equally creative in the emotional domain—just as all people are not equally creative in artistic or scientific domains. Before a person can be creative, regardless of domain, he or she must be prepared, that is, possess relevant knowledge and expertise (Hayes, 1981; Weisberg, 1986). At first, the notion of emotional *preparedness* might seem anomalous—but only if we assume that emotions come "naturally." However, any visitor to another culture may quickly realize how difficult it is to understand, no less to experience and express, emotions indigenous to that culture.

Even within a person's own culture, individuals differ widely in their knowledge and understanding of the fine nuances of emotional experience: This was the point of Samuel Johnson's observation, cited earlier, on the relative capacities of peasants and philosophers to experience happiness. Happiness, it might be said, is like a fine wine; and just as there are connoisseurs of wine, so, too, there may be connoisseurs of happiness. The same is true of other emotions. Consider, for example, the following ways of experiencing the "grapes of wrath": aggrieved, angry, annoyed, arrogant, bilious, bitter, brooding, chagrined, contemptuous, defiant, disdainful, disgruntled, enraged, envious, fractious, fretful, incensed, indignant, irate, irked, irritated, jealous, malevolent, malicious, obstinate, outraged, peevish, perturbed, piqued, resentful, revengeful, revolted, sarcastic, scornful, spiteful, vexed, vindictive, wrathful.

It requires fine discrimination, as well as conceptual knowledge, to distinguish anger from malevolence, arrogance from scorn, chagrin from petulance, envy from jealousy, viciousness from vindictiveness, outrage from fury, to mention a few of many possible combinations. Even more difficult is to be angry while joyful, arrogant while humble, chagrined while elated, fractious while gleeful, envious while tranquil, jealous while exhilarated, outraged while mirthful. It is difficult not simply because anger and joy, say, are seemingly incompatible states. After all, we have little difficulty with such incompatibles as "sweet sorrow." The difficulty is, rather, a lack of preparedness.

Criteria for Evaluating a Response as Creative

Preparedness is necessary but not sufficient for creativity. For a response to be judged creative, it must meet some combination of three criteria: *novelty, effectiveness,* and *authenticity*. That is, the response should be in some fashion different from the norm; it should be of some value to the individual or group; and it should reflect the individual's own self or vision—what Arnheim (1966), in reference to artistic creativity, called the "pregnant sight of reality" (p. 299). Although the three criteria are easy to state, they are difficult to apply (Averill, 2005; Averill & Nunley, 1992). Take the criterion of effectiveness: What is effective in the short term may be ineffective in the long term, and vice versa; and what is effective for the individual may be ineffective for the group, and vice versa. The criteria of novelty and authenticity are similarly dependent on context.

The importance of the criteria of novelty and effectiveness are well recognized; by contrast, authenticity has received less attention. The reasons are partly cultural. The origin of an authentic response lies within the self; hence, an authentic response may also be novel, that is, idiosyncratic to the individual. In individualistic (e.g., Western) societies, therefore, the distinction between novelty and authenticity tends to get blurred. By contrast, in collectivist (e.g., East Asian) societies in which the self is more identified with the group and its traditions, authenticity and novelty may diverge as criteria for creativity (Averill, Chon, & Hahn, 2001). I will have more to say about emotional authenticity in a later section on emotional intelligence and adaptation to real-life situations.

Assessing Emotional Creativity

Based on the above considerations, a 30-item Emotional Creativity Inventory (ECI) has been constructed (Averill, 1999). Seven items assess emotional preparedness (knowledge about and interest in one's emotions); 14 items assess novelty (the tendency to experience unusual and difficult to describe emotions); and 9 items assess perceived effectiveness and authenticity. (Although logically distinct, the criteria of effectiveness and authenticity are difficult to distinguish using simple self-report items.)

The ECI has reasonable construct and discriminative validity. For example, persons who score high on the ECI are rated by their peers as emotionally more creative than others, and they are better able to express unusual emotions in stories and pictures (Averill, 1999; Averill & Thomas-Knowles, 1991; Gutbezhal & Averill, 1996). High scorers are also better able to benefit from solitude, a condition that traditionally has been associated with creative pursuits in a variety of fields (Long, Seburn, Averill, & More, 2003).

In terms of the "Big Five" personality dimensions (Costa & McCrae, 1985), the ECI is most closely related to openness to experience, but it is independent of extraversion and neuroticism, two traits closely related to positive and negative emotionality, respectively. The ECI is also modestly correlated with agreeableness (another of the Big Five), self-esteem, and antiauthoritarian attitudes (Averill, 1999).

Of particular relevance to the present discussion is the relation of emotional creativity to emotional intelligence. Conceptually, there is an obvious overlap between emotional intelligence and emotional creativity; for example, both presume an understanding of emotions (preparedness), sensitivity to one's own and others' emotions (authenticity), as well as the ability to respond appropriately (effectiveness). The major difference is the potential for novel responses in the case of emotional creativity.

Empirically, Ivcevic, Brackett, and Mayer (2007) directly compared emotional creativity and emotional intelligence, using a variety of measures including the ECI and the MSCEIT. Intercorrelations and confirmatory factor analyses suggest that emotional creativity and emotional intelligence are independent abilities, at least in terms of the measures used. Moreover, the ECI was a better predictor of creative writing and artistic activities than was the MSCEIT. This last finding is consistent with the notion that the MSCEIT is a measure of convergent rather than divergent emotional intelligence.

Needless to say, one set of studies is not sufficient to determine whether emotional creativity and emotional intelligence are independent abilities, or whether emotional creativity might best be considered another facet of emotional intelligence. A similar issue has been debated with reference to the relation between cognitive creativity and intelligence, without resolve even after decades of research (Sternberg & O'Hara, 2000).

How Is EI Distinct From Existing Personality and Ability Constructs? Could a Multistratum Psychometric Model Integrate a Dimension or Dimensions of EI With Existing Personality and Ability Constructs?

This question basically asks whether emotional intelligence is a source or surface trait. If it is a surface trait, then it can be replaced, theoretically if not practically, by some combination of other traits (see Table 2.1 presented earlier). Most advocates of emotional intelligence assume it to be a source trait; some critics question that assumption, contending that perhaps emotional intelligence can be reduced to currently existing personality and ability constructs. This is an issue that can be resolved only by further research. Implicit in the controversy, however, is another assumption that deserves brief examination, namely, that source traits can be divided neatly into two kinds: personality (temperament) and ability.

Ability is typically judged by a criterion of success; temperament, by the manner in which a response is made—its expressive aspects. Relatedly, temperamental traits are often linked to the expression of emotion: for example, extraversion, to positive emotions; and neuroticism, to negative emotions. One reason the concept of emotional intelligence seems so radical is because it transcends this traditional divide between temperament and ability traits. But the divide, I would suggest, is more apparent than real.

Like many distinctions in psychology, that between temperament and ability is relative to the context. It is a useful distinction for many purposes; however, when made in the abstract, divorced from context, conceptual confusion is liable to result. To illustrate, consider two people taking a test of cognitive ability. One person approaches the task with energy; another, with lethargy. If both are equally successful in solving problems, they would receive the same score on ability—their style or method of approach being irrelevant in that context. But change the context, and what was considered a temperamental trait may now be regarded as an ability. In the above example, for instance, energy was treated as a temperamental trait. However, if a task requires endurance, as in running a marathon, then the energetic person may be better *able* to succeed than a lethargic person. An even better example might be found in the performing arts (e.g., dance), in which style becomes an all-important criterion for success. Thus, physical gracefulness may be an important ability for a dancer, but only a stylistic trait for a mathematician. Conversely, even such a paradigmatic ability as intelligence can be regarded as a stylistic (temperamental) trait in some contexts, as when a dance critic characterizes a performance as too "intellectual" or "cerebral."

A conception of temperamental traits as abilities or capacities has both methodological and theoretical implications. Methodologically, it means that some of the procedures developed for the assessment of abilities could be fruitfully applied to the assessment of temperament. In ability tests, for example, items are made as unambiguous as possible; the test takers are made aware that some answers are correct, others not; and they are motivated to do their best. Contrast this with the typical personality tests, in which items are made ambiguous by design and test takers may be given instructions such as the following: "Work quickly. There are no right or wrong answers; your first intuitive reaction is often the best." Research by Wallace (1966) and Willerman, Turner, and Peterson (1976) suggest that if temperamental traits were assessed in a manner similar to abilities, predictive validity might actually be increased.

The studies by Wallace and Willerman et al. were conducted decades ago. One might wonder why, if the assessment of temperament as ability enhances predictive validity, so little research has been devoted to the issue. The answer is, in part, methodological (assessing temperamental traits as abilities is labor intensive), and it is, in part, substantive (in many situations, how people typically behave, successfully or not, is of more interest than their capabilities).

What relevance do these considerations have for emotional intelligence? The issue is sometimes raised whether emotional intelligence might be accounted for in terms of a "mixed model"; that is, some combination of ability and temperamental traits. But if temperamental traits can be viewed as abilities, depending on the context, then the model is less mixed than might be assumed. The issue is reduced to the simpler question of whether emotional intelligence is best conceived as a source or surface trait. That question can be answered only with further research, keeping in mind the criteria for a source trait discussed earlier.

An abilities conception of personality traits has more fundamental implications. As Mayer et al. (2000) point out, popular accounts tend to equate emotional intelligence with the more positive attributes of personality (e.g., assertiveness, sociability, empathy, self-control) included in many personality inventories. To the extent that temperamental traits are related both to emotions and abilities, it is tempting to assimilate all such traits into a single, more encompassing category, namely, emotional intelligence. Mayer et al. (2000) criticize this tendency: "The term *emotional intelligence*, when used to designate tests that are not appreciably different from general scales of personality may be more of a distraction than a clarification" (p. 105). They are certainly correct. Many talents (athletic, social, artistic) lend meaning and value to life; to label them all a kind of intelligence can only obfuscate the meaning of intelligence.

Nevertheless, we want to be careful not to throw the intellectual baby out with the temperamental bathwater. As indicated in response to an earlier question (on contemporary theories of intelligence and emotion), g processes, such as an efficient and capacious working memory, may contribute to a wide variety of abilities, not just cognitive intelligence. This does not mean, however, that all such abilities should be mushed together into one broad category of "intelligence," multiple or not. Strategically, it remains to be seen whether emotional intelligence is best recognized as a variety of intelligence in the traditional sense, or as another valuable human talent that draws on some of the same g processes. As a short-term tactical move, however, I believe the notion of emotional intelligence has had a very salutary effect, first, by focusing attention on emotional abilities rather than liabilities, and second, by helping to break down the long-standing division between emotional and intellectual (cognitive) processes.

How Might EI Contribute to Adaptation to Real-World Social Environments?

Cognitive intelligence has been related to a wide variety of outcomes, from petty criminality, on the low end of the IQ spectrum, to socioeconomic success and even physical health, on the high end, with fine gradations in between (e.g., Gottfredson, 2004). Whether emotional intelligence makes a contribution in addition to cognitive intelligence is an open question. Past research has not been particularly kind to suggestions for "multiple intelligences," such as those proposed by Gardner (1993).

When we speak of adaptation to real-world environments, however, a caveat must always be added: Adaptation to what? No trait is adaptive in and of itself, but only within a context. For example, a highly intelligent person is more likely to get away with murder (literally as well as figuratively) than is a person of limited cognitive capacity. Few people would argue that murder is adaptive. Even when intelligent actions are explicitly undertaken for the general good, they may have unintended negative consequences. Again, examples in the domain of cognitive intelligence are easy to find. The drug Thalidomide was the product of scientific research, intentionally undertaken; however, when given to pregnant women to alleviate nausea, the results were sometimes tragic (fetal deformities).

Similar considerations apply in the emotional domain. Giacomo Casanova (1725–1798), whose life spanned most of the eighteenth-century Enlightenment, was an emotional as well as an intellectual genius. He was a prolific writer, an accomplished violinist, a successful entrepreneur, and an occasional diplomat and spy. But today, he is most remembered for seducing more than a hundred women, as recounted in his memoirs (Gribble, 1984). Considering Casanova's accomplishments and chicaneries in multiple domains, I suspect he would have scored well on the MSCEIT and related tests of emotional intelligence. Were his exploits adaptive? That clearly depends on one's perspective. In his own day, he was considered by many to be a scoundrel and a knave. (He was imprisoned once, but escaped.) Today's assessment may be kinder, partly because norms are more forgiving, but largely because threat diminishes with time.

Emotions embody the values of a society: To a large extent, social norms dictate whom we should love and hate, what we should hope and fear, and when we should grieve or rejoice. Emotional exploits, such as those by Casanova, are thus more likely to be met with condemnation than praise among contemporaries concerned with upholding prevailing values (the "moral majority" of whatever age).

Even when accepted social practices are respected, emotional intelligence can have unintended negative consequences. Hochschild (1983) has coined the term *emotional labor* to describe the emotional performance expected by some organizations of their employees, as when an airline stewardess is expected to respond cheerfully even when provoked by a rude and inconsiderate passenger. Emotional labor has its costs, including psychological strain and even physical ill health, for which the employee is not compensated (see Steinberg & Figart, 1999, for a review of relevant research).

Like emotional intelligence, emotional labor involves the ability to understand and use emotions to achieve desired ends, even if those ends are in the service of others. Interestingly, however, little overlap exists between the literature on emotional intelligence and that on emotional labor. The reasons are both disciplinary and ideological. Researchers interested in emotional labor tend to be sociologists, and they often approach the topic from a neo-Marxist or feminist perspective. MacDonald and Sirianni (1996), for example, speak of the exploitation of the "emotional proletariat" (p. 3). By contrast, researchers interested in emotional intelligence tend to be psychologists, and they have focused on the potential benefits of emotional intelligence, including success on the job (e.g., Goleman, 1998).

I raise the issue of emotional labor not simply to illustrate one way in which emotional intelligence might have unintended negative consequences, but also to raise an important theoretical question. Earlier, in discussing emotional creativity as a possible facet of emotional intelligence, I noted how authenticity is an important criterion for judging a response as creative, whether the response is a work of art, a scientific discovery, or an emotion. Emotional labor also raises the issue of authenticity, but in a somewhat different fashion. When theorists talk about emotional labor, the implication is that employees can become estranged from their authentic emotions in the furtherance of corporate interests. But what makes an emotion authentic? When an airline stewardess feels contempt for a boorish passenger but nevertheless smiles and acts in a cheerful manner, the answer is clear, at least as far as her cheerfulness is concerned. But how do we know that her hidden contempt is authentic?

Assume for the moment that we are not dealing with an already socialized adult joining a business organization, as in Hochschild's (1983) analysis, but a child being born into a society. During the normal course of events, the child adopts the beliefs and rules of the society as its own, and experiences as "true" the emotions indigenous to the culture. How are we to judge *those* emotions as authentic?

Authenticity is not an inherent feature of emotion, but a judgment we make about emotions; and like other kinds of judgment, a standard of comparison is implied. As a first approximation, we judge the authenticity of an emotion by its sincerity. But sincerity alone will not suffice, as ample clinical studies attest. For example, the hypomania experienced by a depressed patient is unlikely to be confused with authentic happiness, no matter how sincerely felt at the moment. Sincerity, it might be said, is simply believing in the authenticity of one's own experience. The belief may be wrong.

Salmela (2005) outlines three standards or "problems" that must be addressed when assessing the authenticity of an emotional response. He calls these the problem of rationality, autonomy, and processuality.

The Problem of Rationality

In response to an earlier question (on the relations of EI to current concepts of intelligence and emotion), I discussed how emotional syndromes (i.e., those emotions recognized and named in ordinary language, such as love, anger, and the like) are constituted, in part, by a hierarchy of beliefs and values (rules) about what is and what should be. For an emotion to be authentic, according to Salmela (2005), these beliefs and values must withstand critical inquiry. For example, an anorexic might experience disgust at her presumed fatness. However, her beliefs about her weight are contradicted by readily available evidence; hence, her disgust is inauthentic, no matter how keenly it is experienced.

The Problem of Autonomy

Emotions help map the contours of the self. This leads to the problem of autonomy (literally, "self-rule"). Emotional authenticity presumes guiding principles that lend coherence to life, even when circumstances demand radical change. This standard, as adumbrated by Salmela (2005), can take a variety of forms. For example, an autonomous person is willing to take appropriate action, based on his emotions, even in adverse situations. Thus, the angry person should not shy away from taking corrective action, and the person in love should be willing to assist the other in time of need. More fundamentally, autonomy means that a person's beliefs and rules were adopted for reasons deemed appropriate. A person who has been brainwashed while held hostage, for example, may adopt a set of beliefs consistent with those of his captors. However, we would not normally consider the resulting emotions as authentic, nor would the person who had been held hostage, on reevaluation. (There are exceptions, of course, as in the case of religious or political conversions.)

The Problem of Processuality

Authenticity means being open to change; it is forward, not backward looking. As Salmela (2005) points out, we would find perplexing a person's claim that he has finally, once and for all, achieved authenticity. Such a condition would be more a sign of morbidity than of authenticity. The ancient Greeks had a saying: Count no man happy until he is dead. At first, this expression might seem paradoxical, for a dead person cannot be happy—or unhappy. The implication of the saying, however, has nothing to do with the possibility of emotions in an afterlife. Rather, it means simply that the authenticity of an emotion is subject to reevaluation as circumstances change, and a change in fortune is always possible before death. Most emotions are not as global in their implication as is happiness and hence are subject to more frequent reevaluation. For example, what was once considered the epitome of true love may, with hindsight, be dismissed as mere sexual infatuation. In an even shorter time frame, the events of tomorrow may make today's anger (fear, hope, etc.) seem less than genuine.

To summarize briefly, an emotion is authentic when it is realistically based, consistent with a person's fundamental beliefs and values, and open to change as circumstances change. I emphasize these points because without authenticity, emotional intelligence may degenerate into glib sentimentality. More specifically, emotional authenticity is relevant to each of the four branches of emotional intelligence postulated by Mayer et al., namely, the ability to (1) experience emotions accurately, (2) use emotions to facilitate thought and action, (3) understand the meaning of emotions, and (4) manage emotions in one's self and others. Authenticity is also central to emotional creativity, which, as discussed in response to an earlier question, can be considered another facet of emotional intelligence, if not an independent dimension. Finally, emotional authenticity has implications for adaptation to many real-life situations, in which the regulation of emotions is of prime importance (as in emotional labor).

Concluding Observations

People differ in how adroit they are emotionally: Some people have a captivating sense of humor; others make an art of misery; and just as there are Don Juans of love, there are Cyrano de Bergeracs of anger. It is questionable whether one ability—emotional intelligence, by whatever name—underlies such diverse talents. But assuming that such an ability exists, we must ask whether it is a source or surface trait. From a practical point of view, this may be a difference that makes no difference. Of the thousands of traits recognized in ordinary language (roughly 18,000 in English, according to a count by Allport & Odbert, 1936), only a tiny fraction refer to source traits. Clearly, surface traits provide useful guides to understanding and predicting behavior in everyday contexts. From a theoretical perspective, however, the distinction between source and surface traits is of prime importance; for example, it is primarily with reference to source traits that we investigate underlying mechanisms and trace changes over time (e.g., the life span), place (e.g., across cultures), and even generations (e.g., heritability).

Even if we assume that emotional intelligence is a source trait, we still want to ask why it is an *intelligence* as opposed to some other kind of ability. The answer to this question requires more than a standard of achievement. The ability to do 100 push-ups is an achievement. To count as an intelligence requires the demonstration that cognitive functions—such as the g processes that help account for other forms of intelligence—are also involved, intrinsically and not just contingently. For reasons discussed earlier, I believe such an argument can be made, at least provisionally.

Yet, even after a century of research, the concept of intelligence remains ambiguous. Still greater ambiguity exists with respect to the concept of emotion. This is an area in which ample data lie scattered about, but with little agreed-upon theory by which to integrate them. Particularly vexing from an ability point of view is the setting of standards by which to assess emotional achievement, standards that, on the social level, recognize well-documented cultural differences in emotions, and, on the individual level, do not preclude the possibility of emotional innovation and change (divergent emotionality).

To address issues such as those posed by the editors of this volume, psychometrically adequate measures of emotional intelligence are required; at the same time, the development of such measures depends on the further development of theory. This kind of bootstrapping, in which theory drives measurement and measurement drives theory, each constrained by an expanding body of empirical data, is common in science. Remarkably, in little over a decade and a half, considerable progress has been made in clarifying the problems and promises of the EI concept.

At present, there is a faddishness about emotional intelligence that derives, in part, from an understandable desire to spread psychological wealth more equitably: that the person who is poor at words and numbers may yet succeed emotionally. But behind the fad lie phenomena of undeniable importance. We may thus hope that this latest reconciliation of emotion and intelligence will not end soon, but will be fecund in its theoretical and practical offspring.

Notes

1. This statement about Neanderthal intelligence is disputable. According to Deacon (1997), the Neanderthals were as intelligent and linguistically capable as anatomically modern humans. The demise of the Neanderthals, Deacon speculates, was due to a lack of immunity, not to a lack of intelligence. Living in small, isolated groups, Neanderthals were susceptible to diseases brought by modern humans migrating into Neanderthal territory, much as American Indians were susceptible to diseases brought by Europeans. The present argument does not depend, however, on the Neanderthals; the same point could be made by going back to any of the now-extinct hominid species before the development of language.

References

Allport, G. W., & Odbert, H. S. (1936). Trait-names: A psycho-lexical study. *Psychological Monographs, 47* (1, Whole No. 211).

Arnheim, R. (1966). *Toward a psychology of art.* Berkeley: University of California Press.

Averill, J. R. (1974). An analysis of psychophysiological symbolism and its influence on theories of emotion. *Journal for the Theory of Social Behavior, 4,* 147–190.

Averill, J. R. (1982). *Anger and aggression: An essay on emotion.* New York: Springer-Verlag.

Averill, J. R. (1993). Illusions of anger. In R. B. Felson & J. T. Tedeschi (Eds.), *Aggression and violence: Social interactionist perspectives* (pp. 171–192). Washington, DC: American Psychological Association.

Averill, J. R. (1999). Individual differences in emotional creativity: Structure and correlates. *Journal of Personality, 67,* 331–371.

Averill, J. R. (2004). A tale of two snarks: Emotional intelligence and emotional creativity compared. *Psychological Inquiry, 15*, 228–233.

Averill, J. R. (2005). Emotions as mediators and as products of creative activity. In J. Kaufman & J. Baer (Eds.), *Creativity across domains: Faces of the muse* (pp. 225–243). Mahwah, NJ: Erlbaum.

Averill, J. R., Chon, K. K., & Haan, D. W. (2001). Emotions and creativity, East and West. *Asian Journal of Social Psychology, 4*, 165–183.

Averill, J. R., & Nunley, E. P. (1992). *Voyages of the heart: Living an emotionally creative life.* New York: The Free Press.

Averill, J. R., & Sundararajan, L. (2006). Passion and *qing*: Intellectual histories of emotion, West and East. In K. Pawlik & G. d'Ydwalle (Eds.), *Psychological concepts: An international historical perspective* (pp. 101–139). Hove, England: Psychology Press.

Averill, J. R., & Thomas-Knowles, C. (1991). Emotional creativity. In K. T. Strongman (Ed.), *International review of studies on emotion* (Vol. 1, pp. 269–299). London: Wiley.

Bar-On, R. (2000). Emotional and social intelligence: Insights from the Emotional Quotient Inventory. In R. Bar-On & J. D. A. Parker (Eds.), *Handbook of emotional intelligence* (pp. 363–388). San Francisco, CA: Jossey-Bass.

Boswell, J. (1906). *The life of Samuel Johnson* (2 Vols.). New York: Dutton. (Original work published 1791)

Costa, P. T., Jr., & McCrae, R. R. (1985). *The NEO Personality Inventory manual.* Odessa, FL: Psychological Assessment Resources.

Deacon, T. W. (1997). *The symbolic species: The co-evolution of language and the brain.* New York: Norton.

Demetriou, A. (2002). Tracing psychology's invisible giant and its visible guards. In R. J. Sternberg & E. L. Grigorenko (Eds.), *The general factor of intelligence: How general is it?* (pp. 3–18). Mahwah, NJ: Erlbaum.

Dixon, T. (2003). *From passions to emotions: The creation of a secular psychological category.* Cambridge, England: Cambridge University Press.

Epstein, S. (1998). *Constructive thinking: The key to emotional intelligence.* Westport, CT: Praeger.

Fehr, B., & Russell, J. A. (1984). Concept of emotion viewed from a prototype perspective. *Journal of Experimental Psychology: General, 113*, 464–486.

Finlayson, C. (2004). *Neanderthals and modern humans.* Cambridge, UK: Cambridge University Press.

Flynn, J. R. (1987). Massive IQ gains in 14 nations: What IQ tests really measure. *Psychological Bulletin, 101*, 171–191.

Gardner, H. (1993). *Frames of mind: The theory of multiple intelligences* (10th anniversary ed.). New York: Basic Books.

Goleman, D. (1998). *Working with emotional intelligence.* New York: Bantam Books.

Gottfredson, L. S. (2004). Intelligence: Is it the epidemiologists' elusive "fundamental cause" of social class inequalities in health? *Journal of Personality and Social Psychology, 86*, 174–199.

Gribble, G. D. (Ed.) (1984). *The life and memoirs of Casanova* (A. Machen, Trans.). New York: Da Capo Press.

Griffiths, P. (1997). *What emotions really are: The problem of psychological categories.* Chicago, IL: University of Chicago Press.

Guilford, J. P. (1950). Creativity. *American Psychologist, 5*, 444–454.

Gutbezahl, J., & Averill, J. R. (1996). Individual differences in emotional creativity as manifested in words and pictures. *Creativity Research Journal, 9*, 327–337.

Hayes, J. R. (1981). *The complete problem solver.* Philadelphia: Franklin Institute Press.

Hebb, D. O., & Thompson, W. R. (1954). The social significance of animal studies. In G. Lindzey (Ed.), *Handbook of social psychology* (Vol. 1, pp. 532–561). Cambridge, MA: Addison-Wesley.

Hochschild, A. R. (1983). *The managed heart.* Berkeley: University of California Press.

Ivcevic, Z., Brackett, M. A., & Mayer, J. D. (2007). Emotional intelligence and emotional creativity. *Journal of Personality, 75*, 199–235.

Long, C. R., Seburn, M., Averill, J. R., & More, T. A. (2003). Solitude experiences: Varieties, settings, and individual differences. *Personality and Social Psychology Bulletin, 29*, 578–583.

Lutz, C. A. (1988). *Unnatural emotions: Everyday sentiments on a Micronesian atoll and their challenge to Western theory.* Chicago: University of Chicago Press.

MacDonald, C. L., & Sirianni, C. (1996). The service society and the changing experience of work. In C. L. Macdonald & C. Sirianni (Eds.), *Working in the service society* (pp. 1–26). Philadelphia: Temple University Press.

Matthews, G., Zeidner, M., & Roberts, R. D. (2002). *Emotional intelligence: Science and myth.* Boston, MA: MIT Press.

Mayer, J. D., Salovey, P., & Caruso, D. R. (2000). Emotional intelligence as Zeitgeist, as personality, and as a mental ability. In R. Bar-On & J. D. A. Parker (Eds.), *Handbook of emotional intelligence* (pp. 92–117). San Francisco, CA: Jossey-Bass.

Mayer, J. D., Salovey, P., & Caruso, D. R. (2004). A further consideration of the issues of emotional intelligence. *Psychological Inquiry, 15*, 249–255.

Mayer, J. D., Salovey, P., Caruso, D. R., & Sitarenios, G. (2001). Emotional intelligence as a standard intelligence. *Emotion, 1*, 232–242.

Mayer, J. D., Salovey, P., Caruso, D. R., & Sitarenios, G. (2003). Measuring emotional intelligence with the MSCEIT V2.0. *Emotion, 3*, 97–105.

Mayne, T. J., & Bonanno, G. (Eds.). (2001). *Emotions: Current issues and future directions.* New York: Guilford.

McKeon, R. (Ed.). (1941). *The basic works of Aristotle.* New York: Random House.

Parkinson, B. (1995). *Ideas and realities of emotion.* London: Routledge.

Rosch, E. (1978). Principles of categorization. In E. Rosch & B. B. Lloyd (Eds.), *Cognition and categorization* (pp. 27–48). Hillsdale, NJ: Erlbaum.

Saarni, C. (2000). Emotional competence: A developmental perspective. In R. Bar-On & J. D. A. Parker (Eds.), *Handbook of emotional intelligence* (pp. 68–91). San Francisco: Jossey-Bass.

Salmela, M. (2005). What is emotional authenticity? *Journal for the Theory of Social Behavior, 35*, 219–240.

Salovey, P., Mayer, J. D., & Caruso, D. R. (2002). The positive psychology of emotional intelligence. In C. R. Snyder & S. J. Lopez (Eds.), *The handbook of positive psychology* (pp. 159–171). New York: Oxford University Press.

Scherer, K. R. (2004). Feelings integrate the central representation of appraisal driven response organization in emotion. In A. S. R. Manstead, N. H. Frijda, & A. H. Fischer (Eds.), *Feelings and emotions: The Amsterdam symposium* (pp. 136–157). Cambridge: Cambridge University Press.

Steinberg, R. J., & Figart, D. M. (Eds.) (1999). Emotional labor in the service economy [Special issue]. *The Annals of the American Academy of Political and Social Science, 561*(1).

Sternberg, R. J. (2004). Culture and intelligence. *American Psychologist, 59,* 325–338.

Sternberg, R. J., & O'Hara, L. A. (2000). Intelligence and creativity. In R. J. Sternberg (Ed.), *Handbook of intelligence* (pp. 611–630). New York: Cambridge University Press.

Wallace, J. (1966). An abilities conception of personality: Some implications for personality measurement. *American Psychologist, 21,* 132–138.

Weisberg, R. W. (1986). *Creativity: Genius and other myths.* New York: Freeman.

Willerman, L., Turner, R. G., & Peterson, M. (1976). A comparison of the predictive validity of typical and maximal personality measures. *Journal of Research in Personality, 10,* 482–492.

3

A Neurobiological Approach to Emotional Intelligence

EDMUND T. ROLLS

Emotions may be defined as states elicited by reinforcers (rewards and punishers). This approach helps with understanding the functions of emotion, classifying different emotions, and understanding *what* information processing systems in the brain are involved in emotion and *how* they are involved (Rolls, 2005, 2008). The theory is summarized that brains are designed around reward and punishment evaluation systems, because this is the way that genes can build a complex system that will produce appropriate but flexible behavior to increase their fitness. By specifying goals rather than particular behavioral patterns of responses, genes leave much more open the possible behavioral strategies that might be required to increase their fitness.

This approach leads to a framework for understanding brain systems involved in emotion, including how primary (unlearned) reinforcers are decoded; how associations are learned from previously neutral stimuli to primary reinforcers, and rapidly reversed; and how actions are learned to obtain the goals. This approach also leads to a framework for understanding emotional intelligence, in that the evolution of each of the gene-specified reinforcers (which are independent), and the systems that learn about stimulus-reinforcer associations and action-outcome associations, are likely to be independent in part of general cognition and intelligence. By focusing on the core capacities that are fundamental to emotion, it is possible to identify a set of competencies and processes that might be thought of as a basis for emotional intelligence.

In this chapter I first outline this neurobiological approach to emotion, discussing the theory of emotion, the functions of emotion, an evolutionary approach to emotion and brain design, and implicit versus explicit routes to action. This provides the basis for an approach to emotional intelligence, in which emotional competencies are emphasized as providing ways in which emotion-related processing can be different from that involved in general intelligence. We might characterize this as an emotional competencies approach to emotional intelligence.

A Theory of Emotion, and Some Definitions

What are emotions? Why do we have emotions? What are the rules by which emotion operates? What are the brain mechanisms of emotion, and how can disorders of emotion be understood? What motivates us to work for particular rewards such as food when we are hungry, or water when we are thirsty? How do these motivational control systems operate to ensure that we eat approximately the correct amount of food to maintain our body weight or to replenish our thirst? What factors account for the overeating and obesity that some humans show? Why is the brain built to have reward, and punishment, systems, rather than in some other way?

Emotions can usefully be defined as states elicited by rewards and punishers, including changes in rewards and punishers (Rolls, 1990, 1999, 2005). A reward is anything for which an animal will work. A punisher is anything that an animal will work to escape or avoid. An example of an emotion might thus be happiness produced by being given a reward, such as a pleasant touch, praise, or winning a large sum of money. Another example of an emotion might be fear produced by the sound of a rapidly approaching bus, or the sight of an angry expression on someone's face. We will work to avoid such stimuli. Another example would be frustration, anger, or sadness produced by the omission of an expected reward such as a prize, or the termination of a reward such as the death of a loved one. Another example would be relief produced by the omission or termination of a punisher such as the removal of a painful stimulus, or sailing out of danger.

These examples indicate how emotions can be produced by the delivery, omission, or termination of rewards or punishers, and go some way to indicate how different emotions could be produced and classified in terms of the rewards and punishers received, omitted, or terminated. A diagram summarizing some of the emotions associated with the delivery of a reward or punisher or a stimulus associated with them, or with the omission of a reward or punisher, is shown in Figure 3.1. It should be understood that this diagram summarizes the states that could be produced by manipulation of the reinforcement contingencies for any one reinforcer. The brain is built to have a large set of different primary reinforcers, and the reinforcer space is in this sense high dimensional.

Before accepting this approach, we should consider whether there are any exceptions to the proposed rule. Are any emotions caused by stimuli, events, or remembered events that are not rewarding or punishing? Do any rewarding or punishing stimuli not cause emotions? We will consider these questions in more detail below. The point is that if there are no major exceptions, or if any exceptions can be clearly encapsulated, then we may have a good working definition at least of what causes emotions, and this leads to principled ways for eliciting and studying emotion.

I next consider a slightly more formal definition than rewards or punishers in which the concept of reinforcers is introduced, and show how there has been a considerable history in the development of ideas along this line.

The proposal that emotions can be usefully seen as states produced by instrumental reinforcing stimuli follows earlier work by Weiskrantz (1968), Gray (1975, 1987), and

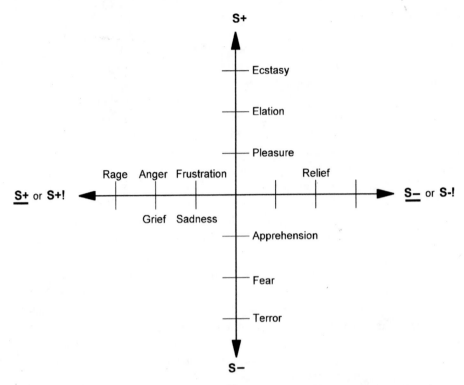

Figure 3.1. Some of the emotions associated with different reinforcement contingencies are indicated. Intensity increases away from the center of the diagram, on a continuous scale. The classification scheme created by the different reinforcement contingencies consists with respect to the action of (1) the delivery presentation of a reward (S+), (2) the presentation of a punisher (S–), (3) the omission of a reward (S+) (extinction) or the termination of a reward (S+!) (time out), and (4) the omission of a punisher (S–) (avoidance) or the termination of a punisher (S–!) (escape).

Rolls (1986a, 1986b, 1990).[1] My argument is that an affectively positive or "appetitive" stimulus (which produces a state of pleasure) acts operationally as a *reward*, which instrumentally when delivered acts as a positive reinforcer, or when not delivered (omitted or terminated) acts to decrease the probability of responses on which it is contingent. Conversely, I argue that an affectively negative or aversive stimulus (which produces an unpleasant state) acts operationally as a *punisher*, which instrumentally when delivered acts to decrease the probability of responses on which it is contingent, or when not delivered (escaped from or avoided) acts as a negative reinforcer.

The link between emotion and instrumental reinforcers being made is partly an operational link. Most people find that it is not easy to think of exceptions to the statements that emotions occur after rewards or punishers are given (sometimes continuing for long after the eliciting stimulus has ended, as in a mood state); or that rewards and punishers, but not other stimuli, produce emotional states. But the link is deeper than this, as we will see, in that the theory has been developed that genes specify primary reinforcers in order to encourage the animal to perform arbitrary actions to seek particular goals, thus increasing the probability of their own (the genes') survival into the next generation (Rolls, 2005). The emotional states elicited by the reinforcers have a number of functions, described below, related to these processes.

This foundation has been developed (Rolls, 1990, 1999, 2005) to show how a very wide range of emotions can be accounted for, as a result of the operation of a number of factors, including the following, all of which can be manipulated to influence the elicitation of emotion:

1. The *reinforcement contingency* (e.g., whether reward or punishment is given or withheld; see Figure 3.1).
2. The *intensity* of the reinforcer (see Figure 3.1).
3. Any environmental stimulus might have a *number of different reinforcement associations*. (For example, a stimulus might be associated both with the presentation of a reward and of a punisher, allowing states such as conflict and guilt to arise.)
4. Emotions elicited by stimuli associated with *different primary reinforcers* will be different.
5. Emotions elicited by *different secondary reinforcing stimuli* will be different from each other (even if the primary reinforcer is similar). For example, if two different people were each associated with the same primary reinforcer, then the emotions would be different. This is in line with my hypothesis that emotions consist of states elicited by reinforcers, and that these states include whatever representations are needed for the eliciting stimulus, which could be cognitive, and the resulting mood change. Moods then may continue in the absence of the eliciting stimulus, or can be produced, as in depression, sometimes in the absence of an eliciting stimulus, perhaps due to dysregulation in the system that normally enables moods to be long lasting.
6. The emotion elicited can depend on whether an *active or passive behavioral response* is possible. (For example, if an active behavioral response can occur to the omission of a positive reinforcer, then anger—a state that tends to lead to action—might be produced, but if only passive behavior is possible; then sadness, depression or grief might occur.)

By combining these six factors, it is possible to account for, and also elicit, a very wide range of emotions (Rolls, 2005). Some examples follow. Fear is a state that might be produced by a stimulus that has become a secondary reinforcer by virtue of its learned association with a primary negative reinforcer such as pain (see Figure 3.1). Anger is a state that might be produced by the omission of an expected reward, frustrative nonreward, when an active behavioral response is possible (see Figure 3.1). (In particular, anger may occur if another individual prevents an expected reward from being obtained.) Guilt may arise when there is a conflict between an available reward and a rule or law of society.

Jealousy is an emotion that might be aroused in a male if the faithfulness of his partner seems to be threatened by her liaison (e.g., flirting) with another male. In this case the reinforcement contingency that is operating is produced by a punisher, and it may be that males are specified genetically to find this punishing because it indicates a potential threat to their paternity and paternal investment (Rolls, 2005). Similarly, a female may become jealous if her partner has a liaison with another female, because the resources available to the "wife" useful to bring up her children are threatened. Again, the punisher here may be gene specified (Rolls, 2005). Envy or disappointment might be produced if a prize is obtained by a competitor. In this case, part of the way in which the frustrative nonreward is produced is by the cognitive understanding that this is a competition in which there will be a winner, and that the person has set himself or herself the goal of obtaining it. The partial list of primary reinforcers, shown in Table 3.1, should provide a foundation for starting to understand the rich classification scheme for different types of emotion that can be classified in this way.

TABLE 3.1. Some primary reinforcers, and the dimensions of the environment to which they are tuned.

Taste	
Salt taste	+ reinforcer in salt deficiency
Sweet	+ reinforcer in energy deficiency
Bitter	– reinforcer, indicator of possible poison
Sour	– reinforcer
Umami	+ reinforcer; indicator of protein; produced by monosodium glutamate and inosine monophosphate; see Rolls et al., 1996b
Tannic acid	– reinforcer; prevents absorption of protein; found in old leaves; probably somatosensory rather than strictly gustatory; see Critchley and Rolls, 1996c
Odor	
Putrefying odor	– reinforcer; hazard to health
Pheromones	+ reinforcer (depending on hormonal state)
Somatosensory	
Pain	– reinforcer
Touch	+ reinforcer
Grooming	+ reinforcer; to give grooming may also be a primary reinforcer
Washing	+ reinforcer
Temperature	+ reinforcer if tends to help maintain normal body temperature; otherwise –
Visual	
Snakes, etc.	– reinforcer for, e.g., primates
Youthfulness	+ reinforcer; associated with mate choice
Beauty	+ reinforcer
Secondary sexual characteristics	+ reinforcers
Face expression	+ (e.g., smile) and – (e.g., threat) reinforcer
Blue sky, cover, open space	+ reinforcer; indicator of safety
Flowers	+ reinforcer (indicator of fruit later in the season?)

TABLE **3.1.** (continued)

Auditory

Warning call	– reinforcer
Aggressive vocalization	– reinforcer
Soothing vocalization	+ reinforcer (part of the evolutionary history of music, which at least in its origins taps into the channels used for the communication of emotions)

Reproduction

Courtship	+ reinforcer
Sexual behavior	+ reinforcer (a number of different reinforcers, including a low waist-to-hip ratio, and attractiveness influenced by symmetry and being found attractive by members of the other sex; discussed in Chapter 8)
Mate guarding	+ reinforcer for a male to protect his parental investment; jealousy results if his mate is courted by another male, because this may ruin his parental investment
Nest building	+ reinforcer (when expecting young)
Parental attachment	+ reinforcer
Infant attachment to parents	+ reinforcer
Infant crying	– reinforcer to parents; produced to promote successful development

Other

Novel stimuli	+ reinforcers; encourage animals to investigate the full possibilities of the multidimensional space in which their genes are operating
Sleep	+ reinforcer; minimizes nutritional requirements and protects from danger
Altruism to genetically related individuals (kin altruism)	+ reinforcer
Altruism to other individuals (reciprocal altruism)	+ reinforcer when the altruism is reciprocated in a "tit-for-tat" reciprocation; – reinforcer when the altruism is not reciprocated
Group acceptance	+ reinforcer (social greeting might indicate this)
Control over actions	+ reinforcer
Play	+ reinforcer
Danger, stimulation, excitement	+ reinforcer if not too extreme (adaptive because practice?)
Exercise	+ reinforcer (keeps the body fit for action)
Mind reading	+ reinforcer; practice in reading others' minds, which might be adaptive
Solving an intellectual problem	+ reinforcer (practice that might be adaptive)
Storing, collecting	+ reinforcer (e.g., food)
Habitat preference, home, territory	+ reinforcer
Some responses	+ reinforcer (e.g., pecking in chickens, pigeons; adaptive because it is a simple way in which eating grain can be programmed for a relatively fixed type of environmental stimulus)
Breathing	+ reinforcer

Many other similar examples can be surmised from the area of evolutionary psychology (Barratt, Dunbar, & Lycett, 2002; Buss, 1999; Ridley, 1993). For example, there may be a set of reinforcers that are genetically specified to help promote social cooperation and even reciprocal altruism. Such genes might specify that emotion should be elicited, and behavioral changes should occur, if a cooperating partner defects or "cheats." Moreover, the genes may build brains with genetically specified rules that are useful heuristics for social cooperation, such as acting with a strategy of "generous tit-for-tat," which can be more adaptive than strict "tit-for-tat," in that being generous occasionally is a good strategy to help promote further cooperation that has failed when both partners defect in a strict "tit-for-tat" scenario (Ridley, 1993). Genes that specify good heuristics to promote social cooperation may thus underlie such complex emotional states as feeling forgiving. As in the other reinforcers specified by genes, genetic variation may lead to differences among individuals.

It is also worth noting that emotions can be elicited by the recall of reinforcing events as well as by external reinforcing stimuli; that cognitive processing (whether conscious or not) is important in many emotions, for very complex cognitive processing may be required to determine whether or not environmental events are reinforcing. Indeed, emotions normally consist of cognitive processing, which analyses the stimulus and then determines its reinforcing valence; and then an elicited mood change if the valence is positive or negative. In that an emotion is produced by a stimulus, philosophers say that emotions have an object in the world, and that emotional states are intentional, in that they are about something. We note that a mood or affective state may occur in the absence of an external stimulus, as in some types of depression, but that normally the mood or affective state is produced by an external stimulus, with the whole process of stimulus representation, evaluation in terms of reward or punishment, and the resulting mood or affect being referred to as emotion.

An external stimulus may be perceived consciously, but stimuli that are not perceived consciously may also produce emotion. Indeed, there may be separate routes to action for conscious and unconscious stimuli (Rolls, 2005). Further, emotional states (i.e., those elicited by reinforcers) have many functions (as described in the next section), and the implementations of only some of these functions by the brain are associated with emotional feelings, that is, with conscious emotional states (Rolls, 2005). There is, for example, evidence for interesting dissociations in some patients with brain damage between actions performed to reinforcing stimuli and what is subjectively reported. In this sense it is biologically and psychologically useful to consider emotional states to include more than those states associated with conscious feelings of emotion (Rolls, 2005).

The Functions of Emotion

The functions of emotion provide insight into the evolution of emotion and lead to the view that particular types of neural processing and brain systems may have evolved for emotion, and thus that some factors involved in what might be termed emotional intelligence may be separable from some processes involved in other types of cognition and intelligence. These functions, described more fully elsewhere (Rolls, 2005), can be summarized as follows:

1. The *elicitation of autonomic responses* (e.g., a change in heart rate) *and endocrine responses* (e.g., the release of adrenaline).
2. *Flexibility of behavioral responses to reinforcing stimuli.* This is a crucial function of emotion in my evolutionary theory of why emotion is so important. Emotional (and motivational) states allow a simple interface between sensory inputs and action systems. The essence of this idea is that goals for behavior are specified by reward and punishment evaluation, and the innate goals are specified by genes. When an environmental stimulus has been decoded as a primary reward or punishment, or (after previous stimulus-reinforcer association learning) a secondary rewarding or punishing stimulus, then it becomes a goal for action. The animal can then perform any action (instrumental response) to obtain the reward, or to avoid the punisher. The instrumental action or "operant" is arbitrary, and could consist of a left turn, or a right turn, to obtain the goal.

   It is in this sense that by specifying goals and not particular actions, the genes are specifying flexible routes to action. This is in contrast to specifying a reflex response, and is also in contrast to stimulus-response, or habit, learning in which a particular response to a particular stimulus is learned. It also contrasts with the elicitation of species-typical behavioral responses by sign-releasing stimuli (such as pecking at a spot on the beak of the parent herring gull in order to be fed [Tinbergen, 1951], in which there is inflexibility of the stimulus and the response, and which can be seen as a very limited type of brain solution to the elicitation of behavior). The emotional route to action is flexible not only because any action can be performed to obtain the reward or avoid the punishment, but also because the animal can learn in as little as one trial that a reward or punishment is associated with a particular stimulus, in what is termed "stimulus-reinforcer association learning." It is because goals are specified by the genes, and not actions, that evolution has achieved a powerful way for genes to influence behavior without having to rather inflexibly specify particular responses.

   An example of a goal might be a sweet taste when hunger is present. We know that particular genes specify the sweet taste receptors, and other genes must specify that only when there is a homeostatic need state for food that the sweet taste is rewarding (Rolls, 2005). Different goals or rewards, including social rewards, are specified by different genes, and each type of reward must not dominate the others if it is to succeed in the phenotype that carries the genes.

   All of these gene-specified reinforcers are primary reinforcers. A preliminary list of these, which is subject to extension and revision, but which is intended to convey the types of stimuli that may be primary reinforcers, was shown in Table 3.1. Each of these genes may be thought of as specifying a different type of emotional competence. To the extent that genes evolve independently, in competition, I thus argue that not only are there many partly independent emotional competencies, but also that they are likely to be partly independent of other types of cognitive processing and general intelligence. Thus the specialized genes for emotion, and the partly specialized brain systems such as the amygdala and orbitofrontal cortex that process the reinforcement-related information as specified by these genes, provide an "emotional competencies" approach to emotional intelligence that separates it in part from other cognitive functions and general intelligence.

Selecting between available rewards with their associated costs, and avoiding punishers with their associated costs, is a process that can take place both implicitly (unconsciously), and explicitly using a language system to enable long-term plans to be made and corrected (Rolls, 2005). These many different brain systems, some involving implicit evaluation of rewards, and others explicit, verbal, conscious, evaluation of rewards and planned long-term goals, must all enter into the selection systems for behavior (see Figure 3.2). These selector or decision systems are poorly understood, but might include a process of competition between all the competing calls on output, and might involve structures such as the cingulate cortex and basal ganglia in the brain, which receive from structures such as the orbitofrontal cortex and amygdala, which compute the rewards (see Figure 3.2 and Rolls, 2005). The decision-making process itself may involve biased competition, with the biasing inputs representing the rewards with their associated costs (Deco & Rolls, 2006).

3. Emotion is *motivating*, as just described. For example, fear learned by stimulus-reinforcement association provides the motivation for actions performed to avoid noxious stimuli. Genes that specify goals for action, for example, rewards, must as an intrinsic property make the animal motivated to obtain the reward, otherwise it would not be a reward. Thus no separate explanation of motivation is required.

4. *Communication*. Monkeys, for example, may communicate their emotional state to others by making an open-mouth threat to indicate the extent to which they are willing to compete for resources, and this may influence the behavior of other animals. This aspect of emotion was emphasized by Darwin (1872), and has been studied more recently by Ekman (1982, 1992). Ekman reviews evidence that humans can categorize facial expressions into the categories happy, sad, fearful, angry, surprised and disgusted, and that this categorization may operate similarly in different cultures. He also describes how the facial muscles produce different expressions. Many different types of gene-specified reward have been suggested by Rolls (2005; see Table 3.1), and include not only genes for kin altruism, but also genes to facilitate social interactions that may be to the advantage of those competent to cooperate, as in reciprocal altruism.

5. *Social bonding*. Examples of this are the emotions associated with the attachment of the parents to their young, and the attachment of the young to their

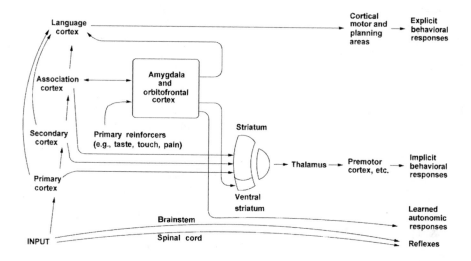

Figure 3.2. Dual routes to the initiation of action in response to rewarding and punishing stimuli. The inputs from different sensory systems to brain structures such as the orbitofrontal cortex and amygdala allow these brain structures to evaluate the reward- or punishment-related value of incoming stimuli, or of remembered stimuli. The different sensory inputs enable evaluations within the orbitofrontal cortex and amygdala based mainly on the primary (unlearned) reinforcement value for taste, touch, and olfactory stimuli, and on the secondary (learned) reinforcement value for visual and auditory stimuli. In the case of vision, the "association cortex," which outputs representations of objects to the amygdala and orbitofrontal cortex, is the inferior temporal visual cortex. One route for the outputs from these evaluative brain structures is via projections directly to structures such as the basal ganglia (including the striatum and ventral striatum) to enable implicit, direct behavioral responses based on the reward- or punishment-related evaluation of the stimuli to be made. The second route is via the language systems of the brain, which allow explicit (verbalizable) decisions involving multistep syntactic planning to be implemented.

parents. The attachment of the parents to each other is also beneficial in species such as many birds, and humans, in which the offspring are more likely to survive if both parents are involved in the care (Rolls, 2005).

6. *The current mood state can affect the cognitive evaluation of events or memories* (Oatley & Jenkins, 1996). This may facilitate continuity in the interpretation of the reinforcing value of events in the environment. A hypothesis that back-projections from parts of the brain involved in emotion such as the orbitofrontal cortex and amygdala to higher perceptual and cognitive cortical areas implement this is described in *Emotion Explained* (Rolls, 2005), and is developed in a formal model of interacting attractor (short-term memory) networks (Rolls & Stringer, 2001). In this model, the weak back-projections from the "mood" attractor can, because of associative connections formed when the perceptual

and mood states were originally present, influence the states into which the perceptual or memory attractor falls.

7. Emotion may facilitate the *storage of memories*. One way this occurs is that episodic memory (i.e., one's memory of particular episodes) is facilitated by emotional states. This may be advantageous in that storing many details of the prevailing situation when a strong reinforcer is delivered may be useful in generating appropriate behavior in situations with some similarities in the future. This function may be implemented by the relatively nonspecific projecting systems to the cerebral cortex and hippocampus, including the cholinergic pathways in the basal forebrain and medial septum, and the ascending noradrenergic pathways (Rolls, 2005). A second way in which emotion may affect the storage of memories is that the current emotional state may be stored with episodic memories, providing a mechanism for the current emotional state to affect which memories are recalled. A third way that emotion may affect the storage of memories is by guiding the cerebral cortex in the representations of the world that are set up. For example, in the visual system it may be useful for perceptual representations or analyzers to be built that are different from each other if they are associated with different reinforcers, and for these to be less likely to be built if they have no association with reinforcement. Rolls and Treves (1998) and Rolls and Deco (2002) discuss ways in which back-projections from parts of the brain important in emotion (such as the amygdala) to parts of the cerebral cortex could perform this function.

8. Another function of emotion is that by enduring for minutes or longer after a reinforcing stimulus has occurred, it may help to produce *persistent and continuing motivation and direction of behavior* to help achieve a goal or goals.

9. Emotion may trigger the *recall of memories* stored in neocortical representations. Amygdala back-projections to the cortex could perform this for emotion in a way analogous to that in which the hippocampus could implement the retrieval in the neocortex of recent (episodic) memories (Rolls & Stringer, 2001; Rolls & Treves, 1998). This is one way in which the memories recalled can be biased by mood states.

Reward, Punishment, and Emotion in Brain Design: An Evolutionary Approach

The implication of this approach to emotion and its evolution (Rolls, 2005) is that operation by animals using reward and punishment systems tuned to dimensions of the environment that increase fitness provides a mode of operation that can work in organisms that evolve by natural selection. It is clearly a natural outcome of Darwinian evolution to operate using reward and punishment systems tuned to fitness-related dimensions of the environment, if arbitrary responses are to be made by the animals, rather than just preprogrammed movements such as taxes and reflexes. Is there any alternative to such a reward/punishment based system in this evolution by natural selection situation? It is not clear that there is, if the genes are efficiently to control behavior by specifying the goals for actions. The argument is that genes can specify actions that will increase their fitness if they specify the goals for action. It would be very difficult for them in general to specify in advance the particular responses to be made to each of a myriad of different stimuli. This may be why we are built to work for rewards, avoid punishers, and to have emotions and needs (motivational states). This view of brain design in terms of reward and punishment systems built by genes that gain their adaptive value by being tuned to a goal for action (Rolls, 2005) offers, I believe, a deep insight into how natural selection has shaped many brain systems, and is a fascinating outcome of Darwinian thought. It also shows how these reinforcer-processing systems could be used to define brain processing for different types of emotional competencies, and how these competencies could be different from other types of cognitive processing and general intelligence.

Dual Routes to Action

It is suggested (Rolls, 1999, 2005) that there are two types of route to action performed in relation to reward or punishment in humans. Examples of such actions include emotional and motivational behavior.

The first (implicit) route is via the brain systems that have been present in nonhuman primates such as monkeys, and to some extent in other mammals, for millions of years. These systems include the amygdala and, particularly well developed in primates, the orbitofrontal cortex. These systems control behavior in relation to previous associations of stimuli with reinforcement. The computation that controls the action thus involves assessment of the reinforcement-related value of a stimulus.

This assessment may be based on a number of different factors. One is the previous reinforcement history, which involves stimulus-reinforcement association learning using the amygdala, and its rapid updating especially in primates using the orbitofrontal cortex. This stimulus-reinforcement association learning may involve quite specific information about a stimulus, for example, of the energy associated with each type of food, by the process of conditioned appetite and satiety. A second is the current motivational state, for example, whether hunger is present, whether other needs are satisfied, and so forth.

A third factor that affects the computed reward value of the stimulus is whether that reward has been received recently. If it has been received recently but in small quantity, this may increase the reward value of the stimulus. This is known as incentive motivation or the "salted nut" phenomenon. The adaptive value of such a process is that this positive feedback of reward value in the early stages of working for a particular reward tends to lock the organism onto behavior being performed for that reward. This means that animals that are, for example, almost equally hungry and thirsty will show hysteresis in their choice of action, rather than continually switching from eating to drinking and back with each mouthful of water or food. This introduction of hysteresis into the reward evaluation system makes action selection a much more efficient process in a natural environment, for constantly switching between different types of behavior would be very costly if all the different rewards were not available in the same place at the same time. (For example, walking half a mile between a site where water was available and a site where food was available after every mouthful would be very inefficient.) The amygdala is one structure that may be involved in this increase in the reward value of stimuli early on in a series of presentations, in that lesions of the amygdala (in rats) abolish the expression of this reward-incrementing process, which is normally evident in the increasing rate of working for a food reward early on in a meal, and amygdala lesions do impair the hysteresis normally built in to the food-water switching mechanism (Rolls, 2005).

A fourth factor is the computed absolute value of the reward or punishment expected or being obtained from a stimulus, for example, the sweetness of the stimulus (set by evolution so that sweet stimuli will tend to be rewarding, because they are generally associated with energy sources), or the pleasantness of touch (set by evolution to be pleasant according to the extent to which it brings animals together [e.g., for sexual reproduction, for maternal behavior, and for grooming], and depending on the investment in time that the partner is willing to put into making the touch pleasurable, a sign that indicates the commitment and value for the partner of the relationship). After the reward value of the stimulus has been assessed in these ways, behavior is then initiated based on approach toward or withdrawal from the stimulus. A critical aspect of the behavior produced by this type of system is that it is aimed directly toward obtaining a sensed or expected reward, by virtue of connections to brain systems such as the basal ganglia, which are concerned with the initiation of actions (see Figure 3.2). The expectation may of course involve behavior to obtain stimuli associated with reward, which might even be present in a chain. This expectation is built by stimulus-reinforcement association learning in the amygdala and orbitofrontal cortex, reversed by learning in the orbitofrontal cortex, from where signals may reach the dopamine system (Rolls, 2005).

Now part of the way in which the behavior is controlled with this first (implicit) route is according to the reward value of the outcome. At the same time, the animal may only work for the reward if the cost is not too high. Indeed, in the field of behavioral ecology, animals are often thought of as performing optimally on some cost-benefit curve (see, e.g., Krebs & Kacelnik, 1991). This does not at all mean that the animal thinks about the rewards and performs a cost-benefit analysis using a lot of thoughts about the costs, other rewards available and their costs, and so forth. Instead, it should be taken to mean that in evolution, the system has evolved in such a way that the manner in which the reward varies with the different energy densities or amounts of food and the delay before it is received, can be used as part of the input to a mechanism that has also been built to track the costs of obtaining the food (e.g., energy loss in obtaining it, risk of predation), and to then select given many such types of reward and the associated cost, the current behavior that provides the most "net reward." Part of the value of having the computation expressed in this reward-minus-cost form is that there is then a suitable "currency," or net reward value, to enable the animal to select the behavior with currently the most net reward gain (or minimal aversive outcome).

The second (explicit) route in humans involves a computation with many "if... then" statements, to implement a plan to obtain a reward. In this case, the reward may actually be *deferred* as part of the plan, which might involve working first to obtain one reward, and only then to work for a second more highly valued reward, if this was thought to be overall an optimal strategy in terms of resource usage (e.g., time). In this case, syntax is required, because the many symbols (e.g., names of people) that are part of the plan must be correctly linked or bound. Such linking might be of the form: "if A does this, then B is likely to do this, and this will cause C to do this..." The requirement of syntax for this type of planning implies that an output to language systems that at least can implement syntax in the brain is required for this type of planning (Rolls, 2004b; see Figure 3.2). Thus the explicit language system in humans may allow working for deferred rewards by enabling use of a one-off, individual, plan appropriate for each situation. Another building block for such planning operations in the brain may be the type of short-term memory in which the prefrontal cortex is involved. This short-term memory may be, for example, in nonhuman primates of where in space a response has just been made. A development of this type of short-term response memory system in humans to enable multiple short-term memories to be held in place correctly, preferably with the temporal order of the different items in the short-term memory coded correctly, may be another building block for the multiple step "if... then" type of computation in order to form a multiple step plan. Such short-term memories are implemented in the (dorsolateral and inferior convexity) prefrontal cortex of nonhuman primates and humans and may be part of the reason prefrontal cortex damage impairs planning and the selection of action (Deco & Rolls, 2005a; Goldman-Rakic, 1996; Rolls & Deco, 2002; Rolls, 2008).

Of these two routes (see Figure 3.2), it is the second, involving syntax and higher order thoughts, that I have suggested above is related to consciousness (Rolls, 2004b, 2005). This second route, with multistep plans, and thoughts about thoughts, may be related to some aspects of general intelligence, and to the extent that this second route can be used for both emotional and nonemotional processing, this aspect of emotional intelligence and general intelligence may be difficult to separate. This type of ability may underlie what contributes to emotional understanding in the sense in which it is used in the context of emotional intelligence (Mayer, Salovey, Caruso, & Sitarenios, 2001).

The question then arises of how decisions are made in animals such as humans, who have both the implicit, direct reward-based, and the explicit, rational, planning systems (see Figure 3.2). One particular situation in which the first, implicit, system may be especially important is when rapid reactions to stimuli with reward or punishment value must be made, for then the direct connections from structures such as the orbitofrontal cortex to the basal ganglia may allow rapid actions. Another is when there may be too many factors to be taken into account easily by the explicit, rational, planning system, when the implicit system may be used to guide action. In contrast, when the implicit system continually makes errors, it would then be beneficial for the organism to switch from automatic, direct action based on obtaining what the orbitofrontal cortex system decodes as being the most positively reinforcing choice currently available, to the explicit conscious control system that can evaluate with its long-term planning algorithms what action should be performed next. Indeed, it would be adaptive for the explicit system to regularly be assessing performance by the more automatic system, and to switch itself in to control behavior quite frequently, as otherwise the adaptive value of having the explicit system would be less than optimal.

Another factor that may influence the balance between control by the implicit and explicit systems is the presence of pharmacological agents such as alcohol, which may alter the balance toward control by the implicit system, allow the implicit system to influence more the explanations made by the explicit system, and within the explicit system alter the relative value it places on caution and restraint versus commitment to a risky action or plan.

There may also be a flow of influence from the explicit, verbal system to the implicit system, in that the explicit system may decide on a plan of action or strategy and exert an influence on the implicit system that will alter the reinforcement evaluations made by and the signals produced by the implicit system. An example of this might be that if a pregnant woman feels that she would like to escape a cruel mate, but is aware that she may not survive in the jungle, then it would be adaptive if the explicit system could suppress some aspects of her implicit behavior toward her mate, so that she does not give signals that she is displeased with her situation.

Another example might be that the explicit system might, because of its long-term plans, influence the implicit system to increase its response to a positive reinforcer. One way in which the explicit system might influence the implicit system is by setting up the conditions in which, when a given stimulus (e.g., person) is present, positive reinforcers are given to facilitate stimulus-reinforcement association learning by the implicit system of the person receiving the positive reinforcers. Conversely, the implicit system may influence the explicit system, for example, by highlighting certain stimuli in the environment that are currently associated with reward to guide the attention of the explicit system to such stimuli.

However, it may be expected that there is often a conflict between these systems, in that the first, implicit, system is able to guide behavior particularly to obtain the greatest immediate reinforcement, whereas the explicit system can potentially enable immediate rewards to be deferred, and longer term, multistep plans to be formed. This type of conflict will occur in animals with a syntactic planning ability (as described above) that is in humans and any other animals that have the ability to process a series of "if...then" stages of planning. This is a property of the human language system, and the extent to which it is a property of nonhuman primates is not yet fully clear. In any case, such conflict may be an important aspect of the operation of at least the human mind, because it is so essential for humans to correctly decide, at every moment, whether to invest in a relationship or a group that may offer long-term benefits, or whether to directly pursue immediate benefits.

A Neurobiological Approach to Emotional Intelligence

Within the framework described above, we now consider whether during evolution special neurobiological systems have been shaped to implement the types of processing involved in emotion. To the extent that they are special and independent of some other brain systems involved in other types of computation, we might have a new approach to understanding how competencies that might underlie emotional intelligence might be separate from other types of intelligence. In the approach described here, *emotional intelligence* would be defined in terms of the special competencies elucidated within the above framework that provide the reinforcer-related processing capacities involved in emotion. These competencies might involve, for example, the ability to respond to a small change of facial expression, and to adjust one's social and emotional behavior accordingly (Kringelbach & Rolls, 2003; Rolls, 2005). A new approach to understanding and even defining emotional intelligence may be particularly useful in view of the evidence that it is difficult to separate current concepts of emotional intelligence (Goleman, 1996; Mayer et al., 2001) from other types of intelligence including general intelligence, and from other constructs (Matthews et al., 2002, 2004).

The concept in the literature of emotional intelligence envisages four processes (Matthews et al., 2002, 2004; Mayer et al., 2001). The first is *emotion perception*. To the extent that this is perception of emotion in others, what I describe in this chapter and elsewhere (Rolls, 2005) related to decoding primary reinforcers such as facial expression and performing stimulus-reinforcer association learning and reversal based on, for example a facial expression associated with subsequent reinforcers, is relevant.

The second is *emotion understanding*. To the extent that this involves emotions produced by external stimuli or events, what I describe in this chapter and elsewhere (Rolls, 2005) about decoding primary reinforcers and stimulus-reinforcer learning is fundamental. These processes correspond in part to primary appraisal in appraisal theory and involve assessing the rewards and punishers that are present (Oatley & Jenkins, 1996). To the extent that emotion understanding might involve thoughts about emotions, this would be part of the higher order syntactic thought system described above under dual routes to action.

The third process is *emotion assimilation*, which involves incorporating one's current emotional circumstances into one's mental life, and this would also seem to involve higher order thoughts and planning for future actions given the emotional context.

The fourth process involves *emotion regulation*, and this could cover a whole host of processes, from autonomic responses through instrumental actions to obtain goals using action-outcome learning, to multistep action planning requiring syntax, and benefiting from higher order thoughts in order to correct the plans. The fourth process, and to some extent the third, may correspond in part to secondary appraisal in appraisal theory. In the next subsections, I describe some of the functions that are involved in emotion when a neurobiological perspective is taken (Rolls, 2005) and show how these functions lead to a new approach to emotional intelligence.

Decoding Primary Reinforcers

A crucial aspect of emotion according to Rolls' theory of emotion (Rolls, 2005) is the ability to respond to primary (unlearned) reinforcers and to treat these as goals for action. There are many emotional competencies of this type. To respond to primary reinforcers, the brain builds special systems that represent different types of reinforcers in terms of their reinforcement value, and this is what I mean by decoding reinforcers.

The concept can be made clear by considering sweet taste. The reward or reinforcing value of the sweet taste is independent of the quality or intensity of the taste, in that the reward value can decrease to zero after eating sucrose to satiety, yet it still tastes as sweet as before feeding to satiety (Rolls, Rolls, & Rowe, 1983). The intensity of the taste is represented in the primary taste cortex in the anterior insula, and the reward value or pleasantness in the secondary taste cortex in the orbitofrontal cortex (Rolls, 2005). Sensory-specific satiety, the process by which the reward value of a particular stimulus consumed to satiety or received for a period in the order of a number of minutes, may decrease relative to other stimuli but independently of the perceived intensity of the stimulus appears to be a general property of reward systems that has the important adaptive function of promoting a variety of goals (Rolls, 2005).

These points, and much other evidence, show that the reward value of different primary reinforcers must be regulated independently (Rolls, 2005). This occurs both on the short timescale of minutes, but also in evolutionary time in the sense that different genes determine which stimuli in the environment are primary reinforcers, and the genes can be seen as promoting their own fitness independently of each other by (selfish) competition (Dawkins, 1986, 1989), but also to some extent by cooperating, in that no one reinforcement system must become so rewarding that it always wins the competition against the other reward systems, as this would be highly maladaptive (Rolls, 2005).

Given that there are specialized systems for decoding primary reinforcers, and that they are genetically, functionally, and in terms of their neural implementation, partly separate, this provides one basis for different processing relevant to emotions to be separable from other types of processing, such as spatial navigation and spatial ability. This is one sense in which some aspects of "emotional intelligence" by virtue of these emotional competencies could be different from other types of intelligence.

Some of the types of primary reinforcers that are relevant were depicted earlier in Table 3.1. They include homeostatically relevant primary reinforcers such as food when hungry, and water when thirsty. They also include specialized perceptual systems for decoding facial expression, which is an important signal in the regulation of emotion and emotional behavior. The systems involved include specialized temporal lobe visual cortical areas with neuronal responses to facial expressions but not facial identity (Hasselmo, Rolls, & Baylis, 1989; Rolls, 2007b), and orbitofrontal cortex regions with selective responses to faces (Rolls, Critchley, Browning, & Inoue, 2006), which if damaged lead to difficulties in recognizing facial (and/or vocal) expressions (Hornak et al., 2003).

The primary reinforcers will also include systems relevant to identifying kin (based perhaps on sensory cues and also on learning) that will be important in kin altruism, and there could be gene-based differences in the extent to which individuals invest in their kin and show family attachment, which could make a contribution to differences in emotional intelligence. They will also include systems relevant to reciprocal altruism, such as being sensitive to whether a particular individual is cooperating or defecting. There appear to be specialized systems important in risk taking and sensation seeking (Zuckerman, 1994; Zuckerman & Kuhlman, 2000), promiscuity (Hamer & Copeland, 1998), and impulsiveness with an implementation in the orbitofrontal cortex (Berlin, Rolls, & Iversen, 2005; Berlin, Rolls, & Kischka, 2004). There may also be more general systems related to personality that reflect sensitivity to punishers including nonreward versus rewards (Gray, 1979, 1987; Matthews & Gilliland, 1999; Matthews et al., 2002).

Concepts of emotional intelligence (Goleman, 1996; Mayer et al., 2001) tend to focus on social reinforcers, but these are just part of the range of reinforcers that contribute to defining emotion and affect (Rolls, 2005).

Learning and Reversing Associations to Primary Reinforcers

Given the importance of rewards and punishers in emotion, the learning of associations from previously neutral stimuli to primary reinforcers is the type of learning that is fundamental in emotion, and that is another type of emotional competency. It is also very important that such associations can be rapidly and flexibly reversed. For example, in social interactions, even a short change in a facial expression may indicate that a change of behavior to the person is appropriate. The processes that underlie this type of associative learning, which is stimulus-stimulus (in that the primary reinforcer is a stimulus), are therefore of considerable interest as emotional competencies and are also of clinical relevance.

It appears that different brain systems, especially the amygdala and orbitofrontal cortex, make different types of contribution to this learning with, as described next, the amygdala playing a special role in learning these associations, and the orbitofrontal cortex in rapidly reversing them. Given that these are systems that are at least partially separate and have evolved differently, with the amygdala present in fish and reptiles, and the orbitofrontal cortex appearing in mammals but developing greatly in primates including humans, it is possible that genetic variation can occur to some extent independently for these systems. This, it is suggested, could lead individuals to differ in their emotional learning and in their ability to respond rapidly to changes in reinforcement contingency, and it is therefore suggested that these could be part of a new neurobiologically based approach to emotional intelligence.

Given the anatomical connections shown in Figure 3.3, there would not seem to be the basis in the high order visual cortical areas, such as the inferior temporal visual cortex, for associations between visual stimuli and primary reinforcers to be learned, in that taste and somatosensory stimuli do not reach these cortical areas. This has been directly demonstrated, in that when the reward that is normally obtained if the monkey

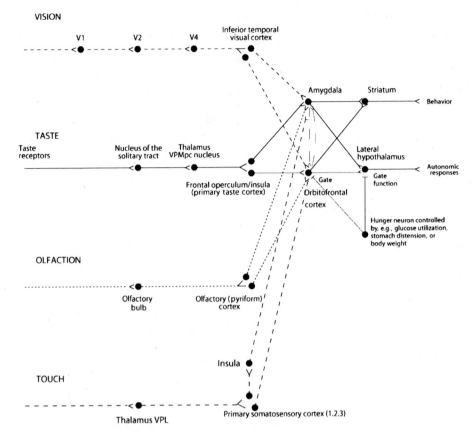

Figure 3.3. Schematic diagram showing some of the gustatory, olfactory, visual, and somatosensory pathways to the orbitofrontal cortex and amygdala, and some of the outputs of the orbitofrontal cortex and amygdala. The secondary taste cortex, and the secondary olfactory cortex, are within the orbitofrontal cortex. V1 = primary visual cortex; V4 = visual cortical area V4.

licks to a visual stimulus is altered in a visual discrimination task so that after reversal the monkey would obtain aversive salt if he licked, there is no alteration of the responses of inferior temporal cortex neurons, which continue to fire to the physical stimulus to which they respond, independently of its affective significance (Rolls, Aggelopoulos, & Zheng, 2003; Rolls, Judge, & Sanghera, 1977).

In contrast, some neurons in the macaque orbitofrontal cortex learn in as little as one trial to respond to a visual stimulus associated with a taste reward, and can reverse this response when the reinforcement contingencies are reversed (Rolls, Critchley, Mason, & Wakeman, 1996; Thorpe, Rolls, & Maddison, 1983). These neurons reflect the reward (or affective) value of the visual stimulus, in that they stop responding to the visual stimulus gradually as the monkey is fed to satiety (Critchley & Rolls, 1996). Also consistent with this, lesions of the macaque orbitofrontal cortex impair stimulus-reward reversal learning and extinction (see Rolls, 2005), and deficits in this type of learning are also found in humans after orbitofrontal cortex lesions (Hornak et al., 2004; Rolls, Hornak, Wade, & McGrath 1994).

In humans, activation of the orbitofrontal cortex can reflect quite abstract rewards (which in the end may be associated with primary reinforcers), such as monetary reward (medially) and loss (laterally; O'Doherty, Kringelbach, Rolls, Hornak, & Andrews, 2001). A probabilistic presentation of the magnitude of reward was used in this investigation, and a complementary investigation with the same task in patients with lesions of the orbitofrontal cortex (Hornak et al., 2004), so that the magnitude of the brain activation could be correlated in a single-event fMRI design with the amount of monetary reward or loss on each trial, and to minimize the use of verbal strategies and encourage the use of implicit associative emotional learning processes.

The special role of the orbitofrontal cortex in rapid reversal of stimulus-reinforcement associations is expressed also in the presence in the orbitofrontal cortex of neurons that respond when an expected reward is not obtained (Thorpe et al., 1983), and these can be called reward error neurons or frustrative nonreward neurons. They may have a special role in reversal (Deco & Rolls, 2005b; Rolls, 2004a, 2005). Consistent with this evidence in macaques, Kringelbach and Rolls (2003, 2004) found activation of a lateral part of the human orbitofrontal cortex specifically when a changed facial expression was used as a cue to signal reversal in a visual discrimination task.

The amygdala receives information about primary reinforcers (such as taste and touch), and also information about visual and auditory stimuli from higher cortical areas (such as the inferior temporal cortex) that can be associated by learning with primary reinforcers (Figure 3.3). Bilateral removal of the amygdala in monkeys produces tameness, a lack of emotional responsiveness, excessive examination of objects, often with the mouth, and eating of previously rejected items such as meat (the Kluver-Bucy syndrome). In analyses of the bases of these behavioral changes, it has been observed that there are deficits in learning to associate stimuli with primary reinforcement, including both punishments and rewards (Rolls, 2005). The association learning deficit is present when the associations must be learned from a previously neutral stimulus (e.g., the sight of an object) to a primary reinforcing stimulus (such as the taste of food).

Further evidence linking the amygdala to reinforcement mechanisms is that monkeys will work in order to obtain electrical stimulation of the amygdala, that single neurons in the amygdala are activated by brain-stimulation reward of a number of different sites, and that some amygdala neurons respond mainly to rewarding stimuli, and others to punishing stimuli (Rolls, 2005). The association learning in the amygdala may be implemented by associatively modifiable synapses from visual and auditory neurons onto neurons receiving inputs from taste, olfactory, or somatosensory primary reinforcers (LeDoux, 2000).

Consistent with this, Davis and Whalen (2001) have found that at least one type of associative learning in the amygdala can be blocked by local application to the amygdala of a NMDA receptor blocker, which blocks long-term potentiation (LTP), which is a model of the synaptic changes that underlie learning (Rolls & Deco, 2002; Rolls & Treves, 1998). Davis and Whalen used a fear-potentiated startle response as a measure of the conditioned fear. Consistent with the hypothesis that the learned incentive (conditioned reinforcing) effects of previously neutral stimuli paired with rewards are mediated by the amygdala acting through the ventral striatum, amphetamine injections into the ventral striatum enhanced the effects of a conditioned reinforcing stimulus only if the amygdala was intact (Cardinal, Parkinson, Hall, & Everitt, 2002).

In an imaging study in humans, Ploghaus et al. (2000) showed that fear conditioning produced activation of the amygdala. A difference between the amygdala and orbitofrontal cortex in stimulus-reinforcement association learning may be that the rapid reversal of the associations may require the orbitofrontal cortex (Rolls, 2005), which may implement this rapid reversal at the neuronal level more efficiently, perhaps because it has rule-based attractor networks that can be rapidly switched by nonreward (Deco & Rolls, 2005b).

Individual variation in the functioning of the orbitofrontal cortex and amygdala could thus result in individuals having different capacities for emotional learning, and in sensitivity to change in reinforcement contingency. This in turn is likely to have implications for personality (Matthews & Gilliland, 1999; Rolls, 2005). Consistent with this, after damage to the human orbitofrontal cortex, there are many changes in emotion (Hornak, Rolls, & Wade, 1996, Hornak et al., 2003; Rolls et al., 1994), and also in impulsiveness, and the impulsiveness is also present in people with borderline personality disorder (Berlin et al., 2004, 2005). It must also be said that the changes in emotion that are produced by bilateral amygdala damage in humans are relatively subtle, with few changes very apparent in their everyday behavior, though there are some deficits in skin conductance response conditioning (Phelps, 2004) and in recognizing fear facial expressions because the eyes are not looked at (Adolphs et al., 2005). It thus appears to be unlikely that the amygdala dominates or controls the orbitofrontal cortex (Goleman, 1996).

Performing Actions to Obtain Emotion-Related Goals—"Emotional Regulation"

As described above, there is evidence for dual routes to action, implicit and explicit. The inherent processes are quite different, and different individuals might be predisposed to utilize these two approaches to different extents. There has to be a decision-making process between the implicit and explicit systems, and this could be biased one way or the other by the relative strengths of the biasing inputs (Deco & Rolls, 2006) in different individuals. Relevant factors that could be related to this are the relative values of short-term versus long-term rewards. The explicit system may enable one to forgo a short-term reward in order to obtain a better outcome in the long term, but this has to depend on the relative values that are placed on short-term versus long-term, discounted, rewards (Rolls, 2005, pp. 441–443). Impulsiveness may increase the value placed on short-term rewards (Rolls, 2005).

When multistep syntactic planning is being used in the explicit system, then this planning and executive function may utilize brain regions such as the dorsolateral prefrontal cortex (McClure, Laibson, Loewenstein, & Cohen, 2004; Rolls, 2005; Shallice &

Burgess, 1996). To the extent that holding and manipulating many items in short-term memory, and syntactic operations (such as "if...then") on them, are required for this rational decision making, then these capacities could in principle be used when making both this type of emotional decision and nonemotional explicit decisions, and we might expect that this aspect of emotional intelligence, and nonemotional intelligence, might operate similarly within an individual. Similarly, theory of mind capability may be very useful, but not for emotion only (Bird, Castelli, Malik, Frith, & Husain, 2004).

When implicit decisions are being taken, instrumental learning of the actions required to obtain a goal is required. There are multiple aspects and processes involved in such instrumental learning, each involving somewhat separate neural systems (Rolls, 2005), and, given that they are separate neural systems, there is presumably the opportunity for variation between individuals, and this variation could allow this neurobiologically defined type of emotional competence or intelligence to differ among individuals. The processes involved in instrumental learning include learning the instrumental contingency between the action and a particular outcome (action-outcome contingency), which can be signaled by a learned discriminative stimulus; and a representation of the outcome as a goal (Cardinal et al., 2002; Rolls, 2005). The representation of the outcome as a goal may involve the orbitofrontal cortex, and this may be related to hedonic assessment (Rolls, 2005). Learning action-outcome associations may involve the anterior cingulate cortex. If the behavior becomes overlearned, it may become implemented by stimulus-response habit learning, implemented in the basal ganglia (Rolls, 2005). These types of processes thus involve different brain systems from those involved in explicit reasoning and planning, and thus some emotional competencies that are part of the new concept of emotional intelligence described here may vary independently of reasoning and general intelligence.

In addition to the systems for instrumental action, there are also multiple neural systems (in the amygdala and orbitofrontal cortex) involved in autonomic responses to learned emotion-provoking stimuli (Rolls, 2005). Differing responsiveness among different individuals might produce variation in the emotional competencies, in that some people might be more sensitive to the autonomic consequences of emotional states. This can occur in people subject to panic attacks.

Alexithymia and Emotional Intelligence

When Daniel Goleman (1996) popularized the concept of emotional intelligence, the rather sweeping definition given was "Emotional intelligence [includes] abilities such as being able to motivate oneself and persist in the face of frustrations, to control impulse and delay gratification; to regulate one's moods and keep distress from swamping the ability to think; to empathize and to hope" (p. 34).

One potential problem with this definition of emotional intelligence as an ability is that different aspects within this definition (such as impulse control and hope) may be unrelated, so a unitary ability described in this way seems unlikely. A critical evaluation of the concept has been produced by Matthews et al. (2002). They note (p. 368) that in a rough and ready way, one might identify personality traits of emotional stability (low neuroticism), extraversion, agreeableness, and conscientiousness/self-control as dispositions that tend to facilitate everyday social interaction and to promote more positive emotion. (Indeed, one measure of emotional intelligence, the EQ-i, has high correlations with some of the Big Five personality traits, especially, negatively, with neuroticism, and the EQ-i may reflect three constructs: self-esteem, empathy, and impulse control [Matthews et al., 2002].) But these personality traits are supposed to be independent, so linking them to a single ability of emotional intelligence is inconsistent. Moreover, this combination of personality traits might well not be adaptive in many circumstances, so the concept of this combination as an "ability" is inappropriate (pp. 368–370).

However, the concept of emotional intelligence does appear to be related in a general way to the usage of the (mainly clinical) term *alexithymia,* in a sense the opposite, which includes the following components: (a) difficulty in identifying and describing emotions and distinguishing between feelings and the bodily sensations of arousal, (b) difficulty in ascribing feelings to other people, (c) constricted imaginal processes, as evidenced by a paucity of fantasies, and (d) a stimulus-bound externally oriented cognitive style, as evidenced by preoccupation with the details of external events rather than inner emotional experiences (Matthews et al., 2002; Taylor & Bagby, 2004). In terms of personality, alexithymia converges with the first three dimensions of the five-factor model of personality (FFM, the Big Five model), with high N (vulnerability to emotional distress), low E (low positive emotionality), and low O (a limited range of imagination; Matthews et al., 2002). Indeed, alexithymia is strongly inversely correlated with measures of emotional intelligence, suggesting that emotional intelligence may be in part a new term that encompasses much of the opposite of what has been the important concept of alexithymia in the clinical literature for more than 20 years (Matthews et al., 2002).

People diagnosed with alexithymia have difficulties in identifying facial expressions (Lane et al., 1996), suggesting some impairments in the fundamental processing of emotion-related information, in particular capacities known to require the orbitofrontal and anterior cingulate cortices (Hornak et al., 2003) and the amygdala (Adolphs et al., 2005). Consistently, it has been found that anterior cingulate cortex activation is correlated across individuals with their ability to recognize and describe emotions induced either by films or by the recall of personal experiences (Lane et al., 1998). Thus, some aspects of alexithymia, and hence of emotional intelligence, may be related to the emotional competencies approach to emotional intelligence developed in this chapter and elsewhere (Rolls, 2005).

Brain Systems Underlying Emotion

The brain systems underlying emotions have been described elsewhere (Rolls, 2005). Some of functions of the amygdala in emotion have been summarized above, and include a role in conditioned emotional responses. The orbitofrontal cortex, in addition to its functions in stimulus-reinforcer learning and reversal, is also important in representing many primary reinforcers, including taste and somatosensory reinforcers. It also represents olfactory, facial expression, visual, monetary, and social reinforcers (Rolls, 2005). Damage to the orbitofrontal cortex, and/or to the anterior cingulate cortex, can impair many aspects of emotional behavior. As noted above, the anterior cingulate cortex may be involved in action-outcome learning and thus in implicit emotional behavior, and the basal ganglia in stimulus-response learning. All of these processes may contribute to emotional competencies, including emotional identification and expression and the elicitation of frequently implicit emotional responses. These processes may be relatively independent of general intelligence, and thus we can propose that there is a neurobiological basis for what we might call emotional competencies as a part of emotional intelligence that is separate from general intelligence.

When it comes to using rational, syntactic processing for multistep planning, the emotional system may be able to use the explicit route to action, but in this case it is likely that the system being used is very similar to the planning system that contributes to general intelligence. Thus this explicit, multistep planning, part of emotional intelligence may be difficult to separate from general intelligence.

The Implications for Emotional Intelligence of This Neurobiological Approach to Emotion

1. *How should EI be conceptualized: as a competence, a skill, an adaptive outcome, a set of cultural beliefs or some other construct?* The neurobiological approach proposed here implies that emotional intelligence is a set of competencies that center on abilities to respond to different rewards and punishers. Within this domain, a first issue is that there are many competencies that are to some extent independent, in that different genes specify different primary reinforcers or goals for action, and the genes operate to some extent independently, in competition with each other. The implication is that gene variation across a population will lead to different patterns of competencies in different individuals.

A second issue is that the competencies to learn different reinforcement contingencies (e.g., that a stimulus is associated with reward vs. that a stimulus is no longer associated with reward; see Figure 3.1) may have a different neurobiological basis. The implication is that the competencies in different individuals may vary in ways that may result in different degrees of sensitivity to reward versus nonreward, to punishment versus nonpunishment, and so forth, in different individuals, leading to, for example, different extents of emotional inhibition versus disinhibition, impulsiveness, and so forth, in different individuals.

A third issue, I have argued, is that there are two main routes to action for emotion, the implicit and explicit (Rolls, 2007a). Much of the reward- and punishment-related processing may take place in the brain by systems specialized for such processing (such as the orbitofrontal cortex and amygdala) and may be separable from other types of cognitive processing (such as spatial ability, multistep planning, and general intelligence), and at least part of this processing is implicit. I have argued that some of the processing in the explicit system is involved with multistep planning, the ability to defer immediate rewards, and so forth, and this type of processing may be useful for both emotional intelligence and general intelligence, and therefore this aspect of emotional intelligence may be difficult to separate from general intelligence.

2. *Is the concept of EI compatible with existing theories of emotion and of cognitive intelligence?* The approach described here has the implications described in question 1. The approach to EI described in this chapter is consistent with Rolls's theory of emotion (Rolls, 2005), and suggests that future work in the area of EI might take into account both the basic emotion competencies described here, which would be expected to show individual variation, and also the explicit multistep planning type of computation which may be more closely related to general intelligence. It is also of interest that maximizing sensitivity to all emotion competencies might not lead to an animal that had optimal survival fitness. Instead, we might consider that each phenotype contains a unique set of values for the different emotion competencies, and that natural selection operating in a particular environment may favor certain combinations of emotion competencies in which each competency is not set to its maximal value. This is neither a Galtonian position (that more is better), nor an Aristotelian position (that there is an optimum intermediate level), but instead a Darwinian position. The position I propose also suggests that there may not be a general EI (apart from the ability to perform multistep planning, which may not be separable from general intelligence), but that instead emotional competencies may exist in a high dimensional space of competencies, which need not have high correlations between different competencies. That is, this is a multifactorial approach.

3. *What are the key components, facets or branches of EI?* The approach described here has the implications described under questions 1 and 2.

4. *How is EI distinct from existing personality and ability constructs?* Could a multistratum psychometric model integrate a dimension or dimensions of EI with existing personality and ability constructs? The approach to emotional intelligence described here is different from existing personality and ability constructs, in that it includes a whole set of emotional competencies that may influence emotional behavior in many ways.

5. *How does EI change over the life span, quantitatively and qualitatively?* The basic sensitivity to different reinforcers is likely to be relatively constant over the life span. Learned associations of previously neutral stimuli to primary reinforcers are likely to change regularly during life, and may even reverse on a single trial, after one pairing. The ability to use planning to help find multistep solutions with the explicit system is likely to be a skill that can develop continuously, though the ability of different individuals to utilize this aspect of emotional intelligence may be different, and may covary with general intelligence in so far as this reflects multistep planning ability.

6. *How might EI contribute to adaptation to real-world social environments?* Competencies such as one-trial stimulus-reward reversal learning provide a mechanism for

continually updating one's social responses (Kringelbach & Rolls, 2003; Rolls, 2005). Competencies such as the abilities involved in reciprocal altruism, tit-for-tat game playing and more efficient strategies, defection detection, and face and voice emotional expression recognition will also be important in real-world social adaptation (Rolls, 2005). Multistep planning, with the ability to correct plans using higher order thoughts, will also make important contributions to adaptation to real-world social environments (Rolls, 2004b, 2005, 2007a).

Notes

The author has worked on some of the experiments described here with I. de Araujo, G. C. Baylis, L. L. Baylis, M. J. Burton, H. C. Critchley, M. E. Hasselmo, J. Hornak, M. Kringelbach, C. M. Leonard, F. Mora, J. O' Doherty, D. I. Perrett, M. K. Sanghera, T. R. Scott, S. J. Thorpe, and F. A. W. Wilson, and their collaboration, and helpful discussions with or communications from M. Davies (Corpus Christi College, Oxford), D. Rosenthal, and M. S. Dawkins, are sincerely acknowledged. Some of the research described was supported by the Medical Research Council. The author is grateful to Moshe Zeidner for comments on an earlier version of this chapter.

1. Instrumental reinforcers are stimuli that, if their occurrence, termination, or omission is made contingent upon the making of an action, alter the probability of the future emission of that action. Rewards and punishers are instrumental reinforcing stimuli. The notion of an action here is that an arbitrary action, for example, turning right versus turning left will be performed in order to obtain the reward or avoid the punisher, so that there is no prewired connection between the response and the reinforcer. Some stimuli are primary (unlearned) reinforcers (e.g., the taste of food if the animal is hungry, or pain); whereas others may become reinforcing by learning, because of their association with such primary reinforcers, thereby becoming "secondary reinforcers."

This type of learning may thus be called "stimulus-reinforcement association," and occurs via an associative learning process. A positive reinforcer (such as food) increases the probability of emission of a response on which it is contingent; the process is termed positive reinforcement, and the outcome is a reward (such as food). A punisher (such as a painful stimulus) can increase the probability of emission of a response, which causes the negative reinforcer to be omitted (as in active avoidance) or terminated (as in escape), and then acts as a positive reinforcer (Rolls, 2005). If a punisher decreases the probability of omission of a response (as in passive avoidance), then the punisher acts as a negative reinforcer. (Negative reinforcement may also be the result produced by the omission or termination of a reward ["extinction" and "time out" respectively], in that both may decrease the probability of responses [Rolls, 2005].)

References

Adolphs, R., Gosselin, F., Buchanan, T. W., Tranel, D., Schyns, P., & Damasio, A. R. (2005). A mechanism for impaired fear recognition after amygdala damage. *Nature, 433,* 68–72.

Barratt, L., Dunbar, R., & Lycett, J. (2002). *Human evolutionary psychology.* Palgrave, UK: Basingstoke.

Berlin, H., Rolls, E. T., & Iversen, S. D. (2005). Borderline personality disorder, impulsivity and the orbitofrontal cortex. *American Journal of Psychology, 162,* 2360–2373.

Berlin, H., Rolls, E. T., & Kischka, U. (2004). Impulsivity, time perception, emotion, and reinforcement sensitivity in patients with orbitofrontal cortex lesions. *Brain, 127,* 1108–1126.

Bird, C. M., Castelli, F., Malik, O., Frith, U., & Husain, M. (2004). The impact of extensive medial frontal lobe damage on "Theory of Mind" and cognition. *Brain, 127,* 914–928.

Buss, D. M. (1999). *Evolutionary psychology: The new science of the mind.* Boston: Allyn & Bacon.

Cardinal, N., Parkinson, J. A., Hall, J., & Everitt, B. J. (2002). Emotion and motivation: The role of the amygdala, ventral striatum, and prefrontal cortex. *Neuroscience and Biobehavioural Reviews, 26,* 321–352.

Critchley, H. D., & Rolls, E. T. (1996). Hunger and satiety modify the responses of olfactory and visual neurons in the primate orbitofrontal cortex. *Journal of Neurophysiology, 75,* 1673–1686.

Darwin, C. (1872). *The expression of the emotions in man and animals.* Chicago: University of Chicago Press.

Davis, M., & Whalen, P. J. (2001). The amygdala: Vigilance and emotion. *Molecular Psychiatry, 6,* 13–34.

Dawkins, R. (1986). *The blind watchmaker.* Harlow, UK: Longman.

Dawkins, R. (1989). *The selfish gene.* Oxford, UK: Oxford University Press.

Deco, G., & Rolls, E. T. (2005a). Attention, short-term memory, and action selection: A unifying theory. *Progress in Neurobiology, 76,* 236–256.

Deco, G., & Rolls, E. T. (2005b). Synaptic and spiking dynamics underlying reward reversal in orbitofrontal cortex. *Cerebral Cortex, 15,* 15–30.

Deco, G., & Rolls, E. T. (2006). A neurophysiological model of decision-making and Weber's law. *European Journal of Neuroscience, 24,* 901–916.

Ekman, P. (1982). *Emotion in the human face.* Cambridge, UK: Cambridge University Press.

Ekman, P. (1992). Facial expressions of emotion: An old controversy and new findings. *Philosophical Transactions of the Royal Society, London B, 335,* 63–69.

Goldman-Rakic, P. S. (1996). The prefrontal landscape: Implications of functional architecture for understanding human mentation and the central executive. *Philosophical Transactions of the Royal Society, London B, 351,* 1445–1453.

Goleman, D. (1996). *Emotional intelligence.* London: Bloomsbury.

Gray, J. A. (1975). *Elements of a two-process theory of learning.* London: Academic Press.

Gray, J. A. (1979). The psychophysiological basis of introversion-extraversion. *Behaviour Research and Therapy, 8,* 249–266.

Gray, J. A. (1987). *The psychology of fear and stress.* Cambridge, UK: Cambridge University Press.

Hamer, D. H., & Copeland, P. (1998). *Living with our genes: Why they matter more than you think.* New York: Doubleday.

Hasselmo, M. E., Rolls, E. T., & Baylis, G. C. (1989). The role of expression and identity in the face-selective responses of neurons in the temporal visual cortex of the monkey. *Behavioural Brain Research, 32,* 203–218.

Hornak, J., Bramham, J., Rolls, E. T., Morris, R. G., O'Doherty, J., Bullock, P. R., & Polkey, C. E. (2003). Changes in emotion after circumscribed surgical lesions of the orbitofrontal and cingulate cortices. *Brain, 126,* 1691–1712.

Hornak, J., O'Doherty, J., Bramham, J., Rolls, E. T., Morris, R. G., Bullock, P. R., & Polkey, C. E. (2004). Reward-related reversal learning after surgical excisions in orbitofrontal and dorsolateral prefrontal cortex in humans. *Journal of Cognitive Neuroscience, 16,* 463–478.

Hornak, J., Rolls, E. T., & Wade, D. (1996). Face and voice expression identification in patients with emotional and behavioural changes following ventral frontal lobe damage. *Neuropsychology, 34,* 247–261.

Krebs, J. R., & Kacelnik, A. (1991). *Decision making.* In J. R. Krebs & N. B. Davies (Eds.), *Behavioural ecology* (pp. 105–136). Oxford, UK: Blackwell.

Kringelbach, M. L., & Rolls, E. T. (2003). Neural correlates of rapid reversal learning in a simple model of human social interaction. *NeuroImage, 20,* 1371–1383.

Kringelbach, M. L., & Rolls, E. T. (2004). The functional neuroanatomy of the human orbitofrontal cortex: Evidence from neuroimaging and neuropsychology. *Progress in Neurobiology, 72,* 341–372.

Lane, R. D., Reiman, E., Axelrod, B., Yun, L.-S., Holmes, A. H., & Schwartz, G. E. (1998). Neural correlates of levels of emotional awareness: Evidence of an interaction between emotion and attention in the anterior cingulate cortex. *Journal of Cognitive Neuroscience, 10,* 525–535.

Lane, R. D., Sechrest, L., Railed, R., Weldon, V., Kaszniak, A., & Schwartz, G. E. (1996). Impaired verbal and nonverbal emotion recognition in alexithymia. *Psychosomatic Medicine, 58,* 203–210.

LeDoux, J. E. (2000). Emotion circuits in the brain. *Annual Review of Neuroscience, 23,* 155–184.

Matthews, G., & Gilliland, K. (1999). The personality theories of H. J. Eysenck and J. A. Gray: A comparative review. *Personality and Individual Differences, 26,* 583–626.

Matthews, G., Roberts, R. D., & Zeidner, M. (2004). Seven myths about emotional intelligence. *Psychological Inquiry, 15,* 179–196.

Matthews, G., Zeidner, M., & Roberts, R. D. (2002). *Emotional intelligence: Science and myth.* Cambridge, MA: MIT Press.

Mayer, J. D., Salovey, P., Caruso, D. R., & Sitarenios, G. (2001). Emotional intelligence as a standard intelligence. *Emotion, 1,* 232–242.

McClure, S. M., Laibson, D. I., Loewenstein, G., & Cohen, J. D. (2004). Separate neural systems value immediate and delayed monetary rewards. *Science, 306,* 503–507.

Oatley, K., & Jenkins, J. M. (1996). *Understanding emotions.* Oxford: Blackwell.

O'Doherty, J., Kringelbach, M. L., Rolls, E. T., Hornak, J., & Andrews, C. (2001). Abstract reward and punishment representations in the human orbitofrontal cortex. *Nature Neuroscience, 4,* 95–102.

Phelps, E. A. (2004). Human emotion and memory: Interactions of the amygdala and hippocampal complex. *Current Opinion in Neurobiology, 14,* 198–202.

Ploghaus, A., Tracey, I., Clare, S., Gati, J. S., Rawlins, J. N., & Matthews, P. M. (2000). Learning about pain: The neural substrate of the prediction error for aversive events. *Proceedings of the National Academy of Sciences of the United States of America, 97,* 9281–9286.

Ridley, M. (1993). *The red queen: Sex and the evolution of human nature.* London: Penguin.

Rolls, E. T. (1986a). Neural systems involved in emotion in primates. In R. Plutchik, & H. Kellerman (Eds.), *Emotion: Theory, research, and experience: Vol. 3. Biological foundations of emotion* (pp. 125–143). New York: Academic Press.

Rolls, E. T. (1986b). A theory of emotion, and its application to understanding the neural basis of emotion. In Y. Oomura (Ed.), *Emotions: Neuronal and chemical control* (pp. 325–344). Basel: Karger.

Rolls, E. T. (1990). A theory of emotion, and its application to understanding the neural basis of emotion. *Cognition and Emotion, 4,* 161–190.

Rolls, E. T. (1999). *The brain and emotion.* Oxford, UK: Oxford University Press.

Rolls, E. T. (2004a). The functions of the orbitofrontal cortex. *Brain and Cognition, 55*, 11–29.

Rolls, E. T. (2004b). A higher order syntactic thought (HOST) theory of consciousness. In R. J. Gennaro (Ed.), *Higher-order theories of consciousness: An anthology* (pp. 137–172). Amsterdam: John Benjamins.

Rolls, E. T. (2005). *Emotion explained.* Oxford, UK: Oxford University Press.

Rolls, E. T. (2007a). The affective neuroscience of consciousness: Higher order linguistic thoughts, dual routes to emotion and action, and consciousness. In P. Zelazo & M. Moscovitch (Eds.), *Cambridge handbook of consciousness* (pp. 829–857). Cambridge, UK: Cambridge University Press.

Rolls, E. T. (2007b). The representation of information about faces in the temporal and frontal lobes. *Neuropsychologia, 45*, 124–143.

Rolls, E. T. (2008). *Memory, attention, and decision-making.* Oxford: Oxford University Press.

Rolls, E. T., Aggelopoulos, N. C., & Zheng, F. (2003). The receptive fields of inferior temporal cortex neurons in natural scenes. *Journal of Neuroscience, 23*, 339–348.

Rolls, E. T., Critchley, H. D., Browning, A. S., & Inoue, K. (2006). Face-selective and auditory neurons in the primate orbitofrontal cortex. *Experimental Brain Research, 170*, 74–87.

Rolls, E. T., Critchley, H. D., Mason, R., & Wakeman, E. A. (1996). Orbitofrontal cortex neurons: Role in olfactory and visual association learning. *Journal of Neurophysiology, 75*, 1970–1981.

Rolls, E. T., & Deco, G. (2002). *Computational neuroscience of vision.* Oxford, UK: Oxford University Press.

Rolls, E. T., Hornak, J., Wade, D., & McGrath, J. (1994). Emotion-related learning in patients with social and emotional changes associated with frontal lobe damage. *Journal of Neurology, Neurosurgery, and Psychiatry, 57*, 1518–1524.

Rolls, E. T., Judge, S. J., & Sanghera, M. (1977). Activity of neurones in the inferotemporal cortex of the alert monkey. *Brain Research, 130*, 229–238.

Rolls, E. T., Rolls, B. J., & Rowe, E. A. (1983). Sensory-specific and motivation-specific satiety for the sight and taste of food and water in man. *Physiology & Behavior 30*, 185–192.

Rolls, E. T., & Stringer, S. M. (2001). A model of the interaction between mood and memory. *Network: Computation in Neural Systems, 12*, 111–129.

Rolls, E. T., & Treves, A. (1998). *Neural networks and brain function.* Oxford, UK: Oxford University Press.

Shallice, T., & Burgess, P. (1996). The domain of supervisory processes and temporal organization of behaviour. *Philosophical Transactions of the Royal Society B, 351*, 1405–1411.

Taylor, G. J., & Bagby, R. M. (2004). New trends in alexithymia research. *Psychotherapy and Psychomatics, 73*, 68–77.

Thorpe, S. J., Rolls, E. T., & Maddison, S. (1983). Neuronal activity in the orbitofrontal cortex of the behaving monkey. *Experimental Brain Research, 49*, 93–115.

Tinbergen, N. (1951). *The study of instinct.* New York: Oxford University Press.

Weiskrantz, L. (1968). Emotion. In L. Weiskrantz (Ed.), *Analysis of behavioural change* (pp. 50–90). New York and London: Harper & Row.

Zuckerman, M. (1994). *Psychobiology of personality.* New York: Cambridge University Press.

Zuckerman, M., & Kuhlman, D. M. (2000). Personality and risk-taking: Common biosocial factors. *Journal of Personality and Social Psychology, 68*, 999–1029.

4

Componential Emotion Theory Can Inform Models of Emotional Competence

KLAUS R. SCHERER

In my view, current conceptualizations and tests of emotional intelligence (EI) suffer from two major problems: an overemphasis on cognitive aspects of *knowledge about emotion* and an overemphasis on adaptive aspects of *personality*. The first problem is directly linked to an attempt to conceptualize emotional competences and skills as "intelligence" and to adopt measurement approaches that are reminiscent of IQ testing (as in the influential work by Mayer & Salovey, 1993). Not surprisingly, there is a lively discussion, based on considerable data (see overviews in Schulze & Roberts, 2005), as to the differential validity of EI and IQ tests and their ability to discriminate different subfactors of cognitive performance. Although I would wholeheartedly agree that cognition plays a major role in emotion and that, in consequence, emotional competence is likely to include cognitive factors, I suggest separating these factors from *knowledge about emotion*, which can be construed as crystallized intelligence in a way that is comparable to many other types of knowledge or content areas. By focusing on cognitive theories of emotion and pertinent research, I will try to show how the cognitive factors involved in emotion elicitation, regulation, and communication could be conceptualized differently, in a way that is perhaps more germane to the emotion mechanism and the competences related to it.

The second problem is linked to the fact that personality, personal adjustment, and psychopathology do have strong affective components. Clearly, emotional disturbance will compromise successful adaptation and adjustment to the contingencies of everyday life. The personality adjustment approach, based on standard self-report methodology and often using items that are directly adapted from standard personality tests, is representative of a more clinically oriented approach (e.g., Bar-On, 2000, 2005; see also Austin, Saklofske, & Egan, 2005; Gannon & Ranzijn, 2005). I claim that this approach does not conceptualize or measure emotional competences as such but, rather, the effects of maladaptive personality syndromes. It may well be that lack of emotional competence is one of the etiological factors involved in such malfunctioning, but it seems virtually impossible to differentiate this determinant from many others that might be involved. In other words, instruments purporting to measure EI with the help of personality scales with strong social and emotional adjustment components may well capture variance that is due to individual differences in EI. However, they measure individuals' self-evaluation of successful adjustment outcomes without identifying the role that EI plays in producing a high level of adjustment. In consequence, the correlations with success and mental health criteria generally reported by proponents of this approach (Bar-On, 2000; Engelberg & Sjoberg, 2004) are not surprising. However, the claim that a personality-based test like the Bar-On EQ inventory has a mean predictive validity coefficient of .59 (Bar-On, 2005) must be taken with more than one grain of salt. Quite apart from the common method variance in the type of self-report measures that are correlated in this type of research, there has been little effort at conceptual clarification and elimination of item overlap. Obviously, good social and emotional adjustment, as measured by self-report, is a good predictor for well-being, as measured by self-report. And good social and emotional adjustment may well be a good predictor for more objective indicators of achievement. But we learn preciously little about EI from this research.

I will illustrate this point with some of our own data. We have developed a computerized assessment system for use by high-level human resource professionals (Computer Assessment of Personal Potential [CAPP]; Scherer & Scherer, 2007a).[1] As part of the validation, we have also used the Management Potential (Mp) special purpose scale of the California Personality Inventory (CPI), consisting of an empirical selection of items that successfully separated groups of people with different degrees of supervisory responsibility (Gough, 1984). Over an N of 1,457 professional participants tested,[2] the scale shows some extremely impressive and highly significant correlations with dimensions measured by instruments assessing personality, coping, emotional regulation, motivation, and values: emotional stability (self-rating, $r = .44$), self-assurance and emotional stability composite dimension (personality test, $r = .38$), emotion regulation (.35), stress resilience (.22), serenity (.16), functional coping (.22), and intellectual values (.25), as well as objective measures of fluid intelligence (.20). Needless to say, with an N of about 1,500, these coefficients are extraordinarily high. Despite this impressive performance, it is hard to say what exactly the Mp scale measures, judging from the item content (items having been empirically selected solely from discrimination performance). Our hunch is that this scale measures general adjustment and "reasonableness," both of which may well be a *consequence* of the effect of the dimensions listed above. I suggest that the correlations of self-report EI scales with success and adjustment measures can be explained in exactly the same fashion.

After having rejected the two dominant approaches to EI conceptualization and measurement, what is the remedy I propose? My suggestion is to drop the potentially misleading term "intelligence" and define the capacity that is at issue, varying over individuals, as differential degrees of *competence in using the emotion mechanism* as it has been shaped by evolution. In consequence, I will refer to *emotional competence* (EC) in this chapter.

It may be useful to specify briefly at the outset how I propose to differentially define *competence* with respect to *ability* on the one hand and *skill* on the other. At one end of a continuum, I suggest using the term *ability* to refer to stable, dispositional capacities that are either genetically endowed or acquired over a long period of socialization. In addition, abilities are general factors, a good example being fluid intelligence, or "*g*," rather than aptitudes for specific performances. I place *skills* at the other end of the continuum, as narrow, highly specific capacities to achieve high-level performance with respect to a particular activity or task. Skills are generally acquired easily, even later in life, through observation or training. Driving a car is a typical example. *Competences* are somewhere between dispositional abilities and concrete skills. They extend over particular domains and may imply a strong component of procedural knowledge that can be generalized across the respective domain. Having a "green thumb" as a gardener may be a good example—a characterization that extends over different types of horticultural success criteria and requires different types of decisions and actions. EC, then, is the particular aptitude to succeed in making the garden of emotion thrive.

Of course, there are links between these three concepts and the levels they occupy: Thus, fluid intelligence may help one to learn about gardening and retain contingencies in memory. Conversely, gardening competence may spawn specific skills such as pruning trees and sowing seeds at just the right time. In a similar vein, we might expect general intelligence to facilitate EC, and the latter to foster the acquisition of specific skills, such as the ability to recognize emotions from a speaker's voice.

In order to measure this competence, we would first need to agree on what the emotion mechanism is. Unfortunately, we are far from such agreement (see Scherer, 2005b). In part this is also the reason for the widespread disagreement about the nature of EI or EC. Elsewhere (Scherer, 2000, 2002), I have compared the different theories of emotion and the dimensions or features on which they vary. It would be tempting to show how each of these conceptualizations engenders a specific type of competence, but space would not be sufficient for this exercise. I will therefore limit the analysis to how a particular type of componential theory, illustrated by my own model, invites a particular type of competence definition.

I will first briefly describe the *component process model* (CPM; Scherer, 1984, 2001, 2004). I will then identify two major aspects of the emotion process, specifically *appraisal* and *regulation*, and evaluate the extent to which they can be considered as being subject to individual differences that could account for differential levels of EC. Finally, I will examine emotion *communication*, including the recognition of emotional expression, as a central component of EC.

A Brief Outline of the Component Process Model of Emotion

Based on the pioneering work of Arnold (1960) and Lazarus (1968, 1991), several models of appraisal have been developed (see Ellsworth & Scherer, 2003; Scherer, 1999; Scherer, Schorr, & Johnstone, 2001). Despite some diversity, consensus on basic assumptions is growing among the different theories. Importantly, for the first time theorists are making clear and empirically testable predictions on the factors that elicit and differentiate emotions and a sizeable number of studies are now providing strong empirical support for the approach. Although much of the earlier work is based on self-report, a number of recent studies use more objective indicators for appraisal processes, for example, physiological measures or facial and vocal expressions (see Part V in Scherer, Schorr, & Johnstone, 2001, for a comprehensive overview of the earlier evidence; see also Aue, Flykt, & Scherer, 2007; Aue & Scherer, 2007; Flykt, Dan, & Scherer, 2007; Grandjean & Scherer, 2007; Johnstone, van Reekum, Hird, Kirsner, & Scherer, 2005; van Reekum, Banse, Johnstone, Etter, Wehrle, & Scherer, 2004).

The component process model (Scherer, 1984, 2001, 2004) is one of the componential appraisal theories postulating that emotion-constituent evaluation is based on a fixed set of criteria or checks. The model postulates that there are *modal*—rather than basic—emotions that seem to be universal because words for them exist in almost every language. Just as we have words to describe objects or events that we regularly deal with, we also label these regularly occurring states. Thus, we have words for joy, happiness, anger, rage, fear, panic, sadness, jealousy and so forth, and these states are modal in the sense that they occur relatively frequently. The existence of such modal emotions confirms Darwin's claim that emotions are adaptive (Darwin, 1872/1998). In contrast to reflexes or instincts, they are optimally suited to help us deal with the situations that occur in everyday life because they are eminently flexible, preparing appropriate behavior tendencies rather than triggering rigid reactions. In consequence, they do not have an invariable profile, or signature, because situations differ and thus call forth emotions that differ accordingly. But, despite their different physiological signatures and expressions, emotions cluster into some major categories or families.

Figure 4.1 shows a simplified graph illustrating the unfolding of appraisal as conceptualized by the component process model (see Sander, Grandjean, & Scherer, 2005; Scherer, 2001, 2004, for more detailed accounts). An event happens, and we will attend to it immediately if it is considered relevant. We will also examine its relevance by drawing from memory and motivation. In addition, we will assess the implications of the event and its consequences for our well-being, drawing from resources such as reasoning and self-concept matching. Then the issue becomes, Can we cope with this event? How much power do we have available? And that again draws from several factors. Highly self-assured people, for example, have different evaluations of their coping abilities than do people who are less assured. Finally, we evaluate the event in terms of its normative significance: Is it legitimate and morally acceptable?

Much of this process occurs unconsciously. Leventhal and Scherer (1987) suggested that appraisal occurs on three levels of emotion processing. On the sensory-motor and schematic levels appraisal tends to be quite rudimentary. In contrast, on the conceptual level appraisal can be highly complex, depending on the goals or plans that are being evaluated, the individual's problem-solving ability, and so forth. Moreover, appraisal processes on different levels work together seamlessly through parallel processing. The

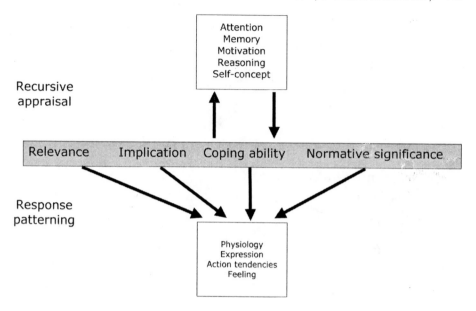

Figure 4.1. A simplified illustration of the Component Process Model of Emotion.

recursive appraisal process changes constantly and so does the nature of the emotion generated by it.

The arrows representing response patterning in Figure 4.1 represent the postulate that once the result of the evaluation is relatively stable, each step in the appraisal process will produce a response, inducing a change in the state of the autonomous and motor systems. When an individual considers something to be relevant and directs attention to it, a number of physiological responses will result. For example, if someone is in danger of being attacked by a bear blood flow to the legs is increased because of the potential need to run away. Note that this physiological response does not yet trigger an action; it is only a preparation for one type of appropriate action. It is not the action that counts; it is the preparation (see also Frijda, 1986). Emotions leave us the choice of behaving one way or another until the last moment, but the beauty of this mechanism is that in a short period of time, it prepares us to react in an adaptive fashion. These intermediate outcomes continuously affect the nervous system, thereby continually preparing the organism for action.

How does the component process model conceptualize feeling? First, *feeling* must be separated from *emotion*. Feeling is a *component* of emotion. The component process model postulates that feeling is the reflection of all changes occurring in the different emotion components in the course of a given episode. This is illustrated in Figure 4.2. Both the cognitive appraisal of the event and the response pattern (physiological symptoms, motor expression, and action tendencies) will be reflected unconsciously (through proprioceptive feedback processes). This monitoring of all ongoing processes produces automatic regulation processes, including the allocation of resources such as attention.

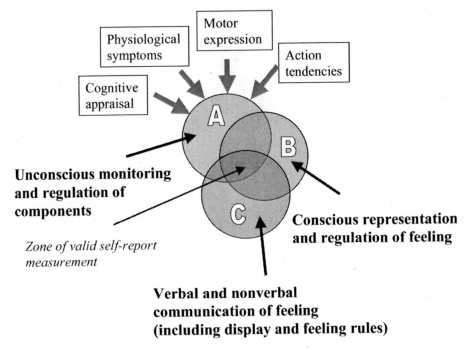

Figure 4.2. The three layers of monitoring of component emotion processes and the resulting feeling states (adapted from Scherer, 2004a).

Some of the responses may eventually become conscious and allow more controlled and effortful regulation processes, such as trying to reduce the degree of arousal through various coping strategies. Finally, the conscious emotional experience can be verbalized and communicated, requiring again a variety of regulation and control processes (such as not speaking of or even not expressing certain feelings because of normative social display rules). As suggested in Figure 4.2, these processes overlap only partially, the nonoverlapping areas of consciousness and verbalization being explained by constructive associations between memory contents or language concepts. Unfortunately, what we can study empirically is only the small area of multiple overlap that represents the verbalized, conscious part of emotion. Clearly, it is only the visible tip of the iceberg, but it is often our only access to feeling and the underlying processes that gave rise to it (see Scherer 2004, 2005a, for further details).

How Does This Theory of Emotion Inform the Conceptualization of EC?

My fundamental assumption is that differences in the competence to *manage* the continuously evolved emotion mechanism, which integrates both psychobiological and sociocultural determinants, need to be defined in terms of *function* or *adaptation*. I suggest that highly emotionally competent individuals are characterized by an optimal functioning of the emotion mechanism with respect to two major domains—emotion production and emotion perception—each of which is constituted by different facets of competence. Emotion production refers to the total pattern of bodily and behavioral changes that characterizes the adaptative function of emotion, allowing the organism to cope with events of major relevance for well-being. These changes are outwardly visible and constitute important social signals for interaction partners, informing about the individual's reaction and probable behavioral intention. Given this important role of emotion signaling in social intercourse, individuals need be able to accurately perceive and interpret the emotional state of others. This is what I will refer to as emotion *perception* competence.

Production Competence

I think the most important facet of EC, and the one that EI theorists seem to have completely neglected so far, is the production of the *most appropriate emotional reaction to different types of events based on adequate appraisal of internal goal states, coping potential, and the probable consequences of events*. If you react with the wrong emotion to a given type of situational meaning, you are not using the potential that this powerful mechanism provides. The second facet is one that all theorists agree on, adaptive *regulation* of one's emotional states, both with respect to internal set points and according to the sociocultural and situational context. And the third facet, again one that most theorists would posit, is efficient emotional *communication* in social interaction through appropriate expression of one's own state.

Appraisal Competence

If, as seems to be almost unanimously accepted these days, emotions in general serve the function of allowing optimal adaptation to important events affecting individuals by preparing a set of appropriate action tendencies, it follows that the significance of the events have to be correctly appraised. If I interpret the bear's approaching me as the desire to be hugged and prepare for a nurturant stance, my action preparation may be suboptimal and my well-being gravely threatened. Similarly, if I wanted to wrestle the bear, I had better correctly estimate my forces. We can distinguish two facets of appraisal competence: (1) appropriate emotion *elicitation* and (2) appropriate emotion *differentiation*.

Appropriate emotion elicitation refers to the ability to rapidly detect significant objects and events that require an emotional response. As shown in Figure 4.1, detecting that something is important is the first, and possibly the most important, step because we are constantly bombarded by stimulation and we have to decide what we want to spend time attending to, as attention is a limited and precious resource; therefore, it is critical not to overreact or underreact. Our relevance detection ability is of paramount importance, especially as it often relies on unconscious processes.

It is one thing to react emotionally when it is required, another to react with the *appropriate emotion*. The claim that an emotional response can be right or wrong depending on the circumstances may strike one as unusual at first glance. Yet, it is an obvious consequence of the generally accepted claim that emotions have evolved to help organisms to adapt to situations that are pertinent to their well-being. What is the criterion for an emotion being inappropriate for a given context? The issue is complex, and I can only briefly mention some elements of a response. One relatively clear-cut case is represented by emotional disturbances such as anhedonia, euphoria, dysphoria, depression, panic attacks, and the like. The fact that there is widespread social consensus that such enduring emotional response dispositions are signals of ill health and require therapy indicates that the emotional reactions of the respective individuals are considered as *pathological* or *abnormal* by society at large. One could argue that such clinical syndromes cannot be used to examine the appropriateness of emotions for "normal" individuals. Yet, the fact that in modern clinical practice a symptom count decides on clinical significance (e.g., *DSM-IV*) suggests that there may well be a continuum between *inappropriate* emotions and clinical disorders. In consequence, one can argue that one criterion for inappropriate emotionality is family or peer judgment that a person's emotional reactivity is inappropriate. In some cases, individuals may be aware of this inappropriateness, either through their own retrospective analysis or by becoming aware of other people's reactions. This approach to the definition of appropriateness is based on the adverse consequences of nonadaptive emotions and general social consensus on "abnormality."

Another approach to defining the appropriateness of an emotional reaction is constituted by the notion of *valid appraisal*. Appropriate emotion differentiation requires evaluating the implications of an event in a realistic fashion and correctly estimating one's coping potential, as shown in the bear example above. In addition, emotions such as pride, shame, guilt, and anger require an accurate representation of social expectations, norms, and moral standards. One essential prerequisite for accurate appraisal is to evaluate each event on its merits and to avoid being influenced by evaluative biases or stereotypical judgments. Let us examine an illustrative example.

In a large-scale actuarial study of daily emotions we asked a quasi-representative sample of about a thousand people in different parts of Switzerland to describe an event that produced the strongest emotion they had *yesterday* and to tell us what that emotion was, using their own words (Scherer, Wranik, Sangsue, Tran, & Scherer, 2004). The numerous labels provided by the respondents were reduced to families or classes with the help of an automatic coding system (GALC; see Scherer, 2005b). Happiness is the most frequent emotion class, with anger being the next most frequent, followed by anxiety, joy, sadness, and so forth. Then we asked, "How often do you experience certain emotions *in your daily life generally?*" and we provided 14 labels. If the respondents said that they frequently experienced happiness in general, the likelihood of experiencing happiness yesterday was higher. We computed the odds ratios to arrive at the mean probability for experiencing happiness, anger, and so on. The findings show that if one has a stable disposition to experience a certain emotion, the likelihood that one will experience that emotion on any given day is significantly higher. I suggest that, in large part, this is due to the operation of *appraisal biases*. Thus, when one is depressed, one is likely to appraise events less optimistically and possibly less accurately or realistically. Conversely, appraisal biases may well have a role in the etiology of depression. If one continuously underestimates one's coping potential, the probability that one will experience sadness, fear, or depression may be much higher. In fact, malfunctioning of appraisal checks ("pathological appraisal") may lead to clinically relevant affective disturbance (see Kaiser & Scherer, 1997).

However, it can be argued that malfunctioning of appraisal is not an etiological, but rather an accompanying or concomitant factor. Evidence on the role of appraisal bias in emotional disorder remains to be collected. As our data on Swiss emotion dispositions and their link to the strongest emotion experienced yesterday was obtained during the same survey, causal mechanisms cannot be identified and the possible operation of response sets remains a problem. We are currently conducting research to disentangle these factors experimentally (Wranik & Scherer, 2007). In any case, appraisal biases are likely to operate as an aggravating factor, or possibly a risk factor.

Here is another example. In the ongoing validation of the CAPP assessment package referred to above (Scherer & Scherer, 2007a), we examined the current database of $N = 1,457$ professionals to find evidence on appraisal competence and its effect on emotional reactions and emotional adjustment. We constructed a scale for "overexternalizers" in causal attribution of the responsibility for emotion-producing events by selecting individuals with extreme scores on "external control" (a scale in the personality test of the assessment package, the Personality-Index, PERS-I) and "external attribution" as measured by an instrument measuring coping strategies, the Coping Index (COP-I; Scherer & Scherer, 2007b). Individuals scoring high on this scale (one standard deviation or more above the mean; $N = 208$ out of a total N of 1,457) scored significantly higher ($p < .05$) on the Worry/Fear scale of a dispositional Emotionality scale (EMOT-I) and reported significantly lower ($p < .001$) emotional stability in a self-rating instrument and in the personality test (PERS-I). It seems reasonable to assume that extreme scores on external attribution might reflect an unrealistic appraisal bias toward overexternalization of causal responsibility to others or to factors beyond control (including the supernatural; see Scherer, 1997). The felt loss of internal control that would tend to accompany this external appraisal bias might produce frequent occurrences of inappropriate emotional reactions that undermine the feeling of emotional stability.

Interestingly, the overexternalizers were also significantly lower ($p < .001$) on a composite coping scale we call Functional Coping (i.e., they had lower scores on self-concept modification, problem redefinition, and problem solving and higher scores on wishful thinking, seeking esteem, and substance use), but significantly higher ($p < .001$) on the composite score Repression (high scores on emotion repression and problem repression; low scores on seeking empathy and seeking social support; see below), as measured by the COP-I. There is also a clue as to one of the factors that might underlie this appraisal bias: Overexternalizers have significantly lower ($p < .001$) scores on scales for Intellectual Challenge and Knowledge/Understanding in instruments assessing life and work values in the assessment package (the Work Value-Index, WORK-I, and the Human Values-Index, VAL-I). It could be that overexternalizers expend less cognitive effort in analyzing the causal structure of emotion-eliciting events.

Another candidate for appraisal bias is an optimistic explanatory style, or the tendency to attribute positive events to the self and to dismiss negative events as attributable to external causes. Although this is generally considered to be beneficial for self-esteem maintenance, physical health, and motivation in individual performance settings, little is known about the effects of this variable in collaborative performance situations. In our laboratory, Tanja Wranik examined the influence of optimism and pessimism on failure explanations and emotions when individuals work together in a series of ingenious laboratory experiments (Wranik & Scherer, 2007). Results from three studies suggest that optimists are more likely than pessimists to blame the interaction partner for failure. Moreover, optimists are more likely to report feeling angry with the interaction partner under certain conditions, whereas pessimists generally report feeling angry with themselves. The results suggest that appraisal biases such as habitual optimism and other-blaming may have negative effects in collaborative settings.

Given the importance of "correctly" appraising events for the probability of responding with an appropriate and functional emotion, it would be useful to assess individual differences with respect to such an ability. To my knowledge, there is currently no validated instrument to assess appraisal competence. Unfortunately, developing such an instrument is no trivial task. A straightforward self-report approach is not very promising, as individuals are generally unaware of their appraisal processes, even though they seem to be able to reconstruct some aspects. The lack of insight into appraisal processes can be demonstrated by using an expert system approach. The system (GENESE; see Scherer, 1993) asks participants to remember a recent emotional experience and then poses 25 questions about the appraisal of the eliciting event. On that basis, it "postdicts" the emotion experienced on the basis of appraisal theory predictions.[3] Although the system achieves respectable accuracy, the results show that people often do not realize what appraisals have contributed to the production of specific emotions. And people differ greatly in terms of how much insight they have into their underlying goal structure. Although emotion psychologists tend to take for granted that specific goals motivate behavior, lay people generally do not analyze their behavior in these categories.

If appraisal competence is high and pertinent events are evaluated realistically, appropriate response preparation should normally follow automatically. As postulated by the component process model outlined above, it is assumed that the results of the individual evaluation checks drive changes in the other emotion components, in other words, autonomous physiology, motor expression, and action tendencies. Ideally, synchronized response patterning appropriately shaped by appraisal should result in the preparation of adaptive action tendencies. However, it is possible that the translation of appraisal results into response patterning and action tendency preparation will malfunction because of "hardware" problems (e.g., lesions in mediating brain circuits) or biases produced by specific learning histories (e.g., a preponderance of a specific kind of response due to strong reinforcement in the past). Thus, when an individual responds in a seemingly incompetent fashion to emotionally arousing events, it may be necessary to examine the appropriateness of the appraisal mechanism and the way in which appraisal results trigger response patterns separately.

Regulation Competence

Virtually all theories of EI or EC assign a central role to emotion regulation ability. One important function of emotion regulation is to correct inappropriate emotional responses that might have been produced by unrealistic appraisals. Often, our social environment will alert us to the fact that an emotional reaction is inappropriate in kind or intensity. Given a certain sluggishness of the response system, especially physiological arousal, emotions cannot be turned on or off like an electric light, and control and management strategies are required. One might think that emotion regulation skills are not needed if one commands exceptional appraisal competence—in that case the emotions triggered by the appraisal results should always be appropriate. However, this is rarely the case. First, fine-tuning is required, as appraisal changes rapidly and abrupt reappraisal as a result of new information requires strong regulation skills. In addition, emotional reactions are subject to strong normative control in most societies. Thus, even though a strong anger reaction to a veiled insult may be an appropriate behavior preparation in an evolutionary sense, rules of politeness might prohibit such reactions. Many authors have described the existence and operation of display and even feeling rules in different societies (Ekman, 1972; Ekman & Friesen, 1969; Hochschild, 1979; Matsumoto, 1990).

Although the importance of emotion regulation is often underlined, relatively little is known about the details of the underlying mechanisms (but see the contributions in Philippot & Feldman, 2004). Based on the layers of feeling and the role of consciousness and verbalization shown in Figure 4.2, I suggest that several determinants of regulation need to be differentiated. A major determinant is *appropriate monitoring* of the emotion process, which I define as (a) appropriate reflection and integration of all emotion components, (b) balanced conscious and unconscious processing, and (c) accurate proprioceptive feedback of peripheral responses to a central monitoring system and their appropriate interpretation. Basically, the idea is that the processes of cross-modality and temporal integration (of appraisal results and the corresponding response patterns; see Scherer, 2004), as well as the interaction between unconscious and conscious processing (see Scherer, 2005a), can operate in a more or less optimal manner. I suggest to refer to this as *monitoring competence*. This sounds more complicated in the abstract than it really is.

Let us take an example. I have a friend who gets easily upset, starting to shout, getting all red in the face, and furiously knitting his brows. When one tries to calm him, his response generally is "I am not at all angry; I just do not agree." This would seem indicative of a certain lack in monitoring competence, implying incomplete proprioceptive feedback from major expressive channels and incomplete integration of appraisal and reaction information. The result is an absence of timely emotion regulation attempts, both on the unconscious and the conscious levels, which may have negative consequences in strategic encounters such as negotiations.

Once the need for emotion management is established, on the basis of appropriate unconscious or conscious monitoring, functional regulation and control strategies need to be available and executable. These come in two types: automatic unconscious regulation and controlled conscious regulation.

Automatic Unconscious Regulation

On the level of unconscious regulation, the automatic allocation of attentional resources is of major importance. Thus, upon detection of potential relevance, the executive space needs to be largely allocated to the further processing of the respective stimulus or event. Individuals differ in the rapidity of reactions, task switching capacity, and parallel processing ability. There are major differences in cognitive ability, specifically with respect to executive processes, which could account for differential competence in automatic regulation. Indeed, there is some evidence in the literature that the automatic regulation of emotion may depend on available executive processing resources (Baumeister, 2002; Derryberry & Reed, 2002; Van der Linden, 2004).

One of the personality factors linked to inefficient executive processing seems to be impulsivity. Whiteside and Lynam (2001) identified four components of impulsive behavior: urgency, (lack of) premeditation, (lack of) perseverance, and sensation seeking. Although empirical proof is currently lacking, at least the first two components might be directly linked to executive processing constraints that limit the capacity for efficient automatic regulation. In any case, the deleterious effects of impulsivity on emotion regulation, in particular anger and aggressiveness, are well known and empirically documented (e.g., Hoaken, Shaughnessy, & Pihl, 2003; Scarpa & Raine, 2000). In our large-scale study with the CAPP assessment instrument, we confirmed this effect: individuals high on impulsivity showed significantly higher frequency of anger experiences ($p < .05$) and higher emotional expressivity ($p < .01$).

Controlled Conscious Regulation

Almost all of the research conducted on emotional regulation to date deals with conscious monitoring and control attempts. In particular, the pioneering work of Gross and his associates (Gross & John, 2002, 2003; John & Gross, 2004) has demonstrated the effects of *reaction suppression* and *cognitive reappraisal*. Reaction suppression refers to the attempt to reduce emotional intensity by controlling or suppressing physiological reactivity and overt motor expression, with the effect being presumably being due to the diminution of proprioceptive feedback. This explanation is consistent with the CPM model, which postulates that subjective feeling is an integration of the complete representation of all component changes, including proprioceptive feedback from the periphery. If less autonomic arousal and motor expression activity is integrated into the total reflection of component changes, subjective feeling will change qualitatively and quantitatively (in terms of intensity).

The effect of reappraisal was early posited and empirically demonstrated by Lazarus and his collaborators (Lazarus, 1968; Lazarus & Alfert, 1964). If the results of appraisal determine the nature of the ensuing emotion, a reappraisal of a central criterion will obviously change the nature of the emotion and consequently of the subjective feeling. Modern componential theories, and particularly the CPM, conceptualize appraisal as a recursive process. In consequence, rather than focusing on single acts of reappraisal, these theorists envisage a constant effort to refine appraisal results and bring them into line with reality. This is achieved by continuous processing of incoming information and continuous search for the most appropriate schemata or criteria for the comparison of currently experienced events and their features to internally stored experiences. The result is a constant change of the qualitative nature and intensity of the resulting emotion (and its subjective experience), something that the notion of emotional states in the sense of a few basic emotions does hardly do justice to. If constant recursive appraisal, and consequently constant reappraisal, is part of the normal emotion process, what is the effect of emotional regulation efforts in this process? This issue has not really been addressed so far, neither on the theoretical nor the empirical level. I would argue that regulation efforts would result in highly effortful and directed appraisal processes, with the individual consciously searching for interpretations of events and their potential implications that are more beneficial than the first evaluation seemed to suggest.

A good example for this type of reappraisal strategy is *wishful thinking*, a regulation strategy that consists of systematically overestimating the probability of appraised causes and consequences that are in line with an individual's desires and thus serve to minimize the impact of threatening events or embellish the hopes for positive outcomes. The example shows that emotion regulation is closely linked to the activity of coping with events and with the emotions they provoke. Given this affinity, it is quite surprising that there seems to be virtually no connection between the conceptualizations of coping and of emotional regulation mechanisms. Clearly, both reappraisal and the active inhibition of reappraisal are coping strategies, as is the suppression of emotional reactions and some of its manifestations by a variety of different control strategies.

I suggest that an attempt to theoretically and empirically integrate coping and emotional regulation research could have very beneficial effects on both domains, especially with respect to defining the functionality of the respective coping or regulation attempts and the type of competences required. The Coping-Index (COP-I; Scherer & Scherer, 2007a), which is used in the CAPP assessment package mentioned above, is well suited for this purpose. The instrument includes not only those strategies that are found in many of the established coping scales, but also additional strategies derived from an overarching theoretical rationale. This rationale is based upon the assumption that coping strategies can vary along three major dimensions:

1. The *functional domain* or modality that is directly affected by the coping attempt—cognition, emotion, the self, or the social domain (other people)

2. The *general orientation* with respect to the emotion-eliciting event, *toward* with an attempt at resolution, problem solving, or abatement versus *away* from the problem as characterized by efforts to avoid dealing with the consequences or repressing them

3. The major *focus of attention,* which can be directed toward the *past,* mainly the causes of the problem or of the state of the person versus a focus on the *future* with respect to options such as active engagement or substitute gratifications

These three dimensions form the $4 \times 2 \times 2$ matrix shown in Table 4.1. Each of the cells of the matrix is characterized by one or more coping strategies corresponding to the characteristics provided by the intersection of the three major dimensions or determinants. Many of these cells represent classic coping strategies as described in the literature, whereas others are less common but plausible and empirically demonstrable. It can be easily seen that these coping strategies represent regulation attempts focusing on different components of the emotion process: the cognitive component (mainly reappraisal of events in terms of agency, consequences, and one's own values and goals in strategies such as problem redefinition, internal or external attribution, self-modification, or wishful thinking), the physiological and expressive component (consisting mainly of the suppression or the enhancement of the respective reactions as in emotion repression, catharsis, emotion substitution, or relaxation), and action tendencies (such as seeking empathy, social support, problem solving, or substance use).

Given these interesting links, a widening of the conceptual definition of emotion regulation by including different forms of coping seems promising. In particular, I suggest a differentiation of the overall concept by addressing (1) the regulation of different components of the emotion process, (2) reappraisals of different aspects of the transaction between event, self, and social context, as well as (3) the nature of the reappraisal tendencies. With respect to the last, the phenomenon of *rumination* is particularly interesting. From the vantage point of appraisal theory one could view this behavior as a compulsive tendency to persevere in recursive reappraisal, being unable to come to some kind of closure. One would expect that extended periods of rumination are quite dysfunctional in terms of effective emotion regulation, as constant reappraisal may prevent a stabilization of emotional experiences (see Segerstrom, Tsao, Alden, & Craske, 2000).

A factor analysis of the individual scales of the Coping-Index for the participants of the CAPP validation study described above, yields the following six orthogonal factors:

1. Functional Coping (+ self-concept modification, problem redefinition, problem solving; – wishful thinking, seeking esteem, substance use)
2. Repression (+ emotion repression, problem repression; – seeking empathy, seeking social support)
3. Rumination (+ rumination, internal attribution; – self-concept bolstering)
4. Problem acceptance (+ problem acceptance; – repression confirmation)
5. Relaxation (+ relaxation, affective resignation; – emotion catharsis)
6. Gratification (+ gratification, emotion substitution)

Composite scales were formed for the six factors and correlated with composite scores for the other instruments in the CAPP assessment package. As expected, Functional

TABLE 4.1. The theoretical model of coping and emotion regulation strategies used in the Coping-Index (COP-I).

	Cognition	Emotion	Self	Social Relations
Orientation toward problem				
Focus: Consequences/ Solutions	Problem solving	Emotion catharsis	Self-concept modification	Seeking social support
Focus: Causes/ Present state	Problem acceptance Problem redefinition Rumination	Affective resignation	Internal attribution	Seeking empathy
Orientation away from problem				
Focus: Consequences/ Solutions	Wishful thinking	Obtaining gratification Relaxation Substance use Emotion substitution	Self-concept bolstering	Seeking esteem
Focus: Causes/ Present state	Problem repression	Emotion repression	External attribution	Repression confirmation

Source: Reproduced from Scherer & Scherer, 2007.

Coping correlates positively with different indices of adjustment such as emotional stability, self-assurance, creativity, and serenity. As reappraisal is a frequent component in the strategies combined under Functional Coping, these results confirm the conclusion reached by John and Gross (2004) as to the beneficial effect of reappraisal compared to suppression. However, in our data, rumination, which has been described above as a dysfunctional urge to persevere in reappraisal, is correlated with less desirable characteristics such as emotional instability, low self-assurance, prevalence of negative emotions, lack of feelings of power and achievement, and a low self-reported ability for leadership. This suggests that we need to further disentangle the mechanisms underlying emotion regulation.

In this context, it is important to underline the issue of the *appropriateness* of particular emotion regulation strategies for different *contexts*. One can define EC in terms of regulation as the competence to use the most appropriate strategy in a given context. As in the case of appropriate emotional reactions, it is not trivial to define the appropriateness of regulation in a particular situation. However, Perrez and Reicherts (1992) have shown that appraisal theory provides the tools to define a "normative" science of coping and emotion regulation. They demonstrate, for example, that given an uncontrollable situation, active problem solving strategies or constant reappraisal of the event and its consequences (e.g., rumination) are not very promising, whereas modification of one's goals and subsequent reappraisal or emotion-focused coping may be more successful (see also John & Gross, 2004).

Communication Competence

Much of the preceding discussion has focused on emotion regulation with respect to the individual's feelings. However, regulation is often an interpersonal affair. If there is any agreement among emotion researchers, it is on the central importance of emotion in social interaction, and in particular the role of emotion *communication*. Communication competence has both a production and a perception part. We will first discuss the former.

Emotional expression informs interaction partners about the way in which an individual has appraised an action or event, the consequent reaction, and, most important, the probability of different behavioral consequences (Scherer, 1984, 2001). Obviously, then, it is part of EC to produce emotional expressions that are optimally suited to that purpose. Thus, it would seem suboptimal to send inappropriate or ambiguous signals about reactions and action tendencies, as this will encourage misunderstanding and seriously complicate interaction processes. If one produces signs toward a partner that he or she can interpret as an anger reaction even though one is worried about the future of the relationship, one is likely to produce unwanted effects of spiraling anger escalation. In some sense, emotion expression always has a strategic aspect that can be more or less pronounced.

It is not surprising then that the appropriate control of emotional expression has been intensively discussed in the literature. Ekman and Friesen (1969) coined the term *display rules* to refer to cultural norms that govern the license to express different emotions in social situations (see also Ekman, 1972, 1993; Matsumoto, 1990). Clearly, this is a competence that needs to be acquired in the socialization process via which a child becomes a well-functioning member of a particular society. Issues concerning both the understanding and the execution of expression control have consequently been an important part of the literature on the socialization of affect (Ceschi & Scherer, 2003; Saarni, 1979). In consequence, one would assume that appropriate consequences of applying display rules to one's expressive behavior are therefore an important part of EI or EC. However, to my knowledge there has been relatively little concern with this important competence in this domain.

But expression control goes much beyond suppression. Ekman and Friesen (1969) differentiated four aspects of using display rules: masking, neutralization, modification, and intensification. Clearly, one needs to add *fabrication*, in other words, showing an emotion one does not feel at all. The strategic use of emotional expression is a central element of emotional skills. A nice example is provided by what may be one of the first formal statements on EC in the history of philosophy and psychology: In his *Nicomachean Ethics*, Aristotle (1941) exhorts us to react to an insult with the appropriate amount of anger, at the appropriate time, directed at the appropriate person, in order to avoid being seen as a social fool. The secret is the measured response, avoiding overreacting (to avoid being seen as hysterical or stressed out) or underreacting (being seen as a "social fool"). The anthropologist Erving Goffman has brilliantly expanded on this important idea by showing the powerful human tendency for positive self-presentation (Goffman, 1959). Importantly, emotional expression, even if strategically regulated or manipulated, needs to be credible and convey the impression of being authentic. One of the essential skills in this respect is to produce congruent expression in different modalities, something that requires important skills, given the difficulty of monitoring and manipulating many different cues at the same time. Ekman's work on deception (Ekman & Friesen, 1969; see review in Ekman, 2003), for example, shows that when you are trying to deceive, the different modalities are often no longer attuned or congruent. In addition, indices of leakage become available for those who can see them.

Perception Competence

In addition to efficient signal production (sending ability), as discussed above, communication competence requires accurate signal *perception* and recognition or interpretation (receiving ability). This implies a high ability to recognize emotional states of others in different modalities such as the face, voice, or body, even though the pertinent cues may be controlled or concealed. For example, accurate emotion recognition is important in negotiations to understand when someone gets edgy or irritated to the point that negotiations may break off. A related competence is the capacity for empathy (Hoffman, 2000).

Clearly, individuals differ greatly in this capacity. Not surprisingly, the issue of "social intelligence," which includes emotion recognition competence, has been early appreciated by the pioneers of intelligence testing, and attempts were made to produce valid tests of these abilities (Moss, Hunt, Omwake, & Ronning, 1927; O'Sullivan & Guilford, 1975; Ruisel, 1992). Later, the field of nonverbal communication produced a large amount of work on *nonverbal sensitivity,* which also concerns emotion recognition ability (Hall & Bernieri, 2001). It is surprising that current efforts to develop tests of EI either completely ignore this important competence (the personality trait/adjustment approach) or deal with it exclusively from the point of socially convergent interpretation. Thus, the facial expression items in the MSCEIT (Mayer, Salovey, Caruso, & Sitarenios, 2003), supposedly a performance test, use ambiguous expressions and score intelligence in terms of response agreement with population means (in the absence of clear criteria, even expert scoring is likely to reflect social agreement). It is surprising that established tests of nonverbal emotion recognition ability based on performance accuracy, which have been available for some time (e.g., for the face, Ekman's Pictures of Facial Affect [PFA] or Ekman & Matsumoto's Japanese and Caucasian Facial Expressions of Emotion [JACFEE][4]; for the voice, Banse & Scherer, 1996; Scherer, Banse, Wallbott, & Goldbeck, 1991), are not used more frequently in this area (but see Biehl et al., 1997; Nowicki & Duke, 1994).

As part of the CAPP assessment package, we developed two tests for competence in recognizing emotional expressions—the Vocal Expression Recognition Index

(Vocal-I) and the Facial Expression Recognition Index (Facial-I). The development and validation of the two tests is documented in Scherer and Scherer (2007c). A summary of some of the major results for the large professional assessment sample is of interest in the current context. As expected on the basis of popular stereotypes and earlier data (Hall, 1984), we also find that women perform significantly better on both facial and vocal recognition. But the effect size is minuscule—a partial eta squared of less than .01, corresponding to less than a two-percentage point difference. There is also a significant age effect, with younger testees (< 40 years) being better than older testees (> 40 years). And there is a powerful interaction effect—the young age advantage is most pronounced for women.

How much overlap is there between vocal and facial recognition competence? The correlation between the total scores of the two tests is $r = .24$ ($N = 1,264$; $p < .001$). The correlations for individual emotions are generally much lower. Thus, although both tests seem to tap into a common facet of perception competence, the joint variance is only about 6% and there are clearly modality-specific competence differences. Can general fluid intelligence explain perception competence (as other facets of EI; see Roberts, Zeidner, & Matthews, 2001)? A composite score for fluid intelligence, based on four appropriate tests, correlates with facial, $r = .12$ ($N = 1,231$; $p < .001$), and with vocal, $r = .18$ ($N = 1,311$; $p < .001$), recognition. Thus, g seems to have a small but reliable effect.

How is emotion recognition competence related to professional performance? Studies of predictive validity are ongoing, but we can report one interesting finding: If we compare candidates in management positions with those in lower echelons, we find more than a three-percentage point advantage (t significant at $p < .01$) for employees in nonmanagement positions for the recognition of vocal anger expression (although there are no differences for other vocal or facial subscores). My favorite explanation for this finding is that managers are rarely exposed to anger expressions on the part of their collaborators and may thus lack sufficient exercise of this skill. On the other hand, it may help to accede to upper level management positions by ignoring the anger of others. This relationship may well be worth exploring.

Most expression tests to date have used single modalities and often static photographs for the visual domain (with the notable exception of the Profile of Nonverbal Sensitivity [PONS]; Rosenthal, Hall, DiMatteo, Rogers, & Archer, 1979). We have recently developed the Multimodal Emotion Recognition Test (MERT), which is based on recordings with professional actors that have been extensively analyzed with the help of microcoding of facial expression and gestures, as well as digital acoustic analysis (Banse & Scherer, 1996; Scherer & Ellgring, 2007a, 2007b; Wallbott, 1998). The development and construct validation of this test, which is available for use in research work, is described in Bänziger, Grandjean, and Scherer (2007). The results support the earlier conclusion that although there is some common variance for different modalities, possibly based on a common communication competence factor, there are also major individual differences in the skills for different communication channels. Such tests can help determine differential abilities for emotion recognition in different modalities or channels and provide the means to increase these abilities.[5]

Criteria of Competence

In addition to identifying the types of competences that are related to efficient use of the emotion mechanism, one needs to define the *criteria* for ability or competence. I will outline two major models (see Figure 4.3). The first, which I call the Aristotelian model, insists on the *appropriateness* of the emotional response. It is also exemplified by Stoic philosophy prescribing the rule of temperance—"not too little, not too much, just right." The upper part of Figure 4.3 shows a hypothetical example: fear disposition. Here, the competence range is situated in the middle of the continuum—the "just right" range. To have a bit more is a sign of "incompetence," for example, of being a "nervous Nelly" or someone who is easily frightened. Still higher scores may indicate a risk for emotional disturbances such as generalized anxiety disorder (GAD) or panic disorder. To have too little fear disposition is also a problem, possibly even more dangerous. In the incompetence range, individuals may be called reckless or irresponsible, a qualification that may entail social sanctions. Individuals that are almost fearless tend to be extreme sensation seekers, with potentially adverse consequences for life and health.

In the second model, which I call the Galtonian, or *ability*, model, the criterion is "the more the better" (lower part of Figure 4.3). The example is emotion recognition ability, a skill that may have perfect accuracy as a ceiling condition. Incompetence occurs only at the lower end, and complete absence may in fact constitute part of a disorder. It could be argued that it is sometimes better not to be able to read one's associates' emotions from their faces or voices; one might be happier being deceived. But it should be noted that happiness or satisfaction is a quite different criterion, one that should not be confused with competence.

Which of the two models is most appropriate for different components of EC outlined above is an empirical question. My hunch is that the Aristotelian model may be more appropriate for regulation competence, whereas the Galtonian model might be better suited to describe appraisal and communication competence. Again, it might be argued that extreme appraisal competence, being accurate and realistic, may not contribute to happiness, as in the frequently quoted notion of depressives being "sadder but wiser" (Alloy & Abramson, 1988; Lewinsohn, Mischel, Chaplin, & Barton, 1980). Apart from the fact that there is a lively discussion about the replicability of the depressive realism effect and the nature of the underlying cognitive mechanism, I would again argue that the happiness criterion should not be confused with the competence criterion. The possibility that lower competence is preferable in some contexts and for some domains does not invalidate the *definition and measurement* of competence. However, it may well be that high EC is not to be aspired to universally.

The actuarial survey of Swiss emotions referred to above nicely illustrates the "moderate is best" rule. Contrary to expectations, participants who experience little anger

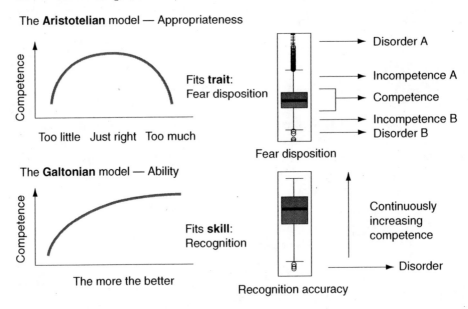

Figure 4.3. The Aristotelian and Galtonian models for criteria of emotional competence.

or irritation are not generally happier and more satisfied with their lives. It seems that a moderate amount of anger and irritation may be beneficial in this respect (Scherer et al., 2004, pp. 550–552).

Another example for the Aristotelian/stoic model of moderation is provided by the attribution of causality in the large professional assessment sample described above. One might think that if overexternalization leads to exaggerated worry and emotional instability, as shown above, it would be better to be biased toward internal attribution. However, our data show that this is just as bad an appraisal bias. We formed an "over-internalization" variable that compared all those participants who scored one standard deviation or higher above the mean for a coping scale measuring "internal attribution" of causes for stressful events. Individuals scoring high on this scale (one standard deviation or more above the mean; $N = 270$ out of a total N of 1,457) also reported significantly lower ($p < .01$) emotional stability in a self-rating instrument and in the personality test (PERS-I). One reason might be that overinternalizers, although being higher on Functional Coping ($p < .001$) and lower on Repression (.001), score significantly higher ($p < .001$) on the Rumination scale—a habit that is described in the literature as having potentially negative consequences for emotional stability (Folkman & Moskowitz, 2004). Clearly then, a bias toward external or internal attribution is a risk factor for emotional stability—a balanced, unbiased appraisal mechanism being much preferable.

One of the problems with curvilinear relationships such as implied by the Aristotelian/stoic model is the difficulty of testing the model statistically. I have attempted to overcome this problem by what I call "centerfolding" the respective scale: This procedure consists of simply computing the z-scores for the scale over all individuals in the sample and then storing the absolute values of these z-scores for all individuals. In the resulting centerfolded scale, values around the mean on the original scale now have low values, and those that were at the high *or* low end now have high values. This has produced interesting results in assessment and predictive validity studies in the human resource domain. For example, in the large professional sample described above, there was a zero correlation between dominance and life satisfaction. Centerfolding the dominance scale produced a correlation of $r = -.12$ ($N = 1,189$; $p < .01$); in other words, individuals who have a moderate score on dominance, as compared with a low or a high score, tend to be more satisfied with their life. A similar result is found for aggressiveness.

The centerfolding technique also yielded interesting results in a study of the personality predictors of training success for air controllers: Candidates with a medium level of dominance are significantly less successful than those with high or low values. On the other hand, candidates with medium extraversion and medium vitality are less likely to resign from the training program.[6]

Conclusion

I hope to have advanced some compelling arguments for EI to be conceptualized and measured as a competence (EC) involving ability, genetically endowed or acquired in the course of socialization, and some skills that can be learned in a relatively short lapse of time. The concept of EC should not only be compatible with widely accepted theories of emotion; it should in fact be *directly based on theoretical models of the emotion mechanism and the available empirical evidence.* I suggested using the component process model as the basis of competence conceptualization, as it is one of the broader theories, encompassing many of the pertinent components, including cognition, and highlighting the dynamic nature of the emotion process. As key components of EC, I identified *appraisal competence* (evaluating pertinent events in an accurate fashion with respect to both the personal implications of the events and one's ability to cope with the consequences), *regulation competence* (the capacity to react in an appropriate fashion both with respect to promising action tendencies and situational contingencies), and, finally, *communication competence* (the ability to produce emotion signals in accordance with strategic aims and cultural norms and to correctly infer the emotions of others on the basis of outward expression and to empathize with others under appropriate circumstances).

A high level of competence in these three facets ought to produce adaptive outcomes; in other words, high EC persons are likely to be resilient in stressful situations, unlikely to suffer from emotional disturbances, and likely to enjoy a high level of life satisfaction. In consequence, high EC should correlate at least moderately with a number of affect-related personality traits and measures of emotional stability. In consequence, it is probable that EC contributes to adaptation to real-world social environments. However, it would be erroneous to deduce from this correspondence that it is sufficient to measure personality and satisfaction constructs with the help of self-report, as it is generally not advisable to measure outcomes in order to understand determinants. Most important, apart from the serious biases and artifacts affecting self-report, EC is only one determinant of adaptive adjustment and the degree of contribution to professional success and well-being is likely to vary over individuals. If one wants to improve EC through appropriate training, it is absolutely essential to diagnose EC directly by assessing emotional performance in order to identify the sources of insufficient competence and to suggest appropriate remedial training.

How does EC change over the life span? Given the importance of cognitive ability in appraisal, the steady increase in cognitive skills from early childhood to adolescence is likely to continuously improve EC. A similar effect is to be expected from the stabilization of the self-concept, providing an important standard of comparison and goal-setting, as well as from increasing acculturation to social norms and values. Across the life span, changes in achievement motivation and standards of comparison, as well as greater experience with social encounters and increased self-knowledge, may, up to a point, increase EC, although losses might be expected in old age.

Much of the copious EI research in past years has, to my mind, started from misconceived preconceptions, focusing too strongly on the intelligence or the personality/adjustment model. Admittedly, the alternative model outline in this chapter is still sketchy and somewhat speculative. Although first steps have been made to develop instruments that could assess the three components of EC, as the examples in this chapter show, much remains to be done. However, a prime condition for method development and research in this domain to flourish is convergent agreement among scholars and practitioners alike that EC can only be reasonably assessed by investigating individual differences with respect to (a) realistic emotion-constituent appraisal and reactions, (b) ability to regulate and control emotion to optimize action preparation and strategic social interaction, and (c) capacity to produce appropriate signals and to infer and empathize with the emotional state of significant interaction partners.

Notes

1. More extensive information on the assessment package and the validation study, as well as detailed tables of results, can be obtained from the author.

2. The *N* shown in this chapter for different analyses from this data set varies due to missing observations for some variables.

3. The GENESE expert system (Geneva Emotion Analyst) can be explored at the following website: http://www.unige.ch/fapse/emotion—then click on Demos.

4. See http://www.paulekman.com/ for further details.

5. See, for example, Ekman's MicroExpression (METT) and Subtle Expression Training Tools (SETT); http://www.paulekman.com/.

6. These data were found as part of a confidential evaluation of air controller training.

References

Alloy, L. B., & Abramson, L. Y. (1988). Depressive realism: Four theoretical perspectives. In L. B. Alloy (Ed.), *Cognitive processes in depression* (pp. 223–265). New York: Guilford Press.

Aristotle (1941). Ethica Nicomachea [Nicomachean ethics]. In R. McKeon (Ed.), *The basic works of Aristotle* (pp. 935–1126). New York: Random House.

Arnold, M. B. (1960). *Emotion and personality: Vol. 1. Psychological aspects*. New York: Columbia University Press.

Aue, T., & Scherer, K. R. (2007). Appraisal-driven somatovisceral response patterning: Effects of intrinsic pleasantness and goal conduciveness. Manuscript submitted for publication.

Aue, T., Flykt, A., & Scherer, K. R. (2007). First evidence for differential and sequential efferent effects of stimulus relevance and goal conduciveness appraisal. *Biological Psychology, 74*, 347–357.

Austin, E. J., Saklofske, D. H., & Egan, V. (2005). Personality, well-being and health correlates of trait emotional intelligence. *Personality and Individual Differences, 38*(3), 547–558.

Banse, R., & Scherer, K. R. (1996). Acoustic profiles in vocal emotion expression. *Journal of Personality and Social Psychology, 70*(3), 614–636.

Bänziger, T., Grandjean, D., & Scherer, K. R. (2007). *The Multimodal Emotion Recognition Test (MERT): Development and validation*. Manuscript submitted for publication.

Bar-On, R. (2000). Emotional and social intelligence: Insights from the Emotional Quotient Inventory (EQ-i). In R. Bar-On & J. D. A. Parker (Eds.), *Handbook of emotional intelligence*. San Francisco: Jossey-Bass.

Bar-On, R. (2005). The Bar-On model of emotional-social intelligence. [Special issue on emotional intelligence]. *Psicothema, 17*.

Baumeister, R. F. (2002). Ego depletion and self-control failure: An energy model of the self's executive function. *Self and Identity, 1*, 129–136.

Biehl, M., Matsumoto, D., Ekman, P., Hearn, V., Heider, K., Kudoh, T., et al. (1997). Matsumoto and Ekman's Japanese and Caucasian facial expressions of emotion (JACFEE): Reliability data and cross-national differences. *Journal of Nonverbal Behavior, 21*(1), 3–21.

Ceschi, G., & Scherer, K. R. (2003). Children's ability to control the facial expression of laughter and smiling: Knowledge and behavior. *Cognition and Emotion, 17*, 385–411.

Darwin, C. (1998). *The expression of emotions in man and animals* (3rd ed., P. Ekman, Ed.). London: HarperCollins. (Original work published 1872)

Derryberry, D., & Reed, M. A. (2002). Anxiety-related attentional biases and their regulation by attentional control. *Journal of Abnormal Psychology, 111*, 225–236.

Ekman, P. (1972). Universals and cultural differences in facial expression of emotion. In J. R. Cole (Ed.), *Nebraska symposium on motivation* (pp. 207–283). Lincoln: University of Nebraska Press.

Ekman, P. (1993). Facial expression and emotion. *American Psychologist, 48*, 384–392.

Ekman, P. (2003). *Emotions revealed*. New York: Times Books.

Ekman, P., & Friesen, W. V. (1969). Nonverbal leakage and clues to deception. *Psychiatry, 32*, 88–105.

Ellsworth, P. C., & Scherer, K. R. (2003). Appraisal processes in emotion. In R. J. Davidson, H. Goldsmith, & K. R. Scherer (Eds.), *Handbook of the affective sciences* (pp. 572–595). New York: Oxford University Press.

Engelberg, E., & Sjoberg, L. (2004). Emotional intelligence, affect intensity, and social adjustment. *Personality and Individual Differences, 37*(3), 533–542.

Flykt, A., Dan, E. S., & Scherer, K. R. (2007). Using a probe detection task to assess the timing of intrinsic pleasantness appraisals. Manuscript submitted for publication.

Folkman, S., & Moskowitz, J. T. (2004). Coping: Pitfalls and promise. *Annual Review of Psychology, 55*, 745–774.

Frijda, N. H. (1986). *The emotions.* Cambridge, England: Cambridge University Press.

Gannon, N., & Ranzijn, R. (2005). Does emotional intelligence predict unique variance in life satisfaction beyond IQ and personality? *Personality and Individual Differences, 38*(6), 1353–1364.

Goffman, E. (1959). *The presentation of self in everyday life.* Garden City, NY: Doubleday Anchor.

Gough, H. G. (1984). A managerial potential scale for the California Psychological Inventory. *Journal of Applied Psychology, 69*, 233–240.

Grandjean, D., & Scherer, K. R. (2007). Unpacking the cognitive architecture of emotion processes. Manuscript submitted for publication.

Gross, J. J., & John, O. P. (2002). Wise emotion regulation. In L. Feldman Barrett & P. Salovey (Eds.), *The wisdom of feelings: Psychological processes in emotional intelligence* (pp. 297–318). New York: Guilford.

Gross, J. J., & John, O. P. (2003). Individual differences in two emotion regulation processes: Implications for affect, relationships, and well-being. *Journal of Personality and Social Psychology, 85*, 348–362.

Hall, J. A. (1984). *Nonverbal sex differences: Communication accuracy and expressive style.* Baltimore: Johns Hopkins University Press.

Hall, J. A., & Bernieri, F. J. (Eds.). (2001). *Interpersonal sensitivity: Theory and measurement.* Mahwah, NJ: Erlbaum.

Hoaken, P. N. S., Shaughnessy, V. K., & Pihl, R. O. (2003). Executive cognitive functioning and aggression, is it an issue of impulsivity? *Aggressive Behavior, 29*, 15–30.

Hochschild, A. R. (1979). Emotion work, feeling rules, and social structure. *American Journal of Sociology, 85*, 551–575.

Hoffman, M. L. (2000). *Empathy and moral development.* Cambridge, England: Cambridge University Press.

John, O. P., & Gross, J. J. (2004). Healthy and unhealthy emotion regulation: Personality processes, individual differences, and lifespan development. *Journal of Personality, 72*, 1301–1334.

Johnstone, T., van Reekum, C. M., Hird, K., Kirsner, K., & Scherer, K. R. (2005). The effect of manipulated appraisals on voice acoustics. *Emotion, 5*(4), 513–518.

Kaiser, S., & Scherer, K. R. (1997). Models of "normal" emotions applied to facial and vocal expressions in clinical disorders. In W. F. Flack, Jr., & J. D. Laird (Eds.), *Emotions in psychopathology* (pp. 81–98). New York: Oxford University Press.

Lazarus, R. S. (1968). Emotions and adaptation: Conceptual and empirical relations. In W. J. Arnold (Ed.), *Nebraska symposium on motivation* (pp. 175–270). Lincoln: University of Nebraska Press.

Lazarus, R. S. (1991). *Emotion and adaptation.* New York: Oxford University Press.

Lazarus, R. S., & Alfert, E. (1964). The short-circuiting of threat. *Journal of Abnormal and Social Psychology, 69*, 195–205.

Leventhal, H., & Scherer, K. R. (1987). The relationship of emotion to cognition: A functional approach to a semantic controversy. *Cognition and Emotion, 1*, 3–28.

Lewinsohn, P. M., Mischel, W., Chaplin, W., & Barton, R. (1980). Social competence and depression: The role of illusory self-perceptions? *Journal of Abnormal Psychology, 89*, 203–212.

Matsumoto, D. (1990). Cultural similarities and differences in display rules. *Motivation and Emotion, 14*, 195–214.

Mayer, J. D., & Salovey, P. (1993). The intelligence of emotional intelligence. *Intelligence, 17*, 433–442.

Mayer, J. D., Salovey, P., Caruso, D. R., & Sitarenios, G. (2003). Measuring emotional intelligence with the MSCEIT V2.0. *Emotion, 3*, 97–105.

Moss, F. A., Hunt, T., Omwake, K. T., & Ronning, M. M. (1927). *Social intelligence test.* Washington, DC: Center for Psychological Service.

Nowicki, S., & Duke, M. P. (1994). Individual differences in the nonverbal communication of affect: The diagnostic analysis of nonverbal accuracy. *Journal of Nonverbal Behavior, 18*, 9–35.

O'Sullivan, M., & Guilford, J. P. (1975). Six factors of behavioral cognition: Understanding other people. *Journal of Educational Measurement, 12*(4), 255–271.

Perrez, M., & Reicherts, M. (1992). *Stress, coping, and health: A situation-behavior approach. Theory, methods, applications.* Seattle: Hogrefe & Huber.

Philippot, P., & Feldman, R. S. (Eds.). (2004). *The regulation of emotion.* Mahwah, NJ: Erlbaum.

Roberts, R., Zeidner, M., & Matthews, G. (2001). Does emotional intelligence meet traditional standards for an intelligence? Some data and conclusions. *Emotion, 1*, 196–231.

Rosenthal, R., Hall, J. A., DiMatteo, M. R., Rogers, P. L., & Archer, D. (1979). *Sensitivity to nonverbal communication: The PONS test.* Baltimore: John Hopkins University Press.

Ruisel, I. (1992). Social intelligence: Conception and methodological problems. *Studia Psychologica, 34*(4–5), 281–296.

Saarni, C. (1979). Children's understanding of display rules for expressive behavior. *Developmental Psychology, 15*(4), 424–429.

Sander, D., Grandjean, D., & Scherer, K. R. (2005). A systems approach to appraisal mechanisms in emotion. *Neural Networks, 18*, 317–352.

Scarpa, A., & Raine, A. (2000). Violence associated with anger and impulsivity. In J. C. Borod (Ed), *The neuropsychology of emotion* (pp. 320–339). New York: Oxford University Press.

Scherer, K. R. (1984). On the nature and function of emotion: A component process approach. In K. R. Scherer & P. Ekman (Eds.), *Approaches to emotion* (pp. 293–317). Hillsdale, NJ: Erlbaum.

Scherer, K. R. (1993). Studying the emotion-antecedent appraisal process: An expert system approach. *Cognition and Emotion, 7*, 325–355.

Scherer, K. R. (1997). The role of culture in emotion-antecedent appraisal. *Journal of Personality and Social Psychology, 73*, 902–922.

Scherer, K. R. (1999). Appraisal theories. In T. Dalgleish & M. Power (Eds.), *Handbook of cognition and emotion* (pp. 637–663). Chichester: Wiley.

Scherer, K. R. (2000). Psychological models of emotion. In J. Borod (Ed.), *The neuropsychology of emotion* (pp. 137–162). New York: Oxford University Press.

Scherer, K. R. (2001). Appraisal considered as a process of multi-level sequential checking. In K. R. Scherer, A. Schorr, & T. Johnstone (Eds.), *Appraisal processes in emotion: Theory, methods, research* (pp. 92–120). New York: Oxford University Press.

Scherer, K. R. (2002). Emotion, the psychological structure of. In N. J. Smelser & P. B. Baltes (Eds.), *International encyclopedia of the social and behavioral sciences* (pp. 4472–4477). Oxford: Pergamon.

Scherer, K. R. (2004). Feelings integrate the central representation of appraisal-driven response organization in emotion. In A. S. R. Manstead, N. H. Frijda, & A. H. Fischer (Eds.), *Feelings and emotions: The Amsterdam symposium* (pp. 136–157). Cambridge: Cambridge University Press.

Scherer, K. R. (2005a). Unconscious processes in emotion: The bulk of the iceberg. In P. Niedenthal, L. Feldman-Barrett, & P. Winkielman (Eds.), *The unconscious in emotion* (pp. 312–334). New York: Guilford.

Scherer, K. R. (2005b). What are emotions? And how can they be measured? *Social Science Information, 44*(4), 693–727.

Scherer, K. R., Banse, R., Wallbott, H. G., & Goldbeck, T. (1991). Vocal cues in emotion encoding and decoding. *Motivation and Emotion, 15,* 123–148.

Scherer, K. R. & Ellgring, H. (2007a). Are facial expressions of emotion produced by categorical affect programs or dynamically driven by appraisal? *Emotion, 7*(1), 113–130.

Scherer, K. R. & Ellgring, H. (2007b). Multimodal expression of emotion: Affect programs or componential appraisal patterns? *Emotion, 7*(1), 158–171.

Scherer, K. R., & Scherer, U. (2007a). *Computer assessment of personal potential (CAPP): Design and validation of a comprehensive human resource assessment package.* Manuscript in preparation.

Scherer, K. R., & Scherer, U. (2007b). The Coping-Index (COP-I): Development and validation of a fuzzy-set measure of preferred coping strategies. Manuscript in preparation.

Scherer, K. R., & Scherer, U. (2007c). *Assessing the ability to recognize facial and vocal expressions of emotion: Construction and validation of the FACIAL-I and the VOCAL-I.* Manuscript submitted for publication.

Scherer, K. R., Schorr, A., & Johnstone, T. (Eds.). (2001). *Appraisal processes in emotion: Theory, methods, research.* New York: Oxford University Press.

Scherer, K. R., Wranik, T., Sangsue, J., Tran, V., & Scherer, U. (2004). Emotions in everyday life: Probability of occurrence, risk factors, appraisal and reaction pattern. *Social Science Information, 43*(4), 499–570.

Schulze, R., & Roberts, R. D. (Eds.) (2005). *Emotional intelligence: An international handbook.* Cambridge, MA: Hogrefe & Huber.

Segerstrom, S. C., Tsao, J. C. I., Alden, L. E., & Craske, M. G. (2000). Worry and rumination: Repetitive thought as a concomitant and predictor of negative mood. *Cognitive Therapy and Research, 24,* 671–688.

Van der Linden, M. (2004). Fonctions exécutives et régulation émotionnelle. [Executive functions and emotional regulation] (pp. 137–153). In T. Meulemans, F. Collette, & M. Van der Linden (Eds.), *Neuropsychologie des fonctions exécutives [Neuropsychology of executive functions].* Marseille, France: Solal.

van Reekum, C., Banse, R., Johnstone, T., Etter, A., Wehrle, T., & Scherer, K. R. (2004). Psychophysiological responses to appraisal responses in a computer game. *Cognition and Emotion, 18*(5), 663–688.

Wallbott, H. G. (1998). Bodily expression of emotion. *European Journal of Social Psychology, 28,* 879–896.

Whiteside, S. P., & Lynam, D. R. (2001). The five factor model and impulsivity: Using a structural model of personality to understand impulsivity. *Personality and Individual Differences, 30,* 669–689.

Wranik, T., & Scherer, K. R. (2007). *The dark side of optimism: Blaming others for failure?* Manuscript submitted for publication.

5

Emotions, Emotionality, and Intelligence in the Development of Adaptive Behavior

CARROLL IZARD, CHRISTOPHER TRENTACOSTA, KRISTEN KING, JUDITH MORGAN, AND MICHELLE DIAZ

In this chapter we will discuss the construct of emotion intelligence in relation to the construct of emotion utilization and the developmental constructs of emotion knowledge and emotion regulation. Differential emotions theory (DET), which emphasizes the adaptive, motivational, and cue-producing properties of emotions, provides the conceptual framework. We see emotion motivation as a key factor in emotion intelligence. Emotions not only motivate or drive behavior, their action tendencies and feeling states provide cues that guide cognition and action, and their expressions may motivate and guide the actions of others (Izard, 1971, 2002). We conceive emotion intelligence as involving both the motivational and informational aspects of emotions and as dependent, in part, on emotionality/temperament/personality and cognitive ability.

Emotion, cognition, and action systems are highly interconnected and interactive. Although these sets of systems influence each other reciprocally and almost continually, the emotion systems sometimes operate relatively independently in generating and guiding thought and action. Thus emotions as both relatively independent and interactive systems play a significant role in intelligent or adaptive behavior. So do cognitive ability and emotionality (as reflected in temperament/personality), both of which join with discrete emotions or patterns of emotions in facilitating the coping strategies involved in adaptive behavior (Izard, Ackerman, Schoff, & Fine, 2000). The latter derives in large part from the effects of emotion motivation as utilized in its interaction with thought and action or thought-action patterns. Emotion utilization involves thought-action patterns

Author note: Preparation of this chapter was supported, in part, by NIMH grant # R21 MH68443. We thank Fran Haskins and Jenny Anderson for their assistance.

and behavior ranging from appropriate self-assertion and conflict resolution to empathy, sympathy, helping, and moral reasoning.

Emotion Utilization, Emotion Adaptiveness, and Emotion Intelligence

Emotionality/temperament, emotion information processing, emotion knowledge, emotion regulation, and intelligence serve as determinants of emotion utilization—effective use of the inherently adaptive functions of emotions. Explicating the construct of emotion utilization may provide an alternative way of conceptualizing what has become widely known as emotional intelligence. Individual differences in emotion information processing, emotion regulation styles as reflected in traits of temperament/emotionality/ personality, and indices of psychometric intelligence correlate substantially with the developmental construct of emotion knowledge. Theoretically, the concept of emotion knowledge has some common ground with the concept of emotional intelligence in the adult literature. From a developmental perspective, we think the terms *emotion intelligence* and *emotion adaptiveness* are better rubrics than *emotional intelligence* for labeling children's emotion-related abilities. Moreover, they are a better fit with available evidence in the developmental literature (Izard, 2001; cf. Zeidner, Matthews, Roberts, & MacCann, 2003).

Below, we describe the core developmental facets of emotion intelligence: emotion knowledge, emotion regulation, and emotion utilization. We discuss the definitional and measurement issues associated with each of these components and describe their developmental predictors and related behavioral outcomes. Throughout the discussion, special attention is paid to the similarities and differences between the facets we describe and traditional definitions and descriptions of EI. We conclude with future research directions to refine and extend the study of emotion intelligence across development, with a particular focus on the measurement of emotion utilization.

Emotion Knowledge

A considerable body of research concerns the development and significance of emotion knowledge (EK) in childhood (Arsenio, Cooperman, & Lover, 2000; Denham & Burton, 2003; Izard, 1971, 2002; Mostow, Izard, Fine, & Trentacosta, 2002; Trentacosta, Izard, Mostow, & Fine, 2006). We define EK in terms of processes relating to emotion activation, emotion expression, emotion experience, emotion labeling, and the relations among emotion, cognitive, and action systems. From our developmental perspective, we assume relative independence between emotion, cognitive, and action systems and have presented supporting evidence from research in early infancy and in psychopathology (Izard, Trentacosta, & King, 2005). Moreover, there is substantial evidence for the existence and relatively frequent operation of noncognitive activators of emotion across the life span (Izard, 1993). Thus normative emotional development in general and emotion intelligence in particular consist largely of the formation and growth of intersystem connections (Izard, 2001; cf. Panksepp, 2001). Effective connections do not necessarily occur easily or automatically. Maladaptive connections (e.g., perceiving anger cues where none exist) may generate aggression or anxious depressed behavior. Genes, environment, and person-environment interactions help determine whether the child forms adaptive or maladaptive intersystem connections and takes a trajectory toward high or low emotion intelligence and positive or negative behavioral outcomes.

Understanding emotion activation requires knowledge of events and situations that elicit particular discrete emotions. More developmentally advanced understanding of emotion activation includes appreciation of individual differences in event- or situation-emotion relations. For example, it includes knowing that an event that angers child A may sadden child B and not activate an emotion in child C. Understanding emotion expressions involves the ability to interpret the behavioral signals of emotions. Knowing about emotion experience or feelings involves some understanding of emotion functions, and knowing how to label emotions requires the ability to acquire and use an emotion vocabulary.

Another important component of EK is the ability to efficiently process emotion information. Furthermore, biased emotion information processing may lead to intense negative emotions, prompt more vigorous emotion-driven reactions, and make the tasks of emotion regulation and adaptive behavior more difficult. Maladaptive emotion information processing also suggests an emotion history that contributes to problems in self-regulation. Factors that adversely influence children's emotion information processing and increase the risk of psychopathology include negative emotionality (Muris, Merckelbach, & Damsma, 2000; Rogosch, Cicchetti, & Aber, 1995; Schultz, Izard, & Bear, 2004), harsh environments, and exposure to physical abuse (Pollak, Cicchetti, Hornung, & Reed, 2000). Emotion perception bias can lead to poor emotion knowledge and negative behavioral outcomes that reflect emotion dysregulation.

A revised model of Crick and Dodge's (1994) social information processing model incorporates emotion processes into the causal chain that leads to aggression or other behavioral outcomes (Lemerise & Arsenio, 2000). The first step of the model, encoding of cues, includes children's ability to accurately recognize their own and others' emotions. The second step of the model, interpretation of cues, encompasses emotion attribution biases (Schultz, Izard, & Ackerman, 2000). In support of EK as a component of earlier social information processing steps, an emotion recognition task predicted later patterns of social information processing, including selection of goals and generation of responses (Dodge, Laird, Lochman, & Zelli, 2002).

Development of Emotion Knowledge

The acquisition of EK requires the development of emotion systems as well as connections between emotion systems and cognitive systems to label and verbalize perceived, expressed, and experienced emotions. Rudimentary EK begins soon after birth as infants selectively respond to emotion information (e.g., smiles) conveyed by their caregivers (Izard et al., 1995; Messinger, 2002). The ability to recognize/label basic emotions (happiness, sadness, anger, fear) begins in the toddler and preschool years, generally starting with the ability to distinguish happy expressions from nonhappy expressions (Izard, 1971). Subsequently, young children begin to grasp distinctions between negative emotions and start to develop an understanding of situations that tend to elicit particular emotions. During the elementary school years, children begin to understand more complex emotions and mixed emotions (i.e., one event eliciting two emotions) as well as display rules and emotion regulation strategies (Garner, 1996; Terwogt, Koops, Oosterhoff, & Olthof, 1986).

The early development of EK appears to support Mayer, Salovey, and Caruso's (2004) conclusion that the developmental trend for an increase in EI supports its viability as a construct. However, because the constructs of EK, temperament, and cognitive ability share common variance (Izard, King, Trentacosta, & Laurenceau, 2005), the wealth of developmental research on EK may not in itself provide evidence that EI is a distinct construct, as defined by Mayer et al. (2004). Data from a study that validated the effectiveness of the Emotions Course, designed to accelerate the development of emotion competence and decelerate the development of behavior problems in economically disadvantaged children, showed that temperament predicted EK longitudinally. Mother-reported temperament factors (surgency, negative affect, and effortful control; Child Behavior Questionnaire; Rothbart, Ahadi, & Evans, 2000) and examiner-reported attentional control (General Assessment of Test Session Behavior; Glutting & Oakland, 1991) predicted time 2 EK after controlling for the effects of age, cognitive ability, time 1 EK, and the emotions course treatment effect. Each of the four predictor variables (age, cognitive ability, time 1 EK, and temperament) accounted for a significant part of the variance in time 2 EK, $\Delta R^2 = .18, .12, .14,$ and $.12$, respectively (p's $\le .001$). Interestingly, in this analysis, cognitive ability and temperament accounted for equal and highly significant parts (12% each) of the variance in time 2 EK. The index of EK included measures of emotion expression knowledge, emotion labeling, and emotion situation knowledge (understanding activators or causes of emotions).

Data like that just described, as well as developmental emotion theory, indicate that temperament, like cognitive ability, is a significant determinant of emotion intelligence or EK as assessed in children. In contrast to researchers who have emphasized the need to show that emotional intelligence must be largely independent of temperament/personality and conventionally measured intelligence (Matthews, Roberts, & Zeidner, 2004; cf. Mayer, 2001; Mayer et al., 2004), we find that emotion intelligence as reflected in child measures of EK is partially determined by temperament and intelligence (cf. Roberts, Schulze, Zeidner, & Matthews, 2005). We consider the variance in EK that is not accounted for by these constructs as an effect of the direct contribution of emotion systems to emotion intelligence or to adaptive cognition and action (Izard, 2001).

These emotion systems, however, do not develop simply as a function of the unfolding of genetic processes. They emerge as a function of genes, environment, and gene-environment interactions. Although emotion expression and emotion perception are present in early infancy, their developmental course is highly dependent on parent-child interactions and other aspects of nurturance. For example, emotion discourse in the home is predictive of emotion understanding, including emotion situation knowledge and understanding of display rules (e.g., Dunn, Brown, & Beardsall, 1991; Garner, Jones, Gaddy, & Rennie, 1997). More specifically, parents who discussed emotions frequently had children with higher emotion knowledge 3 years later (Dunn et al., 1991). Furthermore, parental reactions to emotions (e.g., minimizing, comforting, and problem solving) also influence EK (Eisenberg et al., 1996). Siblings may also play a role in the socialization of emotions and the development of EK as cooperation among siblings has been linked to emotion labeling and perspective taking in young children (Dunn, Brown, Slomkowski, Tesla, & Youngblade, 1991). Complexity of peer play during the preschool years also influences EK (Lindsey & Colwell, 2003). Thus, it would be misleading to characterize EK as an "intelligence" that has a dominant genetic component or as a construct that is largely independent of temperament, cognitive ability, and contextual factors.

Measurement of Emotion Knowledge

Emotion knowledge in young children is usually indexed by measures of the child's ability to label emotions, recognize expressions of emotions, and identify causes of emotions or emotion-eliciting situations. These facets of EK have been studied in children since the resurgence of emotion research in psychology (Izard, 1971), and they are the ones most frequently studied in children (ages 3–11 years). A typical measure of EK in young children focuses on the four basic emotions of joy/happiness, sadness, anger, and fear. In an emotion recognition task, the examiner asks the child to match verbal and pictorial representations of an emotion. In an emotion labeling task, the child is asked to produce a verbal label that matches a photograph of a facial expression of an emotion. The scoring of EK measures allows calculation of not only a child's accuracy at recognizing emotions, but also emotion recognition biases.

Measures of EK for older children often include more complex emotions or assess emotion display rules or the causes and consequences of emotion experiences using vignettes. Tests concerning understanding of activators or causes of emotions ask the child to match a verbal description of a provocative event or situation with an emotion expression or label. A test of understanding of relations among emotion, cognitive, and action systems requires that a child demonstrate knowledge of the functions or uses of emotions in thought and action.

As implied by the descriptions of EK, these measures generally rely on declarative knowledge of emotions. In this way, the measurement of EK is similar to the method Mayer et al. (2004) use to assess the branches of EI that are most similar to EK, perceiving emotions and understanding emotions. Assessing EI in this manner has been criticized by Matthews et al. (2004) because it does not tap into procedural use and execution of EK. Recently, we developed a measure that assesses children's knowledge of emotion utilization strategies, the Emotion Knowledge Interview for Preschoolers (EKIP; Izard, King, & Trentacosta, 2004). This measure includes open-ended questions such as, "What's a good thing to do when you feel sad?" This measure does tap into procedural use of emotion motivation, but, as with other EK measures, EKIP uses a declarative method to assess procedural understanding.

Therefore, a remaining weakness of traditional EK measures as well as the EI measures developed by Mayer and colleagues (e.g., 2004) is that they do not assess the full range of on-line emotion processing. Emotion information processing procedures such as those used by Pollak and colleagues to assess maltreated children come closer to assessing on-line execution of emotion processing abilities. These procedures are somewhat similar to traditional EK assessments because they present participants with standardized emotion cues and measure the participant's response. For example, Pollak, Cicchetti, Klorman, and Brumaghim (1997) measured brain event-related potentials in maltreated and nonmaltreated children, and the maltreated children showed a unique processing pattern when viewing angry faces.

Emotion Knowledge and Longitudinal Behavioral and Academic Outcomes

Unlike EI measures of perceiving and understanding that have been criticized for lacking predictive validity (e.g., Matthews et al., 2004), assessments of EK in childhood consistently predict behavioral and academic outcomes, even when controlling for cognitive ability. Researchers found that accurate emotion information processing led to accurate EK, which contributed to appropriate interpersonal interactions, the development of adaptive social behavior, and academic competence (Denham et al., 2003; Izard et al., 2001; Mostow et al., 2002; Shields et al., 2001; Trentacosta et al., in press). Emotion knowledge mediated the development of social skills, and in turn, level of social skills predicted peer acceptance (Mostow et al., 2002).

Poor EK in early development predicts problem behaviors, particularly internalizing problems (Fine, Izard, Mostow, Trentacosta, & Ackerman, 2003). Some studies also show a link between poor EK and externalizing behaviors, particularly in clinic referred children (e.g., Casey, 1996), although this finding is not consistent in community samples (e.g., Arsenio et al., 2000; Denham et al., 2003; Izard et al., 2001). Furthermore, children who show an emotion labeling bias (e.g., labeling cues as anger in which no veridical anger cues exist) on measures of EK engage in more aggressive and hostile behavior (Fine, Trentacosta, Izard, Mostow, & Campbell, 2004; Pollak et al., 2000; Schultz et al., 2004), suggesting ineffective emotion regulation. The path to these negative behavioral outcomes begins with inaccurate or ineffective information processing patterns and the impact that they have on emotion regulation and emotion functioning. For example, anger-prone children who frequently misperceive or mislabel signals or events in social interactions as anger cues are likely to show increased anger. Their inappropriate anger and inappropriate behavioral responses to false anger cues will likely make matters worse and the application of emotion intelligence more difficult. The net effect could mean further misperception of anger and escalating emotional and behavioral dysregulation.

Children who tend to perceive emotion cues accurately also encounter anger in their social environment. On such occasions, these children could be at risk for emotion dys-regulation. However, the tendency of children with greater emotion knowledge to exhibit higher levels of cognitive abilities (Izard et al., 2001) and more positive emotionality (Schultz et al., 2004) may help protect them from inappropriate anger arousal. Moreover, children with greater emotion knowledge have better social skills and more resources for engaging in appropriate social information processing and effective utilization of the emotion motivation relevant to the adaptive behavior required by the situation (Mostow et al., 2002; Mostow & Izard, 2005).

From the preceding examples, one might expect that EK and emotion regulation (ER) would become closely linked, beginning in early development. We infer that the foregoing positive behavioral outcomes resulted in part from ER, facilitated by effective emotion information processing and accurate EK. These findings suggest that fostering the development of EK would increase children's ability to regulate emotions in social interactions in which interpersonal communication and adaptive behavior depend on accurate detection and interpretation of emotion signals in the expressive behavior of face, voice, and body. Researchers have translated such findings into preventive interventions that increase EK and the ability to regulate negative emotions (Greenberg, Kusche, Cook, & Quamma, 1995; Izard, Trentacosta, King, & Mostow, 2004). However, little basic research has directly examined EK as a predictor of children's ER. The relation between these constructs is not entirely consistent at different points in early childhood, but the magnitude of the relations appears to increase throughout childhood (Denham et al., 2003; Miller et al., in press; Trentacosta, Mostow, Fine, King, & Izard, 2005).

Emotion Regulation

The construct of emotion regulation (ER) is currently a hot topic among developmental psychologists, not all of whom are in agreement on its definition. In a recent discussion of ER, Cole, Martin, and Dennis (2004) defined regulated emotion as "changes in the activated emotion," including "changes in emotion valence, intensity, or time course" (p. 321). Cole and colleagues also suggested that ER might include instances in which emotions regulate behavior or social interaction, but others argue that this expanded conceptualization causes ER to be too ambiguous and broad (Eisenberg & Spinrad, 2004). At the neurological level, ER has been defined by processes in multiple brain structures and regions including the prefrontal cortex, the anterior cingulate cortex, the hypothalamic-pituitary-adrenal (HPA) axis, and the vagal nerve complex (Cicchetti & Tucker, 1994; Davidson, Putnam, & Larson, 2000; Lewis & Stieben, 2004).

Cole et al. (2004) acknowledge, as do we, the conceptual and technical difficulties in separating emotion processes and distinctly different emotion regulatory processes. We propose that one way to circumvent the problem of sorting emotion and emotion regulation is to focus on emotion utilization, measurable phenomena that reflect adaptive utilization of the energy and motivation inherent in the activated emotion. In experimental studies, this approach would entail demonstration of the effectiveness of the individual's emotion-related effort to respond to the emotion and emotion-activating event. In naturalistic or quasi-experimental research, this approach would require evidence of differential gains in behavioral outcomes for a control and treatment group, in which the treatment focused on emotion regulation (cf. Izard et al., 2005).

In keeping with our emphasis on emotion utilization as an evidence of emotion regulation, we conceptualize ER as closely intertwined with effective cognitive processes and adaptive actions. However, as a component of emotion intelligence, ER must also be considered in the context of temperament/emotionality, emotion information processing, and emotion knowledge. ER is most clearly evident when a child responds to emotion eliciting events and situations in an adaptive, age appropriate manner (Izard, 2002; Schultz et al., 2004). Thus, emotion dysregulation is often characterized by intense or extreme levels of emotion arousal that disrupt cognitive and action systems. When overwhelmed by emotion dysregulation, the child cannot effectively utilize her emotion motivation as a means to achieve positive social and behavioral goals. Our definition of ER overlaps considerably with the EI branch called "managing emotions" as described by Mayer and colleagues (2004).

Development of Emotion Regulation

Children's ability to regulate their own emotions increases with age as they become less dependent on caregivers (Denham, 1998; Fabes & Eisenberg, 1992). Infants' and younger children's regulation of emotion is most often externally supported by parents or child care providers, but some self-regulatory skills are evident during this stage, such as proximity seeking to a caregiver or gaze aversion from a disturbing stimulus (Cole et al., 2004). By preschool, children demonstrate an increasing ability to regulate their own emotions, first through efforts at self-soothing followed by more advanced use of the social environment to regulate emotions (Eisenberg & Spinrad, 2004). The progression from externally mediated regulation to primarily self-initiated regulation is closely linked to the rapid growth in motor skills and cognitive processing across early childhood (Cole et al., 2004). Around the time children enter elementary school, the majority of them have begun to master more complex regulation strategies, although ER development continues across childhood and adolescence (Lewis & Stieben, 2004).

Emotionality, like the closely related constructs of temperament and personality, plays a critical role in ER and helps account for a range of individual differences in regulatory processes that affect the development of emotion intelligence. Several theorists suggest that negative emotionality may interfere with the development of effective ER (Calkins, 1994; Fox & Calkins, 2003; Kochanska & Coy, 2002). As early as 10 months of age, negative emotionality predicted temperament factors that related to self-regulation, r's ranged from .13 to .43 (Braungart-Rieker & Stifter, 1996; Gilliom, Shaw, Beck, Schonberg, & Lukon, 2002; Lengua, 2002; Rothbart et al., 2000). Negative emotion expression in 18-month-old toddlers predicted trait neuroticism at age 3.5 years (Abe & Izard, 1999). This relation is probably characterized by bidirectional causality. Negative emotionality may overtax emotion regulatory ability and interfere with developing self-regulation, but in some cases effective ER may also inhibit the manifestation of temperamental tendencies to react with intense negative emotions. In any case, inability to regulate emotions will degrade their motivational properties and interfere with their contribution to intelligent or adaptive behavior.

Although emotionality/temperament and ER influence each other's development, ER independently predicts adaptive social behavior. For example, after controlling for positive emotionality and negative emotionality, third- to fifth-grade children's abilities to self-regulate still predicted positive adjustment, adjustment problems, and vulnerability to risk (Lengua, 2002). These findings and others (e.g., Eisenberg et al., 1997) demonstrate the ability of self-regulation to predict social functioning independent of negative and positive emotionality.

The potentially deleterious effects of negative emotionality on behavior are often moderated in part by regulatory abilities. For example, high levels of infant negative emotionality predicted low social competence at age 3, but only among children with low levels of attentional persistence. Five-month-old infants high in negative emotionality and low in attentional persistence were the most defiant during laboratory tasks (e.g., cleaning up) at 30 months (Stifter, Spinrad, & Braungart-Rieker, 1999). In studies on the prediction of social and behavioral outcomes, researchers also found important interactions between children's negative emotionality and abilities to regulate (Eisenberg et al., 1994, 1995).

Positive emotionality operates as a regulator of negative emotions (for a review, see Tugade & Fredrickson, 2002). Positive emotions help the central nervous system recover from physiological arousal due to negative emotions (Fredrickson & Levenson, 1998). Individuals who are either predisposed to experience positive emotions or able to self-induce positive emotions (via imagery or other techniques) may therefore regulate negative emotions more effectively than others. Consistent with these findings, resilient individuals are characterized by positive emotionality and openness to new experiences (Block & Kremen, 1996; Klohnen, 1996), and are more likely to produce humor in stressful situations (Masten, Best, & Garmezy, 1990).

The emergence of ER depends on many environmental influences other than the more genetically mediated factors such as emotionality/temperament. Parenting techniques and styles are important environmental influences on the child's emerging ER ability. Typically, mothers and children are sensitive to each other's emotion signals and respond in synchronous ways (Field, 1994). Alternately, when maternal emotion is interrupted, it disrupts the exchange between mother and infant (Weinberg, Tronick, Cohn, & Olson, 1999). Not surprisingly, the quality of parent-child interactions is predictive of later self-regulatory functioning (Cole et al., 2004). For example, the quality of emotion discourse in the home and parental warmth relate to children's later emotion self-regulation (Eisenberg, Losoya et al., 2001; Gottman, Katz, & Hooven, 1996).

Poverty and maltreatment are the environmental factors that likely place children at greatest risk for emotion dysregulation. Traumas, which could include tragic negative life events, neglect, or physical and sexual abuse, often lead to emotion dysregulation (Cicchetti & Rogosch, 2001). In one study (Smith & Walden, 1999), maltreated preschool children were less likely to use support-seeking regulatory strategies at home than their nonmaltreated peers. In their preschool classrooms, the maltreated children were more likely than the nonmaltreated to use strategies such as crying to seek emotional support (Smith & Walden, 1999). Research also supports the mediational role of emotion dysregulation in the relation between child maltreatment (particularly physical abuse) and aggression (Shields & Cicchetti, 1998). Within low-income communities, the striking prevalence of peer victimization and violence are partly the consequence of widespread emotion dysregulation. In these communities, adaptive ER during childhood is predictive of resilience in social, academic, and behavioral domains (Buckner, Mezzacappa, & Beardslee, 2003). Not surprisingly, children characterized by both sociodemographic risk factors and poor ER are at the greatest risk for behavior problems (Lengua, 2002).

Measurement of Emotion Regulation

Due to the continual and rapid changes in self-regulatory processes in infants and young children, the measurement of ER presents formidable challenges. Emotion theorists have traditionally used convergent measures including maternal/caregiver reports, observations (e.g., facial expressions, vocal tones, gestures), and physiological assessments (e.g., electromyography, heart rate, vagal tone). The majority of studies conducted during infancy and early childhood employ observational methods. Consequently, emerging support for the construct of ER in early childhood is largely based on inferential evidence (Cole et al., 2004). In order to observe the activation process of specific emotions, some researchers have utilized controlled or quasi-naturalistic conditions, in which strong inferences can be made about efforts to control emotion arousal in direct response to a novel stimulus (Cole et al., 2004). For example, in one study, an averted gaze response in toddlers was associated with attempts to regulate fear (Buss & Goldsmith, 1998).

In looking at the activation process that underlies ER, measures of temperamental effortful control are sometimes used (Eisenberg, Champion, & Ma, 2004). These measures of effortful control are often in the form of ratings made by parents or teachers. Although effortful control is a well-defined and relatively well validated construct (Rothbart, Ellis, Rueda, & Posner, 2003), in the context of ER, its measures suffer from a lack of item content that refers directly to emotion-eliciting situations. Other aspects of temperament, such as emotionality and intensity, can be potential confounds in the measurement of ER (Eisenberg, Fabes, & Losoya, 1997). For example, another well-known parent and teacher rating measure of ER, the Emotion Regulation Checklist (Shields & Cicchetti, 1997), contains two subscales, Lability/Negativity and Emotion Regulation. These subscales correlate highly in most studies and both arguably contain content related to ER. However, the Lability/Negativity subscale contains many items that are similar to those included in measures of temperamental emotionality or emotion intensity.

Another method of measuring ER focuses only on management of a single emotion (e.g., Zeman, Shipman, & Penza-Clyve, 2001). As support for this individual-emotion method, some research demonstrates unique relations between discrete emotion (e.g., sadness) expression and management and specific behavioral outcomes (e.g., internalizing behavior problems; Eisenberg, Cumberland et al., 2001; Zeman, Shipman, & Suveg, 2002). However, support for the broad measurement of ER in childhood psychopathology also exists. For example, an anxiety disorder diagnosis in childhood is associated not only with poor regulation of fear and worry but also with anger and sadness dysregulation (Suveg & Zeman, 2004).

Clearly, the measurement of ER in childhood remains problematic. However, the childhood measures of ER may have distinct advantages over the methods that Mayer and colleagues (2004) and others describe for measuring emotion management in their studies of adult emotional intelligence. The developmentalists' use of observational methods, in which stimuli are utilized to elicit emotions and true regulatory responses are measured and coded, provides an excellent way to study the range of truly adaptive regulatory processes. At the very least, observational methods and ratings from parents, teachers, and peers serve as effective tests of the validity of the self-report methods so commonly used to measure ER in adolescents and adults.

Emotion Regulation, Longitudinal Behavioral, and Academic Outcomes

ER can be characterized by more or less adaptive styles based in part on a child's prior social experiences, which, in turn, will influence that child's future social adjustment. Eisenberg and her colleagues have consistently found longitudinal correlations between emotion dysregulation or excessive negative emotion expression and poor teacher ratings on measures of social competence and internalizing and externalizing behaviors, reflecting a stable developmental pattern in deficient ER abilities (Eisenberg et al., 1995; Eisenberg, Cumberland et al., 2001). A child's ability to regulate emotions and behavior impacts several aspects of social adjustment. In the preschool classroom, peer play can elicit a combination of positive and negative emotions that a child must learn to manage in order to initiate and maintain interpersonal interaction and negotiate (Raver, Blackburn, Bancroft, & Torp, 1999). In social interactions such as peer play, children must effectively interpret, modulate, and utilize their emotions prosocially to develop rapport with their peers. Researchers identify a direct connection between ER skills and peer social status in school-age children, in which higher self-regulatory abilities are predictive of more favorable peer status and acceptance (Denham & Burton, 2003; Hubbard & Coie, 1994). Therefore, the ability to regulate emotions dynamically influences and is influenced by the social and emotional environment. Furthermore, successful ER may lead to a greater ability to sustain positive emotions that mitigate the effects of negative life events and enhance resiliency throughout the life span (Fredrickson, 2001).

Many of the behavioral outcomes associated with ER are closely related to our conceptualization of emotion utilization. In particular, prosocial behavior characterized by empathy, sympathy, and helping actions very often depends on well-regulated emotion (Eisenberg et al., 2003; Izard, 2002). In the next section we will explore how these behavioral outcomes of ER can shed light on emotion intelligence and the adaptiveness of emotions.

Emotion Utilization

Emotion utilization occurs when the properties of discrete emotions or patterns of emotions are harnessed adaptively (Izard, 2001). When emotion motivation and action tendencies are properly regulated, they are able to serve their adaptive purposes. In conjunction with accurate EK and effective ER, emotion motivation promotes "intelligent" behavior. In EU, accurate emotion knowledge and effective ER work with emotion motivation to produce adaptive thought-action patterns. Individual differences in EU are thus due to variation in EK, ER ability, and the adaptiveness of the person's thought-action structures. We expect the processes of EK and ER working together to facilitate EU will result in immediate gains in adaptive behavior as well as long-term benefits in developmental outcomes.

The principles of EU apply to each discrete emotion. For instance, for a child feeling fear at the prospect of walking home from a party alone, effective EU might result in calling a parent for a ride or partnering with a friend who will take the same route. For the emotion of fear to be utilized adaptively, the child must have accurate EK so that she can identify the emotion feeling and properly assess the danger and its implications. The child also requires effective ER to avoid underregulating the fear and refusing to leave the party at all or overregulating the fear and walking home alone despite safety concerns.

We draw some distinctions between ER and emotion utilization (EU), although they are related constructs. In some circumstances (e.g., extremely intense emotion arousal), ER may be a prerequisite of EU. In many if not all circumstances, ER mediates or facilitates EU. ER, but not EU, may result from the presence and behavior of another person. EU often, if not always, reflects successful ER, but ER does not necessarily reflect EU. In addition to the possibility of ER resulting from another's action, an infant may regulate anger by "crying it out" and an older child by unwarranted and maladaptive aggressive behavior. The self-regulation of emotions is by definition emotion focused. EU is typically focused on the context or problem.

In the concept of EU, emotions themselves are the dominant force promoting adaptive behavior and growth, whereas in the concept of emotional intelligence, intelligence seems dominant or equally important. As an example, Mayer, Salovey, and Caruso (2004) conceive of EI as intelligence both working on emotional information and using emotion to enhance cognition. We agree that emotions, particularly the positive emotions of interest-excitement and enjoyment-contentment, can facilitate cognition (the second branch of their emotional intelligence construct), but we also emphasize that all the emotions can motivate adaptive behavior. Our concept of EU seems similar in some respects to the fourth branch of Mayer et al.'s (2004) construct of emotional intelligence, managing emotions. However, emotion management focuses on maintaining or changing emotions appropriately in a situation, whereas EU focuses specifically on capitalizing on the motivation inherent in effectively modulated emotion arousal.

Among the best examples of EU are empathy that leads to sympathy and helping behavior, and guilt (over having harmed another) that leads to reparation or to the internalization of standards for moral behavior. Emotion motivation provides the basis for empathy and prosocial behavior (see discussion in Izard, Ackerman, & Schultz, 1999). Empathy is sometimes used to refer to cognitive awareness of another person's internal state (see Hoffman, 2000). However, we define empathy as dependent on an emotion-related ability or skill, the ability to detect another person's emotion state and share it vicariously. Prosocial utilization of empathy requires, among other capacities, good ER ability; an individual must modulate his or her own level of vicarious emotion in order to stay in the situation and provide comfort. Through down regulation of vicarious negative emotions, an individual is able to look toward the needs of others rather than focus on relieving his or her own distress (Fabes, Eisenberg, Karbon, Troyer, & Switzer, 1994). The importance of ER to the result of empathic arousal of emotion feelings is reflected in the division of empathy by some researchers into personal distress, the aversive emotional reaction, and sympathy, the feeling of concern or sorrow that motivates prosocial behavior (Batson, 1991; Fabes et al., 1994).

Guilt is the most important emotion in the development of the emotion-thought structures of conscience and in emotion-thought-moral behavior pattern (Izard, 1991). Although shame may also lead individuals to conform to the rules of society, the painful experience of shame may bring denial and repression, whereas guilt relates to a sense of personal responsibility for wrongdoing and stimulates thought about reparation (Izard, 1991). A study of self-reported guilt and shame in college students showed that shame correlated with indices of anger arousal, irritability, suspiciousness, resentment, indirect expressions of hostility, and a tendency to blame others, whereas guilt was unrelated or inversely correlated with these (Tangney, Wagner, Fletcher, & Gramzow, 1992). If utilized skillfully through effective ER, guilt prods individuals to follow their internalized moral values, encourages reparations after transgressions, and helps maintain relationships (Izard, 2001). Anticipatory guilt triggered by thoughts of a transgression may encourage following the rules, whereas anticipatory guilt induced by empathy encourages helping behavior (Hoffman, 2000).

Development of Emotion Utilization: The Examples
of Empathy and Moral Behavior

Adaptive utilization of emotion is critical to the development of social and cognitive systems (Abe & Izard, 1999). For example, young children utilize the emotions of interest and joy to engage in the social and physical environment. They utilize shifting patterns of interest-excitement and enjoyment-contentment to drive repetitive play toward task achievement and mastery of skills. The social interactions driven by modulated positive as well as negative emotions (EU) bring advances in social perspective taking and growth in ability to empathize and respond to empathic arousal with prosocial behavior. EU thus promotes the growth of cognitive and social skills (e.g., social perspective taking) in childhood and works with these tools to produce adaptive responses. In order for emotions to perform their developmental tasks, proper emotion-thought-behavior connections must form.

The earliest precursor of empathy, a cry in response to another infant's cry, appears in the first days of life (e.g., Sagi & Hoffman, 1976; Simner, 1971). As cognitive systems advance so that young children can distinguish self from other, they begin showing empathic concern, which they may demonstrate by offering care to others (see Hoffman, 2000). By the toddler and preschool years, children begin to show the capacity to experience guilt and empathy. As early as 22 months, toddlers showed signs of guilt (e.g., averted eyes, suppressed positive emotion) in response to transgressions (Kochanska, Gross, Lin, & Nichols, 2002). Consistent with the sympathy versus personal distress distinction, children with high ER ability (as assessed by heart rate variability and mother-reported coping) were better able than low ER children to respond to a crying infant with comfort rather than distress (Fabes et al., 1994).

As the emotions of guilt and shame form adaptive connections with thoughts and behaviors, the child internalizes moral standards (Abe & Izard, 1999). The development of an adaptive link between empathic arousal and the thought-action pattern of helping behavior is critical for prosocial behavior. A longitudinal study on the structure of the early conscience found that guilt and empathic distress were more strongly related to internalization of rules at age 45 months than at age 33 months, suggesting that the preschool years are a critical time for development of such patterns (Aksan & Kochanska, 2005). In middle and late childhood, utilization of the emotions of guilt, shame, and pride help children form self-concepts and learn from constructive social comparisons and relationships (Abe & Izard, 1999).

Measurement of Emotion Utilization

Although a number of measures have been designed to assess emotional intelligence and the emotion knowledge component of emotion intelligence, we know of no measures that adequately capture our conceptualization of EU. One possible way to assess an individual's EU skills would be to measure the development of empathy. Several self-report measures have been developed to assess empathy in adults, some focusing on the cognitive component of empathy (e.g., the Hogan Empathy Scale; Hogan, 1969) and others assessing the emotion component as well (e.g., the Interpersonal Reactivity Index; Davis, 1983). The Emotional Empathy Questionnaire (EEQ; Mehrabian & Epstein, 1972), a 33-item, self report instrument, measures empathy as the vicarious experience of emotions. A simpler measure of empathy, the Index of Empathy for Children and Adolescents (IECA; Bryant, 1982), was based primarily on items from the EEQ. The IECA consists of 22 true/false items such as "I get upset when I see a boy being hurt" and "Sometimes I cry when I watch TV." It remains for future research to examine the utility of these empathy measures for assessing EU. Such research would have to show a significant relation between scores on an empathy measure and a measure that demonstrates that the empathy leads to prosocial behavior.

Assessing the development of guilt and its consequences on the individual, as a reflection of emotion-related moral internalization, might also provide information on EU. Two well-researched self-report measures of guilt and shame in adults are the Personal Feelings Questionnaire-2 (PFQ-2; Harder & Zalma, 1990) and the Test of Self-Conscious Affect (TOSCA; Tangney, Wagner, & Gramzow, 1989). The PFQ-2 is a checklist of 16 adjectives describing guilt (e.g., "regret") and shame (e.g., "feeling humiliated"). The most recent update of the TOSCA, the TOSCA-3, includes 16 scenarios followed by possible behavioral, emotional, and cognitive responses relating to guilt, shame, pride, detachment/unconcern, and externalization (Tangney, Dearing, Wagner, & Gramzow, 2000). A version of this measure for children ages 8 to 12, the TOSCA-C, has been developed using child-generated scenarios and responses, and an adolescent version is also available (Tangney & Dearing, 2002).

Developing other measures of EU might involve assessing the adaptive (or maladaptive) utilization of specific emotions. For example, measures of self-assertion or aggression in interpersonal conflict situations would provide information on effective utilization of anger. Clearly, we need research on methods of assessing the development of EU.

Emotion Utilization and Social and Behavioral Outcomes

A large body of research indicates that the development of effective regulation and utilization of emotions has broad and important implications for the development of social competence and other forms of adaptive behavior. For example, research on conduct disordered children shows the negative outcomes that can occur when empathy does not develop properly. Children with early-onset conduct disorder who also have callous-unemotional traits are more likely to climb a steep trajectory of aggressive, antisocial behavior (see discussion in Frick & Ellis, 1999).

Most of the research on EU in children has been correlational. A number of studies have shown that empathy relates to prosocial behavior in children and adults (for a review, see Eisenberg, 2000). In a study of 9- and 10-year-old children classified as prosocial, bullies, or victims, the prosocial children showed more empathic awareness than the other two groups (Warden & Mackinnon, 2003). Other researchers showed that empathy in 5-year-olds, as measured by interviews after watching videos of emotion vignettes, related directly to prosocial behavior and inversely to aggression and anger (Strayer & Roberts, 2004). The emotion component of empathy may be particularly important in children's aggression. When 25 aggressive and 27 nonaggressive boys aged 7 to 14 were compared on levels of empathy as measured by statements made during group interviews, the affective, but not the cognitive, component of empathy was higher in the nonaggressive group (Shechtman, 2002). Ineffective socialization of shame and guilt, particularly when linked to difficult temperament and anger perception bias, may also relate to aggression and hostility. In children, adolescents, and adults, shame-prone individuals were more likely to have maladaptive responses to anger, such as hostility and aggression, whereas guilt-prone individuals tended to utilize anger in more constructive ways, such as discussion (Tangney, Wagner, Hill-Barlow, Marschall, & Gramzow, 1996).

Conclusion

As the above description of emotion intelligence and its components suggest, we see the true intelligence of emotions reflected in the adaptive interplay of emotion, thought, and action systems. Emotion intelligence is best demonstrated by emotion knowledge, emotion regulation, and emotion utilization, and, most importantly, through coordination among these facets to meet adaptive and culturally mediated goals and standards. Most previous emotion development research and theory have examined these components separately, but we encourage a coordinated view of these aspects of emotion intelligence in future work.

For example, in our prevention research we teach Head Start preschoolers to practice emotion intelligence when faced with intense or confusing emotions in the classroom or at home. If one child in a classroom is upset that another child ran up and started using her favorite toy during free play time, she might hit the other child and snatch the toy from her. We encourage the child to use an alternative, adaptive method that we call the "hold tight" technique. In order to use the technique, the child must understand through sensing physiological, behavioral, and/or contextual cues (via emotion information processing) that she feels angry, hold herself or hug a pillow, and take three deep breaths to reduce the intensity of the modulated anger arousal (emotion regulation), and use the motivational properties of anger to assert herself in a suitable manner (emotion utilization). For example, the girl could suggest that they share the toy.

This example illustrates the importance of considering the coordination of emotion knowledge, emotion regulation, and emotion utilization when describing emotion intelligence. A child who can understand emotions but has difficulty regulating them or can regulate emotions but does not utilize emotion motivation to share, help, or empathize does not possess adequate emotion intelligence. Similar to the "integrated investment" model outlined by Zeidner et al., (2003), we propose that these emotion processes act reciprocally and interactively. We also emphasize that the coordination of these three emotion processes occurs more or less adaptively, depending on child temperament/emotionality, emotion information processing styles, caregiving relationships, and other interpersonal or social situations.

Unfortunately, few studies actually measure the coordination of emotion knowledge, emotion regulation, emotion utilization, and the relevant contextual factors or examine their combined roles in adaptive social behavior. Thus, innovative and integrated methods to measure adaptive emotion intelligence are a top priority for future research. Using observational methods that elicit emotion and coding child responses for their similarity to theoretical descriptions of emotion utilization is one possible innovation. One study that includes aspects of this innovative approach, the Fabes and colleagues (1994) investigation presented above, simultaneously measured physiological regulation and child responses to distressed infant cries. High heart rate variability, an index of physiological regulation, was related to comforting behavior in response to an infant's cry (Fabes et al., 1994). In our research, we have begun to measure preschool children's knowledge of emotion utilization with an interview, and in future research we hope to assess children's ability to apply or utilize emotion knowledge "on-line" in emotion-eliciting situations.

We expect that participating in an emotion-centered prevention program will promote emotion utilization. We have some preliminary evidence that demonstrated improved emotion intelligence in at-risk (Head Start) children who participated in the Emotions Course (see Izard et al., 2005; Izard et al., 2004). Such emotion-based approaches provide promise for the advancement of emotion intelligence and its status as a legitimate and important developmental construct.

The Nature of Emotion Intelligence: Responses to the Editors' Questions

1. *Conceptualizing EI.* EI derives from the inherently adaptive functions of emotions. The core of EI is emotion processes or emotion functioning that sensitizes, recruits, and interacts with perceptual, cognitive, and action systems for adaptive engagement in the intellectual, social, and physical domains. The motivation inherent in an activated emotion system drives the individual's engagement and transactions. Emotion regulatory abilities, measured in terms of emotionality/personality (including capacity to facilitate or inhibit emotion-driven cognition and action), and perceptual-cognitive abilities, assessed through conventional measures of intelligence, may place restraints on the development and functioning of EI. Facets of EI consist of experientially and culturally influenced emotion-related skills that contribute to intellectual, social, and emotion competence. To assess EI in children, we measure their understanding of the expressions, feeling states, and functions of emotions in the context of measures of cognitive ability and emotionality/temperament and in relation to a criterion that reflects adaptive functioning. We partial out the variance in the index of adaptive functioning that is due to temperament and intelligence and attribute the remainder to EI. In such equations, EI represents the adaptive utilization of emotion processes and emotion motivation, and emotion utilization implies effective interaction of emotion, cognition, and action systems.
2. *The relation of EI to personality and ability.* We view emotionality, temperament, and personality as highly related and overlapping constructs. As explained more fully in the foregoing paragraph item (1), we consider the processes represented by these constructs as contributors and sources of constraints to the development and functioning of EI. We see emotions as a common denominator among all these constructs.

3. *The relation of EI to theories of emotion and intelligence.* Our concept of EI is rooted in differential emotions theory, which is influenced by Darwin's observations on emotions and Tomkin's extensive theorizing. It is compatible, at least in part, with other theories that recognize the emotions as critical motivational systems in development and ongoing adaptation.

4. *EI and real-world social environments.* We have demonstrated that EI, as we define it, is mutable and teachable. The implementation of our emotions course for economically disadvantaged children increased their emotion knowledge (understanding of emotion expressions, feeling states, and functions) and emotion regulation, and decreased their negative emotion expression, aggression, and anxious/ depressed behavior. We have no data on changes in EI or emotion regulation beyond childhood, but we speculate that developmental gains may occur through adolescence and early adulthood, as a function in part of the maturation of prefrontal cortices, and throughout the life span as a function of experience. We expect age-related declines in cognitive ability and increases in negative life events to present challenges to the functioning of EI.

References

Abe, J. A., & Izard, C. E. (1999). A longitudinal study of emotion expression and personality relations in early development. *Journal of Personality and Social Psychology, 77,* 566–577.

Aksan, N., & Kochanska, G. (2005). Conscience in childhood: Old questions, new answers. *Developmental Psychology, 41,* 506–516.

Arsenio, W. F., Cooperman, S., & Lover, A. (2000). Affective predictors of preschoolers' aggression and peer acceptance: Direct and indirect effects. *Developmental Psychology, 36,* 438–448.

Batson, C. D. (1991). *The altruism question: Toward a social-psychological answer.* Hillsdale, NJ: Erlbaum.

Block, J. H., & Kremen, A. M. (1996). IQ and ego-resiliency: Conceptual and empirical connections and separateness. *Journal of Personality and Social Psychology, 70,* 349–361.

Braungart-Rieker, J. M., & Stifter, C. A. (1996). Infants' responses to frustrating situations: Continuity and change in reactivity and regulation. *Child Development, 67,* 1767–1779.

Bryant, B. K. (1982). An index of empathy for children and adolescents. *Child Development, 53,* 413–425.

Buckner, J. C., Mezzacappa, E., & Beardslee, W. R. (2003). Characteristics of resilient youths living in poverty: The role of self-regulatory processes. *Development and Psychopathology, 15,* 139–162.

Buss, K. A., & Goldsmith, H. H. (1998). Fear and anger regulation in infancy: Effects of the temporal dynamics of affective expression. *Child Development, 69,* 359–374.

Calkins, S. D. (1994). Origins and outcomes of individual differences in emotion regulation. *Monographs of the Society for Research in Child Development, 59,* 53–72.

Casey, R. J. (1996). Emotional competence in children with externalizing and internalizing disorders. In M. Lewis & M. W. Sullivan (Eds.), *Emotional development in atypical children* (pp. 161–183). Mahwah, NJ: Erlbaum.

Cicchetti, D., & Rogosch, F. A. (2001). The impact of child maltreatment and psychopathology on neuroendocrine functioning. *Developmental Psychopathology, 13*, 783–804.

Cicchetti, D., & Tucker, D. (1994). Development and self-regulatory structures of the mind. Special Issue: Neural plasticity, sensitive periods, and psychopathology. *Development and Psychopathology, 6*, 533–549.

Cole, P. M., Martin, S. E., & Dennis, T. A. (2004). Emotion regulation as a scientific construct: Methodological challenges and directions for child development research. *Child Development, 75*, 317–333.

Crick, N. R., & Dodge, K. A. (1994). A review and reformulation of social information-processing mechanisms in children's social adjustment. *Psychological Bulletin, 115*, 74–101.

Davidson, R. J., Putnam, K. M., & Larson, C. L. (2000). Dysfunction in the neural circuitry of emotion regulation—a possible prelude to violence. *Science, 289*, 591–594.

Davis, M. H. (1983). Measuring individual differences in empathy: Evidence for a multidimensional approach. *Journal of Personality and Social Psychology, 44*, 113–126.

Denham, S. A. (1998). *Emotional development in young children.* New York: Guilford Press.

Denham, S. A., Blair, K. A., DeMulder, E., Levitas, J., Sawyer, K., Auerbach-Major, S., & Queenan, P. (2003). Preschool emotional competence: Pathway to social competence. *Child Development, 74*, 238–256.

Denham, S. A., & Burton, R. (2003). *Social and emotional prevention and intervention programming for preschoolers.* New York: Kluwer Academic/Plenum.

Dodge, K. A., Laird, R., Lochman, J. E., & Zelli, A. (2002). Multidimensional latent-construct analysis of children's social information processing patterns: Correlations with aggressive behavior problems. *Psychological Assessment, 14*, 60–73.

Dunn, J., Brown, J., & Beardsall, L. (1991). Family talk about feeling states and children's later understanding of others' emotions. *Developmental Psychology, 27*, 448–455.

Dunn, J., Brown, J., Slomkowski, C., Tesla, C., & Youngblade, L. (1991). Young children's understanding of other people's feelings and beliefs: Individual differences and their antecedents. *Child Development, 62*, 1352–1366.

Eisenberg, N. (2000). Emotion, regulation, and moral development. *Annual Review of Psychology, 51*, 665–697.

Eisenberg, N., Champion, C., & Ma, Y. (2004). Emotion-related regulation: An emerging construct. *Merrill-Palmer Quarterly, 50*, 236–259.

Eisenberg, N., Cumberland, A., Spinrad, T. L., Fabes, R., Shepard, S. A., Reiser, M., Murphy, B. C., Losoya, S. H., & Guthrie, I. K. (2001). The relations of regulation and emotionality to children's externalizing and internalizing problem behavior. *Child Development, 72*, 1112–1134.

Eisenberg, N., Fabes, R. A., & Losoya, S. (1997). Emotional responding: Regulation, social correlates, and socialization. In P. Salovey & D. J. Slutyer (Eds.), *Emotional development and emotional intelligence: Educational implications* (pp. 129–163). New York: Basic Books.

Eisenberg, N., Fabes, R. A., Murphy, B., Karbon, M., Smith, M., & Maszk, P. (1996). The relations of children's dispositional empathy-related responding to their emotionality, regulation, and social functioning. *Developmental Psychology, 32*, 195–209.

Eisenberg, N., Fabes, R. A., Murphy, B., Maszk, P., Smith, M., & Karbon, M. (1995). The role of emotionality and regulation in children's social functioning: A longitudinal study. *Child Development, 66*, 109–128.

Eisenberg, N., Fabes, R. A., Nyman, M., Bernzweig, J., & Pinuelas, A. (1994). The relations of emotionality and regulation to children's anger-related reactions. *Child Development, 65,* 109–128.

Eisenberg, N., Losoya, S., Fabes, R. A., Guthrie, I. K., Reiser, M., Murphy, B., Shepard, S. A., Poulin, R., & Padgett, S. J. (2001). Parental socialization of children's dysregulated expression of emotion and externalizing problems. *Journal of Family Psychology, 15,* 183–205.

Eisenberg, N., & Spinrad, T. L. (2004). Emotion-related regulation: Sharpening the definition. *Child Development, 75,* 334–339.

Eisenberg, N., Valiente, C., Morris, A. S., Fabes, R. A., Cumberland, A., Reiser, M., Gershoff, E. T., Shepard, S. A., & Losoya, S. (2003). Longitudinal relations among parental emotional expressivity, children's regulation, and quality of socioemotional functioning. *Developmental Psychology, 39,* 3–19.

Fabes, R. A., & Eisenberg, N. (1992). Young children's coping with interpersonal anger. *Child Development, 63,* 116–128.

Fabes, R. A., Eisenberg, N., Karbon, M., Troyer, D., & Switzer, G. (1994). The relations of children's emotion regulation to their vicarious emotional responses and comforting behaviors. *Child Development, 65,* 1678–1693.

Field, T. (1994). The effect of mother's physical and emotional unavailability on emotion regulation. *Monographs of the Society for Research in Child Development, 59* (2–3, Serial No. 240), pp. 208–227.

Fine, S. E., Izard, C. E., Mostow, A. J., Trentacosta, C. J., & Ackerman, B. P. (2003). First grade emotion knowledge as a predictor of fifth grade self-reported internalizing behaviors in children from economically disadvantaged families. *Development and Psychopathology, 15,* 331–342.

Fine, S. E., Trentacosta, C. J., Izard, C. E., Mostow, A. J., & Campbell, J. L. (2004). Anger perception, caregivers' use of physical discipline, and aggression in children at risk. *Social Development, 13,* 213–228.

Fox, N. A., & Calkins, S. D. (2003). The development of self-control of emotion: Intrinsic and extrinsic influences. *Motivation and Emotion, 27,* 7–26.

Fredrickson, B. L. (2001). The role of positive emotions in positive psychology. *American Psychologist, 56,* 218–226.

Fredrickson, B. L., & Levenson, R. W. (1998). Positive emotions speed recovery from the cardiovascular sequelae of negative emotions. *Cognition and Emotion, 12,* 191–220.

Frick, P. J., & Ellis, M. (1999). Callous-unemotional traits and subtypes of conduct disorder. *Clinical Child and Family Psychology Review, 2,* 149–168.

Garner, P. W. (1996). The relations of emotional role taking, affective/moral attributions, and emotional display rule knowledge to low-income school-age children's social competence. *Journal of Applied Developmental Psychology, 17,* 19–36.

Garner, P. W., Jones, D. C., Gaddy, G., & Rennie, K. M. (1997). Low-income mothers' conversations about emotions and their children's emotional competence. *Social Development, 9,* 29–48.

Gilliom, M., Shaw, D. S., Beck, J. E., Schonberg, M. A., & Lukon, J. L. (2002). Anger regulation in disadvantaged preschool boys: Strategies, antecedents, and the development of self-control. *Developmental Psychology, 38,* 222–235.

Glutting, J. J., & Oakland, T. (1991). *Guide to the assessment of test session behaviors.* San Antonio, TX: The Psychological Corporation.

Gottman, J. M., Katz, L., & Hooven, C. (1996). Parental meta-emotion philosophy and the emotional life of families: Theoretical models and preliminary data. *Journal of Family Psychology, 10,* 243–268.

Greenberg, M. T., Kusche, C. A., Cook, E. T., & Quamma, J. P. (1995). Promoting emotional competence in school-aged children: The effects of the PATHS curriculum. *Development and Psychopathology, 7,* 117–136.

Harder, D., & Zalma, A. (1990). Two promising shame and guilt scales: A construct validity comparison. *Journal of Personality Assessment, 55,* 729–745.

Hoffman, M. L. (2000). *Empathy and moral development: Implications for caring and justice.* New York: Cambridge University Press.

Hogan, R. (1969). Development of an empathy scale. *Journal of Consulting and Clinical Psychology, 33,* 307–316.

Hubbard, J. A., & Coie, J. D. (1994). Emotional correlates of social competence in children's peer relationships. *Merrill-Palmer Quarterly, 40,* 1–20.

Izard, C. E. (1971). *The face of emotion.* New York: Appleton-Century-Crofts.

Izard, C. E. (1991). *The psychology of emotions.* New York: Plenum Press.

Izard, C. E. (1993). Four systems for emotion activation: Cognitive and noncognitive processes. *Psychological Review, 100,* 68–90.

Izard, C. E. (2001). Emotional intelligence or adaptive emotions? *Emotion, 1,* 249–257.

Izard, C. E. (2002). Translating emotion theory and research into preventive interventions. *Psychological Bulletin, 128,* 796–824.

Izard, C. E., Ackerman, B. P., Schoff, K. M., & Fine, S. E. (2000). Self-organization of discrete emotions, emotion patterns, and emotion-cognition relations. In M. D. Lewis & I. Granic (Eds.), *Emotion, development, and self-organization* (pp. 15–36). Cambridge, MA: Cambridge University Press.

Izard, C. E., Ackerman, B. P., & Schultz, D. (1999). Independent emotions and consciousness: Self-consciousness and dependent emotions. In J. Singer & P. Salovey (Eds.), *At play in the fields of consciousness: Essays in honor of Jerome Singer* (pp. 83–102). Mahwah, NJ: Erlbaum.

Izard, C. E., Fantauzzo, C. A., Castle, J. M., Haynes, O. M., Rayias, M. F., & Putnam, P. H. (1995). The ontogeny and significance of infants' facial expressions in the first 9 months of life. *Developmental Psychology, 31,* 997–1013.

Izard, C. E., Fine, S. E., Schultz, D., Mostow, A. J., Ackerman, B. P., & Youngstrom, E. A. (2001). Emotion knowledge as a predictor of social behavior and academic competence in children at risk. *Psychological Science, 12,* 18–23.

Izard, C. E., King, K. A., & Trentacosta, C. J. (2004). *EKIP: Emotion knowledge interview for preschoolers.* Unpublished manuscript, University of Delaware, Newark.

Izard, C. E., King, K. A., Trentacosta, C. J., & Laurenceau, J. P. (2005). *Accelerating the development of emotion competence in Head Start children.* Unpublished manuscript, University of Delaware, Newark.

Izard, C. E., Trentacosta, C. J., & King, K. A. (2005). Brain, emotions, and emotion-cognition relations. *Behavioral and Brain Sciences, 28,* 208–209.

Izard, C. E., Trentacosta, C. J., King, K. A., & Mostow, A. J. (2004). An emotion-based prevention program for Head Start children. *Early Education and Development, 15,* 407–422.

Klohnen, E. C. (1996). Conceptual analysis and measurement of the construct of ego-resiliency. *Journal of Personality and Social Psychology, 70,* 1067–1079.

Kochanska, G., & Coy, K. C. (2002). Child emotionality and maternal responsiveness as predictors of reunion behaviors in the strange situation: Links mediated and unmediated by separation distress. *Child Development, 73,* 228–240.

Kochanska, G., Gross, J. N., Lin, M., & Nichols, K. (2002). Guilt in young children: Development, determinants, and relations with a broader system of standards. *Child Development, 73,* 461–482.

Lemerise, E. A., & Arsenio, W. F. (2000). An integrated model of emotion processes and cognition in social information processing. *Child Development, 71,* 107–118.

Lengua, L. J. (2002). The contribution of emotionality and self-regulation to the understanding of children's response to multiple risk. *Child Development, 73,* 144–161.

Lewis, M. D., & Stieben, J. (2004). Emotion regulation in the brain: Conceptual issues and directions for developmental research. *Child Development, 75,* 371–376.

Lindsey, E. W., & Colwell, M. J. (2003). Preschoolers' emotional competence: Links to pretend and physical play. *Child Study Journal, 33,* 39–52.

Masten, A. S., Best, K. M., & Garmezy, N. (1990). Resilience and development: Contributions from the study of children who overcome adversity. *Development and Psychopathology, 2,* 425–444.

Matthews, G., Roberts, R. D., & Zeidner, M. (2004). Seven myths about emotional intelligence. *Psychological Inquiry, 15,* 179–196.

Mayer, J. D. (2001). Emotion, intelligence, and emotional intelligence. In J. P. Forgas (Ed.), *Handbook of affect and social cognition* (pp. 41–431). Mahwah, NJ: Erlbaum.

Mayer, J. D., Salovey, P., & Caruso, D. R. (2004). Emotional intelligence: Theory, findings, and implications. *Psychological Inquiry, 15,* 197–215.

Mehrabian, A., & Epstein, N. (1972). A measure of emotional empathy. *Journal of Personality, 40,* 525–543.

Messinger, D. S. (2002). Positive and negative infant facial expressions and emotions. *Current Directions in Psychological Science, 11,* 1–6.

Miller, A. L., Fine, S. E., Gouley, K. K., Seifer, R., Dickstein, S., & Shields, A. (in press). Showing and telling about emotions: Interactions between facets of emotional competence and associations with classroom adjustment in Head Start preschoolers. *Cognition and Emotion.*

Mostow, A. J., & Izard, C. E. (2005). *Longitudinal and concurrent prediction of peer acceptance: Direct and indirect effects of emotional, cognitive, and behavioral factors.* Unpublished doctoral dissertation, University of Delaware, Newark.

Mostow, A. J., Izard, C. E., Fine, S. E., & Trentacosta, C. J. (2002). Modeling the emotional, cognitive, and behavioral predictors of peer acceptance. *Child Development, 73,* 1775–1787.

Muris, P., Merckelbach, H., & Damsma, E. (2000). Threat perception bias in nonreferred, socially anxious children. *Journal of Clinical Child Psychology, 29,* 348–359.

Panksepp, J. (2001). The long-term psychobiological consequences of infant emotions: Prescriptions for the twenty-first century. *Infant Mental Health Journal, 22,* 132–173.

Pollak, S., Cicchetti, D., Hornung, K., & Reed, A. (2000). Recognizing emotion in faces: Developmental effects of child abuse and neglect. *Developmental Psychology, 36,* 679–688.

Pollak, S., Cicchetti, D., Klorman, R., & Brumaghim, J. (1997). Cognitive brain event-related potentials and emotion processing in maltreated children. *Child Development, 68,* 773–787.

Raver, C. C., Blackburn, E. K., Bancroft, M., & Torp, N. (1999). Relations between effective emotional self-regulation, attentional control, and low-income preschoolers' social competence with peers. *Early Education and Development, 10,* 333–350.

Roberts, R. D., Schulze, R., Zeidner, M., & Matthews, G. (2005). Understanding, measuring, and applying emotional intelligence: What have we learned? What have we missed? In R. Schulze & R. D. Roberts (Eds.), *Emotional intelligence: An international handbook* (pp. 311–341). Cambridge, MA: Hogrefe & Huber.

Rogosch, F. A., Cicchetti, D., & Aber, J. L. (1995). The role of child maltreatment in early deviations in cognitive and affective processing abilities and later peer relationship problems. *Development and Psychopathology, 7,* 591–609.

Rothbart, M., Ahadi, S., & Evans, D. (2000). Temperament and personality: Origins and outcomes. *Journal of Personality and Social Psychology, 78,* 122–135.

Rothbart, M., Ahadi, S., Hershey, K., & Fisher, P. (2001). Investigations of temperament at three to seven years: The Children's Behavior Questionnaire. *Child Development, 72,* 1287–1604.

Rothbart, M. K., Ellis, L. K., Rueda, M. R., & Posner, M. I. (2003). Developing mechanisms of temperamental effortful control. *Journal of Personality, 71,* 1113–1143.

Sagi, A., & Hoffman, M. L. (1976). Empathic distress in the newborn. *Developmental Psychology, 12,* 175–176.

Schultz, D., Izard, C. E., & Ackerman, B. P. (2000). Children's anger attributional bias: Relations to family environment and social adjustment. *Social Development, 9,* 284–301.

Schultz, D., Izard, C. E., & Bear, G. G. (2004). Children's emotion processing: Relations to emotionality and aggression. *Development and Psychopathology, 16,* 371–387.

Shechtman, Z. (2002). Cognitive and affective empathy in aggressive boys: Implications for counseling. *International Journal for the Advancement of Counselling, 24,* 211–222.

Shields, A., & Cicchetti, D. (1997). Emotion regulation among school-age children: The development and validation of a new criterion Q-sort scale. *Developmental Psychology, 33,* 906–916.

Shields, A., & Cicchetti, D. (1998). Reactive aggression among maltreated children: The contributions of attention and emotion dysregulation. *Journal of Clinical Child Psychology, 27,* 381–395.

Shields, A., Dickstein, S., Seifer, R., Giusti, L., Magee, K. D., & Spritz, B. (2001). Emotional competence and early school adjustment: A study of preschoolers at risk. *Early Education and Development, 12,* 73–96.

Simner, M. L. (1971). Newborn's response to the cry of another infant. *Developmental Psychology, 5,* 136–150.

Smith, M., & Walden, T. (1999). Understanding feelings and coping with emotional situations: A comparison of maltreated and nonmaltreated preschoolers. *Social Development, 8,* 93–116.

Stifter, C. A., Spinrad, T. L., & Braungart-Rieker, J. M. (1999). Toward a developmental model of child compliance: The role of emotion regulation in infancy. *Child Development, 70,* 21–32.

Strayer, J., & Roberts, W. (2004). Empathy and observed anger and aggression in five-year-olds. *Social Development, 13,* 1–13.

Suveg, C., & Zeman, J. (2004). Emotion regulation in children with anxiety disorders. *Journal of Clinical Child and Adolescent Psychology, 33,* 750–759.

Tangney, J. P., & Dearing, R. L. (2002). *Shame and guilt.* New York: Guilford Press.

Tangney, J. P., Dearing, R., Wagner, P. E., & Gramzow, R. (2000). *The Test of Self-Conscious Affect–3 (TOSCA-3).* Fairfax, VA: George Mason University.

Tangney, J. P., Wagner, P., Fletcher, C., & Gramzow, R. (1992). Shamed into anger? The relation of shame and guilt to anger and self-reported aggression. *Journal of Personality and Social Psychology, 62,* 669–675.

Tangney, J. P., Wagner, P. E., Hill-Barlow, D., Marschall, D. E., & Gramzow, R. (1996). Relation of shame and guilt to constructive versus destructive responses to anger across the life span. *Journal of Personality and Social Psychology, 70,* 797–809.

Tangney, J. P., Wagner, P. E., & Gramzow, R. (1989). *The Test of Self-Conscious Affect (TOSCA).* Fairfax, VA: George Mason University.

Terwogt, M. M., Koops, W., Oosterhoff, T., & Olthof, T. (1986). Development in processing of multiple emotional situations. *Journal of General Psychology, 113,* 109–119.

Trentacosta, C. J., Izard, C. E., Mostow, A. J., & Fine, S. E. (2006). Children's emotional competence and attentional competence in early elementary school. *School Psychology Quarterly, 21,* 148–170.

Trentacosta, C. J., Mostow, A. J., Fine, S. E., King, K. A., & Izard, C. E. (2005, April). *The relation between emotion knowledge and emotion regulation.* Poster presented at the meeting of the Society for Research in Child Development, Atlanta, GA.

Tugade, M. M., & Fredrickson, B. L. (2002). Positive emotions and emotional intelligence. In L. F. Barrett & P. Salovey (Eds.), *The wisdom in feeling: Psychological processes in emotional intelligence. Emotions and social behavior* (pp. 319–340). New York: Guilford Press.

Warden, D., & Mackinnon, S. (2003). Prosocial children, bullies and victims: An investigation of their sociometric status, empathy and social problem-solving strategies. *British Journal of Developmental Psychology, 21,* 367–385.

Weinberg, K. M., Tronick, E. Z., Cohn, J. F., & Olson, K. L. (1999). Gender differences in emotional expressivity and self-regulation during early infancy. *Developmental Psychology, 35,* 175–188.

Zeidner, M., Matthews, G., Roberts, R. D., & MacCann, C. (2003). Development of emotional intelligence: Towards a multi-level investment model. *Human Development, 46,* 69–96.

Zeman, J., Shipman, K., & Penza-Clyve, S. (2001). Development and initial validation of the Children's Sadness Management Scale. *Journal of Nonverbal Behavior, 25,* 187–205.

Zeman, J., Shipman, K., & Suveg, C. (2002). Anger and sadness regulation: Predictions to internalizing and externalizing symptoms in children. *Journal of Clinical Child and Adolescent Psychology, 31,* 393–398.

6

Trait Emotional Intelligence

Moving Forward in the Field of EI

K. V. PETRIDES, ADRIAN FURNHAM, AND STELLA MAVROVELI

Two constructs of emotional intelligence (EI) should be distinguished based on the measurement method used in the operationalization process (self-report, as in personality questionnaires, or maximum-performance, as in IQ tests; see Petrides & Furnham, 2000, 2001, 2003). *Trait EI* (or "trait emotional self-efficacy") concerns emotion-related dispositions and self-perceptions measured via self-report, whereas *ability EI* (or "cognitive-emotional ability") concerns emotion-related cognitive abilities that ought to be measured via maximum-performance tests. The conceptual differences between the two constructs are summarized in Petrides, Furnham, and Frederickson (2004; see also Table 6.1). These differences are directly reflected in empirical findings, which reveal very low, often nonsignificant, correlations between measures of trait EI and ability EI, thereby supporting an explicit distinction between the two constructs (Engelberg & Sjöberg, 2004; O'Connor & Little, 2003; Warwick & Nettelbeck, 2004). Findings that are fully in line with our theoretical position have also been reported by researchers who do not seem to espouse it (Brackett & Mayer, 2003; Zeidner, Shani-Zinovich, Matthews, & Roberts, 2005).

Along with others, we have maintained that the operationalization of ability EI is problematic because the subjectivity of emotional experience (e.g., Robinson & Clore, 2002; Watson, 2000) undermines the development of valid maximum-performance (IQ-like) tests. The heart of the problem concerns the inability to create items or tasks that can be scored according to truly objective criteria and that can cover the sampling domain of ability EI *comprehensively*. For example, the entire *intra*personal component of EI seems to be impervious to maximum-performance measurement because the information required to score as correct or incorrect answers to items like "I am aware of my emotions as I experience them" is available only to the individual who provides the answers. The use of alternative scoring procedures designed to create correct responses among a number

TABLE 6.1. Trait EI versus ability EI.

Construct	Measurement	Conceptualization	Expected Relationship to g	Construct Validity	Measures
Trait EI[a, b]	Self-report	Personality trait	Orthogonal Unimportant for construct validity	Consistent with models of differential psychology Discriminant and incremental validity vis-à-vis personality Concurrent and predictive validity with many criteria	TEIQue
Ability EI	Performance-based	Cognitive ability	Moderate-to-strong correlations. Crucial for construct validity	Inconsistent with models of differential psychology Awkward scoring procedures Limited concurrent and predictive validity	MSCEIT

[a] Trait EI and ability EI are unrelated to "mixed" and "ability" models of EI. For more details, see text.
[b] Entries in this row refer specifically to the trait emotional intelligence (trait emotional self-efficacy) conceptualization and do not generalize to other models or to self-report measures other than the TEIQue. For more details, see text.

of equally logical alternatives leads to a host of conceptual, psychometric, and empirical problems that have been repeatedly discussed in the literature (e.g., Day & Carroll, 2004; Roberts, Zeidner, & Matthews, 2001). A succinct analysis from a scientific perspective of the implausibility of EI as a new cognitive ability is given in Brody (2004).

It has been pointed out that it is perfectly possible for trait EI and ability EI to "co-exist" (e.g., Tett, Fox, & Wang, 2005). We would agree that our view of them as different constructs implies that the operationalization of one does not have implications for the operationalization of the other. Indeed, it is irrelevant for our purposes whether ability EI will ever be accepted into the mainstream taxonomies of human cognitive abilities (Carroll, 1993). Nevertheless, our prediction is that this construct will eventually find its place along the ever-growing number of pseudo-intelligences (19 on last count; Furnham, 2005) on the fringes of scientific psychology (Deary, 2001; Gottfredson, 2003).

How Should EI Be Conceptualized: As a Competence, a Skill, an Adaptive Outcome, a Set of Cultural Beliefs, or Some Other Construct?

Any new individual differences construct should be conceptualized in ways that are consistent with existing models of differential psychology. Constructs that contradict established knowledge in a field should be swiftly rejected or fundamentally transformed, unless the theories and data on which they are predicated justify a paradigmatic shift.

We believe that the developing conceptualization of EI as a personality trait (e.g., Petrides et al., 2004; Petrides, Niven, & Mouskounti, 2006) is the one that best fulfills the prerequisite of consistency. Note that trait EI is to be distinguished from other models associated with self-report questionnaires of EI, most of which are psychologically incomplete, incoherent, or both. Prime examples are all those models utilizing self-report questionnaires, but theorizing about abilities, capabilities, and competencies. At present, it is only through the perspective of trait EI theory that the results from self-report questionnaires can be linked to mainstream personality psychology.

Trait EI theory provides an example of how individual differences research can sift through and transform ideas, speculations, and opinions into psychological constructs that can be incorporated into its extant taxonomies. Of course, the resultant constructs may have little in common with the ideas they have sought to operationalize scientifically, as is the case with trait EI and the various notions of Bar-On (1997), Gardner (1983), Goleman (1995), Mayer and Salovey (1997), Thorndike (1920), and others. The trait EI (trait emotional self-efficacy) label helps distinguish this specific construct from other approaches in the field.

Is the Concept of EI Compatible With Existing Theories of Emotion and of Cognitive Intelligence?

If one views EI as an abstract theoretical system (e.g., Greenspan, 1989), then it could be argued that it is, at least partially, compatible with certain approaches to the study of emotion (for example, the dynamic systems approach of Lewis & Douglas, 1988). However, it should be stressed that EI, in most of its forms and guises, is hypothesized to encompass some form of emotion-related *individual differences*. Therefore, as already noted, any operationalization of the construct must be compatible, first and foremost, with existing theories of differential psychology. One explanation for the seeming muddle in the area of EI is that individuals with no significant presence in the scientific literature on differential psychology have suddenly emerged as "pioneers" and "experts" on all aspects of individual differences and psychometrics. The various conceptions of ability EI (e.g., Geher, Warner, & Brown, 2001; Mayer, Salovey, Caruso, & Sitarenios, 2003) are incompatible with existing theories and models of individual differences (see Brody, 2004). The problem that ability EI operationalizations face is as simple as it is fundamental: The subjectivity of emotional experience undermines the development of items or tasks that can be scored according to truly veridical criteria and that can cover the sampling domain of the construct in its entirety. The scoring procedures that ability EI tests utilize in order artificially to objectify emotional experience, thus making it amenable to IQ-type scoring, produce scores that are psychologically meaningless. It follows that correlating these scores with external criteria cannot shed any light on the nature and validity of this construct.

In contrast, the conceptualization of emotional intelligence as a personality trait at the lower levels of trait taxonomies (e.g., Petrides & Furnham, 2001; Petrides, Pita, & Kokkinaki, in press) is consistent with existing models of individual differences. Note that trait EI is explicitly hypothesized to lie outside the realm of human cognitive ability (Carroll, 1993). Hitherto, this hypothesis has been corroborated in many independent studies that have reported near-zero, or even negative, correlations between trait EI questionnaires and IQ tests (Derksen, Kramer, & Katzko, 2002; Newsome, Day, & Catano, 2000; Petrides, Frederickson, & Furnham, 2004; Saklofske, Austin, & Minski, 2003; Van der Zee, Thijs, & Schakel, 2002; Warwick & Nettelbeck, 2004).

As the theory and nomological network of the construct develop and expand, we have little doubt that links and commonalities with existing theories of emotion will become apparent. Indeed, we are hoping that trait EI theory will contribute toward bridging the gap between experimental and correlational accounts of emotion.

What Are the Key Components, Facets, or Branches of EI?

The sampling domain of trait EI (see Table 6.2) was derived from a content analysis of early models of EI and related constructs. The rationale was to include core elements common to more than a single model, but exclude peripheral elements appearing in only one specific conceptualization. This is analogous to procedures used in classical psychometric scale development, whereby the commonalities (shared core) of the various items comprising a scale are carried over into a total (internally consistent) score, with their random or unique components (noise) being canceled out in the process. The systematic nature of this method is to be contrasted with the haphazard procedures

TABLE **6.2**. The adult sampling domain of trait emotional intelligence.

Facets	High scorers perceive themselves as...
Adaptability	flexible and willing to adapt to new conditions.
Assertiveness	forthright, frank, and willing to stand up for their rights.
Emotion expression	capable of communicating their feelings to others.
Emotion management (others)	capable of influencing other people's feelings.
Emotion perception (self and others)	clear about their own and other people's feelings.
Emotion regulation	capable of controlling their emotions.
Impulsiveness (low)	reflective and less likely to give in to their urges.
Relationships	capable of maintaining fulfilling personal relationships.
Self-esteem	successful and self-confident.
Self-motivation	driven and unlikely to give up in the face of adversity.
Social awareness	accomplished networkers with superior social skills.
Stress management	capable of withstanding pressure and regulating stress.
Trait empathy	capable of taking someone else's perspective.
Trait happiness	cheerful and satisfied with their lives.
Trait optimism	confident and likely to "look on the bright side" of life.

on which other models are predicated, whereby the inclusion or exclusion of facets is typically the outcome of unstated or arbitrary decisions. Nevertheless, as we previously noted (Petrides & Furnham, 2001, p. 428):

It cannot be expected that there will be complete consensus as regards the appropriateness of the facets that have been included [in Table 6.2]. Asking what precisely should be part of a construct is like asking what sports should be in the Olympics; neither question can be answered objectively. Consequently, it is possible that some researchers may feel that certain changes need to be made to the above domain. Nevertheless, [Table 6.2] can be used as a guide for the development of comprehensive trait EI inventories. It must also be noted that the facets in this table should be expected to blend through relatively high correlations and therefore they may not be perceived as factors in a statistical sense.

More important, as the theory develops and the empirical base expands, it is inevitable that this sampling domain will have to be amended and adjusted to reflect theoretical and empirical developments. As Zuckerman (1996) pointed out, constructs are not engraved in stone, but chalked on slate and they evolve in response to data and facts.

How Is EI Distinct From Existing Personality and Ability Constructs? Could a Multistratum Psychometric Model Integrate a Dimension or Dimensions of EI With Existing Personality and Ability Constructs?

Trait EI is hypothesized to occupy factor space at the lower levels of personality hierarchies (e.g., Petrides & Furnham, 2001; Petrides et al., in press). Consequently, it is not distinct from personality constructs, but part of them. In a directly relevant paper, De Raad (2005) located trait EI within the Big Five circumplex and concluded that it comprises rather scattered areas of the Big Five domain and correlates with at least four of the five basic personality dimensions. These results are fully in line with Petrides and Furnham (2001) and Petrides et al. (in press), who carried out similar analyses within hierarchical trait structures. At this point, it is worth emphasizing the capacity of trait EI theory, which views the construct as a lower order personality dimension, to provide an explanation for such findings. Indeed, this specific example illustrates the hollow foundations of labels and constructs like "EQ," "self-report EI," and so forth, whose inability to accommodate results like the foregoing has repeatedly led to erroneous conclusions about the construct's alleged lack of discriminant validity.

A related criticism that has been leveled against the operationalization of EI as a personality trait is that it has little or no incremental validity over the basic personality dimensions (e.g., Davies, Stankov, & Roberts, 1998; MacCann, Roberts, Matthews, & Zeidner, 2004; Mayer, Salovey, & Caruso, 2000). There is a lot to be said about the concerted focus on incremental predictive validity, which often diverts attention from the more important issue of variance explanation (as distinct from variance prediction).[1] In any case, a strictly empirical examination of this criticism quickly leads to the conclusion that it is unfounded. There is an expanding body of evidence showing that trait EI has incremental validity vis-à-vis a wide range of criteria both over the Big Five (Extremera & Fernández-Berrocal, 2005; Furnham & Petrides, 2003; Palmer, Donaldson, & Stough, 2002; Saklofske et al., 2003; Van der Zee & Wabeke, 2004) as well as over the Giant Three personality frameworks (Petrides et al., 2004; Petrides et al., in press).

As regards the possibility of integrating a dimension, or dimensions, of EI within existing personality or ability taxonomies, we should like to stress three points. First, we submit that any EI "theory" or "model" that fails to explain how the construct fits within these taxonomies should be seriously questioned. There is a glut of "novel" constructs (usually involving new types of "intelligence," such as emotional, personal, social, etc.) that ignore the structural maps of psychology and impede the accumulation of findings that is crucial to the development of the discipline (Eysenck, 1997). The findings from the trait EI research program suggest that the natural home of the growing number of pseudo-intelligences is within personality trait hierarchies.

Second, we would argue that our goal should be to integrate complete EI theories or models, as opposed to isolated facets or dimensions, into the taxonomies of individual differences. Especially as far as ability EI is concerned, it is tempting to try to reduce elaborate models to narrow and specific facets, such as "emotion recognition" or "emotion perception," that may be more amenable to objective testing (see Austin, 2005; Davies et al., 1998). There should be no doubt, however, that the mere relabeling of, say, "emotion perception" as "emotional intelligence" constitutes semantic wizardry, rather than scientific progress. Still, clear discrepancies between theoretical models and measurement vehicles are manifest even in those cases in which both are developed by the same individuals.

For example, Mayer and Salovey (1997) present a model comprising no fewer than 16 convoluted facets (e.g., "ability to manage emotion in oneself and others by moderating negative emotions and enhancing pleasant ones, without repressing or exaggerating information they may convey"), which are then reduced to four simplistic dimensions in their test (Mayer et al., 2003). Of course, this is a secondary issue compared to the terminal problem of the lack of objectively correct responses in that model, but it does provide a useful illustration of a limitation that is very common in the literature.

The third point we would like to emphasize is that the operationalization of EI as a personality trait is specifically aimed at integrating the construct into the established trait taxonomies. This operationalization is consistent not only with the mainstream theories of personality, but also with the bulk of the available evidence from multiple studies in different domains. Thus, trait EI has consistently shown near-zero correlations with IQ tests (Derksen et al., 2002; Petrides et al., 2004), as expected given the general independence of personality and cognitive ability (Eysenck, 1994; Jensen, 1998) and consistently high correlations with the basic personality dimensions (Tett et al., 2005), as expected given its status as a lower order personality construct (Petrides & Furnham, 2001). Based on our analyses of over three dozen independent data sets using many different instruments, we would estimate that the variance overlap between trait EI and the Big Five is in the order of 65% (range 50%–80%). In light of these facts, any model that views the construct as anything other than a personality trait is problematic.

How Does EI Change Over the Life Span, Quantitatively and Qualitatively?

At this stage, it is not possible to give a complete answer to this question due to a dearth of relevant data. A related and, from the perspective of trait EI theory, more pressing issue concerns the temporal stability of the construct. Conceptualizing EI as a personality trait implies that the constellation of emotion-related self-perceptions and dispositions it comprises is generally stable over time and across situations. Test-retest data over a 1-year period are consistent with the theory, showing global trait EI correlations of about .7–.8 (Petrides, 2001; see also Tett et al., 2005). Parker, Saklofske, Wood, Eastabrook, and Taylor (2005) reported a temporal stability for global trait EI scores in the order of .56. However, this lower value was based on a

3-year period and a sample that consisted exclusively of young adults. It should also be noted that none of the values reported above has been corrected for score unreliability.

For very long periods (e.g., during adulthood), it is possible only to state, but not test due to lack of appropriate data, a prediction stemming from trait EI theory, namely that scores should show some increase with age as people become less emotional and better socialized (Costa et al., 2000). On an earlier normative dataset of the Trait Emotional Intelligence Questionnaire Version 1.50 (TEIQue v. 1.50; $N = 1152$; mean age = 31.58 years; $SD = 11.56$), global trait EI scores correlated at $r = .16$ with age. We have observed effects of similar size with the short form of the TEIQue (TEIQue-SF; Petrides & Furnham, 2006; see also Parker et al., 2005). However, these data do not extend into old age, which prohibits testing for theoretically plausible curvilinear effects (especially quadratic components). Furthermore, the data are cross-sectional and, as a result, they cannot provide clear answers in relation to developmental trajectories.

The part of the question concerning qualitative change is important from a theoretical as well as a practical perspective. The standard practice of adapting psychometric instruments that have been specifically developed with reference to adults for use with children and adolescents involves the fundamental, and virtually always untested, assumption that the construct concerned is developmentally invariant. It is true that even expert psychometricians have sometimes assumed that sampling domains and factor structures derived from adult samples and literatures can be automatically adapted for use with children. However, in light of the profound developmental personality changes during childhood and adolescence, this assumption is probably unwarranted.

We have been working toward the identification of the sampling domain of trait EI for children aged between 8 and 12 years. The early stages of this research suggest there are considerable qualitative differences from the current adult sampling domain. Consequently, the TEIQue measures for children should not simply consist of syntactically simplified items at the appropriate reading level, but, more important, they must be based on a conceptualization and sampling domain that are developmentally suitable for this particular age group. The way forward in this direction is to provide the field with a sampling domain derived from a comprehensive content analysis of the literature on children's temperament and socioemotional development, work that is currently undertaken within the trait EI research program.

Quantitative and qualitative changes in trait EI should be viewed as partial functions of socioemotional development (Abe & Izard, 1999) and of the broader development of the self (see Berk, 2001; Lewis, 2000; Saarni, 1999), both of which emerge from the interaction of maturational processes (Izard, 1991), cognitive development (Kagan, 1978), and social experiences (Dickson, Fogel, & Messinger, 1998). It remains to be seen whether, in terms of its long-term stability, trait EI is more similar to personality traits or to affective traits, which are comparatively more variable (Vaidya, Gray, Haig, & Watson, 2002).

How Might EI Contribute to Adaptation to Real-World Social Environments?

Research that is broadly relevant to this question has revealed clear and replicable associations between trait EI and coping styles (positive with adaptive and negative with maladaptive styles). These associations have held up in the presence of the Giant Three and the Big Five personality dimensions and have also been replicated cross-culturally (Petrides et al., in press).

If we extended the scope of the question to include relationships between trait EI and criteria from the domains of educational, organizational, and child psychology, it is evident that a large empirical base has been emerging over the last few years. For example, it has been found that high trait EI scores are positively related to peer-rated sociability in children (Petrides, Sangareau, Furnham, & Frederickson, 2006), fulfilling interpersonal relationships (Schutte et al., 2001), social network size (Austin, Saklofske, & Egan, 2005), and job satisfaction in employed adults (Petrides & Furnham, 2006).

It needs to be registered, however, that trait EI theory does not view the construct as an ability of any kind. Consequently, it is possible, indeed likely, that there are contexts in which high trait emotional self-efficacy (trait EI) is potentially maladaptive. For example, in Petrides and Furnham (2003), participants with high trait EI scores showed greater mood deterioration following the presentation of a short distressing video segment compared to participants with low scores. Maladaptive effects are more likely to be observed in studies using objective data from laboratory or real-life settings, rather than in questionnaire studies based exclusively on self-report. Questionnaire studies almost invariably find that trait EI is positively correlated with socially desirable variables and negatively correlated with socially undesirable variables. Before results from such studies start to interact with a misunderstanding of trait EI theory to lead to erroneous conclusions (e.g., high scores are always desirable because they have generalized adaptive value), it is important to take into account concerns about item overlap, criterion contamination, and common method variance, all of which inflate the intercorrelations in self-report research.

Proliferation of Questionnaires

Self-report questionnaires of EI continue to proliferate at a rate that has led to requests for a moratorium (Roberts, Schulze, Zeidner, & Matthews, 2005). From our perspective, these questionnaires are best understood as flawed measures of trait EI that share, or can be made to share, variance with the TEIQue.[2] In fact, this is the very reason that trait EI theory can offer a context for the interpretation of the results from these questionnaires. Indeed, it is only through the perspective of trait EI theory that these results can be linked to mainstream differential psychology research.

However, relying on trait EI theory to interpret results from various EI questionnaires can be problematic for several reasons. For example, it increases the likelihood of confounding trait EI theory with the promotional documentation accompanying these measures. The primary basis on which we recommend the TEIQue for use in research and applied settings is that it provides a direct gateway to trait EI theory.[3] The TEIQue aims to capture comprehensively the affective aspects of personality, a goal that gives rise to a particular factor structure and, more important, a particular way or distributing and interpreting variance. The core advantages of trait EI theory, and of the TEIQue as its operationalization vehicle, are to be found at the level of conceptual content and explanatory power, more so than the level of predictive and incremental utility.

Proliferation of Labels

The distinction between trait EI (or "trait emotional self-efficacy") and ability EI (or "cognitive-emotional ability"; Petrides & Furnham, 2000, 2001) is unrelated to Mayer et al.'s (2000) distinction between "ability" and "mixed" models of EI. Our differentiation is based on the method of measurement (self-report versus maximum-performance) and views the resultant constructs as qualitatively different. In contrast, Mayer et al. (2000) attempt to differentiate on the basis of whether a model "mixes" cognitive abilities with other characteristics. If it does, it is a "mixed" model, and if it does not, it is an "ability" model. This confusing differentiation is at odds both with the principles of psychological measurement as well as with all empirical data showing that trait EI measures tend to intercorrelate strongly, irrespective of whether they are based on "mixed" or "ability" models.

Without further belaboring the point, distinguishing between constructs is different from attempting to distinguish between models, and only the former distinction is psychologically meaningful and empirically valid. A corollary of this is that ability EI should not be confused with "ability models" and trait EI should not be confused with "mixed models," as has been the case in the past (e.g., Lyons & Schneider, 2005).

Confusion may also arise from labels mirroring trait EI (e.g., "self-reported EI," "perceived EI," "characteristic EI," "self-perceived EI"). These should not be confused with trait EI theory. That is not to say that research under these labels is not empirically useful. Indeed, the findings of these studies should be closely monitored for their relevance to trait EI theory. On the other hand, without the theoretical framework provided by the trait EI conceptualization, these findings cannot be properly linked to theories of individual differences and, consequently, they cannot be properly interpreted.

The Future of Trait Emotional Intelligence

Trait EI theory is only now beginning to take shape, and it is essential that it be developed in ways that are consistent with established knowledge in psychology. Research will have to be undertaken at many different levels, both basic and applied. As regards basic research, it will be necessary to explore issues pertaining to the identification of the sociobiological bases of the construct (e.g., twin studies), its measurement (e.g., assessment in children), its developmental trajectories (e.g., longitudinal studies), and its universality (e.g., cross-cultural studies). With respect to applications and the areas in which trait EI may have a role to play, we believe they are as broad and diverse as the areas in which emotion-related individual differences are relevant (see Figure 6.1 for an example from the domain of education).

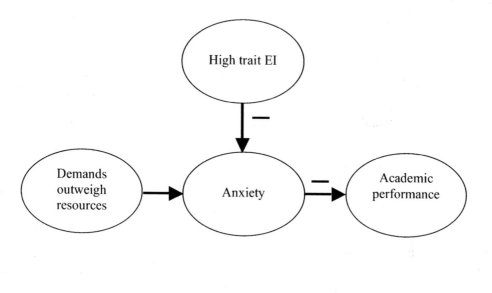

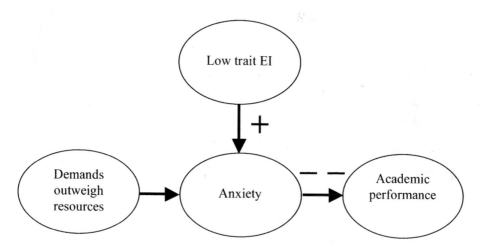

Figure 6.1. The moderating role of trait EI in academic performance. This figure illustrates how trait EI moderates the negative effect of low cognitive ability on academic performance. Low-ability students find themselves in an intellectually demanding environment that overtaxes them cognitively and emotionally. Those high on trait EI are better able to deal with the resultant stress and have larger social networks, both of which help reduce the negative impact of anxiety on performance. In contrast, those low on trait EI find it difficult to deal with stress and are more likely to experience deficits in social support, which compounds the negative impact of anxiety on performance. The process applies to low-cognitive-ability students only (see Petrides et al., 2004).

The ongoing operationalization of emotional intelligence as a personality trait is leading to a general explanatory construct that may open up new avenues of research in emotion-related individual differences and shed new light on existing debates. Early findings from studies in diverse domains, including experimental (Mikolajczak, Petrides, Luminet, & Coumans, 2007), decision making (Sevdalis, Petrides, & Harvey, in press), and child development psychology (Mavroveli, Petrides, Rieffe, & Bakker, in press) corroborate the promising prospects of this research.

Notes

1. The distinction between prediction and explanation is fundamental from a scientific perspective (see, e.g., Scriven, 1959). Anyone can put together a bunch of questions and correlate them with whatever criterion happens to be available, and anyone does. For example, it is entirely possible to achieve predictive correlations of similar magnitude using a personality measure based on Eysenckian theory, one based on obsolete Jungian theory, and one taken from the latest issue of *Cosmo*. It is in the *interpretation* of the results, which requires the existence of a valid theory, that the differences between the instruments will emerge.

2. Needless to stress, the authors of these questionnaires would disagree with this assessment and argue that their instruments measure some type of emotional ability, "emotional intelligence," or "EQ." As Zeidner, Roberts, and Matthews (2004, p. 240) note, "the leading questionnaire developers are quite explicit that they seek to measure an ability that predicts objective behavior." Setting aside the question of what constitutes a "leading questionnaire developer," it should be reiterated that the notion that mental abilities can be assessed by self-reports is psychometrically invalid. As we note elsewhere in the chapter, practitioners and, especially, researchers using these questionnaires must make appeal to trait EI theory for psychologically meaningful interpretations of their results.

3. All TEIQue forms, versions, and adaptations are available, free of charge, for research purposes.

References

Abe, J. A., & Izard, C. E. (1999). A longitudinal study of emotion expression and personality relations in early development. *Journal of Personality and Social Psychology, 77*, 566–577.

Austin, E. J. (2005). Emotional intelligence and emotional information processing. *Personality and Individual Differences, 39*, 403–414.

Austin, E. J., Saklofske, D. H., & Egan, V. (2005). Personality, well-being and health correlates of trait emotional intelligence. *Personality and Individual Differences, 38*, 547–558.

Bar-On, R. (1997). *Bar-On Emotional Quotient Inventory: Technical manual.* Toronto: Multi-Health Systems.

Berk, L. (2001). *Development through the lifespan* (2nd ed.). Needham Heights, MA: Allyn & Bacon.

Brackett, M. A., & Mayer, J. D. (2003). Convergent, discriminant, and incremental validity of competing measures of emotional intelligence. *Personality and Social Psychology Bulletin, 29*, 1147–1158.

Brody, N. (2004). What cognitive intelligence is and what emotional intelligence is not. *Psychological Inquiry, 15*, 234–238.

Carroll, J. B. (1993). *Human cognitive abilities: A survey of factor-analytic studies*. New York: Cambridge.

Costa, P. T., Jr., McCrae, R. R., Martin, T. A., Oryol, V. E., Senin, A. G., Rukavishnikov, A. A., et al. (2000). Personality development from adolescence through adulthood: Further cross-cultural comparisons of age differences. In V. J. Molfese & D. Molfese (Eds.), *Temperament and personality development across the life span* (pp. 235–252). Hillsdale, NJ: LEA.

Davies, M., Stankov, L., & Roberts, R. D. (1998). Emotional Intelligence: In search of an elusive construct. *Journal of Personality and Social Psychology, 75*, 989–1015.

Day, A. L., & Carroll, S. A. (2004). Using an ability-based measure of emotional intelligence to predict individual performance, group performance, and group citizenship behaviours. *Personality and Individual Differences, 36*, 1443–1458.

Deary, I. J. (2001). *Looking down on human intelligence*. Oxford, UK: Oxford University Press.

De Raad, B. (2005). The trait-coverage of emotional intelligence. *Personality and Individual Differences, 38*, 673–687.

Derksen, J., Kramer, I., & Katzko, M. (2002). Does a self-report measure for emotional intelligence assess something different than general intelligence? *Personality and Individual Differences, 32*, 37–48.

Dickson, L. K., Fogel, A., & Messinger, D. (1998). The development of emotion from a social process view. In M. F. Mascolo & S. Griffin (Eds.), *What develops in emotional development?* (pp. 253–271). New York: Plenum Press.

Engelberg, E., & Sjöberg, L. (2004). Emotional intelligence, affect intensity, and social adjustment. *Personality and Individual Differences, 37*, 533–542.

Extremera, N., & Fernández-Berrocal, P. (2005). Perceived emotional intelligence and life satisfaction: Predictive and incremental validity using the Trait Meta-Mood Scale. *Personality and Individual Differences, 39*, 937–948.

Eysenck, H. J. (1994). Personality and intelligence: Psychometric and experimental approaches. In R. J. Sternberg & P. Ruzgis (Eds.), *Personality and intelligence* (pp. 3–31). New York: Cambridge University Press.

Eysenck, H. J. (1997). Personality and experimental psychology: The unification of psychology and the possibility of a paradigm. *Journal of Personality and Social Psychology, 73*, 1224–1237.

Furnham, A. (2005, July). *Exploring no-man's land in differential psychology*. Presidential address presented at the biennial meeting of the International Society for the Study of Individual Differences, Adelaide, Australia.

Furnham, A., & Petrides, K. V. (2003). Trait emotional intelligence and happiness. *Social Behavior and Personality, 31*, 815–823.

Gardner, H. (1983). *Frames of mind: The theory of multiple intelligences*. New York: Basic Books.

Geher, G., Warner, R. M., & Brown, A. S. (2001). Predictive validity of the emotional accuracy research scale. *Intelligence, 29*, 373–388.

Goleman, D. (1995). *Emotional intelligence: Why it can matter more than IQ*. London: Bloomsbury.

Gottfredson, L. S. (2003). Dissecting practical intelligence theory: Its claims and evidence. *Intelligence, 31*, 343–397.

Greenspan, S. I. (1989). Emotional intelligence. In K. Field, B. J. Cohler, & G. Wool (Eds.), *Learning and education: Psychoanalytic perspectives*. Madison, CT: International Universities Press.

Jensen, A. R. (1998). *The g factor*. Westport, CT: Praeger.

Kagan, J. (1978). On emotion and its development: A working paper. In M. Lewis & L. A. Rosenblum (Eds.), *The development of affect* (pp. 11–42). New York: Plenum Press.

Lewis, M. D. (2000). The emergence of human emotions. In M. Lewis & J. M. Haviland-Jones (Eds.), *Handbook of emotions* (2nd ed., pp. 265–280). New York: The Guilford Press.

Lewis, M. D., & Douglas, L. (1998). A dynamic systems approach to cognition-emotion interactions in development. In F. Mascolo & S. Griffin (Eds.), *What develops in emotional development?* (pp. 159–188). New York: Plenum Press.

Lyons, J. B., & Schneider, T. R. (2005). The influence of emotional intelligence on performance. *Personality and Individual Differences, 39,* 693–703.

MacCann, C., Roberts, R. D., Matthews, G., & Zeidner, M. (2004). Consensus scoring and empirical option weighting of performance-based emotional intelligence (EI) tests. *Personality and Individual Differences, 36,* 645–662.

Mavroveli, S., Petrides, K. V., Rieffe, C., & Bakker, F. (in press). *Trait emotional intelligence, psychological well-being, and peer-rated social competence in adolescence. British Journal of Developmental Psychology.*

Mayer, J. D., & Salovey, P. (1997). What is emotional intelligence? In P. Salovey & D. J. Sluyter (Eds.), *Emotional development and emotional intelligence: Educational implications*. New York: Basic Books.

Mayer, J. D., Salovey, P., & Caruso, D. R. (2000). Models of emotional intelligence. In R. J. Sternberg (Ed.), *Handbook of human intelligence*. New York: Cambridge University Press.

Mayer, J. D., Salovey, P., Caruso, D. R., & Sitarenios, G. (2003). Measuring emotional intelligence with the MSCEIT V2.0. *Emotion, 3,* 97–105.

Mikolajczak, M., Petrides, K. V., Luminet, O., & Coumans, N. (2007). *An experimental demonstration of the moderating effects of trait emotional intelligence on laboratory-induced stress.* Manuscript submitted for publication.

Newsome, S., Day, A. L., & Catano, V. M. (2000). Assessing the predictive validity of emotional intelligence. *Personality and Individual Differences, 29,* 1005–1016.

O'Connor, R. M., & Little, I. S. (2003). Revisiting the predictive validity of emotional intelligence: Self-report versus ability-based measures. *Personality and Individual Differences, 35,* 1893–1902.

Palmer, B., Donaldson, C., & Stough, C. (2002). Emotional intelligence and life satisfaction. *Personality and Individual Differences, 33,* 1091–1100.

Parker, J. D. A., Saklofske, D. H., Wood, L. M., Eastabrook, J. M., & Taylor, R. N. (2005). Stability and change in emotional intelligence: Exploring the transition to young adulthood. *Journal of Individual Differences, 26,* 100–106.

Petrides, K. V. (2001). *A psychometric investigation into the construct of emotional intelligence.* Unpublished doctoral dissertation, University College London.

Petrides, K. V., Frederickson, N., & Furnham, A. (2004). The role of trait emotional intelligence in academic performance and deviant behaviour at school. *Personality and Individual Differences, 36,* 277–293.

Petrides, K. V., & Furnham, A. (2000). On the dimensional structure of emotional intelligence. *Personality and Individual Differences, 29,* 313–320.

Petrides, K. V., & Furnham, A. (2001). Trait emotional intelligence: Psychometric investigation with reference to established trait taxonomies. *European Journal of Personality, 15,* 425–448.

Petrides, K. V., & Furnham, A. (2003). Trait emotional intelligence: Behavioural validation in two studies of emotion recognition and reactivity to mood induction. *European Journal of Personality, 17,* 39–57.

Petrides, K. V., & Furnham, A. (2006). The role of trait emotional intelligence in a gender-specific model of organizational variables. *Journal of Applied Social Psychology, 36,* 552–569.

Petrides, K. V., Furnham, A., & Frederickson, N. (2004). Estimates of emotional and psychometric intelligence: Evidence for gender-based stereotypes. *Journal of Social Psychology, 144,* 149–162.

Petrides, K. V., Niven, L., & Mouskounti, T. (2006). The trait emotional intelligence of ballet dancers and musicians. *Psicothema, 18,* 101–107. [Special issue on emotional intelligence].

Petrides, K. V., Pita, R., & Kokkinaki, F. (in press). The location of trait emotional intelligence in personality factor space. *British Journal of Psychology.*

Petrides, K. V., Sangareau, Y., Furnham, A., & Frederickson, N. (2006). Trait emotional intelligence and children's peer relations at school. *Social Development, 15,* 537–547.

Roberts, R. D., Schulze, R., Zeidner, M., & Matthews, G. (2005). Understanding, measuring, and applying emotional intelligence: What have we learned? What have we missed? In R. Schulze & R. D. Roberts (Eds.), *Emotional intelligence: An international handbook* (pp. 311–341). Cambridge, MA: Hogrefe & Huber.

Roberts, R. D., Zeidner, M., & Mathews, G. (2001). Does emotional intelligence meet traditional standards for an intelligence? Some new data and conclusions. *Emotion, 1,* 196–231.

Robinson, M. D., & Clore, G. L. (2002). Belief and feeling: Evidence for an accessibility model of emotional self-report. *Psychological Bulletin, 128,* 934–960.

Saarni, C. (1999). *The development of emotional competence.* New York: Guilford.

Saklofske, D. H., Austin, E. J., & Minski, P. S. (2003). Factor structure and validity of a trait emotional intelligence measure. *Personality and Individual Differences, 34,* 707–721.

Schutte, N. S., Malouff, J. M., Bobik, C., Coston, T. D., Greeson, C., Jedlicka, C., et al. (2001). Emotional intelligence and interpersonal relations. *Journal of Social Psychology, 141,* 523–536.

Scriven, M. (1959). Explanation and prediction in evolutionary theory. *Science, 130,* 477–482.

Sevdalis, N., Petrides, K. V., & Harvey, N. (in press). Predicting and experiencing decision-related emotions: Does trait emotional intelligence matter? *Personality and Individual Differences.*

Tett, R. P., Fox, K. E., & Wang, A. (2005). Development and validation of a self-report measure of emotional intelligence as a multidimensional trait domain. *Personality and Social Psychology Bulletin, 31,* 859–888.

Thorndike, E. L. (1920). Intelligence and its uses. *Harper's Magazine, 140,* 227–235.

Vaidya, J. G., Gray, E. K., Haig, J., & Watson, D. (2002). On the temporal stability of personality: Evidence for differential stability and the role of life experiences. *Journal of Personality and Social Psychology, 83,* 1469–1484.

Van der Zee, K., Thijs, M., & Schakel, L. (2002). The relationship of emotional intelligence with academic intelligence and the big five. *European Journal of Personality, 16,* 103–125.

Van der Zee, K., & Wabeke, R. (2004). Is trait emotional intelligence simply or more than just a trait? *European Journal of Personality, 18,* 243–263.

Warwick, J., & Nettelbeck, T. (2004). Emotional intelligence is…? *Personality and Individual Differences, 37,* 1091–1100.

Watson, D. (2000). *Mood and temperament.* New York: Guilford.

Zeidner, M., Roberts, R. D., & Matthews, G. (2004). The emotional intelligence bandwagon: Too fast to live, too young to die? *Psychological Enquiry, 15,* 239–248.

Zeidner, M., Shani-Zinovich, I., Matthews, G., & Roberts, R. D. (2005). Assessing emotional intelligence in gifted and non-gifted high school students: Outcomes depend on the measure. *Intelligence, 33,* 369–391.

Zuckerman, M. (1996). "Conceptual clarification" or confusion in "The study of sensation seeking." *Personality and Individual Differences, 21,* 111–114.

7

Emotional Intelligence

More Than Personality and Cognitive Ability?

NICHOLAS R. BURNS, VENETA A. BASTIAN,
AND TED NETTELBECK

When preparing this chapter, our brief has been to address key questions about how emotional intelligence (EI) should be conceptualized. Is EI distinct from existing personality and ability constructs? If so, what are the main components that distinguish EI from these constructs and how might EI be included within a multistratum model capable of predicting more favorable adaptation within real-world social environments? Is EI predominantly a single domain or is it multifactorial? If EI is a separate entity, can it be improved by training? Does it change over the life span?

We have preliminary answers to some of these questions; and we are prepared to speculate about others. Our conclusions have largely been shaped by new analyses of a large data set, collected from 458 young and middle-aged adults by Veneta Bastian as part of her PhD, supervised by the other two authors. This research has considered relationships between three different measures of EI, five personality traits, two different cognitive abilities, and several life skills. The main aim has been to test whether EI has predictive validity for these life skills, beyond contributions of personality and cognitive abilities to these outcomes.

Background

Current interest in EI stems from a seminal article by Salovey and Mayer (1990), in which they proposed that EI is an important explanatory construct for improving understanding of individual differences in everyday achievements. Salovey and Mayer were not first to raise this possibility, crediting Payne (1986, cited by Mayer, 2001) with earlier use of *emotional intelligence*. However, Bar-On (2004) has traced the term back to Leuner (1966), while pointing to precursors to current ideas about EI in the earlier concept of *social intelligence* and in Darwin's (1872/1965) inquiries into emotional expression and social behavior.

Social Intelligence

In his recent comprehensive review of the history of ideas about social intelligence, Landy (in press) has traced this term back to Dewey (1909). Landy has plausibly suggested that Dewey's definition of social intelligence as "the power of observing and comprehending social situations" (1909, p. 43) was the basis for E. L. Thorndike's (1920) more familiar concept of social intelligence as the way in which intelligence could be displayed in social situations. Thus, Thorndike's tripartite theory of intelligence included both cognition and behavior, and social intelligence required a different kind of measurement from those employed to assess abstract (academic) intelligence or mechanical (practical) intelligence. He defined social intelligence as "the ability to understand and manage (people and) to act wisely in human relations" (1920, p. 228).

As Landy (in press) has emphasized, Thorndike's ideas differed from those who followed. Thorndike was principally concerned with different behavioral manifestations of intelligence; essentially, how a unitary form of intelligence was expressed in different ways, depending on the cognitive demands of radically different environmental circumstances. Subsequently, however, social intelligence came to be envisaged as a different kind of intelligence from academic ability—and one requiring a hierarchical taxonomy to describe its more specific components. Thus, in his structure-of-intellect model, Guilford included 30 different forms of social intelligence as factors relatively independent from academic abilities, located within the behavioral contents dimension (as cited in Landy, in press; Weis & Süß, 2005; see also O'Sullivan, Chapter 10, this volume).

Gardner and Others

More recently, Gardner (1983, 1993) has speculated about the potential importance to successful everyday adaptation of what he has described as separate intelligences, including interpersonal intelligence (making distinctions based on mood, temperament, and intention when interacting with others) and intrapersonal intelligence (self-perception for feelings and emotions that guides one's own behavior). Similarly, Greenspan (1981) outlined a theory specific to intellectual disability that emphasized the importance of social competencies, over and above considerations of IQ and adaptive behavior.

These ideas all share to some extent the notion, intrinsic to our culture, that social competencies, including control of emotions, can be important to successful activities of daily living. Landy (in press) has traced the way in which ability to judge emotion from facial expression became linked to ideas about social intelligence (see also O'Sullivan, Chapter 10, this volume). Surveys of lay and expert opinion about what intelligence means have typically included social skills, which must include among defining characteristics both regulating personal emotions and responding appropriately to the emotions of others (Sternberg & Detterman, 1986). Indeed, wide acceptance of the plausibility of these ideas undoubtedly reflects intuitions, bolstered by personal experience, that being able to recognize and manage one's own and others' emotions is important to successful interactions with others. And as several authors have recently concluded, attempts to develop definitions for social, and emotional, intelligence have resulted in considerable overlap between these constructs (Austin & Saklofske, 2004; Kang, Day, & Meara, 2004; Weis & Süß, 2005).

Limitations of IQ

Attempts to expand descriptions of intelligence have been motivated by the aim of being better able to predict individual differences in successful real-life adaptation. A century of psychometric endeavor has clearly established that, the utility of IQ tests notwithstanding, being skilled in ways other than those tapped by IQ tests does influence important life outcomes. It is now widely accepted that, although psychometric tests of cognitive abilities generally provide the best available predictors of a diverse range of real-life outcomes, even the most reliable of such tests account for only about 25% of variance in educational achievement and workplace settings (Gottfredson, 1997; Neisser et al., 1996; Schmidt & Hunter, 1998).[1] This degree of predictive validity has considerable practical value, particularly for employment or work training (Schmidt & Hunter, 1998); but it is clear, nonetheless, that success at school, at work, and in other respects, must be influenced by traits and behaviors besides the cognitive abilities measured by IQ-type tests.

These influences will normally include personal motivation, persistence, interests, conscientiousness, background knowledge, learning styles, parental attitudes, peer influences, teaching and training practices. Wechsler (1940) recognized this, allowing that personal "non-intellective" characteristics might influence both test performance and broader life outcomes. However, even including such influences that can be reliably measured, together with tests of cognitive abilities, will leave in excess of 50% of variance in real-life achievements unaccounted for (Matthews, Zeidner, & Roberts, 2002). Moreover, as Schulze, Roberts, Zeidner, and Matthews (2004) have pointed out, despite strong assertions about the fairness of IQ tests across diverse spectra within our culture (Jensen, 1980, 1998), widespread concern about the ecological validity of cognitive testing under some circumstances has motivated some differential psychologists to seek alternative psychological domains that may improve prediction of life achievements.

Sternberg

Personal characteristics may extend to different practical and socially relevant forms of intelligence (Sternberg, 1985); and they may extend also to emotional management skills or to forms of EI. However, it is one thing to speculate about the possible contribution of such influences but another to demonstrate the differential validity of so many different constructs. Nor does it follow that, even if management of emotion was found to contribute to valued lifestyle outcomes, such behaviors should usefully be held to reflect another form of intelligence. They may, for example, reflect context specific competencies, acquired by training rather than being derived from fundamental aptitudes, so that levels of skill vary across different emotions or different situations. However, until the validity of emotion-based constructs for successful outcomes has been firmly established, we prefer not to be drawn into debate about whether EI is better conceptualized as a raft of learned skills, rather than as one or more kinds of intelligence.

Salovey and Mayer

Early attempts to demonstrate the validity and practical efficacy of theories about the relevance of social judgments and competencies for important life outcomes were widely judged in the 1960s and beyond to have been unsuccessful (Cronbach, 1960; Ford, 1994; Keating, 1978; Matarazzo, 1972), although contrary evidence could be found in some quarters. Thus, Landy (in press) has pointed out that Cronbach (1970) reversed his earlier unfavorable assessment of social intelligence research, at least insofar as he regarded as promising the attempt by Guilford and his colleagues to develop tests for "cognition of behavioral relationships" (see also O'Sullivan, Chapter 10, this volume). Carroll (1993) also concluded that, despite limited data, there was sound evidence for a distinct broad domain of demonstrating knowledge about prosodic cues (e.g., recognizing vocal inflections, gestures, facial expressions) that communicate moods, emotions, and intentions in social interactions, consistent with Guilford's "behavioral content."

Nonetheless, earlier researchers did not agree about how to define critical constructs and, lacking consensus about external criteria against which to validate measurement, these efforts to develop procedures that distinguished social intelligence from academic abilities were widely considered to be unsuccessful. Even within the restricted IQ range that characterizes people with a mild intellectual disability, Mathias and Nettelbeck (1992) found only limited evidence for Greenspan's theory, with IQ the most reliable predictor of performance in a range of activities. Salovey and Mayer (1990) should therefore be credited for reviving interest in theory that hitherto had stalled for some time (Jones & Day, 1997).

Growing interest in EI as a potentially important theoretical and practical construct has been dramatic, generating extensive research activity across several disciplines. Yet, despite widespread interest, considerable confusion exists about how to define EI. Although this field is relatively new, Salovey and Mayer have already provided several versions of what they mean by EI. However, their intention, to bring theories about how emotions are perceived, expressed, and regulated in self and others together with theories of cognitive abilities, so as to better predict adaptive behavior, has remained clear. More recently they have defined EI as "the ability to perceive emotions, to access and generate emotions so as to assist thought, to understand emotions and emotional knowledge and to reflectively regulate emotions so as to promote emotional and intellectual growth" (Mayer & Salovey, 1997, p. 10). This reflects their conviction that EI is best conceived as a multifactorial form of intelligence that involves processing information to solve problems that relate to emotions. In this important respect, Mayer and Salovey's theoretical approach has differed from conceptualizations of EI that have included links to personality (Austin & Saklofske, 2004).

Tests

Central to EI research, several different measures have been developed within alternative theoretical conceptions during the past decade (Mayer, Caruso, & Salovey, 2000;

Neubauer & Freudenthaler, 2004). Mixed/trait models have included personality, motivational, and affective dispositions and conceptions for intelligence. These have typically generated self-report scales such as the Emotional Quotient Inventory (EQ-i; Bar-On, 1997). The EQ-i has been designed to draw on "noncognitive capabilities, competencies and skills" (Bar-On, 1997, p. 14), together with personality dispositions and cognitive abilities that Bar-On has argued hold relevance for successful everyday coping.

This all-encompassing approach has been criticized as conceptually confusing and unhelpful for theoretical progress (Matthews, Emo, Roberts, & Zeidner, in press; Matthews et al., 2002; Neubauer & Freudenthaler, 2004). In short, there is now considerable evidence (Ciarrochi, Chan, & Caputi, 2000; Davies, Stankov, & Roberts, 1998; MacCann, Matthews, Zeidner, & Roberts, 2004; Van Rooy & Viswesvaran, 2004) that many self-report EI scales are essentially measures of familiar personality traits, without reliable correlations with cognitive abilities. Plausibly, therefore these scales measure different things than do so-called ability EI scales (see below). This being so, as Austin and Saklofske (2004) have remarked, it might be preferable not only to distinguish between the two forms of measurement but also to avoid referring to both underlying constructs as EI (see also Matthews et al., 2002).

The Trait Meta Mood Scale (TMMS; Salovey, Mayer, Goldman, Turvey, & Palfai, 1995) and the Assessing Emotions Scale (AES; Schutte et al., 1998) are also self-report measures but were based on Salovey and Mayer's initial (1990) conception of EI as a form of intelligence; that is, an ability to process and integrate information about emotional feelings so as to guide thoughts and behaviors. Most recently, this ability theory of EI has generated the Multifactor Emotional Intelligence Scale (MEIS; Mayer, Caruso, & Salovey, 1999) and its amended shorter revision, the Mayer-Salovey-Caruso Emotional Intelligence Test (MSCEIT; Mayer, Salovey, & Caruso, 2000). The aim has been to develop ways by which EI can be assessed in accordance with objective, maximal performance criteria for which there are factually correct answers, analogous to how cognitive abilities have been measured. Consistent with this aim, such items have been described as "performance" measures.

In practice, however, the correctness or otherwise of a response has been determined by "target," "consensus," or "expert" scoring. With the first, correct answers are defined in terms of a target person's self-reported emotions. For the second and third methods, observations obtained from large samples of test respondents or from panels of "experts" (typically those interested in emotion research; see, for example, Mayer, Salovey, Caruso, & Sitarenious, 2003) have been used to produce average or common answers most endorsed as appropriate by the sample. This procedure assumes that some predetermined degree of shared opinion about whether an answer is correct can provide a criterion for response accuracy. Scoring an ability item has therefore reflected the degree of correspondence between a test taker's answer and the extent of consensus about how to answer that item, either within a large sample of respondents or among experts. Thus, when 75% of the normative sample has advocated a particular answer, a test taker selecting this answer would score .75.

Whether these scoring practices are appropriate has certainly attracted considerable debate (e.g., Stankov, 2000). Mayer and Geher (1996) have recognized that target agreement will depend on capacities of the target person to report emotions accurately, without bias. Other researchers have challenged whether consensual agreement or expert opinion can define answers as correct (e.g., Roberts, Zeidner, & Matthews, 2001), whether expertise can be established (MacCann, Roberts, Matthews, & Zeidner, 2004), and pointed out that stated intention does not necessarily translate into behavior (Brody, 2004).

Elsewhere, however, Legree, Psotka, Tremble, and Bourne (2004) have argued that these forms of measurement are appropriate in the absence of a formal body of knowledge that predicts performance in real-life domains, as applies with traditional psychometric tests of intelligence. Legree et al.'s position is essentially pragmatic, arguing that procedural knowledge emerges only with experience and that until objective standards for verification exist, consensual opinion provides a way forward. Nonetheless, they support this argument with evidence that larger samples of nonexperts will converge on outcomes that approximate expert opinion, even when the knowledge base involves cognitive processes rather than behavioral observations.

These developments have captured the interest of increasing numbers of researchers. Computer-based catalogues listing EI research reveal increasingly high levels of activities in this field. Several hundreds of peer-reviewed articles have been published on the topic in psychology, educational, management, and commerce journals during the past 5 years, together with large numbers of books and chapters. These have generated expanding interest among behavioral scientists but have also attracted broad media interest and wide acceptance among lay audiences of the validity of the basic ideas. Although Salovey and Mayer have been appropriately cautious, emphasizing that their research is still a work in progress, others have been less constrained. Most notably, Goleman (1995, 1998) has enthusiastically promoted EI (or EQ for emotional quotient, analogous to IQ) as critically important to both educational and workplace achievements, especially at management and leadership levels within commercial organizations.

Nonetheless, these developments have also attracted considerable debate. Goleman's claims, in particular, have been criticized as speculations beyond available data that are, moreover, rendered untestable because of the diverse range of characteristics aligned to abilities, attitudes, beliefs, social competencies, learned skills, and personality traits included as relevant to EI (Epstein, 1998; Pfeiffer, 2001). As Roberts et al. (2001) have pointed out (see also Schulze et al., 2004), different authors have differently conceptualized EI and, thus far, there is confusion about how to define and measure it. Certainly, if EI is a form of intelligence, then it should fit into the currently best available psychometric model, the Cattell-Horn-Carroll hierarchical model (Carroll, 1993), either as a specific first-order factor or as a broad second-order factor. However, EI has not been confirmed as a distinct general factor and is yet to be adequately located within a comprehensive taxonomic theory of intelligence (MacCann, Matthews et al., 2004). Its status as a form of intelligence is therefore still uncertain.

Proponents for EI can point to evidence that different measures have been found to correlate positively with a wide range of practically useful variables in workplace, educational, and interpersonal situations (e.g., Austin, Saklofske, Huang, & Mc Kenney, 2004; Charbonneau & Nicol, 2002; Ciarrochi, Chan, & Bajar, 2001; Ciarrochi et al., 2000; Dawda & Hart, 2000; Lopes, Salovey, & Straus, 2003; Martinez-Pons, 1998; Mayer et al., 1999; Palmer, Donaldson, & Stough, 2002; Saklofske, Austin, & Minski, 2003; Schutte et al.,

1998; Schutte et al., 2001). Hall, Geher, and Brackett (2004) have recently reported that EI distinguished children with reactive attachment disorder from normally developing children. Negative correlations have also been reported with socially undesirable, illegal, and deviant behaviors (e.g., Brackett, Mayer, & Warner, 2004; Petrides, Frederickson, & Furnham, 2004; Trinidad & Johnson, 2002). However, although acknowledging evidence for the potential utility of EI measures, others have warned against uncritical acceptance of the many claims made for EI, pending clearer theoretical development (Day & Kelloway, 2004; MacCann, Matthews et al., 2004). Importantly, few studies have controlled for the possible effects of personality or cognitive abilities and even in which one or the other has been included, typically both have not. This is an important shortcoming because, ultimately, from both theoretical and practical perspectives, the relevance of EI as a useful construct depends on its incremental predictive validity. In short, it is not sufficient that EI tests predict significant life outcomes. EI is useful only as a separate construct if it adds to knowledge about what influences real-life outcomes, beyond what can be attributed to cognitive abilities and personality.

Van Rooy and Viswesvaran (2004) have attempted to test the incremental validity of EI by conducting a meta-analysis of 57 studies that have explored whether EI predicts academic, employment, and other forms of performance. Some of these studies (theses, laboratory reports) have not been published in refereed journals, and the different studies have involved different measures of trait EI and ability EI. Results suggested that the composite EI derived by combining all measures might account for 4%–5% of performance variance beyond that predicted by the Big Five personality variables but no incremental validity over general intelligence. Moreover, differences between the performance-based MEIS and the other EI measures (all self-report) suggested that different underlying constructs could be involved. Apart from this analysis, and a study by Brackett and Mayer (2003), we know of no investigation that has directly considered whether EI predicts performance, beyond what can be predicted by intelligence and personality. In the next section, therefore, we summarize a recent attempt to test the incremental predictive validity of EI for real-life variables, after controlling for cognitive abilities and several personality domains. EI has been operationalized specifically in terms of Salovey and Mayer's (1990; Mayer & Salovey, 1997) conceptions of EI as an information processing ability.

Bastian's Data

During 2002–2003 Bastian recruited 246 predominantly first-year psychology students (69 males, 177 females) aged 16–39 years (mean 20 years). They completed a battery of tests measuring EI (TMMS, MSCEIT, AES), cognitive abilities (Raven's Advanced Progressive Matrices [APM; Raven, Court & Raven, 1993], the Phonetic Word Association Test [PWAT; Brownless & Dunn, 1958]), personality (Revised NEO Personality Inventory [NEO PI-R; Costa & McCrae, 1992]), life satisfaction (Satisfaction With Life Scale [SWLS; Diener, Emmons, Larsen, & Griffin, 1985]), anxiety (Anxious Thoughts Inventory [ATI; Wells, 1994]), perceived problem solving (Problem Solving Inventory [PSI; Heppner & Petersen, 1982]), and coping (COPE [Carver, Scheier, & Weintraub,

1989]). Self-reported Australian Tertiary Entrance Rank (TER) scores from the final Year 12 of secondary schooling were available for 185 younger participants, to assess their academic achievement. TER is a percentile rank based on school performance relative to other students. It is used to determine competitive entrance to tertiary education.

The aim of Bastian's study was to test whether EI, assessed by self-report (TMMS, AES) and ability EI performance measures (MSCEIT), exhibited incremental predictive validity for real-life outcomes as indicated by academic achievement, problem solving, coping and lower anxiety, and life satisfaction, after controlling for individual differences in personality and cognitive abilities. In summary, the results from this study, published by Bastian, Burns, and Nettelbeck (2005), were that, consistent with previous research (e.g., Dawda & Hart, 2000; Petrides & Furnham, 2000, 2001; Saklofske et al., 2003; Van der Zee, Schakel, & Thijs, 2002), the TMMS and AES measures were more related to personality than was MSCEIT. Cognitive abilities tended to be more closely related to MSCEIT than to TMMS and AES, as reported by others (e.g., Brackett & Mayer, 2003; Lopes et al., 2003; O'Connor & Little, 2003), although this distinction was less clear. EI and academic achievement were not reliably correlated but, consistent with theory, higher EI was low to moderately correlated with higher life satisfaction, problem solving, more positive coping, and lower anxiety. However, after controlling for personality and cognitive abilities, EI predicted only small amounts of variance in these life skills. The MSCEIT shared about 6% of variance with the ATI. Self-report EI (i.e., a combined measure from TMMS and AES) accounted for 4%–6% in life satisfaction and coping.

Bastian's second study in 2004 involved 212 participants aged 40–68 years (mean 52 years) who were widely recruited from the general community. There was therefore no overlap between the ranges of ages in the two studies, but together they provide a continuous but not uniform age distribution from 16 to 68 years. The battery of tests completed by these participants was identical to that in the first study, but indices of academic achievement at the end of secondary education were not available for these older participants.

Bastian's aims were twofold. Principally, she wanted to check whether the pattern of results found in the first study would be found with an older, more heterogeneous IQ sample. In summary, results from this study were markedly similar to those from the first—but with even less evidence of incremental validity beyond personality and cognitive ability for either the separate EI scales or the combined self-report measure (derived from TMMS and AES). Secondly, Bastian was interested in ascertaining whether the older group would score higher on the measures of EI. This question about whether EI changes over the life span will be addressed in a later section.

The main analyses presented here have been made after combining the samples from both of Bastian's studies; in other words, $N = 458$ (130 males, 328 females). Because TER scores were not available for the older group, they have been excluded from most of the analyses that follow, although within the younger group TERs have been included for the one analysis about EI and life outcomes. Similarly, because ATI data were not available for about half of the first cohort, these are not considered here.

Dimensionality of EI Measures

Prior to addressing the questions set for us by the editors (using the data at hand), some comments on our methodology are necessary. We have used exploratory factor analysis (EFA) and confirmatory factor analysis (CFA) at different points. There has been a tendency for use of EFA to be seen as naïve or old-fashioned and for CFA (or, more generally, structural equation modeling, SEM) to be promoted because of the availability of hypothesis testing and statistical significance information within its framework. We believe that this tendency is unfortunate for at least two reasons. First, as Schulze (2005) pointed out, the exploratory-confirmatory dichotomy is somewhat illusory. Much work in the SEM framework is, indeed, exploratory in nature, with liberal use of modification indices for model refinement and generation. Modern EFA techniques, on the other hand, allow confirmation of structural models, and maximum likelihood implementations also provide tests of statistical fit (see also Cudeck, 2000). Second, CFA requires strong a priori models for its effective use (Schulze, 2005). EI research has developed a plethora of models, but whether they can be considered strong is moot. It is one thing to propose a model of EI and then show that data fit it to some arbitrary level acceptable to the proponent for that model; but it is another to demonstrate that model's superiority to other models (including equivalent but substantively distinct models). At various points in what follows, we will take the opportunity to advocate for modern approaches to EFA and raise issues on the use of CFA/SEM in EI research.

For Bastian's TMMS data, EFA of the polychoric correlation matrix for the 30 items from this instrument was conducted. We used polychoric rather than Pearson correlations because it has been amply demonstrated that for categorical data with only a few categories (say two to six), use of the Pearson correlation can lead to artifactual outcomes (Kubinger, 2003). Until recently it was thought that prohibitively large samples were required to use polychoric correlations validly, particularly in CFA, but recent research has shown that it is valid with only moderately large samples (Flora & Curran, 2004). To determine the number of factors, we examined the scree plot, calculated Velicer's minimum average partial, and used a parallel roots analysis (see O'Connor, 2000; a fuller description on the use of the parallel roots procedure is given below). All three methods suggested a four-factor solution.

Again, it is common for researchers in EI to use the eigenvalue greater than unity rule as their sole criterion for determining the number of factors to extract, although it has long been known that this method is often misleading (Cattell, 1978). There are now readily available program extensions (O'Connor, 2000; see also Russell, 2002) that allow researchers to more reliably determine the number of factors in a data set, although experience and knowledge of the research field are still indispensable (Schulze, 2005). Examination of the promax rotated four-factor maximum likelihood solution for TMMS showed that this solution was largely consistent with the three domains identified by Salovey et al. (1995). The relevant items defined the Repair and Clarity domains; the other two factors represented aspects of Attention. Thus, the three domain scores suggested by Salovey et al. (Repair, Attention, and Clarity) were used for this instrument.

Similar analysis for AES defined a two-factor solution, rather than the one- or four-factor solutions reported in the literature (Ciarrochi et al., 2001; Petrides & Furnham, 2000; Saklofske et al., 2003; Schutte et al., 1998). We designated these two factors AES-Competency/Management and AES-Recognition. Summed item scores for these as well as an AES total score are reported in different contexts here. Thus, use of polychoric correlations and applying the parallel roots criterion to determine the number of factors distinguishes our result for AES from that of, for example, Petrides and Furnham (2000). In their exploratory analysis, they used Pearson correlations and reported that the eigenvalues greater than unity rule suggested 10 factors, whereas the scree plot suggested only two. In the end, however, they decided on a four-factor varimax (i.e., orthogonal factors) solution because "it was interpretable, clear, and accounted for a reasonable amount of the total variance" (p. 317).

It is also apposite to compare our exploratory approach with the CFA of the AES by Gignac, Palmer, Manocha, and Stough (2005). They assumed validity of the model on which the AES was based (but see Petrides and Furnham's qualification on Schutte et al.'s methodology); and this model specifies six domains. Gignac et al. assigned 28 items from the AES to these six domains and also included a general EI factor on which all 28 items loaded. They also proposed that an acquiescence factor was required because only 3 of 33 items of the AES are negatively keyed. Thus, their model was complex, containing 2 factors on which all items loaded and 6 other factors defined by between 2 and 7 of the 28 items. Certainly, the argument for the acquiescence factor is weak and its necessity cannot be empirically determined because there are so few negatively keyed items in the AES (see McPherson & Mohr, 2005, for further discussion on item keying and factor analysis). Here it seems clear that an EFA approach is preferable to CFA because demonstrating that data fit a model is not the same thing as providing evidence for that model (Roberts & Pashler, 2000). Our two-factor EFA solution, on the other hand, is parsimonious and interpretable.

For the MSCEIT V2.0 (prerelease version), we have four branch scores and a total EI score provided by the publishers of the instrument (MHS). Following Mayer and Salovey (1997), the four branches are as follows:

1. *Perception, appraisal, and expression of emotion* (Perceiving). This ability has been described as the accuracy with which emotions in self and others can be identified.
2. *Emotional facilitation of thinking* (Using); how emotions are used to guide thinking.
3. *Understanding and analyzing emotions, employing emotional knowledge* (Knowledge); understanding how emotions change.
4. *Reflective regulation of emotions to promote emotional and intellectual growth* (Management). This involves managing both one's own and others' emotions.

However, we also calculated consensus scores based on our own sample. These were calculated by determining the proportion of the sample that gave a particular response to each item. That proportion was then assigned as the score for that item to each individual who made that particular response. Then, for each subtest of MSCEIT, the mean of these scores was calculated for each individual. The branch scores were the mean of the two subtests comprising each branch. These scores are shown in Table 7.1, along with descriptive statistics for our other EI measures. Correlations of our consensus scores with those provided by MHS publishers were moderately high: .64, .67, .64, and .68 for Perceiving, Using, Knowledge, and Management branch scores, respectively, consistent with Legree et al. (2004).

We have used the consensus scores to determine how well the EI model encapsulated by MSCEIT was fit by our data. The four branch scores were each defined by two tasks from the MSCEIT as described by Mayer et al. (2000). This model, shown in Figure 7.1, is referred to hereafter as Model 1. For comparison purposes, we also fitted: (a) a single general factor model in which all eight MSCEIT tasks load a general EI factor (Model 2); (b) a two-factor model in which four tasks load what Mayer et al. refer to as EI areas (specifically, Emotional Experiencing and Emotional Reasoning; Model 3); and (c) a four-factor model in which the tasks were arbitrarily assigned in pairs to define a factor (Model 4). It should be noted that there are other models, including higher order models, that could be fitted to these data (see Schulze, 2005), but these four are sufficient for our current purpose.

Comparing these types of models should be done using a range of fit criteria; specifically, goodness of fit and model complexity should be considered (Kline, 2005). Here we have used the Bayesian Information Criterion (BIC; Raftery, 1995; Schwarz, 1978), the Root Mean Square Error of Approximation (RMSEA; Steiger & Lind, 1980), along with its 90% confidence interval, and the likelihood ratio chi-square. The BIC takes account of sample size and penalizes model complexity; the RMSEA is a parsimony-adjusted index in which values less than about .05 indicate close approximate fit; and RMSEA greater than or equal to .10 suggests poor fit. The likelihood ratio chi-square tests the hypothesis that the model is correct but it is sensitive to the size of correlations and to sample size. Commonly, to overcome these problems, it is divided by the model degrees of freedom and a rule of thumb is that this value should be less than about 2 for a good-fitting model (Kline, 2005).

Table 7.2 shows the fit criteria for the models considered. Several points emerge from examination of this table. First, Model 1, with four correlated factors representing the EI branches proposed by Mayer and colleagues, is clearly the best-fitting model by all criteria, and it is the only model that satisfies the chi-square test for exact fit. Second, Model 4, in which the MSCEIT tasks were arbitrarily assigned in pairs to four factors, provides poor fit to the data. Models 2 and 3 do not satisfy the chi-square criterion but are plausible by the other criteria; the two-factor model, particularly, rivals Model 1 because its fit is not too bad and it is more parsimonious than Model 1. Nonetheless, our data provide strongest evidence for the EI model operationalized by MSCEIT. We now address the question of whether EI is distinct from personality and cognitive ability.

EI, Personality, and Cognitive Ability

In this section we address the question of how EI tests relate to existing personality and ability constructs. Data were the 3 measures from TMMS (Repair, Attention, and

TABLE 7.1. Means and standard deviations for measures from three EI instruments.

	Mean	SD	Range
TMMS[a]			
Repair	22.4	4.1	6–30
Attention	49.5	6.9	20–68
Clarity	39.6	7.0	15–58
AES[b]			
AES-Competency/Management	88.1	9.2	54–112
AES-Recognition	37.1	5.0	16–50
AES-Total	125.2	12.7	78–161
MSCEIT[c]			
MHS-Perception	102.4	15.3	41.9–123.5
MHS-Using	100.9	13.0	41.5–126.7
MHS-Knowledge	104.7	11.4	51.2–123.5
MHS-Management	99.1	12.0	50.9–124.1
MHS-EI	101.5	12.2	32.9–123.6
Consensus-Perception	.499	.089	.13–.62
Consensus-Using	.428	.061	.13–.54
Consensus-Knowledge	.570	.074	.24–.69
Consensus-Management	.396	.057	.12–.50

[a] TMMS is Trait Meta Mood Scale (Salovey et al., 1995).
[b] AES is Assessing Emotions Scale (Schutte et al., 1998).
[c] MSCEIT is Mayer-Salovey-Caruso Emotional Intelligence Test v2.0 (Mayer et al., 2000); MHS scores are those provided by the publishers; consensus scores were calculated on our own sample (see text for details).

Clarity), AES total score, 8 task scores from MSCEIT (based on our consensus scores), the 30 facet scores derived from NEO-PI-R, the APM score, and PWAT score. For reasons discussed above, the approach was exploratory and the Pearson correlation matrix was analyzed via maximum likelihood factoring. The number of factors was determined using a parallel roots analysis, in which 1000 random permutations of the raw data were used to generate the eigenvalues with which those from the observed correlation matrix were compared (O'Connor, 2000). A plot of both the eigenvalues for the observed data and eigenvalues from the random data against factor number showed that between factor 7 and factor 11 the two lines were close together and near parallel and at factor 12 the eigenvalues for observed and random data were indistinguishable (see Figure 7.2). On this basis, we used a 7-factor model, which accounted for 50.5% of variance.

Table 7.3a shows the pattern matrix for the promax rotated 7-factor maximum likelihood solution, and Table 7.3b shows the factor correlation matrix. To summarize, EFA has nicely recovered the 5 domains expected from the NEO-PI-R. The self-report measures in TMMS predominantly loaded on the personality factors Openness and Neuroticism, and there was some overlap between TMMS and AES, but the latter did not

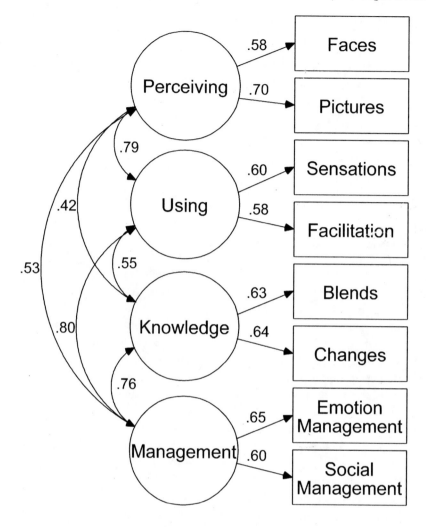

Figure 7.1. Measurement model for MSCEIT showing eight tasks defining four EI branches and showing standardized parameter estimates.

load on any domain other than Openness. The performance measures from the eight MSCEIT tasks, on the other hand, clearly defined an EI factor. Combining this outcome with the CFA described above suggests that MSCEIT captures Mayer and Salovey's (1997) definition in terms of perceiving, using, understanding, and managing emotions. EI, so defined, loaded the two cognitive ability tests to some extent; but the analytical reasoning factor (AR), here solely defined by Raven's APM performance, was relatively independent from EI and the personality dimensions.

TABLE **7.2.** Fit criteria for four measurement models for MSCEIT.

Model	BIC	RMSEA 90% CI	x^2 (df)	p
1	156.2	.03 [.00, .05]	21.5 (14)	.090
2	203.7	.10 [.08, .12]	105.7 (20)	< .001
3	160.8	.07 [.05, .09]	56.7 (19)	< .001
4	232.8	.12 [.09, .14]	98.1 (14)	< .001
Saturated	220.5	—	0 (0)	—
Null	681.1	.22 [.20, .23]	632.1 (28)	< .001

Note: For comparison purposes, the relevant statistics are shown for the saturated model, in which no constraints are imposed and fit is perfect; and for the null model in which population correlations are assumed to be zero. See text for description of the four measurement models. BIC is Bayesian Information Criterion; RMSEA is Root Mean Square Error of Approximation.

To paraphrase Boring's (1923) famous dictum, this analysis has found that EI at this stage is what the Mayer-Salovey-Caruso Emotional Intelligence Test tests. This EI factor is relatively independent from personality, although there was some overlap with Openness and Agreeableness (see Table 7.3b). Further, MSCEIT is independent from cognitive ability as defined for this sample. It is important to note, however, that whereas personality has been well defined in these data, cognitive abilities were defined by only two marker tests, one for each of fluid ability and crystallized ability. Correlations of the AR factor with personality factors were consistent with other research that has found relationships between personality, particularly Openness, and intelligence (Matthews, Deary, & Whiteman, 2003). However, cognitive ability, as defined here, is clearly inadequate to permit a test of where EI may be located within a well-articulated psychometric hierarchical model for intelligence.

This result suggests that future development of performance measures that characterize MSCEIT holds the best prospects for defining EI independently from personality domains. Two caveats to this conclusion should be noted, however. First, as pointed out by Brody (2004), MSCEIT performance items do not measure actual performance and, although answers may test knowledge of perception, use, knowledge, and management of emotions, such answers do not demonstrate how that person would actually behave. Given considerable evidence from diverse circumstances that self-assessment of traits, skills, and achievement are frequently substantially inaccurate (Dunning, Heath, & Suls, 2005), Brody's criticism raises a serious problem about the validity of so-called performance items. Second, and most important, whether the EI factor has incremental predictive validity for practical life outcomes beyond what can be predicted by measures of personality and intelligence is ultimately critical to the usefulness of the construct. We consider this in the next section.

EI and Life Outcomes

Here we report the extent to which measures of EI predict three self-reported measures of positive life outcomes. These life outcome measures were life satisfaction

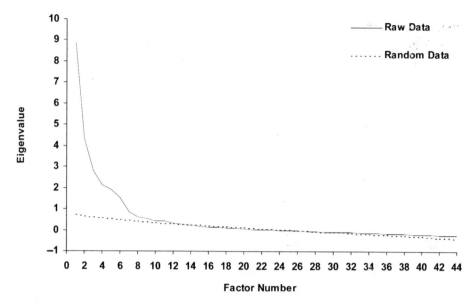

Figure 7.2. Plot of eigenvalues against factor number for 44 variables and for the mean of 1,000 random permutations of the raw data for the same 44 variables. The two lines become nearly parallel at about factor number 7, and eigenvalues are indistinguishable at factor number 12.

(SWLS; Diener et al., 1985), problem solving (PSI; Heppner & Petersen, 1982), and coping (COPE; Carver et al., 1989). We also consider the measure of academic achievement, TER, but this was available only for 185 participants in the younger adult group and this result will therefore be discussed separately. For the SWLS and PSI, we used total scale scores; note that lower scores on the latter indicate superior problem solving. For the COPE, we have factor analyzed the 15 domain scores and identified 3 qualitatively different aspects of coping: Active Coping, Social Coping, and coping by Denial. We report on these separately because, *prima facie*, we expected EI to relate to these aspects of coping differentially. Thus, for example, high EI may predict Active Coping or Social Coping but not coping by Denial. In what follows, therefore, there are five separate life outcome measures.

The summary for a series of multiple regression analyses is set out in Table 7.4. The five measures of life outcome were regressed separately onto each of the EI measures. For TMMS, the three domain scores were used; for AES, the two domains identified by our own factor analyses (Competency/Management and Recognition) were used; and for MSCEIT, the four branch scores were used.[2] TMMS predicted substantial variance in SWLS, PSI and Active Coping (17%, 23%, and 27%, respectively) and lower amounts of variance in Social and Denial Coping (3% and 10%, respectively). AES predicted less than 10% of variance in life outcome measures. MSCEIT predicted only between 1% and 6% of variance in life outcome measures, substantially less than either of the two self-report EI measures. The differential pattern of magnitudes for the standardized regression coefficients within each EI measure is of some interest. Thus, TMMS-Repair predicted

TABLE **7.3a.** Pattern matrix for Promax rotation of seven-factor maximum likelihood solution for EI measures, NEO-PI-R facets, APM, and PWAT.

	N	E	O	A	C	EI	AR	h^2
Neuroticism 1	**-0.94**	0.05	0.09	-0.01	0.17	0.04	-0.03	0.69
2	**-0.46**	-0.14	0.18	**-0.59**	0.04	0.04	-0.11	0.73
3	**-0.93**	-0.01	0.10	0.03	0.02	-0.02	0.01	0.77
4	**-0.84**	-0.05	0.07	0.08	0.05	0.06	0.03	0.60
5	**-0.33**	0.18	**0.32**	-0.33	**-0.28**	0.03	-0.08	0.53
6	**-0.84**	0.04	0.02	0.16	-0.17	-0.02	0.03	0.75
Extraversion 1	0.04	**0.72**	0.18	**0.25**	0.03	-0.01	-0.06	0.78
2	0.00	**0.86**	-0.21	0.05	-0.13	0.10	0.03	0.62
3	**0.48**	**0.30**	0.02	**-0.48**	0.19	0.05	0.04	0.55
4	0.17	**0.31**	0.13	**-0.26**	**0.25**	0.00	0.06	0.35
5	-0.20	**0.63**	-0.16	-0.19	-0.12	0.00	0.23	0.48
6	0.19	**0.55**	**0.25**	0.08	-0.02	-0.01	0.07	0.63
Openness 1	-0.03	0.10	**0.39**	-0.09	**-0.32**	0.00	**0.33**	0.43
2	-0.22	-0.03	**0.60**	0.10	0.11	-0.13	**0.26**	0.42
3	**-0.26**	0.08	**0.79**	-0.15	0.06	0.03	-0.06	0.60
4	**0.25**	0.03	**0.37**	0.11	-0.12	-0.08	0.20	0.35
5	-0.01	-0.06	**0.38**	-0.03	0.23	-0.17	0.60	0.61
6	0.22	-0.16	**0.66**	0.00	-0.16	0.01	0.03	0.47
Agreeableness 1	**0.30**	0.15	0.22	**0.53**	-0.15	0.02	-0.01	0.64
2	-0.13	-0.07	0.12	**0.57**	0.20	0.07	-0.06	0.42
3	-0.19	**0.38**	0.25	**0.41**	**0.28**	0.03	-0.11	0.55
4	0.02	0.10	-0.06	**0.84**	-0.02	-0.02	0.05	0.70
5	**-0.29**	-0.05	0.06	**0.44**	-0.11	0.07	-0.16	0.26
6	0.12	-0.18	0.69	0.17	-0.04	-0.06	-0.06	0.50
Conscientiousness 1	0.21	0.05	0.06	-0.05	**0.69**	0.03	0.07	0.72
2	-0.13	-0.12	-0.05	-0.10	**0.75**	0.05	-0.06	0.47
3	0.02	-0.05	0.00	0.17	**0.74**	0.02	-0.08	0.67
4	-0.17	0.13	0.01	-0.10	**0.88**	-0.06	0.12	0.65
5	0.16	-0.07	0.04	0.00	**0.75**	-0.01	-0.03	0.72
6	-0.04	-0.09	**-0.27**	**0.26**	**0.61**	0.06	0.09	0.48
TMMS-Repair	**0.44**	**0.28**	0.14	0.21	0.00	0.01	-0.08	0.55
TMMS-Attention	-0.13	0.06	**0.69**	-0.02	-0.12	0.08	-0.13	0.47
TMMS-Clarity	**0.61**	-0.19	**0.27**	-0.04	0.09	0.12	-0.19	0.56
AES-Total	0.17	0.15	**0.28**	-0.10	0.08	0.02	-0.12	0.21

TABLE **7.3a** (continued)

MSCEIT-Faces	−0.13	0.11	−0.14	0.00	−0.03	**0.49**	0.00	0.36
MSCEIT-Facilitation	0.08	0.09	−0.14	−0.06	−0.02	**0.57**	−0.10	0.42
MSCEIT-Changes	−0.05	−0.05	0.09	−0.02	−0.01	**0.51**	0.18	0.36
MSCEIT-Emotion Management	0.00	0.03	0.09	0.01	0.08	**0.51**	0.06	0.42
MSCEIT-Pictures	0.10	0.06	−0.14	0.02	−0.01	**0.52**	0.02	0.36
MSCEIT-Sensations	−0.15	0.06	−0.01	0.07	0.12	**0.55**	0.00	0.42
MSCEIT-Blends	0.06	−0.23	0.22	0.04	−0.04	**0.39**	**0.25**	0.36
MSCEIT-Social Management	0.05	0.08	0.12	0.09	−0.01	**0.47**	0.05	0.42
APM	−0.06	0.16	−0.16	−0.04	−0.07	0.24	**0.61**	0.42
PWAT	0.05	**−0.25**	0.22	0.05	0.00	**0.36**	0.21	0.36

Note: Factors are N = neuroticism, E = extraversion, O = openness, A = agreeableness, C = conscientiousness, EI = emotional intelligence, AR = abstract reasoning, h^2 = communality. Loadings ≥ .25 in bold.

SWLS, PSI, and Active Coping, whereas TMMS-Attention did not. However, TMMS-Clarity predicted coping by Denial, but TMMS-Repair and TMMS-Attention did not. Of the MSCEIT branches, Management had the largest regression coefficients.

To summarize, the EI measures, particularly self-report EI, did predict substantial variance in the outcome measures of life satisfaction, problem solving, and active coping. However, the critical question is whether the predictive validities of these EI measures add to the already well established predictive validity of personality and ability measures.

Table 7.5 summarizes a series of hierarchical regression analyses completed to answer this question. The five personality domains from NEO-PI-R, together with PWAT and APM scores, were entered into regression models, as described above. Next, EI measures were entered into the same models. Table 7.5 shows the change in proportion of variance accounted for when the EI measures were added to the models along with the standardized

TABLE **7.3b.** Factor correlation matrix for Promax rotation of seven-factor maximum likelihood solution for eight EI measures, 30 NEO-PI-R facets, APM, and PWAT.

	N	*E*	*O*	*A*	*C*	*EI*
E	0.25					
O	0.34	0.40				
A	0.42	0.00	0.22			
C	0.54	0.11	0.20	0.27		
EI	0.14	0.00	0.35	0.22	0.03	
AR	0.18	−0.05	0.24	−0.05	−0.08	0.13

Note: Factors are N = neuroticism, E = extraversion, O = openness, A = agreeableness, C = conscientiousness, EI = emotional intelligence, AR = abstract reasoning.

TABLE 7.4. Multiple regression of life outcome measures onto EI measures.

	SWLS		PSI		COPE-Active		COPE-Social		COPE-Denial	
TMMS										
R^2_{adj}	.17		.23		.27		.03		.09	
$F (3, 406)$	29.3	$p < .001$	41.7	$p < .001$	50.9	$p < .001$	5.00	$p = .002$	15.0	$p < .001$
β Repair	.35	$p < .001$	-.24	$p < .001$	.37	$p < .001$	.11	$p = .061$	-.04	$p = .469$
β Attention	.01	$p = .774$	.06	$p = .182$	-.06	$p = .208$	.14	$p = .006$	.09	$p = .065$
β Clarity	.12	$p = .024$	-.34	$p < .001$	.25	$p < .001$	-.01	$p = .862$	-.31	$p < .001$
AES										
R^2_{adj}	.05		.09		.09		.02		.00	
$F (2, 407)$	12.6	$p < .001$	19.9	$p < .001$	22.8	$p < .001$	5.05	$p = .007$	1.13	$p = .326$
β Competency/ Management	.30	$p < .001$	-.24	$p < .001$	.33	$p < .001$	.17	$p = .007$	-.05	$p = .461$
β Recognition	-.14	$p = .024$	-.08	$p = .189$	-.02	$p = .716$	-.02	$p = .753$	-.04	$p = .560$
MSCEIT										
R^2_{adj}	.02		.06		.04		.01		.03	
$F (4, 405)$	3.52	$p = .008$	8.04	$p < .001$	5.11	$p = .001$	1.47	$p = .210$	3.79	$p = .005$
β Perception	.01	$p = .811$	.11	$p = .046$	-.11	$p = .045$	-.08	$p = .153$	-.03	$p = .550$
β Using	.02	$p = .706$	.00	$p = .950$	-.01	$p = .801$	.00	$p = .991$	.06	$p = .323$
β Knowledge	.05	$p = .382$	-.13	$p = .011$	.07	$p = .192$	.04	$p = .509$	-.11	$p = .034$
β Management	.15	$p = .006$	-.21	$p < .001$	.20	$p < .001$	.10	$p = .072$	-.13	$p = .020$

TABLE 7.5. Multiple regression of life outcome measures onto EI measures after regression of personality and ability measures showing R^2_{cha} when EI is added and standardized regression coefficients for the EI measures only.

	SWLS		PSI		COPE-Active		COPE-Social		COPE-Denial	
TMMS										
R^2_{cha}	.02		.00		.06		.01		.01	
F_{cha} (3, 399)	3.51	$p=.015$	1.19	$p=.313$	11.1	$p<.001$	1.36	$p=.256$	1.04	$p=.376$
β Repair	.16	$p=.007$	-.02	$p=.678$	.26	$p<.001$	.03	$p=.705$	-.04	$p=.469$
β Attention	.07	$p=.154$	.08	$p=.066$	-.11	$p=.040$	.05	$p=.411$	.09	$p=.065$
β Clarity	-.01	$p=.899$	-.01	$p=.833$	.15	$p=.011$	.09	$p=.164$	-.31	$p<.001$
AES										
R^2_{cha}	.01		.01		.02		.01		.00	
F_{cha} (2, 400)	3.33	$p=.037$	3.02	$p=.050$	5.81	$p=.003$	1.25	$p=.287$	0.13	$p=.880$
β Comp/Manage	.14	$p=.012$	-.06	$p=.187$	.18	$p=.002$	.09	$p=.177$	.02	$p=.712$
β Recognition	-.10	$p=.059$	-.04	$p=.341$	-.03	$p=.521$	-.01	$p=.926$	-.03	$p=.622$
MSCEIT										
R^2_{cha}	.01		.01		.01		.01		.01	
F_{cha} (4, 398)	1.24	$p=.295$	1.07	$p=.373$	1.45	$p=.218$	0.71	$p=.583$	0.92	$p=.450$
β Perception	-.01	$p=.853$	.07	$p=.100$	-.09	$p=.089$	-.08	$p=.170$	-.07	$p=.150$
β Using	.06	$p=.228$	-.03	$p=.414$	.00	$p=.932$	.00	$p=.920$	.06	$p=.264$
β Knowledge	.04	$p=.498$	-.06	$p=.186$	.09	$p=.098$	.05	$p=.364$	-.03	$p=.592$
β Management	.05	$p=.289$	-.02	$p=.959$	.04	$p=.488$	.02	$p=.706$	-.04	$p=.432$

TABLE **7.6.** Correlations of MSCEIT, APM, and PWAT with TER and partial controlling for APM and PWAT *(N = 185).*

	TER Zero-Order		TER Controlling for APM and PWAT	
MSCEIT-Perception	−.05	$p = .51$	−.10	$p = .20$
MSCEIT-Using	−.02	$p = .80$	−.03	$p = .72$
MSCEIT-Knowledge	.33	$p < .001$	.14	$p = .06$
MSCEIT-Management	.17	$p = .02$	.08	$p = .27$
APM	.43	$p < .001$	—	
PWAT	.35	$p < .001$	—	

regression coefficients for the EI measures. The overall outcome is very clear. The EI measures have incremental validity that exceeds 2% for only one of the life outcome measures. TMMS predicted 6% of variance in Active Coping beyond that predicted by personality and ability measures. This outcome extends the conclusions previously drawn by Bastian et al. (2005). For these self-report life outcome measures, none of the EI measures has substantial incremental predictive validity over that of personality and ability.

Because MSCEIT has been shown to be relatively independent from personality measures (see Tables 7.3a and 7.3b) and because the life outcome measures considered so far were all self-report measures, it is important to consider the possibility that MSCEIT may have incremental predictive validity for life outcome measures that do not depend on self-report. In the next analysis we therefore used the TER scores (an independent measure of academic achievement when leaving secondary schooling), available for the younger group. Table 7.6 shows zero-order correlations and second-order partial correlations (controlling for APM and PWAT) between MSCEIT and TER, on one hand, and APM, PWAT, and TER on the other. MSCEIT branches for Knowledge and Management correlated significantly with TER; but these correlations were substantially reduced to unreliable levels when APM and PWAT scores were partialed out. This result reflects the moderately strong correlations between these ability tests and TER. Noting that the participants in this sample were first-year university students, with restricted ranges for scores on these ability tests, this outcome suggests that EI as measured by MSCEIT has little incremental validity beyond that achievable with tests of cognitive abilities.

Does EI Change Over the Life Span?

To address this question the total sample has been divided into two groups: those 21 years or younger (*N* = 206, 54 males, 152 females, 16–21 years) and those 40 years or older (*N* = 211, 60 males, 151 females, 40–68 years). Table 7.7 shows the comparisons between the younger and older groups for all measures of personality, cognitive abilities, and EI. It is clear from inspection of Table 7.7 that the outcomes for personality and ability measures were consistent with previous findings. Thus, as would be expected,

TABLE **7.7.** Comparison of young and middle-aged adults on personality, ability, and EI measures.

	Young (N = 206) Mean (SD)	Middle-Aged (N = 207) Mean (SD)	d^a	$t(411)$	P
NEO-PI-R					
Neuroticism	99.8 (24.1)	79.7 (26.0)	.80	8.15	< .001
Extraversion	119.3 (21.3)	111.1 (20.1)	.40	4.03	< .001
Openness	124.9 (19.1)	129.5 (18.9)	−.24	2.46	.014
Agreeableness	116.3 (19.2)	128.4 (16.2)	−.68	6.94	< .001
Conscientiousness	106.7 (23.3)	121.1 (21.4)	−.65	6.57	< .001
Cognitive Ability					
PWAT	35.9 (8.6)	42.5 (7.4)	−.83	8.42	< .001
APM	23.5 (7.0)	18.8 (6.6)	.69	7.06	< .001
TMMS[b]					
Repair	21.3 (4.3)	23.4 (3.8)	−.53	5.39	< .001
Attention	49.6 (6.5)	49.4 (7.4)	.02	0.25	.807
Clarity	36.7 (6.6)	42.5 (6.3)	−.91	9.20	< .001
AES[c]					
AES-Total	123.5 (12.3)	127.0 (12.7)	−.28	2.89	.004
MSCEIT[d]					
Perception	102.4 (15.2)	102.2 (15.9)	.01	0.15	.883
Using	99.2 (13.6)	102.6 (12.7)	−.26	2.63	.009
Knowledge	103.4 (11.2)	106.1 (10.7)	−.25	2.50	.013
Management	95.2 (11.9)	103.3 (11.3)	−.70	7.13	< .001
EI	99.2 (13.0)	103.8 (11.4)	−.37	3.75	< .001

[a] d is Cohen's d, the difference between means divided by the pooled standard deviation estimate. Negative values indicate higher means for the middle-aged group.
[b] TMMS is Trait Meta Mood Scale (Salovey et al., 1995).
[c] AES is Assessing Emotions Scale (Schutte et al., 1998).
[d] MSCEIT is Mayer-Salovey-Caruso Emotional Intelligence Test v2.0 (Mayer et al., 2000); MHS scores are those provided by the publishers; consensus scores were calculated on our own sample (see text for details).

the younger group scored higher on Neuroticism and Extraversion but lower on Openness, Agreeableness, and Conscientiousness. Again, as would be expected, the older group scored higher on PWAT (i.e., a measure of crystallized ability, Gc) but lower on APM (i.e., a measure of fluid and visuospatial abilities, Gf and Gv). As indicated by the effect sizes, these age-related differences were large.

For the self-report EI measures, differences were largest for TMMS-Repair and TMMS-Clarity and somewhat smaller for AES, with the older group scoring higher. There was no difference between age groups on TMMS-Attention. For MSCEIT there was no difference on Perception, but small differences favoring older adults on Using and Knowledge and a larger difference again favoring older adults on Management. Insofar as Mayer and Salovey's (1997) conception for these four branches was hierarchical, with perception of emotion represented by basic psychological processes and management of emotion requiring the most complex, integrated processes, the increasing effect sizes across the four branches in Table 7.7 suggest that the differences between the groups have increased as the complexity of putative processes underpinning these four branches increases. Whether this is so or not, it is clear that responses among the participants between 40 and 68 years of age have indicated at least higher levels of knowledge about the regulation of emotions, compared to 16 to 21-year-olds. Taken together, these MSCEIT results suggest that more complex aspects of EI described by this instrument continue to develop beyond young adulthood. In this regard, EI would therefore appear to follow a different trajectory to psychometric cognitive abilities, which typically reach maximum levels by early adulthood. Potentially useful future research questions may be whether the levels of EI competence registered by these older participants were attained markedly earlier than 40 years of age; and whether improvement continues into older age bands. We note again, however, that the relevance of such questions will depend on establishing that EI has useful incremental validity, beyond competencies predicted by personality and cognitive abilities.

Conclusions

Our conclusions here should not be interpreted as meaning that we believe that the attempt to develop a valid measure of EI has failed to produce worthwhile outcomes or that future attempts to develop valid tests of EI will not succeed. On the contrary, we accept that the question of whether EI is a useful construct, distinct from personality and cognitive abilities, is still open. Ultimately, this matter can be resolved only by confirmation that EI, measured from tasks that require processing of emotion-relevant information, has significant incremental predictive validity for important life outcomes, beyond what is predicted by personality and intelligence tests. Moreover, an additional important consideration yet scarcely addressed is whether EI's usefulness will depend on the kind of activities involved. As Van Rooy and Viswesvaran (2004) have surmised, EI may influence different kinds of performance to different extents and may even be counterproductive under some circumstances.

Our results have suggested that the best available test of EI (MSCEIT V2.0) cannot yet reliably and substantially improve what can be predicted about life outcomes by tests of personality and cognitive abilities. However, given the relatively short history of interest in this topic, it is expecting a lot to demand that, at this stage, it should. Our results have confirmed that the attempt, initiated by Mayer et al. (1999), to develop performance scoring methods that do not rely on self-report has successfully produced a scale in the MSCEIT V2.0 that is largely independent from the personality domains measured by NEO-PI-R (cf. also Brackett & Mayer, 2003; Lopes et al., 2003) and from cognitive abilities tapped by APM and PWAT. Moreover, recent evidence from

Mayer et al. (2003) has confirmed excellent reliability, a sound fit for the four-branch model that we have relied on here and predictive validity for life satisfaction. And, as our comparison between younger and older participants has shown, MSCEIT is sensitive to changes across the life span.

Although, according to our analyses, the incremental validity of MSCEIT for life outcome measures beyond regression of personality and ability measures was generally not promising, this finding should be interpreted cautiously. In fact, the life outcome measures also suffered from the same shortcomings that apply to the trait measures of EI. They relied entirely on self-report, a procedure that challenges their validity. The validity of TER scores for university entrance is, on the other hand, well established, and confirmed here by moderate correlations with the two cognitive ability tests. Nonetheless, the range of TERs among these participants was obviously restricted to, at most, the upper 25% of more academically able students, which might attenuate correlation with EI constructs, particularly if these were more like threshold variables than continuous variables. It is also obvious that a more fully articulated multifactorial model of intelligence than was available here will be necessary to attempt to test how ability EI aligns with an adequate description of psychometrically defined cognitive abilities.

Finally, although it will pose an enormous challenge, it may be necessary to develop performance measures that rely less on consensual agreement about ways in which people think that they ought to behave but seek instead more direct behavioral measures. As researchers attempt to explore ways of accomplishing this, it would be helpful if they could develop means for protecting their intellectual property without restricting access to scoring procedures. Of course, one understands the concerns of publishers when attempting to maintain the commercial potential of their product. On the other hand, lack of transparency about how scores are derived may hamper attempts to further understanding of underlying constructs. That said, however, we acknowledge that MHS scores provided by the publishers for Bastian's data were sufficiently similar to those that we have calculated from consensus among the 458 participants to engender high confidence in the reliability of the MHS scores.

We remain optimistic about future prospects for EI as a useful construct for better informing understanding of individual differences in important life outcomes. The broad idea is certainly intuitively attractive. The initial enthusiasm in some quarters for a quick solution to the problems of defining and measuring EI—and for far-reaching claims about its relevance—has certainly raised lay expectations for EI among the general community that at this stage cannot be met. Clearly, we prefer an approach to a future research agenda based on the more reserved, cautious position that has been taken by Mayer, Salovey, and their colleagues, who first raised the possible utility of these ideas.

Summary

Based on a sample of 458 participants who completed the same battery of tests for EI, personality traits, cognitive abilities, and real-life outcomes, we have conducted a series of analyses that have addressed key questions about how EI should be conceptualized. We have concluded that EI should be defined as recommended by Mayer and Salovey (1997), in terms of processes that deal with information about emotions, and measured by evaluating performance, rather than by self-report. Currently, MSCEIT provides the only approximation to this standard. As measured by MSCEIT, EI has been found to be relatively independent from well-defined personality and ability constructs, although the range of cognitive abilities included in our analyses has been too narrow to permit an adequate test of independence from intelligence. This is therefore a potentially fruitful area for future research.

Current evidence suggests that EI is multifactorial and well described by four sub-domains ("branches") that capture the perception, use, understanding, and manage-ment of emotions, although such evidence is largely in the hands of the publishers of MSCEIT, and we would advocate independent analyses, as we have done here, to con-firm this conclusion. Cross-sectional improvements in average subdomain scores from younger adults around age 20 years and adults 40 years and older were consistent with the theoretical conception of these subdomains as developmentally hierarchical, with management processes represented as most complex. However, we are not aware of any data that would yet inform on how the trajectory for EI development, through child-hood into adulthood and across the life span, would look. The cross-sectional changes observed in our sample imply that improvement can accompany normal, age-related life experiences; but we cannot comment further about whether EI represents a skill base, subject to improvement by training, or some more fundamental trait. Our main conclusion is that, although EI as measured by MSCEIT correlates with life skills like problem solving, coping, and satisfaction, it has only very limited incremental validity once personality and cognitive abilities have been taken into account.

Whether this outcome constitutes a theoretical or practical advance at this rela-tively early stage of development of such measures depends on one's expectations. Presumably, those initially persuaded by the extravagant enthusiasm of some early proponents for EI may be disappointed to learn that current measures yield so little by way of incremental validity, especially in face of the realization that, after all, IQ re-mains a fairly robust predictor for so many real-life activities. On the other hand, even modest incremental validity will serve a useful purpose, all other things being equal; and it is reasonable to expect that, given improved reliability and veracity of scoring methods, incremental validity will also improve. In our opinion, testing whether the relatively weak incremental validity of the MSCEIT can be overcome may require that successors move away from the current focus on consensual or expert-based scor-ing procedures and, instead, explore whether it is possible to develop reliable behav-ioral measures.

Notes

1. This widely accepted generality might not apply under some circumstances. A recent meta-analysis of the Graduate Record Examinations (GRE) by Kuncel, Hezlett, and Ones (2001)

has found that although verbal, quantitative, and analytical components of the GRE (essentially a proxy for general mental ability) predicted graduate student performance reasonably well, discipline-relevant background knowledge did better. Plausibly, this outcome might reflect more homogeneous levels of ability and higher levels of both interest and declarative knowledge required for graduate selection, compared to most jobs. Nonetheless, Kuncel et al.'s findings have demonstrated that nonspecific, general cognitive tests can prove not to have incremental validity over specific cognitive knowledge, a cautionary reminder against uncritical acceptance of psychological dogma.

2. For this and subsequent analyses, the branch scores from MHS publishers were used. This was justified by comparison between results from EFAs using both our consensus scores and publishers' scores, which yielded substantially similar outcomes. The MHS scores have the advantage of being standardized to a mean of 100, with a standard deviation of 15, thereby permitting direct comparisons with other published data.

References

Arbuckle, J. L. (1999). *AMOS 5*. Chicago, IL: Small Waters.

Austin, E. J., & Saklofske, D. H. (2004). Far too many intelligences? On the communalities and differences between social, practical and emotional intelligences. In R. Schulze & R. D. Roberts (Eds.), *Emotional intelligence: An international handbook* (pp. 107–128). Cambridge, MA: Hogrefe & Huber.

Austin, E. J., Saklofske, D. H., Huang, S. H. S., & McKenney, D. (2004). Measurement of trait emotional intelligence: Testing and cross-validating a modified version of Schutte et al.'s measure. *Personality and Individual Differences, 36*, 555–562.

Bar-On, R. (1997). *Emotional Quotient Inventory (EQ-i): Technical manual*. Toronto, Canada: Multi-Health Systems.

Bar-On, R. (2004). The Bar-On emotional quotient inventory (EQ-I): Rationale, description, and summary of psychometric properties. In G. Geher (Eds.), *Measuring emotional intelligence: Common ground and controversy* (pp. 111–142). Hauppauge NY: Nova Science.

Bastian, V. A., Burns, N. R., & Nettelbeck, T. (2005). Emotional intelligence predicts life skills, but not as well as personality and cognitive abilities. *Personality and Individual Differences, 39*, 1135–1145.

Boring, E. G. (1923). Intelligence as the tests test it. *New Republic, 35*, 35–37.

Brackett, M. A., & Mayer, J. D. (2003). Convergent, discriminant and incremental validity of competing measures of emotional intelligence. *Personality and Social Psychology, 29*, 1147–1158.

Brackett, M. A., Mayer, J. D., & Warner, R. M. (2004). Emotional intelligence and its relation to everyday behavior. *Personality and Individual Differences, 36*, 1387–1402.

Brody, N. (2004). What cognitive intelligence is and what emotional intelligence is not. *Psychological Inquiry, 15*, 234–238.

Brownless, V., & Dunn, S. (1958). *Manual for Shorthand Aptitude Test*. Melbourne, Australia: Australian Council for Educational Research.

Carroll, J. B. (1993). *Human cognitive abilities: A survey of factor-analytic studies*. New York: Cambridge University Press.

Carver, C. S., Scheier, M. F., & Weintraub, J. K. (1989). Assessing coping strategies: A theoretically based approach. *Journal of Personality and Social Psychology, 56*, 267–283.

Cattell, R. B. (1978). *The scientific use of factor analysis*. New York: Plenum.

Charbonneau, D., & Nicol, A. A. M. (2002). Emotional intelligence and leadership in adolescents. *Personality and Individual Differences, 33*, 1101–1113.

Ciarrochi, J., Chan, A. Y. C., & Bajgar, J. (2001). Measuring emotional intelligence in adolescents. *Personality and Individual Differences, 31*, 1105–1119.

Ciarrochi, J., Chan, A. Y. C., & Caputi, P. (2000). A critical evaluation of the emotional intelligence construct. *Personality and Individual Differences, 28*, 539–561.

Costa, P. T., & McCrae, R. R. (1992). *NEO PI-R professional manual.* Odessa, FL: Psychological Assessment Resources.

Cronbach, L. J. (1960). *Essentials of psychological testing* (2nd ed.). New York: Harper & Row.

Cronbach, L. J. (1970). *Essentials of psychological testing* (3rd ed.). New York: Harper & Row.

Cudeck, R. (2000). Exploratory factor analysis. In H. E. A. Tinsley & S. D. Brown (Eds.), *Handbook of applied multivariate statistics and mathematical modeling* (pp. 265–296). San Diego, CA: Academic Press.

Darwin, C. (1965). *The expression of the emotions in man and animals.* Chicago: University of Chicago Press. (Original work published 1872)

Davies, M., Stankov, L., & Roberts R. D. (1998). Emotional intelligence: In search of an elusive construct. *Journal of Personality and Social Psychology, 75*, 989–1015.

Dawda, D., & Hart, S. D. (2000). Assessing emotional intelligence: Reliability and validity of the Bar-On Emotional Quotient Inventory (EQ-i) in university students. *Personality and Individual Differences, 28*, 797–812.

Day, A. L., & Kelloway, E. K. (2004). Emotional intelligence in the workplace. In G. Geher (Ed.), *Measuring emotional intelligence: Common ground and controversy* (pp. 215–237). Hauppauge, NY: Nova Science.

Dewey, J. (1909). *Moral principles in education.* New York: Houghton Mifflin.

Diener, E., Emmons, R. A., Larsen, R. J., & Griffin, S. (1985). The Satisfaction With Life Scale. *Journal of Personality Assessment, 49*, 71–75.

Dunning, D., Heath, C., & Suls, J. M. (2005). Flawed self-assessment: Implications for health, education, and the workplace. *Psychological Science in the Public Interest, 5*, 69–106.

Epstein, S. (1998). *Constructive thinking: The key to emotional intelligence.* Westport, CT: Praeger.

Flora, D. B., & Curran, P. J. (2004). An empirical evaluation of alternative methods of estimation for confirmatory factor analysis with ordinal data. *Psychological Methods, 9*, 466–491.

Ford, M. E. (1994). Social intelligence. In R. J. Sternberg (Ed.), *Encyclopedia of human intelligence* (pp. 974–978). New York: Macmillan.

Gardner, H. (1983). *Frames of mind: The theory of multiple intelligences.* New York: Harper & Row.

Gardner, H. (1993). *Frames of mind: The theory of multiple intelligences* (2nd ed.). New York: Harper & Row.

Gignac, G. E., Palmer, B. R., Manocha, R., & Stough, C. (2005). An examination of the factor structure of the Schutte Self-Report Emotional Intelligence (SSREI) scale via confirmatory factor analysis. *Personality and Individual Differences, 39*, 1029–1042.

Goleman, D. (1995). Emotional intelligence: Why it can matter more than IQ. London: Bloomsbury.

Goleman, D. (1998). *Working with emotional intelligence.* New York: Bantam.

Gottfredson, L. S. (1997). Why *g* matters: The complexity of everyday life. *Intelligence, 24*, 79–132.

Greenspan, S. (1981). Defining childhood social competence: A proposed working model. In B. K. Keogh (Ed.), *Advances in special education* (Vol. 3, pp. 41–82). Greenwich, CT: JAI Press.

Hall, S. E. K, Geher, G., & Brackett, M. A. (2004). The measurement of emotional intelligence in children: The case of reactive attachment disorder. In G. Geher (Ed.), *Measuring emotional intelligence: Common ground and controversy* (pp. 199–217). Hauppauge, NY: Nova Science Publishers.

Heppner, P. P., & Petersen, C. H. (1982). The development and implications of a personal problem-solving inventory. *Journal of Counseling Psychology, 29,* 66–75.

Jensen, A. R. (1980). *Bias in mental testing.* New York: Free Press.

Jensen, A. R. (1998). *The g factor.* Westport, CT: Praeger.

Jones, K., & Day, J. D. (1997). Discrimination of two aspects of cognitive-social intelligence from academic intelligence. *Journal of Educational Psychology, 89,* 486–497.

Kang, S., Day, J. D., & Meara, N. M. (2004). Social and emotional intelligence: Starting a conversation about their similarities and differences. In R. Schulze & R. D. Roberts (Eds.), *Emotional intelligence: An international handbook* (pp. 91–105). Cambridge, MA: Hogrefe & Huber.

Keating, D. P. (1978). The search for social intelligence. *Journal of Educational Psychology, 70,* 218–223.

Kline, R. B. (2005). *Principles and practice of structural equation modeling* (2nd ed.). New York: Guilford.

Kubinger, K. D. (2003). On artificial results due to using factor analysis for dichotomous variables. *Psychology Science, 45,* 106–110.

Kuncel, N. R., Hezlett, S. A., & Ones, D. S. (2001). A comprehensive meta-analysis of the predictive validity for the Graduate Record Examinations: Implications for graduate student selection and performance. *Psychological Bulletin, 127,* 162–181.

Landy, F. J. (2006). The long, frustrating and fruitless search for social intelligence: A cautionary tale. In K. R. Murphy (Ed.), *Critique of emotional intelligence: What are the problems and how can they be fixed?* (pp. 81–123). Mahwah, NJ: Erlbaum.

Legree, P. J., Psotka, J., Tremble, T., & Bourne, D. R. (2004). Using consensus based measurement to assess emotional intelligence. In R. Schulze & R. D. Roberts (Eds.), *Emotional intelligence: An international handbook* (pp. 155–179). Cambridge, MA: Hogrefe & Huber.

Leuner, B. (1966). Emotional intelligence and emancipation. *Praxis der Kinderpsychologie und Kinderpsychiatrie, 15,* 196–203.

Lopes, P. N., Salovey, P., & Straus, R. (2003). Emotional intelligence, personality and the perceived quality of social relationships. *Personality and Individual Differences, 35,* 641–658.

MacCann, C., Matthews, G., Zeidner, M., & Roberts, R. D. (2004). The assessment of emotional intelligence: On frameworks, fissures and the future. In G. Geher (Ed.), *Measuring emotional intelligence: Common ground and controversy* (pp. 19–50). Hauppauge, NY: Nova Science.

MacCann, C., Roberts, R. D., Matthews, G., & Zeidner, M. (2004). Consensus scoring and empirical option weighting of performance-based emotional intelligence (EI) tests. *Personality and Individual Differences, 36,* 645–662.

Martinez-Pons, M. (1998). The relation of emotional intelligence with selected areas of personal functioning. *Imagination, Cognition and Personality, 17,* 3–13.

Matarazzo, J. D. (1972). *Wechsler's measurement and appraisal of adult intelligence.* (5th ed.). New York: Oxford University Press.

Mathias, J. L., & Nettelbeck, T. (1992). Validity of Greenspan's models of adaptive and social intelligence. *Research in Developmental Disabilities, 13,* 113–129.

Matthews, G., Deary, I. J., & Whiteman, M. C. (2003). *Personality traits* (2nd ed.). Cambridge: Cambridge University Press.

Matthews, G., Emo, A. K., Roberts, R. D., & Zeidner, M. (2006). What is this thing called emotional intelligence? In K. R. Murphy (Ed.), *Critique of emotional intelligence: What are the problems and how can they be fixed?* (pp. 3–36). Mahwah, NJ: Erlbaum.

Matthews, G., Zeidner, M., & Roberts, R. D. (2002). *Emotional intelligence: Science and myth.* Cambridge, MA: MIT Press.

Mayer, J. D. (2001). A field guide to emotional intelligence. In J. Ciarrochi, J. P. Forgas, & J. D. Mayer (Eds.), *Emotional intelligence and everyday life* (pp. 3–24). New York: Psychology Press.

Mayer, J. D., Caruso, D. R., & Salovey, P. (1999). Emotional intelligence meets traditional standards for an intelligence. *Intelligence, 27,* 267–298.

Mayer, J. D., Caruso, D. R., & Salovey, P. (2000). Selecting a measure of emotional intelligence: The case for an ability scale. In R. Bar-On & J. D. A. Parker (Eds.), *Handbook of emotional intelligence* (pp. 320–324). San Francisco: Jossey-Bass.

Mayer, J. D., & Geher, G. (1996). Emotional intelligence and the identification of emotion. *Intelligence, 22,* 89–113.

Mayer, J. D., & Salovey, P. (1997). What is emotional intelligence? In P. Salovey & D. Sluyter (Eds.), *Emotional development and emotional intelligence: Implication for educators* (pp. 3–31). New York: Basic Books.

Mayer, J. D., Salovey, P., & Caruso, D. R. (2000). *Mayer-Salovey-Caruso Emotional Intelligence Test (MSCEIT) user's manual.* Toronto, Ontario, Canada: MHS.

Mayer, J. D., Salovey, P., Caruso, D. R., & Sitarenios, G. (2003). Measuring emotional intelligence with the MSCEIT V2.0. *Emotion, 3,* 97–105.

McPherson, J., & Mohr, P. (2005). The role of item extremity in the emergence of keying-related factors: An exploration with the Life Orientation Test. *Psychological Methods, 10,* 120–131.

Neisser, U., Boodoo, G., Bouchard, T. J., Jr., Boykin, A. W., Brody, N., Ceci, S. J., Halpern, D. F., Loehlin, J. C., Perloff, R., Sternberg, R. J., & Urbina, S. (1996). Intelligence: Knowns and unknowns. *American Psychologist, 51,* 77–101.

Neubauer, A. C., & Freudenthaler, H. H. (2004). Models of emotional intelligence. In R. Schulze & R. D. Roberts (Eds.), *Emotional intelligence: An international handbook* (pp. 31–50). Cambridge, MA: Hogrefe & Huber.

O'Connor, P. (2000). SPSS and SAS programs for determining the number of components using parallel analysis and Velicer's MAP test. *Behavior Research Methods, Instrumentation, and Computers, 32,* 396–402.

O'Connor, R. M., & Little, I. S. (2003). Revisiting the predictive validity of emotional intelligence: Self-report versus ability-based measures. *Personality and Individual Differences, 35,* 1893–1902.

Palmer, B. R., Donaldson, C., & Stough, C. (2002). Emotional intelligence and life satisfaction. *Personality and Individual Differences, 33,* 1091–1100.

Petrides, K. V., Frederickson, N., & Furnham, A. (2004). The role of trait emotional intelligence in academic performance and deviant behavior at school. *Personality and Individual Differences, 36,* 277–293.

Petrides, K. V., & Furnham, A. (2000). On the dimensional structure of emotional intelligence. *Personality and Individual Differences, 29,* 313–320.

Petrides, K. V., & Furnham, A. (2001). Trait emotional intelligence: Psychometric investigation with reference to established taxonomies. *European Journal of Personality, 15,* 425–448.

Pfeiffer, S. I. (2001). Emotional intelligence: Popular but elusive construct. *Roeper Review, 23,* 138–142.

Raftery, A. (1995). Bayesian model selection in social research. In P. Marsden (Ed.), *Sociological methodology* (pp. 111–163). Oxford: Blackwell.

Raven, J. C., Court, J. H., & Raven, J. (1993). *Manual for Raven's progressive matrices and vocabulary scales—advanced progressive matrices, Sets I & II.* Oxford: Oxford Psychologists Press Ltd.

Roberts, R. D., Zeidner, M., & Matthews, G. (2001). Does emotional intelligence meet traditional standards for an intelligence? *Emotion, 1,* 196–231.

Roberts, S., & Pashler, H. (2000). How persuasive is a good fit? A comment on theory testing. *Psychological Review, 107,* 358–367.

Russell, D. W. (2002). In search of underlying dimensions: The use (and abuse) of factor analysis in *Personality and Social Psychology Bulletin. Personality and Social Psychology Bulletin, 28,* 1629–1646.

Saklofske, D. H., Austin, E. J., & Minski, P. S. (2003). Factor structure and validity of a trait emotional intelligence measure. *Personality and Individual Differences, 34,* 707–721.

Salovey, P., & Mayer, J. D. (1990). Emotional intelligence. *Imagination, Cognition and Personality, 9,* 185–211.

Salovey, P., Mayer, J. D., Goldman, S. L., Turvey, C., & Palfai, T. P. (1995). Emotional attention, clarity and repair: Exploring emotional intelligence using the Trait Meta Mood Scale. In J. W. Pennebaker (Ed.), *Emotion, disclosure and health* (pp. 125–154). Washington, DC: American Psychological Association.

Schmidt, F. L., & Hunter, J. E. (1998). The validity and utility of selection methods in personnel psychology: Practical and theoretical implications of 85 years of research findings. *Psychological Bulletin, 124,* 262–274.

Schulze, R. (2005). Modeling structures of intelligence. In O. Wilhelm & R. W. Engle (Eds.), *Handbook of understanding and measuring intelligence* (pp. 241–263). Thousand Oaks, CA: Sage.

Schulze, R., Roberts, R. D., Zeidner, M., & Matthews, G. (2004). Theory, measurement and applications of emotional intelligence: Frames of reference. In R. Schulze & R. D. Roberts (Eds.), *Emotional intelligence: An international handbook* (pp. 3–29). Cambridge, MA: Hogrefe & Huber.

Schutte, N. S., Malouff, J. M., Bobik, C., Coston, T. D., Greeson, C., Jedlicka, C., Rhodes, E., & Wendorf, G. (2001). Emotional intelligence and interpersonal relationships. *The Journal of Social Psychology, 141,* 523–536.

Schutte, N. S., Malouff, J. M., Hall, L. E., Haggerty, D. J., Cooper, J. T., Golden, C. J., & Dornheim, L. (1998). Development and validation of a measure of emotional intelligence. *Personality and Individual Differences, 25,* 167–177.

Schwarz, G. (1978). Estimating the dimensions of a model. *Annals of Statistics, 6,* 461–464.

Stankov, L. (2000). Structural extensions of a hierarchical view on human cognitive abilities. *Learning and Individual Differences, 12,* 35–51.

Steiger, J. H., & Lind, J. C. (1980 June). *Statistically-based tests for the number of common factors.* Paper presented at the Annual Spring Meeting of the Psychometric Society, Iowa City.

Sternberg, R. J. (1985). *Beyond IQ: A triarchic theory of human intelligence.* New York: Cambridge University Press.

Sternberg, R. J., & Detterman, D. K. (1986). *What is intelligence? Contemporary viewpoints on its nature and definition.* Norwood, NJ: Ablex.

Thorndike, E. L. (1920). Intelligence and its uses. *Harper's Magazine, 140,* 227–235.

Trinidad, D. R., & Johnson, C. A. (2002). The association between emotional intelligence and early adolescent tobacco and alcohol use. *Personality and Individual Differences, 32*, 95–105.

Van Der Zee, K., Schakel, L., & Thijs, M. (2002). The relationship of emotional intelligence with academic intelligence and the big five. *European Journal of Personality, 16,* 103–125.

Van Rooy, D. L., & Viswesvaran, C. (2004). Emotional intelligence: A meta-analytic investigation of predictive validity and nomological net. *Journal of Vocational Behavior, 65*, 71–95.

Wechsler, D. (1940). Non-intellective factors in general intelligence. *Psychological Bulletin, 37,* 444–445.

Weis, S., & Süß, H.-M. (2005). Social intelligence—A review and critical discussion of measurement concepts. In R. Schulze & R. D. Roberts (Eds.), *Emotional intelligence: An international handbook* (pp. 203–230). Cambridge, MA: Hogrefe & Huber.

Wells, A. (1994). A multi-dimensional measure of worry: Development and preliminary validation of the Anxious Thoughts Inventory. *Anxiety, Stress and Coping, 6*, 289–299.

PART III

EMOTIONAL INTELLIGENCE

Measurement Frameworks

8

Approaches to the Assessment of Emotional Intelligence

RALF SCHULZE, OLIVER WILHELM,
AND PATRICK C. KYLLONEN

It seems reasonable to expect that since the term emotional intelligence (EI) was coined in the modern scientific psychological literature about 16 years ago (by Salovey & Mayer, 1990), EI research would have matured from infancy to adolescence. That is, the field might have resolved or overcome initial problems by now and focused its attention on further development and refinements of established theories, measures, and applications. Unfortunately, this does not seem to be the case (Matthews, Roberts, & Zeidner, 2004; Van Rooy, Viswesvaran, & Pluta, 2005; Zeidner, Matthews, & Roberts, 2001). The manifest signs of an early stage of development are that the field is still mainly concerned with (a) debating fundamentally different conceptualizations of EI (as personality characteristic vs. ability), (b) stockpiling more (predominantly self-report) instruments with theoretical foundations that are insufficiently supported by empirical research, (c) exploring the structure of such measures as well as relationships with a vast array of potentially valuable criteria, and, last but not least, (d) struggling to shake off the bad reputation of disseminating scientifically unfounded claims about the value of the construct for real-world applications.

After little more than a decade of research, a need to take stock seemed to be prevalent in the field. In this climate, one of the major scientific milestones in the field was published, the comprehensive expertise on the status of EI research by Matthews, Zeidner, and Roberts (2002). The science and myth of EI were disentangled in this book and, on the basis of the evidence reviewed, the conclusion was reached that EI was more myth than science (Matthews et al., 2002, p. 548). Landy (2005) recently also drew attention to the

The views expressed here are those of the authors and do not reflect on the Educational Testing Service. We are grateful to the editorial team, and especially Rich Roberts, for constructive comments on an earlier draft of this chapter.

fact that, at least for applications in the workplace, the scientific basis for many of the claims made about the potential impact EI might have is practically nonexistent.

Taking such signs together, it appears legitimate to continuously inquire about the status and progress of the field. This is true in light of the fact that the number of publications in scientific as well as nonscientific journals and books still flourishes, with 175 publications in the scientific literature in 2005 alone.[1] However, notwithstanding this lively activity in the field, the movement has seemingly reached a plateau of innovation. Despite the fact that new measures of EI continue to appear in the literature (e.g., Tett, Fox, & Wang, 2005), they predominantly follow the same (self-report) approach. Hence, more evidence of the same type is accumulated when a need for new developments in theory, measurement, and applications of EI is prevalent.

In the present chapter, a partial reassessment of the current state of EI research will be done. Some gaps in the knowledge about the assessment of EI will also be identified, and untrodden paths in this area will be highlighted. Before this is done in the context of answering a series of questions about the measurement of EI, some general remarks on the theoretical orientation of the chapter authors seem to be in order.

From the outset, we note that from our point of view EI has to be conceptualized as an ability. The reasons for taking this position and focusing as far as possible on this kind of conceptualization are semantic, theoretical, and empirical. The semantic reason is simple. The label *intelligence* is used for a construct if and only if it is a cognitive ability. Without going further into details of semantics (see Carroll, 1993), we then note that it is tautological to say that emotional intelligence is an ability. In fact, it wouldn't be necessary to make this statement concerning semantics here if there weren't conceptualizations of EI that explicitly define the construct in a way that puts it outside the realm of abilities (e.g., Bar-On, 1997).

The case of a schism between personality[2] versus ability approaches in theories (mixed models versus ability models, see Mayer, Salovey, & Caruso, 2000) and measurement of EI (self-report versus maximum performance tests; see Matthews et al., 2002) represents a case of conceptual and theoretical incoherence (see Matthews et al., 2004) and is therefore unfortunate for a further development of the field. The divide itself has attracted considerable attention in the scientific literature (cf. Matthews et al., 2002; Mayer et al., 2000; Pérez, Petrides, & Furnham, 2005; Petrides & Furnham, 2001). The controversy surrounding this schism did not lead to significant progress in the field of EI and probably has been confusing not only for the uninitiated when trying to understand the history, status, and future of the field. Because extant theories that conceptualize EI as an ability (or an array thereof) are at least commensurable with established theories of intelligence (see Carroll, 1993), such EI theories are preferable over personality-like characterizations of EI. Furthermore, they allow for a theoretically stronger top-down approach of theory testing, whereas available personality-like conceptualizations of EI follow a more inductive bottom-up route.

The empirical reasons for preferring an ability conceptualization are that the empirical evidence militates for the dominant four-area theory of EI, which conceptualizes EI as an ability (see, e.g., Neubauer & Freudenthaler, 2005). In contrast, the evidence for the various so-called mixed models (an example is given by the model of

Bar-On, 1997; for an overview, see Mayer et al., 2000) is heterogeneous and weak in terms of general criteria for the evaluation of measurement instruments and their under-lying theoretical conceptualizations (see below). More will be said about the evidence concerning this latter approach in the following subsections. Nevertheless, a few caveats concerning the above statements in this paragraph are indicated.

First, the four-area model and the corresponding measure, the Mayer-Salovey-Caruso Emotional Intelligence Test (MSCEIT; Mayer, Salovey, & Caruso, 2002; Mayer, Salovey, Caruso, & Sitarenios, 2003) are also burdened with problems. Several reviews have pointed to deficits in conceptualization and measurement (see, e.g., Matthews et al., 2002; Roberts et al., 2006; Wilhelm, 2005). Nonetheless, among available theo-ries and measures, the four-area EI model still has the most consistent empirical support, and if any currently available assessment procedure could count as the flagship of EI measurement, it would be the MSCEIT.

Second, although mixed models or so-called trait EI approaches (see Pérez et al., 2005) are not the preferred conceptualizations here, it is noticed that interesting evi-dence for their potential usefulness notably also in applied contexts has been published (see, e.g., McEnrue & Groves, 2006; Parker, Summerfeldt, Hogan, & Majeski, 2004; Petrides & Furnham, 2003). Beyond interesting correlations with valued outcomes re-ported in these publications, constructs within this realm of research might lead to new insights about the structure of personality (see, e.g., McCrae, 2000). Thus, although we support the proclamation of a moratorium to generate new measures for mixed mod-els (Roberts, Schulze, Zeidner, & Matthews, 2005), it is not suggested to dismiss the developments and findings from this strand of research altogether. It is possible that they might lead to advances in theory, measurement, and applications in psychology, though not of EI in particular.

Lastly, it is important to distinguish between the theoretical and the empirical level when evaluating EI theories. The empirical reasons to prefer an ability conceptualiza-tion are at least partly a function of the quality of the measurement instruments and research designs used to evaluate the theories. Insofar as the links between the empirical and the theoretical level are flimsy, the strength of arguments for or against a theoretical concept is weak as well.

To summarize, it is assumed in this chapter that EI as the target of assessment is conceptualized as an ability, though some discussion of personality-like concepts and the corresponding measurement approach of self-reports appears unavoidable given that most assessment procedures allegedly measuring EI are of this type. It is argued that the label *EI* is a misnomer for the latter approach and particularly unfortunate because the same name (EI) is used to designate different constructs (ability versus personality).

After these general statements, six basic questions posed by the editors will be answered in the subsequent sections. The main aim of the chapter is to demarcate the status of current EI measurement and point out approaches to the assessment of EI that might be fruitful to advance the field. A thorough and comprehensive analysis of the many diverse measurement instruments will not be given. The interested reader is referred to the literature (e.g., Matthews et al., 2002) or other chapters in Part III of this book.

What Is the Optimal Approach to the Assessment of EI?

A plethora of reviews of extant measures of EI, both for self-report and ability tests (e.g., McEnrue & Groves, 2006; Pérez et al., 2005), suggest that there is no single optimal approach to the assessment of EI available yet. However, recent publications have reached quite positive conclusions at least for the MSCEIT (e.g., Mayer, Salovey, & Caruso, 2004). In any event, it appears unlikely that a single optimal approach will ever emerge as long as there is no consensus on the theoretical properties of the construct of interest. That is, it only makes sense to consider an approach optimal for the assessment of a construct if a sound scientific theory about the construct was available that clearly specifies the properties of what should be measured.

As explicated in the introduction of this chapter, it is assumed here that EI as the target of assessment is conceptualized as an ability construct. Hence, self-report approaches are certainly not optimal because it has been demonstrated that they provide insufficient proxies for the assessment of abilities (e.g., Paulhus, Lysy, & Yik, 1998). In the next section, a more detailed account of self-report measures will be given. It suffices here to state that only a maximum performance test approach is considered to lead to an optimal measurement approach.

Why are the extant approaches not judged to be optimal? If no optimal assessment approach is currently available, what would be the characteristics of such an approach? The answer to these questions requires a specification of the optimality criteria to satisfy. There are two distinguishable sources for such criteria. First, there are general sets of rules for psychological testing, which can be applied to any form of psychological assessment procedure. Second, there are standards specific for the assessment of an intelligence, which are relevant only for a particular class of constructs. In the following two subsections, both of these sources will be discussed with respect to their relevance for an optimal approach for the assessment of EI and how they might guide the design of better assessment procedures.

General Standards of Psychological Testing

Available common standards of psychological testing (e.g., American Educational Research Association, American Psychological Association, and National Council on Measurement in Education, 1999) offer a series of criteria that should be satisfied to evaluate an instrument as a good, if not optimal, assessment approach of any psychological construct. In a nutshell, these criteria pertain to test construction, test evaluation, fairness, and applications. In the research context, it is often focused on the psychometric test evaluation criteria reliability and validity.

These commonly accepted standards, especially those highlighted in the research context, have found application in most reviews and comparisons of existing EI measures up to date (e.g., Brackett & Mayer, 2003; Matthews et al., 2002; Matthews et al., 2004; McEnrue & Groves, 2006; Pérez et al., 2005; Roberts, Zeidner, & Matthews, 2001). Their stringent application shows that most available EI measures have satisfactory estimates of reliability but associated validity claims are empirically unfounded or questionable (see Matthews et al., 2002). The question arises whether an optimal approach to the assessment of EI would eventually emerge if problems of validity with existing measures could be resolved.

Beyond maximal or at least sufficient reliability and validity, an optimal approach would be one that also facilitates fair and efficient assessment at a large scale. That is, it would go beyond concerns of precision and whether the intended construct is in fact targeted with the assessment procedure to enable efficient assessment, for example, in which the generation of items is coordinated with underlying substantive theories. That is, the whole assessment design would be a concerted effort to coordinate the elements: (a) substantive theory, of which the intended construct(s) is an element, (b) statistical measurement models and scoring procedures, (c) specification of types of tasks and items, and (d) the delivery system for the assessment. Such a framework is provided by evidence-centered design.

Evidence-centered design (ECD; see Mislevy, Almond, & Lukas, 2003; Mislevy, Steinberg, & Almond, 2003) is a principled approach to the design of assessments. In its original formulation, ECD has been developed with applications in the field of education in mind. As a consequence, it also focuses on knowledge, skills, and abilities as types of constructs of interest and instruction to intervene on such constructs. Emotional intelligence falls within this realm, though education is only one field of application of EI (see, e.g., Zeidner, Roberts, & Matthews, 2002). The ECD approach includes many stages, of which the so-called conceptual assessment framework (CAF) is discussed in more detail here. Other stages include domain analysis, domain modeling, and the so-called four-process delivery system (see Mislevy, Steinberg et al., 2003), which, together with the CAF, should lead to claims about examinees' abilities or proficiencies that are evidence-based. These other stages concern (a) the identification and organization of the knowledge about the domain of interest (domain analysis), (b) the derivation of paradigms for proficiencies, gathering evidence, and tasks (domain modeling), and (c) the operational assessment (four-process delivery system). The latter encompasses task selection by the administrator (or an algorithm), presenting the task, scoring tasks, and scoring the test. In order to focus on those parts of ECD that might be most informative with respect to an optimal assessment approach for EI, the following description is focused on the CAF.

The CAF is illustrated in Figure 8.1 in an adapted version for the assessment of EI. It includes examinee models,[3] evidence models, task models, assembly model, and a delivery model. Brief descriptions for each of these models follow.

In the examinee model, the variables of interest in the context of measurement that characterize the examinee are specified, along with their mutual dependencies. From the perspective of the four-area model of EI (e.g., Mayer & Salovey, 1997; Mayer et al., 2000; Neubauer & Freudenthaler, 2005), perceiving emotions would be one of these variables, whereas optimism, part of the model hypothesized to underlie the Emotional Quotient Inventory (EQ-i; Bar-On, 1997), would not be included. From a technical perspective, the variables in the examinee model need not be continuous and might also include ordered categorical variables representing different levels of proficiency.

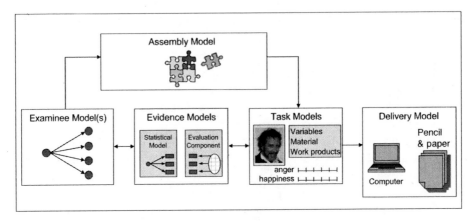

Figure 8.1. Conceptual assessment framework as part of the evidence-centered design.

The joint (multivariate) probability distribution of the variables would represent the available knowledge or belief about the position of an examinee in the multivariate EI ability space. The examinee model for EI need not be a higher-order structure as suggested in Figure 8.1. In fact, Mayer and Salovey (1997) propose a hierarchy of the four areas of EI, each with different sets of skills with individual developmental trajectories.

It can be derived from their model that managing emotions skills at the highest level depend to a certain extent on more basic skills in the perceiving emotions area. Such, in the context of EI measurement, often neglected dependencies would be part of the examinee model to reflect the fact that knowledge about an examinee's perceiving emotions skills changes our beliefs about his or her managing emotion skills. Technically, such dependencies could be part of a Bayesian inference network (see, e.g., Mislevy, 1994) that includes other components of the CAF as well. In sum, the examinee model represents the bridge between the theoretical framework and the measurement machinery.

The evidence models are the psychometric core of the CAF. From the perspective of ECD, much of the discussion about EI measurement approaches has been focused on evidence models. There are two aspects of evidence models: the evaluation component and the statistical (measurement) model. The evaluation component designates the process of evaluating the work products of examinees to arrive at an item score. That is, rules are specified, informed by the underlying psychological theory, to isolate the aspects of an examinee's response or work product that is relevant for the targeted proficiencies. The rules also provide guidance on how to assign scores to different work products. This part of the CAF represents one of the most controversial aspects of EI measurement, namely, how responses should be scored. Because this issue will be dealt with in more detail later in this chapter, it suffices to highlight that it clearly has its place in the CAF. The other aspect of the evidence model in Figure 8.1 is the statistical model. Here, the functional relationship between the observable responses and the latent variables of interest are specified. This may take the form of any of the measurement models available to date (see, e.g., Skrondal & Rabe-Hesketh, 2004). Given that evidence-based claims about the examinees' proficiencies are informed and updated in a Bayesian framework, the measurement model often is some form of item response theory (IRT) model.

In the task models, basically the properties of the universe of tasks and work products are defined. That is, the characteristics of the material that elicits the relevant aspects of responses are specified. The evidence on which claims about examinee characteristics are made is thereby defined. As suggested in Figure 8.1, a task model could be the definition of a task that assesses a skill of the perceiving emotion area by presenting faces and let the examinee rate the presence of a number of basic emotions. Of course, many different task models would have to be specified to gain information about all areas and skills of EI. A theory about EI should provide a rationale or at least some information for the critical task design and work product features. The task models, in turn, enable an assessment that is informative and potentially maximally efficient with respect to the proficiencies of interest. It is therefore easily comprehensible that task models play an important role in assessment in general and in automatic item generation in particular (see Mislevy, Steinberg, & Almond, 2002).

The selection of specific tasks from a universe that constitute a test for an examinee is done in the assembly model. This step could be accomplished, for example, by specifying a design matrix for the task elements in the task model to optimize the precision of measurement in a certain region of the latent variable continuum. Of course, other selection criteria could be implemented as well, such as adaptive testing with or without additional constraints (see, e.g., van der Linden, 2005). The assembly model provides the means to go beyond item selection governed by arbitrary rules, such as to have an equal number of items for each subscale of a test intended to assess a single latent variable. Thereby, it provides another means to coordinate the different aspects for an optimal assessment of the psychological variable of interest.

The final step of actually presenting the test to examinees is dealt with in the delivery model. It includes the scheduling of the tasks and the task environment, for example. This is exemplified in Figure 8.1 with the options computer versus paper and pencil (P&P) as presentation media. Hence, the presentation model is used to specify the boundary conditions and specifics of the presentation process.

In sum, the CAF as part of ECD calls for an integrated approach to assessment design. One of the important features of ECD highlighted in this chapter is its emphasis on coordinating different aspects of assessment design and to avoid taking a fragmented route to designing measures. The current landscape of available EI measures predominantly offers assessment procedures with rather loose connections to theoretical models and rather unsophisticated task and assembly models. Especially in the case of self-report instruments, substantive theories are heterogeneous and have been generated post hoc by induction from empirical results (e.g., for Bar-On's EQ-i; Bar-On, 1997). However, ability tests of EI (the MSCEIT in particular) do not seem to draw on any sophisticated assembly model either. Tasks with a questionable rationale (e.g., designs in the MSCEIT; see Wilhelm, 2005) are included, and the evidence model has its weaknesses both in the evaluation component and in the statistical model. With respect to the latter, it is somewhat irritating that for the MSCEIT as the most prominent EI measure, it still seems unclear which type of measurement model is most appropriate and the data-driven exploratory use of confirmatory methods appears still necessary to arrive at an acceptable model fit (cf. Mayer, Panter, Salovey, Caruso, & Sitarenios, 2005; Mayer, Salovey, Caruso, & Sitarenios, 2003; Palmer, Gignac, Manocha, & Stough, 2005).

The application of the ECD framework has the potential to do the field of EI research, and measurement of EI in particular, great benefits in that it could help approximating an optimal approach to the assessment of EI. More specifically, the benefits could lie in (a) drawing attention to modeling approaches not yet in use in the context of EI assessment (e.g., Bayes nets), (b) encouraging the theory-driven design of tasks that play a specific role in an a priori specified measurement model, (c) enabling more efficient assessment of EI, (d) highlighting the connectedness of several assessment problems (e.g., scoring), and (e) coordinating the various steps in designing assessment procedures.

Specific Standards for the Assessment of an Intelligence

In addition to the general standards described in the previous subsection, specific standards have been proposed for an intelligence and, hence, for EI in particular. These criteria can be gathered from the various approaches to specify and apply them (cf. Austin & Saklofske, 2005; Mayer, Caruso, & Salovey, 1999; Mayer, Salovey, Caruso, & Sitarenios, 2001; Roberts et al., 2001; Wilhelm, 2005). The criteria can be summarized as follows (also see Mayer et al., 1999):

1. EI should be capable of being operationalized as a set of abilities. One corollary of this requirement is that the evaluation component of the evidence model should include unequivocal rules to score the responses as correct or incorrect.

2. EI should show a pattern of relationships with other established constructs that reflects convergent, discriminant, and predictive validity. This is roughly translated in the investigations cited above as follows: EI measures should (a) significantly correlate with general intelligence tests, (b) not correlate significantly and substantially with personality test scales, and (c) show significant incremental variance explained in valued criterion variables over established predictors (cognitive abilities and broadly accepted personality factors in particular).

3. EI should develop over time. In light of the facts that there can be no specific predictions be derived from extant EI theories on the developmental trajectories, and that empirical evidence based on longitudinal designs is nonexistent, this criterion will not be further discussed here. For a recent developmental framework of EI, see Zeidner, Matthews, Roberts, and MacCann (2003).

4. EI should have biological, genetic, and lower level cognitive tasks correlates (see Austin & Saklofske, 2005). Beyond the requirement that these correlates should exist (i.e., correlations should be significant), no further conditions are specified.

These four criteria were introduced into the literature to enable an objective evaluation of the question of whether EI legitimately falls within the realm of intelligence research. In correspondence with the criteria, and assuming they were satisfied at the construct level, EI measures can be evaluated with regard to the question of whether they enable the assessment of a intelligence construct or not.

With regard to the second criterion, it can be noted that the following findings can count as well-replicated in the EI literature (cf. Matthews et al., 2002; Warwick & Nettelbeck, 2004; Zeidner, Shani-Zinovich, Matthews, & Roberts, 2005): (a) (very) strong relationship between scales of different types of self-report EI measures (e.g., EQ-i; Bar-On, 1997) and personality variables, (b) relative absence of a relationship between ability EI measures (the MSCEIT in particular) and personality variables, and (c) small to moderate relationship between ability EI measures (again, MSCEIT in particular) and intelligence (g or reasoning). These findings demonstrate that the ability measure MSCEIT shows better conformity with the second requirement as compared to self-report approaches, though it should be noted that satisfactory evidence for all criteria is not available to date.

In addition to the criteria listed above, it seems plausible to require any theory of an intelligence to make clear statements that enable derivation of a measurement model and, more important in the present context, state how the newly proposed ability structure fits in established models of intelligence structure (e.g., Carroll's three-stratum model; Carroll, 1993). Recently published confirmatory analyses of the measurement models hypothesized to generate the covariance structure of various EI tests (cf. Mayer et al., 2003; Palmer et al., 2005) reveal that the hypothesized underlying four-area EI structure is somewhat volatile. Similar findings have been reported for self-report measures. The results of such analyses have either not been fully reported (e.g., Bar-On, 2004) or show that the proposed structure does not hold (Palmer, Manocha, Gignac, & Stough, 2003). Tests of an integrated model of EI and established models of intelligence are practically nonexistent for both types of measures. Preliminary results for the MSCEIT, however, suggest that the abilities assessed with this instrument cannot be subsumed under Gf and/or Gc (fluid intelligence and crystallized intelligence, respectively; Roberts et al., 2006). These findings allude to suboptimal properties of existing EI as asserted at the beginning of this section.

In addition to addressing the question of whether EI is an appropriate addition to the canon of intelligence constructs, it seems plausible to ask whether EI is an appropriate member of the constructs in emotion research. No such criteria have been established yet, probably because the field of emotion research is more heterogeneous and it is much harder to derive defensible criteria.

Nevertheless, one criterion that could be easily established is that measures with the same target construct from both domains should empirically turn out to measure the same latent variable. In terms of a confirmatory factor analysis as the measurement model, the requirement would be that the correlations between the latent variables of the measures from emotion research with the EI measures are unity. At least for the area perceiving emotion, this claim can be assessed because both domains of research offer measures of this component (e.g., Ekman's standardized database of facial expressions, Ekman, 1973, and the faces subtest in the MSCEIT). Unfortunately, such an approach (see also Roberts et al., 2005) has not been widely applied yet, though a recent study (Roberts et al., 2006) shows that it can be fruitfully applied and that the relation between measures and constructs from both domains of research is quite low.

To summarize, there is no optimal approach available for the assessment of EI. If there will ever be one, it will not be based on self-report data. The catalogue of general and specific criteria to evaluate EI measures seems elaborate enough to use it as a guideline to design new measures with the aim to eventually arrive at optimal ones. The ECD approach appears particularly useful for such an endeavor because it demands integration of assessment design components from theory to delivery. This is something we would expect from an optimal approach.

Can Self-Reports and Questionnaires Ever Provide Assessments of Intelligence and Competence?

The short answer to the question is: It is highly unlikely, if not an impossible event, that self-reports and questionnaires will ever provide reliable and valid assessments of EI. The reasons for such an assertion are manifold and will be elaborated in the following subsections. An important boundary condition to keep in mind, which was introduced at the beginning of this chapter, is that EI is considered to be conceptualized as an ability. Accordingly, the following evaluation of some extant measures allegedly measuring EI will focus on this conceptualization and will only in passing analyze what other construct(s) of potential relevance for EI research these measures might assess.

On the Assessment of Intelligence With Self-Report Measures

In this subsection, the question will be addressed if there is evidence that a self-report format can be used to collect reliable and valid evidence on intellectual performance. In this context, a distinction is made between self-reports and self-estimates. With reference to the literature on intellectual engagement, the question of what kind of interesting information in relation to intelligence could be provided by using self-reports will also be addressed.

Self-Report and Self-Estimates of Intelligence

In principle, it is possible that people can provide information about their intelligence via self-reports. If someone took a fair, reliable, and valid EI test, received numeric feedback and was able to remember this information when prompted for it, then this person is able to report an EI score. Of course, this is true only if no response distortion is coming into play (see below). Can or will people actually provide valid information on their intellectual performance in practice?

A recent meta-analysis shows that information on intellectual performance (grades, class ranks, and test scores like the SAT) collected via self-reports should be interpreted with caution (Kuncel, Credé, & Thomas, 2005). From the results reported in this meta-analysis, it can be concluded that individual differences in self-reported as compared to actual scores are fairly precise, as evidenced by meta-analytic estimates of the correlations of $r = .90$ for GPA (overall; i.e., for both college and high school) and $r = .82$ for SAT total. However, these correlations vary by levels of GPA and ability. For example, lower correlations result for the subpopulation of low GPA students. More important, there are standardized mean differences in self-reported versus actual performance of up to $d = 1.38$ for college GPA, indicating a considerable level of over-reporting for GPA, though much less so for test scores in the SAT ($d = .12$ for SAT-Math). Hence, self-reports of performance scores or ranks do not seem to be viable candidates for an assessment of EI.

The prerequisite that a test score has to be available in memory to use the self-report approach practically rules it out as an assessment procedure of EI because few, if any, examinees will have ever taken such a test before they should report on the result. Hence, they would have to *estimate* their EI. This raises the question of whether people can estimate their intelligence at all, rather than report a score. As already mentioned at the beginning of this chapter, previous research has shown that self-estimates of intelligence provide insufficient (i.e., biased and imprecise) proxies for the assessment of abilities (e.g., Paulhus et al., 1998). Moreover, such estimates vary by levels of background characteristics relevant for the assessment of EI, like culture and gender (Furnham, 2001; Rammstedt & Rammseyer, 2002), which renders them even more dubious as measures of EI.

Beyond the inability of examinees to self-report or self-estimate their (emotional) intelligence, the ease with which responses on such measures can be distorted may be one of the reasons for a dissociation between the responses and actual ability. The literature on measures of noncognitive qualities shows that respondents can fake self-report measures when they are instructed to. This was shown both in studies in which participants were asked afterward whether they did fake (e.g., McFarland, 2003) and in studies in which they were instructed to fake (see Viswesvaran & Ones, 1999). The literature also shows that examinees appear to fake naturally (see Schmit & Ryan, 1993), though the findings concerning this natural tendency appear to be heterogeneous (see, e.g., Barrick & Mount, 1996). Taken together, these findings show that self-report measures are plagued with too many problems to be viable candidates for the assessment of EI.

Self-Motivated Cognition in the Area of Emotions

Although self-report measures do not provide dependable information at the level of an individual's EI, this approach might nevertheless be used to gather valuable information related to the construct. In analogy to similar approaches in research on intelligence and personality (e.g., Ackerman & Heggestad, 1997), it might be possible to assess the motivational tendency of individuals to engage in everyday activities for which EI is relevant. That is, instead of assessing the maximum performance with respect to EI, the typical level of engagement is of interest as an indicator of the self-motivated behavioral tendency to think about emotional issues. The literature on a series of highly redundant, if not identical, constructs from different areas of psychology (openness to ideas, see McCrae, 2000; need for cognition, see Cacioppo, Petty, Feinstein, & Jarvis, 1996; analytical-rational thinking style, Pacini & Epstein, 1999; typical intellectual engagement, Ackerman & Heggestad, 1997), which can be subsumed under the common label of *self-motivated cognition*, suggests that it makes sense to postulate such a construct for the domain of intelligence and, hence, for EI as well.

In fact, there are approaches in EI research drawing on self-report methods (Pérez et al., 2005; Petrides & Furnham, 2000) that refer to the distinction between maximal and typical performance (see Cronbach, 1949). To emphasize the difference between these types of performance, the label *trait EI* has been introduced for the constructs measured with self-report, and *ability EI* for maximum performance measurement (see Pérez et al., 2005). Typical performance in Cronbach's distinction is indeed related to self-motivated cognition. However, such EI approaches go far beyond self-motivated cognition and tap deep into the realm of personality by including dimensions like assertiveness, happiness, and optimism, among others in the self-report measures (see Pérez et al., 2005).

Some Typical Observations in Empirical Findings With Self-Report Measures

In this subsection, only a selection of relatively recent empirical studies on two of the most popular available self-report measures are discussed to illustrate some typical findings with such measures. The reader interested in an overview of most self-report instruments in this area of research is referred to the succinct but comprehensive overview by Pérez et al. (2005; see also Matthews et al., 2002; Tett et al., 2005).

The EQ-i (Bar-On, 1997) consists of 133 self-report items and is considered to be "the main commercial trait EI instrument" (Austin, Saklofske, Huang, & McKenney, 2004, p. 556). It has 15 subscales, which are combined to form five so-called composite scores. The underlying theory was derived post hoc to fit these empirically derived subscales.

One of the typical observations in this area of research is a high degree of overlap between self-report measures allegedly assessing EI and variables from the domain of personality. Although it was claimed that the EQ-i does not assess personality variables (Bar-On, 2004), there is consistent evidence based on different measures of personality that this is the case (cf. Brackett & Mayer, 2003; Dawda & Hart, 2000; Newsome, Day, & Catano, 2000). In addition, it was shown that correlations of the EQ-i subscales with psychopathology (i.e., depression) and desirable responding (i.e., impression management and self-deception) are in the range of .50 to .60 in absolute value (Hemmati, Mills, & Kroner, 2004). The latter findings underscore the relevance of faking for this type of measurement approach. In contrast, the EQ-i does not substantially correlate with intelligence (e.g., Derksen, Kramer, & Katzko, 2002), nor does it substantially correlate with EI as measured by the MSCEIT (at $r = .21$ in the study by Brackett & Mayer, 2003).

Another common phenomenon is the instability of results concerning the structure underlying self-report measures. For the EQ-i, for example, the structure is somewhat volatile, changing from one study to the next (see Bar-On, 2004). Additionally, Palmer et al. (2003) have shown in extensive analyses that the empirical structure of the EQ-i does not match the one proposed by Bar-On (1997).

Yet another consistent observation can be made in the context of trying to establish the predictive validity of such measures. The criteria selected are very heterogeneous (see Bar-On, 2004), and in cases in which significant correlations with criteria are reported, important correlates from personality research are not controlled for (e.g., Parker et al., 2004). Hence, such correlations can be considered to be interesting but their interpretation is equivocal. In contrast, in cases in which personality and intelligence variables are controlled, the relation with criteria disappeared (e.g., O'Connor & Little, 2003).

A measure that surfaced in the last 5 years with more than 100 citations in the scientific literature is the Schutte et al. Self-Report Emotional Intelligence Test (SREIT; Schutte et al., 1998; see Austin et al., 2004, for a recent revision). It is an interesting self-report measure, different from the EQ-i, in that it is claimed to be based on the model by Mayer and Salovey (1997). Note that this model is also hypothesized as the relevant model for the MSCEIT, a maximum performance measure. However, the structural properties of the SREIT are enigmatic. Several studies examining the structure of the scale (cf. Austin et al., 2004; Gignac, Palmer, Manocha, & Stough, 2005; Petrides & Furnham, 2000; Schutte et al., 1998) provided different results. Whatever the structural properties of this scale are, it does not seem to match the proposed structure underlying the MSCEIT. Accordingly, the scales of the SREIT are not related to the corresponding MSCEIT subscales (Goldenberg, Matheson, Mantler, 2006; Petrides & Furnham, 2000).

The EQ-i and the SREIT correlate at $r = .43$ at the total score level (Brackett & Mayer, 2003) and very heterogeneously at the composite level from $r = -.08$ to $r = .61$, for the revised version of the SREIT (Austin et al., 2004). Interestingly, the correlation between the total scores vanished when personal well-being is controlled for (Brackett & Mayer, 2003), suggesting that their correlation might be determined by this third variable. As is typical for the self-report approach, many studies using the SREIT do not control for personality and intelligence when investigating predictive validity (e.g., Schutte et al., 1998). However, when these variables are controlled for, then correlations with criteria ordinarily vanish. Results consistent with this statement are reported, for example, by Brackett and Mayer (2003), who report only one significant negative partial correlation with high school rank, indicating that low academic performance is associated with high scores in the SREIT. It might be added that in carefully controlled studies that simultaneously used self-report and maximum performance EI measures as predictors of academic success, neither type of measure turned out to be potent in prediction models (Barchard, 2003; Barchard & Hakstian, 2004). The results of these studies suggest that after many years of research it might still be true what was stated early on, namely that EI is an elusive construct (Davies, Stankov, & Roberts, 1998).

Overall, the EQ-i, the SREIT, and other self-report measures in this domain do not seem to come anywhere near satisfying the standards explicated in the context of describing an optimal approach to the assessment of EI. Therefore, it is concluded that self-report measures do not and probably will never provide assessments of EI.

What Are the Most Prevalent Scoring Procedures for EI Measures, and Are They Valid for Ability Measures?

In the ECD terminology, scoring concerns the evaluation component of the evidence models. This illustrates that scoring plays a very important role in measurement. It would be ideal if it were fully justified by the properties of the target constructs and the theories they are embedded in. This is neither the case for self-report assessment procedures nor for ability tests of EI. Especially for ability tests of EI, scoring remains a vexing problem. One of the requirements for an ability test (see the specific standards for the assessment of an intelligence) is the availability of scoring rules for the evaluation component. The unavailability of indisputable rules can be considered as the most important problem in the entire field of EI research.

For the case of self-report measures, scaling is commonly done by fiat. That is, values are assigned to responses more or less arbitrarily while conserving the ordinal properties of the response scales. As self-report measures are not considered to be appropriate for the assessment of EI (see above), their scoring is not further discussed here.

The most prevalent scoring procedure for ability measures is probably consensus-based measurement (CBM; see Legree, Psotka, Tremble, & Bourne, 2005). This inference is drawn from the fact that the MSCEIT appears to be the most often used measure of this type and it employs CBM or expert scoring. For the MSCEIT, it has been shown that both of these scoring procedures are highly correlated (Mayer et al., 2003) so that they need not be distinguished here. It is noted, however, that for the predecessor of the MSCEIT, the Multifactor Emotional Intelligence Scale (MEIS; Mayer et al., 1999), this was not the case (Roberts et al., 2001), so that such a high correlation can not be taken for granted.

The basic idea of CBM is to collect responses for the tasks of interest from a large representative sample from the target population and to compute the relative frequencies for each response option. These relative frequencies are then used as a scoring key to score responses on the tasks. There are different variants of CBM (cf. Legree et al., 2005; MacCann, Roberts, Matthews, & Zeidner, 2004), but the basic idea of using responses from such a calibration sample to find a scoring key empirically is the same for all of them.

An empirical comparison between five different variants applied to the two perceiving Emotions subtests of the MSCEIT (Faces and Designs) was done by MacCann et al.

(2004). Using internal consistency estimates as the evaluation criterion, they concluded that the above described variant (using relative frequencies) is one of the two best methods of CBM. The other variant of the two, called mode scoring, is a dichotomous scoring method in which the modal option is assigned a value of 1 and all other options are scored 0. In addition to isolating these two procedures as the best with respect to internal consistency estimates, they pointed to the problem of nonnormal (i.e., skewed) distributions generated by the CBM scoring procedure.

The skewness of score distributions is one of a sizable set of partly more fundamental problems with both CBM and expert scoring that have been discussed in the literature (see Matthews et al., 2002). Of these, the lack of a clear justification for the procedure, especially one that goes beyond pointing to the lack of alternative promising candidates for scoring, is one of the more worrisome problems. However, it is noted that Legree et al. (2005) have recently presented a rationale for CBM that offers a potential justification.

Nevertheless, there remain scoring problems with CBM like the following. Imagine a case with three dichotomous items, an easy one (probability of correct response .80), one with medium difficulty (.50) and a hard one (.20). Let's assume there are two people taking the test, one very emotionally intelligent and one from the lower end of the ability distribution. We expect these two people to receive very different scores corresponding to their difference in ability. Also imagine the test was scored with CBM, so that the probabilities correspond to the scores awarded for a correct response. Now the following observations can be made: First, the item of medium difficulty is uninformative, because not matter what response is given, the respondent always receives a score of .50. Second, assuming the more able person gets the hard item right, and the person low in ability gets it wrong, the less able person receives a higher score (.80 vs. .20). Lastly, if in addition the more able gets the easy item right and the other person does not, then both get the same total score. This certainly does not make sense.

This small example illustrates a problem with CBM that is relevant not only in the context of scoring, but also in the phase of designing a test. Items of medium difficulty would be weeded out because they do not contribute valuable information to the ability score estimation and hard items might be included but would be scored incorrectly. Unfortunately, the extent to which this problem applies to existing tests can not be estimated because an objective answer key is not available.

Are there really no alternatives to CBM? At least for dichotomously scored items for which an answer key is not available there are psychometric models, which have also been generalized to become applicable to multiple-choice items (see Batchelder & Romney, 1988). In a nutshell, these methods can be used to recover a scoring key not known a priori, which is the case in EI research. The basic idea of this approach can be characterized most easily for a situation with two response options A and B and by referring to latent class models. In contrast to the usual application of latent class models, however, the items (instead of respondents) are classified in two classes in this dichotomous case, in which one class represents the items for which response option A is the correct one and for the items in the other class option B is the correct one. This enables the recovery of the scoring key and estimation of the participants' ability, for example. Potential other psychometric candidates, especially for tasks with more than two response options, are forms of test analysis that do not require the availability of continuously scored items, like certain factor-analytic or principal component-type models and IRT (see, e.g., Gifi, 1990; Skrondal & Rabe-Hesketh, 2004). Basically, these models provide scoring of the indicators that is most consistent with a certain postulated measurement model for a set of items. However, such models have not been tried with EI tests yet.

In sum, the problems with CBM referred to here, and the one described with an example, appear to be quite serious. Additionally considering the fact that a solution to the problems raised has not appeared in the literature to date, it is hard to find a definite answer to the question of whether CBM is a valid procedure for EI measurement.

What Are the Prospects for Assessment of EI Using Psychophysiological, Developmental, and Neurological Measures?

Considering evidence from a variety of disciplines and methods of assessment is important to assess the viability of EI and related constructs. Integrating knowledge from different disciplines to develop a broader and more profound understanding of psychological constructs can count as an important general strategy for assessment. In this vein, psychophysiological, developmental, and neurological measures have the potential to add important information in the context of EI assessment, though, at the current state of knowledge, it is hard to imagine that such measures can replace extant EI measures and provide better ones.

Instead, these types of measures might provide valuable information to answer the question of what EI is and what it is not. Across psychological disciplines there are various forms of dissociations between constructs (Oberauer, Wilhelm, & Schmiedek, 2005). Cognitive psychologists consider constructs as distinct when corresponding measures respond differently to experimental manipulations. At a psychophysiological and neurological level, processes are considered different when they are localized in different parts of the brain or can be selectively impaired by brain damage. In individual differences research, two constructs are different when they can be separated in factor analysis. In developmental psychology, constructs are different when they have distinct trajectories over time. Integrating these different strands of research is a worthwhile endeavor to triangulate a construct as elusive as EI.

However, such a triangulation is a complex information integration process that is probably better suited for more advanced fields of study than EI research. In the present section, this contention will be supported and illustrated by focusing on a specific construct for which such different sources of information are available and that has at least a remote association to EI and a more direct one to social intelligence: Memory for names and face-name associations. Results from individual differences research and experimental, neurological, and psychophysiological evidence on this construct that speaks to the distinctiveness of a construct of memory for names will be briefly summarized.

The reader will undoubtedly consider memory for names and face-name associations relevant for personal relations, for example, in a social context of personal importance in which reciprocate recognition of a name or retrieving a face-name association was not possible. However, it is not immediately clear how memory for names would be identified as part of any of the four areas of EI in the model by Mayer and colleagues (e.g., Neubauer & Freudenthaler, 2005). Nevertheless, it is considered to be a good candidate for the purpose of the present illustration.

Memory for names has been subsumed under the construct of social intelligence in the early days of intelligence research (Thorndike, 1920) because of its importance for interpersonal relations. Correspondingly, measures of memory for names were included in early tests of social intelligence (for reviews, see Kihlstrom & Cantor, 2000; Weis & Süß, 2005) and tests of memory for names are included in several well-known intelligence batteries (Jäger, Süß, & Beauducel, 1997; McGrew, 1997; McGrew & Flanagan, 1998). Within intelligence research, the specificities of memory for names have been investigated by Guilford's group in the context of other social ability indicators. However, in most parts of traditional mainstream intelligence research, measures of memory for names and face-name associations are considered as tests of general memory ability.

Some interesting efforts in investigating social intelligence found evidence for a somehow unique social memory factor that included memory for names (Weis & Süß, 2005). Similarly, early research found evidence for specific factors of social intelligence (Hoepfner & O'Sullivan, 1968; O'Sullivan, Guilford, & de Mille, 1965). Within Guilford's group, social intelligence measures were thought to assess abilities in the behavioral domain of the structure-of-intellect model. From the perspective of facet models of intelligence performance on social memory, measures like memory for names or face-name associations can be thought of as being a combination of a specific content (behavioral or social domain) and a specific operation (memory).

Measures of memory for names or face-name associations are rather easy to design. Correct answers can be objectively specified, item difficulties can be manipulated by varying the memory load or other item attributes, and so forth. However, despite a long history of research on such measures, it is still not completely certain what the underlying latent variables of such measures are. Most plausibly a factor of social intelligence and a general memory factor contribute to performance. The social intelligence factor might partly reflect deliberate attention devoted to the task of remembering a name or a face-name association. The general memory factor might reflect a mechanical thinking ability that expresses generalized ability to learn and retrieve information.

In addition to these results from individual differences research, there is some evidence that people can be selectively impaired in generating names of familiar people, regardless of the input being verbal descriptions of persons or displays of their faces. This deficit following lesions can be observed with intact biographical knowledge and with essentially preserved name production for common objects (Lucchelli & De Renzi,

1992; McKenna & Warrington, 1980). These case studies support the possibility that proper name memory can be selectively impaired. Conversely, there is also evidence that proper name memory (production and comprehension) can be selectively spared from lesions (Semenza & Sgaramella, 1993; Warrington & McCarthy, 1983). Although the evidence is limited to several case studies only (but see the fMRI study by Tsukiura et al., 2002), lesions might be specifically affecting memory for names. An objection to the possibility of neural specificity of name memory is that semantic memory might be specialized for storing unique biographies. Other equally unique memory entries might be just as selectively impaired as person identity nodes. Bringing the logic of such lesions studies to individual differences research, it might be interesting to see whether or not two measures of memory for names are more highly associated with each other than say a measure of memory for names of persons with a measure of memory for names of prominent buildings.

In ERP studies on proper name processing with unimpaired subjects, name perception elicited a bilateral P1 on temporo-occipital sites, a left lateralized N1 and a large P2 at vertex (Dehaene, 1995; Müller & Kutas, 1996). More important, ERP differences appearing 260 ms after stimulus onset had a larger left inferior temporal negativity for proper names compared to animal names, numerals, or verbs (Dehaene, 1995). In EEG studies, the N170 for names has been shown to be lateralized to the left hemisphere, whereas the N170 to faces is most pronounced over the right hemisphere (Pfütze, Sommer, & Schweinberger, 2002). The early repetition effect for written names, suggested to represent the activation of name recognition units in long-term memory, is seen at similar latency as for faces but maximal over the left hemisphere (e.g., Pfütze et al., 2002). The topography of the early repetition effect differed between faces and names, indicating that representations of faces and names are at least partially differently stored in memory. Additionally, the difference due to memory, an indicator for encoding specific brain activity, was shown to differ in its distribution across the scalp between faces and names. This finding suggests that there are at least partially distinct mechanisms for encoding of faces and names (Sommer, Komoss, & Schweinberger, 1997).

In neuroimaging studies, faces and names (famous and nonfamous) in a same-different matching task activated a common set of regions including the medial portions of the temporal lobe bilaterally, two areas in the medial surface of the superior frontal cortex, and the medial parietal lobe (Gorno-Tempini et al., 1998). With respect to retrieval of face-name associations, recently an anatomo-temporal model was specified (Joassin et al., 2004) but it is too early to assess whether or not there is convincing evidence supporting the uniqueness for the retrieval mechanisms of face-name associations.

How can this wealth of evidence from different research approaches be summarized to arrive at a consistent synthesis of the state of empirical knowledge about memory for names and face-name associations? It seems evident that this is a daunting task. It is not without irony that this section about the prospects of neurological and psychophysiological EI measurement started with some of the oldest tasks from intelligence research. These tasks are also untypical for EI measures in that there are unequivocally correct solutions. In fact, the intention was to illustrate how difficult and challenging it can be to validate specific tasks with psychophysiological, neurological, and other methods. The selection of available experimental and psychophysiological evidence on memory for names and face-name associations in this chapter served to illustrate the complexity of unequivocally demonstrating the uniqueness of some thought process.

Tasks like memory for names and face-name associations are in use and have been under investigation for about 80 years now. On the basis of the available evidence, it is still not perfectly known what these tasks are actually measuring. It is easy to imagine how hard it will be to provide convincing evidence for the validity and utility of measures that are in use for slightly more than 15 years, usually have no objective answer key, and sometimes use some unusual procedures and stimuli (e.g., designs in the MSCEIT) in the assessment process. Psychophysiological, developmental, and neurological measures are certainly very important to support a deep understanding of a construct. They also provide evidence independent in type from what is most often available from assessments of intelligence. From the perspective of multimethodological assessment, this cannot be overrated in its importance. However, at the current state of theoretical and empirical knowledge about EI, it appears too early for these measures to bear good prospects to provide improved EI assessment procedures in the foreseeable future.

What Are the Prospects for Assessment of EI Using Information-Processing Tasks?

To date, there are only a few maximum performance EI tests available. This is an undesirable state of affairs given the need for multivariate, multimodal, and multimethod approaches to measurement for a thorough investigation of EI. Hence, there is a need for more varied tasks in this domain, preferably tasks with a theoretically justified and rationally derived scoring scheme. The idea to borrow strength from importing information-processing task paradigms developed in more experimentally oriented subdisciplines (cognitive psychology and emotion research) as well as individual differences research (intelligence) to expand the EI measurement spectrum, is certainly a good and promising one.

Measures From the Domain of Cognitive Psychology and Emotion Research

There are a number of measures from experimental psychology that might be successfully embedded in the four-area model of EI. In particular, measures of the ability to recognize emotion in various stimuli have not generally been seen as EI measures, but at least some of them can easily be classified as measures of perceiving emotions, one of the four areas of EI. For example, it appears to be self-evident to classify emotion perception in faces measures developed by Ekman (1973) in this category (see also Chapter 12, by Herzmann et al., in this volume). In addition, there are measures

218 Emotional Intelligence: Measurement Frameworks

in experimental emotion research that include auditory stimuli, like the Index of Vocal Emotion Recognition (Vocal-I; see Chapter 4, by Scherer, in this volume) to assess emotion perception voices that can be used to tap a different modality of perceiving emotions. It has been argued in the present chapter that such measures should converge with subtests from existing EI tests like the MSCEIT due to the same measurement intention. Recent research has shown, however, that this does not always seem to be the case (Roberts et al., 2006). Because many measures from experimental emotion research are not plagued with similar scoring problems as the tasks used to assess EI, such findings are valuable for the validation of existing EI measures to pave the way for their refinement or their substitution.

Beyond the area of perceiving emotions, the classification of existing measures from emotion research into the four EI areas is less clear-cut. As an example, take a measure widely used in psychopathology research, the Emotional Stroop test (EST; for an overview see Williams, Mathews, & MacLeod, 1996). In the EST, words are presented in different colors and the task for the participants is to name the color of the word as fast as possible. The words can be either neutral (e.g., *gate*), positive (e.g., *smile*) or negative (e.g., *death*).[4] The emotional valence of the words, if present, is assumed to affect the response times as an intrusive stimulus in both clinical an nonclinical populations. Hence, there is no response competition between two opposing color names (the color word written vs. the color the word is printed in) as in the classical Stroop task. Instead, the EST is probably better classified as a measure of cognitive interference.

Most research with the EST, which has predominantly focused on clinical populations and threat-related (i.e., negative) words, showed that psychological processes underlying the emotional intrusion effect might be different for different clinical subpopulations and various stimuli under investigation (cf. McKenna & Sharma, 2004; Williams et al., 1996). Notwithstanding such group differences, individual differences in the EST are particularly relevant to EI research insofar as they might be indicative of an ability to protect thinking processes from being affected by irrelevant (emotional) cues. Although it appears evident for such an ability to be classified under the heading of EI, the assignment to one or more of the four areas in the model proposed by Mayer et al. (2000) is not straightforward.

The EST has been used in previous EI studies, but unfortunately only in combination with self-report instruments purportedly assessing EI. Bar-On (2000) reports a correlation between the EST and the EQ-i of $r = .36$. Similarly, the correlation between factor scores for several self-report measures and the EST was estimated at $r = .15$ by Coffey, Berenbaum, and Kerns (2003). What is worrisome about these findings is that the correlations are positive in sign. That is, higher scores in the self-report measures are associated with slower responses to the emotional words (as compared to neutral words). If the self-report measures were assessing an ability, the correlations should be expected to be negative in sign, indicating emotionally intelligent participants are able to protect their cognitive processes from impairments induced by emotions.

What this example illustrates is that the use and interpretation of measures from the domain of cognitive psychology and emotion research can be problematic from the perspective of EI research. Nevertheless, the potential benefits of using such measures seem to outweigh the costs in that their use enforces conceptual clarity in EI research, which has to be consistent with existing cognitive and emotions research.

Measures From the Domain of Intelligence Research

There are various faceted theories of human cognitive abilities (see, e.g., Süß & Beauducel, 2005) that suggest certain contents (such as verbal, figural, and numeric) may be crossed with certain operations (such as knowledge, creativity, working memory, and speed; see Matthews et al., 2002). It is entirely possible that there is a domain of emotional content, which may be distinct from the verbal, numerical, and figural content and which may allow an EI test in all other respects to resemble traditional intelligence measures. If such a model were appropriate for EI, then a host of task types could be used from intelligence research to assess EI.

Unfortunately, an effort to construct corresponding EI tasks has not yet been undertaken systematically. Instead, specific tasks from individual differences have been used with emotionally relevant content and related to measures used in EI research. One example for such a task paradigm from traditional intelligence research is the Inspection Time (IT) paradigm used to assess speed abilities (see, e.g., Danthiir, Roberts, Schulze, & Wilhelm, 2005). In brief, the IT is the time an individual needs to reliably discriminate between two (or more) simple stimuli, like identifying the longer of two vertical lines. This task paradigm has been adapted in an emotional IT by Austin and colleagues (e.g., Austin, 2004; Austin & Saklofske, 2005). The basic idea of the emotional IT is to replace the simple stimuli with faces expressing specific emotions like happiness or sadness, or show a neutral face. The task of the participants is to identify the emotion expressed in faces shown at varying durations (e.g., from 17 ms to 350 ms in the study by Austin, 2004), followed by a mask (i.e., a neutral face). One of the major questions to be answered when adapting such task paradigms is whether the emotion-related content introduces individual differences in scores that are indicative of individual differences in EI. Austin and Saklofske (2005) argue that this is indeed the case on the basis of significant correlations between the emotional IT and a self-report measure purportedly assessing EI.

In sum, these examples illustrate the interesting and potentially useful approach to use or adapt information processing paradigms from cognitive psychology, as well as emotion and intelligence research, for the assessment of EI. However, as shown, an adaptation of such tasks might not always be straightforward, but the potential benefits of following such an approach appear to be sufficiently large to evaluate the prospects as promising.

What Are the Prospects for New Techniques, Such as Application of Advanced Psychometrics and Situational Judgment Methodologies, Leading to Improved Assessment?

The issue of psychometrics, and scoring in particular, was already broached in the context of an optimal EI assessment. Emotional intelligence certainly is a challenging field for advanced psychometrics mainly due to the lack of a scoring key for the ability indicators. Selected approaches mentioned earlier for scoring without an answer key (e.g., Batchelder & Romney, 1988) might indeed help to alleviate or solve one of the most vexing problems in EI assessment. However, it should be clear that even if it would be possible to go beyond consensus-based measurement in the near future by using any advanced psychometric procedure, many other problems related to EI assessment will remain. This is particularly true for assessment issues related to validity. For an improved assessment of EI, more elaborate and specific theories of EI and better assessment approaches would be needed as well.

One candidate for an assessment approach that might lead to improved EI assessment are Situational Judgment Tests (SJTs; for a comprehensive treatment, see Weekley & Ployhart, 2006). What are SJTs? In the classic field of application, industrial-organizational psychology, the SJT technique presents an individual with a description of a problematic or critical situation, followed by a number of possible problem-solving responses to this situation. The situations are usually generated employing an established industrial-organizational technique: the critical incident approach (Flanagan, 1954). Critical incidents are produced from observations, surveys, and interviews of task specialists to specify the nature of the situations and corresponding appropriate behaviors that appear to be pivotal for success in a particular task domain.

The content of SJTs can be varied to capture different aspects of the work environment, like working within a team, various emotional climates, problem situations, communication (and miscommunication) elements, and so forth; although the general design of such SJTs is remarkably similar. A scenario (i.e., description of a critical incident or situation) is given to the participant. This scenario is followed by instructions to the participant to rate the quality of various courses of action associated with this hypothetical situation. The participant is required to make a judgment, for each and every course of action by establishing rank orders, making binary decisions (i.e., appropriate or inappropriate) or making Likert-type ratings (e.g., extremely uncharacteristic to extremely characteristic).

Hence, amongst other approaches, SJTs can be viewed as one of many contextualized procedures to assess problem solving (Kyllonen & Lee, 2005). The contextualization is considered to be one of the virtues of the method that appears to make it appropriate for the assessment of more complex constructs (e.g., EI) and potentially enhances the face validity of the procedure. The procedure is very inexpensive as compared to real-job simulations, and it has been reported to show smaller subgroup score differences for African Americans versus Whites. The latter is particularly true for video-based forms of SJTs as compared to paper-and-pencil versions (see Chan & Schmitt, 1997; McDaniel, Whetzel, Hartman, Nguyen, & Grubb, 2006). Given these potential advantages of the method, it seems to be a promising candidate for an improved assessment of EI.

In fact, SJT-like task types are not entirely new for the assessment of EI. One might argue that already the George Washington Social Intelligence Test included items of this type to assess skills related to EI (see Moss & Hunt, 1927). The Levels of Emotional Awareness Scale (LEAS; see Lane, 2000), the Emotional Accuracy Research Scale (EARS; Geher, Warner, & Brown, 2001; Mayer & Geher, 1996), and the subtest Stories in the MEIS (Mayer et al., 1999), which is a derivative of the EARS, and some subtests of the MSCEIT (e.g., Emotion Management) are more current examples of SJT-like tasks used to assess EI. It should be noted, however, that they are not constructed by using the critical incidents technique from industrial-organizational psychology outlined above. Instead, they follow a developmental rationale in designing and scoring the tasks (LEAS) or they are adapted from stories written by students about real emotional episodes in their life (e.g., EARS, Stories). In addition, the task required from the examinees is not always to make judgments about the appropriateness of different courses of actions but to rate the intensity of emotions of the writer of the stories presented as vignettes (e.g., EARS).

Despite these differences to classical SJTs, available evidence suggests that these tests provide useful measures of EI, though the evidence is sometimes based on relatively small samples (e.g., Geher et al., 2001). It is also noteworthy that the Stories subtest in the MEIS has the highest loading on a general factor of the MEIS, but appears to be misclassified as a perceiving emotions measure as evidenced by its loadings on this factor (see Roberts et al., 2001). In any event, it can be stated that the SJT method appears to be an appropriate approach for the assessment of at least some areas of EI.

One common feature of all SJTs used for the assessment of EI is that they present situations as vignettes, that is, as verbal descriptions of situations. There are several advantages associated with using a different format to present SJTs in a multimedia format (e.g., less adverse impact), and a video-based form in particular (cf. McDaniel et al., 2006; Olson-Buchanan, & Drasgow, 2006). It is also important to note that the use of verbal descriptions (i.e., vignettes) of emotional episodes, which is in widespread use in emotion research, has been criticized for several reasons (see Parkinson & Manstead, 1993). Among the points leveled against the use of verbal SJTs in this domain are (a) doubts that a narrative representation appropriately represents the emotional episodes themselves, (b) the fact that emotional reactions are not necessarily mediated by symbolic processes involved when taking verbal SJTs, and (c) that interactive processes are neglected in such a form of testing. Although the use of video-based SJTs might not appropriately address all these criticisms, they appear to be an improvement of the existing methodology that enables the presentation of a series of stimuli relevant for the assessment of EI (e.g., nonverbal aspects of gait and posture ideally enacted by professional actors) not accessible to the examinee taking a verbal SJT.

In sum, we are inclined to state that the prospects for SJTs are very promising for an improved assessment of EI. However, we also think that this method requires the use of a variety of multimedia techniques in the task design and models to take advantage of its full potential.

Discussion

After little more than 15 years of research, the landscape of EI assessment still seems to be in a state of disarray. Fundamentally different approaches for the assessment of personality characteristics on the one hand and abilities on the other appear to be equally viable alternatives for the assessment of EI. In this chapter, the perspective has been focused on the ability approach to the conceptualization and measurement of EI, which arguably is the more appropriate one. As was elaborated in the comments on the prospects of self-report approaches for an assessment of EI, neither is a personality conceptualization appropriate for EI nor are self-report assessments which can be perfectly appropriate for the assessment of personality characteristics viable candidates for the assessment of EI.

However, an optimal approach for the assessment of EI has also not emerged to date and this is unlikely to happen in the near future. Notwithstanding, there appears to be a fair chance to make considerable progress toward the goal of an optimal assessment procedure for EI. A theme that ran through this chapter is that available procedures and models, both substantive and statistical, have not been exploited entirely to use their full potential. Efforts to draw on theories and knowledge from different psychological subdisciplines, like emotion research (e.g., Ekman, 1973) or even social psychology (e.g., Gilbert & Wilson, 2000), are an obvious as well as promising strategy to make progress in EI theory and assessment development and refinement. Although recent evidence is not encouraging in terms of the convergence of results for emotion perception measures from EI and emotion research (Roberts et al., 2006), such results can inform the design of improved assessment procedures. Similarly, tests of the hypothesized structure underlying major measures of EI (e.g., Mayer et al., 2003; Palmer et al., 2005) have not portrayed a clear picture of what might be the most appropriate measurement model. Again, using modern techniques to establish and test measurement models for abilities (cf. Schulze, 2005; Wilhelm, 2005) might be beneficial for EI assessment, especially when embedding this empirical aspect in a framework like ECD.

Commonly, the evaluation of EI assessment approaches does not only depend on the fit of measurement models. In addition, the strength of relationships with external variables and criteria are taken into consideration to make a judgment about the usefulness of a measure. Traditionally, indicators like job or academic success are used as criteria in studies with intelligence measures and this has also been done in EI research (e.g., Barchard, 2003; Barchard & Hakstian, 2004). Although such criteria appear to be perfectly appropriate for EI research, it makes sense to take a broader look at the criterion space to include variables for which it is easier to make a theory-based case as to why a direct link between EI and these criteria should exist. Besides other more cognitive variables, noncognitive qualities like test anxiety (high EI examinees are better in managing their emotions and therefore experience less test anxiety) or stress state (see Matthews et al., 2006) could be among the variables in such an expanded criterion space. To date, there is not much evidence that EI substantially relates to criteria of this type, but the number of existing studies is still too small to reach any firm conclusions.

In sum, there is reason to be disappointed about the knowns in the field of EI assessment and the quality of existing approaches, especially given the lively research activities in this field in recent years. Nevertheless, we remain optimistic for the foreseeable future that by focusing on an ability conceptualization and by borrowing strength from substantive areas and statistical methods, significant progress will be made in turning unknowns into knowns.

Notes

1. At the time of writing this chapter, the number of publications in PsycINFO as a result of the query " 'emotional intelligence' and '2005 in PY' " was 175.

2. This use of the term *personality* stands in contrast to a recently published new view by Mayer (2005) in which EI is part of personality. In this chapter, personality basically re-fers to the five-factor space (openness, conscientiousness, extraversion, agreeableness, and neuroticism).

3. In the original ECD framework (Mislevy, Steinberg et al., 2003), this model is called student model. To highlight the fact that ECD is not limited to applications in education, the model is given the more general designation examinee model.

4. Note that recent evidence has shown that the choice of specific words is critical for the effect to occur (Larsen, Mercer, & Balota, 2006).

References

Ackerman, P. L., & Heggestad, E. D. (1997). Intelligence, personality, and interest: Evidence for overlapping traits. *Psychological Bulletin, 121*, 219–245.

American Educational Research Association, American Psychological Association, and National Council on Measurement in Education (1999). *Standards for educational and psychological testing*. Washington, DC: American Educational Research Association.

Austin, E. J. (2004). An investigation of the relationship between trait emotional intelligence and emotional task performance. *Personality and Individual Differences, 36*, 1855–1864.

Austin, E. J., & Saklofske, D. H. (2005). Far too many intelligences? On the communalities and differences between social, practical, and emotional intelligences. In R. Schulze & R. D. Roberts (Eds.), *Emotional intelligence: An international handbook* (pp. 107–128). Cambridge, MA: Hogrefe & Huber.

Austin, E. J., Saklofske, D. H., Huang, S. H. S., & McKenney, D. (2004). Measurement of trait emotional intelligence: Testing and cross-validating a modified version of Schutte et al.'s (1998) measure. *Personality and Individual Differences, 36*, 555–562.

Barchard, K. A. (2003). Does emotional intelligence assist in the prediction of academic success? *Educational and Psychological Measurement, 63*, 840–858.

Barchard, K. A., & Hakstian, A. R. (2004). The nature and measurement of emotional intelli-gence abilities: Basic dimensions and their relationships with other cognitive abilities and personality variables. *Educational and Psychological Measurement, 64*, 437–462.

Bar-On, R. (1997). *Bar-On Emotional Quotient Inventory (EQ–i): Technical manual*. Toronto, Canada: Multi-Health Systems.

Bar-On, R. (2000). Emotional and social intelligence: Insights from the Emotional Quotient Inventory. In R. Bar-On & J. D. A. Parker (Eds.), *The handbook of emotional intelligence* (pp. 363–388). San Francisco: Jossey-Bass.

Bar-On, R. (2004). The Bar-On Emotional Quotient Inventory (EQ-i): Rationale, description, and summary of psychometric properties. In G. Geher (Ed.), *Measuring emotional intelligence: Common ground and controversy* (pp. 111–142). Hauppauge, NY: Nova Science.

Barrick, M. R., & Mount, M. K. (1996). Effects of impression management and self-deception on the predictive validity of personality constructs. *Journal of Applied Psychology, 81,* 261–272.

Batchelder, W. H., & Romney, A. K. (1988). Test theory without an answer key. *Psychometrika, 53,* 71–92.

Brackett, M. A., & Mayer, J. D. (2003). Convergent, discriminant, and incremental validity of competing measures of emotional intelligence. *Personality and Social Psychology Bulletin, 29,* 1147–1158.

Cacioppo, J. T., Petty, R. E., Feinstein, J. A., & Jarvis, W. B. G. (1996). Dispositional differences in cognitive motivation: The life and times of individuals varying in need for cognition. *Psychological Bulletin, 119,* 197–253.

Carroll, J. B. (1993). *Human cognitive abilities: A survey of factor-analytic studies.* New York: Cambridge University Press.

Chan, D., & Schmitt, N. (1997). Video-based versus paper-and-pencil method of assessment in situational judgment tests: Subgroup differences in test performance and face validity perceptions. *Journal of Applied Psychology, 82,* 143–159.

Coffey, E., Berenbaum, H., & Kerns, J. G. (2003). The dimensions of emotional intelligence, alexithymia, and mood awareness: Associations with personality and performance on an emotional Stroop task. *Cognition & Emotion, 17,* 671–679.

Cronbach, L. J. (1949). *Essentials of psychological testing.* New York: Harper & Row.

Danthiir, V., Roberts, R. D., Schulze, R., & Wilhelm, O. (2005). Mental speed: On frameworks, fissures, and a platform for the future. In O. Wilhelm & R. W. Engle (Eds.), *Handbook of understanding and measuring intelligence* (pp. 27–46). Thousand Oaks, CA: Sage.

Davies, M., Stankov, L., & Roberts, R. D. (1998). Emotional intelligence: In search of an elusive construct. *Journal of Personality and Social Psychology, 75,* 989–1015.

Dawda, D., & Hart, S. D. (2000). Assessing emotional intelligence: Reliability and validity of the Bar-On Emotional Quotient Inventory (EQ-i) in university students. *Personality and Individual Differences, 28,* 797–812.

Dehaene, S. (1995). Electrophysiological evidence for category-specific word processing in the normal human brain. *Neuroreport, 6,* 2153–2157.

Derksen, J., Kramer, I., & Katzko, M. (2002). Does a self-report measure for emotional intelligence assess something different than general intelligence? *Personality and Individual Differences, 32,* 37–48.

Ekman, P. (1973). *Darwin and facial expressions.* New York: Academic Press.

Flanagan, J. C. (1954). The critical incident technique. *Psychological Bulletin, 51,* 327–358.

Furnham, A. (2001). Self-estimates of intelligence: Culture and gender difference in self and other estimates of both general (g) and multiple intelligences. *Personality and Individual Differences, 31,* 1381–1405.

Geher, G., Warner, R. M., & Brown, A. S. (2001). Predictive validity of the emotional accuracy research scale. *Intelligence, 29,* 373–388.

Gifi, A. (1990). *Nonlinear multivariate analysis.* New York: Wiley.

Gignac, G., Palmer, B. R., Manocha, R., & Stough, C. (2005). An examination of the factor structure of the Schutte Self-Report Emotional Intelligence (SSREI) scale via confirmatory factor analysis. *Personality and Individual Differences, 39,* 1029–1042.

Gilbert, D. T., & Wilson, T. D. (2000). Miswanting: Some problems in the forecasting of future affective states. In J. P. Forgas (Ed.), *Feeling and thinking: The role of affect in social cognition* (pp. 178–197). Cambridge: Cambridge University Press.

Goldenberg, I., Matheson, K., & Mantler, J. (2006). The assessment of emotional intelligence: A comparison of performance-based and self-report methodologies. *Journal of Personality Assessment, 86*, 33–45.

Gorno-Tempini, M. L., Price, C. J., Josephs, O., Vandenberghe, R., Cappa, S. F., Kapur, N., & Frackowiak, R. S. J. (1998). The neural systems sustaining face and proper name processing. *Brain 121*, 2103–2118.

Hemmati, T., Mills, J. F., & Kroner, D. G. (2004). The validity of the Bar-On emotional intelligence quotient in an offender population. *Personality and Individual Differences, 37*, 695–706.

Hoepfner, J. S., & O'Sullivan, M. (1968). Social intelligence and IQ. *Educational and Psychological Measurement, 28*, 339–344.

Jäger, A. O., Süß, H.-M., & Beauducel, A. (1997). *Berliner Intelligenzstruktur-Test (BIS-Test): Form 4* [The Berlin Intelligence Structure Test: Form 4]. Göttingen, Germany: Hogrefe.

Joassin, F., Campanella, S., Debatisse, D., Guerit, J. M., Bruyer, R., & Crommelinck, M. (2004). The electrophysiological correlates sustaining the retrieval of face-name associations: An ERP study. *Psychophysiology, 41*, 625–635.

Kihlstrom, J. F., & Cantor, N. (2000). Social intelligence. In R. J. Sternberg (Ed.), *Handbook of intelligence* (2nd ed.). New York: Cambridge University Press.

Kuncel, N. R., Credé, M., & Thomas, L. L. (2005). The validity of self-reported grade point averages, class ranks, and test scores: A meta-analysis and review of the literature. *Review of Educational Research, 75*, 63–82.

Kyllonen, P. C., & Lee, S. (2005). Assessing problem solving in context. In O. Wilhelm & R. W. Engle (Eds.), *Handbook of understanding and measuring intelligence* (pp. 11–25). Thousand Oaks, CA: Sage.

Landy, F. J. (2005). Some historical and scientific issues related to research on emotional intelligence. *Journal of Organizational Behavior, 26*, 411–424.

Lane, R. D. (2000). Levels of emotional awareness: Neurological, psychological, and social perspectives. In R. Bar-On & J. D. A. Parker (Eds.), *The handbook of emotional intelligence* (pp. 171–191). San Francisco: Jossey-Bass.

Larsen, R. J., Mercer, K. A., & Balota, D. A. (2006). Lexical characteristics of words used in emotional Stroop experiments. *Emotion, 6*, 62–72.

Legree, P. J., Psotka, J., Tremble, T., & Bourne, D. R. (2005). Using consensus based measurement to assess emotional intelligence. In R. Schulze & R. D. Roberts (Eds.), *Emotional intelligence: An international handbook* (pp. 155–179). Cambridge, MA: Hogrefe & Huber.

Lucchelli, F., & De Renzi, E. (1992). Proper name anomia. *Cortex, 28*, 221–230.

MacCann, C., Roberts, R. D., Matthews, G., & Zeidner, M. (2004). Consensus scoring and empirical option weighting of performance-based emotional intelligence (EI) tests. *Personality and Individual Differences, 36*, 645–662.

Matthews, G., Emo, A. K., Funke, G., Zeidner, M., Roberts, R. D., Costa, P. T., Jr., & et al. (2006). Emotional intelligence, personality, and task-induced stress. *Journal of Experimental Psychology: Applied, 12*, 96–107.

Matthews, G., Roberts, R. D., & Zeidner, M. (2004). Seven myths about emotional intelligence. *Psychological Inquiry, 15*, 179–196.

Matthews, G., Zeidner, M., & Roberts, R. D. (2002). *Emotional intelligence: Science and myth.* Boston, MA: MIT Press.

Mayer, J. D. (2005). A tale of two visions: Can a new view of personality help integrate psychology? *American Psychologist, 60,* 294–307.

Mayer, J. D., Caruso, D., & Salovey, P. (1999). Emotional intelligence meets traditional standards for a intelligence. *Intelligence, 27,* 267–298.

Mayer, J. D., & Geher, G. (1996). Emotional intelligence and the identification of emotion. *Intelligence, 22,* 89–113.

Mayer, J. D., Panter, A. T., Salovey, P., Caruso, D. R., & Sitarenios, G. (2005). A discrepancy in analyses of the MSCEIT—Resolving the mystery and understanding its implications: A reply to Gignac (2005). *Emotion, 5,* 236–237.

Mayer, J. D., & Salovey, P. (1997). What is emotional intelligence? In P. Salovey & D. J. Sluyter (Eds.), *Emotional development and emotional intelligence: Educational implications* (pp. 3–31). New York: Basic Books.

Mayer, J. D., Salovey, P., & Caruso, D. R. (2000). Models of emotional intelligence. In R. J. Sternberg (Ed.), *Handbook of intelligence* (pp. 396–420). Cambridge: Cambridge University Press.

Mayer, J. D., Salovey, P., & Caruso, D. R. (2002). *The Mayer, Salovey, and Caruso Emotional Intelligence Test: Technical manual.* Toronto, Canada: Multi-Health Systems.

Mayer, J. D., Salovey, P., & Caruso, D. R. (2004). Emotional intelligence: Theory, findings, and implications. *Psychological Inquiry, 15,* 197–215.

Mayer, J. D., Salovey, P., Caruso, D. R., & Sitarenios, G. (2001). Emotional intelligence as a standard intelligence. *Emotion, 1,* 232–242.

Mayer, J. D., Salovey, P., Caruso, D. R., & Sitarenios, G. (2003). Measuring emotional intelligence with the MSCEIT V2.0. *Emotion, 3,* 97–105.

McCrae, R. R. (2000). Emotional intelligence from the perspective of the five-factor model of personality. In R. Bar-On & J. D. A. Parker (Eds.), *The handbook of emotional intelligence* (pp. 263–276). San Francisco: Jossey-Bass.

McDaniel, M. A., Whetzel, D. L., Hartman, N. S., Nguyen, N. T., & Grubb III, W. L. (2006). Situational judgment tests: Validity and an integrative model. In J. A. Weekley & R. E. Ployhart (Eds.), *Situational judgment tests: Theory, measurement and application* (pp. 183–203). Mahwah, NJ: Erlbaum.

McEnrue, M. P., & Groves, K. (2006). Choosing among tests of emotional intelligence: What is the evidence? *Human Resource Development Quarterly, 17,* 9–42.

McFarland, L. A. (2003). Warning against faking on a personality test: Effects on applicant reactions and personality test scores. *International Journal of Selection and Assessment, 11,* 265–276.

McGrew, K. S. (1997). Analysis of the major intelligence batteries according to a proposed comprehensive Gf-Gc framework. In D. P. Flanagan, J. L. Genshaft, & & P. L. Harrison (Eds.), *Contemporary intellectual assessment: Theories, tests, and issues* (pp. 151–179). New York: Guilford Press.

McGrew, K. S., & Flanagan, D. P. (1998). *The intelligence test desk reference: Gf-Gc cross-battery assessment.* Boston: Allyn & Bacon.

McKenna, F. P., & Sharma, D. (2004). Reversing the emotional Stroop effect reveals that it is not what it seems: The role of fast and slow components. *Journal of Experimental Psychology: Learning, Memory, and Cognition, 30,* 382–392.

McKenna, P., & Warrington, E. K. (1980). Testing for nominal dysphasia. *Journal of Neurology, Neurosurgery, & Psychiatry, 43*, 781–788.

Mislevy, R. J. (1994). Evidence and inference in educational assessment. *Psychometrika, 59*, 439–483.

Mislevy, R. J., Almond, R., & Lukas, J. F. (2003). *A brief introduction to evidence-centered design* (ETS Research Reports, RR-03–16). Princeton, NJ: Educational Testing Service.

Mislevy, R. J., Steinberg, L. S., & Almond, R. G. (2002). On the roles of task model variables in assessment design. In S. H. Irvine & P. C. Kyllonen (Eds.), *Item generation for test development* (pp. 97–128). Mahwah, NJ: Erlbaum.

Mislevy, R. J., Steinberg, L. S., & Almond, R. G. (2003). On the structure of educational assessments. *Measurement: Interdisciplinary Research and Perspectives, 1*, 3–62.

Moss, F. A., & Hunt, T. (1927). Are you socially intelligent? *Scientific American, 137*, 108–110.

Müller, H. M., & Kutas, M. (1996). What's in a name? Electrophysiological differences between spoken nouns, proper names, and one's own name. *NeuroReport, 8*, 221–225.

Neubauer, A. C., & Freudenthaler, H. H. (2005). Models of emotional intelligence. In R. Schulze & R. D. Roberts (Eds.), *Emotional intelligence: An international handbook* (pp. 31–50). Cambridge, MA: Hogrefe & Huber.

Newsome, S., Day, A. L., & Catano, V. M. (2000). Assessing the predictive validity of emotional intelligence. *Personality and Individual Differences, 29*, 1005–1016.

Oberauer, K., Wilhelm, O., & Schmiedek, F. (2005). Experimental strategies in multivariate research. In A. Beauducel, B. Biehl, M. Bosniak, W. Conrad, G. Schönberger, & D. Wagener (Eds.), *Festschrift on multivariate research strategies* (pp. 119–150). Maastricht, The Netherlands: Shaker.

O'Connor, R. M., Jr., & Little, I. S. (2003). Revisiting the predictive validity of emotional intelligence: Self-report versus ability-based measures. *Personality and Individual Differences, 35*, 1893–1902.

Olson-Buchanan, J. B., & Drasgow, F. (2006). Multimedia situational judgment tests: The medium creates the message. In J. A. Weekley & R. E. Ployhart (Eds.), *Situational judgment tests: Theory, measurement and application* (pp. 253–278). Mahwah, NJ: Erlbaum.

O'Sullivan, M., Guilford, J. P., & de Mille, P. (1965). *The measurement of social intelligence.* (Rep. No. 34). Los Angeles, CA: University of Southern California, Psychometric Laboratory.

Pacini, R., & Epstein, S. (1999). The relation of rational and experiential information processing styles to personality, basic beliefs, and the ratio-bias phenomenon. *Journal of Personality and Social Psychology, 76*, 972–987.

Palmer, B. R., Gignac, G., Manocha, R., & Stough, C. (2005). A psychometric evaluation of the Mayer-Salovey-Caruso Emotional Intelligence Test Version 2.0. *Intelligence, 33*, 285–305.

Palmer, B. R., Manocha, R., Gignac, G., & Stough, C. (2003). Examining the factor structure of the Bar-On Emotional Quotient Inventory with an Australian general population sample. *Personality and Individual Differences, 35*, 1191–1210.

Parker, J. D. A., Summerfeldt, L. J., Hogan, M. J., & Majeski, S. A. (2004). Emotional intelligence and academic success: Examining the transition from high school to university. *Personality and Individual Differences, 36*, 163–172 .

Parkinson, B., & Manstead, A. S. R. (1993). Making sense of emotion in stories and social life. *Cognition and Emotion, 7*, 295–323.

Paulhus, D. L., Lysy, D. C., & Yik, M. S. M. (1998). Self-report measures of intelligence: Are they useful as proxy IQ tests? *Journal of Personality, 66*, 525–554.

Pérez, J. C., Petrides, K. V., & Furnham, A. (2005). Measuring trait emotional intelligence. In R. Schulze & R. D. Roberts (Eds.), *Emotional intelligence: An international handbook* (pp. 181–201). Cambridge, MA: Hogrefe & Huber.

Petrides, K. V., & Furnham, A. (2000). On the dimensional structure of emotional intelligence. *Personality and Individual Differences, 29,* 313–320.

Petrides, K. V., & Furnham, A. (2001). Trait emotional intelligence: Psychometric investigation with reference to established trait taxonomies. *European Journal of Personality, 15,* 425–448.

Petrides, K. V., & Furnham, A. (2003). Trait emotional intelligence: Behavioural validation in two studies of emotion recognition and reactivity to mood induction. *European Journal of Personality, 17,* 39–57.

Pfütze, E.-M., Sommer, W., & Schweinberger, S. R. (2002). Age-related slowing in face and name recognition: Evidence from event-related brain potentials. *Psychology and Aging, 17,* 140–160.

Rammstedt, B., & Rammsayer, T. H. (2002). Self-estimated intelligence: Gender differences, relationship to psychometric intelligence and moderating effects of level of education. *European Psychologist, 7,* 275–284.

Roberts, R. D., Schulze, R., O'Brien, K., Reid, J., MacCann, C., & Maul, A. (2006). Exploring the validity of the Mayer-Salovey-Caruso Emotional Intelligence Test (MSCEIT) with established emotions measures. *Emotion, 6,* 663–669.

Roberts, R. D., Schulze, R., Zeidner, M., & Matthews, G. (2005). Understanding, measuring, and applying emotional intelligence: What have learned? What have missed? In R. Schulze & R. D. Roberts (Eds.), *Emotional intelligence: An international handbook* (pp. 311–341). Cambridge, MA: Hogrefe & Huber.

Roberts, R. D., Zeidner, M., & Matthews, G. (2001). Does emotional intelligence meet traditional standards for an intelligence? Some new data and conclusions. *Emotion, 1,* 196–231.

Salovey, P., & Mayer, J. D. (1990). Emotional intelligence. *Imagination, Cognition and Personality, 9,* 185–211.

Schmit, M. J., & Ryan, A. M. (1993). The big five in personnel selection: Factor structure in applicant and nonapplicant populations. *Journal of Applied Psychology, 78,* 966–974.

Schulze, R. (2005). Modeling structures of intelligence. In O. Wilhelm & R. W. Engle (Eds.), *Handbook of understanding and measuring intelligence* (pp. 241–263). Thousand Oaks, CA: Sage.

Schutte, N. S., Malouff, J. M., Hall, L. E., Haggerty, D. J., Cooper, J. T., Golden, C. J., et al. (1998). Development and validation of a measure of emotional intelligence. *Personality and Individual Differences, 25,* 167–177.

Semenza, C., & Sgaramella, T. M. (1993). Production of proper names: A clinical case study of the effects of phonemic cueing. *Memory, 1,* 265–280.

Skrondal, A., & Rabe-Hesketh, S. (2004). *Generalized latent variable modeling: Multilevel, longitudinal, and structural equation models.* Boca Raton, FL: Chapman & Hall/CRC.

Sommer, W., Komoss, E., & Schweinberger, S. R. (1997). Differential localization of brain systems subserving memory for names and faces in normal subjects with event-related potentials. *Electroencephalography and clinical Neurophysiology, 102,* 192–199.

Süß, H.-M., & Beauducel, A. (2005). Faceted models of intelligence. In O. Wilhelm & R. W. Engle (Eds.), *Handbook of understanding and measuring intelligence* (pp. 313–332). Thousand Oaks, CA: Sage.

Tett, R. P., Fox, K. E., & Wang, A. (2005). Development and validation of a self-report measure of emotional intelligence as a multidimensional trait domain. *Personality and Social Psychology Bulletin, 31*, 859–888.

Thorndike, E. L. (1920). Intelligence and its use. *Harper Magazine, 140*, 227–235.

Tsukiura, T., Fujii, T., Fukatsu, R., Otsuki, T., Okuda, J., Umetsu, A., et al. (2002). Neural basis of the retrieval of people's names: evidence from brain-damaged patients and fMRI. *Journal of Cognitive Neuroscience 14*, 922–937.

van der Linden, W. J. (2005). *Linear models for optimal test design.* New York: Springer.

Van Rooy, D. L., Viswesvaran, C., & Pluta, P. (2005). An evaluation of construct validity: What is this thing called emotional intelligence? *Human Performance, 18*, 445–462.

Viswesvaran, C., & Ones, D. S. (1999). Meta-analyses of fakability estimates: Implications for personality assessment. *Educational and Psychological Measurement, 59*, 197–210.

Warrington, E. K., & McCarthy, R. A. (1983). Category specific access dysphasia. *Brain, 106*, 859–878.

Warwick, J., & Nettelbeck, T. (2004). Emotional intelligence is…? *Personality and Individual Differences, 37*, 1091–1100.

Weekley, J. A., & Ployhart, R. E. (Eds.). (2006). *Situational judgment tests: Theory, measurement, application.* Mahwah, NJ: Erlbaum.

Weis, S., & Süß, H.-M. (2005). Social intelligence—A review and critical discussion of measurement concepts. In R. Schulze & R. D. Roberts (Eds.), *Emotional intelligence: An international handbook* (pp. 203–230). Cambridge, MA: Hogrefe & Huber.

Wilhelm, O. (2005). Measures of emotional intelligence: Practice and standards. In R. Schulze & R. D. Roberts (Eds.), *Emotional intelligence: An international handbook* (pp. 131–154). Cambridge, MA: Hogrefe & Huber.

Williams, J. M. G., Mathews, A., & MacLeod, C. (1996). The emotional Stroop task and psychopathology. *Psychological Bulletin, 120*, 3–24.

Zeidner, M., Matthews, G., & Roberts, R. D. (2001). Slow down, you move too fast: Emotional intelligence remains an "elusive" intelligence. *Emotion, 1*, 265–275.

Zeidner, M., Matthews, G., & Roberts, R. D., & MacCann (2003). Development of emotional intelligence: Toward a multi-level investment model. *Human Development, 46*, 69–96.

Zeidner, M., Roberts, R. D., & Matthews, G. (2002). Can emotional intelligence be schooled? A critical review. *Educational Psychologist, 37*, 215–231.

Zeidner, M., Shani-Zinovich, I., Matthews, G., & Roberts, R. D. (2005). Assessing emotional intelligence in gifted and non-gifted high school students: Outcomes depend on the measure. *Intelligence, 33*, 369–391.

9

Measuring Emotional Intelligence as a Set of Mental Abilities

SUSAN E. RIVERS, MARC A. BRACKETT, PETER SALOVEY, AND JOHN D. MAYER

Emotional intelligence (EI) refers to an individual's capacity to process emotional information in order to enhance cognitive activities and facilitate social functioning (Mayer & Salovey, 1997; Salovey & Mayer, 1990). EI is defined as the perception, use, understanding, and management of one's own and others' emotional states to solve problems and regulate behavior. In this chapter, we argue that EI is best described as a set of abilities and therefore best measured by ability-based assessments. First, we present an overview of EI theory. Second, we describe the Mayer-Salovey-Caruso Emotional Intelligence Test (MSCEIT; Mayer, Salovey, & Caruso, 2002a), a theoretically derived and empirically validated assessment tool. In this section, we describe the psychometric properties of the MSCEIT, focusing as well on what EI predicts about a person's life. Third, we review additional ability-based tools that assess a subset of the skills measured by the MSCEIT. Finally, we describe two alternative measurement approaches to EI assessment: self-judgment and information processing tasks. Throughout the chapter, we discuss strengths and limitations in both EI theory and measurement as well as identify areas for future research.

Emotional Intelligence Theory

The initial conceptualization of EI was derived from early psychological research on the three components of the mind: cognition (thought), affect (feeling), and conation (motivation; Mayer & Salovey, 1997; Salovey & Mayer, 1990). Initial writings proposed that EI connects the first two components: cognition and affect. Intelligence belongs to the cognitive component of the mind and refers to how well one engages in tasks pertaining to memory, reasoning, judgment, and abstract thought. Emotion belongs to the affective component that involves emotions themselves (e.g., sadness, anger, and fear), moods, evaluations or preferences, and feeling states (e.g., energy or fatigue). Thus, the theory of EI links cognition and affect by suggesting that emotions make cognitive processes more intelligent and that one can think intelligently about emotions.

In developing the model of EI, we reviewed the literature on emotions and intelligence to identify the abilities linking cognitive processes with emotions and emotions with thinking. Four interrelated emotion abilities emerged: perceiving, using, understanding, and managing emotions. Based on this review, we formally proposed that four dimensions of abilities comprise EI: "the ability to perceive accurately, appraise, and express emotion [perceiving]; the ability to access and/or generate feelings when they facilitate thought [using]; the ability to understand emotion and emotional knowledge [understanding]; and the ability to regulate emotions to promote emotional and intellectual growth [managing]" (Mayer & Salovey, 1997, p. 10). These abilities can be measured and are not captured within conceptualizations or assessments of other constructs such as social competence or temperament/personality.

The abilities constituting each dimension are outlined in Figure 9.1 and are defined more fully elsewhere (Mayer & Salovey, 1997). The four abilities are arranged hierarchically such that more basic psychological processes (i.e., perceiving emotions) are at the base or foundation of the model, and more advanced psychological processes (i.e., managing emotions) are at the top of the model and are thought, to some extent, to be dependent upon the lower level abilities. Abilities within each dimension are expected to develop with experience and age.

The first dimension, perceiving emotions, includes skills related to identifying and differentiating emotions in the self and others. The most basic aspects of this ability are identifying and differentiating emotions in one's physical states (including bodily expressions), feelings, and thoughts. At a more advanced level, this ability enables one to identify emotions in other people, designs, or objects using cues such as sound, appearance, language, and behavior. Appropriately expressing emotions and related needs also represents more complex perceiving abilities. The ability to discriminate between honest and false emotional expressions in others, for example, is considered an especially sophisticated perceiving ability.

The second dimension, using emotions, refers to using or generating emotions to facilitate cognitive activities. The most basic aspects of this ability are prioritizing thinking by directing attention to important information about the environment or others. More advanced ability involves generating vivid emotions to aid judgment and memory processes and generating moods to facilitate the consideration of multiple perspectives. Producing emotional states to foster different thinking styles (e.g., inductive versus deductive reasoning) constitutes an especially high level of ability in this dimension.

The third dimension is understanding the language and meaning of emotions. Basic ability in this area includes labeling emotions with accurate language as well as recognizing similarities and differences between emotion labels and the emotions themselves. Interpreting meanings of emotions (e.g., anger means that one's goal has been blocked, happiness means that one's goal has been attained) and understanding complex feelings

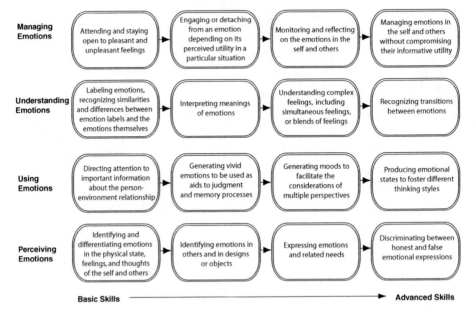

Figure 9.1. Mayer and Salovey's (1997) model of emotional intelligence. Adapted from Mayer and Salovey (1997, figure 1.1).

such as simultaneous moods or emotions (grief and joy), or blends of feelings (e.g., contempt as a combination of disgust and anger) represent more advanced understanding emotion ability. Recognizing transitions between emotions (e.g., frustration may lead to anger which may lead to rage) is an especially sophisticated ability within this dimension.

The fourth dimension, managing emotions, includes the ability to reduce, enhance, or modify an emotional response, as well as the ability to experience a range of emotions while also making decisions about the appropriateness or usefulness of the emotion in a given situation. Indeed, basic emotion regulation ability involves attending and staying open to pleasant and unpleasant feelings, whereas more advanced ability involves engaging or detaching from an emotion depending on its perceived utility in a particular situation. Monitoring and reflecting on the emotions in the self and others (e.g., processing whether the emotion is typical, acceptable, or influential) also represents more complex emotion regulation ability. At an especially advanced level, this dimension involves managing emotions (e.g., reducing, enhancing, or maintaining) in the self and others without compromising the information value of the emotion.

This model of EI is theoretically and empirically distinguishable from other models of EI (trait or "mixed" models) that define and measure the construct as a set of personality attributes and perceived competencies such as empathy, alexithymia, and stress tolerance (e.g., Bar-On, 1997, 2000; Petrides & Furnham, 2001). A more thorough review of the distinctions between these models can be found elsewhere (Brackett & Geher, 2006; Brackett & Mayer, 2003; Day, 2004; Matthews, Zeidner, & Roberts, 2002; Mayer, Caruso, & Salovey, 2000).

Measuring Emotional Intelligence

The ability model of emotional intelligence is operationalized by the Mayer-Salovey-Caruso Emotional Intelligence Test Version 2.0 (MSCEIT; Mayer et al., 2002a). The MSCEIT was designed to measure the four emotion-related abilities delineated by the model—perceiving, using, understanding, and managing emotions—using task-based measures. The test is published commercially by Multi-Health Systems (MHS) and is based on its predecessors, the MSCEIT RV.1, a test of roughly twice the length containing several additional subscales (Mayer et al., 2002a), and the Multifactor Emotional Intelligence Scale (MEIS; Mayer, Caruso, & Salovey, 1999). These instruments are considered performance tests because they rely on task performance and problem solving as opposed to self-reports of ability. These instruments require individuals to use the four EI abilities to solve emotion-related tasks.

The MSCEIT 2.0 is comprised of 141 items that are divided among 8 tasks (2 for each dimension). The test yields seven scores: one for each of the four dimensions, two area scores, and a total EI score. The two area scores are termed: experiential EI (combined scores from the perceiving and using dimensions) and strategic EI (combined scores from the understanding and managing dimensions). A summary of the tasks for each dimension is provided below; more detailed information is provided in the MSCEIT technical manual (Mayer et al., 2002b).

Perceiving Emotions

The ability to perceive emotions is assessed by asking respondents to identify and differentiate emotions expressed in photographs of people's faces (faces task) as well as emotions represented in artistic designs and landscapes (pictures task). Respondents first examine an image and then use a 5-point scale to indicate the extent to which each of five emotions (e.g., happy, sad, fear) are expressed in the photograph, design, or landscape.

Using Emotions

The ability to use emotions to facilitate thinking is assessed by asking respondents to generate an emotion in order to compare it to other sensory modalities like taste, color, and temperature (sensations task). By way of example, respondents are asked to imagine feeling an emotion such as sadness and then use a 5-point scale to rate how much this feeling is similar to adjectives related to other sensory modalities, such as "closed," "dark," and "numb." Second, the ability to identify the feelings that assist or interfere with performing various cognitive and behavioral tasks (facilitation task) is assessed. For example, respondents are asked, "What mood(s) might be helpful to feel when composing an inspiring military march?" Respondents rate a list of possible moods (e.g., anger, excitement) using a 5-point scale.

Understanding Emotions

The ability to understand emotions and employ emotional knowledge is assessed first by one task asking respondents to decompose emotion blends and to construct simple emotions to form complex feelings (blends task). A sample item from the blends task is, "Sadness and satisfaction are both sometimes part of the feeling of…" The second task asks respondents to identify transitions between emotions, such as identifying an event that would have happened to make a woman feel angry and then guilty (changes task). For each task, respondents choose the most appropriate response from a list of response alternatives.

Managing Emotions

The ability to manage emotions in the self and others is assessed first with the emotion management task, which measures the ability to identify the effectiveness of strategies to manage emotions in various situations to achieve a specified intrapersonal goal (e.g., preserving a positive mood). For example, respondents read a short vignette about another person, and then evaluate the effectiveness of several different courses of action to cope with emotions in the story using a 5-point scale. The second task, social management, measures the ability to identify the effectiveness of strategies to manage others' emotions in various situations to achieve a specified interpersonal goal (e.g., maintaining a good relationship with a close friend).

Scoring the MSCEIT

The theory underlying the ability model of EI is that emotions convey information about both people and the environment, and that this information system has evolved biologically and is modified and refined further by culture (Mayer, Salovey, Caruso, & Sitarenios, 2001). The authors of the MSCEIT have argued that assessing the correctness of an answer according to group consensus is one operationalization of EI. The assumption underlying consensual scoring or consensus based measurement (CBM) is that large samples of individuals converge on correct answers (Legree, 1995; Legree, Psotka, Tremble, & Bourne, 2005). CBM relies on a representative sample of individuals to approximate how knowledge is used and applied. CBM is useful when a formal information source is not readily available (Legree et al., 2005). Because the formalization of knowledge related to the perception, use, understanding, and regulation of emotions is emerging and varies according to cultural norms, utilizing CBM is appropriate. For this reason, one way to score the MSCEIT is with consensus scoring (Mayer et al., 2002b). Consensus scores reflect the proportion of people in a heterogeneous normative sample (over 5,000 respondents) who endorsed each MSCEIT response. Thus, an individual's score is computed by comparing her responses to those of the normative sample. For example, if .67 of the normative sample reports that there is a moderate amount of sadness in a face (i.e., chose 3 on the 5-point scale), the score of a respondent who also chose that answer is incremented by .67.

Criticisms of early versions of the MSCEIT (MEIS, MSCEIT research version 1.0) raise the question of whether general consensus would agree with, for example, a consensus among the emotions experts (e.g., Matthews et al., 2002). To test this hypothesis, a second set of consensus scores were calculated, this time based on expert responding. The expert scores reflect the proportion of 21 emotions experts from the International Society Research on Emotions (ISRE) who endorsed each response. The emotions experts were selected to judge the test item responses because they have spent much of their careers investigating facial expressions of emotion, emotional language, the subjective experience of emotion, and emotion regulation. Full-scale MSCEIT scores based on both the consensus norms and expert norms correlate quite highly, $r > .90$ (Mayer et al., 2002a; Mayer, Salovey, Caruso, & Sitarenios, 2003; see also Palmer, Gignac, Manocha, & Stough, 2005).[1] Generally, correlations with external criteria are similar for the two scoring methods. For example, in one study both expert and consensus scores on the MSCEIT predicted outcomes of social importance, including illegal drug use and social deviance (Brackett & Mayer, 2003). There are a number of limitations to scoring performance tests such as the MSCEIT with these methods; these will be addressed later in the chapter.

Psychometric Properties of the MSCEIT

In this section, we present a brief overview of the evidence supporting the psychometric properties of the MSCEIT (for more detailed reviews, see Barchard & Russell, 2004; Brackett & Salovey, 2004; Mayer, Salovey, & Caruso, 2004a; Mayer et al., 2003).

Reliability

The four MSCEIT dimension scores draw on heterogeneous tasks that include different item formats. For example, the ability to perceive emotions is measured by asking respondents to identify the emotions expressed in pictures, whereas the ability to understand emotions is measured by asking respondents to select one response from a list of alternatives. For these reasons, split-half reliability coefficients are employed as they involve the orderly allocation of different item types to the two different halves of the test (Nunnally, 1967).

The reliability of the MSCEIT is acceptable (MacCann, Matthews, Zeidner, & Roberts, 2004). Mayer et al. (2003) reported full-test split-half reliabilities of .93 and .91 for consensus and expert scoring, respectively, using MSCEIT protocols from 2,000 individuals from the standardization sample. The reliability of the two area scores (experiential and strategic EI) were both .90 for consensus scoring, and .88 and .86, respectively, for expert scoring. The reliabilities of the four dimension scores for both methods of scoring ranged from .76 to .91 (see Mayer et al., 2003, Table 1). The reliabilities of the eight individual tasks are somewhat low (.55 to .88) and are not recommended to be used for most analyses. Finally, the test-retest reliability of the full-test MSCEIT over a 3-week interval was $r(59) = .86$ in a college student sample (Brackett & Mayer, 2003). Comparable reliabilities are reported by Palmer et al. (2005).

Factor Structure

Using a large portion of the standardization sample, Mayer et al. (2003) performed confirmatory factor analysis on the eight tasks that make up the MSCEIT, testing for a one-, two-, and four-factor model to examine the range of permissible factor structures. All models fit fairly well, but the best fit was the four-factor solution as evidenced by the following goodness-of-fit indices using consensus and expert scoring methods, respectively: NFI = .98, .97; TLI = .96, .97; RMSEA = .05, .04. Gignac's (2005) re-analysis of Mayer et al.'s (2003) data found similar results for the four-factor solution, but dramatically less good fits for the one- and two-factor solutions than those reported by Mayer etal. (2003). Mayer, Panter, Salovey, Caruso, and Sitarenios (2005) traced the differences to an unpublished change in the algorithm for Amos 4.0 (in his reanalysis, Gignac used Amos 4.2). In a separate study, Palmer et al. (2005) reported that a better one-factor model may be obtained by employing a hierarchical model; their data, however, did not support a four-factor model (there was a high correlation between scores on the using and the managing subscales; $r = .90$). Thus, evidence supporting the factor structure remains equivocal. Additional research is necessary to identify the optimal factor structure of the MSCEIT.

Validity

Even though the MSCEIT was first published in 2002, a fairly large number of studies have provided evidence supporting its validity. These findings indicate that the MSCEIT is measuring something new, as scores on the test correlate only modestly with measures of intelligence and are essentially distinct from most personality measures (including measures of socially desirable responding; e.g., Lopes, Salovey, & Strauss, 2003). The evidence to date supporting the predictive validity of the MSCEIT also is promising. Scores on the test are associated with relevant outcomes across multiple dimensions including academic performance, cognitive processing, social functioning, psychological well-being, psychopathology, and leadership and other behavior in the workplace. Due to limited space, our review of the construct and predictive validity of the MSCEIT primarily focuses on studies using total EI scores (for more thorough reviews see Brackett & Salovey, 2004; Grewal & Salovey, 2005; Mayer et al., 2000; Mayer et al., 2004a; Salovey & Grewal, 2005).

Relation to Cognitive Abilities

EI is hypothesized to predict cognitive functioning because the abilities allow individuals both to garner emotions to facilitate thinking and regulate emotions in order to focus on important information (Mayer & Salovey, 1997). As predicted, total scores on the MSCEIT overlap somewhat with measures of verbal and analytic intelligence showing appropriate convergent validity. For example, MSCEIT scores correlate moderately with verbal SAT scores (Brackett, Mayer, & Warner, 2004; David, 2005; Gil-Olarte Marquez, Palomera Martin, & Brackett, 2006; Lopes et al., 2003), verbal intelligence as measured by the WAIS-III (Lopes et al., 2003), ACT scores (O'Connor & Little, 2003), reasoning (O'Connor & Little, 2003), academic giftedness (Zeidner, Shani-Zinovich, Matthews, & Roberts, 2005), and general intelligence measures (e.g., Factorial General Intelligence; Gil-Olarte Marquez et al., 2006).[2] In their meta-analysis of 18 studies that used the MEIS or the MSCEIT, Van Rooy, Viswesvaran, & Pluta (2005) report a correlation of .34 (after correcting for unreliability in measurement) between EI and assessments of verbal and spatial intelligence (see also Van Rooy & Viswesvaran, 2004).

There is evidence that MSCEIT scores predict the amount of cognitive effort employed to solve problems as well as performance on affectively laden social problems. Specifically, individuals with higher MSCEIT scores used less cognitive effort while problem solving, as assessed by patterns in theta and alpha frequency bands of electroencephalographic activity of the brain (Jausovec, Jausovec, & Gerlic, 2001). In addition, a recent study showed that individuals with higher MSCEIT scores solved social problems that were affective in content more quickly than those with lower scores (Reis et al., 2007). Importantly, there was no difference in reaction time to solving nonaffective social problems. It remains an open question whether EI fosters all types of cognitive processing, or primarily that which is focused on affective or social information.

Relation to Personality

Personality accounts for only a small amount of the variance in MSCEIT scores (Brackett & Mayer, 2003; Gil-Olarte Marquez et al., 2006; Mayer et al., 2004a; Lopes et al., 2003; Van Rooy et al., 2005; Warwick & Nettlebeck, 2004). Across five studies ($N = 1584$) conducted in our lab and in others, EI (as measured by the MSCEIT or MEIS) correlated positively with agreeableness ($r = .21$) and openness ($r = .17$; Mayer et al., 2004a, Table 5). Each correlation reflects a weighted mean over the five studies. The relationship between MSCEIT score and these personality constructs is not surprising. Individuals who are open to experience are intellectually curious and have sensitivity to aesthetics of the world; emotion-related abilities rely, to some extent, on such inclinations. Individuals who are agreeable tend to conform to group norms; performance on the MSCEIT is in part calculated by the extent to which respondents converge with respect to a consensus, though, as mentioned, MSCEIT scores do not correlate with social desirability. The weighted mean correlation for EI with extraversion, neuroticism, and conscientiousness were significant, but lower ($rs = .06$, $-.09$, and $.11$, respectively).

Relation to Other Conceptualizations of EI

Numerous studies show that the MSCEIT does not overlap very much with self-report assessments of EI based on trait or mixed models (Brackett & Mayer, 2003; Gohm & Clore, 2002; Livingstone & Day, 2005; Lopes et al., 2003; O'Connor & Little,

2003). In a meta-analysis of 13 studies (combined sample size of 2,442) that employed both the MSCEIT and one of the measures based on trait or mixed models (e.g., EQ-i; Bar-On, 1997), Van Rooy and colleagues (2005) reported that MSCEIT scores are relatively distinct from these measures ($r = .14$). Assessments of EI derived from trait or mixed models appear to be tapping into a construct separate from the abilities described in Mayer and Salovey's (1997) model.

Relation to Academic Performance

Emotion-related skills are hypothesized to prioritize thinking and enable one to manage emotions in provoking situations such as the anxiety that occurs while taking a test (Lopes & Salovey, 2004). Thus, one would expect MSCEIT scores to correlate positively with academic achievement. The evidence supporting the relationship between EI and school achievement is mixed. Among college students, there is some evidence for positive zero-order correlations between MSCEIT total scores and SAT scores as well as MSCEIT total scores and course grades (Barchard, 2003; Brackett & Mayer, 2003). However, the correlation with grades typically becomes nonsignificant once verbal intelligence (e.g., SAT scores) is statistically controlled (Barchard, 2003; Brackett & Mayer, 2003). Other studies report no correlation between MSCEIT scores and grade point average (O'Connor & Little, 2003).

A new study with a high school student sample reported that the Spanish version of the MSCEIT, administered at the start of the academic year, predicted final grades after controlling for personality and academic intelligence (Gil-Olarte Marquez et al., 2006). It is possible that the findings from high school students are stronger due to a restricted range of IQ scores in college student samples, which would attenuate associations. Gil-Olarte Marquez's findings should be interpreted with caution until replicated. To test the relationship between MSCEIT scores and academic performance more adequately, studies should be conducted recruiting samples with a wide range of IQ scores (e.g., students from public elementary and high schools, students attending nonelite colleges, and adults in the community).

Relation to Social Functioning

EI is postulated to promote positive social functioning by (a) focusing attention on important information in the environment, (b) facilitating the ability to adopt others' perspectives, which leads to increased empathy and provision of social support, (c) enhancing communication about emotions, which leads to fewer misunderstandings, and (d) regulating behavior, which reduces the likelihood of irrational action (Mayer & Salovey, 1997). In several studies with college students, EI was associated with various indicators of positive social relations, even after personality and traditional intelligence were controlled for statistically. MSCEIT scores were positively related to self-perceived supportive relationships with friends and parents, and negatively associated with antagonistic and conflictual relationships with close friends (Lopes et al., 2003), although there is some evidence that this relationship may hold only for men

(Brackett, Rivers, Shiffman, Lerner, & Salovey, 2006). Among male college students, lower EI was associated with maladaptive outcomes, including illegal drug and alcohol use, deviant behavior, and poor relations with friends (Brackett et al., 2004).

A limitation of the studies described above is that they used the MSCEIT primarily to predict the self-reported quality of social relationships. Lopes, Brackett, Nezlek, Schütz, Sellin, and Salovey (2004), however, examined the relationship between individuals' emotional intelligence and reports of their social attributes by their peers. American college students took the MSCEIT and were asked to have their close friends rate their personal qualities. The students who scored higher on the managing emotions dimension of the MSCEIT received more positive ratings from their friends of the quality of their social interactions. Similarly, a follow-up study revealed that college students who scored higher on the managing emotions dimension of the MSCEIT were viewed by their peers as more interpersonally sensitive and prosocially inclined (Lopes, Salovey, Côté, & Beers, 2005). In another study, German students were asked to keep diaries of their daily social interactions (Lopes et al., 2004). Those students who scored higher on the MSCEIT reported greater success in their social interactions with members of the opposite sex. For example, they were more likely to report that they had come across in a competent or attractive manner and that their opposite-sex partner perceived them as having desirable qualities, such as intelligence and friendliness.

In a sample of dating couples, when both partners had low MSCEIT scores, relationship quality was lower and conflict and maladaptive relationship behaviors were higher than when both partners had high MSCEIT scores (Brackett, Warner, & Bosco, 2005; see also Brackett, Cox, Gaines, & Salovey, 2007). In another study, total MSCEIT scores correlated significantly with secure attachment styles, which reflect emotional closeness to others as well as feeling comfortable both depending on others and having others dependent on oneself (Kafetsios, 2004). Finally, when real-time social interactions were observed, male college students with higher MSCEIT scores engaged in more successful social behaviors than those with lower scores, as indicated by behavioral measures and informant reports (Brackett et al., 2006).

Importantly, a number of the studies reviewed in this section replicated earlier findings with the MEIS and the MSCEIT research version 1.1 (see Mayer et al., 2000). For example, Brackett et al.'s (2004) findings with drug use, alcohol consumption, and social deviance replicated and extended an earlier study with comparable outcome variables (Formica, 1998). Children with higher scores on the youth version of the MEIS were rated as being less aggressive by their peers and as more prosocial by teachers than students with lower scores (Rubin, 1999). Finally, in one study with adolescents in California, MEIS scores were associated negatively with tobacco and alcohol use (Trinidad & Johnson, 2002).

Relation to Psychological Well-Being

Because emotions provide information about one's relationship to the environment and others, interpreting and responding to that information can direct action and thought in ways that enhance or maintain well-being (Lazarus, 1991; Parrott, 2002). For this reason, EI is hypothesized to predict well-being and psychopathology. There is some preliminary evidence to support this hypothesis. Among college students, MSCEIT scores correlated positively with well-being as measured by Ryff's (1989) psychological well-being scale (Brackett & Mayer, 2003; Lopes et al., 2003). It is unknown whether this relationship exists in populations other then college students. Livingstone and Day (2005), for instance, did not find associations between subscale scores on the MSCEIT (research version 1.1) and life or job satisfaction among Canadian military personnel. Additional studies are needed to test the extent to which EI skills are lacking among individuals diagnosed with psychopathologies that have roots in emotional disturbances, like unipolar depression, social anxiety disorder, and schizophrenia (Keltner & Kring, 1998). Some preliminary evidence suggests that these correlations may exist. For example, David (2005) reported a negative correlation between MSCEIT scores and depression and anxiety ($rs = -.25$ and $-.24$, respectively). O'Connor and Little (2003) also report that MSCEIT scores correlated negatively with anxiety ($r = -.24$), as assessed by the 16PF.

Relation to Workplace Outcomes

EI is hypothesized to influence the capacity to interact and communicate effectively with others as well as the ability to manage conflict, handle stress, and perform under pressure (Lopes, Côté, & Salovey, 2006). For these reasons, EI is predicted to be instrumental in leadership and workplace behavior. Preliminary findings with the MSCEIT across organizational settings suggest that EI positively contributes to some aspects of job performance. For example, in a Fortune 400 insurance company, analysts and clerical employees from the finance department with higher EI scores received greater merit increases and held higher company rank than their lower EI counterparts. They also received better peer and/or supervisor ratings of interpersonal facilitation, stress tolerance, and leadership potential than their lower EI counterparts. With few exceptions, these associations remained statistically significant after controlling for other predictors, including age, gender, education, verbal ability, and personality traits (Lopes, Grewal, Kadis, Gall, & Salovey, 2006). Among currently or recently employed undergraduates, MSCEIT scores significantly predicted supervisor-rated job performance even after controlling for cognitive intelligence (Janovics & Christiansen, 2002). Finally, the total MSCEIT scores of 41 senior executives predicted leadership effectiveness as rated by managers (Rosete & Ciarrochi, 2005).[3]

Critiques and Limitations of the MSCEIT

Historically, intelligence researchers have been relatively skeptical about the plausibility of an emotional intelligence. Given some of the overblown claims accompanying reports about EI in the popular press, and its relatively recent introduction in the scientific literature, it is not surprising that the field has received a lot of attention and criticism. In this section we review the common themes found in critiques and commentaries on the measurement of EI.

Content Limitations

The MSCEIT was designed as a standardized, easy-to-administer test. This is beneficial for researchers because of its transportability across testing settings (i.e., it can be administered to individuals or groups) and its efficiency (respondents typically complete the tool in less than 45 minutes using a pencil-and-paper or online version of the test). Many EI skills are amenable to assessment vis-à-vis standardized testing procedures, such as the understanding emotions dimension. However, the structure of the test does not allow for the direct assessment of several abilities, especially the higher order skills specified in the Mayer and Salovey (1997) model. These skills include: appropriately expressing emotions (Dimension 1), discriminating between honest and false emotional expressions (Dimension 1), the ability to prioritize thinking by directing attention to important information (Dimension 2), the ability to monitor and reflect on one's own and others' emotions for the purpose of regulating them (Dimension 4), and the ability to manage emotions in the self and other without compromising the information value of the emotions (Dimension 4). Testing these more fluid skills independently of the others—to the extent they may be independent—requires more complex procedures, perhaps using behavioral indicators or interactive tasks. To assess managing the emotions of others, for example, researchers could create an interpersonal task in the laboratory in which an individual must interact with a friend (real or virtual) who is angry. Management ability may be assessed by examining how the individual interacts with the friend and the extent to which the individual effectively manages the friend's emotions. The effectiveness of the regulation technique could be assessed by asking the recipient of the management strategy (the friend) the extent to which the anger remains and what information the emotion provided about the event.

Other commentaries of the MSCEIT's limitations focus on the specific items. For example, O'Sullivan and Ekman (2004) point out that the emotions depicted in the faces task are limited to a few emotions that may not adequately represent a full range of emotional expressions. They propose the incorporation of subscales assessing perception ability for a set of emotions, for example, the basic emotions of anger, sadness, joy, fear, disgust, and surprise. Moreover, they argue that the photographs on the test are not clear expressions of a particular affective state; rather they are subtle expressions and blends of expressions with "idiosyncratic facial displays of the models" (p. 95). Yet items based on pure expressions proved to be too easy to be psychometrically useful. By Ekman's own findings, they are identified correctly more than 80% of the time (Ekman, Friesen, & Ellsworth, 1972).

It also is important to note that the faces and pictures tasks do not focus on the many other nonverbal channels of emotional expression such as gesture, voice, posture, or physiological arousal, which would be difficult to capture in a paper-and-pencil test.

We appreciate the limitations of the MSCEIT to assess each of the skills delineated by the model. Indeed, it may not be appropriate or realistic for this type of paper-and-pencil instrument to assess all relevant EI skills. However, we agree with Gohm (2004) that it is imperative for scores on the MSCEIT to correlate with other measures of emotion-related abilities such as the Levels of Emotional Awareness Scale (LEAS; Lane, Quinlan, Schwartz, Walker, & Zeitlin, 1990) and the Diagnostic Analysis of Nonverbal Accuracy 2 (DANVA2; Nowicki & Carton, 1993). To date, there is limited evidence for the convergent validity of the MSCEIT with conceptually related ability measures.

Critiques of Consensus and Expert Scoring

Because the highest scores on the MSCEIT are obtained by agreeing with an expert or general consensus, it remains unclear whether the MSCEIT, when scored using such methods, assesses EI ability or convergence to popular opinion—the "tendency to respond in a stereotypical, common way" (Geher & Renstrom, 2004, p. 8). Day (2004) poses the question, "Does the high EI individual know what everyone else knows or does the high EI individual know more and know better?" It may be that agreement with the consensus reflects average EI, not high EI (e.g., Day, 2004). In support of this view, Averill (2004) argues that a measure of EI that relies on the convergence of "correct" responses precludes creativity in the experience, understanding, and expression of emotions (i.e., emotional creativity).

O'Sullivan and Ekman (2004) argue that being able to identify how most people interpret a facial expression is different from being able to identify accurately a facial expression. Although there is an advantage to knowing how a facial expression is interpreted by most people, such interpretations may not be accurate. Both skills are important, but they are different skills; "*Accuracy* and *intelligence* both presuppose a *correct* answer, not one generated by group opinion" (p. 97, italics in original). This is an intriguing criticism: Ekman's work is largely responsible for many of the psychoevolutionary assumptions underlying the idea of emotional information, including emotional information in the face. To date we are unaware of studies indicating that expertise in emotions yields a defined set of answers that are different than consensually derived answers. As described above, scores computed using expert and consensus scoring are correlated highly. Indeed, the basis of expert answers in the emotions area seems to be knowing the consensus as well or better than the average person (Mayer et al., 2001). Theoretically, it is possible that an expert answer is different than the consensus.

Although there is convergence between consensus and expert scores on the MSCEIT, this overlap may indicate that the experts are identifying the most popular or stereotypical answer, not the correct one (Day, 2004; Geher & Renstrom, 2004). One way to address this issue may be by using tasks that rely on veridical scoring (i.e., tasks that have a true or real answer; Geher & Renstrom, 2004). Most questions on the SAT, for example, have a correct answer—vocabulary definitions, answers to algebra problems, and so forth. MacCann and colleagues (2004) reviewed studies using measures of emotion perception ability that relied on veridical scoring. On these tasks, respondents receive credit to the extent that they identify the emotion that is actually expressed on the face as determined by a standardized assessment of the configuration of the facial muscles. MacCann and colleagues (2004) found that emotion ability measures using veridical scoring converge more with other measures of intelligence than those using consensus-based scoring, providing initial evidence for the validity of veridically scored tests. If the MSCEIT, as scored by consensus and experts, is tapping into EI, then scores should be correlated highly with related tests of emotion-abilities that use veridical scoring. There are, however, few tests available that are amenable to using veridical scoring. One central concern in identifying or developing veridically scored EI tests is that there may not be one "correct" answer to emotion-related tasks. Indeed, there might be multiple correct answers to test items. It may be instructive to use more flexible scoring, perhaps with experts ranking response alternatives (Mayer et al., 2004a).

Future Directions

EI research is in its beginning stages, as is work on its measurement. There likely will be improvements made to the content and structure of the MSCEIT based on the limitations noted here. Nevertheless, the psychometric properties of the MSCEIT are promising given that it is a recently developed test designed to assess a relatively new construct. Some critics argue that EI, as assessed by the MSCEIT, is of little use because most of the variance in MSCEIT performance can be predicted by cognitive ability, agreeableness, and gender (Schulte, Ree, & Carretta, 2004). Given their small sample size ($N = 102$) and the accumulating evidence demonstrating the usefulness of the construct, Schulte et al.'s findings seem unlikely to be robust.

Despite the burgeoning of EI research, many unaddressed questions remain. A primary tenet of EI theory is that emotion skills develop with age and experience (Mayer & Salovey, 1997; Salovey & Mayer, 1990), thus next steps in EI research should focus on developmental changes in EI. Although there is some evidence to support this postulate (e.g., Mayer et al., 1999), most of the research described in this section was conducted with college student samples. Additional research in younger and older samples is needed. A youth version of the MSCEIT (MSCEIT-YV) has been developed recently (Mayer, Caruso, & Salovey, 2005), and we are currently testing its psychometric properties in adolescent samples (Rivers, Brackett, & Salovey, in press).

There is little research examining the role of EI in ongoing emotional situations. EI should be especially influential in predicting outcomes in circumstances in which the skills are required—during a relationship conflict, before an important exam, confronting peer pressure, when making a decision about a career change or choice of college, or during a traumatic event. To understand better the processes by which EI influences optimal performance across life dimensions, it is necessary to examine when and how individuals access and utilize emotion skills. In addition, there are no studies that look at whether performance on the MSCEIT assesses what a person *can* do or what a person *will* do. An effective assessment of EI should assess both a person's abilities to process and integrate emotional information when thinking critically about emotions *and* what a person will do in the context of daily emotional events (Van Rooy & Viswesvaran, 2004).

Finally, it is important to recognize and attend to the gender differences in the predictive validity of the MSCEIT. The presence of gender differences in MSCEIT performance is interesting and an important area for future work to examine. Women typically outperform men on the MSCEIT (e.g., Barchard, 2003; Brackett & Mayer, 2003; Brackett et al., 2004; Brackett et al., 2006; Schulte et al., 2004) and its predecessor tests (Mayer et al., 1999). These gender differences provide additional support for the construct validity of the test as the emotions literature reliably shows that women perform better on emotion-related tasks, like decoding and encoding facial expressions of emotion (Brody, 2000).[4]

The meaning of these gender differences is not well understood. It may be that women as a group are more emotionally intelligent than men. Or, it may be that men, as a group, do not take the test as seriously as women. Another possibility is that because the emotional worlds that men and women inhabit may be quite different, EI may operate differently in men and women (e.g., Shields, 2002). Indeed, there is some evidence that MSCEIT scores, for example, correlate significantly with negative social outcomes for men but not for women (Brackett et al., 2004; Brackett et al., 2006). Why is it that MSCEIT scores, in some cases predict outcomes, especially negative ones, for men only? To identify the behaviors in which gender moderates the relationship between MSCEIT scores and outcomes, researchers should conduct analyses separately by gender when sample sizes are large enough to do so (Brackett et al., 2004). The consistent gender difference should be considered seriously if EI testing is to be employed in high-stakes assessment, such as evaluating potential employees for hire or promotion. Men, as a group, may be unjustly penalized for their lower scores. Clearly, this issue deserves further investigation and attention.

Other Ability-Based Assessments

Although there are other ability-based assessments of the different components of EI, to date the MSCEIT remains the only available instrument that assesses skills across the four theoretically described dimensions. Nevertheless, in this section we present an overview of instruments that assess at least one of the emotion-related abilities captured by the MSCEIT (for a more thorough review, see MacCann et al., 2004). Table 9.1 presents these instruments as they map onto three of the four dimensions of EI. We did not identify any ability-based measures that assess use of emotions to facilitate thinking. The instruments reviewed here focus on assessment in adults. There exist many assessments of emotion-related abilities in children and adolescents (e.g., Denham et al., 2003; Greenberg, Kusche, Cook, & Quamma, 1995; Izard, Trentacosta, King, & Mostow, 2004), but these instruments are beyond the scope of this chapter.

TABLE 9.1. Ability-based measures of EI.

Dimension	Instrument	Brief Measure Description	Scoring
Perception, appraisal, and expression of emotion	MSCEIT	*Faces task.* Identify the emotions expressed on targets' faces. *Pictures task.* Identify the emotions expressed in images of artistic designs and landscapes.	Consensus; expert
	JACBART	Identify the emotions expressed on the faces of Caucasian and Japanese targets.	Veridical
	CARAT	Identify the emotions expressed on targets' faces.	Target
	DANVA2	Identify four basic emotions (happiness, sadness, anger, and fear) in the facial and vocal expressions of adults and children.	Veridical
	PONS	Identify the content of emotional situations using one of four communication channels: face, full body, body only (no head), and voice.	Expert
	IPT	Identify the content of interpersonal situations using nonverbal behavioral cues.	Veridical
	EARS	Identify the feelings of targets in several emotionally laden stories.	Consensus; target
	Vocal expression	Identify emotions of targets as expressed vocally.	Target; expert
Emotional facilitation of thinking	MSCEIT	*Sensations task.* Compare emotions to other sensory modalities (e.g., taste, color, temperature). *Facilitation task.* Identify feelings that assist or interfere with performance on cognitive and behavioral tasks.	Consensus; expert

(continued)

245

TABLE 9.1 (continued)

Dimension	Instrument	Brief Measure Description	Scoring
Understanding and analyzing emotions; employing emotional knowledge	MSCEIT	*Blends task.* Decompose emotion blends; construct simple emotions to form complex feelings. *Changes task.* Identify transitions between emotions.	Consensus; expert
	LEAS	Use written emotion language (i.e., appropriate use of emotion language to describe one's own and others' emotion, as well as the variability of emotion language) in response to a series of emotionally evocative interpersonal scenes.	Structured coding
	Emotion differentiation card-sorting task	Sort cards with emotion terms into separate categories or groups of similar terms.	Structured coding
Reflective regulation of emotions	MSCEIT	*Emotion management task.* Identify the effectiveness of strategies to manage emotions to achieve specified intrapersonal goals. *Social management task.* Identify the effectiveness of strategies to manage others' emotions to achieve specified interpersonal goals.	Consensus; expert
	Management of negative mood	Manage negative mood through structured writing task.	Structured coding

Note: MSCEIT = Mayer-Salovey-Caruso Emotional Intelligence Test (Mayer et al., 2002a); JACBART = Japanese and Caucasian Brief Affect Recognition Test (Matsumoto et al., 2000); CARAT = Communication of Affect Receiving Ability Test (Buck, 1976); DANVA2 = Diagnostic Analysis of Nonverbal Accuracy 2 (Nowicki & Carton, 1993); PONS = Profile of Nonverbal Sensitivity (Rosenthal et al., 1979); IPT = Interpersonal Perception Task (Costanzo & Archer, 1989); EARS = Emotional Accuracy Research Scale (Mayer & Geher, 1996); Vocal expression (Scherer et al., 2001); LEAS = Levels of Emotional Awareness Scale (Lane et al., 1990); Emotion differentiation card-sorting task (Kang & Shaver, 2004); Management of negative mood (Ciarrochi et al., 2001).

Perceiving Emotions

Emotion perception is the best studied of the four EI dimensions, but skills in this dimension still are not well-understood (Boone & Buck, 2004; O'Sullivan & Ekman, 2004). Valid criteria for "correct" attributions of emotions are lacking. We rely on multiple criteria (e.g., antecedent events, behavioral indicators, physiological responses, self-reports, or expert judgments) to garner information about the emotional states of the self and others; but these criteria often do not converge, making it difficult to identify a valid measure of emotion perception (Boone & Buck, 2004). Nevertheless, there are multiple instruments available to assess this ability.

The most cited measures of emotion perception of facial expression include the Japanese and Caucasian Brief Affect Recognition Test (JACBART; Matsumoto et al., 2000), the Communication of Affect Receiving Ability Test (CARAT; Buck, 1976), the Profile of Nonverbal Sensitivity (PONS; Rosenthal, Hall, DiMatteo, Rogers, & Archer, 1979), and the Diagnostic Analysis of Nonverbal Accuracy 2 (DANVA2; Nowicki & Carton, 1993). The DANVA2 and the PONS also assess the ability to recognize emotions in vocal expressions, as does a measure developed by Scherer and colleagues (Scherer, Banse, & Wallbott, 2001; for reviews, see Scherer, 2003). The PONS assesses recognition of emotions in body posture as well. The Interpersonal Perception Task (IPT; Costanzo & Archer, 1989) assesses the ability to interpret nonverbal behaviors that are not confined to emotional expressions, such interpersonal expressions of power and closeness. Finally, the Emotional Accuracy Research Scales (EARS; Geher, Warner, & Brown, 2001) assess the ability to recognize emotions in written descriptions of emotionally laden situations. Descriptions of the tasks comprising these instruments, as well as the scoring methods, are provided in Table 9.1.

Although most of these tests have shown some success when predicting relevant outcomes (e.g., Archer, Costanzo, & Akert, 2001; Buck, 1976; Hall, 2001; Matsumoto et al., 2000; Mayer & Geher, 1996; Nowicki & Duke, 2001), the intercorrelations among tests of emotion perception tend to be low (Boone & Buck, 2004; Hall, 2001). These tests may not be ecologically valid as emotion signals are much more likely to occur in ongoing social interactions and rarely are received passively (Boone & Buck, 2004).

Understanding Emotions

The Levels of Emotional Awareness Scale (LEAS; Lane et al., 1990) is one measure of emotional understanding described in the literature. On the LEAS, written responses to a series of emotionally evocative interpersonal scenes are coded using specified criteria for emotional awareness, including the appropriate use of emotion language to describe one's own and others' emotion as well as the variability of emotion language. The reliability of the LEAS is acceptable and is related to, but discriminable from, relevant measures of cognitive development (Lane & Pollermann, 2002). The relationship between the LEAS and EI (as measured with the MEIS) is $r = .15$, with modestly higher correlations in the emotional understanding area (Ciarrochi, Caputi, & Mayer, 2003).

Another measure of emotional understanding is a card-sorting task design to assess emotion differentiation (Kang, Day, & Meara, 2005; Kang & Shaver, 2004; Shaver, Schwartz, Kirson, & O'Connor, 1987). Kang and Shaver (2004, Study 2) showed that individuals who were better able to differentiate between emotional terms were more empathic and had greater interpersonal adaptability.

Managing Emotions

We identified only one additional ability-based assessment of emotion management (Ciarrochi, Chan, & Bajgar, 2001); there are many self-report scales, of course. After inducing a negative mood using short video segments, participants were presented with an ambiguous photograph from the Thematic Apperception Test and wrote a story about the image. Written responses were coded for their positive and negative tone. There were individual differences in tone that were related to postwriting mood. Individuals who wrote more positively toned stories recovered more quickly from the mood induction than those individuals who wrote more negatively toned stories. This task may be valuable to test the construct validity of the MSCEIT. It would be expected that the stories of higher EI individuals include emotions that serve to modify (i.e., dampen) their negative mood.

Summary

The MSCEIT is the only available ability-based instrument that simultaneously assesses skills across each of the four EI dimensions. Testing the correlations among the MSCEIT and the measures described in this section may be useful to assess the generalizability and convergent validity of the MSCEIT. Alas, there are few studies available comparing the current version of the MSCEIT with these instruments (see MacCann et al., 2004).

Alternative Measurement Methods

Researchers long have been sensitive to the fact the one must collect the correct kind of data to assess a specific aspect of personality (Mayer, 2004). Test design centrally includes the consideration of the specific type of data that is appropriate to assessing the attribute at hand. For example, self-judgment data are a preferred means of obtaining information about a person's current emotional experience; criterion report (ability) data are preferred in the intelligence area; and for some researchers, thematic-report data (e.g., projective data) are preferred for the measure of motivation. In recent years, psychologists have become more closely attuned to the fact that each of these kinds of data yield different information about personality. Contemporary systems have been developed for classifying these kinds of data (Funder, 2001; Mayer, 2004). There are limited methods for assessing the ability model of EI beyond the MSCEIT. In the following section, we review the feasibility of other measurement methods for operationalizing EI, including self-judgment indices and information processing measures.

Self-Judgment Indices

A self-judgment scale that maps onto the ability model of EI would be valuable because it would be less costly than performance tests both in terms of time to administer and fees charged by test publishers (Brackett et al., 2006). However, the limitations of self-judgment measures of mental abilities may render such an instrument invalid. As an analogy, intelligence researchers depend on performance tests because intelligence generally pertains to the actual ability to perform well at mental tasks, not just one's self-reported beliefs about those abilities (Carroll, 1993; Neisser et al., 1996). Even though individuals would appear to be in the best position to assess their mental skills, self-judgments are often problematic due to impression management, self-deception, question misinterpretation, and inaccurate memories (DeNisi & Shaw, 1977; Paulhus, Lysy, & Yik, 1998). Indeed, with respect to mental abilities, most people make inaccurate self-judgments and tend to overestimate their performance on objective tests (Alicke, 1985; Dunning, Johnson, Ehrlinger, & Kruger, 2003; Mabe & West, 1982).

Recently, the Self-Rated Emotional Intelligence Scale (SREIS) was developed to map onto the four emotion-related skills assessed by the MSCEIT (Brackett et al., 2006). A confirmatory factor analysis of the 19-item SREIS yielded a four-factor solution that mapped onto the four-dimension model (Brackett, 2004), providing some evidence that the four basic dimensions of EI can be detected with both self-judgment and performance tests. Three studies comparing the validity of the SREIS to the MSCEIT, however, strongly suggest that performance measures of EI remain optimal for three reasons: (1) there is a lack of correspondence between self-ratings and performance (i.e., the correlation between the SREIS and the MSCEIT was low), (2) the SREIS, like other self-report inventories, overlaps with personality measures but the MSCEIT, for the most part, does not, and (3) the MSCEIT demonstrates incremental validity with respect to social outcomes, as measured by self-judgment and real-time behavioral indices, but the SREIS does not (Brackett et al., 2006). This set of studies provided initial evidence that emotion-related abilities operate in a similar way to other mental abilities in that individuals are poor evaluators of their ability (Dunning et al., 2003; Paulhus et al., 1998) and that performance measures of ability are more predictive of outcomes than are self-reports of ability.

A large number of researchers favor self-judgment inventories of EI (e.g., Bar-On, 1997; Boyatzis, Goleman, & Rhee, 2000; Petrides & Furnham, 2003). Such self-judgment measures include the Emotion Quotient Inventory (EQ-i; Bar-On, 1997) and the Self-Report EI Test (SREIT; Schutte et al., 1998). In contrast to Mayer and Salovey's (1997) ability approach, these researchers promote a mixed model of EI, including self-reported traits and competencies. Researchers have sometimes referred to these mixed models as "trait" models, but even those who proposed this label acknowledge that it relies on an idiosyncratic use of the term *trait* (Petrides & Furnham, 2003). For example, almost all psychologists consider intelligences, and therefore EI measured as an ability, to be a trait. Mixed models generally include three classes of constructs by definition: perceived emotion-related (and other) cognitive abilities; perceived social and emotional tendencies, qualities, and competencies; and more general personality traits. One concern is that these self-report scales often have little to do with *emotion* or *intelligence* and consequently fail to map conceptually and empirically on to the ability model (Brackett & Geher, 2006). These scales often seem based on depictions of EI targeted to the general public (e.g., Goleman, 1995, 1998).

Although the utility of self-judgment indices is not adequate to measure emotional intelligence itself, it would be interesting to examine discrepancies between EI ability (measured with the MSCEIT or other measures) and perceptions of ability (measured with a self-judgment instrument like the SREIS) to investigate the consequences of perceiving one's ability as higher or lower than it actually is.

Information Processing Tasks

There are few tasks that examine memory capacity or general processing speed with regard to emotional information and emotion-related abilities. Austin (2004) developed an information processing task to assess the ability to perceive emotions in faces. Participants were presented with computerized images of happy or sad faces that were partially covered by a mask, and then they were instructed to indicate whether the face was happy or sad as the mask partially disappeared. Austin showed that there were individual differences in emotional information processing speed, and that these differences were not explained by general information processing speed. Speed in detecting happy and sad faces was correlated even after controlling for speed of processing nonemotional information. Petrides and Furnham (2003) also developed an information processing task to assess ability to perceive emotions in six facial expressions of emotions. In their task, the intensity of the emotional expression progressed from neutral to a maximum. Response times for correctly identifying the target emotion were recorded. For both emotion perception information processing tasks, it would be expected that individuals with higher EI would detect the expression on the faces more quickly and with more of the mask still present than individuals with lower EI. It is unknown whether or not response times are related to relevant outcomes (e.g., social functioning).

Using information processing tasks to assess the ability to distinguish between facial expressions of emotions may be effective as there are true correct and incorrect answers (Ekman & Friesen, 1975). Translating information processing tasks to the other EI dimensions is more challenging because responses may not be verifiable as correct in the same way. To be useful, measurement instruments need to assess skills within each of the four dimensions of EI.

Conclusion

In our view, the term *EI* and its measurement should be limited to a set of mental abilities that rely on joint operation of the emotion and cognitive systems to solve emotion-laden problems. Currently, the MSCEIT is the only test available that requires test takers to apply their emotion-related skills in solving emotion-based problems across the four dimensions of EI. Although research on the MSCEIT is still in a relatively early stage, what we know about the test and its validity is promising. The tasks on the MSCEIT are by no means exhaustive of EI abilities. For example, tasks assessing the ability to perceive emotions on the MSCEIT do not measure the ability to express emotions, to detect honest versus dishonest emotional expressions, or to detect emotions in music, voice, or posture. In order to validate the ability model of EI, it is important for other new assessment instruments to be developed so that evidence of the construct can be shown to exist beyond one particular measurement instrument (Van Rooy et al., 2005). Nevertheless, the limitations of the tests outlined in this chapter are important to consider as our knowledge of EI is accumulating. Currently, EI researchers are considering the addition of subtests to tap into skills that are not currently included in the MSCEIT (Gignac, 2005; Mayer, Panter, et al., 2005). Ideally, researchers interested in the measurement of EI will collaborate with experts in diverse fields such as psychometrics, intelligence, emotions, expert systems, and graphic design to build the next generation of EI tests that mimic real-life, emotion-laden situations and fluid, real-time emotional responses.

Notes

1. Test reliabilities are higher when expert scoring is used for the perceiving and understanding branch items (e.g., Palmer et al., 2005), due, most likely, to more institutionalized knowledge in these areas. Further, Palmer et al. report that scores were higher on the perceiving and understanding subscales with expert scoring than with consensus scoring, suggesting that expert scoring may be optimal for domains in which there is more formalized knowledge.

2. Scores on the understanding subscales of the MSCEIT do correlate significantly with verbal intelligence measures (e.g., Lopes et al., 2003). This is not surprising given that the understanding tasks rely on emotional vocabulary.

3. Day and Carroll (2004), however, report that only scores on the perceiving subscales of the MSCEIT (research version 1.0) correlate significantly (positively) with workplace performance.

4. With earlier versions of the MSCEIT (research version 1.1), gender differences were less systematic. Livingstone and Day (2005) report that women score higher than men on the perceiving emotion subscale of the research version of the MSCEIT (v1.1) but not on the other subscales. However, Day and Carroll (2004) report that women score higher than men on all subscales of the MSCEIT v1.1.

References

Alicke, M. D. (1985). Global self-evaluation as determined by the desirability and controllability of trait adjectives. *Journal of Personality and Social Psychology, 49*, 1621–1630.

Archer, D., Costanzo, M., & Akert, R. (2001). The interpersonal perception task (IPT): Alternative approaches to problems of theory and design. In J. A. Hall & F. J. Bernieri (Eds.), *Interpersonal sensitivity: Theory and measurement* (pp. 161–182). Mahwah, NJ: Erlbaum.

Austin, E. J. (2004). An investigation of the relationship between trait emotional intelligence and emotional task performance. *Personality and Individual Differences, 36*, 1855–1864.

Averill, J. R. (2004). A tale of two snarks: Emotional intelligence and emotional creativity compared. *Psychological Inquiry, 15, 228–233.*

Barchard, K. A. (2003). Does emotional intelligence assist in the prediction of academic success?
Educational and Psychological Measurement, 63, 840–858.

Barchard, K. A., & Russell, J. A. (2004). Psychometric issues in the measurement of emotional
intelligence. In G. Geher (Ed.), *Measuring emotional intelligence: Common ground and
controversy* (pp. 51–70). Hauppauge, NY: Nova Science.

Bar-On, R. (1997). *Bar-On Emotional Quotient Inventory: Technical manual.* Toronto, Canada:
Multi-Health Systems.

Bar-On, R. (2000). Emotional and social intelligence: Insights from the Emotional Quotient Inventory. In R. Bar-On & J. D. A. Parker (Eds.), *The handbook of emotional intelligence* (pp.
363–388). San Francisco: Jossey-Bass.

Boone, R. T., & Buck, R. (2004). Emotion receiving ability: A new view of measuring individual
differences in the ability to accurately judge others' emotions. In G. Geher (Ed.), *Measuring emotional intelligence: Common ground and controversy* (pp. 71–87). Hauppauge, NY:
Nova Science.

Boyatzis, R. E., Goleman, D., & Rhee, K. S. (2000). Clustering competence in emotional intelligence:
Insights from the Emotional Competence Inventory. In R. Bar-On & J. D. A. Parker (Eds.),
*The handbook of emotional intelligence: Theory, development, assessment, and application at
home, school, and in the workplace* (pp. 343–362). San Francisco, CA: Jossey-Bass.

Brackett, M. A. (2004). The four-domain self-report emotional intelligence scale (SREIS). Unpublished data, Yale University.

Brackett, M. A., Cox, A., Gaines, S. O., & Salovey, P. (2007). Emotional intelligence and relationship quality among heterosexual couples. Manuscript submitted for publication.

Brackett, M. A., & Geher, G. (2006). Measuring emotional intelligence: Paradigmatic shifts and
common ground. In J. Ciarrochi, J. P. Forgas, & J. D. Mayer (Eds.), *Emotional intelligence
and everyday life* (pp. 27–50, 2nd ed.). New York: Psychology Press.

Brackett, M. A., & Mayer, J. D. (2003). Convergent, discriminant, and incremental validity of competing measures of emotional intelligence. *Personality and Social Psychology Bulletin, 29,*
1147–1158.

Brackett, M. A., Mayer, J. D., & Warner, R. M. (2004). Emotional intelligence and its relation to
everyday behaviour. *Personality and Individual Differences, 36,* 1387–1402.

Brackett, M. A., Rivers, S. E., Shiffman, S., Lerner, N., & Salovey, P. (2006). Relating emotional
abilities to social functioning: A comparison of self-report and performance measures of
emotional intelligence. *Journal of Personality and Social Psychology, 91,* 780–795.

Brackett, M. A., & Salovey, P. (2004). Measuring emotional intelligence with the Mayer-
Salovey-Caruso Emotional Intelligence Test (MSCEIT). In G. Geher (Ed.), *Measuring emo-
tional intelligence: Common ground and controversy* (pp. 179–194). Hauppauge, NY: Nova
Science.

Brackett, M. A., Warner, R. M., & Bosco, J. S. (2005). Emotional intelligence and relationship
quality among couples. *Personal Relationships, 12,* 197–212.

Brody, L. R. (2000). The socialization of gender differences in emotional expression: Display
rules, infant temperament, and differentiation. In A. H. Fischer (Ed.), *Gender and emotion:
Social psychological perspectives* (pp. 24–47). New York: Cambridge University Press.

Buck, R. (1976). A test of nonverbal receiving ability: Preliminary studies. *Human Communication
Research, 2,* 162–171.

Carroll, J. B. (1993). *Human cognitive abilities: A survey of factor-analytic studies.* New York: Cambridge University Press.

Ciarrochi, J., Caputi, P., & Mayer, J. D. (2003). The distinctiveness and utility of a measure of trait emotional awareness. *Personality and Individual Differences, 34,* 1477–1490.

Ciarrochi, J., Chan, A. Y. C., & Bajgar, J. (2001). Measuring emotional intelligence in adolescents. *Personality and Individual Differences, 31,* 1105–1119.

Costanzo, M., & Archer, D. (1989). Interpreting the expressive behavior of others: The interpersonal perception task. *Journal of Nonverbal Behavior, 13,* 225–245.

David, S. A. (2005). Emotional intelligence: Developmental antecedents, psychological and social outcomes. Unpublished doctoral dissertation, University of Melbourne, Australia.

Day, A. L. (2004). The measurement of emotional intelligence: The good, the bad, and the ugly. In G. Geher (Ed.), *Measuring emotional intelligence: Common ground and controversy* (pp. 239–264). Hauppauge, NY: Nova Science.

Day, A. L., & Carroll, S. A. (2004). Using an ability-based measure of emotional intelligence to predict individual performance, group performance, and group citizenship behaviors. *Personality and Individual Differences, 36,* 1443–1458.

Denham, S. A., Blair, K. A., DeMulder, E., Sawyer, K., Auerbach-Major, S., & Queenan, P. (2003). Preschool emotional competence: Pathway to social competence. *Child Development, 74,* 238–256.

DeNisi, A. S., & Shaw, J. B. (1977). Investigation of the uses of self-reports of abilities. *Journal of Applied Psychology, 62,* 641–644.

Dunning, D., Johnson, K., Ehrlinger, J., & Kruger, J. (2003). Why people fail to recognize their own incompetence. *Current Directions in Psychological Science, 12,* 83–87.

Ekman, P., & Friesen, W. V. (1975). *Unmasking the face: A guide to recognizing emotions from facial clues.* Oxford, England: Prentice-Hall.

Ekman, P., Friesen, W. V., & Ellsworth, P. (1972). *Emotion in the human face.* New York: Pergamon Press.

Formica, S. (1998). *Describing the socio-emotional life space.* Unpublished senior honor's thesis, University of New Hampshire.

Funder, D. C. (2001). *The personality puzzle* (2nd ed.). New York: Norton.

Geher, G., & Renstrom, K. L. (2004). Measurement issues in emotional intelligence research. In G. Geher (Ed.), *Measuring emotional intelligence: Common ground and controversy* (pp. 1–17). Hauppauge, NY: Nova Science.

Geher, G., Warner, R. M., & Brown, A. S. (2001). Predictive validity of the Emotional Accuracy Research Scale. *Intelligence, 29,* 373–388.

Gignac, G. E. (2005). Evaluating the MSCEIT V2.0 via CFA: Comment on Mayer et al. (2003). *Emotion, 5,* 233–235.

Gil-Olarte Márquez, P., Palomera Martín, R., & Brackett, M. A. (2006). Relating emotional intelligence to social competence and academic achievement in high school students. *Psicothema, 18,* 118–123.

Gohm, C. L. (2004). Moving forward with emotional intelligence. *Psychological Inquiry, 15,* 222–227.

Gohm, C. L., & Clore, G. L. (2002). Four latent traits of emotional experience and their involvement in well-being, coping, and attributional style. *Cognition and Emotion, 16,* 495–518.

Goleman, D. (1995). *Emotional intelligence.* New York: Bantam Books.

Goleman, D. (1998). *Working with emotional intelligence.* New York: Bantam Books.

Greenberg, M. T., Kusche, C. A., Cook, E. T., & Quamma, J. P. (1995). Promoting emotional competence in school-aged children: The effects of the PATHS curriculum. *Development and Psychopathology, 7*, 117–136.

Grewal, D. D., & Salovey, P. (2005). Feeling smart: The science of emotional intelligence. *American Scientist, 93*, 330–339.

Hall, J. A. (2001). The PONS Test and the psychometric approach to measuring interpersonal sensitivity. In J. A. Hall & F. J. Bernieri (Eds.), *Interpersonal sensitivity: Theory and measurement* (pp. 143–160). Mahwah, NJ: Erlbaum.

Izard, C. E., Trentacosta, C. J., King, K. A., & Mostow, A. J. (2004). An emotion-based prevention program for Head Start children. *Early Education and Development, 15*, 407–422.

Janovics, J., & Christiansen, N. D. (2002). *Emotional intelligence in the workplace.* Paper presented at the 16th Annual Conference of the Society of Industrial and Organizational Psychology, San Diego, CA.

Jausovec, N., Jausovec, K., & Gerlic, I. (2001). Differences in event-related and induced electro-encephalography patterns in the theta and alpha frequency bands related to human emotional intelligence. *Neuroscience Letters, 311*, 93–96.

Kafetsios, K. (2004). Attachment and emotional intelligence abilities across the life course. *Personality and Individual Differences, 37*, 129–145.

Kang, S., Day, J. D., Meara, N. M. (2005). Social and emotional intelligence: Starting a conversation about their similarities and differences. In R. Schulze & R. D. Roberts (Eds.), *Emotional intelligence: An international handbook* (pp. 91–105). Cambridge, MA: Hogrefe & Huber.

Kang, S., & Shaver, P. R. (2004). Individual differences in emotional complexity: Their psychological implications. *Journal of Personality, 72*, 687–726.

Keltner, D., & Kring, A. M. (1998). Emotion, social function, and psychopathology. *Review of General Psychology, 2*, 320–342.

Lane, R. D., & Pollermann, B. Z. (2002). Complexity of emotion representations. In L. F. Barrett & P. Salovey (Eds.), *The wisdom in feeling: Psychological processes in emotional intelligence* (pp. 271–293). New York: Guilford Press.

Lane, R. D., Quinlan, D. M., Schwartz, G. E., Walker, P. A., & Zeitlin, S. B. (1990). The Levels of Emotional Awareness Scale: A cognitive-developmental measure of emotion. *Journal of Personality Assessment, 55*, 124–134.

Lazarus, R. S. (1991). *Emotion and adaptation.* New York: Oxford University Press.

Legree, P. J. (1995). Evidence for an oblique social intelligence factor established with a Likert-based testing procedure. *Intelligence, 21*, 247–266.

Legree, P. J., Psotka, J., Tremble, T., & Bourne, D. R. (2005). Using consensus based measurement to assess emotional intelligence. In R. Schulze & R. D. Roberts (Eds.), *Emotional intelligence: An international handbook* (pp. 155–179). Cambridge, MA: Hogrefe & Huber.

Livingstone, H. A., & Day, A. L. (2005). Comparing the construct and criterion-related validity of ability-based and mixed model measures of emotional intelligence. *Educational and Psychological Measurement, 65*, 757–779.

Lopes, P. N., Brackett, M. A., Nezlek, J. B., Schütz, A., Sellin, I., & Salovey, P. (2004). Emotional intelligence and social interaction. *Personality and Social Psychological Bulletin, 30*, 1018–1034.

Lopes, P. N., Côté, S., & Salovey, P. (2006). An ability model of emotional intelligence: Implications for assessment and training. In V. Druskat, F. Sala, & G. Mount (Eds.), *Linking emotional intelligence and performance at work* (pp. 53–80). Mahwah, NJ: Erlbaum.

Lopes, P. N., Grewal, D., Kadis, J., Gall, M., & Salovey, P. (2006). Evidence that emotional intelligence is related to job performance and affect and attitudes at work. *Psicothema, 18,* 132–138.

Lopes, P. N., & Salovey, P. (2004). Toward a broader education: Social, emotional and practical skills. In J. E. Zins, R. P. Weissberg, M. C. Wang & H. J. Walberg (Eds.), *Building academic success on social and emotional learning: What does the research say?* (pp. 76–93). New York: Teachers College Press.

Lopes, P. N., Salovey, P., Côté, S., & Beers, M. (2005). Emotion regulation abilities and the quality of social interaction. *Emotion, 5,* 113–118.

Lopes, P. N., Salovey, P., & Straus, R. (2003). Emotional intelligence, personality, and the perceived quality of social relationships. *Personality and Individual Differences, 35,* 641–658.

Mabe, P. A., & West, S. G. (1982). Validity of self-evaluation of ability: A review and meta-analysis. *Journal of Applied Psychology, 67,* 280–296.

MacCann, C., Matthews, G., Zeidner, M., & Roberts, R. D. (2004). The assessment of emotional intelligence: On frameworks, fissures, and the future. In G. Geher (Ed.), *Measuring emotional intelligence: Common ground and controversy* (pp. 19–50). Hauppauge, NY: Nova Science.

Matsumoto, D., LeRoux, J., Wilson-Cohn, C., Raroque, J., Kooken, K., Ekman, P., et al. (2000). A new test to measure emotion recognition ability: Matsumoto and Ekman's Japanese and Caucasian Brief Affect Recognition Test (JACBERT). *Journal of Nonverbal Behavior, 24,* 179–209.

Matthews, G., Zeidner, M., & Roberts, R. D. (2002). *Emotional intelligence: Science and myth.* Cambridge, MA: MIT Press.

Mayer, J. D. (2004). A classification system for the data of personality psychology and adjoining fields. *Review of General Psychology, 8,* 208–219.

Mayer, J. D., Caruso, D. R., & Salovey, P. (1999). Emotional intelligence meets traditional standards for an intelligence. *Intelligence, 27,* 267–298.

Mayer, J. D., Caruso, D. R., & Salovey, P. (2000). Selecting a measure of emotional intelligence: The case for ability scales. In R. Bar-On & J. D. A. Parker (Eds.), *The handbook of emotional intelligence: Theory, development, assessment, and application at home, school, and in the workplace* (pp. 320–342). San Francisco, CA: Jossey-Bass.

Mayer, J. D., Caruso, D., & Salovey, P. (2005). *The Mayer-Salovey-Caruso Emotional Intelligence Test–Youth Version (MSCEIT-YV).* Toronto, Canada: Multi Health Systems.

Mayer, J. D., & Geher, G. (1996). Emotional intelligence and the identification of emotion. *Intelligence, 22,* 89–114.

Mayer, J. D., Panter, A., Salovey, P., Caruso, D. R., & Sitarenios, G. (2005). A discrepancy in analyses of the MSCEIT—Resolving the mystery and understanding its implications: A reply to Gignac (2005). *Emotion, 5,* 236–237.

Mayer, J. D., & Salovey, P. (1997). What is emotional intelligence? In P. Salovey & D. J. Sluyter (Eds.), *Emotional development and emotional intelligence: Educational implications* (pp. 3–34). New York: Basic Books.

Mayer, J. D., Salovey, P., & Caruso, D. (2002a). *The Mayer-Salovey-Caruso Emotional Intelligence Test (MSCEIT), Version 2.0.* Toronto, Canada: Multi Health Systems.

Mayer, J. D., Salovey, P., & Caruso, D. (2002b). *MSCEIT technical manual.* Toronto, Canada: Multi Health Systems.

Mayer, J. D., Salovey, P., & Caruso, D. R. (2004). Emotional intelligence: Theory, findings, and implications. *Psychological Inquiry, 15,* 197–215.

Mayer, J. D., Salovey, P., Caruso, D. L., & Sitarenios, G. (2001). Emotional intelligence as a standard intelligence. *Emotion, 1*, 232–242.

Mayer, J. D., Salovey, P., Caruso, D. R., & Sitarenios, G. (2003). Measuring emotional intelligence with the MSCEIT V2.0. *Emotion, 3*, 97–105.

Neisser, U., Boodoo, G., Bouchard, T. J., Jr., Boykin, A., Brody, N., Ceci, S. J., et al. (1996). Intelligence: Knowns and unknowns. *American Psychologist, 51*, 77–101.

Nowicki, S., & Carton, J. (1993). The measurement of emotional intensity from facial expressions. *Journal of Social Psychology, 133*, 749–750.

Nowicki, S., & Duke, M. P. (2001). Nonverbal receptivity: The Diagnostic Analysis of Nonverbal Accuracy (DANVA). In J. A. Hall & F. J. Bernieri (Eds.), *Interpersonal sensitivity: Theory and measurement* (pp. 183–198). Mahwah, NJ: Erlbaum.

Nunnally, J. C. (1967). *Psychometric theory*. New York: McGraw-Hill.

O'Connor, R. M., & Little, I. S. (2003). Revisiting the predictive validity of emotional intelligence: Self-report versus ability-based measures. *Personality and Individual Differences, 35*, 1893–1902.

O'Sullivan, M., & Ekman, P. (2004). Facial expression recognition and emotional intelligence. In G. Geher (Ed.), *Emotional intelligence: Common ground and controversy.* (pp. 89–109). Hauppauge, NY: Nova Science.

Palmer, B. R., Gignac, G. E., Manocha, R. & Stough, C. (2005). A psychometric evaluation of the Mayer-Salovey-Caruso Emotional Intelligence Test. *Intelligence, 33*, 285–305.

Parrott, W. G. (2002). The functional utility of negative emotions. In L. F. Barrett & P. Salovey (Eds.), *The wisdom in feeling: Psychological processes in emotional intelligence* (pp. 341–359). New York: Guilford Press.

Paulhus, D. L., Lysy, D. C., & Yik, M. S. M. (1998). Self-report measures of intelligence: Are they useful as proxy IQ tests? *Journal of Personality, 66*, 525–554.

Petrides, K. V., & Furnham, A. (2001). Trait emotional intelligence: Psychometric investigation with reference to established trait taxonomies. *European Journal of Personality, 15*, 425–448.

Petrides, K. V., & Furnham, A. (2003). Trait emotional intelligence: Behavioural validation in two studies of emotion recognition and reactivity to mood induction. *European Journal of Personality, 17*, 39–57.

Reis, D. L., Brackett, M. A., Salovey, P., & Gray, J. R. (2007). Emotional intelligence predicts individual differences in social exchange reasoning. *NeuroImage, 35*, 1385–1391.

Rivers, S. E., Brackett, M. A., & Salovey, P. (in press). Measuring emotional intelligence as a mental ability in adults and children. In G. J. Boyle, G. Matthews, & D. H. Saklofske (Eds.), *Handbook of personality theory and testing*. London, UK: Sage Publications.

Rosenthal, R., Hall, J. A., DiMatteo, M. R., Rogers, P. L., & Archer, D. (1979). *Sensitivity to nonverbal communication: A profile approach to the measurement of individual differences.* Baltimore, MD: The Johns Hopkins University Press.

Rosete, D., & Ciarrochi, J. (2005). Emotional intelligence and its relationship to workplace performance outcomes of leadership effectiveness. *Leadership and Organizational Development Journal, 26*, 388–399.

Rubin, M. M. (1999). Emotional intelligence and its role in mitigating aggression: A correlational study of the relationship between emotional intelligence and aggression in urban adolescents. Unpublished manuscript, Immaculata College, Immaculata, PA.

Ryff, C. D. (1989). Happiness is everything, or is it? Explorations on the meaning of psychological well-being. *Journal of Personality and Social Psychology, 57*, 1069–1081.

Salovey, P., & Grewal, D. (2005). The science of emotional intelligence. *Current Directions in Psychological Science, 14,* 281–285.

Salovey, P., & Mayer, J. D. (1990). Emotional intelligence. *Imagination, Cognition and Personality, 9,* 185–211.

Scherer, K. R. (2003). Vocal communication of emotion: A review of research paradigms. *Speech Communication, 40,* 227–256.

Scherer, K. R., Banse, R., & Wallbott, H. G. (2001). Emotion inferences from vocal expression correlate across languages and cultures. *Journal of Cross Cultural Psychology, 32,* 76–92.

Schulte, M. J., Ree, M. J., & Carretta, T. R. (2004). Emotional intelligence: Not much more than g and personality. *Personality and Individual Differences, 37,* 1059–1068.

Schutte, N. S., Malouff, J. M., Hall, L. E., Haggerty, D. J., Cooper, J. T., Golden, C. J., et al. (1998). Development and validation of a measure of emotional intelligence. *Personality and Individual Differences, 25,* 167–177.

Shaver, P., Schwartz, J., Kirson, D., & O'Connor, C. (1987). Emotion knowledge: Further exploration of a prototype approach. *Journal of Personality and Social Psychology, 52,* 1061–1086.

Shields, S. A. (2002). *Speaking from the heart: Gender and the social meaning of emotion.* New York: Cambridge University Press.

Trinidad, D. R., & Johnson, C. (2002). The association between emotional intelligence and early adolescent tobacco and alcohol use. *Personality and Individual Differences, 32,* 95–105.

Van Rooy, D. L., & Viswesvaran, C. (2004). Emotional intelligence: A meta-analytic investigation of predictive validity and nomological net. *Journal of Vocational Behavior, 65,* 71–95.

Van Rooy, D. L., Viswesvaran, C., & Pluta, P. (2005). An evaluation of construct validity: What is this thing call emotional intelligence? *Human Performance, 18,* 445–462.

Warwick, J., & Nettelbeck, T. (2004). Emotional intelligence is…? *Personality and Individual Differences, 37,* 1091–1100.

Zeidner, M., Shani-Zinovich, I., Matthews, G., & Roberts, R. D. (2005). Assessing emotional intelligence in gifted and non-gifted high school students: Outcomes depend on the measure. *Intelligence, 33,* 369–391.

10

Trolling for Trout, Trawling for Tuna

The Methodological Morass in Measuring Emotional Intelligence

MAUREEN O'SULLIVAN

> Popular interest in EI has at times tended to obscure definitional clarity....The term is too often used in the most all-encompassing and protean of ways, thus leaving it bereft of conceptual meaning.
> —Zeidner, Roberts, & Matthews, 2002, p. 215

This chapter addresses questions about the appropriateness of various cognitive approaches in assessing emotional intelligence (EI). The value of any methodology, however, is inextricably wedded to the variable being measured. Construct validity pertains not just to a particular test but to the construct or attribute it is supposed to measure. Validity is not about "a property of tests but about a property of test score interpretation...about the complex question of whether test score interpretations are consistent with a nomological network involving theoretical and observational terms (Cronbach & Meehl, 1955) and with an even more complicated system of theoretical rationales, empirical data, and social consequences of testing" (Borsboom, Mellenbergh, & van Heerden, 2004, p. 1061).[1] Obviously, if the construct is incomplete or overly inclusive, trying to establish the validity of tests designed to measure it is rather like trying to catch trout with a bathtub. Very difficult; and not likely to yield fish in time for dinner. Therefore, this chapter will also consider some of the assumptions underlying a few of the many EI measures currently in use.

Many methods have been suggested for assessing emotional intelligence. This chapter will emphasize two of them: (1) understanding the emotions of other adults from facial expressions and (2) understanding complex social-emotional scenarios or situations involving information from a variety of sources. These limitations will exclude interesting EI-relevant work done in related fields such as dyadic empathic accuracy (Ickes, 1993), emotional accuracy within couples (Levenson & Ruef, 1992), the dialectical relation between emotion and cognition (Forgas & Ciarrochi, 2002; Gohm, 2003), the consequences of variance partitioning in round-robin paradigms (Kenny, 2004), the processes involved in dispositional inferences (Trope & Higgins, 1993), and social cognition (Fiske, 1992) as well as the many self-report measures of "emotional intelligence" (e.g., Bar-On, 2004) that probably measure facets of personality rather than facets of intelligence.

In examining cognitive assessment of EI, we are considering whether two fields with different historical trajectories can inform one another (Schweizer, 2005). Traditionally, those interested in intelligence have been interested in individual differences (who is really good or really bad) in some ability relevant to an important life activity (e.g., school performance or job productivity; recall that IQ tests arose from Binet's practical desire to assign schoolchildren to the proper classes). *Individual differences* implies testing many people in order to demonstrate and reify a score distribution related to an attribute or trait and to classify individuals according to where they fall on that distribution. This concern for the ways in which people differ is the hallmark of clinical and educational applications of psychological knowledge. Cognition, on the other hand, suggests a descriptive (rather than a prescriptive) interest in the typical processes involved in thinking. Cognitive scientists are usually concerned with the midpoint of the distribution rather than the tails. They are interested in what is usually the case, rather than what is problematic or outstanding. Cognitive studies usually involve only a few subjects, at least when compared with the triple-digit N's associated with individual differences research.

Certainly, findings in one field inform those in the other, but the emphases and concerns of researchers in these two areas are often divergent. Where they may converge is in studying people at the tails of the distribution—the truly maladroit by virtue of mental illness or injury or the truly expert by reason of native talent and/or motivated experience. Within the emotional intelligence realm, both those concerned with individual differences and those concerned with basic processes should be interested in social-emotional geniuses or social-emotional "cretins," because an examination of "how they do it" may shed light on the processes involved in the social-emotional intelligence of all people.

Are We Talking Bricks, or Are We Talking Cathedrals?

Although a cathedral may be built of bricks, the two are not identical and close examination of the bricks alone will not reveal the shape of the cathedral. That depends on the talent of the architect and the mastery of the brick masons. In the realm of EI, we often vacillate between bricks and cathedrals, and often confuse bricks and stones. Because this medieval metaphor may not resonate with some readers, let's consider two modern behaviors that, like EI, involve both knowledge (understanding) and action (managing or self-regulating) based on that knowledge, namely, budgeting money and budgeting calories. Many slim people have equally slim bank accounts. They know about calories and the calorie/exercise ratios and act, either consciously, or unconsciously, on that knowledge. There is often no generalization, however, from budgeting calories to budgeting cash. They may understand the relationship between capital and spending, intellectually, but they are unable or unwilling to act on the knowledge. Other people have enviable bank accounts and less enviable physiques. Their knowledge and self-management skills operate in different arenas. On a multiple-choice test, both groups might show similar abstract knowledge of calories and credit. This information will be utilized differently, however, depending on their motivations, life experiences, and discipline, as well as their self-management abilities in these two different areas. The same bricks will result in two quite different cathedrals, or perhaps, in a gym and a bank.

Clinical practitioners, business consultants, popular writers, serious researchers, and scores of other groups use the term *EI* to refer to anything related to understanding one-self and other people, even if the "emotional" connection is rather tenuous (O'Sullivan, 2002). In some cases, they are referring to the EI equivalent of calories; in others, to the EI equivalent of cash. Should we be surprised that findings in different realms differ? And if cognitive knowledge of calories and cash is only marginally related to whether one eats sensibly or spends sensibly, why should we expect tests of the ability to recognize facial expressions, for example, to predict complex social behaviors?

Why most of us expect this nowadays is why Thorndike (1920) and Guilford (1929) expected it long ago. Vocabulary is at the core of general intelligence, or *g*. In our early work, we (O'Sullivan, Guilford, & de Mille, 1965) thought that understanding the behavioral units of communication (i.e., facial expression, gestures, prosody, body postures) would provide a similar Rosetta stone in measuring what Guilford called behavioral intelligence (Guilford, 1956). What we (O'Sullivan & Guilford, 1975) found, however, was that facial expressions were either too easy (everyone got them right—to be expected if such expressions are universal [Ekman et al., 1987; Izard, Chapter 5, this volume]), or too difficult, so idiosyncratic to the person showing them that no one got them right (see also O'Sullivan & Ekman, 2004, for other issues involved in measuring the ability to recognize facial expressions of emotion).

Certainly, as knowledge of cash or calories is a necessary, but not sufficient, contributor to wise life choices, so, too, knowledge of emotional expression may be a necessary, but certainly not a sufficient, contributor to understanding other people.[2] For example, although Ekman and O'Sullivan (1991) and Frank and Ekman (1997) found that facial expression recognition correlated significantly with the ability to tell whether others were lying, these correlations were moderate, accounting for less than 20% of the variance. In other work, we (O'Sullivan, 2005; O'Sullivan & Ekman, 2005) have reported that "expert" (i.e., highly accurate) lie detectors, although very sensitive to a wide variety of facial emotional behaviors, also attend to other, nonfacial and nonemotional clues.

Response Variability = Attribute Variability?

Because many of the "basic" human emotions have universal, easily recognizable facial expressions, variability in recognizing them is not likely to provide much useful score variance for an individual difference test. Unlike vocabulary words, which must be learned in one's cultural language group, recognition of basic facial expressions may be so biologically hardwired, so "innate," so easy for normal people that they fail to provide discriminating items. Asking young children to describe the difference between a dog and a horse may provide information about their verbal and abstract reasoning skills. This question might be useful in discriminating among adults with mental retardation or other abnormalities of mind, but it provides little discrimination among normal and high-functioning people.

This easy recognizability of basic facial expressions (the stimuli) may be why many researchers have increased the difficulty of the response required for facial expression recognition tests—either presenting the stimulus very rapidly (Matsumoto et al., 2000), blending two or more facial expressions (O'Sullivan, 1983), using subtle or idiosyncratic facial expressions (Ekman, 2003b; Mayer, Salovey, & Caruso, 2002) or consensual scoring (Mayer et al., 2002; Nowicki & Duke 2001).

But if the score variance is the result of the response format rather than the information in the face, can we really call it recognizing facial emotion? Is this why so few facial expression measures provide convergent validity for one another? With the MSCEIT (Mayer et al., 2002), the authors' intention is to measure *sensitivity* to the feelings of others. Sensitivity may not be the same as accuracy. The items of the MSCEIT Faces subtest relating to this "sensitive to the feelings of others" "ability" include complex, subtle, and idiosyncratic facial expressions as well as emotion-related paintings. It is not clear whether the Faces subtest converges with more "classic" measures of accuracy in facial expression recognition, although a recent unpublished Finnish study (Ekman, personal communication, August 23, 2005) found a significant correlation between MSCEIT and Ekman's Subtle Expression Training Tool.

Most emotion researchers (Ekman et al., 1987) assume the existence of a few basic, biologically based emotions. There are exceptions (Carroll & Russell, 1996) as well as interest in other kinds of feelings that may be more susceptible to environmental variation. No emotion theorist, however, conflates identification of facial expressions with identification of the emotion in art. (Chamorro-Premuzic and Furnham [2004–2005], however, found that art judgment was significantly correlated with both personality and IQ.) The MSCEIT's blend of faces and art judgments is an innovative test construction procedure, but it does remove scores on this subtest from the realm of facial expression recognition tests at a conceptual as well as at an empirical level because little evidence has been offered of correlation between this subtest and tests that are limited to recognizing facial expressions of emotion accurately. Sensitivity to feelings of various sorts, in various stimuli, may be a mark of an emotionally intelligent, or at any rate, an emotionally sensitive person, but whether this is "accuracy" as the test authors argue, or consensually shared feeling-sensitivity remains to be seen.

Scores on the total MSCEIT, however, have convergent validity with a variety of emotion-related behaviors, such as drug use and relationship success (Brackett & Mayer, 2003), so the test has criterion validity if one wishes to predict those social outcomes and construct validity depending on how one defines emotional intelligence. It may be that sharing the emotional perceptions of one's cultural group, whether they are actually correct or not, is a predictor of social success. Some evidence for this interpretation is suggested by Brackett and Mayer's (2003) finding that NEO agreeableness loaded on the MSCEIT EI factor. If one wishes to claim that this subtest of the MSCEIT relates to the ability to recognize facial expressions of emotion, however, significant correlations with other facial expression measures using other stimuli and other responses are needed.

Another example of the impact of response type on attribute validity is the Profile of Nonverbal Sensitivity (PONS; Rosenthal, Hall, DiMatteo, Rogers, & Archer, 1979). Although the PONS predates the current interest in what is now called emotional intelligence, by attempting to measure nonverbal or interpersonal sensitivity (Hall, 2001), the concerns of the authors place it directly in the shade of the EI umbrella. The PONS consists of 220 10-second videotaped clips of a single woman (Judith Hall) posing a variety of situations, such as admiring nature or talking to a lost child. Most of the emotional communication in the facial expression items is quite clear. It is obvious that the emotion intended is happy or angry, for example. The task, however, is not labeling the emotion shown, but rather, choosing the one of two social situations in which the emotion is likely to occur.

Because Americans and other English-speaking examinees did better on this task than members of other cultures (Hall, 2001), it is likely that the social appropriateness of the facial expression for a particular situation is a significant contributor to obtaining a correct score. This is no trivial skill. In fact, it may be more highly correlated with real-life social ability than the disembodied "decoding" of "pure" facial expressions of emotions. In fact, Rosenthal and his colleagues (1979) conducted many creative studies demonstrating that the PONS was significantly correlated with life situations requiring social or emotional intelligence, such as success as a Foreign Service officer, being the mother of a preverbal as opposed to an older child. So, as a measure of social skill, the PONS has convergent validity. But scores on the facial expression subtest did not correlate with other facial expression measures (O'Sullivan, 1982) or with other social skill tests such as the IPT (Costanzo & Archer, 1993; Hall, 2001).

On the other hand, Nowicki and Duke (2001) have reported a significant correlation between the DANVA and the PONS. The DANVA uses photographs of prototypic emotions, but photographs are included in the test only if 80% of 10-year-old children agreed with the key. And the correct answer is determined by consensus. Again, it may be that such scores reflect social appropriateness rather than accurate identification of facial expressions of emotion. Consider the analogue in the abstract intelligence area. Would a teacher construct a test of geography including only items that 80% of 10-year-olds got correct, regardless of whether the items were accurate on the basis of physical reality? Suppose such scores correlated with interest in travel or success as a travel agent? Would we conclude that this result was due to knowledge of geography or some other aspect of human functioning?

Nowicki and his colleagues (e.g., Nowicki & Duke, 1994; Nowicki & Mitchell, 1998) report that scores on DANVA correlate significantly with peer popularity and adult judgments. They attribute this to the ability to recognize facial expressions correctly. Given the DANVA response format, an alternative hypothesis is that high scorers see other people in ways similar to those of other test takers. Similarity is a basis for interpersonal attraction or popularity, and this similarity may be the reason for their popularity with peers and adults, rather than emotion recognition ability.

In cognitive studies, particularly those involving brain imaging, the stimuli presented and the response required are usually quite limited. The previous analysis of the meaning of scores based on facial expression recognition tests is offered in order to maximize the success of such neurological studies. Tests can have criterion validity for important real-life behaviors without being correctly named. The precision of our construct labeling must be improved if we wish to increase our understanding of how people use their emotions to lead successful lives.

Stimulus Specification—The Case of the Smile

Understanding what the impact of the required response is on score distribution is only part of the picture; comprehension of the stimuli used is also necessary. Although Ekman and Friesen (1978) developed a reliable system for describing facial behavior, including emotional facial behavior, it is rare that constructors of facial expression recognition tests provide this rather rudimentary description of the stimuli used in their tests. Why this is important is suggested by the value added in distinguishing true enjoyment smiles (what has been called "Duchenne" smiles by Ekman, Davidson, & Friesen, 1990) from nonenjoyment smiles (which can include masking, mixed, or polite smiles). Although truth tellers and liars can be distinguished on the basis of the kinds of smiles they show (Ekman, Friesen, & O'Sullivan, 1988), deception researchers continue to collapse both kinds of smiles, and then report no significant difference between lying and truthful smile behavior (DePaulo et al., 2003). Obviously, if amount of smiling is the same in lying and truthful conditions, but the kind of smile shown (felt enjoyment vs. nonfelt enjoyment) is not, using only the total number of smiles is misleading. By analogy, if false smiles are shown in an EI test and a consensus is reached that the person is happy, the truly astute facial expression observer who can distinguish fake from felt smiles will receive a lower score.

Another example of this necessary specification of the elements of facial behavior involved in smiling is given by Woodzicka and LaFrance (2005), who reported no difference in the amount of overall smiling of sexually harassed and nonharassed job applicants, but significant differences in the amount of Duchenne smiling. In addition, women showing non-Duchenne smiles (caused by the harassing experimental situation) were rated as less likely to be hired by judges shown just their video with no information about the experimental paradigm. In other words, a slight difference in a single nonverbal emotional communication had a profound impact on whether one would be hired.

Total amount of smiling does not differentiate deception and truth, or harassment from nonharassment, but kind of smile does. By ignoring such slight, but important differences, nonresults result. If nonverbal behaviors are going to be used in expensive cognitive imaging studies, such differences must be calibrated and appropriate stimuli used.

Can Self-Reports and Questionnaires Ever Provide Assessments of Intelligence and Competence?

Yes, if examinees are asked to report on abilities for which they have received feedback or confirmation. Most people know whether they can lift heavy weights or sing well. In the social behavioral realm, Ekman (2001) suggests that people know whether they are good liars because they know whether they have gotten away with their lies, are too afraid to attempt to lie, or have failed miserably when they did undertake to dissemble. Furnham and Chamorro-Premuzic (2004) have reported moderate correlation ($r = .30$) between self-rated and measured IQ, perhaps because of the relationship between school grades (available information) and IQ.

On the other hand, when feedback is unavailable or imperfect (as in the case of knowledge about some personality traits and other dispositions), correlations between self-reports and objective measures are essentially zero (Ekman & O'Sullivan, 1991; Patterson, Foster, & Bellmer, 2001). Because most people think they have a good sense of humor, self-ratings in this area are also uncorrelated with objective measures of sense of humor (Abad & O'Sullivan, 2001).

Kolar, Funder, and Colvin (1996) found that the ratings of acquaintances were more accurate than self-ratings of general personality attributes based on a videotaped interview. Spain, Eaton, and Funder (2000) refined this finding: People's ratings of their daily emotional experiences and their extroverted behavior in a laboratory setting were more accurate than ratings made by acquaintances. Acquaintances, however, were more accurate in rating laboratory behavior related to neuroticism. They concluded that "self-reports are clearly better for the prediction of emotional experience, while for (overt) behavior the picture is mixed" (p. 838).

Ratings of others, however, can be useful in assessing the competence of targets. Davis and Krauss (1997) did a meta-analysis of the relationship between 30 different interpersonal accuracy measures and 32 different individual differences measures. One of the highest individual effect sizes was for reputational social sensitivity. (Other significant relationships were found for intelligence, cognitive style, positive adjustment, social intelligence, interpersonal trust, acting ability, extraversion and other-directedness.)

The question of self-reports of competence, of course, relates to the many "EI" self-report scales (e.g., Bar-On, 2004) that have rather conclusively been shown to measure factors essentially indistinguishable from those measured by personality tests (Barchard & Hakstian, 2004; MacCann, Matthews, Zeidner, & Roberts, 2003). There are, however, behavior-related skills for which the individual concerned may be the best source of information. In the case of "trait" EI or personality-related social behavior, one's self-perception may be reliably related to the extrafamilial contexts one chooses (Pike & Plomin, 1997). These contexts may reinforce or strengthen different aspects of the self, thereby validating one's self-perception. This increased confidence in self-view may then affect the judgments of others.

Such self-ratings may predict socially important outcomes. If a person reports preferring to be alone, it is unlikely that he or she will be perceived as sociable. Insofar as a job or an activity involves sociability, that will affect performance in the situation. There are many introverts who are highly competent managers, although the social interactions involved in managing others depletes their ego resources (Baumeister, Bratlavsky, Muraven, & Tice, 1998) more than it would if they were extroverted. Prediction of managerial success in this instance will be less related to self-reported EI or to extroversion or introversion than to the motivation to succeed at the job. The EI-competent introvert, if sufficiently motivated by needs for status, security, or a host of other job-relevant motives, can choose to manage his or her preference for reduced stimulation through meditation or other self-management tools. The less–EI-talented extrovert, on the other hand, with little ego depletion caused by social stimulation, can use his or her energy to compensate for a lesser degree of job or emotional competence.

In other words, it is not the method, self-report or performance-based, that is the difficulty, but what is asked about. As indicated above, people know whether they are good liars, but not how accurate they are in detecting deception. Although. research with several groups of expert lie detectors (Ekman, O'Sullivan, & Frank, 1999) as well as with a small group of "truth wizards" (O'Sullivan & Ekman, 2004), suggests that most of these highly accurate, but rare, individuals knew beforehand that they were good at detecting deception.

Another example of the possibility that some self-report measures may reflect competence rather than personality is suggested by research with the Social Skills Inventory (Riggio, 1989), a self-report measure of communication skill in six areas: emotional expressivity, social expressivity, emotional sensitivity, social sensitivity, emotional control, and social control. Eaton, Funder, and Riggio (2005) found that scores on the social control scale (which they interpreted as an aspect of savoir-faire) predicted differential social behavior in cooperative and competitive interactions with strangers. Acquaintances also rated high "savoir-faire" individuals as high in social poise. We know whether we have handled a social interaction well. Information about whether we have been accurately "sensitive" or "expressive" of our emotions may not be as veridical.

There is significant evidence that personality characteristics are predictive of social success and the ability to understand others (Riggio, Salinas, & Tucker, 1988; Riggio, Tucker, & Throckmorton, 1987). Personality may help us understand how EI functions (Lieberman & Rosenthal, 2001), but we have more explanatory power if we keep these concepts separate. For example, Shipe, Rosser, and Sidhu (1973) divided 462 nonacademic high school students into four groups based on whether they were high or low on need for affiliation and high or low on social-emotional intelligence using some of the O'Sullivan-Guilford (1975) tests. Those high on both need for affiliation *and* behavioral intelligence were those who received the highest peer ratings and the most sociometric choices.

Is Consensus Scoring Valid for Ability Measures?

It depends on what kind of ability one is interested in. Legree, Psotka, Tremble, and Bourne (2005) have argued eloquently for the use of consensus-based scoring in ability measures in situations in which expert judges or some other criterion is unavailable, as well as for the more extreme position, that "diverse groups of novices may have a more accurate reflection of truth than experts" (p. 163).

Although Legree and his colleagues presented data showing that the correlation between real-life accuracy and consensus scoring in a test of driving skill was highly correlated, experience with tests of the ability to detect deception suggests that the opposite is the case. Consensus about what honesty and deceptiveness looks like is often incorrect and is one of the many cognitive inaccuracies that contribute to most people's inability to tell when others are lying (O'Sullivan, 2003a).

In addition to Legree, many theorists have commented on the pros and cons of consensus scoring. They also have suggested several different interpretations of what such scores might mean. Over fifty years ago, Cronbach (1955), in attempting to clarify that era's attempt to measure interpersonal sensitivity, argued that if an accuracy score is based on the correlation between John's ratings of Mary and Mary's ratings of herself, whether John receives a high or a low score will be affected by the following factors:

1. Projection—insofar as John thinks everyone is like him, and Mary is in fact like him, he will get a spuriously high score on ratings of Mary, but do less well on people who are dissimilar to him.
2. Stereotypic accuracy—John may have a good idea of what most people are like, and he rates Mary based on that knowledge of other people. If John's ideas about "most people" are correct, and Mary is, indeed, like most people, this bias will also increase his accuracy in judging Mary. He will do less well, however, with the one-third of people who are not typical.
3. Elevation bias—people may tend to routinely rate others as very high or very low. Insofar as the individuals being rated actually are very high or very low, accuracy scores will be artificially increased.
4. Differential accuracy—this is what most researchers want to measure: Is John able to differentiate Mary from himself (not projection), from most other people (not stereotypic accuracy), and to do so within a wide variation of ratings (no elevation bias)?

At the time, Cronbach's critique of interpersonal sensitivity research was so convincing and so thorough that the field essentially collapsed.

By the late 1980s, advances in computer technology and statistics encouraged researchers to control for these biases through statistical and experimental paradigms. Kenny's (1996, 2005) work in this area was particularly influential. He proposed a model of dyadic relationship in which analyses were done not only on the scores generated by the observer, but also on the characteristics of the person judging and the person being judged. By changing the unit of analyses and by identifying the various components of influence, Kenny was able to identify the sources of variance underlying the ratings.

Funder (2001) discussed other ways of controlling for biases such as consensus bias, essentially by statistically partialing it out or removing it from the score. This penalizes the individual with good stereotypic or consensus accuracy (as noted above) and as Funder (2001) wrote,

> If a judge of personality attains some of his or her accuracy through a profound understanding of general human nature, should this be held against him or her? It seems reasonable to expect that an understanding of human nature is part of judging particular humans, and that if one is interested in the difference between judges who are more and less accurate then one would want to include not "correct for" this understanding. (p. 326)

Sternberg, Wagner, Williams, and Horvath (1995) used consensus scoring for theoretical purposes to measure Wagner and Sternberg's concept of tacit knowledge or succeeding in different contexts (sometimes called "street smarts"). Because consensus is a conceptually compelling basis for keying such a test, it provides another example of a situation in which consensus scoring is useful.

It is ironic, therefore, that we have come not merely full circle, but are peeling through a veritable Mobius strip with respect to consensus scores. Consensus or stereotypic accuracy has gone from a bias to be avoided (Cronbach), to an error to be controlled or identified (Kenny), to a potential source of information about understanding people in the absence of specific information (Funder), to the criterion for accuracy (Sternberg), not only for items for which no veridical criterion is available, and therefore consensus is a stopgap measure (Nowicki) or a desirable one (Mayer), to arguments that consensus scoring is actually superior to known truth as the criterion for accuracy test items (Legree).

As in most things, moderation is probably preferable. Knowledge of general human traits, or agreement with what most people believe, may provide useful insights into understanding other people. As such, it is an ability clearly within the domain of emotional intelligence. Test constructors, however, should be clearer about what they are attempting to measure. Consensus can be an approximation to veridical reality or a substitute for it. But without compelling evidence, it does not guarantee a reflection of ground truth or provide a criterion for determining the accuracy of responses. (Also see earlier discussion of facial expression recognition with consensual scoring.)

What Are the Prospects for Assessment of EI Using Psychophysiological and Neurological Measures?

If one extends the scope of emotional intelligence somewhat, there is already quite extensive psychophysiological and neurological literatures related to how people identify, experience, and manage emotions. Levenson and Gottman (1983) hypothesized psychophysiological linkage between happy as opposed to distressed couples. Levenson's research (Levenson & Ruef, 1992), however, highlights the often counterintuitive findings that may result with biologically based methods, as with any other. In Levenson's view, people who are "in tune" with each other should show highly correlated (i.e., synchronous) psychophysiological patterns of response. But husbands and wives in his study showed the most synchronicity or physiological matching during negative emotional events, such as discussion of disagreements or other negative topics. When couples were sharing positive news, or neutral day-to-day information, their physiologies were not synchronous. This replicates work in the early '60s by Kaplan, Burch, and Bloom (cited in Levenson & Ruef, 1992) in which groups of people who disliked each other showed greater similarity in their physiological responding than groups of people who liked each other. What does this mean? Although synchronicity may be ideal for some social or emotional situations, it may not be ideal for all, as psychotherapy research by Krause and Merton (1999) suggests.

Krause and Merton operationalized transference as synchronicity of facial expressions (measured by FACS coding) between individuals with mental disorders and their therapists. Other family members often reflect (are synchronous with) the affect states of mentally ill family members. In the therapy situation, some synchronicity or mirroring is desirable in the early stages of treatment as a method to establish rapport. What Krause and Merton found, however, was that after the beginning therapy sessions, less-expert therapists continued to be synchronous (to mirror the facial expressions of the patients) but the more-expert therapists did not. Lack of synchronicity was more predictive of therapeutic success than continuing synchronicity was.

In the last 10 years, neurological techniques such as fMRI have become increasingly cost effective. The cognitive neuroscience literature is burgeoning with findings, theories, and insights about how human beings think. But as with the psychophysiological literature referred to above, a sophisticated understanding of the methods and the psychological processes being studied is necessary. Scientists often show a magpie mentality, leaping on the newest, most glittery method in the toolbox. But technology alone does not a science make. Understanding the psychological phenomena involved is paramount.

Research by Mertens and Allen (2002) demonstrates this premise. They examined the use of the P300 signal in EEG recordings as a potential lie detection methodology. Most people will show a P300 spike when exposed to a word (such as their name) that they are familiar with. So P300 spiking can be used to distinguish real knowledge from faked knowledge, or actual knowledge from lies about that knowledge. However, if people *think* they have heard a word previously, they will show a P300 spike even though the word was not included in the list they were exposed to. They *thought* they had seen the word because they expected to. So, as with physiological measures, understanding underlying psychological processes is more, not less, important in doing technologically sophisticated neurological work.

A selective reading of several fMRI studies suggests that they provide a particularly good method for understanding how individuals manage emotion at the level of brain functioning (Hare, Tottenham, Davidson, Glover, & Casey, 2005; Ochsner, Bunge, Gross, &

Gabrieli, 2002; Phan et al., 2005), as well as the centrality of the amygdala in processing sadness-related and violence-related emotions (Wang, McCarthy, Song, & LaBar, 2005) and fear and surprise (Whalen et al., 2004). Recent fMRI research has addressed clinically relevant questions such as, Do people high in alexithymia show more change in the posterior cingulate cortex when imagining past emotional experiences than people low in alexithymia (Mantani, Okamoto, Shirao, Okada, & Yamawaki, 2005)? Do individuals who have recovered from depression show differential activation in the dorsolateral prefrontal cortex in response to maternal praise and criticism when compared with individuals who have not been diagnosed with depression (Hooley, Gruber, Scott, Hiller, & Yurgelun-Todd, 2005)? Sex differences and age differences have also been examined. Are there sex differences in the parts of the brain activated during emotional episodic autobiographical memory (Piefke, Weiss, Markowitsch, & Fink, 2005) and other emotional memory tasks (Cahill, Uncapher, Kilpatrick, Alkire, & Turner, 2004)? Do older and younger adults show different amygdala responses to emotionally valenced stimuli (Mather et al., 2004)?

As these studies suggest, fMRI is useful for determining what part of the brain is activated during various psychological states, including emotional ones, and this information can be used, both to increase our knowledge of the brain and how humans function and to diagnose and, potentially, treat individuals with various kinds of behavioral pathologies.

The hardware costs and complexity of using neurological techniques such as EEG, fMRI, and PET will surely plummet in the next 10 years, but given the lack of measurement sophistication that characterizes most existing paper-and-pencil measures of emotional intelligence, there are few indications that the talent and refinement necessary to use such instruments well will be matched by equal refinement in the psychological stimuli used. As an example, the Whalen et al. (2004) study cited above hypothesized that the larger size of fearful and surprised eye whites would be a sufficient trigger for amygdala activation (i.e., the whole fear or surprise expression was not necessary). A neutral face mask was preceded by either larger or smaller eye whites (meant to represent happy). They found that signal intensity within the ventral amygdala was greater for fearful than happy eye whites. One cannot argue with the fact of greater activation for larger versus smaller eye whites, but the meaning of this finding is unclear. Anger facial expressions (also known to show amygdala activation) have small eyes, as does disgust and sadness (which also causes amygdala activation). It exceeds the operationalization to claim that it is fear that is activating the ventral amygdala, especially in the light of previous work (Levenson, Ekman, & Friesen, 1990) showing different physiological responses to partial versus full facial expressions.

Earlier, the different goals of individual differences researchers and cognitive researchers were highlighted. Current neurological techniques provide exciting methods to learn more about how the brain works when humans are in the process of thinking and feeling. Findings from this research can guide the development of individual differences measures, but at the present time, the use of such technologies to assess unselected groups for differences in EI seems unlikely. For groups already identified by reason of some EI-related deficiency (such as depression or schizophrenia) or some EI-related superiority (such as individuals identified as successful CEOs or accurate lie catchers), neurological investigation of their mind at work could be extremely informative. But again, such information seems to fall more within the realm of experimental cognitive studies than correlational individual differences ones.

What Are the Prospects for Assessment of EI Using Computer-Based Assessments and Information-Processing Tasks Such as Implicit Reasoning Tasks?

Earlier, some distinctions between intelligence research and cognitive research were drawn. Recently, however, researchers have begun investigating the overlap in the two realms. Schweizer (2005) described several different areas of research that suggest a cognitive basis for intelligence. He outlined five different areas of cognitive study that provided good candidates for the cognition-intelligence bridge: mental speed, attention, working memory, memory access, and transfer of learning. Schweizer's remarks pertain to general intelligence, not EI, but his outline will be used to organize the cognitive research (broadly defined) that has relevance for the EI field.

The metamorphosis of Ekman and Friesen's Brief Affect Recognition Test (BART) (1974) is an example of one attempt to test mental speed in the area of emotional intelligence. They devised a 70-item test containing exemplars of each of the 6 basic facial expressions and 10 neutral photographs; each photograph was easily identified if presented for 1 second. Because of their interest in microexpressions, as well as to increase the difficulty of the test, they presented the stimuli tachistoscopically, so that examinees saw them at 1/60th of a second. Because tachistoscopic proficiency was, at that time, regarded as an error to be controlled, Ekman devised the Facial Interpretation Test, 30 schematic drawings of faces that were shown for speeds varying from 1/30th to 1/125th of a second. The drawings were not of emotion, but showed schematic faces with the eyes open or closed, and the mouths opened or closed. The test served as a warm-up, pre-test for BART and provided scores for tachistoscopic proficiency that were used to partial this variance out of the BART scores. The test worked well and suggested differences between patients diagnosed with depression or schizophrenia (Shannon, 1970) when the patients were tested individually. When O'Sullivan and her students (Fields & O'Sullivan, 1976) attempted to use BART in a group format, however, the administration problems (ambient light, afterimages, angle of reflection, etc.) proved overwhelming and they abandoned further studies with the measure.

In 2000, with the development of video technology, Matsumoto, Ekman, and others developed a new version of BART (JACBART) using Japanese and Caucasian facial expressions. A neutral photograph was shown before and after a rapidly presented facial expression of emotion. In 2003, Ekman produced a self-instructional training CD (the MicroExpression Training Tools—METT; 2003a) using the JACBART items. METT contains a pretest and a posttest in addition to training modules and practice items.

Because it is self-instructional, anyone able to run a CD on a computer can operate it. Notice that the ability to see images rapidly is no longer regarded as error, but is considered to provide reliable variance in the ability to recognize rapidly occurring facial expressions of emotion. Micromomentary facial expression recognition is significantly related to the ability to detect deception (Ekman, O'Sullivan, & Frank, 1999) and as such is a skill within the emotional intelligence domain (O'Sullivan, 2005). Tests like this, with a considerable mental or perceptual speed component, would be likely candidates for some of the neurological procedures mentioned previously.

The attention approach suggested by Schweizer (2005) is exemplified by the Implicit Association Test (IAT; Greenwald, McGehee, & Schwartz, 1998) and various versions of the Emotional Stroop test. Depending on how they are scored, these measures also assess mental speed, or, more accurately, relative mental speed. Implicit cognition tasks have demonstrated remarkable power in distinguishing manifest and latent social attitudes, particularly with respect to explicit and implicit racism (Richeson & Shelton, 2005). In the IAT, words related to racism, sexism, or affective threat are presented along with neutral words. Reaction times to the different groups of words are evaluated using a rather labyrinthine algorithm. Differences in explicit and implicit attitude scores determined in this way have been related to differences in prejudice toward outgroups after anger was primed, but, as predicted, not following the sadness or neutral conditions (DeSteno, Dasgupta, Bartlett, & Cajdric, 2004). Rudman and Heppen (2003) demonstrated that woman's implicit romantic fantasies, but not their explicit ones, were significantly related to interest in personal power, as reflected in self-reported career and educational goals, projected income, and desire for leadership roles. Other studies have demonstrated differences in attention (i.e., reaction times) for relevant versus non-relevant words in areas ranging from psychopathy (Snowden, Gray, Smith, Morris, & MacCulloch, 2004) to consumer responses (Brunel, Tietje, & Greenwald, 2004).

The IAT is not simple to administer, however, and many methodological difficulties have been discussed in the literature. These include what kind of score to use, how to present the stimuli, how many blocks of stimuli need to be presented, the effect of the order of presentation (Cai, Sriram, Greenwald, & McFarland, 2004; Nosek, Greenwald, & Banaji, 2005), the impact of stereotype threat due to the testing procedure (Frantz, Cuddy, Burnett, Ray, & Hart, 2004), salience (Rothermund & Wentura, 2004), and other idiosyncratic cognitions (Olson & Fazio, 2004). Because the IAT procedure assesses extremely rapidly occurring mental processes, it is thought to be less susceptible to faking.

Some evidence (Steffens, 2004), however, suggests that although the IAT is much less susceptible to faking than questionnaires, with even limited experience with the IAT, faking can occur. It should also be noted that although the IAT was first proposed as an individual differences measure, data relative to ordinary requirements of reliability and validity have not been presented. Validity often is described in terms of internal coherence rather than in terms of alignment with other attributes of interest. As with many experimental studies, the face validity of the measure and the appeal of the empirical findings generated sometimes override critical analysis of what the scores actual mean. Certainly there are differences in people's reaction time to various groups of words. And those differences are predicted beforehand, but the generalization of those differences to important life behaviors has not been adequately demonstrated.

For example, in a study comparing the IAT with facial electromyography (EMG) readings related to subtle facial muscle movements involved in smiling or frowning (Vanman, Saltz, Nathan, & Warren, 2004), racial bias assessed through the EMG procedures correlated with bias in a hiring task, whereas IAT bias did not. Whether this is due to the relative importance of emotion versus cognition in the criterion task used or to the relative reliability or validity of the measures is unclear.

The original Stroop test (1935) was used in clinical testing for many years. It presented words such as *green, red,* and *blue* printed in either the corresponding color, i.e., green, red, and blue, or a contrasting one. If the word *blue* was printed in green ink, rather than in blue ink, most people had difficulty not saying "green" when told to read the word, although some people could. The Emotional Stroop does the same thing except that the words are emotion words rather than color names and the contrast in speed of response is with neutral or nontarget words. The Emotional Stroop is used to determine whether subjects have equal difficulty with words related to all emotions, or just some emotions. Obviously, differences in reaction time are much more easily determined using a computer.

Versions of the Emotional Stroop (researchers tend to develop their own homegrown variants) have been used to examine the effects of drug treatments on depressed patients (Booj et al., 2005) and to demonstrate that violent versus nonviolent offenders respond differently to aggressive words (Smith & Waterman, 2004). A study of explicit/implicit differences in anxiety suggested that for both the IAT and the Emotional Stroop, women's implicit scores were higher than men's, as predicted, but not higher than their explicit scores (Egloff & Schmulke, 2004).

As with the IAT, there are questions about the meaning of the scores obtained from these procedures. Although differences in anxiety are usually reflected in differences in Emotional Stroop scores, differences in depression are found less consistently (Yovel & Mineka, 2005). The impact of experimental requirements is also of concern. Putman, Hermans, and van Honk (2004) found predicted responses to anger and anxiety stimuli with a masked Stroop task but not with an unmasked one, whereas van Honk, Tuiten, and van den Hout (2001) found that anxiety was not related to attentional bias, but that anger was for both masked and unmasked faces.

Other research has suggested that the Stroop task consists of different components (McKenna & Sharma, 2004) and that the results are due to the task presented rather than the Stroop method itself (Algom, Chajut, & Lev, 2004). Questions have also been raised about the intensity of the emotions studied (Jones, Stacey, & Martin, 2002). Kindt, Bierman, and Brosschot (1996) reported low test-retest reliability for both the Stroop and the Emotional Stroop tests, with little convergent validity between them. Interest in the Stroop, is rather like a flame that flickers interminably, never quite dying. Feeble, not shedding much light, but still there. The Emotional Stroop seems no more hardy.

Other information processing tasks potentially relevant to EI include memory and conditional probability reasoning. Although none of the currently popular EI tests feature social or emotional memory, one of the George Washington Social Intelligence tests did (Moss, Hunt, Omwake, & Woodward, 1955). The Memory for Faces subtest presented a sheet of facial photographs,[3] under each of which was a name. After a memorization period, another set of photographs, only some of which were on the previous page, was given to the examinee, who then indicated recall by writing the correct name under the photographs that had been shown. Guilford (1956) also hypothesized that behavioral memory was an important part of social-emotional intelligence, comprising one-fifth of his behavioral intelligence factors in the structure of intellect model. Obviously, emotional memory tasks, varying in terms of length of memory, would be particularly easy to administer with computers, and particularly suitable for neurological studies, similar to those mentioned earlier.

Conditional reasoning tasks examine the kinds of logical errors made when solving social problems. Of particular interest has been the use of such paradigms in assessing proclivity toward aggression. James and his colleagues (2005) reported a substantial correlation between scores on their Conditional Reasoning Measurement System and behavioral indicators of aggression in a series of studies.

Other research (Blanchette & Richards, 2004) suggests that reasoning about emotional statements is much more likely to be logically invalid than reasoning about neutral statements. A voluminous literature on reasoning in general and conditionally probabilistic reasoning in specific could certainly inform thinking about emotional intelligence. Many clinical researchers use the Rogers Decision Making Test (Rogers et al., 1999), a logical reasoning task, to study the differing cognitive deficiencies of individuals with a variety of drug-related disorders with emotional consequences, such as amphetamine and cocaine abuse (Monterosso, Ehrman, Napier, O'Brien, & Childress, 2001). Whether such deficiencies are due to a general intellectual defect in reasoning, which is manifested in emotional difficulties, or whether there are specific failures relative to their emotional pathology is the subject of ongoing investigation. A related question is whether some kinds of tasks, such as cheater detection, depend on a domain specific ability (Cosmides & Tooby, 1989) or a more general kind of reasoning ability (Lawson, 2002). This question also awaits further research.

Other kinds of experimental paradigms relevant to cognitive aspects of emotional intelligence are those studying the impact of cognitive overload and cognitive busyness in interfering with (Crisp, Perks, Stone, & Farr, 2004) and enhancing the processing of emotional stimuli. Gilbert, Pelham, and Krull (1988) suggested that person perception involves many levels of cognitive activity and that these levels differ in terms of their susceptibility to disruption. For example, Pontari and Schlenker (2000) found that cognitive busyness had different effects depending on the congruence of the behavior involved. Cognitively busy extroverts, who attempted to appear introverted, were less effective, but cognitively busy introverts acting as though they were extroverts were more effective, perhaps because the cognitive busyness decreased their self-consciousness.

The final cognitive approach suggested by Schweizer (2005) is transfer. If EI is an intelligence, rather than a personality disposition, then people with more EI should be able to learn EI-related tasks more readily than those who are low in EI. Although there are many popular books purporting to teach people to read faces, to never be lied to again, or to become better managers, the empirical evidence supporting such claims is meager. Rosnow, Skleder, Jaeger, and Rind (1994) conducted an elaborate analysis of Gardner's (1985) theory of intelligence, but the measures in the EI domain were self-reports. M. G. Frank and P. Ekman (personal communication, June 3, 2005) demonstrated an improvement in lie detection ability following training with law enforcement professionals. O'Sullivan (2003b) demonstrated a training effect for accurate lie detection with college students, but only for those with particular intellectual and dispositional characteristics. These studies suggest that at least some aspects of emotional intelligence can be improved through training or education for some people.

All the advantages of computer-assisted test administration in any realm can devolve to EI tests. It is theoretically possible to do adaptive testing, give instantaneous feedback, provide more life-like scenarios, and allow sequential intervention more easily than is possible in paper-and-pencil measures. The same economic limitations of other adaptive tests, however, also hold for EI tests. Given the enormous market in video gaming, it is surprising that so little research has addressed social skills and emotional foibles in that arena, as they relate to differences in emotional intelligence. Insofar as such games include strategic planning related to social outcomes, they provide an engrossing and complex stimuli set that could be used to study such interactions.

What Are the Prospects for New Techniques Such as Situational Judgment Methodologies?

Although the term *situational judgment methodologies* is new, situational judgment tests are at least as old as the George Washington Test of Social Intelligence, which included a subtest called Judgment of Social Situations. For his 1935 dissertation published in 1947, Wedeck devised "problematical situations," much like those in Chapin's Social Insight Scale (1942). Sternberg's (1988) theory of practical intelligence is based on his deep understanding of the importance of context and situations to emotional intelligence (in his term, *practical intelligence*) and good social outcomes. His research on tacit knowledge (of situations) is among the most sophisticated in this realm. If *situational judgment methodologies* means a test in which the problem concerns a social situation involving two or more people, or in which the test item requires knowledge of group mores as a basis for the correct answer, then all of these tests fulfill that requirement. Legree and his colleagues (2005) have proposed a more extensive set of requirements, namely, that a variety of alternative answers be provided, that Likert scaling be used, and so forth.

Given the complexity of situational tests, we need a common language to discuss them, to communicate what we believe they are assessing, and to clarify the construct of interest and demonstrate that variation in the test scores aligns with variation in the attribute (Borsboom et al., 2004). Lacking anything better, Guilford's (1956) description of the elements of behavioral intelligence can be used to deconstruct some of the existing situational tests. Although Guilford's structure of intellect model is no longer widely used in research (but see Weis & Süß, 2005), it provides a framework that can be used to describe almost any ability test and so has merit in that regard.

Guilford identified five intellectual operations: cognition (recognition or understanding), evaluation (choosing the best alternative), convergent production (generating the single best or most appropriate answer), divergent production (producing many different answers), and memory. The five operations interact with six kinds of intellectual products: units, classes, relations, systems, transformations, and implications. In the verbal or semantic arena, for example, cognition of semantic units refers to understanding the meaning of individual words (as is required by a vocabulary test).

In the behavioral intelligence realm, a *behavioral unit* is a single expression— a facial expression, hand gesture, body posture, or vocal sound. This division was also widely used in the nonverbal literature on channels in the 1970s and 1980s and is still in use by researchers in the field of deception detection (DePaulo et al., 2003). Insofar as the items of a test reflect recognizing an emotion that is actually present in the stimulus, the test would be *cognition* (understanding) of behavioral units. Insofar as the emotional expression is ambiguous and the correct answer reflects consensus rather than some other criterion, it would be *evaluation* of behavioral units, or if the answer depends on remembering a similar expression, *memory* of behavioral units. Note that, conceptually, depending on the stimulus, at least in Guilford's model, a different intellectual ability is being assessed in each of these three tasks. Whether there is empirical proof for this theory in the behavioral realm is arguable but, certainly, logically, the distinction can be made.

Behavioral classes refers to groups of related units, such as expressions, showing a variety of anger-related faces or gestures, ranging from irritation to murderous rage. An example of a convergent production of behavioral classes test might be the MSCEIT items that require labeling a group of verbally described affect states. These two types of intellectual products, units and classes, measured purely, would not constitute situational tests. The other four product types (relations, systems, transformations, and implications) would.

Behavioral relations refers to interactions between two people. Understanding the relationship between two individuals requires knowledge of the social status between them as well as what the appropriate range of emotional expression might be in their relationship. Many researchers have constructed ability-based measures of such dyadic situations. Some of the items of Costanzo and Archer's (1993) Interpersonal Perception Task (IPT), for example, show pairs of people who are related by family membership, work hierarchy, or friendship. After watching two people talk, or describe a recent athletic competition, examinees decide who the supervisor is or who won the competition. Knowledge of work and competitive situations is required, as well as knowledge of appropriate social roles, dominance-submission hierarchies, and expected affect among family members. This task is far more complex than merely saying whether a face shows one of six or seven emotions, or whether a group of expressions belongs together or not. Four tests of cognition of behavioral relations were constructed by O'Sullivan and Guilford (1975). One of them showed silhouettes of men and women with differing status relationships; another showed pairs of cartoon faces. The task was to choose the statement that best reflected the feelings of both people in the relationship.

Another type of behavioral relation paradigm is the dyadic interactions that occur in Ickes's (1993) empathic accuracy paradigm in which two individuals talk together. The actual behavior they emit in the interaction may show ability in the convergent or divergent production area, in terms of how well each member of the dyad participates in it. Following the interaction, Ickes then asks each member of the dyad to observe and rate his or her videotaped behavior. This task probably also draws on the intellectual operations of behavioral memory and evaluation.

When an item has a story line and it occurs over time, then behavioral *systems* are being assessed. Many of Sternberg's tests of tacit knowledge fall in this category. Many of the items of the PONS also illustrate what behavioral systems look like. Although only a single nonverbal channel was given, as argued above, the correct answers for this test depend not only on sensitivity to the nonverbal clues provided (facial expressions, vocal intonations, etc.) but on choosing the situation that is appropriate for the nonverbal behavior. The woman's relationship to a social system is described although not shown (e.g., comforting a lost child, asking for help in a department store).

Although Guilford's theory hypothesizes that behavioral systems should be independent of other behavioral products, practically speaking, systems are composed of units, classes, and relations, and underlie behavioral implications and transformations. To illustrate the issues involved in disentangling some of the processes involved in understanding a behavioral system item, let us consider a sample item from one of the O'Sullivan-Guilford (1975) CBS tests, Missing Cartoons.

The task in this test is to look at three panels of a four-panel cartoon strip and then pick the one of four alternative cartoons that completes it, taking into account the characters' thoughts and feelings (i.e., behavioral units), the relationships between them (behavioral relations) and the role expectations of the characters (what would usually be expected in the middle-class world depicted in the cartoon strip). The first cartoon shows Ferd'nand, sweating after completing a tree house for his smiling son. The second cartoon shows Ferd'nand cleaning up in the kitchen. The third cartoon is missing. The fourth cartoon shows Ferd'nand standing by the house, looking sad and thinking about dinner. His wife and son are reading in the tree house. His wife looks annoyed. The alternatives for the missing third cartoon are: (1) the wife returns from grocery shopping and places the groceries on the kitchen counter; (2) the wife returns from shopping, and her son signals her to join him in the tree house; (3) Ferd'nand proudly displays the tree house to his wife, who smiles; (4) the wife returns from shopping to a dirty kitchen; she looks angry. The only alternative that makes sense of the wife's angry expression while reading in the tree house is alternative 4. The other alternatives make logical sense. Any of them could have happened, but only alternative 4 also accounts for the feelings of all of the characters.

This item shows the many pieces of information that must be analyzed and understood in order to arrive at the correct answer for a situational judgment task, in which "correct" means making sense of all the nonverbal elements depicted, as well as the interconnected relationships of those involved in the scenario.

Other examples of behavioral systems or situational judgment tasks are the lie detection tests developed by Ekman and Friesen (1974) and Frank and Ekman (1997). Research with these tests suggest that knowledge of nonverbal leakage of emotion is important in determining whether people are lying or being truthful about their opinion, about stealing money, and about what kind of film they are watching. These situational tests were developed using high-stakes lies in which the participants were motivated by large rewards and significant punishments. This is necessary if the items are to have any behavioral clues (units) that contain information about their truthfulness. Ongoing research (O'Sullivan, 2005; O'Sullivan & Ekman, 2004) about the processes used in obtaining very high scores on these tests suggests that expert lie detectors also pay attention to the relationship between the person being interviewed for the test and the person doing the interview, as well as the social status and ethnicity of both participants. Situational judgment tasks, then, are useful, because they require knowledge in several different areas of emotional intelligence. As such, they are more likely to simulate the kind of social-emotional information processing that occurs in complex life situations. They are less likely to define pure factors in a factor analysis, however.

What Is the Optimal Approach to Assessment of EI?

In general, and with tongue firmly in cheek, I offer the following suggestions:

1. All EI researchers must pass a test in History of Psychology.
2. All EI researchers must pass a multiple-choice exam in which they demonstrate their knowledge of existing tests of EI and the differences among them; current research on emotion; current research on intelligence and current standards in test construction.
3. All EI researchers must write a research-based essay distinguishing personality from intelligence. Alternately, they may argue that there is no empirical or theoretical value in distinguishing ability from disposition, and provide evidence contradicting 100 years of research, that such a distinction is useful.
4. Everyone should snigger when the terms *ability EI* and *trait EI* are used. Otherwise, we are condoning the redundancy of a label that says "ability emotional ability" or the inaccuracy of one that suggests that only dispositions are traits (i.e., intelligence may also be viewed as a trait).
5. EI researchers must be certified as EI researchers. If they devise a test of an ability or a disposition related to EI, they must give it a name other than "EI." Only Greenspan (1989), Salovey, Mayer, and Caruso may use the term *EI*,

and in the interest of clarity even they might consider referring to their construct as MSCEIT EI. They may wish to expand what they include as they continue their interesting research program, but at least we would all realize that they are studying a particular domain, with no established overlap with other seemingly relevant abilities, such as facial expression recognition. We should also recognize that the view of EI popularized by Goleman (1995) owes its wide appeal to the broad and overly inclusive array of abilities and applications he suggested. There is little other than the name, EI, in common with the more nuanced and restricted definition and measures suggested by Salovey and Mayer.

These suggestions are offered facetiously and with the rueful acknowledgment that I satisfy only a couple of them. But these suggestions reflect some of the difficulties limiting scientific progress in the EI field.

Recently, Landy (2005) presented an elegant analysis of Thorndike's (1920) article in a popular magazine on a topic (social intelligence) on which Thorndike had done no research. Nonetheless, historical, political, and intellectual forces at that time, combined with Thorndike's status, caused an upswell of interest in the topic. Landy suggested similarities between the rise and fall of social intelligence in the first half of the century and the foment and ferment surrounding EI at the present time. Many thoughtful scientists have decried the state of EI research (Davies, Stankov, & Roberts, 1998; Roberts, Zeidner, & Matthews, 2001).

We all know that like the blind men examining the elephant, part of our morass in the EI realm is not only that some of us are talking about tails and some of us are talking about trunks, but that some of us are interested in studying elephant hairs, whereas others are selling rings made of those hairs. And let's not forget the interest in *Dumbo* cartoons. All parts of the elephant are of interest and contribute to our understanding of elephantness. But elephant rings and *Dumbo* cartoons are located in different sections of the emporium. We need to be clear about this and to be clear about what we are measuring and for what purpose. So when we ask, "What is the optimal way to measure EI?" we must first determine what the focus of the optimal is: Optimal to predict a criterion like job success or drug behavior? Optimal for choosing who is good at telling when others are lying or telling the truth? Optimal for accurately judging the personality of another? Optimal for allowing an examination of the brain activation of a person with schizophrenia during a stress exam? Optimal for increasing a company's profits? Optimal for understanding sex differences? Optimal for understanding the relatedness of different intellectual factors? Optimal for exploring cultural similarities and differences in emotional processing? Each of these endpoints will require a different set of measures although there may be dispositional similarities across situations.

After determining the goal of the effort and clarifying the definition of what one is interested in, two principles may help to identify the optimal method to measure EI: (1) isomorphism and (2) contrasted groups.

Isomorphism

The more refined the experimental technique, the more specific and refined the stimulus of interest should be. Neurological studies require specification. There is evidence (Levenson et al., 1990) that physiology is different when people activate only part rather than the entire facial expression and that not all people are equally good or equally bad at recognizing all emotions (O'Sullivan, 1983). Therefore, when studying physiological or neurological reactions to affective stimuli, there must be a clear understanding of what the stimulus is. Many computer experts have a sophisticated and subtle understanding of the machines they use, but their understanding of issues in social psychology and human emotion research is similar to my understanding of how to build an fMRI machine. In these investigations, an interdisciplinary group effort is necessary, so that the level of understanding of the technical requirements of brain assaying is matched by the understanding of the social-emotional stimuli used.

At the other end of isomorphism is the use of EI-related measures to predict complex life behaviors—job success, relationship duration, drug use, or health behavior. In this realm, because what is likely at play is a mix of dispositional and ability variables, either a mix of measures or measures like the MSCEIT, which attempts to cast a wide net, should be examined. The interest in situational judgment tests is also consistent with this suggestion. Current research programs using this approach include Funder's Riverside Accuracy Project, Ickes's work on empathic accuracy, and O'Sullivan and Ekman's work on expert lie detectors' accuracy.

This chapter is titled "Trolling for Trout, Trawling for Tuna" to suggest that different sorts of fish require different methods of fishing. The concept of isomorphism also suggests that the method fit the goal. Attempts to understand the entire domain of EI will require different strategies for testing (Barchard & Hakstian, 2004) than those focused on a particular skill within the broader EI realm, such as correctly distinguishing fearful and angry faces.

Contrasted Groups, or the Tale of the Tails

Many interesting results have come from research programs in which deviant individuals are examined. The clinical literature contains many findings relevant to the errors made by pathologic individuals. At the other end of the ability distribution, Ericcson's (1996) work on expertise, Sternberg's work on tacit knowledge, and O'Sullivan and Ekman's work on "truth wizards" illustrate how intense examination of highly gifted people in a domain can illuminate the functioning of those less gifted. What is interesting about this approach is that despite very different starting points, their descriptions of their high achievers, whom we can safely assume are highly emotionally intelligent in at least some of the ways in which people are interested, share common characteristics, not unlike those reported by Davis and Krauss (1997) in the meta-analysis noted earlier.

Identifying deviant individuals requires large groups of people or an environment in which they naturally occur, such as a hospital or a prison. A large sample is necessary because differences among normal individuals may not yield sufficient variance to distinguish the socially adroit from the rest of us. As an example, we (Ekman & O'Sullivan, 1991) tested many groups of law enforcement personnel before finding a group of Secret Service agents who, as a group, were above chance in their ability to detect lies. It took many more years, and testing many more professional groups, before we and Mark Frank (Ekman et al., 1999) were able to find a few more groups of highly accurate truth discerners. After many years of sequential testing of thousands of people, more than 45 individuals have been identified who are at least 80% accurate in distinguishing truth and deception on at least two different tests in which most people's accuracy is about chance (50%; Malone & DePaulo, 2001). We believe (O'Sullivan & Ekman, 2004) that these highly gifted lie detectors represent the upper 5 to 10 % of talent in this area. The downside of such a research program, of course, is its cost and its duration. But how many Mozarts or Tiger Woods are there? And what is it worth to find them?

Interest in the concept of emotional intelligence and related constructs, such as social intelligence, interpersonal perception, nonverbal sensitivity, and empathy, has survived, despite quite unimpressive psychometric support for the many measures that have been proposed in the domain. Consumer groups of many sorts assume such abilities exist, and believe they are related to important life outcomes. As we fish in the sea of knowledge, let us be clear about our goal: Are we seeking trout or tuna? What technique is best to snare our prey? Where are our icythmatomous friends likely to reside? And like all successful fishermen, we need, patience, experience, taut lines, fine bait, and the company of good men (and women, of course).

Notes

1. These authors do not agree with this definition of validity, offering instead what they consider a "simpler" one. This quotation is used out of context because it reflects the orientation to validity on which my remarks are based. Borsboom and his colleagues argue for establishing a directional and causal relationship between a test and an attribute. This may be possible within more restricted or established domains in psychology. The criterion is too arduous to be met at the present time in the field of emotional intelligence.

2. A highly successful charismatic administrator remarked that he had no understanding of the emotions of others, but succeeded by copying the behavior of the administrator immediately above him. Obviously, he was astute about some aspects of behavior, if not emotion, and as a former media personality, was able to simulate them successfully.

3. All the photographs were of Caucasian men in business suits.

References

Abad, M., & O'Sullivan, M. (2001, February). Emotional intelligence and humor: Convergent and discriminant validity. Poster presented at the meeting of the Society for Personality and Social Psychology, San Antonio, TX.

Algom, D., Chajut, E., & Lev, S. (2004). A rational look at the Emotional Stroop phenomenon: A generic slowdown not a Stroop effect. *Journal of Experimental Psychology*, 133, 323–338.

Barchard, K. A., & Hakstian, A. R. (2004). The nature and measurement of emotional intelligence abilities: Basic dimensions and their relationships with other cognitive ability and personality variables. *Educational and Psychological Measurement, 64*, 437–462.

Bar-On, R. (2004). The Bar-On Emotional Quotient Inventory (EQ-i): Rationale, description and summary of psychometric properties. In G. Geher (Ed.), *Measuring emotional intelligence* (pp. 115–146). Hauppauge, NY: Nova Science.

Baumeister, R. F., Bratlavsky, E., Muraven, M., & Tice, D. M. (1998). Ego depletion: Is the active self a limited resource? *Journal of Personality and Social Psychology, 74*, 1252–1265.

Blanchette, I., & Richards, A. (2004). Reasoning about emotional and neutral materials: Is logic affected by emotion? *Psychological Science, 25*, 745–752.

Booj, L., Van de Does, A. J., Haffmans, P. M., Riedel, W. J., Fekkes, D., & Blom, M. J. (2005). The effects of high-dose and low-dose tryptophan depletion on mood and cognitive functions of remitted depressed patients. *Journal of Psychopharmacology, 19*, 267–275.

Borsboom, D., Mellenbergh, G. J., & van Heerden, J. (2004). The concept of validity. *Psychological Review, 111*, 1061–1071.

Brackett, M. A., & Mayer, J. D. (2003). Convergent, discriminant, and incremental validity of competing measures of emotional intelligence. *Personality and Social Psychology Bulletin, 29*, 1147–1158.

Brunel, F. F., Tietje, B. C., & Greenwald, A. G. (2004). Is the Implicit Association Test a valid and valuable measure of implicit consumer social cognition? *Journal of Consumer Psychology, 14*, 385–404.

Cahill, L., Uncapher, M., Kilpatrick, L., Alkire, M. T., & Turner, J. (2004). Sex-related hemispheric lateralization of amygdale function in emotionally influenced memory: An fMRI investigation. *Learning & Memory, 11*, 261–266.

Cai, H., Sriram, N., Greenwald, A. G., & McFarland, S. G. (2004). The Implicit Associations Test's D measure can minimize a cognitive skill confound: Comment on McFarland and Crouch (2002). *Social Cognition, 22*, 673–684.

Carroll, J. M., & Russell, J. M. (1996). Do facial expressions signal specific emotions? Judging emotion from the face in context. *Journal of Personality and Social Psychology, 70*, 205–218.

Chamorro-Premuzic, T., & Furnham, A. (2004–2005). Art judgment: A measure related to both personality and intelligence? *Imagination, Cognition & Personality, 24*, 3–24.

Chapin, F. S. (1942). Preliminary standardization of a social insight scale. *American Sociological Review, 7*, 214–225.

Cosmides, L., & Tooby, J. (1989). Evolutionary psychology and the generation of culture: II. Case study: A computational theory of social exchange. *Ethology and Sociobiology, 10*, 51–97.

Costanzo, M., & Archer, D. (1993). *The Interpersonal Perception Task-15 (IPT-15).* Berkeley, CA: University of California Center for Media and Independent Learning.

Crisp, R. J., Perks, N., Stone, C. H., & Farr, M. J. (2004). Cognitive busyness and the processing of evaluative information in intergroup contexts. *Journal of Social Psychology, 144*, 541–544.

Cronbach, L. J. (1955). Processes affecting scores on "understanding of others" and "assumed similarity." *Psychological Bulletin, 52*, 177–193.

Cronbach, L. J., & Meehl, P. E. (1955). Construct validity in psychological tests. *Psychological Bulletin, 52*, 281–302.

Davies, M., Stankov, L., & Roberts, R. D. (1998). Emotional intelligence: In search of an elusive construct. *Journal of Personality and Social Psychology, 75,* 989–1015.

Davis, M. H., & Krauss, L. A. (1997). Personality and empathic accuracy. In W. Ickes (Ed.), *Empathic accuracy* (pp. 144–168). New York: Guilford.

DePaulo, B. M., Lindsay, J. J., Malone, B. E., Muhlenbruck, L., Charlton, K., & Cooper, H. (2003). Cues to deception. *Psychological Bulletin, 129,* 74–118.

DeSteno, D., Dasgupta, N., Bartlett, M. Y., & Cajdric, A. (2004). Prejudice from thin air: The effect of emotion on automatic intergroup attitudes. *Psychological Science, 15,* 319–324.

Eaton, L. G., Funder, D. C., & Riggio, R. E. (2005). *Skill in social role-playing: The essence of savoir-faire.* Unpublished manuscript.

Egloff, B., & Schmukle, S. C. (2004). Gender differences in implicit and explicit anxiety measures. *Personality and Individual Differences, 36,* 1807–1815.

Ekman, P. (2001). *Telling lies: Clues to deceit in the marketplace, politics, and marriage* (3rd ed.). New York: Norton.

Ekman, P. (2003a). *The microexpression training tools.* Available from: http://www.emotionsrevealed.com.

Ekman, P. (2003b). *The subtle expression training tools.* Available from http://www.emotionsrevealed.com.

Ekman, P., Davidson, R. J., & Friesen, W. V. (1990). The Duchenne smile: Emotional expression and brain physiology. *Journal of Personality & Social Psychology, 58,* 342–353.

Ekman, P., & Friesen, W. V. (1974). Detecting deception from body or face. *Journal of Personality and Social Psychology, 29,* 288–298.

Ekman, P., & Friesen, W. V. (1978). *Facial action coding system.* Palo Alto, CA: Consulting Psychologists Press.

Ekman, P., Friesen, W. V., & O'Sullivan, M. (1988). Smiles when lying. *Journal of Personality and Social Psychology, 54,* 414–420.

Ekman, P., Friesen, W. V., O'Sullivan, M., Chan, A., Diacoyanni-Tarlatzis, I., Heider, K., et al. (1987). Universals and cultural differences in the judgments of facial expressions of emotion. *Journal of Personality and Social Psychology, 53,* 712–717.

Ekman, P., & O'Sullivan, M. (1991). Who can catch a liar? *American Psychologist, 46,* 913–920.

Ekman, P., O'Sullivan, M., & Frank, M. G. (1999). A few can catch a liar. *Psychological Science, 10,* 263–266.

Ericsson, K. A. (1996). The acquisition of expert performance: An introduction to some of the issues. In K. A. Ericsson (Ed.), *The road to excellence: The acquisition of expert performance in the arts and sciences, sports, and games* (pp. 1–50). Hillsdale, NJ: Erlbaum.

Fields, B., & O'Sullivan, M. (1976, April). Convergent validation of five person perception measures. Paper presented at the meeting of the Western Psychological Association, Los Angeles, CA.

Fiske, S. T. (1992). Thinking is for doing: Portraits of social cognition from daguerreotype to laser photo. *Journal of Personality and Social Psychology, 63,* 877–889.

Forgas, J. P., & Ciarrochi, J.V. (2002). On managing moods: Evidence for the role of homeostatic cognitive strategies in affect regulation. *Personality and Social Psychology Bulletin, 28,* 336–345.

Frank, M. G., & Ekman, P. (1997). The ability to detect deceit generalizes across different types of high-stake lies. *Journal of Personality and Social Psychology, 72,* 1429–1439.

Frantz, C. M., Cuddy, A. J. C., Burnett, M., Ray, H., & Hart, A. (2004). A threat in the computer: The race implicit association test as a stereotype threat experience. *Personality and Social Psychology Bulletin, 30,* 1611–1624.

Funder, D. C. (2001). In J. A. Hall & F. J. Bernieri (Eds.), *Interpersonal sensitivity: Theory and measurement* (pp. 319–332). Mahwah, NJ: Erlbaum.

Furnham, A., & Chamorro-Premuzic, T. (2004). Estimating one's own personality and intelligence scores. *British Journal of Psychology, 95,* 149–160.

Gardner, H. (1985). *Frames of mind: The theory of multiple intelligences.* New York: Basic Books.

Gilbert, D. T., Pelham, B. W., & Krull, D. S. (1988). On cognitive busyness: When person perceivers meet persons perceived. *Journal of Personality and Social Psychology, 54,* 733–740.

Gohm, C. L. (2003). Mood regulation and emotional intelligence: Individual differences. *Journal of Personality and Social Psychology, 84,* 594–607.

Goleman, D. (1995). *Emotional intelligence.* New York: Bantam Books.

Greenspan, S. I. (1989). Emotional intelligence. In K. Field & B. J. Cohler (Eds.), *Learning and education: Psychoanalytic perspectives* (pp. 209–243). Madison, CT: International Universities Press.

Greenwald, A. G., McGhee, D. E., & Schwartz, J. L. K. (1998). Measuring individual differences in implicit cognition: The implicit association test. *Journal of Personality and Social Psychology, 74,* 1464–1480.

Guilford, J. P. (1929). An experiment in learning to read facial expressions. *Journal of Abnormal and Social Psychology, 24,* 191–202.

Guilford, J. P. (1956). The structure of intellect. *Psychological Bulletin, 53,* 267–293.

Hall, J. A. (2001). The PONS Test and the psychometric approach to measuring interpersonal sensitivity. In J. A. Hall & F. J. Bernieri (Eds.), *Interpersonal sensitivity: Theory and measurement* (pp. 143–160). Mahwah, NJ: Erlbaum.

Hare, T. A., Tottenham, N., Davidson, M. C., Glover, G. H., & Casey, B. J. (2005). Contributions of amygdale and striatal activity in emotion regulation. *Biological Psychiatry, 57,* 624–632.

Hooley, J. M., Gruber, S. A., Scott, L. A., Hiller, J. B. & Yurgelun-Todd, D. A. (2005). Activation in dorsolateral prefrontal cortex in response to maternal criticism and praise in recovered depressed and healthy control participants. *Biological Psychiatry, 57,* 809–812.

Ickes, W. (1993). Empathic accuracy. *Journal of Personality, 61,* 587–610.

James, L. R., McIntyre, M. D., Glisson, C. A., Green, P. D., Patton, T. W., LeBreton, J. M., Frost, B. C., et al. (2005). A conditional reasoning measure for aggression. *Organizational Research Methods, 8,* 69–99.

Jones, G. V., Stacey, H., & Martin, M. (2002). Exploring the intensity paradox in Emotional Stroop. *Cognitive Therapy and Research, 26,* 831–839.

Kenny, D. A. (1996). The design and analysis of social-interaction research. *Annual Review of Psychology, 47,* 59–86.

Kenny, D. A. (2004). PERSON: A general model of interpersonal perception. *Personality and Social Psychology Review, 8,* 265–280.

Kindt, M., Bierman, D., & Brosschot, J. F. (1996). Stroop versus Stroop: Comparison of a card format and a single-trial format of the standard color-word Stroop task and the Emotional Stroop task. *Personality and Individual Differences, 21,* 653–661.

Kolar, D. W., Funder, D. C., & Colvin, C. R. (1996). Comparing the accuracy of personality judgments by the self and knowledgeable others. *Journal of Personality, 64,* 311–337.

Krause, R., & Merten, J. (1999). Affects, regulation of relationship, transference and counter-transference. *International Forum of Psychoanalysis, 8*, 103–114.

Landy, F. (2005, May). *The pursuit of emotional intelligence: A cautionary tale.* Invited address presented at the meeting of the American Psychological Society, Los Angeles, CA.

Lawson, A. E. (2002). The origin of conditional logic: Does a cheater detection module exist? *Journal of Genetic Psychology, 163*, 425–444.

Legree, P., Psotka, J., Tremble, T., & Bourne, D. R. (2005). Using consensus based measurement to assess emotional intelligence. In R. Schulze & R. R. Roberts (Eds.), *Emotional intelligence: An international handbook* (pp. 155–180). Cambridge, MA: Hogrefe & Huber.

Levenson, R. W., Ekman, P., & Friesen, W. V. (1990). Voluntary facial action generates emotion-specific autonomic nervous system activity. *Psychophysiology, 27*, 363–384.

Levenson, R. W., & Gottman, J. M. (1983). Marital interaction: Physiological linkage and affective exchange. *Journal of Personality and Social Psychology, 45*, 587–597.

Levenson, R. W., & Ruef, A. M. (1992). Empathy: A physiological substrate. *Journal of Personality and Social Psychology, 63*, 234–246.

Lieberman, M. D., & Rosenthal, R. (2001). Why introverts can't always tell who likes them: Multitasking and nonverbal decoding. *Journal of Personality and Social Psychology, 80*, 294–310.

MacCann, C., Matthews, G., Zeidner, M., & Roberts, R. D. (2003). Psychological assessment of emotional intelligence: A review of self-report and performance based testing. *The International Journal of Organizational Analysis, 11*, 247–274.

Malone, B. E., & DePaulo, B. M. (2001). Measuring sensitivity to deception. In J. A. Hall & F. J. Bernieri (Eds.), *Interpersonal sensitivity: theory and measurement* (pp. 103–124). Mahwah, NJ: Erlbaum.

Mantani, T., Okamoto, Y., Shirao, N., Okada, G., & Yamawaki, S. (2005). Reduced activation of posterior cingulated cortex during imagery in subjects with high degrees of alexithymia: A functional magnetic resonance imaging study. *Biological Psychiatry, 57*, 982–990.

Mather, M., Canli, T., English, T., Whitfield, S., Wais, O., Ochsner, K., et al. (2004). Amygdala responses to emotionally valenced stimuli in older and younger adults. *Psychological Science, 15*, 259–263.

Matsumoto, D., LeRoux, J., Wilson-Cohn, C., Raroque, J., Kooken, K., Ekman, P., et al. (2000). A new test to measure emotion recognition ability: Matsumoto and Ekman's Japanese and Caucasian Brief Affect Recognition Test (JACBART). *Journal of Nonverbal Behavior, 24*, 179–209.

Matthews, G., Zeidner, M., & Roberts, R. D. (2003). *Emotional intelligence: Science and myth.* Boston, MA: MIT Press.

Mayer, J. D., Salovey, P., & Caruso, D. (2002). *Mayer-Salovey-Caruso Emotional Intelligence Test user's manual.* Toronto, Canada: Multi-Health Systems.

McKenna, F. P., & Sharma, D. (2004). Reversing the Emotional Stroop effect reveals that it is not what it seems: The role of fast and slow components. *Journal of Experimental Psychology: Learning, Memory and Cognition, 30*, 382–392.

Mertens, R., & Allen, J. J. B. (2002, October). Erroneous classification of false memories as veridical: Possible limits of ERP based memory assessments. Poster presented at the meeting of the Society of Psychophysiological Research, Washington, DC.

Monterosso, J., Ehrman, R., Napier, K. L., O'Brien, C. P., & Childress, A. R. (2001). Three decision-making tasks in cocaine-dependent patients: Do they measure the same construct? *Addiction, 96*, 1825–1837.

Moss, F. A., Hunt, T., Omwake, K. T., & Woodward, L. G. (1955). *Social Intelligence Test.* Washington, DC: George Washington University.

Nosek, B. A., Greenwald, A. G., & Banaji, M. R. (2005). Understanding and using the Implicit Association Test: II. Method variables and construct validity. *Personality and Social Psychology Bulletin, 31,* 166–180.

Nowicki, S., Jr., & Duke, M. (1994). Individual differences in the nonverbal communication of affect: The Diagnostic Analysis of Nonverbal Accuracy Scale. *Journal of Nonverbal Behavior, 18,* 9–35.

Nowicki, S., Jr., & Duke, M. (2001). Nonverbal receptivity: The Diagnostic Analysis of Nonverbal Accuracy (DANVA). In J. A. Hall & F. J. Bernieri (Eds.), *Interpersonal sensitivity: Theory and measurement* (pp. 183–198). Mahwah, NJ: Erlbaum.

Nowicki, S., Jr., & Mitchell, J. (1998). Accuracy in identifying affect in child and adult faces and voices and social competence in preschool children. *Genetic, Social and General Psychology Monographs, 124,* 39–59.

Ochsner, K. N., Bunge, A. S., Gross, J. J., & Gabrieli, J. D. E. (2002). Rethinking feeling: An fMRI study of the cognitive regulation of emotion. *Journal of Cognitive Neuroscience, 14,* 1215–1229.

Olson, M. A., & Fazio, R. H. (2004). Reducing the influence of extrapersonal associations on the Implicit Associations Test: Personalizing the IAT. *Journal of Personality and Social Psychology, 86,* 653–667.

O'Sullivan, M. (1982). Measuring the ability to recognize facial expressions of emotion. In P. Ekman (Ed.), *Emotion in the human face* (2nd ed., pp. 281–317). Cambridge, UK: Cambridge University Press.

O'Sullivan, M. (1983, May). Recognizing facial expressions of emotion: *The Affect Blend Test.* Symposium titled Social Intelligence Revisited: New Approaches to Old Problems (Chair: L. B. Sechrest) conducted at the American Psychological Association Convention, Anaheim, CA.

O'Sullivan, M. (2002, February). *Emotion and intelligence in emotional intelligence.* Poster session presented at the annual meeting of the Society for Personality and Social Psychology, Savannah, GA.

O'Sullivan, M. (2003a). The fundamental attribution error in detecting deceit: The boy-who-cried-wolf effect. *Personality and Social Psychology Bulletin, 29,* 1316–1327.

O'Sullivan, M. (2003b, May). Learning to detect deception. Poster session presented at the annual convention of the *Western Psychological Association,* Vancouver, BC.

O'Sullivan, M. (2005). Emotional intelligence and detecting deception: Why most people can't "read" others, but a few can. In R. Riggio & R. Feldman (Eds.), *Applications of nonverbal communications* (pp. 215–253). Mahwah, NJ: Erlbaum.

O'Sullivan, M., & Ekman, P. (2004). Facial expression recognition and emotional intelligence. In G. Geher & K. L. Renstrom (Eds.), *Measuring emotional intelligence: Common ground and controversy* (pp. 91–111). Hauppauge, NY: Nova Science.

O'Sullivan, M., & Ekman, P. (2004). The wizards of deception detection. In P. A. Granhag & L. Strömwell (Eds.), *Detecting deception in forensic context* (pp. 269–286). Cambridge, UK: Cambridge University Press.

O'Sullivan, M., & Guilford, J. P. (1975). Six factors of behavioral cognition: Understanding other people. *Journal of Educational Measurement, 12,* 255–271.

O'Sullivan, M., Guilford, J. P., & de Mille, R. (1965). *The measurement of social intelligence: Report from the Psychology Laboratory, No. 34.* Los Angeles: University of Southern California.

Patterson, M. L., Foster, J. L., & Bellmer, C. (2001). Another look at accuracy and confidence in social judgments. *Journal of Nonverbal Behavior, 25,* 207–219.

Phan, K. L., Fitzgerald, D. A., Nathan, P. J., Moore, G. J., Uhde, T. W., & Tancer, M. E. (2005). Neural substrates for voluntary suppression of negative affect: A functional magnetic resonance imaging study. *Biological Psychiatry, 57,* 210-219.

Piefke, M., Weiss, P. H., Markowitsch, H. J., & Fink, G. R. (2005). Gender differences in the functional neuroanatomy of emotional episodic autobiographical memory. *Human Brain Mapping, 24,* 313–324.

Pike, A., & Plomin, R. (1997). A behavioral genetic perspective on close relationships. *International Journal of Behavioral Development, 21,* 647–667.

Pontari, B. A., & Schlenker, B. R. (2000). The influence of cognitive load on self-presentation: Can cognitive busyness help as well as harm social performance? *Journal of Personality and Social Psychology, 78,* 1092–1108.

Putman, P., Hermans, E., & van Honk, J. (2004). Emotional Stroop performance for masked angry faces: It's BAS, not BIS. *Emotion, 4,* 305–311.

Read, S. J., & Miller, L. C. (1993). Rapist or "regular guy": Explanatory coherence in the construction of mental models of others. *Personality and Social Psychology Bulletin, 19,* 526–540.

Richeson, J. A., & Shelton, J. N. (2005). Brief report: Thin slices of racial bias. *Journal of Nonverbal Behavior, 29,* 75–86.

Riggio, R. E. (1989). *Social Skills Inventory.* Palo Alto, CA: Consulting Psychologists Press.

Riggio, R. E., Salinas, C., & Tucker, J. (1988). Personality and deception ability. *Personality and Individual Differences, 9,* 189–191.

Riggio, R. E., Tucker, J., & Throckmorton, B. (1987). Social skills and deception ability. *Personality and Social Psychology Bulletin, 13,* 568–577.

Roberts, R. D., Zeidner, M., & Matthews, G. (2001). Does emotional intelligence meet traditional standards for an intelligence? Some new data and conclusions. *Emotion, 1,* 196–231.

Rogers, R. D., Everitt, B. J., Baldacchino, A., Blackshaw, A. J., Swainson, R., Wynne, K., et al. (1999). Dissociable deficits in the decision making cognition of chronic amphetamine abusers, opiate abusers, patients with focal damage to prefrontal cortex, and tryptophan-depleted normal volunteers: evidence for monoaminergic mechanisms. *Neuropsychopharmacology, 20,* 322–339.

Rosenthal, R., Hall, J. A., DiMatteo, M. R., Rogers, P., & Archer, D. (1979). *Sensitivity to nonverbal communication: A profile approach to the measurement of individual differences.* Baltimore: Johns Hopkins University Press.

Rosnow, R. L., Skleder, A. A., Jaeger, M. E., & Rind, B. (1994). Intelligence and the epistemics of interpersonal acumen: Testing some implications of Gardner's theory. *Intelligence, 19,* 93–116.

Rothermund, K., & Wentura, D. (2004). Underlying processes in the Implicit Association Test: Dissociating salience from associations. *Journal of Experimental Psychology: General, 133,* 139–16.

Rudman, L. A., & Heppen, J. A. (2003). Implicit romantic fantasies and women's interest in personal power: A glass slipper effect? *Personality and Social Psychology Bulletin, 29,* 1357–1370.

Salovey, P., & Mayer, J. D. (1989–1990). Emotional intelligence. *Imagination, Cognition, & Personality, 9,* 185–211.

Schweizer, K. (2005). An overview of research into the cognitive basis of intelligence. *Journal of Individual Differences, 26,* 43–51.

Shannon, A. (1970). Differences between depressives and schizophrenics in the recognition of facial expressions of emotion. Unpublished doctoral dissertation, University of California, San Francisco.

Shipe, D., Rosser, M. & Sidhu, R. (1973). Social intelligence, affiliation motivation, and inter-personal effectiveness in non-academic youth. Proceedings of the annual convention of the American Psychological Association, Montreal, Quebec.

Smith, P., & Waterman, M. (2004). Processing bias for sexual material: The Emotional Stroop and sexual offenders. *Sexual Abuse: Journal of Research and Treatment, 16,* 163–171.

Snowden, R. J., Gray, N. S., Smith, J., Morris, M., & MacCulloch, M. J. (2004). Implicit affective associations to violence in psychopathic murderers. *Journal of Forensic Psychiatry and Psychology, 15,* 620–641.

Spain, J. S., Eaton, L. G., & Funder, D. C. (2000). Perspectives on personality: The relative accu-racy of self versus others for the prediction of emotion and behavior. *Journal of Personality, 68,* 837–867.

Steffens, M. C. (2004). Is the Implicit Association Test immune to faking? *Experimental Psychol-ogy, 51,* 165–179.

Sternberg, R. J. (1988). *The triarchic mind: A new theory of human intelligence.* New York: Penguin Books.

Sternberg, R. J., Wagner, R. K., Williams, W. M., & Horvath, J. A. (1995). Testing common sense. *American Psychologist, 50,* 912–927.

Stroop, J. R. (1935). Studies of interference in serial verbal reactions. *Journal of Experimental Psychology, 18,* 643–662.

Thorndike, E. L. (1920). Intelligence and its uses. *Harper's Magazine, 140,* 227–235.

Trope, Y., & Higgins, E. T. (1993). The what, when, and how of dispositional inferences: New answers and new questions. *Personality and Social Psychology Bulletin, 19,* 493–500.

van Honk, J., Tuiten, A., & van den Hout, M. (2001). Selective attention to unmasked and masked threatening words: Relationship to trait anger and anxiety. *Personality and Individual Difference, 30,* 711–720.

Vanman, E. J., Saltz, J. L., Nathan, L. R., & Warren, J. R. (2004). Racial discrimination by low-prejudiced Whites' facial movements as implicit measures of attitudes related to behavior. *Psychological Science, 15,* 711–714.

Wang, L., McCarthy, G., Song, A. W., & LaBar, K. S. (2005). Amygdala activation to sad pictures during high-field (4 Tesla) magnetic resonance imaging. *Emotion, 5,* 12–22.

Wedeck, J. (1947). The relationship between personality and "psychological ability." *British Journal of Psychology, 37,* 133–151.

Weis, S., & Süß, H. (2005) Social intelligence—a review and critical discussion of measurement concepts. In R. Schulze & R. R. Roberts (Eds.), *Emotional intelligence: An international handbook* (pp. 203–230). Cambridge, MA: Hogrefe & Huber.

Whalen, P. J., Kagan, J., Cook, R. G., Davis, F. C., Kim, H., Polis, S., et al. (2004). Human amyg-dale responsivity to masked fearful eye whites. *Science, 306,* 2061.

Woodzicka, J. A., & LaFrance, M. (2005). Working on a smile: Responding to sexual provoca-tion in the workplace. In R. E. Riggio & R. S. Feldman (Eds.), *Applications of nonverbal communication* (pp. 141–160). Mahwah, NJ: Erlbaum.

Yovel, I., & Mineka, S. (2005). Emotion-congruent attentional biases: The perspective of hierarchical models of emotional disorders. *Personality and Individual Differences, 38,* 785–795.

Zeidner, M., Roberts, R. D., & Matthews, G. (2002). Can emotional intelligence be schooled? A critical review. *Educational Psychologist, 37,* 215–231.

11

Why Emotional Intelligence Needs a Fluid Component

ANDREW ORTONY, WILLIAM REVELLE,
AND RICHARD ZINBARG

There is something intuitively appealing and "right" about the idea of emotional intelligence (EI), but what is that something? Before we can answer this question, and especially before we raise issues about what exactly the construct of EI is or ought to be and the problem of how to measure it, it will be helpful to address the question of how to characterize the presupposed notion of "emotion." There is much disagreement among emotion theorists as to exactly what emotions are (and even as to which psychological conditions are emotions), and insofar as different theorists have different conceptions of what an emotion is, their instincts as to what EI is are likely to be different. Certainly this is the case with respect to our own conception of EI as compared to the one introduced, elaborated, and extensively investigated by Mayer and Salovey and their colleagues (e.g., Mayer & Salovey, 1995, 1997; Salovey & Mayer, 1990). We believe that differences in conceptions of EI ultimately come to rest in different conceptions of emotions. Once we have addressed the question of what an emotion is, we review Mayer and Salovey's construct of EI and its measurement, suggesting that, at least in principle, both could be strengthened by introducing an additional, critical, ingredient.

What Is an Emotion?

We view emotions as states that result from value-laden appraisals of a person's environment. Of course, this is a very broad, general statement, and it turns out to be

We gratefully acknowledge extensive discussions on these issues with Nisha Moody and helpful comments on an earlier version of this chapter from Shlomo Hareli. This chapter is based in part on a talk given by the first author at a symposium on "Computing With Emotions" held in Haifa, Israel, in June 2005.

not so easy to reach consensus on a more specific characterization. Some theorists (e.g., Ortony, Clore, & Collins, 1988; Roseman, 1984; Scherer, 1984) focus on what one might call the "input" side of emotions by attending to the cognitive and perceptual aspects. Others (e.g., Frijda, 1986) devote more attention to the "output" side by concentrating on action tendencies. Yet others (e.g., Ekman, 1982; Izard, 1971) have undertaken extensive studies of the facial expressions of emotions. Finally, the rapidly expanding field of affective neuroscience reflects a growing interest in the brain structures and mechanisms that underlie emotion processes (e.g., Lane & Nadel, 2000; LeDoux, 1996; Panksepp, 1998). These different approaches are best thought of as representing emphases on different aspects of emotion rather than as competing theories of emotion. Viewing them in this way allows for the possibility of finding a characterization of emotion that is compatible with all of them.

Our attempt at such a characterization is illustrated in Figure 11.1. We suspect that most emotion theorists would agree that under normal conditions, emotions have the components indicated in the figure, namely, a *somatic component* having to do with the feeling of bodily disturbance or change (we think of this as "raw" affect), a *cognitive component* wherein the emotion-inducing aspects of the environment (including the "internal" environment of memories, representations of bodily and mental states, etc.) are (often consciously) appraised and "made sense of," and a *motivational component* comprising the inclinations to act (or not act). In addition, each of these three components has associated with it (observable) *behavioral manifestations*, ranging from fully automatic "behaviors," such as flushing or grimacing, to complex planful acts such as taking revenge for a perceived harm. Finally, the interaction of the three components and their behavioral manifestations gives rise to an integrated holistic phenomenological *experience* of emotion, represented in the figure by the central "experiential whole."

With respect to emotion theory in general, the virtue of a model of this kind is that it can accommodate both the similarities and differences among the various proposals found in the literature. With respect to the issue of EI in particular, its value is that it forces us to develop an account of EI that does justice to some of the basic facts about emotions. These basic facts, simply put, are that an emotion is normally *an experience that involves bodily feeling, thinking, wanting, and doing*. These aspects are all represented in the model, but not, we think, in the account of emotion upon which Mayer and Salovey appear to base their conception of EI.

Consider how the model plays out in the case of, say, a person walking across a deep gorge on a shaky suspension bridge. In order for an effectively functioning individual to get across, the four ingredients or "modes" of what we (Ortony, Norman, & Revelle, 2005) call "effective functioning" need to work in concert. These modes—affect, cognition, motivation, and behavior—are analogous but not identical to the four components of emotions just described, namely, the somatic, cognitive, motivational, and behavioral.[1] From the effective functioning perspective, the affective mode for our hesitant bridge crosser is an emotional state of (high) anxiety (pun intended). From the emotion perspective, his fear or anxiety has its own internal structure, including such bodily (somatic) feelings as a tensing of the body and a pounding heart. From

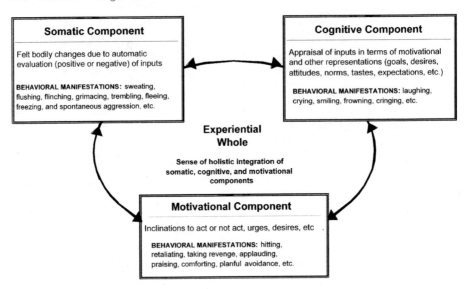

Figure 11.1. The components of a typical, "full-fledged" emotion.

the effective functioning perspective, the would-be bridge crosser, like the proverbial chicken, is motivated to get to the other side, but from the emotion perspective, his fear incorporates an opposing motivation, namely the inhibitory motivation to avoid crossing the bridge. The attendant cognitions are equally complex and include things like a belief in the utility of getting to the other side and the knowledge that there's a risk of falling, with painful and perhaps even fatal consequences. All of these features, along with their tensions, have to be resolved and integrated if the resultant behavior is to be in the service of effective functioning (e.g., successfully crossing the bridge).

One can see from this example how optimal functioning is likely to be enhanced by some (albeit not excessive) level of emotion. A modicum of fear will increase vigilance and care, and thus help protect the person from the potentially disastrous consequences of carelessness. Excessive fear, on the other hand, is likely to be as dysfunctional as fearlessness. In general, and as we will discuss later, of particular importance in the context of EI, *optimal functioning requires an optimal level of affect.*

In contrast to our view of emotions as the product of value-laden appraisals, Mayer and Salovey take a rather different tack, apparently equating emotions with emotional relationships. Specifically, they claim that emotional information is information about (aspects of) relationships. However, it is not clear what exactly they mean in saying this. Presumably they do not intend "relationships" to be taken in a weak sense, for that sense tells us little about what emotions are (or what emotional information is). In the weak sense, most things are (ultimately) about relationships—color is about the relation between objects and reflected light, distance is about the relation between two points, intelligence is about the relationship between people and problems, and so on. If, on the other hand, we take "relationships" to mean *interpersonal* relationships, which we suspect is what Mayer and Salovey have in mind, then we are faced with the problem that emotions often arise without the involvement of others. Again, to take the example of the person crossing the shaky bridge, by hypothesis, that person would be quite scared, but presumably there would be nothing *interpersonal* about his fear.

The source of Mayer and Salovey's focus on relationships is the fact that emotions *frequently* occur in relationships. However, frequency is not necessity: The fact that emotions frequently arise in relationships does not mean that they always or necessarily do, and thus it does not entail that "emotional information is information about [certain forms of these] relationships" (Mayer, Salovey, Caruso, & Sitarenios, 2001, p. 234). It might be, sometimes, but it need not be.

Mayer and Salovey's Construct of EI

It is our contention that Mayer and Salovey's emphasis on emotions and emotional information as being about relationships has problematic consequences for their construct of EI because it takes the focus off what goes on *inside* the individuals in those relationships. In fact, we think that their definition of EI as "the ability to *recognize* the meanings of emotions and their relationships and to use them as a basis in *reasoning* and problem solving" (italics added) (Mayer, Salovey, Caruso, & Sitarenios, p. 234), with its emphasis on recognizing and reasoning provides some evidence for our contention. These two (cognitive) abilities—recognizing and reasoning—become the basis for operationalizing their construct of EI as *perceiving*[2] emotions and emotional relationships and using them for *facilitating thinking* (i.e., to use them in reasoning).

We are cognitivists, so it is perhaps ironic that we find this account of EI to be a little too cognitive![3] But given our componential view of emotions in which emotions involve somatic, cognitive, motivational, and behavioral constituents, our own conception of EI is one that necessarily involves not only the ability to perceive and reason about emotions and emotional reactions, but also *the ability to experience emotions* (in contextually appropriate ways). That is, it involves *all* of the components of emotions that we laid out in the previous section. Thus our concern is that the Mayer and Salovey account tends to neglect the "experiential whole" and the contribution of, especially, the motivational and somatic components to that whole. By focusing on the admittedly important role in EI of recognizing, perceiving, and thinking about and with emotions, it is easy to lose sight of the possibility that a critical part of EI has to do with the ability to appropriately *experience* emotions in their full richness.

But matters are not so simple—some things are easier said than done. A consequence of insisting that emotional experience is a crucial aspect of EI is that the task of measuring EI becomes even more difficult than it already is, and unlike us, Mayer and Salovey and colleagues were constrained by the practical problems of devising a measure. Measuring emotional experience is a daunting challenge, especially given the fact that the most intuitively appealing route to doing it, namely using physiological correlates, does not appear to be a promising approach. Emotion theorists are in fair agreement that discrete emotions cannot be finely differentiated on the basis of physiological "signatures." There is little convincing evidence of a one-to-one relationship between discrete emotions and associated patterns of physiological activity (but see Ekman, Levenson, & Friesen, 1983), even though such patterns, as well as those of arousal and brain activation, can be found at grosser levels of affect-related phenomena (e.g., approach and avoidance motivation are associated with somewhat distinct patterns of brain activation; Davidson, 1992; Fox, 1991). However, if one's ultimate goal is to develop a valid measure of EI, the fact that there are serious practical problems associated with measuring all of the constituents of emotion does not reduce the desirability of doing so. It remains true that to the extent that what we call "full-fledged" emotions—as opposed to generalized, undifferentiated affect—involve the integration of somatic, cognitive, motivational, and behavioral components into an experiential whole, and to the extent that integration of this kind is part of EI, then ideally a measure of EI should assess people's ability to effect such integration.

Mayer and Salovey's Measure of EI: The MSCEIT

So far we have noted that there seems to be something right about the general idea of EI, but we have suggested that a crucial part of this something, the capacity to appropriately experience emotions, is not a focus of Mayer and Salovey's conception of EI. This is especially clear with respect to the EI construct as manifested in the MSCEIT (Mayer, Salovey, & Caruso, 2001), which we consider to be the most extensively investigated and best validated measure of EI that there is.[4] We believe that any test of EI that fails to incorporate an assessment of emotional experience or feeling would be a test on which intelligent, albeit nonsentient, computer programs could (in principle) demonstrate as high a level of EI as emotionally sensitive people. Yet it would be odd if an artificial intelligence (AI) system could exhibit high EI while the current state of AI is such that few if any would be willing yet to say that computers "have" emotions. How could a test of EI that was unable to discriminate between an emotionless AI system and an emotionally well adjusted person be an adequate test of EI? We could make the same argument replacing AI systems with psychopaths, whose trait profile according to Cleckley (1988) includes a lack of remorse, incapacity for love, failure to learn from punishment despite adequate reasoning abilities including reasoning about emotional matters and general poverty in major affective reactions. A test of EI ought to be able to distinguish individuals who are appropriately emotionally warm and empathetic from computers or from humans who superficially appear to react with normal emotions but are loveless, remorseless, emotionally shallow, and incapable of using negative affect to motivate behavioral adaptations. Emotional intelligence presupposes emotional feelings.

What the MSCEIT Measures: A Thought Experiment

We have just implied that, at least in principle, current AI technology is good enough to produce tolerable performance on the MSCEIT, as though an inability to distinguish human from machine performance on the MSCEIT comprised an acceptable criterion for an "emotional Turing test" (Turing, 1950).[5] But does it? We take it as a given that computers as we know them today, regardless of how much AI they embody, do not have feelings. If this is right, and if the MSCEIT is a valid test of EI, then the MSCEIT should be capable of differentiating humans from (emotionless) machines. In this section, as a kind of thought experiment, we sample items from four sections of the MSCEIT with a view to examining this question. Even if there are as yet no systems that can produce humanlike responses to the different kinds of items on the MSCEIT, maybe we can articulate the kind of the design and information-processing principles that would be needed to do so. Accordingly, we examine the MSCEIT to see if its items are in principle amenable to algorithmic solutions. Because neither we nor anyone else knows of any algorithmic way in which to capture emotional experience or feelings, if a machine could generate reasonable responses, those responses could not be dependent on the ability to experience emotions.

The MSCEIT is comprised of eight subtests, or sections (see Figure 11.2), two for each of four "branches": (1) *perceiving* emotions (the faces task, section A; and the pictures task, section F), (2) *facilitating thought* through emotions (the facilitation task; section B; and the sensations task, section E), (3) *understanding* emotions (the changes task, section C; and the blends task, section G), and the fourth branch, (4) *managing* emotions (the management task, section D; and the relationships task, section H). In this brief review, we seek only to give the flavor of representative items, together with suggestions as to what kind of algorithmic procedures we think could in principle generate sensible responses to them. We focus in particular on the faces task, the pictures task, and (only) two of the language-based tasks (the facilitation task and the sensations task) because the kind of mechanisms needed to accomplish any one of the language-based tasks could be used for all of them.

In the faces task, respondents have to rate the intensity of facial expressions on each of five psychological state dimensions on a scale ranging from no emotion to extreme emotion. There are four items covering a total of seven different states. As already indicated, we assume that if a computer could perform this or any task, then feeling-based experience cannot be a prerequisite for successful task completion. In the case of facial expressions, accurate machine recognition of emotions is routine. For well over a decade, computer scientists have been developing a variety of techniques for automatically classifying facial expressions, typically into one of the six "basic" emotions proposed by Ekman, Levinson, and Friesen (1983) (although, see Ortony & Turner, 1990, for a challenge to the notion of "basic" emotions). The results of these efforts are dozens of algorithms that do a remarkably good job of classifying emotional expressions (typically with recognition accuracy between about 75% and 95%) using both static images and dynamic emotional expression displays (see Fasel & Luettin, 2003, for a review). Furthermore, some of the systems that do this even do well at estimating the intensity of the expressions. So, we can conclude with confidence that the faces task is well within the capacity of modern computer systems. Computers with no experiential knowledge of emotions or emotional feelings can learn to classify facial expressions of emotions quite easily.

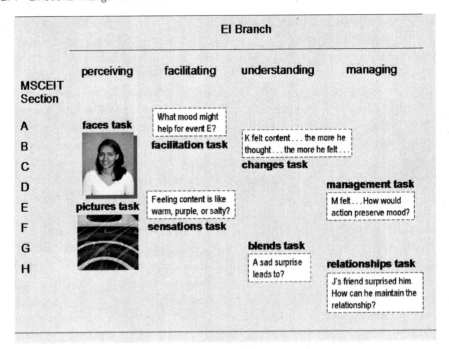

Figure 11.2. Relation between sections and the branches of the MSCEIT.

The pictures task is the second of the two tasks designed to tap the *perceiving* branch. In this task, respondents have to estimate the intensity of five states "expressed" [*sic*] by pictures of naturalistic scenes or of abstract art ("How much of each feeling is expressed by the picture?"). Consider how this might be done for a scenic picture of blue-green water with rocks in and around it, assuming for the sake of argument that the input is a crude description of the scene.[6] Given such a description, reference to an associative thesaurus (e.g., the *Edinburgh Word Association Thesaurus;* Wilson, 1988) could easily generate some basic concepts such as *peaceful* and *beautiful* (it really doesn't matter much which). From these, one could extract the affective valence and strength— for example, positive concepts, but not excessively so—enabling a response of, say, a moderate level of happiness and no sadness, and no fear, anger, or disgust. Notice that accuracy here is not important, because there is no "correct" answer. But such a simple procedure would result in a reasonable response, not too different, presumably, from the responses that many people would give.

In the cases of abstract pictures, the same mechanism could be employed, although the starting point would require the basic shapes to be described using adjectives such as *hard, sharp, jagged,* and the colors as *saturated, bright, strong contrast, red, green, yellow,* and *blue.* The associations to and affective connotations of these words could be processed using the kind of algorithm described in Ortony and Radin (1989) operating on a database with semantic differential ratings (see Heise, 2001). Descriptors such as *hard*, *sharp*, and *jagged* would presumably be associated with some moderate level of negative affect, whereas some of the descriptors relating to the colors would be associated with positive affect and some with negative affect. The color terms themselves could also elicit affect through conventional cross-modal mappings relating to "warm" and "cold" or "cool" colors ("soft" reds, blues, etc.). Some sort of associative process like this is psychologically plausible precisely because pictures of this kind are abstract (that is, they lack referential semantic content) so that associative mechanisms of one kind or another are the only basis upon which picture descriptions can be built in the first place.

Having a set of associatively derived affective markers is only half of what is needed to complete this kind of task. The other half of the process involves selecting a response from the response alternatives. In the case of the abstract picture, in the first column of Figure 11.2, the response scales are amount of happiness, sadness, fear, anger, and disgust. Selecting an appropriate response again requires an ability to *reason* about emotion concepts. One might, for example, reason that *happiness* and *sadness* are very general forms of affect respectively, with *fear*, *anger*, and *disgust* being more specific kinds of negative affect—they are particular ways of being unhappy (Ortony & Turner, 1990) and there is no semantically based reason for selecting them. This might lead to the selection of a small amount of *happiness* (e.g., a rating of 2) and a larger amount of *sadness* (e.g., a rating of 4), because there were more descriptors activating negative as opposed to positive affect. The fact that there is no semantically based reason for selecting specific emotions does not preclude the possibility of their being selected on the basis of associative connections. Such associations might result in slight activation of *fear* (sharp jagged edges can be dangerous), and a slight activation of *anger* (one meaning of *sharp* is associatively related to *anger*, as is *harsh*). In this case, small amounts of the expression of *fear* and *anger* might also be endorsed.

"If you had to create new, exciting decorations for a birthday party, what mood or moods might be helpful?" This is one of the five items that comprise Section B. Each item has three mood states to rate for their usefulness on a 5-point scale ranging from not useful to useful. In this case, the mood states are *annoyance*, *boredom*, and *joy*. Again, once one has a reasonable representation of the underlying structure of moods and emotions, it is easy to envisage a procedure that would generate a reasonable response. Everything in the context description points to positive affect (birthday party, exciting, decorations). The simple heuristic of matching the mood to the (demands of) the context will result, in this example, in the endorsement of a positive mood as helpful, and the rejection of negative ones. Rejecting a mood state means assigning it a value of "not useful." The only remaining decision, in positive cases, is what value to assign. The simplest heuristic for value assignment would be to choose moderate values (3 or 4) except if there is only one candidate, in which case one might assign the maximum value on the usefulness scale. Again, we suspect these details are not crucial for generating a reasonable pattern of responses.

Finally, one might think that at least the sensations task (Section F) tries to get at the experiential component, but it really doesn't succeed because it too can be solved by matching associatively related affective values—"content" is mildly positive, as is "warm" (but not "purple" or "salty"). One knows this by knowing the language, so not even items like these necessarily tap into emotional experience.

The crucial point, and one that applies to the items on all the other subtests in the MSCEIT (for which reason we will not review them further), is that responses are made by *reasoning* about emotions in a way that can be accomplished provided only that one has a *cognitive* (and linguistic) representation of emotions. No direct experience of emotions is necessary, and that, we think, is the problem not just for the MSCEIT, but probably with any pencil-and-paper test that one could imagine.

None of the above is to deny that an important feature of EI is the ability to understand and reason about emotions and emotional reactions. This ability, which by analogy with measures of general intelligence, G, and its components (Horn & Cattell, 1966), we can call crystallized EI, or EIc, is well measured by the MSCEIT. But our point is that if a measure of EI also has to assess people's abilities in the domain of emotional *experience*, then there will need to be a component of the measure that assesses the fluid (affective), experiential component of emotion, EIf.

In this section, we have tried to show that responses to the MSCEIT could be generated by algorithmic processes that do not require any emotional experience. But there are also empirical reasons derived from a structural analysis of the MSCEIT that lead to the same conclusion. Factor analyses tend to show a hierarchical structure of four correlated factors (the "branches") nested in two higher order factors, which themselves are correlated (Mayer et al., 2003).[7] When we apply an analysis of hierarchical structures to the disattenuated correlations reported in the manual (Mayer et al., 2001) for the MSCEIT (i.e., a Schmid-Leiman transformation of an oblique factor solution to produce a general factor and orthogonal residual factors; Schmid & Leiman, 1957), we find support for a general factor of EI, but, as can be seen from Table 11.1, it is a factor that is primarily associated with the last five sections of the MSCEIT. That is, it appears that the sections with the highest loadings on the general factor common to all of the sections, EIg, are those that are most cognitively oriented.

Administering the MSCEIT to psychopaths and appropriate controls would provide a further empirical test of whether the MSCEIT is primarily a measure of EIc. Given that psychopaths are widely recognized as being emotionally shallow and deficient in inhibiting behavior that has previously led to punishment and negative affect, it is clear that they are deficient in EIf. On the other hand, regarding the psychopath's ability to reason about emotion, Cleckley observed, "He also shows no evidence of a defect. So long as the test is verbal or otherwise abstract, so long as he is not a direct participant, he shows that he knows his way about" (1988, p. 346). Although as yet there are no data directly bearing on the performance of psychopaths on the MSCEIT, there is evidence suggesting that they would not be deficient on the faces task. That is, whereas some studies have found psychopaths to be deficient at recognizing a particular emotional expression (e.g., Blair, Colledge, Murray, & Mitchell, 2001; Blair et al., 2004; Kosson, Suchy, Mayer, & Libby, 2002), there has been inconsistency across studies in terms of whether psychopaths are deficient in recognizing disgust, sadness, or fear. Moreover, these studies have all failed to find significant group differences in recognizing the vast

TABLE 11.1. Schmid-Leiman orthogonalization of factors from the MSCEIT.

	EI_g	Factor1	Factor2	Factor3	Factor4	h2	u2
Faces	**0.44**	0.02	**0.54**	0.00	0.04	0.43	0.57
Pictures	**0.51**	0.03	**0.30**	0.02	0.16	0.22	0.78
Facilitation	**0.55**	0.01	**0.42**	0.10	0.09	0.30	0.70
Sensations	**0.79**	0.04	0.08	0.03	**0.44**	0.63	0.37
Changes	**0.71**	**0.63**	0.06	0.01	0.02	0.93	0.07
Blends	**0.72**	**0.57**	0.08	0.03	0.04	0.79	0.21
Manage	**0.76**	0.03	0.08	**0.55**	0.05	0.88	0.12
Relations	**0.76**	0.00	0.08	**0.51**	0.08	0.77	0.23

Note: Factors 1–4 are orthogonal to each other and to the general factor. Correlations from the MSCEIT manual were corrected for attenuation and then factored.

majority of expressions included, and Kosson et al. even reported that under some conditions, psychopaths were superior to normal controls at recognizing anger.

An Alternative Construct of EI: Emotional Fit

If EI is indeed an ability, then it should possess one of the defining features of abilities, namely that the measure of the ability should have the property that that higher observed scores indicate more of that ability. In the context of EI, one thing this cannot mean is that the more emotion a person experiences the more emotionally intelligent that person is. Somebody who committed suicide out of sympathy for a friend who lost $20 would have evidenced plenty of emotion, but we would hardly want to call such a response an emotionally intelligent one. Similarly, one would not want to say that the more a highly emotionally aware and sensitive army general "feels" for the pain and suffering of his troops, the more effective he is. What about his sensitivities apropos innocent civilians, or even his opponents? To the extent that such sensitivities were to lead to inaction or inappropriate military action, one would not argue that the general was emotionally intelligent or functionally effective, but rather that he was hypersensitive and ineffective. So, it would appear that one can have "too much" emotional sensitivity, yet a measure of emotional sensitivity surely ought somehow to figure in a measure of EI.[8]

This problem is exacerbated by the fact that very many of the ingredients of EI are likely to be noncognitive personality traits. A characteristic of such traits (e.g., Big Five traits, conscientiousness, agreeableness, neuroticism, openness, and extraversion) is that like the general's emotional sensitivity, their value or utility is generally best described by an inverted U-shaped function so that for optimal functioning (relative to any given context), it is not effective to be at one end of the scale or the other. Consider, for example, neuroticism. At the low (emotionally stable) end, such individuals tend to be unresponsive to threat and lacking in emotions such as remorse, whereas at the high end, they are overreactive neurotics. Neither is optimal. Similarly, too much boldness can lead to excessive self-confidence, but too little can lead to indecisiveness (see Hogan & Kaiser, 2005, for further examples of how extreme levels of personality traits can lead to suboptimal performance). Thus, whereas for *cognitive* abilities, more is clearly better, so that (cognitive) intelligence is always monotonically related to optimal functioning, for many (perhaps all) of the constituents of EI, this is not the case. The relation between the quantity of these constituents and their utility is a curvilinear (inverted U) rather than a monotonic function.

So if we want to treat EI as an ability, how can we satisfy the more-is-better requirement? To the degree that the construct of EI is conceived as a cognitive ability, it is in principle capable of accommodating such a requirement. But what of our demand that EI incorporates an experiential component with its predominantly curvilinear components? As we have already suggested, we can think about the experiential component by analogy to the distinction between fluid and crystallized cognitive intelligence (Gf and Gc), making the same fluid-crystallized distinction for EI. The fluid, experiential component of EI, EIf, would be the ability to "appropriately" *respond* to emotion-inducing situations, whereas crystallized EI, EIc, would be the measure of how much a person *knows* about emotions and about the appropriateness of emotional responses (which the MSCEIT already measures).

We could then view EIf as having to do with how well a person's emotional experiences are appropriate to, or "fit," the conditions. In other words, we could think in terms of trying to assess the extent to which affective reactions and sensitivities contribute to or interfere with people's capacity to optimize the physical and social functioning in the environmental conditions in which they find themselves. Viewed in this way, part of the EI construct becomes a "goodness of emotional fit" notion having to do with the qualitative and quantitative appropriateness of emotional responses to situations. In this way, EIf would be monotonically related to fit, and the measure of it would be a measure of the *ability to maintain (qualitatively and quantitatively) optimal affect for effective functioning*. This would resolve the more-is-better problem, a problem that is even more serious when viewed in light of the much discussed question of the appropriateness of consensus scoring of the MSCEIT, because consensus scoring has the curious property that the more average a set of responses, the better the ability.[9]

However, introducing a fluid component into the construct of EI to accommodate the need to take account of emotional experience still leaves unaddressed the question of what the principle constituents of the fluid component might be. As a first approximation, we suggest that it is comprised of four partially independent abilities deriving from the model of emotion presented at the beginning of this chapter, and all focusing on aspects of how a person *responds* to emotion-inducing situations rather than on what a person *knows or believes* about (the appropriateness) of such responses. The constituent abilities we have in mind are (1) responding to diverse situations with (only) *appropriate emotions*, (2) responding to situations with emotions of *appropriate intensity* (i.e., having an optimal level of emotionality), (3) responding to situations with emotions having (only) *appropriate motivational components* (wants), and (4) responding to situations with emotions having (only) *appropriate behavioral expressions* ([in]actions).

The idea behind the first of these, *responding to diverse situations with (only) appropriate emotions*, is to capture the emotion *identity* aspect of EI. Emotionally intelligent people have the "right" emotions at the right time. Except under extraordinary conditions, a woman who has just been informed that she has won a prestigious prize is more likely at that moment to experience gratitude than jealousy toward the person who nominated her. The reference to "diverse situations" is intended to provide a metric for emotion identity. In the case of gratitude, for example, there are many and varied kinds of situations in which gratitude would be an appropriate emotion. The idea would be that the measure of the identity constituent increases as diversity of gratitude responses in gratitude-appropriate situations increases.

Associated with the emotion identity constituent is a corresponding quantitative aspect, *responding to situations with emotions of appropriate intensity*. Other things being equal, the *intensity* of an emotion has to fit the situation and the perceived significance of the initiating event. One would not attribute much EI to a person who experienced the same level of distress from a minor inconvenience such as getting slightly damp from a light spring shower as from a major personal catastrophes such as the tragic unexpected death of a loved one.

The third constituent, *responding to situations with emotions having (only) appropriate motivational components,* also has to be further analyzed into its qualitative and quantitative facets. The idea is that EI precludes incongruous qualitative aspects of motivation such as wanting to viciously attack a cherished friend because she just did exactly what you had asked her to do. It also precludes inappropriate quantitative aspects of motivation such as wanting to seek bloody revenge upon someone for some trivial infraction such as forgetting to pick up milk as promised from the grocery store.

Finally, the fourth constituent ability, *responding to situations with emotions having (only) appropriate behavioral expressions*, has to do with self-regulation of the actual behaviors. Even when the motivations "fit" the situation, emotionally intelligent individuals are able to modulate their behaviors to make them better fit the situation. More emotionally intelligent individuals should be better able than less emotionally intelligent individuals to resist acting on a desire to drop everything and run in the face of a threat when the cost of running could be expected to far outweigh the benefits of doing so.

Viewing EIf as being comprised of these four (and probably several other) constituent abilities in terms of the "appropriateness" of (facets of) emotions across heterogeneous situations satisfies the requirement that higher levels of EI be associated with higher levels of functionally effective emotional responses. Viewed in this way, more is better. One reason for suspecting that this might be a profitable way of thinking about EI is that when constituent abilities of the kind we have laid out are absent in individuals, those individuals are likely to be characterizable as suffering from emotional disorders of one kind or another. For example, the psychopath who fails to experience empathy under conditions that would warrant empathy is failing to respond to a situation with (only) appropriate emotions, phobics respond to situations with inappropriately intense fear emotions, and so on.

Finally, we need to ask what kind of assessment procedure might enable one to measure a revised construct of EI along the lines we have suggested. One possibility might be to devise virtual reality environments with a view to monitoring how individuals respond to various simulated, albeit realistic, emotion-inducing situations and thus assessing individual differences in fluid EI. But even such a new age solution would have its limitations—limitations that are identical to those that sometimes plague us in the real world. Ultimately, one can never have access to the internal lives of others. The best one could hope for would be converging evidence from an array of externally observable signs—correlates of emotional experience ranging from self-reports, to physiological data (for gross aspects such as intensity), to actual behaviors and behavioral expressions.

In addition, a "portfolio" approach to assessment might be useful. That is, individuals could be interviewed to ascertain whether they have consistently responded to diverse situations with appropriate emotions of appropriate intensities and with appropriate motivational inclinations and behavioral expressions. One might even conduct interviews with collateral informants, especially if there were reason to doubt the veracity of a respondent's report. Of course, obtaining converging evidence across a battery of measures using multiple methods or EI interviews would undoubtedly be far more resource intensive to administer than the MSCEIT.

On the other hand, such approaches are more likely to help us distinguish genuinely emotionally responsive individuals from highly skilled psychopaths in a way in which we think a paper and pencil test could never do. Indeed, numerous studies have found abnormalities in the physiological responses of psychopaths to affective stimuli (e.g., Forth, 1992, Study 2; Hare & Quinn, 1971; Levenston, Patrick, Bradley, & Lang, 2000; Patrick, Bradley, & Lang, 1993). Similarly, Hare and his colleagues (Hare, 1980, 1985; Harpur, Hakstian, & Hare, 1988; Harpur, Hare, & Hakstian, 1989) have shown that interviews (and reviews of institutional records) can reliably and validly distinguish psychopaths from controls.

Conclusion

The hypothesis that there are reliable individual differences in the ability to perceive, understand, and manage emotions in the service of effective functioning is very appealing to us. Others in this book and elsewhere (e.g., Matthews, Zeidner, & Roberts, 2002) have addressed the relationship of these abilities to the more traditional cognitive abilities. Although we do not want to confuse the measurement of a construct (e.g., the MSCEIT) with the construct itself (EI), we have suggested that the MSCEIT, the best validated test of EI, probably cannot distinguish the responses of a sensitive human from those of a well-programmed computer or of a psychopath. That the subtests with the highest loadings on the general factor of the MSCEIT (EIg) are the ones that are most easy to imagine being answered by computers adds credence to our view that the MSCEIT is really only half of the story, measuring as it does primarily EIc. Ultimately, one would like to find some feasible way of assessing EIf that in combination with the MSCEIT could provide a measure of a richer construct of EI—one that incorporated an experiential component having to do with the ability to respond appropriately emotionally to heterogeneous situations. Although we have offered some preliminary suggestions as to what the principal constituents of a fluid component of EI might be, we would be the first to acknowledge that it is much easier to criticize an existing measure than it is to construct and validate a better one, and certainly we have not even begun to address the question of how one might operationalize our notion of "appropriateness," a notion upon which we lean rather heavily.

Notes

1. An important cautionary note is needed: The notion of effective functioning, although having some intuitive appeal, especially when pertaining to threats to basic needs, is not without its problems at the more complex level of social behavior. We recognize that the construct is underconstrained and possibly problematic. Ironically, our account of effective functioning could be said to suffer from some of the same problems that we attribute to the construct of EI. Nevertheless, we find it helpful as an organizing framework for thinking about the kinds of issues we are addressing here.

2. Presumably the move from recognizing emotions and emotional relationships to perceiving them is based on the entirely reasonable assumption that recognition depends on perception—that in order to recognize an emotion, one must first, in some sense, perceive it.

3. We freely admit that some of our own work (e.g., the so-called OCC model of Ortony, Clore, & Collins, 1988) has just this feature: It focuses (albeit intentionally) on only the cognitive aspect, paying little or no attention to the feeling component (Arbib, 1992).

4. There are, of course, other tests of EI, most notably the "EQ" test described in Bar-On and Parker (2000), but we prefer to examine the measure of EI designed by those who developed the construct.

5. Of course, the logic here is rather different. For the original Turing test, the idea was that an inability to distinguish the responses of a human from those of a machine would warrant the inference that machines can "think." For our "emotional Turing test," the starting point is the "fact" that machines can't emote, so that an inability to distinguish the responses of a human from those of a machine mean that the test (in this case the MSCEIT) is not actually assessing the ability to emote.

6. We need not concern ourselves with the question of whether current work on scene understanding can generate such a description because that is an aspect of the problem that has absolutely nothing to do with emotion. This simplifying strategy is analogous to that made for the Turing test with respect to speech understanding and generation. In both cases, the assumption is that the focus has to be on the *content* of what is being expressed, not on giveaway surface features, such as voice quality, that have no necessary connection to that content.

7. The Mayer and Salovey concept of a hierarchy appears to be an inclusion hierarchy: Managing emotions *includes* understanding emotions, which *includes* using emotions, which *includes* perceiving emotions (Mayer et al., 2003). This seems to imply an ordering of necessity: Without

the ability to *perceive* emotions, one cannot *use* emotions, and without the ability to *use* emotions, one cannot *understand* them, and without the ability to *understand* emotions, one cannot *manage* them. Such a "Russian dolls" nested hierarchy implies a simplex correlational structure, that is, when the subtests are appropriately ordered, the greatest correlations are nearest the diagonal and systematically fall off as one moves away from the diagonal. This is very different from the traditional treelike hierarchy seen in analyses of mental abilities (e.g., Carroll, 1993), in which subtests may be grouped into nonoverlapping clusters, which themselves may be grouped into higher order clusters.

8. Issues that warrant further discussion, but not here, include the question of how much of the variance in EI is accounted for by curvilinear constituents such as emotional sensitivity, and the extent to which actions (or inactions) are determined solely by EI (as opposed to EI together with practical reasoning capacities).

9. In this connection, we note that consensus scoring is not likely to be a useful way to measure abilities. A majority of the population in the United States believes in scientifically implausible explanations for natural phenomena. Consensus scoring would reject the last 150 years of biology, physics, and geology.

References

Arbib, M. A. (1992). Review of the book *The Cognitive Structure of Emotions. Artificial Intelligence, 54,* 229–240.

Bar-On, R., & Parker, J. D. A. (Eds.). (2000). *The handbook of emotional intelligence.* San Francisco: Jossey-Bass.

Blair, R. J. R., Colledge, E., Murray, L., & Mitchell, D. G. V. (2001). A selective impairment in the processing of sad and fearful expressions in children with psychopathic tendencies. *Journal of Abnormal Child Psychology, 29,* 491–498.

Blair, R. J. R., Mitchell, D. G. V., Peschardt, K. S., Colledge, E., Leonard, R. A., Shine, J. H., et al. (2004). Reduced sensitivity to others' fearful expressions in psychopathic individuals. *Personality and Individual Differences, 37,* 1111–1122.

Carroll, J. B. (1993). *Human cognitive abilities: A survey of factor analytic studies.* Cambridge, UK: Cambridge University Press.

Cleckley, H. (1988). *The mask of sanity* (5th ed.). St. Louis: Mosby.

Davidson, R. J. (1992). Anterior cerebral asymmetry and the nature of emotion. *Brain and Cognition, 20,* 125–151.

Ekman, P. (Ed.). (1982). *Emotion in the human face.* New York: Cambridge University Press.

Ekman, P., Levenson, R. W., & Friesen, W. V. (1983). Autonomic nervous system activity distinguishes between emotions. *Science, 221,* 1208–1210.

Fasel, B., & Luettin, J. (2003). Automatic facial expression analysis: A survey. *Pattern Recognition, 36*(1), 259–275.

Forth, A. E. (1992). *Emotion and psychopathy: A three-component analysis.* Unpublished doctoral dissertation, University of British Columbia, Vancouver, Canada.

Fox, N. A. (1991). If it's not left, it's right: Electroencephalograph asymmetry and the development of emotion. *American Psychologist, 46,* 863–872.

Frijda, N. (1986). *The emotions.* New York: Cambridge University Press.

Hare, R. D. (1980). A research scale for the assessment of psychopathy in criminal populations. *Personality and Individual Differences, 1,* 111–119.

Hare, R. D. (1985). Comparison of the procedures for the assessment of psychopathy. *Journal of Consulting and Clinical Psychology, 53*, 7–16.

Hare, R. D., & Quinn, M. J. (1971). Psychopathy and autonomic conditioning. *Journal of Abnormal Psychology, 77*, 223–235.

Harpur, T. J., Hakstian, A. R., & Hare, R. D. (1988). Factor structure of the Psychopathy Checklist. *Journal of Consulting and Clinical Psychology, 56*, 741–747.

Harpur, T. J., Hare, R. D., & Hakstian, A. R. (1989). Two-factor conceptualization of psychopathy: Construct validity and assessment implications. *Psychological Assessment: A Journal of Consulting and Clinical Psychology, 1*, 6–17.

Heise, D. R. (2001). Project Magellan: Collecting cross-cultural affective meanings via the internet. *Electronic Journal of Sociology, 5*(3).

Hogan, R., & Kaiser, R. B. (2005). What we know about leadership. *Review of General Psychology, 9*, 169–180.

Horn, J. L., & Cattell, R. B. (1966). Refinement and test of the theory of fluid and crystallized intelligence. *Journal of Educational Psychology, 57*, 253–270.

Izard, C. E. (1971). *The face of emotion.* New York: Appleton Century-Crofts.

Kosson, D. S., Suchy, Y., Mayer, A. R., & Libby, J. (2002). Facial affect recognition in criminal psychopaths. *Emotion, 2*, 398–411.

Lane, R. D., & Nadel, L. (Eds.). (2000). *Cognitive neuroscience of emotion.* New York: Oxford University Press.

LeDoux, J. E. (1996). *The emotional brain: the mysterious underpinnings of emotional life.* New York: Simon & Schuster.

Levenston, G. K., Patrick, C. J., Bradley, M. M., & Lang, P. J. (2000). The psychopath as observer: Emotion and attention in picture processing. *Journal of Abnormal Psychology, 109*, 373–385.

Matthews, G., Zeidner, M., & Roberts, R. D. (2002). *Emotional intelligence: Science and myth.* Cambridge, MA: MIT Press.

Mayer, J. D., & Salovey, P. (1995). Emotional intelligence and the construction and regulation of feelings. *Applied and Preventive Psychology, 4*, 197–208.

Mayer, J. D., & Salovey, P. (1997). What is emotional intelligence? In P. Salovey & D. Sluyter (Eds.), *Emotional development and emotional intelligence: Implications for educators* (pp. 3–31). New York: Basic Books.

Mayer, J. D., Salovey, P., & Caruso, D. R. (2001). T*he Mayer-Salovey-Caruso Emotional Intelligence Test (MSCEIT): Technical manual.* Toronto: Multi Health Systems.

Mayer, J. D., Salovey, P., Caruso, D. R., & Sitarenios, G. (2001). Emotional intelligence as a standard intelligence. *Emotion, 1*, 232–242.

Mayer, J. D., Salovey, P., Caruso, D. R., & Sitarenios, G. (2003). Measuring emotional intelligence with the MSCEIT V 2.0. *Emotion, 3*, 97–105.

Ortony, A., Clore, G. L., & Collins, A. (1988). *The cognitive structure of emotions.* New York: Cambridge University Press.

Ortony, A., Norman, D. A., & Revelle, W. (2005). Affect and proto-affect in effective functioning. In J. M. Fellous & M. A. Arbib (Eds.), *Who needs emotions: The brain meets the machine.* New York: Oxford University Press.

Ortony, A., & Radin, D. I. (1989). SAPIENS: Spreading activation processor for information encoded in network structures. In N. Sharkey (Ed.), *Models of cognition: A review of cognitive science.* Norwood, NJ: Ablex.

Ortony, A., & Turner, T. J. (1990). What's basic about basic emotions? *Psychological Review, 97*, 315–331.

Panksepp, J. (1998). *Affective neuroscience: The foundations of human and animal emotions.* New York: Oxford University Press.

Patrick, C. J., Bradley, M. M., & Lang, P. J. (1993). Emotion in the criminal psychopath: Startle reflex modulation. *Journal of Abnormal Psychology, 102,* 82–92.

Roseman, I. J. (1984). Cognitive determinants of emotions: A structural theory. In P. Shaver (Ed.), *Review of personality and social psychology* (Vol. 5). Beverly Hills, CA: Sage.

Salovey, P., & Mayer, J. D. (1990). Emotional intelligence. *Imagination, Cognition, and Personality, 9,* 185–211.

Scherer, K. R. (1984). On the nature and function of emotion: A component process approach. In K. R. Scherer & P. Ekman (Eds.), *Approaches to emotion* (pp. 293–317). Hillsdale, NJ: Erlbaum.

Schmid, J., & Leiman, J. M. (1957). The development of hierarchical factor solutions. *Psychometrika, 22,* 52–61.

Turing, A. (1950). Computing machinery and intelligence. *Mind, 59,* 433–460.

Wilson, M. D. (1988). The MRC Psycholinguistic Database: Machine Readable Dictionary, Version 2. *Behavioral Research Methods, Instruments and Computers, 20*(1), 6–11.

12

Face Memory

A Cognitive and Psychophysiological Approach to the Assessment of Antecedents of Emotional Intelligence

GRIT HERZMANN, VANESSA DANTHIIR, OLIVER WILHELM,
WERNER SOMMER, AND ANNEKATHRIN SCHACHT

Overview

In this chapter, we illustrate what we hold to be an appropriate approach to measure individual differences in cognitive abilities, such as specific aspects of emotional intelligence (EI). Instead of concentrating on the broad concept of EI, we will focus on what we deem to be neglected issues in research concerning EI: individual differences in face perception and memory. Concerning faces, EI—as defined in the four branches model—is conceptualized only with regard to individual differences in recognizing facially expressed emotions, independent from perception, learning, and recognition of faces. Currently, the assumption of functionally independent systems for the processing of facial identity and facially expressed emotions are being challenged; recent evidence suggests that emotion recognition is different for unfamiliar as compared to familiar faces. We therefore argue that it is necessary to consider and measure both individual differences in emotion recognition and face perception and memory in order to understand their connection.

Concentrating on face perception and memory, we demonstrate how functional and neurophysiological models of face processing, as well as important behavioral and neuroscientific evidence, can be used as a productive path along which to proceed with the development of measures of individual differences in face memory. We propose that the measurement of face memory, or of any other cognitive process related to EI, must be anchored in (a) established functional models of cognition, (b) sound experimental and neuroscientific evidence, and (c) multivariate psychometric data.

Measurement of Emotional Intelligence (EI) and Related Constructs

Our answers to the editors' questions could hardly be more diverse in length, with some being addressed very shortly, others at length and in detail. More precisely, this chapter will essentially focus on the prospects of EI assessment with information-processing tasks and with psychophysiological measures. Rather than providing *ex cathedra* advice, we will attempt to illustrate and exemplify our recommendation with a specific example—face memory. We will present this example in some detail, highlighting its relevance for EI and many aspects we deem critical to deriving indicators of EI-related abilities.

The core of this chapter will therefore delineate a research agenda for measuring individual differences in face memory. This research agenda is based on the integration of experimental, psychophysiological, and correlational research. Meeting the challenge of an integrated measurement approach is difficult and is most feasible if the analysis is restricted to circumscribed cognitive abilities, such as face memory. In developing our framework, we will start by summarizing functional and neurophysiological models of face processing. In addition, we will present available evidence for three proposed abilities of face memory: perceiving, learning, and recognizing faces. These abilities are discussed from an experimental and psychophysiological viewpoint, and from the perspective of differences between individuals. Each section is concluded by discussing measurement issues and proposing measurement instruments. Finally, we briefly summarize our expectations concerning such a proposed approach and conclude with special attention to measurement implications and the potential impact on EI research.

Question 1. What Is the Optimal Approach to Assessment of EI?

This question is based on two important presuppositions: First, EI is assumed to exist as a coherent epistemological entity, and second, EI is supposed as causal to observable individual differences. Once these presuppositions are made, it is obviously of interest to identify approaches best suited for the measurement of this entity. However, we hesitate to make these presuppositions. Obviously this hesitation makes it hard to legitimately answer the question. So, we wish to firstly explain our position.

Rather than classifying ourselves as believers or contenders of the dominating model—the four-branches model underlying the MSCEIT (Mayer, Salovey, & Caruso, 1999; Mayer, Salovey, Caruso, & Sitarenios, 2003)—we prefer to be agnostic regarding whether EI exists and causes individual differences. This is, of course, not to say that the concepts and considerations underlying the MSCEIT are irrelevant. Indeed, we think that performances related to concepts like the perception of emotions can hardly be overrated in their relevance for everyday life and for research on cognitive processes.

We wish to refrain from extensively discussing more or less well-suited approaches in the assessment of EI because we doubt that the proposed cognitive processes of EI should be subsumed under one overarching construct. Potentially, after long and laborious research, there will be compelling evidence for a general factor of EI—just as for general intelligence. It is thus hard to make claims about optimal approaches to the measurement of a construct if one thinks that current conceptions of that constructs are not adequately substantiated. However, research on measuring the intensity of some psychological disposition in persons does need psychological substantiation. Hopefully, our own research can serve as an instance of contribution to such substantiation.

Our research in the area of EI might be labeled atomistic, hands-on, and down-to-earth, in focusing on something rather specific and then looking at it from a variety of perspectives, namely cognitive, psychophysiological, and correlational. Once a broad variety of such work in a field has accumulated, only then might it be instrumental to reconsider the structure of individual differences in it. From this perspective, an optimal measurement approach is one that allows answering underlying research (or an applied) questions optimally. The answers to questions 4 and 5 will hopefully provide an illustration of what we deem to be an optimal or appropriate approach in testing the structure of individual differences in important aspects of face cognition. Instead of addressing very general and broad ideas of emotional intelligence, we restrict ourselves to a highly specific set of cognitive abilities that we believe are directly relevant to aspects of EI—those involved in face perception and memory—to illustrate how the theoretical derivation and content-valid grounding of new measures can proceed.

In the four branches model, EI is defined as including the abilities to perceive, assess, understand, and modify one's own and also other people's emotions. The ability to perceive emotions is concerned only with the recognition of emotions and does not take into account the recognition of person identity. Conceptually, it is obvious that the perception and correct identification of faces incorporates the perception and recognition of facially expressed emotions as one specific aspect. Only if we know about facial features and their configurations can we perceive and interpret changes in them and relate these to emotional states. At just as fundamental a level, if we are unable to recognize a person's face because we cannot access the stored facial structures in memory (or did not adequately learn the face previously), this would inhibit our ability to correctly interpret the subtleties of emotions expressed on a familiar person's face (allowing, of course, for idiosyncrasies in expression).

Recent evidence indeed shows that emotions are recognized differentially in unfamiliar as compared to familiar faces (Baudoin, Stansone, & Tiberghien, 2000; Schweinberger & Soukup, 1998). Thus, when asked to judge whether a face expresses happiness or disgust, participants were quicker and more accurate when the face shown was personally familiar, that is, when participants knew these people from previous social encounters (Wild-Wall, 2004). Conversely, the emotional expression influences the ease of recognizing identity (e.g., Baudouin, Gilibert, Sansone, & Tiberghien, 2000). Therefore, the assumption of functionally independent systems (e.g., Bruce & Young, 1986) for the processing of facial identity and facial expression may not hold. Recently, Calder and Young (2005) proposed that the bifurcation of the corresponding processing streams takes place only after a common structural encoding phase, suggesting a strong connection between face perception and memory and emotion recognition.

Taken together, it seems reasonable to assume that face perception and memory are a necessary requirement for other cognitive abilities, such as EI, and more specifically, for the ability of perceiving emotions: Identity specific information, including the name of a face, can be retrieved only if the respective person is familiar. Emotions expressed in a familiar face are recognized faster and more accurately. It is therefore interesting to investigate individual differences in face perception and memory in order to explore its connection to EI-related abilities like emotion recognition. Approaches to emotion recognition that do not consider other aspects of face processing might be flawed because there is a serious threat that instead of emotion recognition, more general aspects of face processing were measured. We do not think that individual differences in face processing are noise or measurement error. In an effort to develop an understanding of individual differences in a construct such as emotion recognition, it will be not only instrumental but also necessary to develop an understanding of components involved in such processes.

Our perspective on the importance of face perception and memory to the construct of EI, as broadly conceived, rests on the notion that faces are visual objects of special social and emotional significance. Faces are the most distinctive and widely used keys to our conspecifics' identities. They convey highly important socially relevant information such as age, gender, emotional and other expressions, mate and social attractiveness, lip speech, and gaze direction. In addition, faces are a primary gateway to semantic knowledge about familiar people, such as the person's occupation or social status, and his or her name. To perceive, learn, understand, and recognize information that a face provides is therefore crucial for successful interpersonal interaction.

We have all experienced occasional failures in performing these processes, which can lead to awkward social moments. A friend unwittingly introduces us to someone whom we have already met a number of times, but despite the previous encounters, we fail to recognize the person. We say the usual pleasantries about how nice it is to meet, only to hear in return, "But we've met before. *Twice.*" The role one plays in such situations partly depends on individual differences in remembering faces. Individual differences in the speed and accuracy of face perception and memory can be considered important input for further information processing—specifically, cognitive activities subsumed under the label emotional or social intelligence.

Theoretical approaches to face processing (e.g., Bruce & Young, 1986) have identified three different classes of information that can be derived from faces: (a) perceptual structural aspects, (b) knowledge about a person, and (c) changeable aspects. Perceptual structural aspects of faces are necessary for the recognition of a face as familiar, which requires the perception of a face as a face and furthermore, the recognition of facial structures that were stored in memory from previous encounters; we will herein refer to the combination of these processes as face memory. Perceptual structural aspects might also be, as explained above, relevant for emotion recognition. Knowledge about a person refers to semantic information associated with the face (social status, occupation, etc.) and the retrieval of their name. Changeable aspects involve facial expressions, lip speech, and other visually derived information (age, gender, etc.) and are independent from the familiarity of the face. The relation of changeable aspects, or more specifically, facial expressions, to EI is apparent and discussed in detail in this volume (O'Sullivan, Chapter 10, this volume). However, faces comprise much more information than facially expressed emotions that can be relevant for EI, such as the information required for face memory—the perception of specific features of a face (i.e., eyes, nose, and mouth) and their configurations that will be employed to learn and later recognize a particular face, and the emotion expressed in it.

In answering questions 4 and 5, we will present a theoretical model of individual differences in face memory that incorporates the perception, learning, and recognition of faces. The derivation of indicators for these proposed factors hopefully goes beyond the vagueness surrounding the underlying performance models of most currently available EI measures.

One plausible, theoretically derived measurement model for individual differences in face perception and memory is shown in Figure 12.1. This model is solely concerned with face perception and memory and does not explicitly mention emotion recognition, because as yet the precise connection between the two is not known. Three successive stages, perceiving faces, learning faces, and recognizing faces, are considered necessary to successfully remember a face.

In order to recognize a person's face—as well as its emotional expression—we must first be able to visually analyze the facial structure into its features, as well as their configuration. *Perceiving faces* thus refers to the perception and extraction of variable and invariant aspects of faces and their maintenance in memory for a short period. After a visual stimulus is successfully recognized as a face, we can correctly recognize it as familiar only if we have seen the face and stored it in memory during previous encounters. It can therefore be assumed that *learning faces* depends on the analysis of structural codes of perceived faces and the encoding of relevant and unchangeable features into memory, in order to preserve them for a short or longer period. It should be noted that we use the term "learning," herein, to refer to the process necessary to encode structural codes into memory, independently of how long they are stored. Finally, given the existence of stored facial structures in memory and successful perceptual and structural analysis of the actual face, the recognition of a perceived face as familiar still requires the activation of the correct representations of the facial structures stored in memory.

In sum, *recognizing faces* requires, at a minimum, the extraction of the invariant facial structural features from the perceived visual stimulus, the existence of representations stored in memory, and the successful comparison of stored facial structures with those currently seen. Thus, in our model, face memory is depicted as a general factor, with perception, learning, and recognizing faces as narrower factors. Face memory was used here and will be used in subsequent sections to illustrate our measurement approach.

All this being said, we will return to the editors' question on optimal approaches to the measurement of EI and make the two presuppositions for the sake of providing a hopefully clear answer.

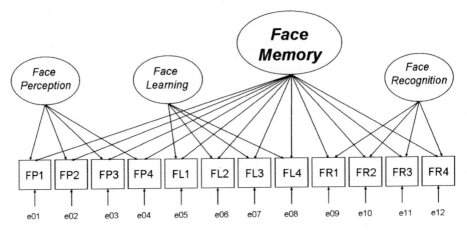

Figure 12.1. A hierarchical measurement model for individual differences in face memory. In line with convention, ellipses represent latent constructs, rectangles represent task indicators, single-headed arrows represent causal paths, and e represents residual variance. FP1 through FP4, FL1 through FL4, and FR1 though FR4 are indicators for Face Perception, Face Recognition, and Face Learning, respectively.

An optimal approach to the assessment of EI related cognitive processes should have a variety of features. The assessment of validity, viability, and utility of EI, as a construct of individual differences research, is essentially an empirical issue, and the standards for assessing and weighing empirical evidence have methodological as well as psychological aspects. It is critical that our measurement devices satisfy the well-established psychometric criteria. Establishing new, broad, and general constructs that predict important real-life criteria is a very difficult job. Sound measurement procedures, careful consideration of method artifacts, and convincing incremental validity including assessment of redundancy with established instruments and constructs are obvious methodological desiderata. Satisfying these and related methodological issues is necessary but not sufficient for establishing new constructs. Psychological theory is the core issue in deriving measurement instruments, and the section "Empirical Foundation of Face Memory" aims to outline such a theory for face memory as one important aspect of EI.

We have discussed practice and standards for the measurement of EI elsewhere (Wilhelm, 2005), and various skeptical comments exist concerning available assessments approaches (i.e., Schulze et al., Chapter 8, this volume, and various contributions from the editorial team). Thus, there are numerous answers as to what classify as sub-optimal approaches to the assessment of EI, from within a psychometric context.

It is easier to specify what qualifies an approach to be suboptimal than to detail what makes an approach optimal. Apart from the rather obvious (but nevertheless far from trivial) conformance to psychometric standards, assessment of EI should also reflect knowledge from relevant psychological disciplines. Two examples of measures with at least some of the desired background in experimental psychology are the Japanese and Caucasian Brief Affect Recognition Test (JACBART; Matsumoto & Ekman, 1992) and the Levels of Emotional Awareness Scale (LEAS; Lane, Quinlan, Schwartz, Walker, & Zeitlin, 1990). The JACBART (Matsumoto et al., 2000) is firmly grounded in research on emotion recognition, and it is unique with respect to the validity of the expressions used to portray emotions. One concern with the JACBART is that it is an indicator that is essentially a speed measure of emotion recognition ability; exposition of the stimuli, to be classified with respect to the emotion displayed, is strictly time limited and the level of difficulty dramatically changes if exposition time is modified. Variants of emotion recognition measures probably can provide indicators that jointly could serve as an emotion recognition ability test battery, thereby allowing a multivariate assessment approach that—other things being equal—would be a better, though not necessarily optimal, approach to EI assessment.

We consider it too early to assess the quality of other attempts to assess EI-related individual differences that are based upon theories of information processing (such as the Emotional Stroop Test; Coffey, Berenbaum, & Kerns, 2003). To the extent that theories about ongoing cognitive processes gain support, such approaches are worth being pursued in the future. Taken together, we think there is a strong need for more measures of maximal performance with sound conceptual and empirical grounding in experimental work.

In the section on empirical foundation of face memory, some EI-related constructs and related measures will be discussed that meet the psychometric criteria as well as the demand of strong grounding in relevant psychological knowledge.

Question 2. Can Self-Reports and Questionnaires Ever Provide Assessments of Intelligence and Competence?

Our answer to this question is an unequivocal NO. Measures that do not tap maximal behavior cannot qualify as tests of ability constructs. Furnham (2001, 2002) has investigated the relation between self-ratings of intelligence and the results from traditional intelligence assessments and found only small to moderate correlations between both measures. We expect that self-ratings of EI are likely to be the form of self-report assessment that is most highly correlated with ability EI. However, we anticipate the magnitude of such relations to be no higher than small or moderate, and obviously too small to justify substituting self-rating questionnaires for ability measures of EI.

Question 3. Is Consensus Scoring Valid for Ability Measures?

Although there are some interesting methodological developments (Legree, Psotka, Tremble, & Bourne, 2005; MacCann, Roberts, Matthews, & Zeidner, 2004; see also Schulze, Wilhelm, & Kyllonen, Chapter 8, this volume), there are also several persistent problems in consensus scoring (MacCann et al., 2004; McDaniel, Morgeson, Finnegan, Campion, & Braverman, 2001). The answer to the question of whether consensus scoring is valid for EI ability measures depends critically on the strength of the relation of such measures with those scored by objective standards.

In this chapter, we will describe a variety of measures that do have objectively correct responses. It is highly implausible that researchers or practitioners, who have a choice between consensus and objectively scored measures purportedly assessing individual differences in the same construct, would choose the consensus-scored test. Thus, consensus scoring is justified whenever the measures satisfy a practical need and there are no competing measures with objectively scored responses that assess the same construct with the same fidelity and reliability. Consensus-scored measures of EI are methodologically superior to self-reports of EI—although such measures do not reflect the same construct.

The Prospects of Information-Processing Tasks and Psychophysiological Measures—Answers to Questions 4 and 5

Cognitive and psychophysiological research is highly relevant for the measurement of EI. Measurement of cognitive abilities in general and EI in particular benefit greatly from an anchorage in (a) information-processing models and experimental investigations and (b) psychophysiological paradigms and knowledge about manifestations of ongoing processes in the brain. Answers to questions 5 and 4 will highlight our overall assessment of the situation before going into more detail by considering the measurement of individual differences in face memory. For a better understanding of our approach we answer first question 5 and then 4.

Question 5. What Are the Prospects for Assessment of EI Using Information-Processing Tasks?

Information-processing models are often the result of long-term, fruitful research in various fields and can thereby provide detailed information about processes underlying cognitive abilities. Behaviors captured by EI measures are considered caused by a latent construct reflecting individual differences in a specified information-processing ability. Thus, relating extant as well as prospective EI measures to a theory of information processing should be considered necessary (at least eventually). A relatively new construct benefits from being grounded in information-processing theories through the concomitant knowledge base that can lead to the identification of processes underlying a proposed ability. Such grounding offers a starting point for operational definitions for measures of individual differences in these processes. Therefore, the assessment of EI using information-processing tasks is a promising and desirable avenue for EI research. However, developing valid and profound ideas of the information processing underlying broad ability constructs is no small feat and requires collaboration with experts from particular content areas to anchor the measures in established and tested theories of information processing. This is what we attempt in the following sections, with regard to face memory.

Question 4. What Are the Prospects for Assessment of EI Using Psychophysiological and Neurological Measures?

Psychophysiological data add evidence for mechanisms and substrates underlying human information processing—an important and critical layer of facts—that facilitates assessment of the viability and theoretical soundness of behavioral measures. Event-related potential (ERP) amplitudes and latencies can reflect consequences of experimental manipulations, in many instances similar to behavioral data like speed and accuracy of responses. Similarly, individual differences in speed or accuracy of performance may be reflected in ERPs as well. In other words, if individual differences in ERPs reflect distinctions and similarities between tasks that are also found with traditional ability indicators, then these psychophysiological data should have an equivalent or highly similar structure. This, however, is not a given but an empirical question.

In this chapter, we will consider ERPs as indicators of processes related to face memory and discuss evidence supporting this conceptualization. We do, however, draw an important distinction between behavioral and psychophysiological data. Behavioral data, as discussed here, index whether or not a person meets the instructions to respond quickly and/or accurately, and responding as per the instructions is the ultimate criterion. ERPs accompanying behavior have a different status. ERPs—like other psychophysiological data—are measures of what goes on in the brain while a person is performing a task, and this should not be confused with task performance itself.

In many instances, there are direct and close relationships between ERP parameters, such as amplitude and latency of a specific component, and the speed and quality of performance. In fact, the information provided by ERPs may be more pure and less dependent upon response strategies than information provided by behavioral measures, because the latter provide us only with the end product of processing, whereas ERPs give us a relatively direct insight into specific processes underlying the final performance. Because ERPs can be indicators of specific processes, which may differ in accuracy and speed between persons, they could be considered as specific assessment tools. Such measures should index the intended processes, correlate with corresponding behavioral measures, and satisfy psychometric criteria. We will discuss these issues further when we consider such ERP indices in the section on the empirical foundation of face memory.

Theoretical Foundation of Face Memory

Due to its complexity, face processing involves the interplay of a number of different functional components. The following sections will outline how functional models conceptualize the cooperation of the different components in face processing and some of their neuroanatomical underpinnings.

Functional Models

On the basis of error reports concerning everyday face recognition and identification, and neuropsychological and experimental investigations, Bruce and Young (1986) developed the most widely held theoretical model of the components involved in face processing. The model specifies seven distinct codes, derived during the perception of faces and the retrieval of information related to the particular face, as products of the functional components in the face-processing system and their interaction. Here we will confine the description of the model to the codes and functional components relevant to face memory.

If a face or a portrait of a face is seen, *pictorial codes* are derived from the retinal input. These pictorial codes are represented in the initial stage of face processing, in which perceptual characteristics of a face are processed, termed *structural encoding* in Bruce and Young's model (Figure 12.2, panel A). Such codes are relatively raw images that contain much irrelevant information for face memory, such as lighting, flaws in the picture and its grain, and the pose of the person. Still within the structural encoding stage, pictorial encoding is followed by the extraction of viewpoint- and expression-independent descriptions of the structure of the perceived face (i.e., *structural codes*). Structural codes are suggested to mediate everyday recognition of familiar faces because they incorporate the facial features and their specific arrangement (configuration), required to distinguish faces from each other. For each familiar face, Bruce and Young postulate the existence of a *face recognition unit* (FRU), that is, interconnected sets of structural codes—some containing the details of particular facial features, some encompassing the configuration of these features. If the seen face is familiar, the structural codes derived during perception will match those stored within the corresponding FRU.

According to Bruce and Young, when an FRU is activated by matching structural codes, it gives rise to a feeling of familiarity but not yet to recognition of that face. In the third stage of the model, activation from the FRU feeds into a *person identity node* (PIN). PINs are *identity-specific semantic codes*, that is, information about the person, such as occupation, nationality, and other biographical facts. In contrast to FRUs, which depend solely on visual input, PINs can also be accessed via voice, gait, or the name of the person. Bruce and Young postulate that it is the access of identity-specific semantic codes in the PINs that give rise to the feeling of recognizing and identifying a person. Their final stage in identifying a person involves the retrieval of the person's name—the *name code*—which is assumed to be stored separately from other semantic knowledge.

Although the Bruce and Young model does not specify how information about unfamiliar people is learned, it is likely that as people become familiar, structural codes for their faces will be extensively elaborated through frequent exposure and will become represented within new FRUs, just as semantic and name information are stored in new PINs and name recognition units. Yet, it has to be said that much less is known about the acquisition of face- and person-related knowledge than about the recognition of already familiar people.

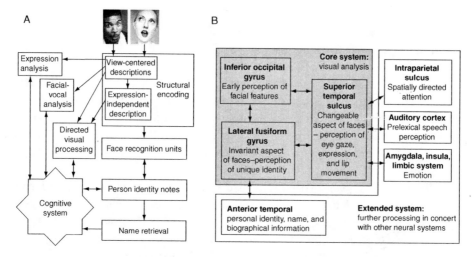

Figure 12.2. Bruce and Young's (1986) functional model of face processing (panel A) contains separate parallel routes for recognizing facial identity and changeable facial aspects. Face recognition is considered as matching a seen face to its stored representations, at the level of face recognition units, which exist only for known faces and contain their view-independent structural codes. The Bruce and Young framework is compatible with the distributed human neural system for face perception proposed by Haxby et al. (2000; panel B). This identifies the neural structures that are involved in recognizing changeable and invariant information of faces. This model is divided into a core system for the visual analysis of faces, which comprises three occipital-temporal regions, and an extended system that includes neural systems that are involved in other cognitive functions.

A major extension, subsequently added to the Bruce and Young model, shows the close connection between emotion recognition and face memory. Breen, Caine, and Coltheart (2000) and Ellis and Lewis (2001) implemented another affective process into the face-processing model in addition to the analysis of emotional facial expressions. They proposed a second pathway bifurcating after the FRUs, toward a system that is responsible for the generation of affective responses to familiar faces, a feeling of familiarity. This affective response is presumably generated by the amygdala and can be measured, for example, with skin-conductance responses (e.g., Herzmann, Schweinberger, Sommer, & Jentzsch, 2004). Patients suffering from Capgras delusion (e.g., Ellis & Lewis, 2001) fail to develop an affective response to familiar faces. Although they are still able to—cognitively—recognize familiar people, they hold the very strong belief that these people are replaced by imposters, doubles, or aliens.

Neuroanatomical Underpinnings

Following the Bruce and Young model, and integrating findings from neuropsychological, neurophysiological, and brain imaging studies, Haxby, Hoffman, and Gobbini (2000) proposed a neuroanatomical model for the organization of the face-processing system, which distinguishes between invariant and changeable aspects of faces (Figure 12.2, panel B). The representations of invariant aspects of faces support the recognition and identification of individuals, whereas the representations of changeable aspects of faces, such as eye gaze, expression, and lip reading, convey information facilitating social communication. The model is organized into a core system for the visual analysis of faces, which is connected to an extended system for processing the meaning of information gleaned from the face. The core system consists of three bilateral brain regions, with an anatomical configuration that suggests a hierarchical organization in which the inferior occipital region may provide input to the lateral fusiform and superior temporal sulcal regions (Figure 12.3).

The inferior occipital gyri are supposed to process facial features in the initial stages of face perception. Thereafter, invariant aspects of faces, which represent their unique identities, are processed in the lateral fusiform gyrus. In this region, the activity in response to faces has been found to be greater than that evoked by the perception of nonsense stimuli or nonface objects, especially in the right hemisphere (e.g., Kanwisher, McDermott, & Chun, 1997). On the basis of such findings, some authors have proposed a so-called fusiform face area, situated in the fusiform gyrus and conceived as a specialized module for face perception (e.g., Kanwisher et al., 1997; McCarthy, Puce, Gore, & Allison, 1997). The lateral fusiform gyrus is active during passive viewing of faces and when attention is directed toward invariant aspects of the facial configuration. In contrast, attending to changeable aspects of faces, like gaze direction, emotional expression, or lip movement, preferentially activates the superior temporal sulcus (e.g., Hoffman & Haxby, 2000). Therefore, the superior temporal sulcus is suggested to process changeable aspects of faces.

In the extended system, as conceived by Haxby et al. (2000), neural systems that perform other cognitive functions are considered to act in concert with face-responsive regions. For example, access to semantic and biographical information during face processing (corresponding to the PINs proposed by Bruce & Young, 1986) appears to be mediated by anterior temporal regions (Sergent, Ohta, & MacDonald, 1992).

Thus, distinct aspects of face processing are supported by multiple brain regions that are spatially disparate yet act together in a coordinated way. However, Haxby et al. (2000) point out that the degree of functional separation of the different regions in the face-processing system is unclear. For example, the fusiform face–responsive regions may play a supportive role also in expression analysis, because persons may have characteristic facial expressions, associated solely with them. Haxby et al. (2000) emphasized that brain systems for face processing may work not in isolation but might participate in other cognitive functions such as object recognition, especially when demands are similar to those for face processing.

Empirical Foundation of Face Memory

In face-processing research, a variety of experimental paradigms are used that can be related to individual components of face recognition models. More recently, the

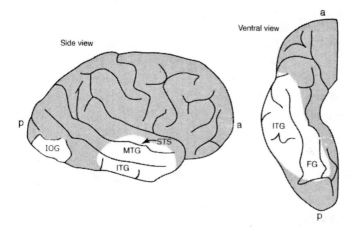

Figure 12.3. The human brain from ventral and side view, showing the brain regions relevant for face processing: inferior occipital gyrus (IOG), fusiform gyrus (FG), superior temporal sulcus (STS), and medial temporal gyrus (MTG). The anterior side of the brain is indicated by an "a," the posterior by a "p."

neurophysiological and neuroanatomical concomitants of these processes have been explored by combining some of these paradigms with psychophysiological data or brain imaging recordings. The implementation of these paradigms in individual differences research is still in its infancy. In this section, we will briefly outline the progress that has been made in research on perception, learning, and recognition of faces. On this foundation, we will introduce both existing and conceivable instruments, derived from experimental and psychophysiological paradigms, for assessing individual differences on a behavioral and psychophysiological level in these three areas.

We include ERP components in the measurement section that have been shown to be related to specific processes underlying face memory. We wish to emphasize that for ERPs to be potentially useful as measures of individual differences, they must (a) reliably index brain activity, (b) be stable across time, and (c) be sensitive to differences in the processes that they are supposed to measure. It is an empirical issue for future research to more fully investigate the prospects for the assessment of cognitive processes such as face memory or components of EI using psychophysiological and other neuroscientific measures, along with behavioral indicators. We suggest that such investigations are promising, under the abovementioned provisos, and we will sketch their potential relevance in the following sections.

Perceiving Faces

Perceiving faces comprises several processes that, together, enable the perception of a face as a general gestalt. Important aspects of this high-level visual processing of faces are the analysis of (a) first-order features, (b) second-order or configural features, and (c) the holistic perception and representation of faces. First-order features are facial elements that can be referred to in relative isolation, such as the size and shape of the eyes, nose, mouth, and chin. Configural information refers to the spatial relationships among first-order features, such as the distance between the nose and the mouth. The notion of holistic perception and representation specifies that faces are perceived as undifferentiated wholes or gestalts (Farah, Wilson, Drain, & Tanaka, 1998). Both configural and holistic processing are contrasted with part- or feature-based processing, in which local information (e.g., eye color and lip shape) supports perception and recognition.

Experimental Evidence

Evidence suggesting the importance of configural information in face perception is derived from the performance effects of turning faces upside-down, coined an *inversion effect*, and from the effect of spatially manipulating facial features (e.g., Freire, Lee, & Symons, 2000). Support for holistic processing in face perception is seen in the so-called "part-whole recognition effect" (e.g., Tanaka & Farah, 1993) as well as the "composite face effect" (e.g., Young, Hellawell, & Hay, 1987). Tasks eliciting these latter effects typically also compare the difference between inverted and upright face stimuli on the effect under consideration. The utility of such difference measures as individual differences indicators of the quality of face memory is currently uncharted territory.

The face inversion effect is a robust phenomenon that can be observed when photographs or drawings of inverted faces are to be named, classified, or matched to other faces (Valentine, 1988). When focusing solely on the inversion effect, two types of tasks are typically used: One such task requires the recognition of upright or inverted faces that have been studied in upright or inverted conditions, and the other is a matching task that requires deciding whether upright or inverted faces, presented simultaneously, are the same or different.

Many studies have shown that turning a face upside-down has two important outcomes. One outcome is that the face becomes more difficult to perceive and recognize, evidenced by a decrease in accuracy in recognition tasks or a slowing of response speed in matching tasks (e.g., Diamond & Carey, 1986). Importantly, this detrimental effect of inversion on the perception and recognition of faces is disproportionately greater than the effect of inverting objects (for review, see Valentine, 1988). The second result is that even striking spatial distortions of the features in the face, such as the eyes and mouth being inverted within a face, are much less perceptible when the face as a whole is shown upside-down than when it is upright (e.g., the Margaret Thatcher illusion; Thompson, 1980). Studies that have manipulated the spatial relations between facial features have found much greater detrimental effects of inversion on discrimination and recognition than those in which only local features were changed (e.g., Freire, Lee, & Symons, 2000). These findings of disproportionately stronger inversion-induced impairments for the processing of spatial relations, as opposed to featural or part-based information, support the notion that configural relations between facial features represent important information used in normal face perception.

Taken together, the face inversion effect is thought to result mainly from a disruption to processing of configural information, which is held to be sensitive to face orientation and restricted to upright faces. Inversion does not affect the processing of featural, or part-based information, to the same extent as configural and holistic information, as evidenced by the considerably smaller inversion effect found for objects (Diamond & Carey, 1986) and the fact that the part-whole and composite faces effects (to be mentioned below) do not occur in the inverted condition. It is thus generally accepted that the visual processing of faces is special, not least because face perception and recognition relies more heavily upon configural information than does object recognition (Valentine, 1988). The face inversion effect is now taken as diagnostic for configural processing (Maurer, Le Grand, & Mondloch, 2002). It is possible, however, to argue that visual processing of objects relies on the same type of visual processing as faces, and that differences in findings between face and object perception are simply due to human expertise with faces. Apparently, there is only limited evidence supporting this position (e.g., Diamond & Carey, 1986).

We now turn to evidence in support of the importance of holistic processing in face perception. In the part–whole paradigm (Tanaka & Farah, 1993), a particular facial feature (e.g., Larry's nose) is recognized more accurately in the context of the whole, originally studied face (e.g., Larry's nose in Larry's face vs. Harry's nose in Larry's face) than when tested as an isolated feature (e.g., Larry's nose vs. Harry's nose). This advantage provided by the whole-face context is not found for other objects such as scrambled faces[1] or houses, and is eradicated by inverting the face. Similarly, the composite face effect (Young et al., 1987) refers to the phenomenon whereby upper and lower face halves derived from different faces appear to fuse into a new face when the halves are aligned, impeding, for example, recognition or naming of one half face as compared to when the halves are horizontally misaligned or inverted. Both effects suggest that upright faces are usually processed as a gestalt, making it more difficult to focus on individual features.

Psychophysiological and Neuroimaging Evidence

Psychophysiological and neuroimaging studies provide evidence for the mechanisms underlying face perception along with their neuroanatomical substrates. The N170 component, which appears around 150–200 ms after stimulus onset as a negative peak over occipitotemporal areas, is sensitive to faces but absent, attenuated, or changed in hemispheric laterality for visual stimuli other than faces (e.g., Bentin, Allison, Puce, Perez, & McCarthy, 1996). The N170 is delayed and enhanced by inversion of faces (Rossion et al., 1999), but unaffected either by familiarity of the face (e.g., Rossion et al., 1999) or by directed attention (Séverac-Cauquill, Edmonds, & Taylor, 2000). The N170 has thus been suggested to reflect perceptual encoding processes of faces. The delayed and enhanced N170 found for inverted faces is thought to reflect a more difficult encoding of inverted than upright faces, due to the diminished availability of holistic and configural information in the inverted condition. The N170 has also been found in response to stimuli such as isolated eyes and combinations of inner facial features presented without a face contour (e.g., Bentin et al., 1996), providing evidence that feature-based processes can also elicit an N170.

There is considerable evidence that the perception of faces is mediated by the visual extrastriate cortex. As described in the neuroanatomical model of face perception (Haxby et al., 2000), areas in the middle lateral fusiform gyrus (Kanwisher et al., 1997) and in the inferior occipital gyrus (e.g., Halgren, Raij, Marinkovic, Jousmaki, & Hari, 1999) have been found to respond more strongly and with a right hemispheric preponderance during the presentation of faces as compared to other object categories. These brain regions have been found to be related to the discrimination between faces and other object categories (i.e., "face detection"; Rossion, Schiltz, & Crommelinck, 2003). Interestingly, faces and nonface objects are not processed in discrete, segregated brain areas; instead, they are associated with their own specific pattern of brain activity in widely distributed but overlapping areas (Ishai, Ungerleider, Martin, & Haxby, 2000).

The face inversion effect has also been investigated with fMRI (Haxby et al., 1999). Contrary to the assumption that inverted faces would be processed by mechanisms utilized for the perception of other objects, rather than by specialized face perception mechanisms, Haxby et al. (1999) found that face-selective brain regions were activated equally for upright and inverted faces. However, in response to inverted faces, cortical areas involved in normal object perception were also activated, suggesting that the face perception systems alone are inadequate for dealing with inverted faces, leading to the recruitment of processing resources from object perception systems.

Correlational Evidence

Individual differences in face perception have been studied predominantly in patients with prosopagnosia. Prosopagnosia constitutes two broad classes of deficits: failures to form accurate facial percepts, that is, to employ configural and holistic processing (apperceptive prosopagnosia); and the inability to match facial percepts to face representations in memory (associative prosopagnosia). In most cases, prosopagnosia is a clinical condition following brain damage or neurological diseases. Recently, congenital prosopagnosia has received some attention, referring to a chronic impairment in face processing apparent from birth despite intact basic visual and intellectual functions (e.g., Kress & Daum, 2003a). It is unclear to what extent congenital prosopagnosia overlaps with acquired prosopagnosia; some recent evidence suggests a differentiation into apperceptive and associative types for congenital prosopagnosia also (e.g., Kress & Daum, 2003a).

Patients with prosopagnosia do not exhibit the normal advantage in processing upright compared to inverted faces (e.g., Behrmann, Avidan, Marotta, & Kimchi, 2005), and in face matching tasks they seem to meticulously compare every single feature of the faces (Kress & Daum, 2003a). Furthermore, patients with prosopagnosia do not show a larger N170 for faces compared to other nonface objects, as seen in normal people (e.g., Eimer & McCarthy, 1999; Kress & Daum, 2003b). It has therefore been suggested that patients with prosopagnosia cannot extract configural information from faces nor process faces holistically, but might instead employ feature-based processing strategies.

In normal participants the N170 has recently been shown to be responsive to perceptual sensitivity, measured as d' (hits minus false alarms), in an identity decision task (Yoon, Halit, & Csibra, 2005). Participants were shown two faces in immediate succession. The first face was presented in three-quarter view; the second was seen in frontal view. Half of the faces were from the same ethnic group (race) as the participants; the other half were from a different race. The task was to decide whether both faces belonged to the same person. The outcome of interest was that participants showed a significantly higher d' and N170 for own race faces. The difference of the N170 amplitude for own minus other race faces correlated ($r = .74$, $p < .01$) with the magnitude of own-race d', indicating that neural processes serving identity discrimination may be reflected in relative differences in N170 amplitude.[2]

Measurement

Measuring the perception of faces has long been of great importance for neuropsychological research investigating patients with deficits in face processing, like in prosopagnosia. The Benton and Van Allen Test (Benton & Van Allen, 1968) is an unspeeded, unfamiliar-face matching task, in which decisions are made about the identity (i.e., same or different person) of simultaneously presented faces, seen either under the same condition or in different viewpoints or lighting. The rationale behind the test is that faces can be correctly matched only if the relevant facial structures can be extracted. However, the Benton and Van Allen Test has been criticized because people with prosopagnosia can score within the normal range on this test presumably by using feature-matching strategies.

When measuring face perception, two important requirements must be met: (a) The demands on memory must be minimized, and (b) the possibility of fulfilling the task requirements through a reliance on feature-matching must also be minimized. The Cambridge Face Perception Task (CFPT; Dingle, Duchaine, & Nakayama, 2005) has been proposed as a test of perceptual face processing fulfilling these requirements. The CFPT employs the morphing method that creates a new face (morph) out of two different faces by combining and averaging the facial and configural features of both faces. In the CFPT, a target face is separately morphed with six other faces, creating six new faces, which vary in the proportion to which the target face has contributed (e.g., 10%–60%). All morphs are presented together with the target face and are to be ordered according to their similarity to the target face, in both upright and inverted conditions. The advantage of configural and holistic processing is expressed by a performance advantage in the upright compared to the inverted condition. Because morphs and target faces do not share the exact same features, feature-matching strategies cannot be employed. Furthermore and importantly, the memory load is abrogated due to the simultaneous presentation of target and morphs.

Like face inversion, other established experimental effects can be implemented within a simultaneous-matching paradigm to investigate face perception. For instance, tasks can be devised to assess configural processing and holistic processing, respectively, by combining the inversion effect with the manipulation of spatial configurations of features within a face (e.g., Freire et al., 2000) or the composite effect (Young et al., 1987), within a simultaneous matching task.

Apart from performance data, psychophysiological parameters like the N170 might be promising measures to express individual differences in face perception processes.

Learning Faces

Learning faces is conceived, for the present purposes, as the establishment of new representations of facial structures (i.e., relevant, unchangeable features and their configuration) in memory, independently of how long they are stored. The importance of learning new faces for many social tasks is emphasized by everyday problems seen in patients with Alzheimer's disease. These patients have severe deficits in the learning of new faces, fail to recognize them, and are therefore substantially impaired in their social lives.

Evidence from the normal population suggests that familiar and unfamiliar faces are processed rather differently (e.g., Hancock, Bruce, & Burton, 2000). Still, comparatively little is known about the transition from unfamiliar to familiar faces. One reason for this lack of knowledge arises due to the difficulty in separating learning and recognition processes in face-learning tasks. When attempting to investigate solely the learning of faces, it is not easy to find a measure of learning success that is independent from the recognition process. It is therefore uncertain if phenomena like facial distinctiveness or the own-race advantage, which will be discussed below, are due to learning, recognition, or both.

Experimental Evidence

Humans appear to rely on different types of facial information when recognizing familiar and unfamiliar faces. Although there are obviously degrees of familiarity, for our current purposes we will use the term *unfamiliar* to denote a face that has been seen either never or once, thereby allowing for the apparent contradiction in the concept of recognizing an unfamiliar face. Attributes that are considered as external features of a face (hair, hairline, ears, and face outline) tend to be more dominant in the recognition of initially unfamiliar faces, whereas internal features (eyes, nose, mouth, and their configuration) tend to be more important when recognizing familiar faces (e.g., Ellis, Shepherd & Davies, 1979). Bonner, Burton, Jenkins, McNeill, and Bruce (2003) have shown that when unfamiliar faces became familiar, external features diminish in importance while internal features become more salient for recognition. This finding suggests that the initial representations in memory for a face—serving recognition of unfamiliar faces—are predominantly external facial features. Thus, the learning process concerns representations of unchangeable internal facial features to a greater extent than external features.

Several authors have investigated how newly acquired facial representations are organized in memory. To this end, they have examined the *distinctiveness effect* and the *own-race bias*. The distinctiveness effect refers to a cluster of findings suggesting that distinctive faces appear to be processed somewhat differently than typical faces. To assess the distinctiveness of faces, people are asked to judge how likely it is that they would recognize a given face, for example, in a crowd at a train station. Distinctive faces, according to such ratings, are usually better recognized than typical faces (e.g., Valentine, 1991). Also, distinctive familiar faces are usually judged more quickly as being familiar than typical familiar faces (Valentine & Bruce, 1986). In addition, when people are asked to classify a stimulus as a face or a "nonface," they respond slower for distinctive faces (Valentine & Bruce, 1986).

These findings have been integrated into a theory postulating the existence of a *face space* (Valentine, 1991)—a multidimensional space, defined by dimensions that serve to encode and discriminate faces, with the origin of the space as the central tendency of the dimensions. Typical faces are therefore assumed to be clustered around the center of the face space, with faces becoming more sparsely distributed as one moves toward the poles of the dimensions, where distinctive faces are located. It is suggested that because there are many more faces near the center of the face space than at the periphery, matching or recognition processes for typical faces are more likely to be confused by the many representations of other typical faces nearby. Hence, distinctive faces are better recognized and judged more quickly as being familiar, but it is easier to classify a typical face as being a face. An alternative suggestion that bears the same explanations is the prototype hypothesis (Valentine & Bruce, 1986). It assumes that a general face prototype might be abstracted from previously encountered faces and used as a basis for encoding faces in the future. Such a face prototype could be proposed to be at the center of the face space.

The concept of face space can also account for the own-race bias (also referred to as the cross-race or other-race effect). This bias refers to the findings that unfamiliar faces from one's own race are better recognized than faces from another race (for review, see Bothwell, Brigham, & Malpass, 1989) and that people are quicker in making face/nonface decisions for own-race than for other-race faces (Valentine, 1991). For most people, the overwhelming majority of people encountered are from their own race. It has therefore been suggested that the face space is finely tuned to own-race faces and other-race faces are poorly represented. As a result, other-race faces would not only be represented farther away from the center or prototype but would also be more tightly clustered as they are less individuated than own-race faces (Valentine, 1991). Similar to the explanation of the distinctiveness effect, it would be much more difficult both to recognize other-race faces and to classify them as faces. Please note that the own-race bias is not an indicator of racism or ethnocentrism but likely reflects the comparatively small amount of exposure to, and resulting (un)familiarity with, other-race faces. When investigating individual differences in the own-race bias, the exposure to other-race faces could be used as a very relevant covariate.

As yet, it is not completely clear whether the distinctiveness effect or the own-race bias has its inception in processes at the learning or recognition stage, or both. Walker and Tanaka (2003) propose that the own-race bias occurs at the learning stage of face processing. They showed that an own-race advantage was still present when using a same/different matching task, in which essentially no memory load is necessary to complete the task. Distinctiveness has been found to influence both learning and recognition by increasing the hit rate as well as the rate of correct rejections of distracter faces, respectively (Deffenbacher, Johanson, Vetter, & O'Toole, 2000).

Psychophysiological and Neuroimaging Evidence

Psychophysiological studies bear particular importance for distinguishing between learning and recognition because these methods allow assessment of brain activity during learning, that is, while the unfamiliar face is seen for the first time. The Dm (difference due to memory) is a component in the ERP elicited in the subsequent memory paradigm (Sommer, Komoss, & Schweinberger, 1997; Sommer, Schweinberger, & Matt, 1991) and, most important, shown to be predictive of later recognition. In the subsequent memory paradigm, the EEG is recorded while participants are learning faces. ERPs for faces from the learning session are later sorted and averaged according to memory performance (i.e., recognized or forgotten) in the test session, and the difference between the ERPs is derived.

The resulting Dm is described as a larger positivity over central-parietal areas for subsequently recognized compared to subsequently forgotten faces. The Dm is independent of fluctuations in attention and perceptual factors, such as differences in contrast or lighting in the pictures, during the study phase (Sommer et al., 1991), but is related to facial distinctiveness (Sommer, Heinz, Leuthold, Matt, & Schweinberger, 1995). This suggests that the Dm reflects processes of encoding involved in face memory, rather than perception. Further evidence for this suggestion was found also by Sommer et al. (1997). They showed that the Dm for names reveals a different distribution of brain activity across the scalp than the Dm for faces, indicating that memory encoding for faces and names is mediated by at least partially different brain systems.

Imaging studies have explored brain activation during the acquisition of new facial representations (see Otten & Rugg, 2002, and Paller & Wagner, 2002, for reviews). These studies showed that in the subsequent memory paradigm, faces that were later recognized elicited higher activations during learning in the inferior frontal areas, the bilateral medial temporal lobe (specifically in its anterior sections, hippocampus, and perirhinal cortex), and in the fusiform face-selective regions, indicating these areas' importance for face learning.

Correlational Evidence

In everyday life, individual differences in learning faces are very prevalent. Some, predominantly psychophysiological, studies have investigated these differences systematically. Alexander et al. (1999) found that better performance in a face-matching task was associated with relatively greater brain activity in the ventral visual association areas of the bilateral occipito-temporal cortex as well as in several subcortical and limbic regions. In contrast, better performance was correlated with relatively less activity in the anterior cingulate cortex, several areas of bilateral prefrontal cortex, temporal cortex, and right inferior parietal cortex.

The amplitude of the Dm has been reported to be uncorrelated with memory performance measured in the same experiment (Guo, Voss, & Paller, 2005). However, we have recently demonstrated that different measures of the Dm correlate positively, to varying degrees, with memory performance (Herzmann & Sommer, 2006).

Measurement

Measuring the learning of new faces is very often confounded with the recognition of faces because the success of encoding new facial representations can be seen only after they are retrieved during the recognition process. We envisage two major options to disentangle the contributions of learning (as defined previously) and recognition processes. The first option is to use tasks with a low memory load, which we suggest would primarily measure the contribution of learning processes; for example, paradigms in which faces have to be encoded in memory and maintained there for a short period of time (some seconds to a few minutes) before they are tested for recognition. In contrast, tasks that primarily assess the contribution of recognition processes should use longer delays between learning and test or use already familiar faces like celebrities (see the section on face recognition measurement, pages 328–329). The second option is the recording of ERPs (such as the Dm, see above) or other physiological parameters that directly measure the activity of the brain during learning, when faces are seen for the first time.

A possible measure of individual differences in the learning of faces, adhering to the first prescription, would be a delayed matching or nonmatching task with a short interval between learning and test. Such a task should have a greater memory load than simultaneous matching tasks, which are used to investigate perception processes, but not an overly long delay, which would account for mainly recognition processes.

Recently, the Cambridge Face Memory Test (CFMT; Duchaine & Nakayama, 2006) was established partly on the basis of a short delay between learning and recognition. Directly following the learning of three viewpoints of a target face, participants are tested on recognition of the face from each viewpoint, with three alternative forced-choice items. Participants review the targets' frontal views and are again tested for recognition using items depicting novel viewpoints of the targets. The novel-viewpoint condition is then repeated with Gaussian noise added to the faces. Importantly, the novel-viewpoint condition and the noise condition, separately and together, make feature-based processing difficult. This enforces a reliance primarily on configural and/or holistic processing for recognition. Duchaine and Nakayama (2006) have demonstrated that patients with prosopagnosia performed remarkably poorer on the CFMT than healthy controls, suggesting that the test is an effective instrument for assessing face learning.

Other indicators of face learning could combine the distinctiveness effect and the own-race bias with a typical short-term memory paradigm, in which faces are learned and memorized for a short time before they are tested for recognition. For example, if the faces that are to be learned differ in their rated distinctiveness or race, distinctive compared to typical faces and own-race compared to other-race faces should lead to better performance. Hence, apart from an overall accuracy measure, the magnitude of a person's distinctiveness effect and own-race bias can also be assessed. The psychometric quality of such difference variables is obviously an issue (Muthén, Collins, & Horn, 1991).

The difference due to memory (Dm), derived from the EEG, has been demonstrated to measure brain activity during learning (e.g., Sommer et al., 1997). Recently we demonstrated that the Dm shows high split-half reliability and is positively correlated with face recognition performance (Herzmann & Sommer, 2006). The magnitude of the Dm, that is, the magnitude of the difference between brain activities for later recognized and for later forgotten faces, might therefore serve as a possible psychophysiological measure for learning faces.

Recognizing Faces

Successful recognition of a face relies on the extraction of invariant facial structural features from visual stimuli and the correct reactivation of the corresponding FRU, that is, the successful comparison of stored with currently seen facial structures. Thus, there are two aspects of face recognition: (a) the perceptual process that allows mapping of a visual image onto a given representation by extracting invariant facial structures and (b) the cognitive process of activating memory representations for the seen stimulus. Here we concentrate on the cognitive aspect of face recognition. Perceptual aspects of face recognition were considered in the section on perceiving faces (pp. 317–322). Being able to access stored facial structures in memory is the final stage of face recognition because it enables us to use these representations to recognize a given face as familiar.

Experimental Evidence

Face recognition has been investigated with implicit and explicit memory tasks. For faces, explicit (or direct) memory tasks require the recognition of a face that was, for example, seen previously in a study list. In contrast, implicit (sometimes referred to as indirect) memory tasks do not require conscious recognition of a previous event (e.g., priming tasks). Instead, they typically require memory-unrelated tasks, for example, gender or face/nonface decisions. Nevertheless, performance in such tasks is often improved by the fact that a given event (face presentation) had been processed previously. Face recognition research has relied to a great extent on such priming paradigms to provide support, for example, for the existence and reactivation of FRUs. Although priming traditionally has been related to implicit memory, it can also be induced with an explicit instruction when the familiarity of the face is directly relevant for the task.

Using the familiarity decision task in a repetition priming paradigm, it has been shown that recognition of a face as familiar is facilitated by earlier presentation of the same face but not by earlier presentation of the person's name, indicating that priming does not act on semantic stages in face processing (e.g., Bruce & Valentine, 1985). The priming effect for familiar faces is smaller when a different picture of the same familiar person's face is used as prime, suggesting that priming relies not only on pictorial codes but more importantly on view-independent representations of the facial structures in memory (e.g., Bruce & Valentine, 1985). Bruce and Young (1986) therefore proposed that repetition priming is mediated by residual activation of the FRU resulting from the first presentation of a familiar face. Facilitation of the familiarity decision for unfamiliar faces is substantially smaller and was completely absent when different pictures of the same unfamiliar person were used, indicating that pictorial codes of facial structures additionally contribute to the mechanisms established in repetition priming paradigms (e.g., Böhm, Klostermann, Sommer, & Paller, 2006; Bruce & Valentine, 1985).

Psychophysiological and Neuroimaging Evidence

Psychophysiological studies using the repetition priming paradigm in a familiarity decision task have found support for the suggestion that priming effects for familiar faces are mediated by residual FRU activation (e.g., Herzmann et al., 2004; Pfütze, Sommer, & Schweinberger, 2002). These studies identified an ERP component, around 250 ms after target onset, as a stronger negativity across inferior temporal brain areas for repeated compared to unrepeated stimuli. This difference wave between repeated and unrepeated stimuli was termed the *early repetition effect* (ERE, also referred to as N250r). The ERE is larger for personally familiar faces in comparison to famous faces (Herzmann et al., 2004) and reduced or even absent for unfamiliar as compared to famous faces (e.g., Pfütze et al., 2002), suggesting that it is mediated by an existing memory representation. Because the ERE is absent when a familiar face is preceded by its name or a related person (e.g., seeing Bill Clinton after Hillary Clinton; Schweinberger, 1996), it is assumed that it is linked to perceptual (i.e., facial structures) rather than postperceptual (i.e., identity-specific semantic) representations. The ERE is therefore taken to indicate transient activation of FRUs.

Psychophysiological studies often employ the old/new effect to investigate the recognition of faces within an explicit memory task (e.g., Paller, Gonsalves, Grabowecky, Bozic, & Yamada, 2000). In these studies, participants are asked to learn faces for which they are later tested for recognition, together with completely unfamiliar faces, while the EEG is recorded. Correct responses to old (i.e., familiar) faces elicit a larger positivity over central brain areas than correctly rejected new faces—this difference is referred to as the old/new effect. Comparing old/new effects to named and unnamed faces, Paller et al. (2000) found the old/new effect for unnamed faces only at posterior areas, whereas for named faces it was evident also at anterior areas. The posterior portion of the old/new effect was interpreted as a neural correlate for the retrieval of visual facial information and the anterior portion as an indicator for the retrieval of person-specific semantic information. It could also be argued that the posterior portion of the old/new effect represents FRU activation.

Imaging studies have shown that the right lateral fusiform gyrus, the right inferior occipital cortex, and regions in the temporal lobe are not only involved in distinguishing faces from non-face objects, but are also differentially activated for familiar and unfamiliar faces (e.g., Rossion et al., 2003). These findings illustrate that these brain areas play a role in the distinction between unfamiliar and familiar faces, and provide evidence for the overlap between visual and presemantic memory-related representations of unfamiliar and familiar faces, respectively, in the brain (e.g., Rossion et al., 2003). Recent dipole source modeling was consistent with a generator of the ERE in the fusiform gyrus (Schweinberger, Pickering, Jentzsch, Burton, & Kaufmann, 2002).

Correlational Evidence

Age-related differences are one form of available evidence for individual differences in face recognition. Pfütze et al. (2002) found that the ERE is delayed with age, indicating that with increasing age it becomes more difficult to access FRUs. Imaging studies have shown that contrary to findings with young adults, activity in the medial temporal cortex of older adults is not correlated with memory performance, whereas positive correlations have been found for the right prefrontal and pariet al regions and have been taken to indicate their compensatory role in face recognition (Grady, Bernstein, Beid, & Siegenthaler, 2002).

In a recent study, we investigated the correlation of the ERE amplitude with memory performance (Herzmann & Sommer, 2007) and found the expected negative correlation of the priming effect in reaction times and the ERE amplitude with memory performance. In the same experiment we also investigated the posterior old/new effect, thought to reflect familiarity processes in face recognition. In line with the ERE findings, we found the expected negative correlation of the posterior old/new effect (i.e., the difference wave between old and new faces) with memory performance. This indicates that smaller differences between brain activity for old and new faces are related with better memory performance.

Research on gender differences has made wide use of face recognition paradigms and has revealed conflicting conclusions: Shapiro and Penrod (1986) concluded that there are no sex differences, whereas Hall (1984) concluded that women score higher on face recognition tasks. Findings from more recent studies lean in favor of a female advantage, both in person identification (e.g., Lindholm & Christianson, 1998) and face recognition (e.g., Herlitz & Yonker, 2002). Herlitz and Yonker (2002) found that face recognition performance is unrelated with intelligence in women but that it is positively correlated with intelligence in men—a finding emphasizing the importance of uncovering the relations between face recognition and basic cognitive processes as well as aspects of emotional intelligence.

Measurement

Impairment in face recognition is consistently found in older adults and in patients with dementia. It is therefore not surprising that face recognition tests are used in clinical and aging research. Test batteries like the Wechsler Memory Scale (Wechsler, 1997), the Denman Neuropsychological Memory Scale (Denman, 1984), and the Warrington Recognition Memory Test (Warrington, 1984) include subtests for the assessment of face recognition. The tests are procedurally similar in that all require participants to learn a number of faces and be tested for recognition immediately after learning.

A problem with this procedure is that the assessment of face recognition is contaminated with face learning (as discussed in the section on learning faces, pages 322–326). One possibility to disentangle, to some extent, face recognition from face learning is the use of a delay of, for instance, at least 1 hour between learning and recognition. A second possibility is to use faces that are already familiar, such as portraits of celebrities. Tests measuring recognition of known famous faces are available (e.g., the Famous Face Test; Hodges & Ward, 1989; the Bielefeld Famous Faces Test; Fast, Fujiwara, & Markowitsch, 2004). However, an important drawback of famous face recognition is that there are vast individual differences in the frequency and duration of exposure, as well as in availability and type of additional information for already familiar faces. Such artifacts are difficult to control and certainly cause substantial unwanted variance in test performance. Taken together, tests assessing recognition of faces should therefore ideally use unfamiliar faces that have been learned within an experimental setting at least 1 hour prior to being tested for recognition.

A measure of face recognition could be based on the priming effect for learned faces, which is suggested to tap the reactivation of FRUs. In such a task, experimentally learned familiar and completely unfamiliar faces would be employed as target faces in a repetition priming paradigm (see the section on experimental evidence of perceiving faces, pages 318–319) in which participants complete familiarity decisions for the target faces and make no response to the prime faces. The difference in reaction times between familiar faces primed with themselves or preceded by an unfamiliar face (i.e., the priming effect for learned faces) would be a potential measure of face recognition (see above for requirements such indicators should meet). Better face recognition performance would be expected to be associated with smaller priming effects (Herzmann & Sommer, 2007).

In terms of ERP components, we have recently shown that 1 week after learning, experimentally learned faces elicited an ERE that was comparable to the ERE for famous faces (Herzmann & Sommer, 2007). Additionally, in the test session, learned faces showed an old/new effect as found in experiments that integrated learning and recognition phases within the same experiment (Paller et al., 2000). Both the ERE and the old/new effect in the ERP revealed high retest reliabilities (Herzmann & Sommer, 2007) and, more important, correlated with face recognition performance. The ERP components might therefore be useful psychophysiological measures of individual differences in face recognition.

Putting It All Together

In this chapter, we have outlined what we consider as an optimal or, more modestly, appropriate approach to measure individual differences in face memory. We suggest that face memory is relevant to, and in some instances necessary for, specific aspects of emotional intelligence, especially emotion recognition. We proposed that this approach should be based on profound theoretical knowledge about processes of face memory, derived from evidence within areas such as experimental psychology and psychophysiology. We began with the separation of face memory into three successive stages, representing three possible abilities: face perception, face learning, and face recognition. This division is somewhat complicated by the fact that later stages partly rely on successful completion of earlier stages. However, the division is psychologically meaningful and we tried to substantiate it with theoretically derived measures. The next step required is to empirically test such a suggested structure of face memory.

A substantial body of experimental, psychophysiological, and correlational evidence was presented for the proposed abilities, and it was shown how experimental paradigms have provided insights into their underlying cognitive mechanisms. This foundation was then elaborated upon by psychophysiological and neuroimaging studies that have provided evidence for their principal neural generators. The correlational evidence clearly lags behind the other forms of evidence, and remarkably little is known about individual differences in the proposed abilities. There are manifold interesting and relevant questions about face memory that cannot be adequately answered with currently available knowledge. For instance, Are there differential preferences in the processes employed in perceiving faces (i.e., feature-based, configural, and holistic)? Are there individual differences in people's ability to learn faces that go beyond general learning ability? Are there individual differences between face spaces within a culture? Do humans recognize faces in different ways? Do they show differential brain activity when perceiving, learning, or recognizing faces?

The benefit of addressing these questions, conceptually and empirically, is not only a broader understanding of individual differences in face perception and memory. Answering these questions provides the platform for answering further questions: Is the use of primarily holistic processing correlated with better memory performance when recognizing faces? Is a superior ability for learning faces always correlated with better face recognition? Does more (e.g., brain activity) always mean better face memory? The answers to these questions will lead us to an understanding of how the proposed abilities in face perception and memory work together to form the complex picture of individual performance in face processing in everyday life. It will provide the basis of a measurement model of individual differences in face memory, thereby yielding a new aspect from which to examine the relationship between face memory and other abilities such as, for instance, the recognition of emotional facial expressions or other factors from the four branches model.

Measures for the three proposed abilities suggested to underlie a model of face memory were derived from experimental and psychophysiological studies. Three lines of research are critical to establish a model for face memory. The first and most critical line of research is to test the measurement model (see Figure 12.1) with a diverse group of participants. The second line is to make sure that there is nontrivial uniqueness to the estimated factors. That is, it should be empirically established that face recognition cannot be completely regressed on general recognition ability. Similarly, face perception and face learning should not be perfectly correlated with general perceptual abilities and general learning abilities, respectively. The third line should aim to establish relations with constructs and outcome variables of interest. Prominent and saliently related constructs are emotional and also social intelligence. Despite our skepticism toward such denominations, relating compilations of indicators subsumed under such labels with indicators of face cognition discussed herein can be very instructive. In terms of interesting outcome variables, a relevant endeavor would be the prediction of performance variables, for example, in jobs or situations in which face memory is crucial (e.g., eyewitness testimony, security, police, public relations, and the hospitality industry). For such jobs, we would obviously also predict that face cognition is incrementally valid, over and above established predictors, in the prediction of relevant criteria (i.e., criteria that represent job performance and require face perception, face learning, or face recognition performance).

It seems reasonable to suggest that any construct dealing with interactions between humans, whether they are related more to emotional or social interactions—if indeed these different aspects are so readily disentangled as suggested by the proposal of different constructs for emotional and social intelligence—are related in a crucial way to memory for faces and names, as well as the ability to recognize emotions. At the least, these components form an integral layer of our interactions with familiar people, and those to become familiar. We therefore suggest that the investigation of processes like these, in relation to constructs associated with human interactions, should not be ignored and indeed might form an alternative path to understand these constructs, as opposed to more intangible concepts such as the management of emotions.

Notes

1. In scrambled faces, the internal facial features are unnaturally disarranged (e.g., the mouth where the eyes are normally positioned). Because they contain all the same features of faces, these stimuli are often used as control conditions in face recognition experiments.

2. We use the term *correlational evidence* as summarizing nonexperimental empirical evidence here. Hence, apart from traditional correlational studies, we also refer to group differences if group membership is not assigned experimentally.

References

Alexander, G. E., Mentis, M. J., Van Horn, J. D., Grady, C. L., Berman, D. F., Furey, M. L., et al. (1999). Individual differences in PET activation of object perception and attention systems predict face matching accuracy. *NeuroReport, 10,* 1965–1971.

Baudouin, J. Y., Gilibert, D., Sansone, S., & Tiberghien, G. (2000). When the smile is a cue to familiarity. *Memory, 8,* 285–292.

Behrman, M., Avidan, G., Marotta, J. J., & Kimchi, R. (2005). Detailed exploration of face-related processing in congenital prosopagnosia: 1. Behavioral findings. *Journal of Cognitive Neuroscience, 17,* 1130–1149.

Bentin, S., Allison, T., Puce, A., Perez, E., & McCarthy, G. (1996). Electrophysiological studies of face perception in humans. *Journal of Cognitive Neuroscience, 8*, 551–565.

Benton, A. L., & Van Allen, M. W. (1968). Impairment in facial recognition in patients with cerebral disease. *Cortex, 4*, 344–358.

Böhm, S. G., Klostermann, E. C., Sommer, W., & Paller, K. A. (2006). Dissociating perceptual and representation-based contributions to priming of face recognition. *Consciousness and Cognition, 15*, 163–174.

Bonner, L., Burton, A. M., Jenkins, R., McNeill, A., & Bruce, V. (2003). Meet the Simpsons: Top-down effects in face learning. *Perception, 32*, 1159–1168.

Bothwell, R. K., Brigham, J. C., & Malpass, R. S. (1989). Cross-racial identifications. *Personality and Social Psychology Bulletin, 15*, 19–25.

Breen, N., Caine, D., & Coltheart, M. (2000). Models of face recognition and delusional misidentification: A critical review. *Cognitive Neuropsychology, 17*, 55–71.

Bruce, V., Burton, A. M., & Craw, I. (1992). Modelling face recognition. *Philosophical Transactions of the Royal Society London B, 335*, 121–128.

Bruce, V., & Valentine, T. (1985). Identity priming in the recognition of familiar faces. *British Journal of Psychology, 76*, 373–383.

Bruce, V., & Young, A. (1986). Understanding face recognition. *British Journal of Psychology, 77*, 305–327.

Calder, A. J., & Young, A. W. (2005). Understanding the recognition of facial identity and facial expression. *Nature Reviews, 6*, 641–651.

Coffey, E., Berenbaum, H., & Kerns, J. G. (2003). The dimensions of emotional intelligence, alexithymia, and mood awareness: Associations with personality and performance on an Emotional Stroop task. *Cognition & Emotion, 17*, 671–679.

Deffenbacher, K. A., Johanson, J., Vetter, T., & O'Toole, A. J. (2000). The face typicality-recognizability relationship: Encoding or retrieval locus? *Memory & Cognition, 28*, 1173–1182.

Denman, S. B. (1984). *Denman neuropsychology memory scale*. Charleston, SC: Author.

Diamond, R., & Carey, S. (1986). Why faces are and are not special: An effect of expertise. *Journal of Experimental Psychology: General, 115*, 107–117.

Dingle, K. J., Duchaine, B. C., & Nakayama, K. (2005). A new test for face perception [Abstract]. *Journal of Vision, 5*, 40a.

Duchaine, B., & Nakayama, K. (2006). The Cambridge Face Memory Test: Results for neurologically intact individuals and an investigation of its validity using inverted face stimuli and prosopagnosic participants. *Neuropsychologia, 44*, 576–585.

Eimer, M., & McCarthy, R. A. (1999). Prosopagnosia and structural encoding of faces: Evidence from event-related potentials. *Neuroreport, 10*, 255–259.

Ellis, H. D., & Lewis, M. B. (2001). Capgras delusion: A window on face recognition. *Trends in Cognitive Sciences, 5*, 149–156.

Ellis, H. D., Shepherd, J. W., & Davies, G. M. (1979). Identification of familiar and unfamiliar faces from internal and external features: Some implications for theories of face recognition. *Perception, 8*, 431–439.

Endl, W., Walla, P., Lindinger, G., Lalouscheck, W., Barth, F. G., Deecke, L., et al. (1998). Early cortical activation indicates preparation for retrieval of memory for faces: An event-related potential study. *Neuroscience Letters, 240*, 58–60.

Farah, M. J., Wilson, K. D., Drain, M., & Tanaka, J. N. (1998). What is "special" about face perception? *Psychological Review, 105*, 482–498.

Fast, K., Fujiwara, E., & Markowitsch, H. J. (2004) *Famous Faces Test Ein Verfahren zur Erfassung semantischer Altgedächtnisleistungen*. Göttingen: Hogrefe.

Freire, A., Lee, K., & Symons, L. A. (2000). The face-inversion effect as a deficit in the encoding of configural information: Direct evidence. *Perception, 29*, 159–170.

Furnham, A. (2001). Self-estimates of intelligence. *Personality and Individual Differences, 31*, 1381–1405.

Furnham, A. (2002). Self-rated intelligence: Specific abilities and demographic variables. *Social Behaviour and Personality, 30*, 185–194.

Grady, C. L., Bernstein, L. J., Beid, S., & Siegenthaler, A. L. (2002). The effects of encoding task on age-related differences in the functional neuroanatomy of face memory. *Psychology and Aging, 17*, 7–23.

Guo, C., Voss, J. L., & Paller, K. A. (2005). Electrophysiological correlates of forming memories for faces, names, and face-name associations. *Cognitive Brain Research, 22*, 153–164.

Halgren, E., Raij, T., Marinkovic, K., Jousmaki, V., & Hari, R. (2000). Cognitive response profile of the human fusiform face area as determined by MEG. *Cerebral Cortex, 10*, 69–81.

Hall, J. A. (1984). *Nonverbal sex differences: Communication accuracy and expressive style*. Baltimore, MD: Johns Hopkins University Press.

Hancock, P. J. B., Bruce, V., & Burton, A. M. (2000). Recognition of unfamiliar faces. *Trends in Cognitive Science, 4*, 330–337.

Haxby, J. V., Hoffman, E. A., & Gobbini, M. I. (2000). The distributed human neural system for face perception. *Trends in Cognitive Sciences, 4*, 223–232.

Haxby, J. V., Ungerleider, L. G., Clark, V. P., Schouten, J. L., Hoffman, E. A., & Martin, A. (1999). The effect of face inversion of activity in human neural systems for face and object perception. *Neuron, 22*, 189–199.

Herlitz, A., & Yonker, J. E. (2002). Sex differences in episodic memory: The influence of intelligence. *Journal of Clinical and Experimental Neuropsychology, 24*, 107–114.

Herzmann, G., Schweinberger, S. R., Sommer, W., & Jentzsch, I. (2004). What's special about personally familiar faces? A multimodal approach. *Psychophysiology, 41*, 1–14.

Herzmann, G., & Sommer, W. (2006). The reliability of the Dm as a measure of face encoding into memory. Journal of Psychophysiology, 20 (Suppl. 1), S46.

Herzmann, G., & Sommer, W. (2007). Memory-related ERP components for experimentally learned faces and names: Characteristics and parallel-test reliabilities. *Psychophysiology, 44*, 262–276.

Hodges, J. R., & Ward, C. D. (1989). Observation during transient global amnesia. *Brain, 112*, 595–620.

Hoffman, E. A., & Haxby, J. V. (2000). Distinct representations of eye gaze and identity in the distributed human neural system for face perception. *Nature Neuroscience, 3*, 80–84.

Ishai, A., Ungerleider, L. G., Martin, A., & Haxby, J. V. (2000). The representation of objects in the human occipital and temporal cortex. *Journal of Cognitive Neuroscience, 12*, 35–51.

Kanwisher, N., McDermott, J., & Chun, M. M. (1997). The fusiform face area: A module in human extrastriate cortex specialized for face perception. *Journal of Neuroscience, 17*, 4302–4311.

Kress, T., & Daum, I. (2003a). Developmental prosopagnosia: A review. *Behavioural Neurology, 14*, 109–121.

Kress, T., & Daum, I. (2003b). Event-related potentials reflect impaired face recognition in patients with congenital prosopagnosia. *Neuroscience Letters, 352*, 133–136.

Lane, R., Quinlan, D., Schwartz, G. E., Walker, P., & Zeitlin, S. (1990). The levels of emotional awareness scale: A cognitive-developmental measure of emotion. *Journal of Personality Assessment, 55,* 124–134.

Legree, P. L., Psotka, J., Tremble, T., & Bourne, D. R. (2005). Using consensus based measurement to assess emotional intelligence. In R. Schulze & R. D. Roberts (Eds.), *Emotional intelligence: An international handbook* (pp. 155–180). Göttingen: Hogrefe & Huber.

Lindholm, T., & Christianson, S.-A. (1998). Gender effects in eyewitness accounts of a violent crime. *Psychology, Crime and Law, 4,* 323–339.

MacCann, C., Roberts, R. D., Matthews, G., & Zeidner, M. (2004). Consensus scoring and empirical option weighting of performance-based emotional intelligence (EI) tests, *Personality and Individual Differences, 36,* 645–662.

Matsumoto, D., & Ekman, P. (1992). *Japanese and Caucasian Brief Affect Recognition Test (JACBART), I, II, III* [Videotapes]. (Available from Culture and Emotion Research Laboratory, Department of Psychology, San Francisco State University, 1600 Holloway Avenue, San Francisco, CA, 94132)

Matsumoto, D., LeRoux, J., Wilson-Cohn, C., Raroque, J., Kooken, K., Ekman, P., et al. (2000). A new test to measure emotion recognition ability: Matsumoto and Ekman's Japanese and Caucasian Brief Affect Recognition Test (JACBART). *Journal of Nonverbal Behavior, 24,* 179–209.

Maurer, D., Le Grand, R., & Mondloch, C. J. (2002). The many faces of configural processing. *Trends in Cognitive Sciences, 6,* 255–260.

Mayer, J. D., Salovey, P., & Caruso, D. R. (1999). *The Mayer, Salovey, and Caruso Emotional Intelligence Test: Technical manual.* Toronto: Multi-Health Systems.

Mayer, J. D., Salovey, P., Caruso, D. R., & Sitarenios, G. (2003). Measuring emotional intelligence with the MSCEIT V2.0. *Emotion, 3,* 97–105.

McCarthy, G., Puce, A., Gore, J. C., & Allison, T. (1997). Face-specific processing in the human fusiform gyrus. *Journal of Cognitive Neuroscience, 9,* 605–610.

McDaniel, M. A., Morgeson, F. P., Finnegan, E. B., Campion, M. A., & Braverman, E. P. (2001). Use of situational judgment tests to predict job performance: A clarification of the literature. *Journal of Applied Psychology, 86,* 730–740.

Muthén, B., Collins, L., & Horn, J. (1991). *Best methods for the analysis of change.* Washington, DC: American Psychological Association.

Otten, L. J., & Rugg, M. D. (2002). The birth of memory. *Trends in Neuroscience, 25,* 279–281.

Paller, K. A., Gonsalves, B., Grabowecky, M., Bozic, V., & Yamada, S. (2000). Electrophysiological correlates of recollecting faces of known and unknown individuals. *NeuroImage, 11,* 98–110.

Paller, K. A., & Wagner, A. D. (2002). Observing the transformation of experience into memory. *Trends in Cognitive Science, 6,* 93–102.

Pfütze, E.-M., Sommer, W., & Schweinberger, S. R. (2002). Age-related slowing in face and name recognition: Evidence from event-related brain potentials. *Psychology and Aging, 17,* 140–160.

Rossion, B., Campanella, S., Gomez, C. M., Delinte, A., Debatisse, D., Liard, L., et al. (1999). Task modulation of brain activity related to familiar and unfamiliar face processing: An ERP study. *Clinical Neurophysiology, 110,* 449–462.

Rossion, B., Schiltz, C., & Crommelinck, M. (2003). The functionally defined right occipital and fusiform "face areas" discriminate novel from visually familiar faces. *NeuroImage, 19,* 877–883.

Schweinberger, S. R. (1996). How Gorbachev primed Yeltsin: Analyses of associative priming in person recognition by means of reaction times and event-related brain potentials. *Journal of Experimental Psychology: Learning, Memory, and Cognition, 22*, 1383–1407.

Schweinberger, S. R., Pickering, E. S., Jentzsch, I., Burton, A. M., & Kaufmann, J. M. (2002). Event-related brain potential evidence for a response in inferior temporal cortex to familiar face repetitions. *Cognitive Brain Research, 14*, 398–409.

Schweinberger, S. R., & Soukup, G. R. (1998). Asymmetric relationships among perceptions of facial identity, emotion, and facial speech. *Journal of Experimental Psychology-Human Perception and Performance, 24*, 1748–1765.

Sergent, J., Ohta, S., & MacDonald, B. (1992). Functional neuroanatomy of face and object processing: A positron emission tomography study. *Brain, 115*, 15–36.

Séverac-Cauquill, A. S., Edmonds, G. E., & Taylor, M. J. (2000). Is the face-sensitive N170 the only ERP not affected by selective attention? *NeuroReport, 11*, 2167–2171.

Shapiro, P. N., & Penrod, S. (1986). Meta-analysis of facial identification studies. *Psychological Bulletin, 100*, 139–156.

Sommer, W., Heinz, A., Leuthold, H., Matt, J., & Schweinberger, S. R. (1995). Metamemory, distinctiveness, and event-related potentials in recognition memory for faces. *Memory & Cognition, 23*, 1–11.

Sommer, W., Komoss, E., & Schweinberger, S. R. (1997). Differential localization of brain systems subserving memory for names and faces in normal subjects with event-related potentials. *Electroencephalography and clinical Neurophysiology, 102*, 192–199.

Sommer, W., Schweinberger, S. R., & Matt, J. (1991). Human brain potential correlates of face encoding into memory. *Electroencephalography and clinical Neurophysiology, 79*, 457–463.

Tanaka, J. W., & Farah, M. J. (1993). Parts and wholes in face recognition. *Quarterly Journal of Experimental Psychology, 46A*, 225–245.

Thompson, P. (1980). Margaret Thatcher—A new illusion. *Perception, 9*, 483–484.

Valentine, T. (1988). Upside-down faces: A review of the effect of inversion upon face recognition. *British Journal of Psychology, 79*, 471–491.

Valentine, T. (1991). A unified account of the effects of distinctiveness, inversion, and race in face recognition. *Quarterly Journal of Experimental Psychology, 43A*, 161–204.

Valentine, T., & Bruce, V. (1986). The effect of race, inversion and encoding activity upon face recognition. *Acta Psychologica, 61*, 259–273.

Walker, P. M., & Tanaka, J. W. (2003). An encoding advantage for own-race versus other-race faces. *Perception, 32*, 1117–1125.

Warrington, E. K. (1984). *Manual for Recognition Memory Test*. Windsor, England: NFER-Nelson.

Wechsler, D. (1997). *Wechsler Memory Scale—Third Edition*. San Antonio, TX: Harcourt Assessment.

Wild-Wall, N. (2004). *Is there an interaction between facial expression and facial familiarity? An investigation using performance data and event-related potentials*. Unpublished doctoral dissertation, Humboldt University of Berlin, Institute for Psychology. Retrieved May 10, 2006, from http://edoc.hu-berlin.de/dissertationen/wild-wall-nele-2004-05-28/HTML/

Wilhelm, O. (2005). Measures of emotional intelligence: practice and standards. In R. Schulze, & R. D. Roberts (Eds.), *International handbook of emotional intelligence* (pp. 131–154). Seattle, WA: Hogrefe & Huber.

Yoon, J., Halit, H., & Csibra, G. (2005). N170 peak amplitude differences correlate with individuals' magnitude of same-race advantage in an identity judgment task. *Journal of Cognitive Neuroscience* (Suppl. S), 145–145.

Young, A. W., Hellawell, D., & Hay, D. C. (1987). Configurational information in face perception. *Perception, 16,* 747–759.

PART IV

EMOTIONAL INTELLIGENCE

Applications

13

The Clinical Utility
of Emotional Intelligence

Association With Related Constructs,
Treatment, and Psychopathology

DAVID D. VACHON AND R. MICHAEL BAGBY

For many, the idea of emotional intelligence (EI) is intuitively appealing. Despite a great deal of excitement about the potential of emotional intelligence, however, there remains very little evidence that EI offers a unique conceptualization of the mechanisms, processes, behaviors, and outcomes associated with emotion. The issue of discriminant validity—that is, whether EI is useful and different from other, well-established constructs—is of particular concern to those mental health professionals who already find themselves struggling to employ a number of empirically correlated and conceptually overlapping constructs to organize and guide their interactions with mental disorder. Accordingly, the purpose of this chapter is to compare EI to related constructs and consider the relationship between EI, psychopathology, and clinical treatment. To the extent that EI varies from other constructs, we will discuss the practical application of EI to the mental health field and speculate about the theoretical advances necessary to support these applications.

EI and Related Constructs

There are several constructs conceptually related to EI, including alexithymia (Sifneos, 1973; Taylor, 1984), psychological mindedness (Silver, 1983), self-awareness (Bloch, 1979), social intelligence (Thorndike, 1920), personal intelligences (intrapersonal and interpersonal intelligence; Gardner, 1983), and ego strength (Lake, 1985). Some of these constructs are quite closely related to particular conceptualizations of the EI construct (Matthews, Zeidner, & Roberts, 2002). Parker, Taylor, and Bagby (2001), for example, used a large nonclinical sample (N = 734) and reliable measures of both alexithymia (the Twenty-Item Toronto Alexithymia Scale [TAS-20]; Bagby, Parker, & Taylor, 1994) and emotional intelligence (the Bar-On Emotional Quotient Inventory [EQ-i]; Bar-On, 1997) to investigate the relationship between EI and alexithymia. Although Parker, Taylor, and Bagby (2001) did not investigate the role of personality in this relationship—a function that will almost certainly be examined in the near future—they did find EI and alexithymia to be strongly correlated ($r = -0.72, p < 0.01$). Furthermore, certain EI-related constructs, such as psychological mindedness and alexithymia, are of considerable clinical relevance and have generated a vast clinical literature (McCallum & Piper, 2000; Taylor & Bagby, 2000; Taylor, Bagby, & Parker, 1997); accordingly, a discussion of the relationships between EI, psychological mindedness, and alexithymia will precede our speculative analysis of the clinical utility of EI.

Before making these comparisons, however, it is important to specify between EI as conceived by Bar-On and measured by the self-report EQ-i (Bar-On, 1997), and EI as conceived by Mayer, Salovey, and Caruso and measured by the ability-based MEIS and its updated version, the MSCEIT (Mayer, Salovey, & Caruso, 2002). Although many researchers have used the EQ-i as a measure of EI, we believe that EI as measured by the MSCEIT is a more appropriate conceptualization, particularly when studying the clinical utility of emotional intelligence. Because the research on EI that employs self-report methodology (e.g., mixed models such as Bar-On's EQ-i) is plagued by a number of problems and serious omissions (Matthews, Roberts, & Zeidner, 2004), and because EI measures should minimally satisfy the four standard psychometric criteria—content validity, reliability, predictive validity, and construct validity—set out by Anastasi and Urbina (1997), we endorse the use of ability-based measures of EI. The MSCEIT is a reliable ability-based measure with some predictive validity, and although it currently fails to meet all of Anastasi and Urbina's (1997) validity criteria, its emphasis on internal mood regulation and comparatively focused parameters make it a more useful model of EI than the more wide-ranging mixed models (e.g., EQ-i) that can include generic facets of personality and coping. Herein, EI will refer to undifferentiated emotional intelligence, EI-EQ-i will refer to emotional intelligence as measured by Bar-On's (1997) EQ-i, and EI-MSCEIT will refer to emotional intelligence as measured by Mayer, Salovey, and Caruso's (2002) MSCEIT.

Psychological Mindedness and Emotional Intelligence

Some individuals respond quite poorly to psychotherapy, especially insight-oriented therapy, and from the start of treatment are often difficult to manage, frustrated with the pace and progress of therapy, and likely to prematurely terminate treatment (Parker, 2000). An early study by Owen and Kohutek (1981), for example, reported that dropout rates from psychotherapy can be as high as 80%–90%. As a result of the frustration and Freudian countertransference often associated with treating these individuals (Taylor, 1977), and in conjunction with a set of abilities frequently linked with successful outcomes from psychotherapy (Conte et al., 1990), the construct of psychological mind-edness emerged in the clinical literature and has since been championed primarily by psychoanalysts (see Bachrach & Leaff's [1978] review of the "analyzability" literature; McCallum & Piper, 2000).

Psychological mindedness (PM) has been described by Appelbaum (1973) as "a person's ability to see relationships among thoughts, feelings, and actions, with the goal of learning the meanings and causes of his experience and behaviour" (p. 36). Conte et al. (1990) and Conte, Buckley, Picard, and Karasu (1995) have since developed an operational definition and measure of PM that identifies four facets to the construct: (1) access to one's feelings, (2) willingness to talk about one's intrapersonal or interpersonal problems, (3) a capacity for behavioral change, and (4) an interest in why people behave the way they do (Conte et al., 1990). In contrast to emotional intelligence—which is considered to be a general construct that can encompass emotional, intrapersonal, and interpersonal abilities, processes, and outcomes—PM is often considered to be a concept specific to the identification of suitable candidates for psychotherapy (though PM has been studied in nonclinical settings, where it was found to be related to mindfulness, private self-consciousness, and both cognitive and affective indices of empathy; Beitel, Ferrer, & Cecero, 2005).

Thus, the primary difference between EI and PM is that the conceptual parameters of PM are more limited and focused (McCallum & Piper, 2000). Despite this difference, however, there is considerable conceptual overlap between PM and EI, and regardless of the dimensions used to describe the theoretical territory of either construct, an individual with limited PM is generally expected to have limited EI (Taylor et al., 1997). Preliminary research seems to support such an expectation—Taylor et al. (1997), for example, found a strong positive relationship between psychological mindedness and EI-EQ-i. This research is in its infancy, however, and the current scarcity of data on the relationship between PM and EI—especially EI-MSCEIT—makes expectations about such relationships somewhat premature.

Despite the fact that most clinicians value PM in their patients, and despite the many positive events associated with PM (e.g., increased tolerance for others, appreciation for life events, freedom from the tyranny of unconscious impulses; Farber & Golden, 1997), disadvantages associated with high levels of PM have also been documented (Fenigstein & Vanable, 1992). Psychological mindedness can exacerbate depression, anxiety, and paranoia, and has been associated with lower self-esteem. Furthermore, those with high PM are less able to "allow people and things to be simple," tend to feel lonelier, and are often disappointed with the seeming superficiality of nonpsychologically minded people (Farber & Golden, 1997; Fenigstein, 1994; McCallum & Piper, 2000; Park, Imboden, Park, Hulse, & Unger, 1992). McCallum and Piper (2000) refer to those with high PM as "wiser but sadder."

Interestingly, recent evidence seems to suggest that high levels of EI may also be related to negative events; specifically, Ciarrochi, Deane, and Anderson (2002) used an objective measure of emotion perception (Mayer & Geher, 1996) and a subjective, self-report measure of EI (Schutte et. al, 1998) to study the relationship between EI, life stress, and mental health, and found that participants high in emotional perception reported greater levels of depression, hopelessness, and suicidal ideation. Ciarrochi and colleagues did not, however, study EI using the EQ-i or MSCEIT, and without further study it is impossible to know whether certain interpersonal dimensions of EI are related to heightened levels of negative affect. It may be possible, for example, that those high in emotional perception—a common facet of EI—resemble those "wiser but sadder" individuals high in psychological mindedness who tend to be depressed, anxious, and disappointed with the superficiality of others.

Perhaps, like psychologically minded individuals, those with particularly high EI are less able to "allow people and things to be simple," are more likely to feel disappointed, alone, and depressed when those people and things are undeniably simple, and tend to be distanced from the experience in favor of the process. This is, admittedly, rather speculative on our part, but the notion of unrequited insight and a constant appraisal and reappraisal of experience seems at odds with the principles behind—and the benefits associated with—the mindfulness movement in positive psychology.

Perhaps an important empirical question is whether extremely high EI is less adaptive or effective than high EI. Alternatively, if EI has several components that are somewhat independent of one another (e.g., MSCEIT components of emotional perception, use, understanding, and management), perhaps the combination of certain high and low EI abilities leads to negative outcomes. One would imagine, for example, that being able to perceive emotions without the ability to use them, or being able to understand emotions without the ability to manage them, might lead to a sort of cognitive-emotional dissonance. The distress and alienation potentially caused by this kind of unregulated or unmanageable dissonance may help explain the difference between the "wiser but sadder" and the wise—one cannot help but think of the anguish experienced by *Amadeus's* Salieri, whose ability to perceive and understand music greatly exceeded his ability to use or manage it.

Alexithymia and Psychological Mindedness

Alexithymia is a personality construct that reflects a deficit in the experiencing, regulation, and expression of emotions (Parker, Taylor, & Bagby, 1993). The term *alexithymia,* stemming from the Greek for "lack of emotion" (*a* = lack, *lexis* = word, *thymos* = emotion), was first coined by Sifneos (1972) and represents a significant disorder of affect that has been implicated in a range of clinical disorders, including eating disorders, panic disorders, substance abuse, somatoform disorders, posttraumatic stress disorder, and other illnesses (Krystal, 1978; Taylor et al., 1997). The alexithymia construct, as currently construed, includes the following four components: (1) difficulty identifying feelings and distinguishing between feelings and the bodily sensations of arousal, (2) difficulty describing feelings to other people, (3) constricted imaginal processes, as evidenced by a paucity of fantasies, and (4) a stimulus-bound, externally oriented cognitive style, as evidenced by preoccupation with the details of external events rather than inner emotional experiences (Parker et al., 2001; Taylor et al., 1997).

Unlike psychological mindedness—which can focus solely on the self (intrapersonal; Bagby et al., 1994; Fenigstein, Scheier, & Buss, 1975), solely on others (interpersonal; Dollinger, 1985), or on both the self and others (intrapersonal and interpersonal; Conte et al., 1990; Menna & Cohen, 1997; Park & Park, 1997)—alexithymia is a much more narrowly defined construct, concerned exclusively with the intrapersonal processing and regulation of affect (McCallum & Piper, 2000). Despite this difference, however, both PM and alexithymia have been found to be related to the "openness to experience" (O) dimension of the five-factor model of personality (McCrae & Costa, 1985, 1987; Taylor et al., 1997). Furthermore, because PM is related to O and EI-EQ-i (Taylor et al., 1997), alexithymia is negatively related to O (Taylor, 1994) and EI (Taylor, Parker, & Bagby, 1999), and alexithymia is strongly and negatively related to PM (Bagby et al., 1994), there appears to be some overlap between alexithymia and psychological mindedness. The precise nature of the relationship between alexithymia and psychological mindedness, however, remains speculative in the absence of empirical data.

Alexithymia and Emotional Intelligence

Although EI is better known in the popular press, alexithymia is a concept that has generated far more empirical research and is widely known in the scientific literature (Taylor et al., 1997). When Salovey, Hsee, and Mayer (1993) conceptualized EI as a multidimensional construct involving a set of processes, skills, and outcomes related to the appraisal, expression, and regulation of emotion, they placed alexithymia at the extreme lower end of the EI continuum (Parker, 2000). Furthermore, and as mentioned above, Parker et al. (2001) found a strong negative correlation ($r = -0.72$, $p < 0.01$) between EI-EQ-i and alexithymia, suggesting a relationship between alexithymia and low EI-EQ-i.

The relationship between alexithymia and EI, however, may not be quite so simple. Alexithymia, for example, is a much more narrowly defined construct than either EI-EQ-i or EI-MSCEIT. Alexithymia is related to disordered affect, encompasses only the lower end of the emotional ability continuum, and has an etiology based on biology and development. Moreover, alexithymia conceptually overlaps the lower pole of Gardner's (1983) intrapersonal intelligence concept—the ability to identify, label, and discriminate among feelings and represent them symbolically—whereas both EI-EQ-i and EI-MSCEIT are related to the entire range of Gardner's intrapersonal and interpersonal concepts, and, in the case of EI-EQ-i, can include outcome variables such as stress management, adaptability, and general mood.

Despite the fact that difficulty in monitoring the feelings and emotions of others is not included in the definition of alexithymia, there is clinical and empirical evidence that alexithymia is related to difficulties in accurately identifying the emotions and facial expressions of others (Lane et al., 1996; Parker, Taylor, Bagby, & Acklin, 1993), limited capacity for empathizing with the emotional states of others (Davies, Stankov, & Roberts, 1998; Krystal, 1979), low interpersonal intelligence, low stress management, low adaptability, and negative mood (Parker et al., 2001). Ultimately, then, the degree to which alexithymia and EI are empirically correlated and conceptually overlapping is a function of how EI is constructed, how the conceptual parameters of alexithymia relate to this construction, and whether the empirical association between the two constructs is representative of their respective theoretical relationship.

Emotional Intelligence, Psychological Mindedness, Alexithymia, and Personality

Because an individual with limited PM is generally expected to have limited EI (Taylor et al., 1997), PM is conceptually related to EI. Also, because the PM construct can focus solely on the self (Bagby et al., 1994; Fenigstein et al., 1975), solely on others (Dollinger, 1985), or on both the self and others (Conte et al., 1990; Menna & Cohen, 1997; Park & Park, 1997), EI and PM can overlap in intrapersonal, interpersonal, or both intra- and interpersonal domains. In contrast, alexithymia is conceptually related to both EI and PM, but this relationship is negative and mostly limited to intrapersonal processes.

In addition to a conceptual relationship, EI, PM, and alexithymia have been related empirically. Although monitoring the feelings and emotions of others is not included in the definition of alexithymia, empirical studies have shown that alexithymia relates to a lack of empathy and awareness for others (Parker et al., 2001). Beyond what one would predict on theoretical grounds, therefore, alexithymia (Bagby et al., 1994) correlates strongly and negatively to the total score, the interpersonal factor, *and* the intrapersonal factor of the EQ-i (Taylor & Bagby, 2000). Furthermore, alexithymia is significantly and negatively correlated with the second-order factors of the EQ-i—stress management, adaptability, and general mood—despite these factors seeming more related to the *outcomes* of EI rather than essential *components* of the construct (Taylor & Bagby, 2000).

Without the use of more sophisticated structural modeling to distinguish outcomes from causal factors, however, the nature of these relationships are uncertain, and the question of how EI relates to alexithymia may be better answered with the MSCEIT. As of yet, only two unpublished studies (Lumley et al., 2002; Parker, Bagby, & Taylor, 2003) have used the MSCEIT to study this relationship: Each study used an undergraduate student sample and the TAS-20 and MSCEIT measures, and found moderate negative associations between alexithymia and EI-MSCEIT (Parker, 2005).

Psychological mindedness, on the other hand, is positively related to EI-EQ-i (Taylor et al., 1997), positively related to intra- and interpersonal intelligences (Beitel et al., 2005; Farber & Golden, 1997), and negatively related to alexithymia (Bagby et al., 1994; McCallum & Piper, 2000). The relationship between PM and the other second-order factors of the EQ-i—stress management, adaptability, and general mood—is less clear, though sufficient evidence exists to suggest a negative relationship between PM and

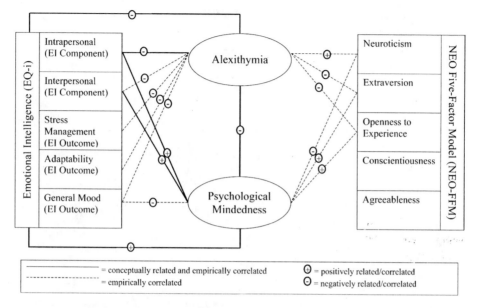

Figure 13.1. Conceptual relationship and empirical correlations between EI-EQ-I, alexithymia, psychological mindedness, and personality.

general mood (Farber & Golden, 1997; Fenigstein, 1994; McCallum & Piper, 2000). Like alexithymia, research needs to be conducted comparing PM to EI-MSCEIT. Finally, both PM and alexithymia are related to a variety of personality variables, suggesting that they may be influenced by basic temperamental factors. Alexithymia, for example, converges with certain dimensions of the five-factor model of personality; specifically, vulnerability to emotional distress (high N), low positive emotionality (low E), and limited imagination (low O) are all related to alexithymia (Taylor, 1994; Taylor et al., 1997). Conversely, PM is related to low N, high E, and high O (Beitel & Cecero, 2003; Taylor et al., 1997). Figure 13.1 presents a summary of these conceptual relationships and empirical correlations, whereas Table 13.1 summarizes the definitions of EI, alexithymia, and PM.

EI and Psychopathology

Before discussing the relationship between EI and the onset, maintenance, and treatment of psychopathology, it is important to note that both the meaning of emotional intelligence and the content of EI tests vary greatly (see Mayer, Caruso, & Salovey, 2000). Moreover, the match between what a test is supposed to measure and the content of that test (content validity) is sometimes imperfect. Thus, depending on the theory behind EI (see Chapters 1–6, this volume), the meaning of EI, and how it is assessed (see Chapters 7–11), the relationship between EI and psychopathology will be more or less mediated by genetics, neurobiology, temperament, development, cognitive ability,

TABLE 13.1. Definitions of emotional intelligence, alexithymia, and psychological mindedness.

Construct	Definition
Emotional intelligence	Emotional Intelligence (EI) has been defined a number of ways. In *Emotional Intelligence*, Goleman (1995) describes EI as having five parts: knowing emotions, managing emotions, motivating oneself, recognizing emotions in others, and handling relationships (p. 43), though later in the book, Goleman adds "self-awareness, impulse control and delaying gratification, and handling stress and anxiety" (p. 259). Bar-On (1997), alternatively, characterizes EI as "an array of noncognitive capabilities, competencies, and skills that influence one's ability to succeed in coping with environmental demands and pressures" (p. 14), and went on to develop the EQ-i, which has as components intrapersonal EQ, interpersonal EQ, adaptability EQ, stress management EQ, and general mood EQ (pp. 43–45). More recently, Goleman (1998) broke EI these five dimensions down into 25 emotional competencies. Finally, Mayer and Salovey's (1997) ability model of EI, as measured by the MEIS and its successor, the MSCEIT, includes four branches: (1) emotional perception, (2) emotional integration, (3) emotional understanding, and (4) emotional management. (For more about assessing EI, see Chapters 7–11, this volume, and Mayer, Caruso, and Salovey, 2000).
Alexithymia	According to Taylor, Bagby, and Parker (1997), alexithymia is a construct "composed of the following salient features: (1) difficulty identifying feelings and distinguishing between feelings and the bodily sensations of emotional arousal; (2) difficulty describing feelings to other people; (3) constricted imaginal processes, as evidenced by a paucity of fantasies; and (4) a stimulus-bound, externally orientated cognitive style" (p. 29).
Psychological mindedness	The capacity for psychological mindedness includes "the patient's desire to learn the possible meanings and causes of his internal and external experiences as well as the patient's ability to look inwards to psychical factors rather than only outwards to environmental factors . . . [and] to potentially conceptualize the relationship between thoughts, feelings, and actions" (Silver, 1983, p. 516).

learning, motivation, personality, and situational variables. Additionally, the extent to which EI is related to clinically significant constructs (e.g., alexithymia) and describes the kind of emotional regulation that affects one's vulnerability to mental disorder is largely a function of the particular brand of EI concerned. Because very little clinical research exists related to EI, and almost no research exists related to EI-MSCEIT, any conclusions we draw about EI and psychopathology are highly speculative. Only by comparison to alexithymia and PM—well-researched and clinically relevant constructs—can we speak with any degree of certainty.

EI and *DSM-IV-TR* Diagnoses

Emotional disturbance is a common criterion for many *DSM-IV-TR-IV* diagnoses, and it is difficult to confine emotional problems to any small number of diagnostic categories. For example, emotional symptoms are a central feature of mood disorders (i.e., major depressive disorder, dysthymic disorder, cyclothymic disorder, and bipolar disorder) and anxiety disorders (i.e., phobias, panic disorder, generalized anxiety disorder, obsessive-compulsive disorder, posttraumatic stress disorder, and acute stress disorder). The inability to regulate distressing emotions through mental processes is also a major feature of hypochondriasis and somatization disorder, in which a limited awareness and cognitive processing of emotions can lead to the amplification and misinterpretation of the somatic sensations that accompany emotional arousal (Taylor et al., 1997).

Furthermore, because EI often refers to the awareness and management of emotion rather than to an emotional state per se, some disorders (disorders associated with poor impulse control, such as antisocial personality disorder, kleptomania, explosive disorder, pyromania, etc.) may be more aligned with the theory of EI than others. Because impulse control is related to EI-MSCEIT (i.e., to the "managing emotions" branch) much more than it is to PM or alexithymia, a potentially important area for future research is whether emotional management provides EI-MSCEIT with discriminant validity over related concepts. Certainly, the management of emotion—above and beyond the ability to perceive, use, and understand emotions—may be related to the onset, maintenance, and treatment of several disorders. Until such research is completed, the unique role of EI-MSCEIT in psychopathology will remain unknown.

Finally, disorders characterized by a lack of insight of other's motives and feelings are also related to EI-EQ-i (interpersonal facet) and EI-MSCEIT (understanding emotions branch); specifically, social dysfunction associated with the inaccurate evaluation of others may often be experienced by those with schizophrenia and related spectrum disorders (e.g., schizotypal), and other Axis II personality disorders, especially Cluster B disorders (i.e., narcissistic, borderline, antisocial, and histrionic personality disorders). Conversely, if extremely high EI does sometimes lead to negative outcomes, then high EI may also be related to social dysfunction, but dysfunction associated with the *accurate* evaluation of others rather than the inaccurate evaluation of others. If this is the case, then dysfunction associated with the accurate evaluation of others would most likely be associated with a different set of DSM categories than that dysfunction associated with the inaccurate evaluation of others.

EI and Psychotherapy

Although a number of mental disorders are related to direct or indirect expressions of negative affect, the diversity of these disorders mitigates against any straightforward relationship between low EI and psychopathology. Moreover, EI fails to emerge from the *DSM-IV-TR* as a clear diagnostic criterion, and employing a categorization based on emotional pathology may obscure the fact that many of the disorders related to low EI have distinct etiologies and require different treatments. Nevertheless, low EI is associated with vulnerability to a range of clinical pathologies, and if low EI plays a role in the etiology of certain mental disorders, then "treating" EI may be therapeutically effective.

Unfortunately, there is currently very little evidence that addresses this issue directly, though some clinicians have developed a number of therapeutic modifications to conventional forms of psychotherapy for treating clients with alexithymia (Parker, 2000). The general purpose of these modifications is to help clients better recognize and discuss emotions, and understand how their emotional processes and experiences are related to their intra- and interpersonal difficulties. This approach contrasts sharply with traditional psychotherapy because it "attempts to elevate emotions from a level of perceptually bound experience (a world of sensation and action) to a conceptual representational level (a world of feelings and thoughts) where they can be used as signals of information, thought about, and sometimes communicated to others" (Taylor et al., 1997, p. 252).

According to Krystal (1979, 1988) and Taylor (1977, 1987), however, this type of modified psychotherapy can be slow and tedious, especially for those alexithymics who assume a dependent role and expect therapy to "cure" them of their problems. Given enough time and the appropriate training, however, even these alexithymic clients can learn to discriminate between emotional states, better understand their feelings, and develop a larger range of verbal and behavioral expressions for conveying information about their emotional experiences (Krystal, 1988; Taylor, 1977). This process can be facilitated by directing the client's attention to behavioral expressions of emotion as a means of communicating feelings (Greenberg & Safran, 1989) and by teaching the client to pay attention to their dreams as a means of teaching them to focus on inner feelings (Cartwright, 1993).

Alternatively, Flannery (1978), Schraa and Dicks (1981), and Taylor, Bagby, and Parker (1991) suggest the use of pharmacologic, cognitive-behavioral, or multiple modes of therapeutic intervention. An integrated treatment approach is consistent with the psychobiological nature of emotions, and well-aligned with Taylor et al.'s (1997) view that "the etiology and pathogenesis of disorders of affect regulation involve complex interactions between psychosocial and neurobiological factors" (p. 256). Furthermore, although alexithymics respond poorly to insight-oriented therapy, a combination of psychotherapy and behavioral techniques—such as biofeedback or relaxation training— has been found to foster greater introspective awareness and enhance the capacity to self-regulate different physiological states (Taylor, 1987). Finally, a wide variety of psychoactive drugs are useful in the treatment of disorders of affect regulation; benzodiazepines, tricyclic antidepressants, MAO inhibitors, selective serotonin reuptake inhibitors (SSRIs), mood stabilizers (such as lithium carbonate, carbamezapine, and valprate), and neuroleptics are examples of medications selected to target specific symptoms such as depression, anxiety, panic, instability of mood, irritability, impulsivity, or intrusive thoughts (Taylor et al., 1997). Because the specificity of different neurotransmitter subsystems and selectivity of drug treatments is far from absolute, however, the relationship between psychoactive drugs and emotional pathology is far from clear (Dubovsky & Thomas, 1995).

As a practical and effective alternative to individual psychotherapy, several researchers have suggested group therapy for some clients with alexithymia (e.g., Apfel-Savitz, Silvermann, & Bennett, 1977; Swiller, 1988). Although individual sessions are ideal for educating patients about their difficulties in regulating affect, there are some unique therapeutic benefits that the structured social environment of a group setting can provide, including a broader range of interpersonal situations for alexithymic patients to experience, learn about, and model emotions (Apfel-Savitz et al., 1977; Swiller, 1988). On the other hand, although group therapy is considered a useful alternative or adjunct to individual psychotherapy for many alexithymic clients, the mediocre interpersonal skills of these clients may ultimately generate feelings of frustration and boredom in other group members and increase the likelihood that members without alexithymia will drop out of the group (Swiller, 1988). It is important, therefore, to avoid placing more than two or three individuals with alexithymia in the same group at one time; even then Swiller (1988) recommends that these individuals be at different stages of treatment.

Key Questions

Although emotional intelligence is of obvious relevance to clinical psychology, we must emphasize that virtually all of the published research on the construct has examined nonclinical populations. With this in mind, we will attempt to address specific questions related to the clinical utility of emotional intelligence in a manner that minimizes speculation.

In Which Real-World Domains Will EI Be Most and Least Useful?

As clinical researchers, it is difficult to know whether EI is more or less useful in clinical psychology than it is in other applied fields, but what we do know is that psychopathology is often related to disordered affect, and that EI as described by ability-based measures is potentially related to a host of clinically relevant perceptions, processes, attitudes, and behaviors. Furthermore, affect regulation—a core component of EI-MSCEIT but not of related constructs, such as alexithymia and PM—is almost certainly more relevant to clinical psychology than it is to other real-world domains. The ability, or lack of ability, to manage emotions is a key component in the onset, maintenance, and treatment of several mental illnesses related to disordered affect.

What Theoretical Advances Are Necessary to Support Practical Applications?

In order to understand how EI overlaps with similar constructs, is related to an array of biological, developmental, and social influences, and can be treated in conjunction with related emotional pathology, it is first necessary to develop a well-defined theory of EI. Ideally, the theory of EI would identify a specific set of emotional processes evident at the various levels of normal personality, abnormal personality, and diagnosis. Moreover, there is a general need for the EI to become theory-based; alexithymia, for example, is clearly defined as a deficit in the cognitive processing of emotion, and is thought to be the result of an arrest in early development. On the other hand, if the theoretical foundation of EI continues to fluctuate—sometimes limited to certain intrapersonal facets, other times encompassing alexithymia, psychological mindedness, social skills, and outcome variables—EI will remain a vague concept with a good name.

Once the theoretical foundation of emotional intelligence is secure, and once a measure of that construct is developed such that it meets the reliability and validity criteria set out by Anastasi and Urbina (1997), it will be possible to match clients with appropriate therapeutic interventions, monitor the progress of clients during psychotherapy, and investigate whether EI is related to psychopathology in a way that is unique and worthwhile. Moreover, once EI is clearly defined and measurable, the developmental antecedents, personality correlates, and neurobiological underpinnings of EI can be studied—the result of these efforts will allow us to gauge the extent to which EI is modifiable.

Finally, in order to more firmly establish EI as an essential construct, it is also critical to conduct (1) an investigation of how the expression of the EI-MSCEIT diathesis may be modulated by situational factors, (2) a series of prospective, longitudinal studies, including large epidemiological studies to compare the prevalence of alexithymia and/or pathologically low EI-MSCEIT in different cultures, and (3) an evaluation of the relationship between EI-MSCEIT and various psychotherapy outcome variables (Salminen, Saarijarvi, & Aarela, 1995; Taylor et al., 1991).

Can EI Be Trained?

In our opinion, there is a minimum level of EI required to train or improve EI. Those with alexithymia/low EI may lack the required EI to benefit from various cognitive therapies (e.g., insight-oriented therapy); instead, therapy that helps to educate those with extremely low EI/alexithymia about their condition and teach them ways of adjusting to or coping with it may be more effective. Also, as mentioned above, therapeutic modifications to conventional forms of psychotherapy for treating clients with alexithymia, combined with behavioral techniques (e.g., biofeedback, relaxation training), may also be effective for those with low EI. In these circumstances, it is not necessarily EI itself that is trained; rather, through education and behavioral modification the individual is taught how to adjust to his or her level of ability. This is not to say that EI cannot be trained—with enough EI, training can become useful (as seen in the coaching movement), and cognitive/insight-oriented therapies become increasingly effective. If our assumptions are valid, research is required to discover the minimum level of EI necessary for various therapies and training programs to be effective, what the function is between the level of EI and the ability to train EI, and whether certain components of EI are more responsive to training.

Is There Any Practical Advantage to Focusing on EI, Rather Than on Specific Contextualized Skills, Such as Skills for Assertiveness, Impulse Control, Stress Management, and So Forth?

As discussed above, there may be a practical advantage to focusing on EI in individuals whose EI is high enough to benefit from such efforts. The decision to focus on EI, rather than on specific contextualized skills, is also a function of whether EI is discriminantly valid—if so, if EI is a unique and useful conceptualization related to psychopathology in ways not captured by other constructs, then focusing on EI rather than contextualized skills is worthwhile to the extent that the training programs and therapy produced by this focus are different from those that coach contextualized skills.

What Are the Cultural, Social, and Economic Factors That May Constrain or Facilitate Applications Based on EI?

Without a reliable and valid measure of EI, and without a sufficient EI clinical literature, it is difficult to understand how EI is related to psychopathology, and how EI can be applied clinically; as a result, it is difficult for us to comment on the cultural, social, and economic factors that affect applications based on EI. What we do know is that basic emotions are universally expressed, and that emotion has neurological correlates. Thus, the universality of emotion implies at least a partial independence from cultural, social, and economic factors. These factors may, and almost certainly do, affect emotional intelligence; exactly how and when they affect emotional intelligence, and the ways in which they constrain or facilitate applications based on EI, remain a function of our growing ability to describe and measure EI.

Conclusion

When so many mental illnesses are related, directly or indirectly, to emotional pathology, a broad theory of emotional intelligence could have an almost unparalleled impact on clinical practice. As it stands, however, there is little evidence that EI is a useful way of discriminating processes at either the diagnostic or individual case level. What the evidence does show is the pervasiveness of N (neuroticism) as a vulnerability factor for many disorders (Costa & McCrae, 1985; Cox, Borger, Asmundson, & Taylor, 2000; Deary, Wilson, & Kelly, 1995; Martin & Sher, 1994), though the causal role of N is uncertain (e.g., N scores drop as alcoholism is treated; Shaw, Waller, Latham, Dunn, & Thompson, 1997). Ultimately, the application of a construct to clinical practice requires the development of relatively narrow constructs (e.g., alexithymia), not some lack of generalized EI. At the moment, alexithymia may be a more useful construct than EI precisely because it is a narrowly constructed, theory-based, well-researched condition that clinicians can recognize, measure, and treat. Until the same can be said for EI—and there is a great deal of interdisciplinary, longitudinal, and multicultural research to be

conducted before such an event occurs—emotional intelligence will remain an ineffective and specious conceptualization of emotional pathology.

References

Anastasi, A., & Urbina, S. (1997). *Psychological testing.* Upper Saddle River, NJ: Simon & Schuster.

Apfel-Savitz, R., Silvermann, D., & Bennett, M. I. (1977). Group psychotherapy of patients with somatic illnesses and alexithymia. *Psychotherapy and Psychosomatics, 28,* 323–329.

Appelbaum, S. A. (1973). Psychological-mindedness: Word, concept, and essence. *International Journal of Psychoanalysis, 54,* 35–45.

Bachrach, H. M., & Leaff, L. A. (1978). "Analyzability": A systematic review of the clinical and quantitative literature. *Journal of the American Psychoanalytic association, 26,* 881–920.

Bagby, R. M., Parker, J. D. A., & Taylor, G. J. (1994). The Twenty-Item Toronto Alexithymia Scale: I. Item selection and cross-validation of the factor structure. *Journal of Psychosomatic Research, 38,* 23–32.

Bar-On, R. (1997). *Bar-On Emotional Quotient Inventory (EQ-I): Technical manual.* Toronto: Multi-Health Systems.

Beitel, M., & Cecero, J. J. (2003). Predicting psychological mindedness from personality style and attachment security. *Journal of Clinical Psychology, 59,* 163–172.

Beitel, M., Ferrer, E., & Cecero, J. J. (2005). Psychological mindedness and awareness of self and others. *Journal of Clinical Psychology, 16*(6), 739–750.

Bloch, S. (1979). Assessment of patients for psychotherapy. *British Journal of Psychiatry, 135,* 193–208.

Cartwright, R. D. (1993). Who needs their dreams? The usefulness of dreams in psychotherapy. *Journal of the American Academy of Psychoanalysis, 21,* 539–547.

Ciarrochi, J., Deane, F. P., & Anderson, S. (2002). Emotional intelligence moderates the relationship between stress and mental health. *Personality and Individual Differences, 32,* 197–209.

Conte, H. R., Buckley, P., Picard, S., & Karasu, T. B. (1995). Relationships between psychological mindedness and personality traits and ego functioning: Validity studies. *Comprehensive Psychiatry, 36,* 11–17.

Conte, H. R., Plutchik, R., Jung, B. B., Picard, S., Karasu, T. B., & Lotterman, A. (1990). Psychological mindedness as a predictor of psychotherapy outcome: A preliminary report. *Comprehensive Psychiatry, 31,* 426–431.

Costa, P. T., & McCrae, R. R. (1985). *The NEO Personality Inventory manual.* Odessa, FL: Psychological Assessment Resources.

Cox, B. J., Borger, S. C., Asmundson, G. J. G., & Taylor, S. (2000). Dimensions of hypochondriasis and the five-factor model of personality. *Personality & Individual Differences, 29,* 99–108.

Davies, M., Stankov, L., & Roberts, R. D. (1998). Emotional intelligence: In search of an elusive construct. *Journal of Personal and Social Psychology, 75,* 989–1015.

Deary, I. J., Wilson, J. A., & Kelly, S. W. (1995). Globus pharyngis, personality, and psychological distress in the general population. *Psychosomatics, 36,* 570–577.

Dollinger, S. J. (1985). Sagacious judgment via word association. *Journal of Personality and Social Psychology, 49,* 1738–1752.

Dubovsky, S. L., & Thomas, M. (1995). Serotonergic mechanisms and current and future psychiatric practice. *Journal of Clinical Psychiatry, 56*, 38–48.

Farber, B. A., & Golden, V. (1997). Psychological mindedness in psychotherapists. In M. McCallum & W. E. Piper (Eds.), *Psychological mindedness: A contemporary understanding* (pp. 211–236). Mahwah, NJ: Erlbaum.

Fenigstein, A. (1994). Paranoia. In V. S. Ramachandran (Ed.), *Encyclopedia of human behaviour.* San Diego: Academic Press.

Fenigstein, A., Scheier, M. F., & Buss, A. H. (1975). Public and private self-consciousness: Assessment and theory. *Journal of Consulting and Clinical Psychology, 43*, 522–527.

Fenigstein, A., & Vanable, P. A. (1992). Paranoia and self-consciousness. *Journal of Personality and Social Psychology, 62*, 129–138.

Flannery, J. G. (1978). Alexithymia II. The association with unexplained physical distress. *Psychotherapy and Psychosomatics, 30*, 193–197.

Gardner, H. (1983). *Frames of mind: The theory of multiple intelligences.* New York: Basic Books.

Goleman, D. (1995). *Emotional intelligence.* New York: Bantam.

Goleman, D. (1998). *Working with emotional intelligence.* New York: Bantam.

Greenberg, L. S., & Safran, J. D. (1989). Emotion in psychotherapy. *American Psychologist, 44*, 19–29.

Krystal, H. (1978). Trauma and affects. *The Psychoanalytic Study of the Child, 33*, 81–115.

Krystal, H. (1979). Alexithymia and psychotherapy. *American Journal of Psychotherapy, 33*, 17–31.

Krystal, H. (1988). *Integration and self-healing: Affect, trauma, alexithymia.* Hillsdale, NJ: Analytic Press.

Lake, B. (1985). Concept of ego strength in psychotherapy. *British Journal of Psychiatry, 147*, 471–478.

Lane, R., Sechrest, L., Reidel, R., Weldon, V., Kaszniak, A., & Schwartz, G. (1996). Impaired verbal and nonverbal emotion recognition in alexithymia. *Psychosomatic Medicine, 58*, 203–210.

Lumley, M. A., Davis, M., Labouvie-Vief, G., Gustavson, B., Clement, R., Barry, R., et al. (2002, March). *Multiple measures of emotional abilities: Their interrelationships and associations with physical symptoms.* Presentation at the annual meeting of the American Psychosomatic Society, Barcelona, Spain.

Martin, E. D., & Sher, K. J. (1994). Family history of alcoholism, alcohol use disorders, and the five-factor model of personality. *Journal of Studies on Alcohol, 55*, 81–90.

Matthews, G., Roberts, R. D., & Zeidner, M. (2004). Seven myths about emotional intelligence. *Psychological Inquiry, 15*(3), 179–196.

Matthews, G., Zeidner, M., & Roberts, R. D. (2002). *Emotional intelligence: Science and myth.* Cambridge, MA: MIT Press.

Mayer, J. D., Caruso, D. R., & Salovey, P. (2000). Selecting a measure of emotional intelligence: The case for ability scales. In R. Bar-On & J. D. A. Parker (Eds.), *The handbook of emotional intelligence: Theory, development, assessment, and application at home, school, and in the workplace* (pp. 320–342). San Francisco: Jossey-Bass.

Mayer, J. D., & Geher, G. (1996). Emotional intelligence and the identification of emotion. *Intelligence, 22*, 89–113.

Mayer, J. D., & Salovey, P. (1997). What is emotional intelligence? In P. Salovey & D. Sluyter (Eds.), *Emotional development and emotional intelligence: Implications for educators* (pp. 3–31). New York: Basic Books.

Mayer, J. D., Salovey, P., & Caruso, D. R. (2002). *Mayer-Salovey-Caruso Emotional Intelligence Test (MSCEIT) user's manual.* Toronto, Ontario: Multi Health Systems.

McCallum, M., & Piper, W. E. (2000). Psychological mindedness and emotional intelligence. In R. Bar-On & J. D. A. Parker (Eds.), *The handbook of emotional intelligence: Theory, development, assessment, and application at home, school, and in the workplace* (pp. 118–135). San Francisco: Jossey-Bass.

McCrae, R. R., & Costa, P. T. (1985). Openness to experience. In R. Hogan & W.H. Jones (Eds.), *Perspectives in psychology: Theory, measurement and interpersonal dynamics,* (Vol. 1, pp. 145–172). Greenwich: JAI Press.

McCrae, R. R., & Costa, P. T. (1987). Validation of a five-factor model of personality across instruments and observers. *Journal of Personality and Social Psychology, 52,* 81–90.

Menna, R., & Cohen, N. J. (1997). Social perspective taking. In M. McCallum & W. E. Piper (Eds.), *Psychological mindedness: A contemporary understanding* (pp. 189–210). Mahwah, NJ: Erlbaum.

Owen, P., & Kohutek, K. (1981). The rural mental health dropout. *Journal of Rural Community Psychology, 2,* 38–41.

Park, L. C., Imboden, J. B., Park, T. J., Hulse, S. H., & Unger, H. T. (1992). Giftedness and psychological abuse in borderline personality disorder: Their relevance to genesis and treatment. *Journal of Personality Disorders, 6,* 226–240.

Park, L. C., & Park, T. J. (1997). Personal intelligence. In M. McCallum & W. E. Piper (Eds.), *Psychological mindedness: A contemporary understanding* (pp. 133–167). Mahwah, NJ: Erlbaum.

Parker, J. D. A. (2000). Emotional intelligence: Clinical and therapeutic implications. In R. Bar-On & J. D. A. Parker (Eds.), *The handbook of emotional intelligence: Theory, development, assessment, and application at home, school, and in the workplace* (pp. 490–500). San Francisco: Jossey-Bass.

Parker, J. D. A. (2005). The relevance of emotional intelligence for clinical psychology. In R. Schulze & R. D. Roberts (Eds.), *Emotional intelligence: An international handbook* (pp. 271–287). Göttingen: Hogrefe & Huber.

Parker, J. D. A., Bagby, R. M., & Taylor, G. J. (2003, August). *Twenty-Item Toronto Alexithymia Scale: Is it distinct from basic personality?* Presented at the annual meeting of the American Psychological Association, Toronto, Canada.

Parker, J. D. A., Taylor, G. J., & Bagby, R. M. (1993). Alexithymia and the recognition of facial expressions of emotion. *Psychotherapy and Psychosomatics, 59,* 197–202.

Parker, J. D. A., Taylor, G. J., & Bagby, R. M. (2001). The relationship between emotional intelligence and alexithymia. *Personality and Individual Differences, 30,* 107–115.

Parker, J. D. A., Taylor, G. J., Bagby, R. M., & Acklin, M. W. (1993). Alexithymia in panic disorder and simple phobia: A comparative study. *American Journal of Psychiatry, 150,* 1105–1107.

Salminen, J. K., Saarijarvi, S., & Aarela, E. (1995). Two decades of alexithymia. *Journal of Psychosomatic Research, 39,* 803–807.

Salovey, P., Hsee, C. K., & Mayer, J. D. (1993). Emotional intelligence and the self-regulation of affect. In D. M. Wegner & J. W. Pennebaker (Eds.), *Handbook of mental control* (pp. 258–277). Englewood Cliffs, NJ: Prentice Hall.

Schraa, J. C., & Dicks, J. F. (1981). Hypnotic treatment of the alexithymic patient: A case report. *American Journal of Clinical Hypnotherapy, 23,* 207–210.

Schutte, N., Malouff, J., Hall, L., Haggerty, D., Cooper, J., Golden, C., & Dornheim, L. (1998). Development and validation of a measure of emotional intelligence. *Personality and Individual Differences, 25,* 167–177.

Shaw, G. K., Waller, S., Latham, C. J., Dunn, G., & Thompson, A. D. (1997). Alcoholism: A long-term follow-up study of participants in an alcohol treatment programme. *Alcohol & Alcoholism, 32*, 527–535.

Sifneos, P. E. (1972). *Short-term psychotherapy and emotional crisis.* Cambridge, MA: Harvard University Press.

Sifneos, P. E. (1973). The prevalence of "alexithymic" characteristics in psychosomatic patients. *Psychotherapy and Psychosomatics, 22*, 255–262.

Silver, D. (1983). Psychotherapy of the characterologically difficult patient. *Canadian Journal of Psychiatry, 28*, 513–521.

Swiller, H. I. (1988). Alexithymia: Treatment utilizing combined individual and group psychotherapy. *International Journal of Group Psychotherapy, 38*, 47–61.

Taylor, G. J. (1977). Alexithymia and the counter-transference. *Psychotherapy and psychosomatics, 28*, 141–147.

Taylor, G. J. (1984). Alexithymia: Concept, measurement, and implications for treatment. *American Journal of Psychiatry, 141*, 725–732.

Taylor, G. J. (1987). *Psychosomatic medicine and contemporary psychoanalysis.* Madison, CT: International Universities Press.

Taylor, G. J. (1994). The alexithymia construct: Conceptualization, validation, and relationship with basic dimensions of personality. *New Trends in Experimental and Clinical Psychiatry, 10*, 61–74.

Taylor, G. J., & Bagby, R. M. (2000). An overview of the alexithymia construct. In R. Bar-On and J. D. A. Parker (Eds.), *The handbook of emotional intelligence: Theory, development, assessment, and application at home, school, and in the workplace* (pp. 40–67). San Francisco: Jossey-Bass.

Taylor, G. J., Bagby, R. M., & Parker, J. D. A. (1991). The alexithymia construct: A potential paradigm for psychosomatic medicine. *Psychosomatics, 32*, 153–164.

Taylor, G. J., Bagby, R. M., & Parker, J. D. A. (1997). *Disorders of affect regulation: Alexithymia in medical and psychiatric illness.* Cambridge, UK: Cambridge University Press.

Taylor, G. J., Parker, J. D. A., & Bagby, R. M. (1999). Emotional intelligence and the emotional brain: Points of convergence and implications for psychoanalysis. *Journal of the American Academy of Psychoanalysis, 27*, 339–354.

Thorndike, E. L. (1920). Intelligence and its uses. *Harper's Magazine, 140*, 227–235.

14

Emotional Intelligence in Organizational Behavior and Industrial-Organizational Psychology

PETER J. JORDAN, NEAL M. ASHKANASY,
AND KAYLENE W. ASCOUGH

Since the introduction of emotional intelligence (EI) by Salovey and Mayer (1990) and its subsequent popularization by Goleman (1995), the construct has garnered intense interest from both scientists and practitioners and, as illustrated in this volume, it has been broadly applied. Chapters in this volume examine its application in education (Zins, Payton, Weissberg, & O'Brien, Chapter 15), and clinical psychology (Vachon & Bagby, Chapter 13), as well as its links to artificial intelligence (Picard, Chapter 16). The area in which the EI construct has really grown in popularity, however, is in its applications in the workplace. The growth of interest in EI in the workplace can be attributed to two factors, (1) the desire of businesses to find new ways of gaining performance improvements, and (2) the desire of managers to be able to predict behavior in the workplace. A search of PsycINFO for "emotional intelligence" and "organizational behavior" (October 8, 2005) found 297 peer-reviewed journal articles and 59 books. And, of course, this does not include the many books and articles published outside of the domain accessed by PsycINFO, especially in the popular management literature (e.g., Cooper & Sawaf, 1996; Goleman, 2001; Goleman, McKee, & Boyatzis, 2002).

During its relatively short existence, EI has generated intense controversy in organizational behavior (OB) and industrial and organizational (I/O) psychology, illustrated by the debates at international conferences (e.g., see Daus & Ashkanasy, 2003) and in leading journals (see Spector, 2005). So strong is the debate, the topic has even resulted in the publication of whole volumes dedicated to the controversy in general (e.g., Matthews,

Acknowledgments: This chapter was partially funded by a grant from the Australian Research Council.

Zeidner, & Roberts, 2002) and in OB and I/O psychology in particular (e.g., see Murphy, in press). Indeed, in giving a keynote address at the 2005 Industrial and Organizational Psychology Conference in Australia, Kevin Murphy listed *emotional intelligence* as one of the top 10 misses of industrial and organizational psychology over the last 10 years (Myors, 2005)—and there is probably some justification in this assertion, particularly in relation to issues surrounding varying construct definitions and well-discussed measurement problems.

Critics of EI (e.g., Landy, 2005; Locke, 2005) have focused in particular on the shortcomings of the more popular models of emotional intelligence. This includes some of the more extravagant claims made by advocates such as Goleman (1995) for the construct and perceptions that EI is based in discredited theories of "social intelligence," first advocated by Thorndike (1920) over 80 years ago. Although initially strident in their criticism, we acknowledge that some of these critics have become more sanguine in their responses, acknowledging that there is some merit in a scientific approach to research investigating emotional intelligence.

We argue that, although there is mixed evidence about the link between EI and workplace applications, steadily maturing research in the field is providing increasing confidence regarding the predictive ability of emotional intelligence. In this chapter, we provide a broad overview of EI in OB research and I/O psychology, including a review of applications and coverage of some of the contentious issues in the field. We conclude by placing emotional intelligence research within the context of the wider framework of research on the role of emotions in organizational settings.

Constructs of Emotional Intelligence in the Workplace

Mayer, Salovey, and Caruso (2000a) identified a distinction between *mixed* and *ability* models of emotional intelligence. The mixed models include personality variables as a part of the emotional intelligence construct, whereas the ability models relate to specific abilities that link emotion and cognition. As indicated in Jordan, Ashkanasy, and Härtel (2003), we have concerns over evidence provided by researchers who use mixed models of emotional intelligence, on the basis that the efficacy of EI research may be diminished if the construct is confounded with personality variables such as empathy, self-confidence, or conscientiousness. Nonetheless, although we agree with Ashkanasy and Daus (2005) and Mayer et al. (2000a) that the results of research using the mixed models may be open to question, we also acknowledge that there is continuing research and interest in these models of the emotional intelligence construct. Consequently, we include discussion of the mixed models in this chapter.

The emotional abilities associated with Mayer and Salovey's (1997) model of EI are not new. Rather, these authors drew together the previous literature concerning links between emotion and cognition, coalescing this knowledge into a comprehensive model that they called emotional intelligence. More specifically, the Mayer and Salovey model acknowledges that emotion and cognition are virtually inseparable in an individual's reaction to situations and thus should not be separated in studies of human decision making. As such, they identified EI as the ability to be aware of emotions in self and others, and the ability to modify our reactions to situations accordingly. The four related emotion-processing abilities (or "branches") they identified are (a) emotion perception, (b) emotion facilitation, (c) emotion understanding, and (d) emotion management (Mayer & Salovey, 1997). Each of these branches has been outlined in detail elsewhere in this volume. We thus examine specifically the application of emotional intelligence in the workplace within the reference framework of the Mayer and Salovey model.

At this point, we need also to address measurement, on the basis that measurement has a direct impact on the application of emotional intelligence in the workplace. Although this issue is dealt with in some detail elsewhere in this volume (see Petrides, Furnham, & Mavroveli [Chapter 6]; Schulze, Wilhelm, & Kyllonen [Chapter 8]; Rivers, Brackett, Salovey, & Mayer [Chapter 9]), it is nonetheless important for us to point out that we take no firm stance on the debate between ability versus self-report measures. Although traditional intelligence research supports ability testing as the most appropriate approach, we note that emotions are generally very personal experiences. From this viewpoint, although we acknowledge the complications involved in self-assessment bias, we consider self-report to be an appropriate measurement method in particular contexts, especially in field and group applications (e.g., Jordan & Troth, 2004).

Research suggests that emotional awareness can be reasonably accurately assessed using self-report. Davis (1994), for example, found that individuals were able to identify their own emotional reactions to situations and place them in categories ranging from personal distress to perspective taking. More recently, Jordan and Ashkanasy (2006) reported that self- and peer-report measures of emotional intelligence could be combined to provide a measure of emotional self-awareness in teams. Consequently, at this relatively early stage of the development of EI measures, and so long as a particular measure has been shown to be psychometrically validated, it seems reasonable to accept the legitimacy of self-report measures of emotional intelligence.

In order to determine how EI is being applied in the workplace, we examine empirical data to support the claims that have been made by researchers working in this field. Jordan and his colleagues (2003) note that many of the potential applications have not been extensively tested by empirical data owing to the infancy of EI research. Although more research has been published in the intervening years, it is clear that emotional intelligence research is still in its infancy when compared to the more established research in personality and intelligence. Furthermore, in many cases, data and claims have been based on models of EI that are inconsistent with the construct of emotional intelligence described by Mayer and Salovey (1997). In other cases, this research has incorporated personality variables that expand the potential impact of the construct beyond its original definition (Mayer et al., 2000a). Indeed, this is a major deficiency in the arguments of the detractors of emotional intelligence—insofar as their criticisms are generally about research conducted without a distinctive definition of emotional intelligence (see Ashkanasy & Daus, 2005). In this chapter, we report on research that includes measures of emotional self-awareness and emotional management, and we avoid conclusions that draw on broader personality variables such as conscientiousness or empathy.

In summary, and consistent with Ashkanasy and Daus (2005), we note three "streams" of research and application on emotional intelligence in organizations. Stream 1 comprises research that conforms closely to the EI model first proposed by Salovey and Mayer (1990), which was subsequently refined by Mayer and Salovey (1997) and is measured using the Mayer-Salovey-Caruso Emotional Intelligence Test (MSCEIT; Mayer, Salovey, Caruso, & Sitarenios, 2001). Stream 2 includes research that, although based on the Mayer and Salovey model, uses measures other than the abilities-oriented MSCEIT to measure the construct, typically based on self-reports (e.g., Jordan, Ashkanasy, Härtel, & Hooper, 2002; Schutte et al., 1998; Wong & Law, 2002). Finally, Stream 3 includes conceptualizations and measures that differ from the Mayer and Salovey model but have some common ground. As a general rule, these include factors that tend to overlap with personality constructs and have been characterized by Mayer et al. (2000a) as "mixed models" of emotional intelligence. Examples include research conducted using the EQ-i developed by Bar-On (1997), which is based in the idea that emotional intelligence is a form of psychological/emotional well-being; the Emotional Competency Index (ECI; Sala, 2002), which is founded in Goleman's (1998) broadly based construct of emotional intelligence as a form of social and interpersonal competence (see also Goleman et al., 2002); and other self-report measures including, for example, the measure developed by Dulewicz, Higgs, and Slaski (2003).

In order to be comprehensive in this chapter, we report on the broad range of research from Streams 1, 2, and 3 but note that the results from Stream 3 may need further testing to make sure that the findings do not confound EI with other personality variables. Additionally, we should point out that a number of the studies we use in this chapter report the relationship between dependent variables and total EI, rather than exploring individual branches of emotional intelligence. In this chapter, we use these findings to indicate a connection between the variables and EI that requires further detailed research in relation to the individual branches of emotional intelligence.

Emotional Intelligence and Workplace Applications

Given the widespread interest in emotional intelligence in OB and I/O psychology, it is not surprising that the construct has found application across a broad range of subtopics in the workplace. In Tables 14.1, 14.2, and 14.3, we provide a comprehensive overview of empirical research that has examined the links between EI and workplace applications, categorized as Stream 1, 2, or 3, respectively (see above). Of course, it is beyond the scope of this chapter to discuss the results of each and every one of these studies. Instead, we discuss in detail a selection of studies that have investigated the role of EI in workplace settings.

Recent publications that have examined evidence of the links between EI and workplace applications include Daus and Ashkanasy (2005), Druskat, Sala, and Mount (2006), Jordan, Ashkanasy, and Ashton-James (2006), and Zeidner, Matthews, and Roberts (2004). In assessing some of the major claims made for the emotional intelligence construct, Jordan and his colleagues (2006) examined the links between EI and

TABLE 14.1. Stream 1 emotional intelligence research (i.e., using the MSCEIT) involving workplace variables.

Author	EI Measure	N	Dependent Variables	Findings
Day & Carroll (2004)	MSCEIT v1.1; Mayer, Salovey, & Caruso (2000b)	246	Personality, performance, and citizenship behavior	Some dimensions of EI are linked to experience and individual task performance, but not overall group performance or citizenship behavior.
Brotheridge (2003)	MSCEIT v2.0; Mayer, Salovey, & Caruso (2002)	188	Emotional labor	EI is positively linked to deep acting, but not surface acting. Surface acting is linked only to awareness of emotions.
Lyons & Schneider (2005)	MSCEIT v2.0	126	Cognitive appraisals and performance	Specific dimensions of ability-based EI predict stressor appraisals and performance.
Lopes, Salovey, Côté, & Beers (2005)	MSCEIT v2.0	76	Emotion regulation ability and quality of social interactions	Emotion regulation abilities are related to indicators of the quality of social interactions over and above variance accounted for by the Big Five personality traits and verbal and fluid intelligence.
Leban & Zulauf (2004)	MSCEIT v2.0	24	Transformational leadership and performance	EI is linked to inspirational motivation, idealized influence, and individual consideration components of transformational leadership.
Feyerherm & Rice (2002)	Multifactor Emotional Intelligence Scale (MEIS); Mayer, Salovey, & Caruso (1997)	164	Team EI, team leader EI, and team performance	Team leader EI is linked with performance through manager rankings and ratings, but not through team performance assessment. Manager ratings and team member performance ratings produce negative correlations between team EI and performance.
Thi Lam & Kirby (2002)	MEIS	304	General intelligence and individual cognitive-based performance	EI contributes to individual cognitive-based performance.

TABLE 14.2. Stream 2 emotional intelligence research (i.e., self-reports based on the Mayer and Salovey model) involving workplace variables.

Author	EI Measure	N	Dependent Variables	Findings
Palmer, Walls, Burgess, & Stough (2001)	Trait Meta Mood Scale; Salovey, Mayer, Goldman, Turvey, & Palfai (1995)	43	Transformational leadership	Transformational leadership is linked with EI. However, transformational leaders are not necessarily higher in EI than transactional leaders.
Jordan, Ashkanasy, Härtel, & Hooper (2002)	WEIP-3; Jordan, Ashkanasy, Härtel, & Hooper (2002)	448	Team performance	Teams high in EI operate at higher levels of performance.
Moriarty & Buckley (2003)	WEIP-5	80	Team learning and team process	Undertaking a program in developing team skills and being taught from the perspective of the process increases EI.
Jordan & Troth (2004)	WEIP-6	350	Team problem solving and conflict resolution	EI was linked with team performance and conflict resolution methods but not performance at an individual level.
Jordan & Troth (2002)	WEIP-6	139	Conflict resolution style	Individuals with higher levels of EI are more likely, or more able, to engage in collaborative conflict resolution and reject forcefulness and avoidance.
Sue-Chan & Latham (2004)	WEIP-6	75	Situational interview, teamplaying behavior	Emotional intelligence mediated the relationship between the SI and team-playing behavior.
Wong, & Law (2002)	Wong, & Law (2002)	149/146	Emotional labor, job satisfaction, organizational commitment, turnover intention, job performance, job perception, in-role and extra-role behavior, and education and tenure with organization	EI in followers is related to job performance and job satisfaction, but not to organizational commitment and turnover, with the EI–job performance relationship and the EI organizational commitment relationship moderated by the emotional labor required in the job. However, the EI–job satisfaction relationship was not moderated by emotional labor. The EI of supervisors has an effect on the job satisfaction of subordinates and their extra-role behaviors, but not on their job performance.

(Continued)

TABLE 14.2. (continued)

Author	EI Measure	N	Dependent Variables	Findings
Foo, Anger Elfenbein, Tan, & Aik (2004)	Emotional Intelligence Scale (EIS); Wong, Law, & Wong (2004)	164	Personality and subjective experience in negotiation	Individuals high in EI reported more positive experiences in negotiation, and having a partner high in EI is related to better objective outcomes.
Carmeli (2003)	Schutte et al. (1998)	256	Work outcomes, work behavior, and work attitudes	Senior managers with high EI develop high affective commitment to their organization and high commitment toward their career, report higher job satisfaction, and perform the job better than senior managers with low EI. They also can effectively control work-family conflict and display higher levels of altruistic behavior.
Schutte, Schuettpelz, & Malouff (2001)	Schutte et al. (1998)	38	Performance on cognitive tasks	Individuals with higher EI perform better on a cognitive task and are better able to ward off the detrimental emotional effects of the difficulties and persist at the task.
Rozell, Pettijohn, & Parker (2002)	Schutte et al. (1998)	103	Organizational commitment, and performance, selling orientation/customer orientation	A salesperson's customer orientation is positively related to EI and performance, but not with organizational commitment.
Abraham (2000)	Schutte et al. (1998)	79	Job control, job satisfaction, and organizational commitment	EI predicted a variance in job satisfaction and organizational commitment and exerted influence in conjunction with job control.
Vakola, Tsaousis, & Nikolaou (2004)	Emotional Intelligence Questionnaire (EIQ); Tsaousis (2003)	137	Personality and attitude toward change	There is a relationship between personality traits and employees' attitudes toward change, along with EI relating to positive attitudes to willingness toward change, turnover intentions, and increased job satisfaction.
Nikolaou & Tsaousis (2002)	EIQ	212	Gender, family status, educational background, job description, stress, and organizational commitment	EI is linked to occupational stress and organizational commitment. Workers higher in EI have significantly lower occupational stress.

362

TABLE 14.3. Stream 3 emotional intelligence research (i.e., self-reports based on models other than Mayer and Salovey) involving workplace variables.

Author	EI Measure	N	Dependent Variables	Findings
Rapisarda (2002)	Self-Assessment Questionnaire (SAQ); Boyatzis (1982). Emotional Competence Inventory (ECI); Boyatzis & Goleman (1998)	91	Work team cohesiveness and performance	EI competencies were linked to the group's self-reported cohesiveness, and the self-reported study group cohesiveness showed a stronger relationship with EI than with study group performance.
Offermann, Bailey, Vasilopoulos, Seal, & Sass (2004)	ECI-U; Boyatzis & Goleman (2002)	425	Cognitive ability, personality, individual performance, and team performance	Cognitive ability (CA) predicts individual academic performance. Emotional competence (EC) was more effective at predicting team performance and is associated with team attitudes.
Slaski & Cartwright (2003)	EQ-i; Bar-On (1997)	120	General health, psychological outcomes, stress, and management performance	EI can be taught and learned, and may be useful in reducing stress and improving health, well-being, and performance.
Langhorn (2004)	EQ-i	161	Profit performance data, team satisfaction, team turnover, customer satisfaction, appraisal rating, gender, and age.	Managerial EI is positively related to employee satisfaction, customer satisfaction, and profit performance, though profit performance is not related to gendered EI or age-related EI.
Sivanathan & Fekken (2002)	EQ-i	232	Moral reasoning, transformational leadership, and effectiveness	Followers' evaluations of leaders' transformational behaviors were linked to leaders' self-reports of EI and followers' ratings on leadership effectiveness but not to self-reports of moral reasoning or supervisor ratings of leader effectiveness.
Douglas, Frink, & Ferris (2004)	EQ-i	205	Conscientiousness, performance, and self-monitoring	Among highly conscientious workers, those high in EI had higher performance scores than those low in EI.

(Continued)

TABLE 14.3. (continued)

Author	EI Measure	N	Dependent Variables	Findings
Mandell & Pherwani (2003)	EQ-i	32	Transformational leadership	Transformational leadership style could be predicted from EI scores, but no gender differences were found.
Barling, Slater, & Kelloway (2000)	EQ-i	60	Transformational leadership	EI is associated with three aspects of transformational leadership (idealized influence, inspirational motivation, and individualized consideration), and contingent reward. Active and passive management-by-exception and laissez-faire management were not associated with EI.
Gardner & Stough (2002)	SUEIT: Palmer & Stough (2001)	110	Leadership styles: transformational, transactional, and laissez-faire	A strong relationship exists between transformational leadership and overall EI. A negative relationship exists between laissez-faire leadership and EI.
Palmer, Gardner, & Stough (2003)	SUEIT	210	Personality and effective leadership	EI is higher in executive populations than those working in more general roles in organizations.
Rahim & Minors (2003)	EQ Index; Rahim (2002)	222	Quality concern and problem solving	Components of EQ are positively associated with concern for quality and problem solving.
Ferres & Connell (2004)	EQ Index	448	Organizational change cynicism and dispositional trust	Employees would report less change cynicism if managed by leaders whom they rated as high in EI.
Higgs (2004)	EIQ: Dulewicz & Higgs (2000)	289	Call center agents and performance	Overall EI is significantly related to center agent performance.

364

job performance, EI and career progression, and EI and leadership, and found mixed support for the substantial claims made in these areas. Zeidner et al. (2004) attempted to untangle the claims from empirical evidence and, although they were encouraged by the potential of EI to add to our understanding of work encounters, they concluded that there is still a need for more scientifically validated studies to advance the area. Finally, Daus and Ashkanasy (2005) examined the links between EI and leadership, job performance, and emotional labor and came to a conclusion similar to that reached by Zeidner and his associates.

In terms of performance, authors such as Goleman (1998) argue that EI predicts a broad spectrum of work performance. Jordan et al. (2006), however, examined the extant research and concluded that, despite these sweeping claims, the empirical evidence points only to links between EI and performance for tasks in which there is a *clear emotional skill* required for successful task completion. For instance, Brotheridge (2003) found emotional intelligence measured using the MSCEIT was linked to deep acting in individuals undertaking emotional labor. Her data, however, revealed that only emotional awareness of emotions was linked to surface acting.

In the area of leadership, Daus and Ashkanasy (2005) discussed recent Stream 1 research that found evidence of links between EI and leadership emergence and transformational leadership. Jordan et al. (2006), on the other hand, who looked at the spectrum of EI measures and definitions, suggested caution in interpreting any broad assertions made about the link between EI and leadership. They did nonetheless acknowledge that there is an emotional element to leadership (see Humphrey, 2002) and point to theoretical research that supports links between emotional awareness and transformational leadership. Jordan and his coauthors concluded that the links between EI and specific forms of leadership require more rigorous theoretical development, followed by appropriate tests to establish the veracity of these claims.

Leban and Zulauf (2004), in a Stream 1 study that examined the links between transformational leadership and emotional intelligence, found that EI was linked to idealized influence and individual consideration. Sivanathan and Fekken (2002) found links between a Stream 3 (EQ-i; Bar-On, 1997) measure of EI and followers' evaluations of transformational leadership behaviors as well as evaluations of leader effectiveness. In another study using the EQ-i, Mandell & Pherwani (2003) reported that transformational leadership style could be predicted from scores gained on an emotional intelligence test.

In relation to research into claims that individuals with high emotional intelligence will have better career paths, Jordan et al. (2006) found no evidence to support this claim. They do acknowledge, however, that, if an employee's workplace performance is contingent solely or largely upon social skills, it may be that emotion perception and emotion management (two branches of the Mayer-Salovey model of EI) can contribute to higher levels of performance, and thus to career success. Jordan et al. comment also that EI is only one of many predictors of career success. Given the proven track record of alternate predictors such as intelligence and conscientiousness, it is unlikely that emotional intelligence alone can play the sort of role in career success predicted by Goleman (1998) and others (e.g., Cooper & Sawaf, 1996).

Overall, although Jordan et al. (2006) and Daus and Ashkanasy (2005) concluded that emotional intelligence does indeed provide additional explanatory power regarding behavior in organizations, they agree with Zeidner and his colleagues (2004) that additional and more focused research is required to extend this knowledge and to explain the processes that underlie emotional intelligence and its effects.

In the remainder of this chapter, we focus on the link between EI and three areas in which other major claims regarding workplace applications have been made: (1) positive organizational behaviors such as organizational commitment, reduced turnover, and organizational citizenship behaviors; (2) dealing with others in the organization and outside the organization (customers and clients), and (3) the ability to deal with conflict in the workplace.

Emotional Intelligence and Positive Organizational Behaviors

We define positive organizational behaviors as those actions in the workplace that benefit working relationships and contribute to a positive working climate. In particular, there is a broad range of literature that predicts a link between high EI and positive organizational behaviors. Abraham (2005) argues that both organizational citizenship behaviors and organizational commitment are enhanced by emotional intelligence. Jordan, Ashkanasy, and Härtel (2002) suggest that organizational commitment is moderated by emotional intelligence, so that individuals with high EI are going to be more likely to generate high affective commitment even during times of stress and instability. Cherniss (2001) contends that EI contributes to organizational effectiveness though increased commitment, improved morale, and better health of individuals.

In an empirical study of some of these variables, based on a Stream 2 model of emotional intelligence, Carmeli (2003) found that EI was positively linked to altruistic behavior, career commitment, job satisfaction, and affective commitment to the organization. He also found that EI was negatively related to work/family conflict and intentions to withdraw from the organization (turnover intention). Discussing his findings, Carmeli (2003) noted that emotional intelligence can augment contextual performance (Motowidlo, Borman, & Schmit, 1997) and is therefore a valuable commodity to the organization.

Wong and Law (2002) conducted a Stream 2 study that examined the EI of leaders and followers, and found that results depended on whether the individual studied was a leader or a follower. For followers, Wong and Law (2002) found that EI was linked to job satisfaction. Emotional intelligence also was linked to the satisfaction of leaders and to their propensity to do extra-role activities that supported their employees. Their data also provided support for relationships between EI and organizational commitment and reduced turnover intention for followers. An interesting outcome of the Wong and Law (2002) study was that individuals with high EI were found to be more likely to leave the organization if they were in jobs that did not allow them to utilize their emotional intelligence.

Vakola, Tsaousis, and Nikolaou (2004) examined links between emotional intelligence and change attitudes, and found EI relates to positive attitudes, willingness to change, reduced turnover intentions, and increased job satisfaction. Although this study showed interesting results, the findings need to be viewed with caution, however, as the measure of EI, while conforming to the Stream 2 Mayer and Salovey (1997) model of emotional intelligence, also had a high correlation to the Big Five personality dimensions. The authors noted, however, that their measure of emotional intelligence did appear to provide incremental validity over the effect of personality (Vakola et al., 2004).

In a series of Stream 2 studies of emotional intelligence training, Murray, Jordan, and Ashkanasy (2005) found that participants not only experienced an increase in overall EI, but that there was a commensurate rise in organizational citizenship behaviors. These finding were similar to those of Slaski and Cartwright (2003), who found, using the EQ-i (Stream 3), an increase in morale and perceptions of the quality of work life, and a decrease in distress following emotional intelligence training. Slaski and Cartwright noted that these are preliminary results only. Their research methodology did not allow them to identify which parts of the training influenced EI or determine whether the training provided actually reduced distress. They further suggest that reduced distress may enable individuals to think in an emotionally intelligent way.

Emotional Intelligence and Working With Others

Abraham (2005) argues that individuals with high EI are more likely to have harmonious relationships in the workplace. Although this may be seen as an overly optimistic and altruistic statement, according to Mayer and Salovey (1997), the skills associated with EI enable individuals to recognize, to understand, and to manage emotions in themselves and others, and this in turn may contribute to better relationships in the workplace. Cherniss (2001) contends in particular that, based on these skills, EI contributes to organizational effectiveness though improved teamwork.

In support of these theoretical models, Lopes, Salovey, Côté, and Beers (2005) found that Stream 1 emotional intelligence was positively linked to interpersonal sensitivity and prosocial tendencies. They also asked participants in their study to rate their peers and found that EI was linked to more positive peer nominations and the identification of reciprocal friendships. These findings were still significant even after the researchers controlled for personality and intelligence. Based on this study, it seems reasonable to conclude that interpersonal skills and relationship management are skills that are linked to emotional intelligence. Consequently, it is also reasonable to predict that these skills can be linked to better working relationships and better team performance.

One area that has attracted a good deal of research is the links between EI and team performance—from both a theoretical and an empirical perspective. Jordan et al. (2002), for example, examined the links between Stream 2 emotional intelligence and team performance in a longitudinal study. Performance in this study was measured in terms of independent raters' scores on two variables: team process effectiveness and team goal focus. Results were that average team emotional intelligence predicted team performance before training, but that the low emotional intelligence teams were performing at the same level as the high emotional intelligence teams after 9 weeks of training. The implications of their findings are that high emotional intelligence teams are able to perform at a high level without training, but that low emotional intelligence teams need specific training programs to be able to reach the same levels of performance.

In a separate Stream 2 study, Jordan and Troth (2004) found that EI *did not* predict individual performance during a cognitive problem-solving task but did predict team performance in the same task. Clearly, from this study there is an indication that the nature of a task changes at the team level when group decisions are required. Jordan and Troth (2004) suggest that there is an emotional element in team decision making that results in teams with high emotional intelligence having an advantage over teams with low emotional intelligence.

In a similar study, but using a Stream 3 measure of EI, Offermann, Bailey, Vasilo-poulos, Seal, and Sass (2004) found EI was not linked to individual performance but was linked to group performance (the results of a group written assignment). In another Stream 2 study, Moriarty and Buckley (2003) found that by using an experiential learning methodology, they were able to increase some aspects of EI and improve group outcomes, thereby preparing individuals for working with others in the workplace. Based on these studies, the evidence seems to support the idea that emotional intelligence does have an effect on team performance.

In looking beyond the effect of EI on relationships in teams, there is also evidence that the EI plays a role in service provider interactions with customers, and therefore plays a role as a determinant of customer satisfaction. Although some of this research is in the early stages of development, Rozell, Pettijohn, and Parker (2002) report significant relationships between Stream 2 emotional intelligence and customer orientation and sales performance.

Emotional Intelligence and Conflict in the Workplace

Following the popularization of emotional intelligence by Goleman (1995), there have been a number of authors who have claimed that individuals with high EI have superior conflict resolution skills. Weisinger (1998), for example, identified emotional management as a prime ability required to manage conflict in the workplace and improve relationships in organizations. Goleman (2001) subsequently listed conflict management as a core competency in his EI model, noting that effective conflict management is critical for maintaining business relationships. Lubit (2004) stated that EI is a competence that enhances the individual's ability to deal with "toxic" managers through enhanced conflict resolution skills. The empirical evidence to support these strong assertions, however, is less than voluminous.

Nonetheless, there is growing evidence of the positive impact of EI on conflict resolution in organizations. To date, researchers have typically categorized conflict in organizations into task, affective (relationship), and process conflict (Jehn, 1995). Task conflict focuses on conflict over work content or task. Within this literature, task conflict is typically resolved using "rational" argument (Jehn, 1995). Relationship (affective) conflict, on the other hand, refers to an emotional disagreement between individuals that generates strong negative emotions such as anger or hostility, which must be dealt with before "rational" arguments can be employed (Dick, 1984). Finally, process conflict refers to disagreements over the team's approach to the task, its methods, and its group processes.

Relationship conflict is consistently differentiated from task conflict and process conflict (e.g., see Pelled, Eisenhardt, & Xin, 1999). Although relationship conflict is seen as inherently emotional, task and process conflict have been portrayed as cognitive rather than emotional processes. Jordan and Troth (2002, 2004), on the other hand, argue that all conflict is inherently emotional, because it involves the perception of threats to individual or group goals. They argue that the emotional management skills of individuals in a group will determine if task conflict remains beneficial and whether the group's inability to resolve such conflict degenerates into relationship or process conflict and subsequently poor performance. This opinion has been supported in the development of a theoretical model by Yang and Mossholder (2004), who argue the beneficial nature of task conflict is influenced by the extent to which negative emotionality is constrained in the group. Based on this evidence, it is appropriate to conclude that emotional awareness and emotional management skills contribute to better conflict resolution.

Researchers have also provided evidence of a link between EI and preferred conflict resolution styles of individuals. For example, Jordan and Troth (2002) showed that individuals with higher levels of (Stream 2) emotional intelligence were more likely to seek collaborative solutions when confronted with conflict and prefer not to use avoidance strategies. They argued that for the emotionally intelligent individual, collaboration in the appropriate circumstances may be a sign of their ability to recognize and regulate emotions. Consequently, collaboration serves to enhance employees' relationships with their fellow workers and serves to achieve their goals during times of change. Indeed, in advancing their research, Jordan and Troth (2004) showed that groups with higher levels of EI were more likely to report using collaborative conflict resolution behavior to resolve an actual decision-making task. On the other hand, those teams with less ability to deal with their own emotions were more likely to engage in greater use of avoidance tactics resulting in lower performance.

In examining the links between (Stream 2) emotional intelligence and negotiation, Foo, Anger Elfenbein, Tan, and Aik (2004) found that individuals with high EI were able to establish a more positive affective tone in negotiations. In particular, Foo et al. concluded that emotional intelligence was a significant factor in reaching an integrative negotiation outcome. Somewhat surprisingly, however, they also found that individuals with high EI actually ended up with lower performance in the negotiation. This was apparently because these individuals conceded ground to achieve an integrative solution. Foo and his colleagues noted, however, that these findings need to be approached with some caution as the study was conducted using student groups in a simulated negotiation.

Conclusion

Based on the evidence discussed in this chapter, we can only agree with Ashkanasy and Daus (2005) that the death of emotional intelligence has been prematurely announced by some critics. Particularly with regard to applications in the workplace, we have demonstrated that EI has a range of positive applications across the three streams of research we identified. Although certainly not a comprehensive list, we have argued that EI can be linked to positive work behaviors such as organizational citizenship behaviors, higher morale, lower turnover, higher job satisfaction, higher affective commitment to organizations, and lower work/family conflict. Similarly, in relation to working with others, we have discussed research linking EI to better customer relations, higher levels of customer orientation, higher levels of customer satisfaction, better working relationships in teams, more effective processes, and more harmonious relationships within organizations. Finally, with respect to conflict, the research evidence suggests that individuals with high EI not only prefer to use collaborative solutions, but actually use this technique in negotiating outcomes. The research also reveals less use of avoidance techniques by those with high emotional intelligence. An important point to note here is that we have drawn our conclusions from a broad range of research. In line with Ashkanasy and Daus (2005) we note that this is drawn from research using ability models of EI (Stream 1), models based on Mayer and Salovey (Stream 2), and mixed models of EI (Stream 3). We argue that in future research there should be at least a requirement to demonstrate that EI measures have an incremental validity over variables that could be more appropriately categorized as personality differences.

In linking back to our introduction, we noted some sympathy for the opinion expressed by Kevin Murphy that EI was one of the top 10 misses of industrial and organizational psychology (Myors, 2005). From the research outlined in this chapter, Murphy seemed to be referring to a substantial amount of research linked to what Ashkanasy and Daus (2005) called "Stream 3" models of emotional intelligence. Clearly, there is a growing body of evidence, and importantly in Stream 1 and Stream 2 research, to suggest that EI does have an important a role in workplace research. Research has shown that EI contributes incremental validity beyond a broad range of existing constructs in both areas of individual differences and intelligence that enables academics to better understand human behavior at work. Nonetheless, and in line with Jordan et al. (2003), we see EI research in the workplace to be at a watershed. There needs to be some convergence of EI research particularly in the area of construct development.

References

Abraham, R. (2000). The role of job control as a moderator of emotional dissonance and emotional intelligence–outcome relationships. *Journal of Psychology, 134*, 169–184.

Abraham, R. (2005). Emotion intelligence in the workplace: A review and synthesis. In R. Schulze & R. D. Roberts (Eds.), *Emotional intelligence: An international handbook* (pp. 255–270). Cambridge, MA: Hogrefe & Huber.

Ashkanasy, N. M., & Daus, C. S. (2005). Rumors of the death of emotional intelligence in organizational behavior are vastly exaggerated. *Journal of Organizational Behavior, 26,* 441–452.

Barling, J., Slater, F., & Kelloway, E. K. (2000). Transformational leadership and emotional intelligence: An exploratory study. *Leadership & Organization Development Journal, 21,* 157–162.

Bar-On, R. (1997). *Bar-On Emotional Quotient Inventory: A measure of emotional intelligence.* Toronto, Ontario: Multi-Health Systems.

Boyatzis, R. E. (1982). *The competent manager: A model for effective performance.* New York: Wiley.

Boyatzis, R. E., & Goleman, D. (1998). *Emotional competence inventory.* Boston: Authors and Hay McBer.

Boyatzis, R. E., & Goleman, D. (2002). *The emotional competency inventory.* Boston: Hay Group.

Brotheridge, D. (2003). *Predicting emotional labor given situational demands and personality.* Paper presented at the Society for Industrial and Organizational Psychology, Chicago, IL.

Carmeli, A. (2003). The relationship between emotional intelligence and work attitudes, behavior and outcomes: An examination among senior managers. *Journal of Managerial Psychology, 18,* 788–813.

Cherniss, C. (2001). Emotional intelligence and organizational effectiveness. In C. Cherniss & D. Goleman (Eds.), *The emotionally intelligent workplace.* (pp. 3–12). San Francisco: Jossey Bass.

Cooper, R. K., & Sawaf, A. (1996). *Executive EQ: Emotional intelligence in leadership and organizations.* New York: Grosset/Putnam.

Daus, C. S., & Ashkanasy, N. M. (2003). Will the real emotional intelligence please stand up? On deconstructing the emotional intelligence "debate." *The Industrial and Organizational Psychologist, 41,* 69–72.

Daus, C. S., & Ashkanasy, N. M. (2005). The case for the ability based model of emotional intelligence in organizational behavior. *Journal of Organizational Behavior, 26,* 453–466.

Davis, M. H. (1994). *Empathy: A social psychological approach.* Dubuque, IA: Brown and Benchmark.

Day, A. L., & Carroll, S. A. (2004). Using an ability-based measure of emotional intelligence to predict individual performance, group performance, and group citizenship behaviours. *Personality and Individual Differences, 36,* 1443–1458.

Dick, R. N. (1984). *Helping groups to be effective: Skills, processes and concepts for group facilitation.* Chapel Hill, Queensland, Australia: Interchange Press.

Douglas, C., Frink, D., & Ferris, G. R., (2004). Emotional intelligence as a moderator of the relationship between conscientiousness and performance. *Journal of Leadership and Organizational Studies, 10,* 2–13.

Druskat, V. U., Sala, F., & Mount, G. (Eds.). (2006). *Linking emotional intelligence and performance at work: Current research evidence with individuals and groups.* Mahwah, NJ: Erlbaum.

Dulewicz, S. V., & Higgs, M. J. (2000). *EIQ-Managerial user guide.* Windsor, UK: NFER-Nelson.

Dulewicz, V., Higgs, M., & Slaski, M. (2003). Measuring emotional intelligence: Content, construct and criterion-related validity. *Journal of Managerial Psychology, 18,* 405.

Ferres, N., & Connell, J. (2004). Emotional intelligence in leaders: An antidote for cynicism towards change? *Strategic Change, 13*, 61–71.

Feyerherm, A. E., & Rice, C. L., (2002). Emotional intelligence and team performance: The good, the bad and the ugly. *International Journal of Organizational Analysis, 10*, 343–362.

Foo, M. D., Anger Elfenbein, H., Tan, H. H., & Aik, V. C. (2004). Emotional intelligence and negotiation: The tension between creating and claiming value. *International Journal of Conflict Management, 15*, 411–436.

Gardner, L., & Stough, C. (2002). Examining the relationship between leadership and emotional intelligence in senior level managers. *Leadership and Organization Development Journal, 23*, 68–78.

Goleman, D. (1995). *Emotional intelligence: Why it can matter more than IQ*. New York: Bantam Books.

Goleman, D. (1998). *Working with emotional intelligence*. New York: Bantam Books.

Goleman, D. (2001). An EI based theory of performance. In C. Cherniss & D. Goleman (Eds.), *The emotionally intelligent workplace* (pp. 27–44) San Francisco: Jossey Bass.

Goleman, D., McKee, A., & Boyatzis, R. E. (2002). *Primal leadership: Realizing the power of emotional intelligence*. Cambridge, MA: Harvard University Press.

Higgs, M. (2004). A study of the relationship between emotional intelligence and performance in UK call centres. *Journal of Managerial Psychology, 19*, 442–454.

Humphrey, R. H. (2002). The many faces of emotional leadership. *Leadership Quarterly, 13*, 493–504.

Jehn, K. (1995). A multimethod examination of the benefits and determinants of intragroup conflict. *Administrative Science Quarterly, 40*, 256–282.

Jordan, P. J., & Ashkanasy, N. M. (2006). Emotional intelligence, emotional self-awareness, and team effectiveness. In V. U. Druskat, F. Sala, & G. J. Mount (Eds.), *Linking emotional intelligence and performance at work: Current research evidence with individuals and groups* (pp. 145–164). Mahwah, NJ: Erlbaum.

Jordan, P. J, Ashkanasy, N. M., & Ashton-James, C. E. (2006). Evaluating the claims: Emotional intelligence in the workplace. In K. R. Murphy (Ed.), *A critique of emotional intelligence: What are the problems and how can they be fixed?* Mahwah, NJ: Erlbaum.

Jordan, P. J., Ashkanasy, N. M., & Härtel, C. E. J. (2002). Emotional intelligence as a moderator of emotional and behavioral reactions to job insecurity. *Academy of Management Review, 27*, 1–12.

Jordan, P. J., Ashkanasy, N. M., & Härtel, C. E. J. (2003). The case for emotional intelligence in organizational research. *Academy of Management Review, 28*, 195–197.

Jordan, P. J., Ashkanasy, N. M., Härtel, C. E. J., & Hooper, G. S. (2002). Workgroup emotional intelligence: Scale development and relationship to team process effectiveness and goal focus. *Human Resource Management Review, 12*, 195–214.

Jordan, P. J., & Troth, A. C. (2002). Emotional intelligence and conflict resolution: Implications for human resource development. *Advances in Developing Human Resources, 4*, 62–79.

Jordan, P. J., & Troth, A. C. (2004). Managing emotions during team problem solving: EI and conflict resolution. *Human Performance, 17*, 195–218.

Landy, F. J. (2005). Some historical and scientific issues related to research on emotional intelligence. *Journal of Organizational Behavior, 26*, 411–424.

Langhorn, S. (2004). How emotional intelligence can improve management performance. *International Journal of Contemporary Hospitality Management, 16*, 220–230.

Leban, W., & Zulauf, C. (2004). Linking emotional intelligence abilities and transformational leadership styles. *Leadership & Organization Development Journal, 25,* 554–564.

Locke, E. A. (2005). Why emotional intelligence is an invalid concept. *Journal of Organizational Behavior, 26,* 425–431.

Lopes, P. N., Salovey, P., Cote, S., & Beers, M. (2005). Emotion regulation abilities and the quality of social interaction. *Emotion, 5,* 113–118.

Lubit, R. H. (2004). *Coping with toxic managers, subordinates, and other impossible people.* Upper Saddle River, NJ: FT Prentice Hall.

Lyons, J. B., & Schneider, T. R. (2005). The influence of emotional intelligence on performance. *Personality and Individual Differences, 39,* 693–703.

Mandell, B., & Pherwani, S. (2003). Relationship between emotional intelligence and transformational leadership style: A gender comparison. *Journal of Business and Psychology, 17,* 387–404.

Matthews, G., Zeidner, M., & Roberts, R. D. (2002). *Emotional intelligence: Science and myth.* Cambridge, MA: MIT Press.

Mayer, J. D., & Salovey, P. (1997). What is emotional intelligence? In P. Salovey & D. J. Sluyter (Eds.), *Emotional development and emotional intelligence: Educational implications* (pp. 3–31). New York: Basic Books.

Mayer, J. D., Salovey, P., & Caruso, D. R. (1997). *Emotional IQ test* [CD-ROM]. Needham, MA: Virtual Entertainment.

Mayer, J. D., Salovey, P., & Caruso, D. R. (2000a). Models of emotional intelligence. In R. J. Sternberg (Ed.), *Handbook of human intelligence* (2nd ed., pp. 396–420). New York: Cambridge University Press.

Mayer, J. D., Salovey, P., & Caruso, D. R. (2000b). *Test manual for the Mayer, Salovey, Caruso Emotional Intelligence Test: Research version 1.1* (3rd ed). Toronto, Canada: Multi-Health Systems.

Mayer, J. D., Salovey, P., & Caruso, D. R. (2002). *Mayer-Salovey-Caruso Emotional Intelligence Test (MSCEIT): User's manual.* Toronto, Ontario, Canada: Multi-Health Systems.

Mayer, J. D., Salovey, P., Caruso, D. R., & Sitarenios, G. (2001). Emotional intelligence as a standard intelligence. *Emotion, 1,* 232–242.

Moriarty, P., & Buckley, F. (2003). Increasing team emotional intelligence through process. *Journal of European Industrial Training, 27,* 98–110.

Motowidlo, S. J., Borman, W. C., & Schmit, M. J. (1997). A theory of individual differences in task and contextual performance. *Human Performance, 10,* 71–83.

Murphy, K. R. (Ed.). (in press). *A critique of emotional intelligence: What are the problems and how can they be fixed?* Mahwah, NJ: Erlbaum.

Murray, J. P., Jordan, P. J., & Ashkanasy, N. M. (2005). Emotional intelligence training: Theoretical and practical issues. In P. Jordan and S. Lawrence (Eds.), *Abstracts of the Third Brisbane Symposium on Emotions and Worklife.* Nathan, Queensland, Australia: Griffith University.

Myors, B. (2005). The abstracts of the 6th Australian Industrial and Organisational Psychology Conference [Editorial]. *Australian Journal of Psychology, 57*(Suppl.), 116.

Nikolaou, I., Tsaousis, I. (2002). Emotional intelligence in the workplace: Exploring its effects on occupational stress and organizational commitment. *International Journal of Organizational Analysis, 10,* 327–343.

Offermann, L. R., Bailey, J. R., Vasilopoulos, N. L., Seal, C., & Sass, M. (2004). The relative contribution of emotional competence and cognitive ability to individual and team performance. *Human Performance, 17,* 219–243.

Palmer, B. R., Gardner, L., & Stough, C. (2003, June). *The relationship between emotional intelligence, personality and effective leadership.* Paper presented at the 5th Australian Industrial & Organisational Psychology Conference, Melbourne.

Palmer, B. R., & Stough, C. (2001). *Workplace SUEIT: Swinburne University Emotional Intelligence Test–Descriptive Report.* Melbourne, Australia: Organisational Psychology Research Unit, Swinburne University.

Palmer, B., Walls, M., Burgess, Z., & Stough, C. (2001). Emotional intelligence and effective leadership [Electronic version]. *Leadership & Organization Development Journal, 22,* 5.

Pelled, L. H., Eisenhardt, K. M., & Xin, K. R. (1999). Exploring the black box: An analysis of work group diversity, conflict, and performance. *Administrative Science Quarterly, 44,* 1–28.

Raham, A. (2002). *The measurement of emotional intelligence: preliminary findings from six countries.* Paper presented at the Ninth International Conference on Advances in Management, Boston. Centre of Advanced Studies in Management, Bowling Green, KY.

Rahim, A. M., & Minors, P. (2003). Effects of emotional intelligence on concern for quality and problem solving. *Managerial Auditing Journal, 18,* 150–156.

Rapisarda, B. A. (2002). The impact of emotional intelligence on work team cohesiveness and performance. *The International Journal of Organizational Analysis, 10,* 363–379.

Rozell, E. J., Pettijohn, C. E., & Parker, R. S. (2002). An empirical evaluation of emotional intelligence: The impact on management development. *The Journal of Management Development, 21,* 272–289.

Sala, F. (2002). *Emotional Competence Inventory: Technical manual.* Boston: McClelland Center For Research, Hay Group.

Salovey, P., & Mayer, J. D. (1990). Emotional intelligence. *Imagination, Cognition, and Personality, 9,* 185–211.

Salovey, P., Mayer, J., Goldman, S., Turvey, C., & Palfai, T. (1995). Emotional attention, clarity, and repair: Exploring emotional intelligence using the Trait Meta-Mood Scale. In J. W. Pennebacker (Ed.), *Emotion, disclosure and health* (pp. 125–154). Washington, DC: American Psychological Association.

Schutte, N. S., Malouff, J. M., Hall, L. E., Haggerty, D. J. Cooper, J. T., Golden, C. J., & Dornheim, L. (1998). Development and validation of a measure of emotional intelligence. *Personality and Individual Differences, 25,* 167–177.

Schutte, N. S., Schuettpelz, E., & Malouff, J. M. (2000). Emotional intelligence and task performance. *Imagination, Cognition and Personality, 20,* 347–354.

Sivanathan, N., & Fekken, G. C. (2002). Emotional intelligence, moral reasoning and transformational leadership. *Leadership & Organization Development Journal, 23,* 198–205.

Slaski, M., & Cartwright, S. (2003). Emotional intelligence training and its implications for stress, health and performance. *Stress and Health, 19,* 233–239.

Spector, P. E. (2005). Introduction: Emotional intelligence. *Journal of Organizational Behavior, 26,* 409–410.

Sue-Chan, C., & Latham, G. P. (2004). The situational interview as a predictor of academic and team performance: A study of the mediating effects of cognitive ability and emotional intelligence. *International Journal of Selection and Assessment, 12,* 312–302.

Thi Lam, L., & Kirby, S. L. (2002). Is emotional intelligence an advantage? An exploration of the impact of emotional and general intelligence on individual performance. *The Journal of Social Psychology, 142,* 133–143.

Thorndike, E. L. (1920). Intelligence and its uses. *Harper's Magazine, 140*, 227–235.

Tsaousis, I. (2003). *Measuring emotional intelligence: Development and psychometric characteristics of the emotional intelligence questionnaire (EIQ)*. Manuscript submitted for publication.

Vakola, M., Tsaousis, I., & Nikolaou, I. (2004). The role of emotional intelligence and personality variables on attitudes toward organizational change. *Journal of Managerial Psychology, 19*, 88–110.

Weisinger, H. (1998). *Emotional intelligence at work*. San Francisco: Jossey-Bass.

Wong, C. S., & Law, K. S. (2002). The effect of leader and follower emotional intelligence on performance and attitude: An exploratory study. *Leadership Quarterly, 13*, 243–274.

Wong, C. S., Law, K. S., & Wong, P. M. (2004). Development and validation of a forced choice emotional intelligence measure for Chinese respondents in Hong Kong. *Asia Pacific Journal of Management, 21*, 535–559.

Yang, J. X., & Mossholder, K.W. (2004). Decoupling task and relationship conflict: The role of intra-group emotional processing. *Journal of Organizational Behavior, 25*, 589–605.

Zeidner, M., Matthews G., & Roberts, R. D. (2004). Emotional intelligence in the workplace: A critical review. *Applied Psychology: An International Review, 53*, 371–399.

15

Social and Emotional Learning for Successful School Performance

JOSEPH E. ZINS, JOHN W. PAYTON, ROGER P. WEISSBERG,
AND MARY UTNE O'BRIEN

This volume proposes that there are a number of potential applications of the emerging science of emotional intelligence (EI) that will enhance the daily functioning of children and adults. This chapter focuses specifically on school-based programming that promotes the social and emotional learning (SEL) of children and youth. SEL represents a rapidly growing movement in preschool through high school education (Elias & Arnold, 2006; Elias et al., 1997; Zins, Weissberg, Wang, & Walberg, 2004). Although EI and SEL have much in common, they also differ in certain respects. Most notably, SEL builds from the field of social competence promotion research and emphasizes educational strategies to enhance children's capacities to coordinate emotion, cognition, and behavior to deal effectively with daily challenges and achieve positive developmental outcomes (Consortium on the School-Based Promotion of Social Competence, 1994; Payton et al., 2000).

This chapter begins by defining SEL and describing applications of SEL principles in elementary and secondary schools. Next, it highlights some components of effective programming and benefits of SEL, and then identifies some current theoretical, empirical, and conceptual issues that will help advance the field. Finally, it addresses key questions posed by the editors to all volume contributors.

What Is Social and Emotional Learning?

The need to prepare students to be responsible, knowledgeable, caring, ethical, nonviolent, healthy, and productive members of society is well established (Elias et al., 1997). Indeed, the general public believes that the primary reason the public schools were created is to prepare students to be responsible citizens (Rose & Gallup, 2000).

However, simply raising academic standards without also giving substantial attention to students' social-emotional and instructional needs is likely to be unsuccessful and harmful, especially for groups at risk (Becker & Luthar, 2002). Dryfoos (1994) warned that a significant number of children will fail to grow into productive adults unless there are major changes in how they are educated.

Implementing evidence-based SEL programming enables schools to carry out this mandate to prepare responsible citizens and productive adults. Through SEL, children learn to integrate their cognition, affect, and behavior, and are provided with opportunities to practice and apply social and emotional skills that mediate competence in dealing with a wide range of developmental tasks in the context of their respective cultures and communities (Consortium on the School-Based Promotion of Social Competence, 1994). By promoting the development of students who are responsible and productive citizens through SEL programming, schools also help build strong and sustainable communities.

Within the context of schools, SEL involves an approach to education that integrates two interrelated strands to promote successful school performance and youth development (see Figure 15.1). The first involves instruction in processing, integrating, and selectively applying social and emotional skills in developmentally appropriate and culturally sensitive ways. Quality SEL instruction also provides students with opportunities to contribute to their schools and experience the satisfaction, sense of belonging, and enhanced motivation that comes from such involvement. Second, SEL programming establishes a safe, supportive, and caring learning environment. Together these components provide conditions in which students feel valued and respected, experience enhanced intrinsic motivation to achieve, and develop a wide range of related social-cognitive skills, knowledge, and prosocial attitudes that mediate valued educational outcomes such as high academic performance, health-promoting behavior, and community engagement (Elias, 2006; Elias et al., 1997).

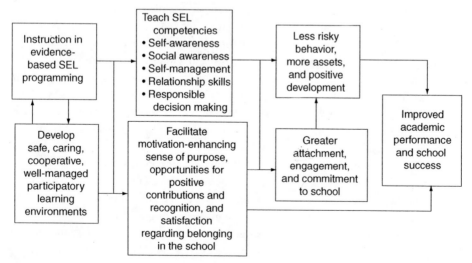

Figure 15.1. Paths to success in school and role of social and emotional learning.

Instruction to Promote Social and Emotional
Competencies

The Collaborative for Academic, Social, and Emotional Learning (CASEL, 2005)
identified the following integrated clusters of core SEL competencies:

- *Self-awareness:* Recognizing one's emotions and values and their influence on
choices and behaviors, plus accurate self-assessment of one's personal qualities;
- *Self-management:* Coordinating and regulating one's emotions, cognitions, and
behaviors to manage stress, control impulses, motivate oneself, nd set and work
toward the achievement of personal and academic goals;
- *Social awareness:* Taking the perspective of and empathizing with others, regardless of whether the others are similar or different from oneself;
- *Relationship skills:* Being able to listen reflectively to and communicate clearly
with others, to resist negative social pressures to engage in destructive or risky
behaviors, and to establish positive relationships and manage conflicts with others; and
- *Responsible decision making:* Making responsible and ethical personal and academic decisions based on a clear understanding of a problem, consideration of
alternative solutions and the consequences of each, and monitoring the implementation of choices made.

Through planned, systematic, and evidence-based classroom instruction, SEL skills
are explicitly taught, modeled, practiced, and applied to diverse situations so that students internalize them as a part of their repertoire of behaviors. In addition, many SEL
programs help student apply SEL skills in preventing specific maladaptive behaviors
such as interpersonal violence, bullying, alcohol and drug use, and truancy (CASEL,
2005). Increasingly, SEL programs also include a component that applies these skills to
academic learning areas (Elias, 2004) with parents as partners in these efforts. In teaching this cluster of social and emotional skills in an integrated, sequential manner across
developmental levels from prekindergarten through high school, SEL adds value to the
teaching of specific social and emotional skills in isolation from one another.

From a developmental perspective, SEL specifies what children's social-emotional
competence might look like at various grade levels. Developmental progression involves
a shift from being increasingly controlled by external factors to acting in accordance
with one's internalized beliefs and values, making good decisions, and taking responsibility for one's choices and behaviors (Bear, 2005).

With regard to the *self-awareness* skill cluster, children in the elementary grades
might be expected to recognize and accurately label simple emotions such as sadness,
anger, and happiness. Middle school students should be able to analyze factors that
trigger their stress reactions, and those in high school might be expected to analyze
how various expressions of emotion affect others. At the elementary school level,
self-management includes an ability to describe the steps of setting and working toward
goals. In middle school, this includes setting and making a plan to achieve a short-term

personal or academic goal, whereas high school students should be able to identify strategies to make use of available school and community resources and overcome obstacles in achieving a longer term goal.

In the area of *social awareness*, elementary students should be able to identify verbal, physical, and situational cues indicating how others feel, and those in middle school should be able to predict others' feelings and perspectives in various situations. High school students should be able to evaluate their ability to empathize with others. In elementary school, *relationship skills* include the ability to describe approaches to making and keeping friends. Middle school students might be expected to demonstrate cooperation and teamwork to promote group goals, and at the high school level they would be expected to evaluate uses of communication skills with peers, teachers, and family members. Finally, elementary school students might be taught to identify a range of decisions they make at school in terms of *responsible decision making*. Middle school students should be able to evaluate strategies for resisting peer pressure to engage in unsafe or unethical activities, and high school students should be able to analyze how their current decision making affects their college and career choices.

Learning Environments That Provide Opportunities
for Positive Contributions

A related component of the SEL approach to education is development and maintenance of a safe, supportive, and well-managed learning environment where children feel cared for, respected, and challenged, and where adults model and provide opportunities for them to practice and apply SEL skills both in class and throughout the school. Such an environment uses interactive, engaging, and participatory instructional methods. Teachers infuse learning activities for students with a sense of purpose and belonging by providing them with opportunities to be recognized for making contributions to their schools and experiencing the satisfaction that comes from such involvement. As Wentzel and Asher (1995) recognized, student perspectives of teacher support and high expectations are related to positive achievement outcomes. Accordingly, students' bonding, connections, and engagement in school are enhanced, which results in greater receptivity to learning and higher motivation to achieve (Becker & Luthar, 2002; Elias, 2006).

The teaching and reinforcement of SEL competencies in a supportive learning environment leads to student asset building, reduction of risky behaviors, enhancement of healthy behaviors, greater attachment to and engagement in school, and better academic performance (Greenberg et al., 2003; Zins et al., 2004). Conversely, socially and emotionally competent students contribute to maintenance of a positive school environment. Enhancing students' self-management, problem-solving, and relationship skills better prepares them for learning. The application of SEL decision-making skills in teaching literature, history, and other subjects also promotes greater subject mastery by deepening students' understanding of the material. When learning takes place in a relationship-centered, nurturing environment, it promotes greater student engagement in learning.

There is solid evidence demonstrating that students' bonding to school and engagement in learning are strongly influenced by a supportive learning environment, and that these variables in turn positively impact student academic performance (McNeely, Nonnemaker, & Blum, 2002; Osterman, 2000). Finally, these interventions help students develop the SEL competencies to avoid engaging in high-risk, negative behaviors such as inhibiting impulsive behavior, delinquency, dropping out of school, and using illegal drugs (Wilson, Gottfredson, & Najaka, 2001; Zins & Elias, 2006).

SEL's Relationship to Emotional Intelligence

As illustrated in the previous section, SEL builds upon and overlaps with the abilities to accurately perceive, manage, understand, and use emotions to facilitate judgment, memory, and problem solving as found in EI theory. Although the focus of EI on an individual's ability to accurately and efficiently process information about his or her emotions is the basis for effective social interaction, many EI theorists do not explicitly address social awareness skills such as taking the perspectives of others, recognizing individual and group differences, and demonstrating a range of interpersonal skills, as does SEL. Nor does EI emphasize social problem solving and decision making, which build several SEL skills into a sequence of steps that is central to understanding SEL. Moreover, EI research has been based primarily on research with adults, whereas an important source of SEL knowledge is child and adolescent developmental psychology and education.

A broad comparison of SEL with the major EI theories and descriptions can be found in Table 15.1. The columns of the table are based on the five skill clusters of SEL. To facilitate comparisons across models, similar elements from various models have been moved to the same columns, which in some cases has necessitated their being separated from other elements in the model component that they comprise. In other cases, model components appear in more than one column because their elements map on to more than one of the SEL skill clusters. As can be seen, SEL emphasizes social skills and responsible decision making more than the models of Mayer, Salovey, and Caruso (2004) or Matthews, Zeidner, and Roberts (2003).

In contrast, Mayer et al. and Matthews et al. place greater focus on the role that emotions play in influencing personal functioning. Although SEL overlaps with the intrapersonal, interpersonal, stress management, and adaptability skills of the Bar-On (1997, 2000) model of emotional intelligence, the latter incorporates many more personality traits (e.g., assertiveness, optimism, self-actualization, and independence) than CASEL's SEL model. Both CASEL (2005) and Goleman (2001) include the core competencies of self-awareness, self-management, social awareness, and social management as explicit features of their models. The main points of difference between the SEL and the Goleman models are that CASEL emphasizes responsible decision making as a core skill, and Goleman highlights several emotional and social competencies that are developmentally appropriate for adults.

TABLE 15.1. Models of emotional intelligence and social and emotional learning.

Model	Component				
CASEL (2005)	*Self-awareness:* • Know what one is feeling • Assess strengths accurately • Sense of self-confidence	*Self-management:* • Regulate emotions for stress management, impulse control • Motivate oneself to overcome obstacles • Set and monitor progress toward achievement of personal and academic goals	*Social awareness:* • Take the perspectives of and empathize with others • Recognize individual and group similarities and differences	*Relationship skills:* • Demonstrate cooperation • Resist inappropriate social pressure • Manage conflict constructively	*Responsible decision making:* • Consider all relevant factors (including the feelings of self and others, safety, ethics) in making decisions • Generate alternative solutions and anticipate the consequences of each • Select the best solution and monitor implementation
Mayer, Salovey, & Caruso (1997)	*Emotional perception and expression, ability to:* • Identify emotions in one's physical and psychological states *Emotional understanding, ability to:* • Understand relationships among emotions • Perceive causes and consequences of emotions • Understand complex feelings, emotional blends, contradictory states	*Emotional facilitation of thought, ability to:* • Generate emotions to facilitate judgment and memory • Capitalize on mood changes to appreciate multiple points of view *Emotional management, ability to:* • Be open to feelings, positive and negative • Monitor and reflect on emotions • Engage, prolong, or detach from an emotional state	*Emotional perception and expression, ability to:* • Identify emotions in other people *Emotional understanding, ability to:* • [See entries in first column under this component]	*Emotional perception and expression, ability to:* • Express emotions and related needs accurately *Emotional management, ability to:* • Manage emotions in others	*Emotional facilitation of thought, ability to:* • Use emotional states to facilitate problem solving and creativity

(Continued)

381

TABLE 15.1. (continued)

Model	Component				
Mayer, Salovey, & Caruso (1997)		Manage emotions in oneself	Understand transitions among emotions		
Bar-On (1997, 2000)	*Intrapersonal intelligence:* • Emotional self-awareness • Self-regard *Adaptability:* • Reality testing *General mood:* • Happiness • Optimism	*Stress management:* • Stress tolerance • Impulse control *Intrapersonal intelligence:* • Self actualization • Independence *Adaptability:* • Flexibility	*Interpersonal intelligence:* • Empathy	*Intrapersonal intelligence:* • Assertiveness *Interpersonal intelligence:* • Interpersonal relationships	*Adaptability:* • Problem solving *Interpersonal intelligence:* • Social responsibility
Goleman (2001)	*Self-awareness:* • Emotional self-awareness • Accurate self-assessment • Self-confidence	*Self-management:* • Emotional self-control • Trustworthiness • Conscientiousness • Adaptability • Achievement drive • Initiative	*Social awareness:* • Empathy • Service orientation • Organizational awareness	*Relationship management:* • Developing others • Influence • Communication • Conflict management • Leadership • Change catalyst • Building bonds • Teamwork and collaboration	
Matthews, Zeidner, & Roberts (2003)	*Identify and express emotions* *Understand emotions*	*Regulate both positive and negative emotions in self*	*Understand emotions*	*Regulate both positive and negative emotions in others*	*Assimilate emotions in thought*

SEL Applications in School and Community Settings

School and community psychologists have multiple opportunities to contribute to the implementation of SEL interventions. Many applications are directed by school and community psychologists toward students from prekindergarten through high school, as the skills and knowledge developed are important for school success, demanded by employers, and essential for lifelong success. These interventions have been applied to address a number of issues including the prevention of substance abuse, interpersonal violence, depression, unintentional injury, bullying, and unwanted teen pregnancy (Greenberg et al., 2003; Weissberg, Gullotta, Hampton, Ryan, & Adams, 1997). School organizations also benefit from the increased productivity of students and staff as they work more cooperatively, have greater commitment, and exhibit better skills in emotional regulation, understanding, and expression.

School and community psychologists can also serve as champions for SEL, which is essential for its sustainability (Elias, Zins, Graczyk, & Weissberg, 2003). Another major avenue for their contribution to the field is as program evaluators, an increasingly important function in the high priority placed on accountability in today's educational environment, and data generated from such SEL program activities are critical to their sustainability. These professionals also can serve as leaders or coleaders of instructional sessions or as consultants to teachers who directly provide SEL programs, as in the examples that follow. These examples of how SEL is taught utilize many techniques that draw on, integrate, and potentiate much of what already has been recognized as effective educational practice (Zins et al., 2004). Among the approaches to introducing SEL, there are specific curricula such as Second Step: A Violence Prevention Curriculum (Committee for Children, 2004) that teach empathy, impulse control, and anger management in regular class sessions throughout the school year.

In contrast, the Caring School Community (CSC) program (Schaps, Battistich, & Solomon, 2004) is infused into the regular academic curriculum through activities such as careful selections of literary works that provide specific examples of social-emotional lessons relevant to the students' lives (e.g., characters experience and display various emotions and make decisions that are examined in class). CSC also enhances protective factors such as school climate and social bonding. Responsive Classroom (Kriet, 2006; www.responsiveclassroom.org) teachers eat lunch with their students and spend time with them on the playground to take advantage of the many informal opportunities they provide to learn social and emotional skills as part of the school's informal curriculum (e.g., dealing with a situation in which a student is excluded from a game).

Other examples demonstrate that the pedagogy of sound SEL is not distinct from that of effective teaching generally, which means that teachers do not need to make dramatic changes in their instruction to implement SEL. One example is the widespread use of cooperative learning strategies in SEL programs (Johnson & Johnson, 2004). This technique has been adopted by many SEL programs to encourage cooperation rather than competition, and to facilitate interactions and teamwork among students of varying backgrounds and ability levels. Another example comes from the Social Decision Making/Social Problem Solving program (Elias & Bruene Butler, 2005), which uses SEL problem-solving and decision-making strategies to deepen students' understanding of literature, historical and contemporary events, and mathematical reasoning.

The school-community learning projects of some SEL programs involve students in providing guided service. These experiences are useful in engaging students actively and experientially in the learning process to increase empathy, bonding, and attachment. A final example comes from extracurricular activities, including sports, which can offer ample opportunities to reinforce and teach SEL principles, such as emotional self-regulation and self-efficacy during practice and actual competition. Additional case descriptions are found in Elias et al. (1997) and Elias and Arnold (2006).

Components of Effective Programming

Over the past 2 decades we have learned a great deal through research, experience, and observing programs in operation about what it takes to make SEL interventions effective. The 39 guidelines for effective programs developed by CASEL reflect the depth of this knowledge (Elias et al., 1997). We know that programs that enhance SEL competencies promote positive behaviors while also preventing or reducing problem behaviors. The best results occur with behavioral and cognitive-behavioral strategies that promote interaction rather than knowledge acquisition only, and with efforts that are coordinated across and within grades. The use of structured manuals for teachers promotes program fidelity. Also essential is the support of educational leaders for maintaining positive classroom and school climates and the reinforcement of classroom lessons through school-family partnerships (e.g., Elias et al., 1997).

Other important structural features of effective SEL include (a) use of instructional materials with demonstrated effectiveness in promoting social and emotional skills; (b) infusing skill instruction throughout the curriculum; (c) implementing programming across multiple years, from prekindergarten through high school; and (d) reinforcing adult and peer norms that convey high expectations and support for high-quality academic performance (Greenberg et al., 2003).

Given the fact that the average school conducts 14 prevention activities (Gottfredson & Gottfredson, 2001), the issue of how these multiple interventions are implemented is vitally important. Whereas fragmented programming results in inconsistent messages, confusion about expectations, decreased sense of common purpose, fewer connections, and less bonding, programs that are linked by an SEL framework and whose efforts are cooperative may result in an improved climate, a view of the school as supportive and safe, mutual support, and greater bonding. Thus, students who experience these more consistent and reinforced messages might have a higher level of engagement, participate in more community service, show better attendance, engage in fewer disruptive behaviors, and experience a greater sense of safety (e.g., Elias et al., 1997).

Known and Likely Positive Outcomes

There is a rapidly growing body of research literature on the outcomes of promotion and prevention programs such as SEL. Narrative and meta-analytic reviews have shown that effective programs consistently produce, on average, substantial measurable benefits (Weisz, Sandler, Durlak, & Anton, 2005).

Evidence-based support for SEL can be organized into three major categories: attitudes (motivation, commitment), behavior (participation, study habits), and performance (grades, subject mastery; Zins et al., 2004). For instance, students who participate in high-quality SEL programs have improved *attitudes* toward school such as a better sense of community and view of the school as caring (Schaps et al., 2004) and higher academic motivation (Johnson & Johnson, 2004). They also have positive school *behaviors*, including more prosocial interactions (Johnson & Johnson, 2004), fewer absences and suspensions (Christenson & Havsy, 2004), and reductions in aggression, disruptions, and interpersonal violence (Greenberg, Kusché, & Riggs, 2004). Finally, students' *performance* in school may be enhanced in terms of improved skills in math, language arts, and social studies (Brown, Roderick, Lantieri, & Aber, 2004) and better problem solving and planning (Greenberg et al., 2004). Other summaries of research on the positive outcomes of SEL programs can be found in many sources (e.g., CASEL, 2005; Durlak & Weissberg, 2005; Elias et al., 1997; Greenberg et al., 2003; Hawkins, 1997; Zins et al., 2004).

A recent meta-analysis encompassing 270 school-based prevention and youth development interventions by Durlak and Weissberg (2005) reported highly consistent results with those presented above. Durlak and Weissberg included studies that focused on the promotion of one or more SEL competencies and targeted children between 5 and 18 years of age. They found that these interventions produced a range of positive benefits to participating children and youth, including enhanced personal and social competencies, decreased antisocial behavior and aggression, and fewer serious discipline problems and school suspensions. They also indicated that students who participated in SEL programs compared to nonprogram peers liked school more, had significantly better attendance records, had higher grade point averages, and ranked at least 10 percentile points higher on academic achievement tests.

In sum, these results illustrate that providing students with good social-emotional skills may lead to enhanced academic achievement and physical and psychological health, and avoidance of health-damaging behaviors. For these reasons SEL is now recognized as an essential element of schooling by increasing numbers of schools in the United States and elsewhere (see Elias, 2004). A recent report sponsored by the Center for Mental Health Services on school-based mental health services indicated that 59% of schools have implemented classroom programs that address children's social and emotional functioning (Foster et al., 2005). Indeed, Second Step has been implemented in over 70% of the schools in Denmark.

Not all programs addressing social-emotional development are equal. Another consideration in evaluating them is the return in benefits compared to the costs of implementation (Aos, Lieb, Mayfield, Miller, & Pennucci, 2004). Aos reported that the

Seattle Social Development Program had a very high cost per student serviced, a whopping $4,590. But, it had benefits of $14,426 for each student, or $3.14 per dollar spent. Examples of demonstrated benefits include improved educational outcomes (e.g., test scores, graduation rates), reduced crime, lowered substance abuse, and decreased teen suicide attempts. Similarly, the Child Development Project (CSC; Schaps et al., 2004), mentioned earlier, provided benefits of $28.42, and Life Skills Training (Botvin, 2002), benefits of $25.61, for each dollar spent. On the other hand, the popular Drug Abuse Resistance Education program (D.A.R.E; www.dare.com), cost $99 per student served but resulted in no measured benefit (Aos et al., 2004).

Identifying Effective Programs

Given the extensive number of SEL-related programs available and the differences in their foci, contents, costs, age levels, intended outcomes, and theoretical bases (see CASEL, 2005; Zeidner, Roberts, & Matthews, 2002), it is challenging for schools to decide what program to implement. Fortunately, a number of organizations reviewed many of the nationally available ones that are SEL-related and provided ratings and other descriptive information about them (see Table 15.2). This information is invaluable as schools select programs to meet their local needs.

The groups that rate programs establish their own inclusion criteria for which programs to assess and which features to rate. For that reason there is variation among the organizations' listings of programs rated and their actual ratings. For example, the primary criteria for inclusion in the federal agency lists of ratings in Table 15.2 are the intended *outcomes* of the programs, such as the prevention of substance abuse, tobacco, violence, and delinquency. On the other hand, CASEL's SEL program rating guide, *Safe and Sound* (2005), focuses on the underlying mechanisms of prevention or *mediators* of SEL skills, whether they teach the five core social and emotional competencies as part of their prevention instruction, and their evidence of effectiveness in well-designed evaluation research. CASEL's ratings examine other program features as well, such as whether they were multiyear in their scope (because single-year interventions are unlikely to have long-term impacts), target the general school population and not only students with special needs or those at high risk, and make professional development available to program implementers.

Advances Necessary for the Continued Development of the Field

Applications of SEL in schools continue to grow. Recently, for instance, Illinois passed the Children's Mental Health Act (Public Law 93–0495), in which social-emotional development is identified as integral to the mission of schools and as essential to children's school success (see relevant links at www.casel.org). This legislation requires all Illinois school districts to adopt a policy specifying how they will incorporate social and emotional development into their educational program. Also in compliance

TABLE 15.2. Ratings of social and emotional learning programs.

Programs	Rating Organization				
	Center for Substance Abuse Prevention (CSAP)	Collaborative for Academic, Social, and Emotional Learning (CASEL)	National Institute on Drug Abuse (NIDA)	Office of Juvenile Justice and Delinquency Prevention (OJJDP)	U.S. Department of Education
Al's Pals: Kids Making Healthy Choices	Model				Promising
Caring School Community		Select	Effective		Promising
I Can Problem Solve	Promising	Select		Promising	Promising
Life Skills Training	Model		Effective	Blueprints Model	Exemplary
Lions-Quest (Skills Series)	Model	Select			Promising
Michigan Model for Comprehensive School Health Education		Select			Promising
Olweus Bullying Prevention	Model			Blueprint Model	
Promoting Alternative Thinking Strategies	Effective	Select		Blueprints Model	Promising
Project Achieve	Model	Select			
Project Northland	Model			Promising	Exemplary
Second Step: A Violence Prevention Curriculum	Model	Select			Exemplary
Resolving Conflict Creatively Program		Select			
Social Decision Making and Social Problem Solving	Promising	Select			Promising

Note: These ratings are subject to change as programs are revised and reassessed.

From Zins, J. E., & Elias, M. J. (2006). *Social and emotional learning*. Copyright 2006. National Association of School Psychologists. Reprinted with permission.

with the new law, the Illinois State education agency adopted social and emotional learning standards that all students are expected to meet. Although such efforts make social-emotional instruction available to more students, this success points to the continuing need for additional development of the field and investigations of many aspects of practice. A few examples follow.

Few comprehensive preschool through high school curricula are available, thus necessitating the coordination of several programs to provide a continuum of instruction across grades. Because the content, techniques, and messages of these programs may not be well aligned with one another, instructional continuity across grades may be compromised. Because programs are implemented in widely varying school settings and in differing instructional contexts, decisions must be made about how to adapt them to meet local conditions and needs while still maintaining program integrity.

Although successful interventions require fidelity in implementing core program components, we also "need a better understanding of how educators make decisions to combine, adapt, and assimilate evidence-based programs" (Greenberg et al., 2003, p. 472), and a better understanding of what constitutes "positive" adaptations that enhance program outcomes. As mentioned earlier, core intervention components that lead to positive outcomes also need to be identified. That is, elements essential to success need to be determined so that the intervention can be provided efficiently while making accommodations to real-world conditions. Likewise, it would be helpful to gain a better understanding of which groups and under what conditions a particular SEL intervention may be beneficial, as evidence indicates that most are not successful in all situations (Weisz et al., 2005). Related to this point, progress in the field might ensue if there were more consistency across studies with respect to mediators and outcomes measured and in actual instruments used to measure these dimensions.

A key to the successful implementation of educational innovations is the active involvement and support of educators, particularly those in leadership positions (Elias et al., 2003). Yet, few educators receive adequate preservice preparation in preventive interventions, and in-service training on this topic likewise has not met demand. Consequently, there is a need to develop high quality, research-based training and technical assistance that align well with national teacher preparation requirements (Fleming & Bay, 2004) and school psychology (National Association of School Psychologists, 2000) practice standards. Ideally, such training would be available at both pre- and in-service levels, although we recognize the challenge of introducing another training topic.

Ensuring that interventions continue after initial program implementation is a major challenge and has been discussed in detail elsewhere (Elias et al., 2003). Having champions, ongoing professional development, support from educational leaders, and policies that promote SEL is likely to lead to more enduring efforts.

As increasing numbers of schools implement prevention and promotion programs, systems for coordinating and integrating these programs with other prevention/promotion, early intervention, and treatment services are required. "Prospects for synchronous operation of prevention and treatment services obviously improve to the extent to which both strategies can be embedded within the same setting" (Weisz et al., 2005, p. 634).

Another need for the field is research demonstrating the impact on SEL programs of being implemented within a coordinated service delivery system, rather than in relative isolation from other prevention and support services.

A substantial body of theory and research underlies the various components of social and emotional learning (Elias et al., 1997). To enable the field to continue its development, greater conceptual clarity regarding related work in the fields of metacognition, social information processing, emotional development, and brain development is needed, as demonstrated in the following examples.

Metacognition helps explain some of the learning processes that occur in SEL. In developing competence in problem solving and decision making, for example, students use metacognition in identifying the skills, strategies, and resources needed for a task, and in determining how and when to use them. They also use it in monitoring performance variables such as planning the means to accomplish a task, predicting outcomes, and assessing the effectiveness of their efforts (Schunk, 1996).

From social information processing, models of children's social behavior serve to advance our understanding of their social adjustment (e.g., Crick & Dodge, 1994; Dodge & Crick, 1990). As noted by the Consortium on the School-Based Promotion of Social Competence (1994), this knowledge helps explain cognitive styles that improve or impair social adjustment. For example, it describes processes that children learn in developing competence in self- and social awareness that promote their ability to enter peer group activities and resolve conflicts (Dodge, 1986).

Findings from research on emotional development demonstrate the impact of emotions on perception, cognition, motivation, critical thinking, and behavior, and that they also serve an adaptive function (Izard, 2002; Kusché & Greenberg, 2006; Lazarus, 1991; Sroufe, 1996). We also know from studies on motivation that children are more likely to develop intrinsic motivation when classroom topics are related to their own lives, needs, and feelings (Ormrod, 1999), an approach commonly used in SEL interventions.

Recent brain development research shows great promise for the effective implementation of SEL in schools. Kusché and Greenberg (2006) drew a number of implications related to SEL from findings about brain organization and processes. They noted that the quality of the emotional attachment of a child and his or her teacher, and whether teachers listen to their students and respect their feelings and ideas, impact the quality of attention, learning, and brain development. Education can strengthen neocortical control and self-awareness, suggesting that the manner in which subject matter is taught (e.g., giving consideration to social-emotional aspects of learning) may have greater impact than the subject matter itself (Sylwester, 1995).

Another consideration with respect to instruction is that teaching SEL is influenced by the fact that it is an adult behavior change process with the target of change being the teacher who instructs the students. Changes in teacher behavior may in turn affect changes in students, but that is a secondary issue moderated by diverse variables such as match of the SEL program with needs of the children, resistance to intervention, competing demands on children, and acceptability of the intervention. For these reasons, issues such as treatment integrity and determining which outcomes to evaluate have added dimensions of complexity.

Further, the educational value of SEL is enhanced when it is used as a framework for organizing all of a school's prevention efforts (Elias et al., 1997). SEL can coordinate these efforts by addressing the risk factors shared by a wide range of behaviors that can compromise children's educational and psychological readiness and their engagement in and adjustment to school. It does so in a coordinated, developmentally appropriate, and culturally sensitive manner that promotes reinforcement and consistency of messages across the curriculum. This approach avoids addressing risk factors in a piecemeal, fragmented, and categorical way that may lead to inconsistency of messages, competition for resources, a decreased sense of common purpose, and fewer connections among faculty and students.

In this still developing field, the integration of the social-emotional variables in the definition of SEL is to some degree conceptual and theoretical rather than purely empirical (i.e., the psychometric properties of SEL as a construct need to be investigated). Another challenge for the field is to identify the factors that mediate specific educational outcomes (Greenberg et al., 2003). A better understanding of this process would contribute to the development of better targeted and more sustainable interventions. Nor have the potential contributions of noncognitive processes such as temperament and emotions been fully investigated with respect to their influence on children's SEL domain (Izard, 2002).

Izard's proposed set of principles for preventive interventions is a contribution to this effort. With regard to the first of these principles, "activation and utilization of positive emotions to increase sociability, personal well-being, and constructive behavior" (p. 798), he notes that few current programs emphasize positive emotions and capitalize on their benefits. Instead they emphasize self-regulation and control of negative emotions. Izard proposes that developing positive emotions may be a better means for enhancing well-being, as well as for regulating negative emotions and their harmful influence on self-control.

It should be noted that some widely adopted prevention and intervention programs ignore both emotion and cognition, and focus almost exclusively on changing student behavior using operant or social control strategies (e.g., Positive Behavioral Interventions and Supports, PBIS; www.pbis.org). Though some educators consider PBIS to be an SEL program, it does not fit the definition of SEL described earlier because of the lack of focus on developing the core SEL competencies or the intrinsic motivation-enhancing aspects characteristic of SEL. Nonetheless, these approaches have many advocates, and evaluation studies have shown positive associations between PBIS and such indicators as decreases in the numbers of student disciplinary referrals. PBIS may, therefore, have a place in creating a more orderly environment in which to implement SEL.

Concluding Comments

Our discussion concludes by addressing the key questions posed by the editors that also serve as a summary of the chapter.

In Which Real-World Domains Will EI Be Most and Least Useful?

Elsewhere we made the case that schools are ideal settings in which to reach children (Consortium on the School-Based Promotion of Social Competence, 1994). Because competence in SEL has implications throughout one's life, instruction in it is a crucial aspect of the education of all children. Moreover, if children develop these competencies early in life, they are more likely to use them as adults and may be more amenable to further training for applications in work- and faith-based settings.

What Theoretical Advances Are Necessary to Support Practical Applications?

Among the areas discussed in the chapter in which the field would benefit from additional advances is identification of the active ingredients in SEL interventions. That is, increasing our knowledge of the key elements that lead to behavioral, cognitive, and affective change is needed. A better understanding of implementation and sustainability issues likewise would move the field forward and keep SEL from becoming the latest educational innovation to fall from sight. Generalization across settings is a problem is many areas of applied psychology, including SEL. Finally, learning how to best position SEL so that it is integrated throughout schools and linked to other prevention, early intervention, and treatment services is needed.

Is There Any Practical Advantage to Focusing on EI, Rather Than on Specific Contextualized Skills, Such as Skills for Assertiveness, Impulse Control, Stress Management, and So Forth?

As part of SEL instruction, students are taught the skills that prepare them to be effective learners (e.g., listening). SEL is not a unitary construct. Rather, it involves the mutual reinforcement of instruction in the five competencies described previously and maintenance of a supportive learning environment. Together, these elements give added value to each of the five SEL skills. Moreover, each of the five skill clusters builds upon and contributes to mastery of the others as part of an integrated whole that is more than the sum of its individual parts. Thus, students may receive direct training in the key competencies (some of which are similar to EI), but they also need the benefits associated with a safe, caring, and challenging learning environment. Competence in the five clusters of SEL skills also constitutes the common basis for prevention of various risky behaviors and the promotion of developmental assets.

What Are the Cultural, Social, and Economic Factors That May Constrain or Facilitate Applications Based on EI?

SEL interventions are more likely to succeed when they are congruent with the values, beliefs, norms, and histories of the children and families served: Schools select

SEL programs that they believe are appropriate culturally, socially, and economically for their students and families. The challenge is to identify these issues and to figure out how they might be reflected in SEL programming. However, exploring human differences also provides many rich opportunities for practicing and applying SEL skills. Natasi, Moore, and Varjos (2004) developed a culturally specific school mental health services program intended to facilitate its provision in a wide range of settings with diverse populations. This model has potential applications with respect to the delivery of SEL and EI interventions.

Can EI Be Taught?

There is some overlap in EI and SEL competencies. Considerable evidence was presented demonstrating that SEL skills can be taught and that in the context of an SEL intervention as shown in Figure 15.1, they lead to better academic achievement, improved prosocial skills, and decreased negative behaviors. What is critical to ensuring successful training for social-emotional competence is to utilize the specific guidelines for promoting SEL discussed by CASEL (2005; Elias et al., 1997).

References

Aos, S., Lieb, R., Mayfield, J., Miller, M., & Pennucci, A. (2004). *Benefits and costs of prevention and early intervention programs for youth.* Olympia: Washington State Institute for Public Policy.

Bar-On, R. (1997). *The Emotional Intelligence Inventory (EQ-i): Technical manual.* Toronto: Multi-Health Systems.

Bar-On, R. (2000). Emotional and social intelligence: Insights from the Emotional Quotient Inventory. In R. Bar-On & J. D. A. Parker (Eds.), *The handbook of emotional intelligence* (pp. 363–388). San Francisco: Jossey-Bass.

Bear, G. G. (with Cavalier, A., & Manning, M.). (2005). *Developing self-discipline and preventing and correcting misbehavior.* Boston: Allyn & Bacon.

Becker, B. E., & Luthar, S. S. (2002). Social-emotional factors affecting achievement outcomes among disadvantaged students: Closing the achievement gap. *Educational Psychologist, 37,* 197–214.

Botvin, G. J. (2002). *Life skills training.* White Plains, NY: Princeton Health Press.

Brown, J. L., Roderick, T., Lantieri, L., & Aber, J. L. (2004). The Resolving Conflict Creatively Program: A school-based social and emotional learning program. In J. E. Zins, R. P. Weissberg, M. C. Wang, & H. J. Walberg (Eds.), *Building school success on social and emotional learning: What does the research say?* (pp. 151–169). New York: Teachers College Press.

Christenson, S. L., & Havsy, L. H. (2004). Family-school-peer relationships: Significance for social, emotional, and academic learning. In J. E. Zins, R. P. Weissberg, M. C. Wang, & H. J. Walberg (Eds.), *Building school success on social and emotional learning: What does the research say?* (pp. 59–75). New York: Teachers College Press.

Collaborative for Academic, Social, and Emotional Learning. (2005). *Safe and sound: An educational leader's guide to evidence-based social and emotional learning (SEL) programs, Illinois edition.* Chicago, IL: Author.

Committee for Children. (2004). *Second Step: A violence prevention curriculum*. Seattle: Author.

Consortium on the School-Based Promotion of Social Competence. (1994). The promotion of social competence: Theory, research, practice, and policy. In R. J. Haggerty, L. Sherrod, N. Garmezy, & M. Rutter (Eds.), *Stress, risk, resilience in children and adolescents: Processes, mechanisms, and interaction* (pp. 268–316). New York: Cambridge University Press.

Crick, N. R., & Dodge, K.A. (1994). A review and reformulation of social information-processing mechanisms in children's social adjustment. *Psychological Bulletin, 115,* 74–101.

Dodge, K. A. (1986). A social information processing model of social competence in children. In M. Perlumutter (Ed.), *The Minnesota symposium on child psychology* (Vol. 18, pp. 77–125). Hillsdale, NJ: Erlbaum.

Dodge, K. A., & Crick, N. R. (1990). Social information processing bases of aggressive behavior in children. *Personality and Social Psychology Bulletin, 16,* 8–222.

Dryfoos, J. G. (1994). *Full-service schools: A revolution in health and social services for children, youth, and families.* San Francisco, CA: Jossey-Bass.

Durlak, J. A., & Weissberg, R. P. (2005, August). *A major meta-analysis of positive youth development programs.* Presentation at the Annual Meeting of the American Psychological Association, Washington, DC.

Elias, M. J. (2004). Strategies to infuse social and emotional learning into academics. In J. E. Zins, R. P. Weissberg, M. C. Wang, & H. J. Walberg (Eds.), *Building academic success on social and emotional learning: What does the research say?* (pp. 113–134). New York: Teachers College Press.

Elias, M. J. (2006, January). *Putting the pieces together: Improving academic outcomes and school climate, safety, and civility.* Presentation at the Developing Safe and Civil Schools Initiative, New Brunswick, NJ.

Elias, M. J., & Arnold, H. (Eds.). (2006). *The educator's guide to emotional intelligence and academic achievement: Social-emotional learning in the classroom.* Thousand Oaks, CA: Corwin.

Elias, M. J., & Bruene Butler, L. (2005). *Social decision making/social problem solving curriculum for grades 2–5.* Champaign, IL: Research Press.

Elias, M. J., Zins, J. E., Graczyk, P. A., & Weissberg, R. P. (2003). Implementation, sustainability, and scaling up of social–emotional and academic innovations in public schools. *School Psychology Review, 32,* 303–319.

Elias, M. J., Zins, J. E., Weissberg, R. P., Frey, K. S., Greenberg, M. T., Haynes, N. M., Kessler, R., Schwab-Stone, M. E., & Shriver, T. P. (1997). *Promoting social and emotional learning: Guidelines for educators.* Alexandria, VA: Association for Supervision and Curriculum Development.

Fleming, J. E., & Bay, M. (2004). Social and emotional learning in teacher preparation standards. In J. E. Zins, R. P. Weissberg, M. C. Wang, & H. J. Walberg (Eds.), *Building school success on social and emotional learning: What does the research say?* (pp. 94–112). New York: Teachers College Press.

Foster, S., Rollefson, M., Doksum, T., Noonan, D., Robinson, G., & Teich, J. (2005). *School mental health services in the United States 2002–2003* (DHHS Publication No. SMA 05–4068). Rockville, MD: Center for Mental Health Services.

Goleman, D. (2001). Emotional intelligence: Issues in paradigm building. In C. Cherniss & D. Goleman (Eds.), *The emotionally intelligent workplace* (pp. 13–26). San Francisco: Jossey-Bass.

Gottfredson, G. D., & Gottfredson, D. C. (2001). What schools do to prevent problem behaviors and promote safe environments. *Journal of Educational and Psychological Consultation, 12,* 313–344.

Greenberg, M. T., Kusché, C. A., & Riggs, N. (2004). The PATHS curriculum: Theory and research on neurocognitive development and school success. In J. E. Zins, R. P. Weissberg, M. C. Wang, & H. J. Walberg (Eds.), *Building academic success on social and emotional learning: What does the research say?* (pp. 170–188). New York: Teachers College.

Greenberg, M. T., Weissberg, R. P., O'Brien, M. U., Zins, J. E., Fredericks, L., Resnik, H. et al. (2003). Enhancing school-based prevention and youth development through coordinated social and emotional learning. *American Psychologist, 58,* 466–474.

Hawkins, J. D. (1997). Academic performance and school success. In R. P. Weissberg, T. P. Gullotta, R. L. Hampton, R. A. Ryan, & G. R. Adams (Eds.), *Healthy children 2010: Enhancing children's wellness* (pp. 278–305). Thousand Oaks, CA: Sage.

Izard, C. E. (2002). Translating emotion theory and research into preventive interventions. *Psychological Bulletin, 128,* 796–824.

Johnson, D. W., & Johnson, R. T. (2004). The three Cs of promoting social and emotional learning. In J. E. Zins, R. P. Weissberg, M. C. Wang, & H. J. Walberg (Eds.), *Building academic success on social and emotional learning: What does the research say?* (pp. 40–58). New York: Teachers College Press.

Kriet, R. (2006). Morning meeting: Teaching the art of caring conversation. In M. J. Elias & H. Arnold (Eds.). *Emotional intelligence and academic achievement* (pp. 109–118). Thousand Oaks, CA: Corwin.

Kusché, C. A., & Greenberg, M. T. (2006). Brain development and social-emotional learning: An introduction for educators. In M. J. Elias & H. Arnold (Eds.), *Emotional intelligence and academic achievement* (pp. 35–42). Thousand Oaks, CA: Corwin.

Lazarus, R. S. (1991). *Emotion and adaptation.* New York: Oxford University Press.

Matthews, G., Zeidner, M., & Roberts, R. D. (2003). *Emotional intelligence: Science and myth.* Cambridge, MA: MIT Press.

Mayer, J. D., Salovey, P., & Caruso, D. R. 2004). Models of emotional intelligence. In P. Salovey, M. A. Brackett, & J. D. Mayer (Eds.), *Emotional intelligence: Key readings on the Mayer and Salovey Model* (pp. 81–119). Port Chester, NY: Dude.

National Association of School Psychologists. (2000*). Standards for training and field placement programs in school psychology.* Bethesda, MD: Author.

McNeeley, C. A., Nonnemaker, J. M., & Blum, R. W. (2002). Promoting school connectedness: Evidence from the National Longitudinal Study of Adolescent Health. *Journal of School Health, 72*(4), 138–146.

Natasi, B. K., Moore, R. B., & Varjos, K. M. (2004). *School-based mental health services: Creating comprehensive and culturally specific programs.* Washington, DC: American Psychological Association.

Ormrod, J. E. (1999). *Human learning* (3rd ed.). Upper Saddle River, NJ: Merrill.

Osterman, K. F. (2000). Students' need for belonging in the school community. *Review of Educational Research, 70,* 323–367.

Payton, J. W., Graczyk, P. A., Wardlaw, D. M., Bloodworth, M., Tompsett, C. J., & Weissberg, R. P. (2000). Social and emotional learning: A framework for promoting mental health and reducing risk behavior in children and youth. *Journal of School Health, 70,* 179–185.

Rose, L. C., & Gallup, A. M. (2000). *The 32nd Annual Phi Delta Kappa/Gallop Poll of the Public's Attitudes Toward the Public Schools.* Retrieved July 7, 2002, from http://www.pdkintl.org/kappan/kpol0009.htm

Schaps, E., Battistich, V., & Solomon, D. (2004). Community in school as key to student growth: Findings from the Child Development Project. In J. E. Zins, R. P. Weissberg, M. C. Wang, & H. J. Walberg (Eds.), *Building academic success on social and emotional learning: What does the research say?* (pp. 189–205). New York: Teachers College Press.

Schunk, D. H. (1996). *Learning theories* (2nd ed.). Englewood Cliffs, NJ: Merrill.

Sroufe, L. A. (1996). Emotional development: The organization of emotional life in the early years. New York: Cambridge University Press.

Sylwester, R. (1995). *A celebration of neurons: An educator's guide to the human brain.* Reston, VA: Association for Supervision and Curriculum Development.

Weissberg, R. P., Gullotta, T. P., Hampton, R. L., Ryan, R. A., & Adams, G. R. (Eds.). (1997). *Healthy children 2010: Enhancing children's wellness.* Thousand Oaks, CA: Sage.

Weisz, J. R., Sandler, I. N., Durlak, J. A., & Anton, B. S. (2005). Promoting and protecting youth mental health through evidence-based prevention and treatment. *American Psychologist, 60,* 628–648.

Wentzel, K. R., & Asher, S. R. (1995). The academic lives of neglected, rejected, popular, and controversial children. *Child Development, 66,* 754–763.

Wilson, D. B., Gottfredson, D. C., & Najaka, S. S. (2001). School-based prevention of problem behaviors: A meta-analysis. *Journal of Quantitative Criminology, 17,* 247–272.

Zeider, M., Roberts, R. D., & Matthews, G. (2002). Can emotional intelligence be schooled? A critical review. *Educational Psychologist, 37,* 215–231.

Zins, J. E., & Elias, M. J. (2006). Social and emotional learning. In G. G. Bear, K. M. Minke, & A. Thomas (Eds.), *Children's needs III: Development, problems, and alternatives* (pp. 1–14). Bethesda, MD: National Association of School Psychologists.

Zins, J. E., Weissberg, R. P., Wang, M. C., & Walberg, H. J. (Eds.). (2004). *Building academic success on social and emotional learning: What does the research say?* New York: Teachers College Press.

16

Toward Machines With Emotional Intelligence

ROSALIND W. PICARD

For half a century, artificial intelligence researchers have focused on giving machines linguistic and mathematical-logical reasoning abilities, modeled after the classic linguistic and mathematical-logical intelligences. This chapter describes new research that is giving machines (including software agents, robotic pets, desktop computers, and more) skills of emotional intelligence. Machines have long been able to appear as if they have emotional feelings, but now machines are also being programmed to learn when and how to display emotion in ways that enable the machine to appear empathetic or otherwise emotionally intelligent. Machines are now being given the ability to sense and recognize expressions of human emotion such as interest, distress, and pleasure, with the recognition that such communication is vital for helping machines choose more helpful and less aggravating behavior. This chapter presents several examples illustrating new and forthcoming forms of machine emotional intelligence, highlighting applications together with challenges to their development.

Introduction

Why would machines need emotional intelligence? Machines do not even have emotions: They don't feel happy to see us, sad when we go, or bored when we don't give them enough interesting input. IBM's Deep Blue supercomputer beat grandmaster and world champion Gary Kasparov at chess without feeling any stress during the game, and without any joy at its accomplishment, indeed without feeling anything at all.

I would like to thank Shaundra Bryant Daily for helpful comments on this manuscript. This research was supported in part by the MIT Media Lab's Things That Think Consortium, Digital Life Consortium, and by the National Science Foundation ITR 0325428. Any opinions, findings, conclusions, or recommendations are those of the author and do not necessarily reflect the views of the NSF.

Nobody worried that it would feel intimidated or get flustered. With the steady hassle of dealing with viruses, spyware, operating system updates, hardware failures, network delays, forgotten passwords, and a host of other computer-related ills, who wants to add worries about their machine acting in any way emotional? Just imagine that you might have to wait for it to have a certain emotional state before you could use it: "Thelma, can you please come calm down my computer so it will let me read my e-mail?" "Thelma, can you calm me down now, too?" This scenario is so unpleasant, that a machine with a sticker labeled "emotions inside" sounds more like a joke from late-night comedy television than like anything we want to see in stores, much less in our office.

This chapter is not about giving machines emotional intelligence to make them more "emotional." Instead, it is about how emotional intelligence could address several problems that exist today, while enabling better technologies for the future. To illustrate, consider the following scenario.

Please imagine that you are the main character in the scenario, and that you are not reading this chapter, but imagine you are in your office, working very hard on a problem of great concern and importance to you. Suppose that you have an urgent deadline tomorrow, and it means a lot to you to make this deadline. Thus, you are in your office working very hard, when the following sequence of events unfolds:

> Someone whose name you don't know enters your office. You are polite, but also slightly annoyed by the interruption, and your face is not welcoming. This individual doesn't apologize; perhaps you express a little bit of annoyance. He doesn't seem to notice. Then, he offers you advice that is useless. You express a little more annoyance. He doesn't show any hint of noticing that you are annoyed. You try to communicate that his advice is not helpful right now, but he cheerily gives you more useless advice. Perhaps when he first came in, you started off with a very subtle expression of negativity, but now (you can use your imagination given your personal style) let's say, "the clarity of your emotional expression escalates." Perhaps you express yourself verbally, or with a gesture. In any case, it doesn't matter: He doesn't get it. Finally, you have to tell him explicitly to go away, perhaps directly escorting him out. Fortunately he leaves, but first he winks and does a happy little dance.

Is this interrupting individual someone that you would eagerly invite back to your office? The annoyance he caused (when this situation happened to me) was not exactly helpful to my productivity. I do not consider his behavior to be intelligent, and he would not last long on the job if I were his boss and if this annoying behavior persisted. Nonetheless, the behavior above is widespread—for it is that of the most successful and most famous, or infamous, computer software agent known to date, "Clippit," the talking, dancing, smiling cartoon paperclip office assistant, a piece of "intelligent" software that ships standard with Microsoft Office.

Many people complain that Clippit is not very intelligent. Actually, Clippit *is* very intelligent when it comes to some things: He probably "knows" more facts about Microsoft Office than 95% of the people at MIT. He is also very good at recognizing your actions, such as whether you are writing a letter or not. He is not good at knowing what you are *intending* to do, but most people are also far from perfect at this. People don't always have the best timing when they interrupt you, and they also don't always understand your problem or how to fix it. Researchers know that recognizing intent is a hard problem for machines, and they are working on it. What, then, is so annoying about the above scenario and about so many people's daily experiences with this modern "intelligent" technology?

Although Clippit is a genius about Microsoft Office, he is an idiot about people, especially about handling emotions. Consider three of the skills of emotional intelligence that Clippit does not have:

1. *He doesn't notice you are annoyed (doesn't detect or recognize your emotion).* Even a dog can see if you are annoyed, such as when the dog is on the sofa, where he knows he is not allowed, and you yell at him to get down. He notices when you yell and are upset, and he changes his behavior, putting his ears back and tail down, as well as doing the right thing by getting down (eventually). Although a dog may not know your intent, he does know you are upset, and he also knows how to respond under such conditions. He responds in such a way that you want to see him again. The dog may not be as smart as Clippit when it comes to Microsoft Office, but he knows how to handle your frustration in a way that helps you feel better, not worse.

2. *You express more annoyance; he ignores it (doesn't respond appropriately to emotion).* People don't respond to every emotion they see, and neither should computers. There is a time to ignore emotion. However, there is also a time to respond, especially when the emotive individual is your valued customer, associate, friend, or family member, and when that individual is expressing increasing aggravation or annoyance toward you. To repeatedly ignore their feelings is to invite escalation of those feelings, possibly even eliciting hatred and destroying the relationship. Computers that repeatedly ignore human expressions of irritation toward them are likely to be significantly less liked as a product than those that respond intelligently to people under duress. Companies that care about their customer's feelings will pay attention to these skills in designing their technology's interactions.

3. *He winks and does a happy little dance before exiting (stupid about displaying emotion).* Winking, smiling, and happy dancing can be charming and entertaining in the right context. When Microsoft tested Clippit with users in its usability lab, these behaviors may have been enjoyable, especially for users who were delighted to serve as testers and felt excited about seeing a cutting-edge, new technology. Clippit was probably not tested under stressful, long-term conditions of personal significance to the users, taking into account variations in mood of users, in other words, under continuous real-world use in which feelings of genuinely significant duress occur. Although it is easy to make computers look like they are having emotions (even though they are not) such as by having the machine display a happy face or dance, it is hard to give computers the ability to know when, where, and how to appropriately display emotions—and when *not* to display them. Responding gleefully after you have annoyed somebody thrice in the last 5 minutes is stupid. Machines with emotional intelligence would be programmed to show emotions only if appropriate. Machines that have the potential to show emotion will also need the intelligence to know when not to show it.

The scenario above illustrates three skills of emotional intelligence with some of the problems they can cause when they are missing from technology. There are many other scenarios, as well, that arise when technology interacts with medical staff, call center workers, drivers, students, and more, all in cases that impact people's feelings, productivity, and performance in measurable ways. As technology is increasingly applied to situations in which it must interact with everyone—not just with its designers and creators, who are experts in how it works—it is all the more vital that it does so in a way that is courteous and respectful of people's feelings.

When reading the scenario above, people tend to initially think that the intruder is a person. I deliberately worded the scenario to try to lead people to think "person," not "computer." This exercise of mentally substituting "person" for "computer" and vice-versa grew out of the work of Cliff Nass and Byron Reeves, whose book *The Media Equation* argues that human-computer interaction is inherently natural and social (Reeves & Nass, 1996). Although their argument may be easily believed if the computer is a humanoid robot, or perhaps a conversational software character with a face and a body, they also show that the tendency of people is to behave toward a computer as if it were a person, even if the computer has no face or lifelike body, and even if it refers to its unit as "this computer" instead of "I." Their work takes studies from sociology, replaces at least one of the persons with a computer, and then tests (in a physical interaction, not just in a thought experiment as in the scenario above) if the results still hold. Although the results are not always identical, the tendency to behave toward the computer *as if* it were a person is true in an enormous number of cases, confirmed not just in their work, but also by others. Thus, it can be a useful exercise when designing a new technology to ask, "What would happen if a person were to do what I'm designing this technology to do?" It is useful to pretend, for a moment, that the computer is a person. If what would happen is annoying and aggravating, then probably the technology should not be built that way.

Based on the theory of Nass and Reeves, elements of human-human interaction that are enjoyable and contribute to productivity and positive experiences have a good chance of similar outcomes when incorporated into human-computer interaction. Thus, to the extent that emotional intelligence is useful and important in human-human interaction, it is also likely to be useful and important in human-computer interaction.

Computers That Sense and Recognize Emotion

Can computers know what you are feeling? I remember the look of one of my non-technical colleagues one day when she overheard some dialogue about computers that could sense people's emotion. She rolled her chair over to me, rotating so that the nearest machine was behind her back, and said to me, with a hushed but deeply worried voice, brow furrowed, and with one hand against her face to hide it from the machine and the other hand pointing over her shoulder to the machine, "Does it know that I don't like it?"

Computers do not know our innermost feelings, and there are good reasons to keep it that way (e.g., Picard & Klein, 2002; Reynolds & Picard, 2005). Many people feel their emotions are private, and concerns about violations of privacy are every bit as valid when machines have access to our emotional information as when they have access to your Social Security number, banking transactions, web browsing patterns, and doctor's notes about your last visit. However, there is also a balance to be achieved, and although there are times when emotions are best kept internal, there are also times when people overtly express their feelings, and it is quite clear to everyone in the vicinity, and sometimes beyond, what they are feeling. In some cases, especially when the feelings are directed to the computer, it can be unintelligent for the computer not to recognize them. If you are cursing at the top of your lungs at the office assistant, and it doesn't flinch, but it smiles and dances and winks at you in response, then it has not only responded with a lack of emotional intelligence, it has responded stupidly. It has failed egregiously to treat its customer well. But how could it know if it can't see, hear, or otherwise sense that which is obvious to every person in the room? Computer scientists have designed technology that can know all your personal financial and health information, all your social communication, e-mail, and entertainment preferences, your personal web browsing patterns, and more; however, they neglected to instruct the machine to see if it has upset its most important customer.

The situation could become worse when emotionally unintelligent technology is in our kitchens, cars, and living rooms, "ubiquitous," and in new forms, such as household robots. If it is smart enough to try to help us, then it should also be smart enough to adapt to our wishes, changing its behavior if we don't like it. Computers can adapt and learn how to behave in ways that we like better, but the interface for such learning and adaptation has not been a social and natural one—usually, it can be operated only by people who know a lot about computers. We are trying to change this so that machines can interpret the feedback people naturally provide to them. People might naturally praise or scold, and we are enabling the machine to see the difference. Machines can be equipped to recognize praising or scolding, or general forms of positive and negative feedback, and to respond. There is no reason why computers have to always ignore all the feelings that are expressed at them.

What affective states should computers be enabled to recognize? Although emotion theorists have developed understanding of a small set of "basic emotions" and also have developed dimensioned representations for emotion, none of the available theories provide comprehensive models for representing the states that tend to arise in interaction with computers. For example, the dominant models neglect states such as boredom, interest, and frustration. My students and I have thus not relied on these dominant theories, but have instead started with observations of a variety of interactions that occur with technology. We have been motivated by applications in learning, health, and usability, in which we need to recognize what is being communicated in those contexts. Here, there is a dearth of theory, and new breakthroughs are needed in order to make useful instantiations of emotional intelligence. Our approach to developing new theory and applications is data-driven: First observe which states naturally are communicated from people to computers, then build and test models that can predict what is measured and reflected in the data. In one of our long-term projects, the building of a computerized *learning companion*, two of the key affective states found from the data are interest and boredom—two states that are not on most theorists' "basic emotions" list. However, discriminating these states is vital to the machine's ability to adapt the pedagogy to help keep the learning experience going, and our model addresses them.

The Computing Research Association has listed the "building of an autonomous teacher for every learner" as one of its grand 5-year research challenges. The vision for this future application is that a personalized "Socrates" or similar tutor could be available for every child to have an ideal, customized learning experience. But we all know that each child is different, and a human tutor senses these differences and adapts continuously to the child.

What will a learning companion need to sense? One key is sensing when to intervene in a child's learning exploration. Being able to determine the difference between students who are making mistakes while being interested and pleasurably engaged versus students who are making mistakes and showing increasing signs of frustration or distraction, like they are ready to quit, is really important if the system is deciding whether or not to intervene. Technology without emotional intelligence would tend to interrupt based only on the action of making a mistake, because it wouldn't be able to recognize the learner's affective state. The result is that the student who was curious and exploring may be annoyed, and thus may be discouraged from future exploration. However, if the technology waits too long before interrupting, the student who is frustrated may have already quit. What is needed is the ability to discriminate relevant emotions of the student.

Although there is currently no one signal that can be read from your brain or the rest of your body to reliably tell a computer what you are feeling, there are a variety of modalities through which a computer can begin to infer information about your emotional state, especially when you are trying to communicate it clearly. The specific modalities used by a person (face, voice, gesture, etc.) may vary with context (e.g., office or home), personality (e.g., introverted or not), culture (e.g., Japanese or Italian), and other factors. We thus choose to construct a large number of tools that can be adapted to different situations.

The following are some examples of tools that we have been developing at the MIT Media Laboratory for recognizing the affective state of a person using a computer, and some of the applications that motivate their development. After the examples, a discussion illustrates several of the current capabilities, as well as challenges researchers in this area face. The discussion is not an exhaustive one—there are many ongoing efforts and the research area is a rapidly moving one.

Recognizing Affective State in Postural Movements
While Seated

There's a popular belief that leaning forward is an indication of interest, whereas slumping lower and lower into one's chair may indicate otherwise. However, we all know that the distinction is not that simple, and there are counterexamples, such as how a student may keep leaning forward toward her computer, nudging closer and closer to the monitor, to the extent that she falls asleep with her head on the keyboard. Nonetheless, we thought that there might be some information about affective state in the posture as a function of time, so we conducted experiments to quantify any changes that might be affectively informative, developed a new tool to automate recognition of affective information from postural changes, and conducted evaluations of the tool. Although the details of the work appear elsewhere (Mota & Picard, 2003), the basic idea is briefly described here.

We collected data on the posture modality from children while they were seated at a computer using state-of-the-art learning software. We knew from the work of Tan, Lu, and Pentland (1997) that postures can be sensed from a commercially available set of 42×48 pressure sensors placed on the back of a chair and on the seat of a chair. Using custom pattern recognition software, the pressure patterns can be reliably discriminated for nine states, including the four illustrated in Figure 16.1: a person sitting up straight (very little action on the back of the chair, but with their weight fairly nicely distributed across the two thighs), leaning forward (no pressure on the back, more pressure toward the knees), leaning back (more pressure on the back, very little on the knees), and leaning right (more pressure on the corresponding side of the back and seat).

Selene Mota and I designed and built a new algorithm that could recognize not only nine static postures of the learner, but also analyze structure in how these postures changed as a function of time (Mota & Picard, 2003). This analysis enabled the computer for the first time to use postural movements over time to classify the learner into a level of high interest, low interest, or a new state that appears to increase in frequency before boredom, which we called "taking a break." Although the latter is arguably not an emotional state, we found it useful to define and recognize it as part of the challenge of recognizing the learner's affective state. Although classification accuracy for the machine

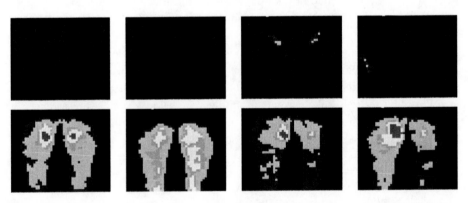

Figure 16.1. Sensor output images. Pressure patterns (top row) from the back of the chair and (bottom row) seat of the chair. Left to right: sitting upright, leaning forward, leaning back, and leaning to the right.

to recognize these three states (high interest, low interest, and taking a break) was not perfect, it was significantly better than random (~33%), attaining levels from 72% to 80% accuracy, depending upon whether the system had seen the child before. With greater exposure to a person, the machine becomes more accurate (up to a point, the limits of which have not been carefully explored).

Although the chair cannot recognize your innermost feelings, it provides a modality of sensing that can be useful for the computer to know. In particular, for children seated comfortably in front of state of the art educational software, this information was found to be one of the most useful channels of feedback in discriminating their interest level (Kapoor, Picard, & Ivanov, 2004), and when combined with other modalities, the accuracy of the inference improves further (Kapoor, Ahn, & Picard, 2005).

Recognizing Facial Expressions

The most widely addressed area of research in automated emotion recognition, and the one in which there has been the most progress, is the recognition of facial expressions. Dozens of researchers have developed methods of trying to recognize complete facial expressions such as "angry" or "sad" or to recognize individual "facial action units" that can be used to make any expression such as "inner eyebrow raise" and "eye widening" (see Pantic & Rothkrantz, 2003, for a nice overview of this area of research). Our approach has been to focus on a mixture of these, recognizing individual action units around the eyes and coarser movements around the mouth, and to also use a special kind of camera, the IBM Blue Eyes camera.

The Blue Eyes camera simplifies the problem of finding the facial movements when the head is moving by tracking the eyes. The principle used is the "red-eye effect," which takes advantage of the fact that the pupils are very good infrared mirrors, and that the pupils will thus "light up" in the image when the camera is surrounded by a ring of infrared LEDs. These LEDs blink on and off at the same time that two adjacent strips of LEDs blink off and on, with the latter strips lighting up the face but not causing the red-eye effect. Subtracting the images where the pupils are "red" from the ones where they are not gives a quick pupil detector, which works robustly even with frequent movement in front of the camera. Although the tracking fails when one blinks or when both eyes are obstructed from the view of the camera, the system recovers them very quickly as soon as they are visible again. Thus, the system is useful as the first step of a real-time facial expression recognition system.

Once the eyes are found, we apply various algorithms from computer vision and pattern recognition, which were developed in our lab by Ashish Kapoor to try to recognize other facial movements relative to the eyes, cheeks, and mouth. Although we have emphasized real-time tracking and recognition of only a subset of expressions, others have restricted head movements and allowed for some manual marking of facial features, and have attained high recognition accuracy—in the 90% range—for many facial expression components. The main problem with the methods, however, is that large and/or rapid head movements and lighting changes can ruin the ability for the system to find facial features, and thus the accuracy can drop dramatically. Our fully automatic system's accuracy, when tested on recognition of upper facial action units in the presence of a lot of natural head movements, is just under 70% accurate (Kapoor, Qi, & Picard, 2003).

Rana el Kaliouby (2005) presented a comparison of the features of many different systems for facial expression recognition, including many systems that claim accuracy rates higher than 70%. Most of these require some kind of manual intervention, and the rates are only reported on cases in which the tracking of the facial expressions was successful. Computer vision is still far from perfect when it comes to finding and tracking faces in natural imagery, where people are free to move and the sun is free to shine (or not) through the window, or outdoors, changing dramatically the appearance of the digital imagery received by the computer. Additionally, to date there have been no systems built that recognize expressions while people are moving their faces for other reasons—talking, chewing gum, bouncing to music, and so forth.

Although research from psychology such as "face of interest" (Reeves, 1993) suggests that faces are indicators of affective states such as interest, our findings measured from children in learning situations using the computer indicate that some children are very facially expressive, whereas others show almost no facial expressions. Analyzing a dozen children who were using a state-of-the-art educational software program (Fripple Place), we found that there were no significant correlations between any of the facial features as marked by a certified facial action coding expert and ratings of the children's levels of interest, as agreed upon by three veteran teachers. However, for some children this channel is useful and can help the computer to be more intelligent about how it interacts with the child. Thus, one of the challenges in giving computers the ability to recognize emotion is that of knowing when a channel's lack of signal is meaningful or not.

Stronger results can sometimes be obtained by combining multiple channels, for example, face with voice (Huang, Chen, & Tao, 1998), face with chair, or mouse and task (Kapoor et al., 2005). Different kinds of sensing (use of a chair, mouse, camera, etc.) may be more or less natural in different kinds of environments, and confidence that the computer has properly recognized the person's affective state tends to increase with more than one mode of sensing. There is also new pioneering research on automated recognition of facial expression and on head gestures to discern states such as "concentrating," "disagreement," "thinking," "unsure," and "interested"(el Kaliouby & Robinson, 2005a, 2005b), all of which could also be helpful to a machine trying to appear more caring by adjusting its responses to those of the person with whom it is interacting. El Kaliouby has additionally described potential applications of her algorithms to assist people with autism spectrum disorder, who routinely have difficulty recognizing others' cognitive-emotional states (el Kaliouby & Robinson, 2005).

Recognizing Emotion From Physiology

In some contexts, for example, medical monitoring or use of other wearable systems, it can be natural and comfortable to work with physiological sensors, sensing information such as changes in heart rate, muscle tension, temperature, skin conductance, and more.

For example, if a patient is wearing a heart monitor, for health monitoring or for fitness tracking, then the technology can potentially measure heart rate variability changes associated with cognitive and emotional stress as well. Physiological information has been shown to carry information that changes with different emotions (Ekman, Levenson, & Friesen, 1983), and such information can be used to build classifiers for an individual's affective state. One of the challenges in building a physiology-based emotion recognition system is that emotion is only one of the factors that affects physiology: Diet, exercise, sleep, basic personality characteristics, environmental context, activity, and more also affect physiological changes, and separating out the effects due to emotion involves significant technical hurdles.

We designed, built, and tested what appears to have been the first physiology-based emotion recognition system for recognizing an individual's emotions over time. This system used four physiological signals that learned patterns for an individual over many weeks and then achieved 81% recognition accuracy classifying which one of eight states (anger, joy, sadness, hatred, platonic love, romantic love, reverence, and neutral) that the individual was having (Picard, Vyzas, & Healey, 2001). (The person was seated in a relatively quiet space, and deliberately focusing on having each of the eight emotions.) Although the results of physiology-based recognition are promising, this work remains very technically challenging, and there is a lot of physiological understanding that still needs to be developed before large repertoires of emotion can be sensed. Also, there will probably be limits regarding how far this work will scale—at some level the physiological differentiation in emotions may become minute and possibly only available at a biochemical level that also involves knowing spatial locations of such activity. Sensors of such information are far from portable and can be very invasive. This is a wide-open area of research, which will need to be informed by cultural, social, and ethical guidelines as well as by scientific inquiry. There are probably certain levels of feelings that are best to keep from revealing to others, including your personal computer.

Signals such as skin conductance and heart rate variability have also been shown to be indicators of stress in natural situations, for example, measured from people while they were driving in Boston (Healey & Picard 2005). Recently it has also been shown that a computer software agent's empathetic responses can influence skin conductance in a way that is associated with decreased stress (Prendinger, Mori, & Ishizuka, 2005). In the latter case, physiological sensing of affect provides evidence that some computer behaviors can be less stressful than others. In the future, computer applications may choose behaviors based on your personal response—choosing to adapt in ways that reduce your stress, instead of always doing the same thing for everyone regardless of the stress it causes them.

What Is a Natural Set of Sensors?

Lots of factors contribute to deciding whether a sensor of emotion is perceived as natural, comfortable, intrusive, or otherwise acceptable or not. Although sometimes using an explicit sensor (such as a physiological sensing system, with skin-surface contact sensors) is valuable, say for knowing that you are being sensed and for giving you control over when this does and does not happen, it is also the case that such an apparatus can require extra effort and thus can be seen as "too much work to use." Some people see any kind of visible sensor as intrusive. In a medical context, however, in which such sensors might naturally be present for other useful functions, they are less likely to be seen as intrusive. Sometimes it is desirable to integrate sensors into the natural environment and see what can be learned about emotions from information they gather. However, sometimes such sensors can be seen as even more invasive, because they can gather information without your knowledge.

A compromise is to make sensors that are visible so that you can tell they are there, but also to integrate them naturally into the environment, so that the person using them doesn't have to do anything special (like attaching electrodes) to communicate through the sensors. The chair sensor, described earlier, falls into this category. Similarly, IBM researchers (Ark, Dryer, & Lu, 1999) placed physiological sensors into computer mice and used a function of those sensors to classify several basic emotions. Although the mouse is comfortable in many ways, our own experience with the IBM mouse was that it picked up a lot of motion artifacts on the electrodes placed on its surface, but that the varying pressure applied to the mouse might itself be useful as a sign of stress or frustration for many users.

Carson Reynolds (1999) designed, built, and tested a pressure-sensitive mouse, examining differences in pressure among users doing the same task, with low stress and with slightly higher stress, and finding some preliminary evidence of stress-related pressure changes. Inspired by this work, Jack Dennerlein at the Harvard School of Public Health decided to look more carefully at stress induced by mild occurrences of bad usability while people filled out forms on the computer. We helped Dennerlein automate his health demographics intake form so that people had to use the mouse to fill it out. Also, unbeknownst to the subjects, we made the forms slightly annoying to fill out, with subtle bad usability in the form's design, such as the use of pull-down menus and requiring commas between numbers. Some people found the forms to be very frustrating to fill out, whereas others did not find them frustrating at all. Comparing the most frustrated top half to the bottom half (according to people's self-reported frustration level), the top half was found to apply significantly more force to the mouse than the bottom half, especially right after being notified that they made an error on the previous page and had to go back and fix it. When they went back to fix it, they found that it had erased all of their answers on that page and they had to reenter them.

Analyzing the data later, Dennerlein found that frustration did co-occur with greater force, and also the specific muscles activated were those causally related to wrist injuries (Dennerlein, 2003). This finding suggested a new application: a mouse that "squeaks" or notifies you in a subtle way when you might be pressing it harder than necessary for some length of time. Thus, the technology could help you become aware of behaviors, possibly linked to stress, which are also associated with medical injury, so that you could better regulate those behaviors and their associated feelings before such an injury develops.

The mouse is just one example of placing affective sensing into devices that we are in ordinary physical contact with. Steering wheels, telephones, keyboards, and more present opportunities for computers to make more accurate inferences not only about what a person is trying to do, but also *how* smoothly (or not) the task is progressing. Although none of these techniques allows a computer to know your innermost feelings, they are channels that can be used to help you communicate a few of the adverbs that might help a machine better customize its interaction with you.

Sensing Emotion From Dialogue

At times it is appropriate to just ask somebody, "How are you feeling?" Although somebody may say, "I'm fine" (even when they are clearly miserable), the self-report of feelings is the de facto standard among psychology researchers when it comes to assessing emotion. Psychologists routinely give people forms to fill out, where they check off items on 7-point scales or use other expressive metrics such as the Self-Assessment Manikin (Bradley & Lang, 1994). Machines can also ask people what they are feeling on a questionnaire, or they can do so in a more conversational way, as indicated in the simple dialogue boxes shown in Figure 16.2.

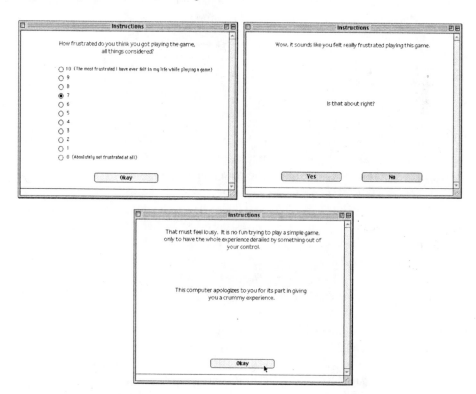

Figure 16.2. Screen shot. Klein et al. used simple dialogue boxes to ask about emotion and to convey the impression of active listening, empathy, and sympathy to help frustrated computer users feel better.

In this dialogue, we aim to go beyond just collecting self-report data. Here, the computer also responds to the user's statement in a way that tries to show that the machine is "listening" and "trying to understand" what the user has said. The machine does this by attempting to paraphrase the user's response, and by giving the user a chance to correct it if the paraphrase is wrong: to say "actually the feelings were a little worse than that" or "they were a little better." Thus, the machine not only collects the user's self-reported feelings, but it also attempts to help the user manage negative emotions by empathizing when things are not going well.

The technique in Figure 16.2 was part of the first "empathetic" agent built by Jonathan Klein. After measuring the behavior and responses of 66 people who were either users of this agent or users of one of two controls, the agent's empathetic approach was argued to have a positive influence on the user's behavior. The controls included a similar dialogue-based agent that simply ignored people's emotions, and another one that let people vent about their emotions but did not otherwise respond to them (Klein, Moon, & Picard, 2002).

Although machines remain very limited in their ability to understand most of language, they can already engage successfully in quasi-scripted dialogues about feelings (Bickmore & Picard, 2005; Klein et al., 2002; Liu & Picard, 2005). The dialogues can reveal feelings in a way that is natural and comfortable for people, as seen in the following example:

Computer: "How's it going?"
Person: "Not so great."
Computer: "Oh dear. Sorry to hear. Anything I can do to help?"
Person: "I don't know, I just feel terrible about…"

Dialogue systems have a chance to sense words selected by a person and to reason about the associated affect using either classic rule-based reasoning tools from artificial intelligence or using new "commonsense reasoning" tools (Elliott, 1992; Liu, Lieberman, & Selker, 2003; Ma, Osherenko, Prendinger, & Ishizuka, 2005). Using new tools of the latter ilk, Shaundra Daily (2005) has built a new technology that tries to help teen girls reason about the emotion of themselves and others in their life. The tool helps girls compose and illustrate stories about events of personal significance, and the commonsense reasoning makes suggestions about possible emotions that may have been present in the events the girl is writing about. After the system suggests, "Perhaps this made you feel angry?" if the girl says, "Yes, that's how I felt," then the system also has the opportunity to subtly empathize, helping validate the girl's feelings as well as reinforce her reflection on them. An initial study of use of this system by girls in a poor-performing school showed that their incorporation of emotional words in their stories increased over time, compared to a control group which used the storytelling system without the computer's emotion suggestions (Daily, 2005). This particular application of the technology also illustrates how even when the technology cannot always accurately infer the true feelings, it can still offer suggestions in a considerate way, which may in turn lead to productive outcomes.

Sometimes feelings are not communicated through *what* is said as much as *how* it is said, for example, "Good Morning!" can be spoken out loud with genuinely cheery enthusiasm or with annoyance, disdain, and other kinds of inflection that may clearly belie the meaning of the words. Machines also have the opportunity to listen to para-linguistic aspects of speech for indications of a person's feelings. Emotion recognition in speech is an active area of research (Douglas-Cowie, Cowie, & Campbell, 2003; Fernandez & Picard, 2005).

Systems that can intelligently sense the affective intent of language can be of immediate use in call centers and in other applications in which the intelligent man-agement of emotion has important business implications, as well as implications for managing the health of the workers who take the calls. Call centers tend to have high turnover of staff, and their cost to companies is enormous in continuously training and in managing these stressful enterprises. If the worker were to have an empathetic system warning her, "This one sounds like it may be tough, so you might want to take a deep breath first..." and showing concern for her feelings afterward if it looks like it may have indeed been stressful, "Was that caller as difficult as I guessed?" and if she answers, "Yes, almost the worst I've ever had," then it's time for a little empathy, and perhaps even some congratulations to her or some encouragement for maintaining her own composure.

Although managing feelings is no substitute for skilled training in how to handle a customer's mishap, skilled training alone is also not enough. Fixing the problem with-out regard for how it has made the customer feel can leave a customer still dissatisfied, whereas sometimes even when a problem is beyond fixing, a customer can feel like the company cares and did their best, engendering loyalty. As technology becomes a greater part of the customer service interaction, it too must be taught about this important dance between fixing problems and managing feelings.

Computers That Respond Appropriately to Human Emotion

Computers usually ignore emotion. Most of them can't sense it, and even if they can sense some aspects of it, the rates are still not perfect, and the theory of emotion is still such a poor fit to reality that it can be risky to assume too much in responding. How-ever, in some cases there are appropriate ways that computers can respond, and there is evidence that it can be productive to do so.

In our work, we have been particularly concerned with how to respond to emotions that occur most frequently around computers. In current business and home uses, these include emotions such as frustration, distress, and even anger. A 1999 survey by U.K. research firm Mori entitled "Rage Against the Machine" found that of 1,250 work-ers questioned, four out of five have "seen colleagues hurling abuse at their personal computers," three-quarters admit that they swear at their computers, and nearly half of all people working with computers feel frustrated or stressed because of information technology problems. Lest people think that the current generation is overreacting, and these problems will disappear with the next generation of youth, they also found that a quarter of all users under 25 admit they have kicked their computer.

Suppose that a computer infers with high probability that you are frustrated. When should it ignore this, and when should it respond? If it should respond, then how should it respond? Handling of emotions, in others as well as in oneself, involves emotional intelligence. This is a difficult challenge for many people, and even more so for machines. Machines have a very long way to go before they can recognize emotions as well as people, much less be smart about how they can respond to them without causing negative emotions to escalate. Nonetheless, the topic is an important one to tackle, and successful handling of emotion is critical to good customer service.

We have begun to give computers a limited range of abilities when it comes to helping handle the emotions of people with whom they are interacting. Our first efforts in this area have been to respond to negative emotions with a little bit of active listening, empathy, and sympathy. As illustrated in Figure 16.2, these responses do not have to involve faces, voices, or other visual effects (dancing, etc.) It is also the case that the computer need not refer to itself as having feelings or even refer to itself as "I" (note that there is no embodied character and no "self" referencing in the empathetic dialogues by Klein et al.).

Brave, Nass, and Hutchinson (2005) compared the use of empathic facial displays and text messages by an embodied computer agent (using images of a person's face with different emotional displays) with self-oriented emotional displays and messages. They found that the empathic agent was given more positive ratings, including likability and trustworthiness, as well as greater perceived caring and felt support, compared to either an agent that used self-oriented displays and messages or an agent that performed no emotion-oriented behavior. Drawing from human-human interaction, such findings are no surprise. Comparing the potential applications in human-computer interaction to existing ones in human-human interaction, we find that in many cases there are important outcomes related to use of empathy. For example, in physician-patient interactions, the physician's empathy for a patient plays a significant role in prescription compliance, and a physician's *lack* of empathy is the most frequent source of complaints (Frankel, 1995). A variety of computer scientists and interaction designers have started to imbue computers with various empathetic and even "caring" behaviors, especially for applications in health and education (Lisetti, Nasoz, LeRouge, Ozyer, & Alvarez, 2003; Liu & Picard, 2005; Paiva, Dias, Sobral, & Aylett, 2004; Prendinger & Ishizuka, 2005; Prendinger et al., 2005).

Relational Computers

Affective responses play an important role in long-term relationships between people and have recently become a topic of study in the development of "relational agents," computer characters that are programmed to develop long-term social-emotional relationships with people (Bickmore, 2003). These agents would have application in areas such as health maintenance or addiction treatment, in which long-term compliance is improved by ongoing interaction with an expert helper (and in which spiraling health care costs make it out of the reach of most people to have such a full-time helper).

In one study, an embodied conversational agent, "Laura," was developed to assist people who wanted to walk 30 minutes a day and weren't succeeding yet at this goal yet knew it was important to get exercise (see Figure 16.3). Two versions of the agent were built: one that was friendly, social in its greetings (and farewells), and talked with you about your goals and progress, trying to motivate you in ways that were derived from observations of a human fitness trainer, and a second (the condition of most interest to us) that was identical to the first, but that also tried to develop a social-emotional long-term relationship with you. The latter was always happy to see you, and after some initial interaction it would begin its sessions by asking how you were feeling and responding empathetically with both words and appropriate facial expressions. It also would "move closer" (the animation was zoomed) when you talked about personal topics such as about your feelings, and over time it changed its language in subtle ways, similar to how people change theirs as they get to know you. (Details of all the differences can be found in Bickmore's PhD thesis; Bickmore, 2003.)

Subjects were randomly placed into a group that either interacted with no agent, or with the nonrelational or the relational Laura approximately daily on their home computers for 1 month. The Laura agents "chatted" with them for about 5 minutes a day, giving feedback on their exercise behavior, discussing any obstacles they mentioned about exercise, providing educational content related to exercise, and obtaining and following up on commitments to exercise. The task and goal structure of the dialogues were the same across the two agent conditions, as was the interface and the animations of Laura. The non-agent control condition did not show any agent or conduct a dialogue, but simply presented web forms for filling out information about their walking.

About a hundred people were recruited for a 6-week study in which one-third interacted with nonrelational Laura, one-third interacted with relational Laura, and one-third interacted with a no-agent control. In all cases, subjects were encouraged to log in to the system daily (the average rate of log-in was every other day) and report on their activity, pedometer readings, and (in the two agent conditions) have a short chat with the agent. The principal outcome measure in comparing the relational and nonrelational agent conditions was the Working Alliance Inventory, a 36-item, self-report question-naire used in psychotherapy that measures the trust and belief that the therapist and patient have in each other as team members in achieving a desired outcome (Horvath & Greenberg, 1989). This inventory has three subscales: Bond, Task, and Goal. Although there were no statistically significant differences in the Task and Goal measures after 1 week and after 1 month of interaction with Laura, there were important and statisti-cally significant differences in the Bond subscale. This measure is of particular interest in thinking about emotional intelligence, as it assesses the emotional bond between the helper (software agent) and the helpee (person).

Thirty-three subjects completed the month of interactions with the relational agent, and twenty-seven subjects completed interactions with the nonrelational agent. Subjects were mostly (69%) students and were 60% female (balanced across the two

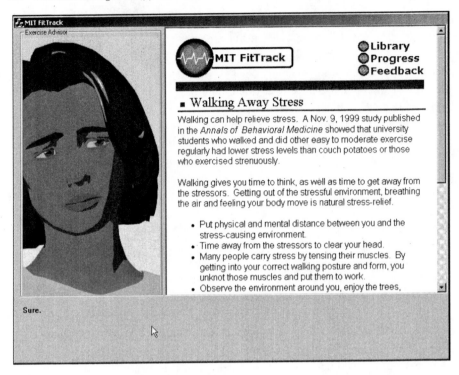

Figure 16.3 Screen shot. Relational agent, "Laura," displaying a look of concern after a user expresses feeling bad.

conditions). Although a full description of the results (including exercise-related outcomes where the two agent groups did better than the control) can be found elsewhere (Bickmore, 2003), key findings relating to emotional intelligence included these significant differences found between the relational and non-relational groups in the predicted direction: in perception that Laura liked them, $t(60) = 2.56$, $p < 0.05$; in trusting Laura and feeling trusted by Laura, $t(50) = 2.05$, $p < 0.05$; in feeling Laura was concerned about them, $t(60) = 2.19$, $p < 0.05$; and in feeling Laura cared about them ("in her own unique way," a clause that was added so that people would not feel entirely silly answering these questions about a software agent that had told them on Day 1 that it was just a computer program), $t(60) = 2.39$, $p < 0.05$. When asked at the end of the month if they would like to continue working with Laura, subjects in the relational condition also responded much more favorably than the nonrelational group, $t(57) = 2.43$, $p = .009$. This measure is of particular importance because the aim is long-term interaction with a technology, and in health-related applications, continuing with a treatment program is related to outcome, and desire to continue with a treatment is likely to facilitate that result as well.

In this study, Bickmore and Picard also obtained a behavioral measure while assessing subjects' feelings of caring toward the agent. Throughout the daily interactions, the agent spoke to the subject, while the subject clicked on text responses to talk to the agent. In the closing session, the text responses for the subjects to bid farewell comprised two choices: "Bye" and "Take care Laura, I'll miss you." Significantly more subjects in the relational group (69%) chose the most sentimental farewell ("Take care Laura, I'll miss you") than in the nonrelational condition (35%), $t(54) = 2.80$, $p = .004$. This behavioral finding is consistent with the interpretation that the relational agent was more successful in eliciting a sense of bond and caring in the people interacting with it. Thus, it suggests that the skills given to the relational agent may bode well for maintaining longer term interactions than when the agent was lacking relational skills (the nonrelational condition).

Summary and the Future

Machines are beginning to be able to sense and recognize human emotion, to respond to emotion with better skills so that negative feelings are less likely to escalate, and to use other skills that can help people develop and assess various abilities and behaviors that contribute to emotional intelligence. These skills are changing the way applications interact with people—agents will show consideration of human feelings and take steps to be less annoying, and applications that deal with customers will show respect for their feelings by acknowledging them and adjusting their behavior in response. The rates at which people curse at their machines, report observations of "colleagues hurling abuse at their machines," and kick their machines should all drop. Experiences with information technologies should become less frustrating and more productive. A variety of new applications will be enabled technology that helps aid individuals in reflection on emotions, and in learning about and developing emotional skills, as well as technology that helps assess such skills.

Motivated by progress building affective agents we have recently begun considering a project to build an Assessment Companion for Emotional Intelligence. This system would target the assessing of how people *behave* in situations that demand emotional intelligence versus testing what they cognitively infer about such situations as in current tests of emotional intelligence such as the MSCEIT (Mayer, Salovey, Caruso, & Sitarenios, 2003). This distinction between knowing and doing, with respect to emotion in cognition, was illustrated by Damasio's (1994) patients, who had frontal lobe and other damage to emotional areas in their brain and yet were able to reason fine about emotional situations. Although they could score fine on pencil-and-paper tests, the situation was quite different when it came to how they behaved. When these patients had to act appropriately, or do the right thing, in real time, in complex social situations, their behavior was far from normal. Although their cognitive reasoning about emotion was fine, their ability to use emotion in action selection was impaired.

Scientists can now begin to build interactive experiences (virtual or virtually augmented environments, social games, and more) that could put emotional intelligence to tests involving behavior, not merely cognitive reasoning. These environments would be engaging, unlike the taking of a long test, which was found to be a problem with teen subjects (Daily, 2005), who indicated that the test was much too long and boring for them to take it seriously.

Although some future testing environments could be built without giving machines emotional abilities, rich assessments with computer role-playing and more could be constructed if the technology could also sense and respond to certain kinds of emotional cues. Thus, giving machines emotional sensing could help them to assess human non-verbal behaviors, and respond to these in ways that "push the boundaries" of people's feelings, allowing for a rich exploration of how they behave in different emotional states. Such machines might have goals quite opposite to those that we are giving to office equipment: In the latter, we aim to reduce frustration, but the assessing companion could aim to maximize it and test how an individual manages himself or herself in the face of difficulty. The computer could deliberately provoke frustration and irritation, and examine its influence on the person's ability to perform under stress.

Our machines will undoubtedly continue to improve in their ability to calm, comfort, and soothe us, to earn our trust and rapport, and to help us in a greater variety of situations. Machines can make use of increasingly sophisticated techniques in how they address our problems. For example, rather than offering just canned empathetic messages or messages indexed to degree of emotional upset (as in Bickmore, Gruber, & Picard, in press; Bickmore & Picard, 2005b; Brave et al., 2005; Klein et al., 2002), they can offer comforting messages that are formulated according to a more fine-grained set of emotional criteria, such as the extent to which a user's feelings are explicitly acknowledged, elaborated, and legitimized; the extent to which the messages are centered on the user's emotions (vs. the computer's actions or the causes of the upset); and whether the empathic messages also contain a cognitively oriented explanation of the user's emotions (Burleson, 1985; Burleson & Picard, 2004). These interventions can also help users reexamine the events that gave rise to their negative emotions in the first place. The aim is not just to build machines that have emotional intelligence, but to build tools that help people boost their own abilities at managing emotions, both in themselves and in others.

References

"Costly computer rage." (1999, May 27). *BBC News.*

Ark, W., Dryer, D. C., & Lu, D. J. (1999). *The emotion mouse.* Munich, Germany: HCI International.

Bickmore, T. (2003, February). *Relational agents: Effecting change through human-computer relationships.* Unpublished PhD thesis, MIT Program in Media Arts and Sciences. Cambridge, MA.

Bickmore, T., Gruber, A., & Picard, R. (in press). Establishing the computer-patient working alliance in automated health behavior change interventions. *Patient Education and Counseling, 59*(1), 21–30.

Bickmore, T., & Picard, R. (2005a). Establishing and maintaining long-term human-computer relationships. *ACM Transactions on Computer Human Interaction, 12*(2), 293–327.

Bickmore, T., & Picard, R. W. (2005b). Future of caring machines. *Future of Intelligent and Extelligent Health Environment, 118,* 132–145.

Bradley, M. M., & Lang, P. J. (1994). Measuring emotion: The self-assessment manikin and the semantic differential. *Journal of Behavior Therapy and Experimental Psychiatry, 25*(1), 49–59.

Brave, S., Nass, C., & Hutchinson, K. (2005). Computers that care: Investigating the effects of orientation of emotion exhibited by an embodied computer agent. *International Journal of Human-Computer Studies, 62,* 161–178.

Burleson, B. (1985). The production of comforting messages: Social-cognitive foundations. *Journal of Language and Social Psychology, 4*(3–4), 253–273.

Burleson, W., & Picard, R. W. (2004). *Affective agents: Sustaining motivation to learn through failure and a state of stuck.* Social and Emotional Intelligence in Learning Environments: Workshop in conjunction with the 7th International Conference on Intelligent Tutoring Systems, Maceio-Alagoas, Brazil.

Costly computer rage. (1999, May 27). *BBC News Online.* Retrieved January 26, 2007, from http://news.bbc.co.uk/2/low/business/353563.stm

Daily, S. B. (2005). Digital Story Explication as it Relates to Emotional Needs and Learning. Unpublished thesis, MIT Program in Media Arts and Sciences, Cambridge, MA.

Damasio, A. R. (1994). *Descartes' error: Emotion, reason, and the human brain.* New York: Avon Books.

Dennerlein, J., Becker, T., Johnson, P., Reynolds, C., & Picard, R. W. (2003). *Frustrating computer users increases exposure to physical factors.* Proceedings of the International Ergonomics Association, Seoul, Korea.

Douglas-Cowie, E., Cowie, R., & Campbell, N. (2003). Speech and emotion [Special Issue]. *Speech Communication, 40.*

Ekman, P., Levenson, R. W., & Friesen, W. V. (1983). Autonomic nervous system activity distinguishes among emotions. *Science, 221,* 1208–1210.

Elliott, C. (1992). The affective reasoner: A process model of emotions in a multi-agent system. Northwestern University.

Fernandez, R., & Picard, R. (2005). *Classical and novel discriminant features for affect recognition from speech.* Interspeech 2005—Eurospeech—9th European Conference on Speech Communication and Technology, Lisbon, Portugal.

Frankel, R. (1995). Emotion and the physician-patient relationship. *Motivation and Emotion 19*(3), 163–173.

Healey, J., & Picard, R. W. (2005). Detecting stress during real-world driving tasks using physiological sensors." *IEEE Transactions on Intelligent Transportation Systems, 6,* 156–166.

Horvath, A. O., & Greenberg, L. S. (1989). Development and validation of the working alliance inventory. *Journal of Counseling Psychology, 36*(2), 223–233.

Huang, T. S., Chen, L. S., & Tao, H. (1998). *Bimodal emotion recognition by man and machine.* ATR Workshop on Virtual Communication Environments.

el Kaliouby, R. (2005). *Mind-reading machines: Automated inference of complex mental states.* University of Cambridge Computer Laboratory.

el Kaliouby, R., & Robinson, P. (2005a). The emotional hearing aid: An assistive tool for children with Asperger syndrome. *Universal Access in the Information Society, 4*(2), 121–134.

el Kaliouby, R., & Robinson, P. (2005b). Real-time inference of complex mental states from facial expressions and head gestures. In B. Kisacanin, V. Pavlovic, & T. S. Huang (Eds.), *Real-time vision for human-computer interaction* (pp. 181–200). New York: Springer-Verlag.

Kapoor, A., Ahn, H., & Picard, R. W. (2005). *Mixture of Gaussian processes for combining multiple modalities.* Proceedings of the Multiple Classifier Systems, 6th International Workshop, MCS 2005, Seaside, CA.

Kapoor, A., Picard, R. W., & Ivanov, Y. (2004). *Probabilistic combination of multiple modalities to detect interest.* International Conference on Pattern Recognition, Cambridge, UK.

Kapoor, A., Qi, Y., & Picard, R. W. (2003). *Fully automatic upper facial action recognition*. IEEE International Workshop on Analysis and Modeling of Faces and Gestures (AMFG 2003) held in conjunction with ICCV 2003, Nice, France.

Klein, J., Moon, Y., & Picard, R. W. (2002). This computer responds to user frustration: Theory, design, results, and implications. *Interacting with Computers, 14,* 119–140.

Lisetti, C., Nasoz, F., LeRouge, C., Ozyer, O., & Alvarez, K. (2003). Developing multimodal intelligent affective interfaces for tele-home health care. *International Journal of Human-Computer Studies, 59*(1–2), 245–255.

Liu, H., Lieberman, H., & Selker, T. (2003). *A model of textual affect sensing using real-world knowledge*. International Conference on Intelligent User Interfaces, Miami, Florida.

Liu, K. K., & Picard, R. W. (2005). *Embedded empathy in continuous interactive health assessment*. CHI Workshop on HCI Challenges in Health Assessment, Portland, OR.

Ma, C., Osherenko, A., Prendinger, H., & Ishizuka, M. (2005). *A chat system based on emotion estimation from text and embodied conversational messengers (Preliminary Report)*. 2005 IEEE International Conference on Active Media Technology (AMT-05), Takamatsu, Kagawa, Japan.

Mayer, J. D., Salovey, P., Caruso, D. R., & Sitarenios, G. (2003). Measuring emotional intelligence with the MSCEIT V2.0. *Emotion, 3,* 97–105.

Mota, S., & Picard, R. (2003). *Automated posture analysis for detecting learner's interest level*. IEEE Workshop on Computer Vision and Pattern Recognition for Human-Computer Interaction, CVPR HCI, Madison, WI.

Paiva, A., Dias, J., Sobral, D., & Aylett, R. (2004). Caring for agents and agents that care: Building empathic relations with synthetic agents. *Proceedings of the Third International Joint Conference on Autonomous Agents and Multi Agent Systems (AAMAS-04)*. New York: ACM Press.

Pantic, M., & Rothkrantz, L. J. M. (2003). Toward an affect-sensitive multimodal human-computer interaction. *Proceedings of the IEEE, 91*(9), 1370–1390.

Picard, R., & Klein, J. (2002). Computers that recognize and respond to user emotion: Theoretical and practical implications. *Interacting With Computers, 14,* 141–169.

Picard, R. W., Vyzas, E., & Healey, J. (2001). Toward machine emotional intelligence: Analysis of affective physiological state. *IEEE Transactions Pattern Analysis and Machine Intelligence, 23*(10), 1175–1191.

Prendinger, H., & Ishizuka, M. (2005). The empathic companion: A character-based interface that addresses user's affective states. *International Journal of Applied Artificial Intelligence, 19*(3–4), 267–285.

Prendinger, H., Mori, J., & Ishizuka, M. (2005). Using human physiology to evaluate subtle expressivity of a virtual quizmaster in a mathematical game. *International Journal of Human-Computer Studies, 62,* 231–245.

Reeves, B., & Nass, C. (1996). *The media equation*. New York: Cambridge University Press.

Reeves, J. M. (1993). The face of interest. *Motivation and Emotion, 17*(4), 353–375.

Reynolds, C. (1999). *Measurement of frustration with computers*. Cambridge, MA: MIT Media Arts and Sciences. (Master of Science thesis)

Reynolds, C., & Picard, R. W. (2005). *Evaluation of affective computing systems from a dimensional metaethical position*. First Augmented Cognition Conference, in conjunction with the Eleventh International Conference on Human-Computer Interaction, Las Vegas, NV.

Tan, H. Z., Lu, I., & Pentland, A. (1997). The chair as a novel haptic user interface. *Proceedings of the Workshop on Perceptual User Interfaces,* Banff, Alberta, Canada.

PART V

CONCLUSIONS

17

Emotional Intelligence

Knowns and Unknowns

RICHARD D. ROBERTS, MOSHE ZEIDNER,
AND GERALD MATTHEWS

In this concluding commentary, we set about the task of reconciling the various perspectives offered by the expert contributors to this edited volume, especially the various answers given to the questions that we posed in Chapter 1. This undertaking is by no means an easy or trivial task as the authors often represent conflicting views on conceptualization, assessment, and applications of emotional intelligence (EI). Even so, we point out how each chapter contributes to the state of the art, the knowns, if you will, of this emerging scientific discipline. We also highlight some areas that seemingly need more detailed consideration (i.e., the unknowns) in order to enhance current knowledge and understanding of EI.

To facilitate the reader's task, we adopt analogous subtitles and reference systems in this chapter as used for the introduction, so that the reader may cross-reference these chapters, if he or she so desires. Wherever possible, we intersperse this review with our own perspective, and in certain instances, additional literatures. It is our intention in these passages to not only distill the various perspectives offered by our expert panel, but also provide some guidelines that will move the program of research concerned with emotional intelligence forward. Of course, this implies a similar systematic approach to the three key areas—conceptualization, assessment, and applications—as used in Chapter 1. Thus, we begin with syntheses and critical analyses of the various contributors who tackled questions posed to them concerning conceptualization.

The views expressed here are those of the authors and do not reflect on the Educational Testing Service.

Key Issues I: Conceptualization of Emotional Intelligence

How Should EI Be Conceptualized? Should It Be a Competence, a Skill, an Adaptive Outcome, a Set of Cultural Beliefs, or Some Other Construct?

Views on conceptualization are diverse. The contributors appear to fall into two main camps. Petrides, Furnham, and Mavroveli, and Burns, Bastian, and Nettlebeck favor the operational, data-driven approach traditional in differential psychology, which emphasizes structural over process models, at least in the early stages of construct validation. We will return to operational definitions in the next section, which addresses the role of emotion theory. The remaining—distinguished emotion, rather than differential—researchers prefer an approach that works forward from emotion theory. We will comment here on two critical issues that emerge from the various chapters: the causal status of EI, and the relationship between EI and adaptation. We cover adaptation in more detail later, but the two issues are intertwined.

EI: Source or Surface Trait?

A persistent difficulty in research on EI is resolving whether we are measuring some superficial expression of more fundamental personal qualities (i.e., adaptive outcomes) or causal entities that influence outcomes (cf. Brody, 2004). In the latter case, is EI some basic aptitude, akin to fluid intelligence, or does it reflect learned competencies and skill that may be molded by culture? As Averill puts it, the key issue is whether EI represents a source or surface trait. The jury is still out on extant operationalizations: Averill's answer to the question posed above is "Any of the above." Indeed, questionnaire assessments have been criticized for criterion contamination; in other words, including items that assess outcomes such as happiness and well-being (Matthews, Zeidner, & Roberts, 2006). In other words, these constructs may blend source traits, surface traits, and outcomes, impeding the prospects for testing causal models.

The "emotions theorists" favor conceptualizations that reflect source traits derived from theory, whether these traits reflect neurological modules for emotion (Rolls), adaptive emotion processes (Izard, Trentacosta, King, Morgan, & Diaz), or emotion competencies (Scherer). These authors seem willing to entertain both innate facets of EI, reflecting genes rather directly, and acquired skills. Averill goes further than these authors in emphasizing the cultural matrix for emotion. Scherer's definition of competence seems especially apt to us. Competencies, like a gardener's "green thumb," generalize across a domain and allow for transfer of skill to new applications. Such a definition of EI allows it to be rather more dependent on learning (and culture) than traditional IQ, and also more than some very specific skill set, like the instructions for watering plants given to a house sitter. The rather catholic conceptualizations of these authors leaves open important questions about the interrelationships of basic aptitudes, competencies, and specific skills (Matthews, Roberts, & Zeidner, 2004), although, as Averill indicates, we may simply need to wait and see which approaches work best.

Adaptation and Self-Regulation

We deal with the issue of EI and adaptation further, below. However, it is worth introducing the topic at this point because adaptation is so central to definition, as stated most explicitly by Izard et al.: "EI derives from the inherently adaptive functions of emotions." The mind has a set of routines for regulation of perception, cognition, and action (e.g., Gross & John, 2003; Kanfer & Heggestad, 1999); EI resides in the effectiveness of these routines. To the extent that adaptive self-regulation is a general psychological function (like perception or memory), EI is a capability that all people share. To the extent that people differ in their competencies for self-regulation, we can seek measurable individual differences in EI. Scherer and Rolls also emphasize the adaptive functions of EI; indeed, Rolls, and to some degree Izard et al., conceptualize EI in a Darwinian sense.

Where do our contributors differ? One of the disparities concerns the functions that support adaptation. Adaptation in some general sense depends on (perhaps many) separate routines for processing emotion and generating action tendencies—routines that must be specified. Indeed, the four-branch model (see Rivers, Brackett, Salovey, & Mayer) starts by specifying four key classes of routine. There is a commonality in the models of Rolls, Scherer, and Izard et al. in that all three relate EI to both lower level (subcortical) and higher level (cortical) processes. However, the attribution of EI to processes including associative learning (Rolls) and primitive sensorimotor appraisals (Scherer) may prove controversial, at least to the extent that insight and self-understanding are central to EI. We may wonder whether EI is exclusively human, or whether lower animals may possess some of the rudiments, as Rolls's analysis suggests. The counterpoint is Hebb's dictum that humans are both the most intelligent and most emotional animals (Averill).

The relationship between emotion and cognition remains problematic. Scherer stresses the importance of distinguishing EI from (cognitive) knowledge about emotion. The four-branch model has been criticized for focusing too much on abstract knowledge of how to regulate emotion, as opposed to procedural skills for actually dealing with emotion (Brody, 2004). Izard et al., too, are at pains to separate emotional from cognitive processes. By contrast, Averill does not support a sharp distinction: "Concepts such as "emotion" and "intelligence" refer to molar behavior interpreted within a social context. Such molar distinctions do not necessarily imply differences in underlying processes" (p. 59).

Averill's chapter is also unique in emphasizing divergent, "creative" elements of EI. Much current work on EI defines it as a "convergent" process. Scherer, for example, claims that we can create criteria for an emotion being appropriate or inappropriate for a given context—there is a "correct" way to feel in a given situation. Averill, however, describes the facility of generating novel, authentic (and somewhat provisional) emotions that may be unique to the person concerned. The idea resonates with Oatley's (2004) call to look more closely at the expertise of real-life paragons of emotional excellence, including creative artists. In cognition, it is claimed (somewhat controversially) that intelligence and creativity appear to become increasingly distinct at higher levels of ability (Sternberg & O'Hara, 2000). Perhaps a similar view may apply to EI. Emotional illiteracy may constrain the full range of emotional functioning, both divergent and convergent processes. At higher levels of emotional competence, the individual's freedom to choose from a range of potentially appropriate emotional stances may become increasingly important.

Is the Concept of EI Compatible With the Existing Theories of Emotion and of Cognitive Intelligence?

Answers to this question hinge on choices of research strategy, in other words, whether contributors favor a theory- or data-driven path. The theory-driven approach is to use a detailed emotional or cognitive theory to identify functions or processes that may vary across individuals, influencing their adaptation to social-emotional challenges. In this case, EI is not just compatible with existing theory, but actively derived from it. For example, Scherer's (2001) appraisal theory explicitly describes processes that plausibly (1) vary across individuals, and (2) influence adaptation. Rolls's (2005) theory does the same from a neurobiological standpoint.

The theory-driven approaches differ in the specifics of how they relate EI to emotion and cognition. Rolls suggests that the explicit system for multistep planning governs cognitive intelligence (and perhaps some cognate aspects of EI), whereas purely emotional competencies may be distributed across a variety of mainly implicit processes. Scherer is careful to differentiate EI from the kind of knowledge that might correspond to crystallized intelligence. Instead, the basic argument is that appraisal is a privileged form of cognition that binds with physiological processes, action tendencies, and so forth to support emotion (see Scherer, Figure 4.1). Izard et al. see emotion and cognition as separate, although interacting, systems. Emotional knowledge is the product of both. The different theories all appear to specify mappings between traits and underlying systems that at least partially discriminate EI from general intelligence, with some overlap. Developing the empirical support for these propositions and testing the theories against one another would seem an important task for future research.

The data-driven approach is to define a construct operationally, as advocated by Burns et al. and Petrides et al. Notably, as these contributions illustrate, operational definitions have advanced from the "laundry-list" approach that exemplified some of the initial attempts at test development. Validation studies map the construct's nomological network and work downward toward its roots and sources. The approach is familiar in personality and intelligence research, but less so in emotion research, in which strong empirical convergence between different responses such as subjective feelings, autonomic arousal, and expressive behaviors is harder to establish (e.g., Eysenck, 1997). Lacking binding theoretical constraints, the operational approach has given us a menu of constructs that are rather differently related to intelligence and emotion. Petrides et al. claim that the Trait Emotional Intelligence Questionnaire (TEIQue) operationalizes EI as a set of personality traits to which emotion is central, without the need to refer in detail to emotion theory. Intelligence theory is irrelevant as EI is definitively allocated to the domain of personality. Conversely, Burns et al. locate the Mayer-Salovey-Caruso Emotional Intelligence Test (MSCEIT) within the ability domain, and their factor analysis demonstrates its status in relation to standard intelligence and personality measures.

Which approach more effectively integrates research on EI with related constructs and theory? In fact, the answer is not clear-cut. The theory-driven approach appears initially more appealing in providing a solid theoretical basis for research from the outset. If, like Rolls, we have a theory that encompasses both emotion and cognition, then the relationship between EI, emotion, and cognitive intelligence should follow naturally. The difficulty is moving from theory to valid measures of individual differences, although the chapters of Scherer and Izard et al. show what can be done in this regard. However, much more work is needed to show whether the actual tests for facets of EI correspond to the processes specified by theory.

At least in principle, the data-driven approach should give us measures that are distinctive from existing individual difference constructs, although, as we have argued in previous critiques (MacCann, Matthews, Zeidner, & Roberts, 2004; Matthews, Zeidner, & Roberts, 2002; Matthews et al., 2004), questionnaire developers have frequently neglected the problem of adequate convergence and divergence. The MSCEIT and Multifactor Emotional Intelligence Scale (MEIS) appear stronger in this regard (e.g., Mayer, Salovey, Caruso, & Sitarenios, 2001), as substantiated by Burns et al.'s data.

A more profound issue is that the mappings between molar traits/abilities and specific processes (of the kind specified by emotion and cognitive theories) may not be straightforward. Personality traits such as neuroticism and extraversion emerge from multiple, discrete psychobiological and cognitive processes (e.g., Zuckerman, 2005). Tracing any single component process for the trait, such as autonomic arousability or sensitivity of reward and punishment systems, does not lead straightforwardly either to the trait or to its behavioral expressions. We need to work with the trait as an independent entity that is resistant to any simple reductionism. Although it is critical to develop approaches founded in strong theories such as those of Rolls, Scherer, and Izard et al., the complexity of process-trait mappings may limit the extent to which the theory will reveal the major individual difference factors. Indeed, both theory- and data-driven approaches confront serious problems in bridging the gap between measured constructs and theory. Perhaps the last word on this issue belongs to Averill. To paraphrase, he states that a practically useful scale for EI, even if conceptually fuzzy, will certainly attract the attention of theoreticians that will lead to scientific advance.

What Are the Key Components, Facets, or Branches of EI?

Discrimination of key components depends critically on whether EI is treated as an ability, or whether it seen as a part of the personality domain. We see partial convergence between some of the ability-minded authors (Scherer, Izard et al., and Burns et al.), as shown in Table 17.1. There are descriptive correspondences between

TABLE 17.1. Correspondences between functional accounts of emotional intelligence or competence.

Mayer-Salovey	Scherer	Izard et al.
Perception	Appraisal	Knowledge (labeling)
Understanding		
Assimilation		Utilization
Regulation	Regulation	Regulation
	Communication	

the three models, along with some notable differences. Regulation is agreed to be a core element of EI. The first row of the table represents the centrality of encoding processes to EI, although appraisal follows perception in information-processing models, and Izard et al. classifies perception as part of the broader category of emotion knowledge. The table expresses Izard et al.'s statement that "the branches of EI that are most similar to emotional knowledge [are] perceiving emotions and understanding emotions" (p. 131). The use of emotions to promote thinking (assimilation, utilization) is a feature of the Mayer-Salovey model and of Izard et al., but not Scherer (although Izard et al. relates utilization to Mayer-Salovey's regulation branch). Scherer appears to be alone in promoting communication as a distinct facet, although Izard et al. briefly refers to expression as a part of emotion knowledge, and the communicative function is an important element of emotions theory (Oatley & Johnson-Laird, 1996).

Table 17.1 suggests some reasonable convergence for the key components and hence a source of optimism. It should be feasible to integrate the models shown into some definitive ability model. Averill's emotional creativity construct might also be added to the list, assuming it could be translated into a behavior-based test. Unfortunately, achieving integration may not be so simple. One concern—to be addressed further in the section on measurement—is whether constructs derived from the different models actually converge. Would Scherer's multimodal recognition tests correlate with MSCEIT scales for emotion perception? The outcome is far from certain. Thus, Roberts et al. (in press) showed that the MSCEIT failed to predict various objective tests related to perception and processing of emotions, including the Japanese and Caucasian Brief Affect Recognition Test (JACBART), Scherer's Vocal-I (a measure of recognition in the tone of voice), and the Emotional Stroop.

Apart from the difficulties of finding a measurement model for the latent constructs, there are conceptual barriers to overcome as well. Rolls's Darwinian analysis suggests that there may be many, more or less independent competencies that contribute to EI, beginning with simple conditioning processes, that may be difficult to accommodate in any coherent taxonomy. Furthermore, the list of major components may not be exhaustive. Weiss and Süß (2005) report on some very careful studies of objective tests for social intelligence, supporting a structural model including factors for social knowledge, social memory, and social understanding (including interpersonal perception). Boone and Buck (2004) also review various measures of decoding the emotions of others. Should we add social constructs to the list of key functions?

A more general difficulty is that listing *functions*—things people can do with emotions—neglects the different processes that may contribute to those functions (Matthews et al., 2004). For example, multiple mechanisms allow us to perceive emotions, including the subcortical pattern recognition facility of the amygdala, explicit and implicit learning of cues to emotion in a given context ("John drinks whisky only when he is unhappy"), and rational analysis ("Xiaoming must be feeling angry given what she's just experienced"). The models reviewed assume that we can carve up emotion at its functional joints, but the multiple processes supporting each function may, in fact, vary independently. To give a simple example, perhaps we should subdivide EI into explicit and implicit components that cut across the functions. Perhaps there are some people who are skilled in the conscious analysis of emotions, and voluntary selection and communication of actions, whereas others have keen intuitions and, seemingly instinctively, connect well with others despite lacking conscious insight.

The Scherer model comes closest to addressing these concerns in differentiating multiple evaluative processes that support the appraisal function (Leventhal & Scherer, 1987). Scherer states that the three levels of processing work together seamlessly, but this may not always be the case; conflicts may arise between lower level "gut feelings" and conceptual analysis. (We also cannot assume that one level is necessarily more reliable than the other; neither gut feelings nor reason are infallible). Echoing Zuckerman's (2005) isomorphism problem, it may also be the case that a given process may contribute to multiple functions. Scherer points out the importance of emotion perception for communication (as well as encoding/appraisal). A final difficulty is that, although each model deals with emotion in the generic sense, there is no obligation for competencies in the different emotions to be directly related. A person may be an emotional genius at acting appropriately when happy but behave like an emotional idiot when angry.

Turning to questionnaire approaches, Petrides et al., on the basis of the "sampling domain" shown in Table 6.2, argue that their trait EI model is superior to its competitors in its discrimination of the key components, although they also note that the inclusion of facets is somewhat arbitrary. It is not our purpose in this chapter to evaluate the respective merits of the TEIQue in relation to other questionnaires for EI. However, we will note that, despite the TEIQue's undoubted merits, it is unlikely that Petrides et al.'s case will end debate. Arguments may be made that the listing in Table 6.2 is both too long and too short. We might wish to exclude some of the facets listed as belonging to other domains. Self-esteem is difficult to distinguish from low neuroticism, for example (Judge, Erez, Bono, & Thoresen, 2002), and assertiveness may be seen as a facet of extraversion (Costa & McCrae, 1992). Other facets, such as happiness, might better be seen as outcomes rather than source traits. There are also constructs that perhaps should be added to the list. For example, what arguably appears as one of the more thorough questionnaire development programs (Tett, Fox, & Wang, 2005) discriminated 10 factors that differ somewhat from those of Petrides et al., falling into three clusters of self-orientation, other-orientation, and emotion sharing.

We cannot resolve the dimensionality of EI without comparing the different instruments empirically. Burns et al. provide an unusually systematic example of work of this kind. Their factor analysis (Table 7.7) recovered the Big Five, a MSCEIT factor, and a cognitive intelligence factor. Of the two questionnaire measures used, the Trait Meta-Mood Scale (TMMS) overlapped substantially with the Big Five, whereas the Schutte et al. (1998) scale was not substantially related to any factor. It is a concern that there seems to be no agreement across studies on the dimensionality of this scale; as Burns et al. discuss, one-, two- and four-factor solutions have all been suggested. Regrettably, questionnaire researchers have been reluctant to perform joint factor analyses of this kind (see Barchard & Hakstian, 2004; Brackett & Mayer, 2003; Gohm & Clore, 2002, for exceptions), but establishing the dimensionality of self-reports should be a relatively tractable problem. However, given the potential problem of overlap and redundancy with existing trait measures, such an effort needs to develop overarching trait models, as further discussed in the passages that follow.

How Is EI Distinct From Existing Personality and Ability Constructs? Could a Multistratum Psychometric Model Integrate a Dimension or Dimensions of EI With Existing Personality and Ability Constructs?

The answer to this question naturally depends on the variant of EI at issue. It is accepted that questionnaire measures tend to overlap substantially with personality, whereas the MSCEIT correlates to a moderate degree with general intelligence. Beyond these findings, the issue is more pressing for the "top-down" theorists than for those working upward from emotion theory. On other occasions we have criticized such theorists for failing to follow through the logic of the operational approach by determining how EI constructs align with personality and ability to an adequate degree (e.g., Matthews et al., 2002). In the present volume, both Burns et al. and Petrides et al. provide informative data.

The study described by Burns et al. shows good convergence between the different MSCEIT branches, and also clearly differentiates the MSCEIT from personality and ability, although the authors caution that a wider range of intelligence tests is needed to fully test the independence of the MSCEIT from intelligence. Indeed, the near-independence of the MSCEIT from cognitive ability is somewhat at variance from other studies that suggest moderate to high correlations between the MSCEIT and intelligence measures (e.g., Barchard & Hakstian, 2004; Schulte, Ree, & Caretta, 2004). The data confirm previous results (e.g., Brackett & Mayer, 2003) showing that the MSCEIT is not redundant with other measures, but it remains unclear how the MSCEIT could be integrated into some general multistratum model of the kind advocated by Carroll (1993).

Specifically, it is unclear whether the MSCEIT is a "one-of-a-kind" test isolated out in the left field of differential psychology, or whether future research will show convergence between the MSCEIT and other ability tests for EI. Lack of convergent evidence remains an issue for this test.

Petrides et al. provide a very clear answer to the question, although one that may be unpalatable to other questionnaire researchers. According to these authors, trait EI is a personality construct, and models of EI should be integrated with dimensional models of personality. This view is supported by the typical linear independence of trait EI from objective ability tests and their estimation that around 70% of the variance in trait EI overlaps with the five factor model. The next step appears to be the development and testing of an explicit multistratum model. Although trait EI scales overlap with several of the Big Five, the precise mappings between the "primary" factors corresponding to Petrides et al.'s Table 6.2 and the "secondary" constructs of the five factor model (FFM) remain unclear.

Development of an overarching personality model also requires attention to other questionnaire assessments that, as we have noted, may add to the variance explained by the TEIQue (e.g., Tett et al., 2005). Burns et al. show that the TMMS overlaps with the Big Five, but the status of the Schutte et al. (1998) scale is in doubt. We suggest that what is needed is a systematic effort to explore the primary factor space of the better trait EI scales, followed by an effort to integrate robust primary factors into the FFM or other general personality models.

Of the remaining contributors, we note that some are reluctant to commit to any position other than the general one that EI constructs derived from theory are liable to overlap with both ability and personality constructs, and these associations require investigation (Averill, Scherer, and Rolls). Rolls adds the interesting point that to the extent that EI depends on his explicit system for multistep planning, it may be hard to separate this aspect of EI from general intelligence. If, as Burns et al. note, the MSCEIT assesses explicit knowledge of emotion (Brody, 2004), it follows that the construct should be brought into general intelligence theory.

Izard et al. have collected data on the interrelationship of their emotional knowledge (EK) and emotional regulation (ER) measures and temperament (personality) and intelligence in their child samples, using longitudinal designs to advantage (e.g., Izard et al., 2001). They accept that both the EK and ER overlap with these constructs, although they can be shown to have independent effects on emotional development. Indeed, there may be bidirectional causal pathways between ER and temperament. Two questions remain. First, as in the case of adult personality, there is a need for detailed structural models interrelating EK, ER, temperament, and ability. Emotional utilization (EU) should also be accommodated once suitable tests have been devised. Second, it remains to be seen how constructs validated in children underpin or correspond to adult constructs. It would be orderly, and scientifically meaningful, if, for example, ER related to emotion management as assessed by the MSCEIT. However, as noted earlier, conceptual correspondences may or may not prove to be supported by future empirical studies.

How Does EI Change Over the Life Span, Quantitatively and Qualitatively?

Broadly, EI increases during childhood as a facet of emotional development, as Izard et al. and Scherer comment. However, as stated in the introductory chapter, there is little hard evidence available on changes in EI during adulthood, although some (e.g., Mayer, Salovey, & Caruso, 1999) have made age-related increases in EI a defining feature of the construct. Against the view that emotional wisdom increases with age, we may point to the decline in fluid cognitive intelligence in adulthood (Horn & Hofer, 1992), and evidence for affective blunting and loss of openness to feelings in old age (Terracciano, McCrae, Brant, & Costa, 2005).

The authors are generally rather noncommittal on this issue. The most direct response is provided by Burns et al., who report a series of comparisons for young and middle-aged adults that suggest higher EI in later life, as measured both by self-report and the MSCEIT. The effect sizes for some facets of EI are quite substantial. The changes in self-report may be connected to the age differences in personality that Burns et al. also report, including reduced neuroticism and increased conscientiousness and agreeableness. The directions of change in the Big Five are consistent with previous findings, although the effect sizes appear to be larger than those usually reported (e.g., Terracciano et al., 2005). The self-report data also contrast with the Petrides et al.'s finding of a 0.16 correlation between age and global trait EI. The MSCEIT data appear to be consistent with other studies (e.g., Kafetsios, 2004).

Burns et al. rightly point out that the data are cross-sectional, and so may be vulnerable to cohort effects. We may wonder whether there are generational differences in norms for emotion management (the most age-sensitive branch) that influence results. Petrides et al. cite studies showing fairly substantial 1-year test-retest reliabilities for trait EI, similar to other personality traits. They also state that there is a lack of longer duration studies, and a lack of data from older age groups. These issues require further data collection.

Izard et al.'s review demonstrates that studies of children appear to be considerably ahead of work on adults. They cite several longitudinal studies, conducted by their own group and others, that show predictive validity for emotion knowledge, even after intelligence and temperament are controlled. The longitudinal studies of Eisenberg and her colleagues (e.g., 2005) provide validation for emotion regulation, although her work often operationalizes regulation as the temperamental factor of "effortful control," calling into question its distinctiveness from temperament. In our view, the next priority for research of this kind is to further probe the underlying neural, emotional, and cognitive processes that mediate the long-term benefits of the various facets of EI in children. For example, there might be several reasons why young children, able to identify and label emotions in faces, effectively go on to develop superior social skills. Izard et al.'s suggestion that emotion knowledge promotes effective communication is plausible, but it leaves open the extent to which the child's knowledge is explicit or implicit. Perhaps emotion knowledge also serves as a proxy index of the emotional supportiveness of the family environment; it may be a by-product of an environment in which parents discuss and train emotional functioning explicitly.

We agree with Izard et al., that there is dynamic interaction between emotion, cognition, and temperament, but—although the task is challenging—the dynamic process might usefully be further specified. Zeidner, Matthews, Roberts, and Mac-Cann (2003) proposed an investment model that, similar to the theory of fluid and crystallized intelligence, describes how temperamental qualities may bias the acquisition of generic, rule-based emotional skills, and, later in development, the acquisition of metacognitive and self-regulative skills, as shown in Figure 17.1. Two features of the model are relevant here. First, EI becomes increasingly multileveled with increasing age. In adolescents and adults, temperamental factors and different sets of skills may become increasingly differentiated, so that there is no strong overarching general factor of EI, consistent with the psychometric evidence. Second, to the extent that acquired skills or competencies are central to EI, a key issue is the degree to which other individual difference factors constrain learning. Figure 17.1 indicates how temperament, ability, and metacognition may impinge on the acquisition of the different elements of emotional competency within a biosocial developmental process. However, as Zeidner et al. (2003) acknowledge, much has to be done to operationalize the constructs and pathways of the model.

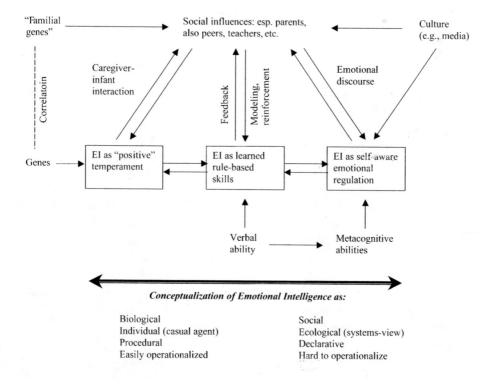

Figure 17.1. An integrated investment model for the development of emotional intelligence.

How Might EI Contribute to Adaptation to Real-World
Social Environments?

Central to Goleman's (1995) popularization of the construct was the notion that
EI is unequivocally adaptive: for communities, for society, and for individuals. This
rosy picture was echoed in some of the early attempts to develop systematic tests for
EI also (e.g., Bar-On, 2000). The selling of EI as a panacea for the ills of the world has
been severely criticized, and it is generally accepted that the overblown claims that followed Goleman's book have no credibility (Murphy, 2006). An especially telling result
comes from Van Rooy and Viswesvaran's (2004) meta-analysis, showing that EI is only
modestly correlated with job performance ($\rho = 0.23$), an effect size similar to those
found for standard personality traits. Other failures to support the grand claims initially
made for EI are documented by Matthews et al. (2002).

The disintegration of Goleman's vision leaves open several more viable possibilities—pessimism, cautious optimism, and a nuanced view of adaptation:

1. EI—at least as assessed by existing instruments—may in fact have only a minor
   role in adaptation, at best. Burns et al.'s failure to find much incremental validity
   for the MSCEIT over intelligence and personality might support a pessimistic
   case, at least for this instrument.
2. EI may indeed be generally adaptive across many areas of life, but its impact
   may often be relatively modest. This perspective is best represented here by
   Rolls, Izard et al., and Scherer.
3. Conceptualizing EI as a personality trait implies that it may confer both benefits
   and costs (Petrides et al.). A related view is that the adaptiveness of EI may
   be evaluated only within specific contexts, rather than in some global sense
   (Averill).

We will explore each one of these possibilities next.

Doom and Gloom?

We will cover the pessimistic standpoint tersely, because our brief here is to
look constructively at prospects for EI research, and we have presented our own critiques of the field elsewhere (Matthews et al., 2002). Even if it is assumed that EI is a
fundamentally misconceived construct, the idea would be hard to kill. Failures to confirm
predictions may be attributed to weaknesses of the specific test used, rather than to the
nonexistence of the underlying latent construct. Hydra-like, there seems no limit to the
proliferation of tests (cf. Petrides et al.). A persistent difficulty has been that when ability and personality confounds are controlled, the incremental validity of both objective
and self-report tests of EI often appears weak (Brody, 2004; Day, 2004). Indeed, even
supporters of the tests have difficulties in demonstrating incremental validity (Brackett &
Mayer, 2003).

The analyses presented by Burns et al. are consistent with a degree of pessimism
(although these authors believe it is worth persisting with EI research). They conclude

that "although EI as measured by MSCEIT correlates with life skills like problem solving, coping, and satisfaction, it has only very limited incremental validity once personality and cognitive abilities have been taken into account" (p. 190). Specifically, Table 7.5 presents 15 incremental R^2 values, crossing five criteria with three EI measures. Five—not one of which involves the MSCEIT—attain significance; additional variance explained by EI measures ranged from 0%–6%. Although several studies suggest some incremental validity for the MSCEIT (e.g., Mayer, Salovey, & Caruso, 2004), its contribution to overall adaptation seems limited.

Petrides et al. include an account of the predictive and incremental validity of trait EI measures. One might raise concerns about the modest variance increments reported in some relevant studies (e.g., Austin, Saklofkse, & Egan, 2005; Saklofske, Austin, & Minski, 2003), failures of trait EI measures to predict as expected (Day, 2004; Fellner, Matthews, Warm, Zeidner, & Roberts 2006), and the reliance of most studies on self-report criteria that may not adequately partition predictor and criterion variance. Also, if we reconceptualize EI as a personality trait, we are left with the oxymoron of examining personality effects with personality controlled. In fact, the issue is how much variance EI explains with higher order traits of the FFM controlled. Primary traits normally explain more variance in criteria than secondary traits, so we should not be surprised to find incremental validity for primary EI traits over the Big Five. The more profound issue is whether we have here anything fundamentally new and different, given that systems of personality primary traits already include dimensions for empathy, impulse control, assertiveness, and so forth. In other words, the challenge is for proponents of EI to show that trait EI defines a coherent subfield of study that can be reasonably separated from the wider world of personality research.

Reasons to Be Cheerful

Evidently, a true ability or competency will be primarily adaptive. It would be difficult to argue with Scherer that accurate appraisals and effective communication are not adaptive, for example. Likewise, a Darwinian analysis (Rolls) also defines adaptive benefits. However, to go beyond mere plausibility, several lines of evidence require development. First, touching on the measurement issues to be discussed in the next section of this chapter, the constructs at issue require solid operationalization. Without valid tests of abilities, no validation is possible. Izard et al.'s work is the most advanced in this respect, although varying for different facets of his model (best for emotional knowledge). Scherer also describes some promising measurement strategies, although further evidence on validity and convergence with other tests is needed. Psychobiological constructs, as described by Rolls, are perhaps the most conjectural at this point. Personality theorists, notably, in recent years, McNaughton and Corr (2004), have made some concerted efforts to identify stable individual differences in brain systems supporting emotion and motivation, with rather mixed results (see Matthews, in press, for a critique).

Second, supposing we have a test showing criterion validity, a sense of its range of relevance is needed. A dubious legacy of Goleman's (1995) thinking is that EI should be important in virtually all areas of life. This need not be so; what may be lacking in research on the MSCEIT and other ability measures is an understanding of the contexts to which the construct is relevant and irrelevant (cf. Averill's comments on context). Similarly, personality research expresses the importance of interactionism in trait expression, leading to a methodological focus on moderator factors. In the EI context, do we really expect that a higher scorer on some test of communication competence will be equally good at inspiring coworkers, at sharing intimacies with a life partner, and setting boundaries for children? Perhaps, but the issue has been largely neglected. We may note also that a competency as defined by Scherer implies some specific context in which the competency is expressed.

Third, caution is needed in discriminating abilities from qualitative styles of emotion processing. Izard et al.'s tests for EK illustrate how some facets of EI are readily operationalized as abilities. Appraisals, too, may be evaluated for "appropriateness" according to a theory of appraisal and emotion (Scherer). Other facets may be more questionable. In particular, emotion regulation is a core feature of most definitions, but it is still unclear what is meant by an *ability* for emotion regulation. We can measure styles of regulation referring to constructs such as suppression, reappraisal, and rumination, for example, but if we evaluate these as more or less competent on the basis of outcomes, the argument is circular.

Fourth, we should be cautious in inferring normal abilities from abnormal findings. Clearly, there are styles of appraisal, emotion management, and communication that are maladaptive in clinical patients (see Scherer). But it does not follow that milder forms of pathological emotion regulation are necessarily maladaptive in nonclinical populations. For example, worry—and especially metacognitive "worry about worry"—plays a central role in generalized anxiety disorder, but normal worries that do not perseverate may be adaptive in focusing problem-solving efforts (Matthews & Funke, 2006; Wells, 2000). Similarly, neuroticism is a vulnerability factor for mental disorder, but many high neuroticism individuals live successful lives in which heightened awareness of threat supports a functional adaptation for anticipation and avoidance of danger (Matthews, 2004).

Thus, an optimistic stance is defensible but raises many unanswered questions, both about the extent to which EI confers substantial, global mechanisms, and about the processes that mediate the benefits of EI. As mentioned earlier, functional descriptions of EI are vague about mediating processes, and there is no guarantee that individual differences in, for example, explicit and implicit processes are mutually aligned.

Nuances and Complexities

A different perspective is that individual differences in emotion processing and regulation are (in fully functioning individuals) rarely adaptive or maladaptive in any general sense (cf. Averill). Research on the impact of coping strategies on stress and well-being demonstrates that strategies are rarely generically harmful or beneficial (Lazarus, 1999;

Zeidner & Saklofske, 1995), despite the tendency of researchers to think "problem-focus good; emotion-focus/avoidance bad." Indeed, it is difficult even to establish sound outcome criteria for evaluating strategies, given that coping has multiple consequences operating over different timescales (Matthews & Zeidner, 2000; Zeidner, Matthews, & Roberts, 2006). Averill rightly indicates the extent to which outcome criteria may be socially and culturally relative. Recent work on coping flexibility (Cheng & Cheung, 2005) captures the notion that appropriate matching of strategy to circumstances may be critical for adaptation, although we are again left with the problem of defining "appropriate."

The various facets of EI may have both benefits and costs. Such an argument is easier to make in the case of personality traits than for abilities. Cost-benefit analyses of traits, as styles of adaptation, provide a means for understanding various standard traits (Matthews & Zeidner, 2004). Petrides et al. make a similar argument for trait EI. For example, high EI may elevate negative mood response to distressing scenes (Petrides & Furnham, 2003); although it should not be taken for granted that negative mood is maladaptive. It may be noted that there is a dark side to many of the facets of trait EI, such as self-esteem (Baumeister, Campbell, Krueger, & Vohs, 2003) and expression of negative emotions (Bonanno, 2004). Furthermore, qualities attributed to low EI may at times be adaptive, including impulsivity (Dickman, 1990) and defensive pessimism (Norem, 2001).

Context-dependence also focuses attention on dynamic interaction between person and environment. Lazarus (1999) has emphasized how the benefits and costs of emotional functioning play out over time, during dynamically unfolding encounters. Figure 17.2 shows how EI may be conceptualized as an "umbrella" covering a set of loosely

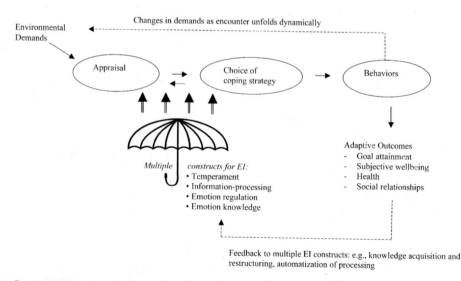

Figure 17.2. A dynamic conception of emotional intelligence within the transactional model of stress.

interrelated influences on the transactional stress processes described by Lazarus (Zeidner et al., 2006). Two forms of dynamic process are distinguished. First, the person's active efforts at coping with the environment feed back to influence his or her emotional competencies, as he or she garners experience with a specific context or challenge; for example, implicit or automatic skills may develop to handle familiar problems. Second, coping behaviors force changes in the external pressures themselves, alleviating or exacerbating demands depending on the adaptive success of coping.

The developmental literature (see Izard et al.) has addressed dynamic issues in more depth than research on adults has done. Children have emotional difficulties not only because of basic temperamental qualities or lack of ability, but because they are exposed to unsupportive family environments, they elicit maladaptive behaviors from caregivers, and, as they grow older, they choose unsuitable friends (Zeidner et al., 2003). As we have suggested, EI is in part a matter of person-environment fit: whether the person's styles of emotion regulation are compatible with external pressures and challenges. The supposedly emotionally illiterate individual may simply have failed to find a compatible emotional niche. Conversely, adaptation may reflect not only the person's competencies as an individual, but the extent to which they share the beliefs and values of those around them (Matthews et al., 2004).

A final nuance that Averill raises is a novel one for EI: emotional authenticity. Is it adaptive to fake the emotions required for the immediate demands of a job or to conform to social norms? If forced to fake, should the person try to believe his or her emotions are authentic or should he or she accept the need to put on an act? Such dilemmas tax emotional creativity. Indeed, professional actors differ in whether they try to authentically experience the emotions of a character (method acting), or whether they focus on more superficial expressions. Cultures may also be sophisticated in handling layers of reality and unreality. Few people believe there is much authentic rage in professional wrestling, but followers of the "sport" presumably manage to suspend disbelief, sometimes knowingly so. It is tempting to say that once the emotionally creative faculties come into play, the adaptive value of the creative interpretation becomes a personalized matter that is difficult to evaluate in an objective way.

Conceptualization: Concluding Remarks

The issues we have covered above underscore the diversity of conceptual approaches to the construct of EI and the vitality of the debate in this area. We will finish this section with just two brief concluding comments.

First, there is diversity not only in conceptualization but in *how* to conceptualize. Table 17.2 lists five alternative strategies for conceptualization that we have covered here (to varying degrees):

1. We can seek to conceptualize EI in terms of its place in *causal models* of emotion (see Averill and Scherer). There remain persistent uncertainties over the extent to which EI depends on some basic aptitudes or learned skills, and the extent to which tests for EI pick up outcomes or antecedents to adaptation.

TABLE 17.2. Five different approaches to conceptualizing EI.

Type of Conceptualization	Key Distinctions
Causal	Source trait, competencies, skills, surface traits
Functional	Perception, assimilation, understanding, regulation, communication, creativity
Operational	Self-report, knowledge about emotions, behavioral
Processing	Neurological, informational, declarative knowledge, procedural knowledge, strategic self-regulation
Contextual	Work, education, intimate relationships, peer relationships

2. Perhaps the most popular approach is *functional*: the specification of how the facets of EI accomplish explicit purposes and goals. There is a partial convergence between different functional models but also numerous unresolved issues.
3. *Operational* definitions seek to develop valid tests for EI that are often rather loosely tied to theories of emotion and cognition. Some progress has been made both with questionnaire and objective assessment of knowledge, but there is a dearth of behavioral measures.
4. *Processing-based* accounts of EI have been rather neglected; we have already signaled the ambiguity of functional accounts in this respect. There is increasing knowledge of relevant neural (Rolls) and cognitive (Scherer) architectures, together with developmental processes (Izard et al.). A marriage between functional and processing-based accounts, in the cognitive science tradition, appears natural. So far, we see flirtation with such notions but no attempts to develop a comprehensive model.
5. Finally, *contextual* accounts of EI have also been rather overlooked. It may be that we need distinct models for understanding emotionally intelligent behaviors at work, in intimate relationships, and in other contexts. Such models may provide better accounts of dynamic person-situation interaction than we currently have, but the challenge is to find general nomothetic principles without degeneration into a sterile social constructivism or entirely idiographic accounts of EI.

Second, this diversity in conceptualizations challenges the prevailing notion that there is some overarching EI waiting to be discovered. Perhaps there are multiple constructs that are largely independent of one another. Matthews, Zeidner, and Roberts (2005) discriminated four elements of "EI" that may merit separate investigation (see Table 17.3): temperament, specific information-processing routines, emotion regulation, and contextualized knowledge and skills. Correlations between the measures we have linked to temperament, information processing, and emotion knowledge rarely exceed 0.3 (e.g., Austin, 2005; Brackett & Mayer, 2003). The distinctiveness of emotion regulation assessed via questionnaire from standard dimensions of temperament is moot; Petrides et al. would likely wish to collapse these two categories. However, we feel that the effort to differentiate elements of styles of monitoring and control over emotion is

TABLE 17.3. Four distinct types of EI construct.

Construct	Possible Current Measure	Equivalent in IQ Research	Key Processes	Adaptive Significance	Developmental Influences
Temperament	Scales for Big Five; TEIque scales	None	Neural and cognitive processes controlling arousal, attention, and reinforcement sensitivity	Mixed: Most temperamental factors confer a mixture of costs and benefits	Genetics and early learning
Information processing	JACBART: Emotional Stroop; DANVA; RAFL	Choice RT, inspection time, working memory	Specific processing modules	Uncertain: Is speed of processing necessarily adaptive?	Genetics and early learning
Emotion regulation	Selected scales from TMMS and TEIQue; Tett et al. scales	Self-assessed intelligence	Self-concept and self-regulation	Predominantly but not exclusively positive	Learning and socialization: e.g. mastery experiences, modeling, direct reinforcement (in emotive contexts)
Context-bound emotional knowledge and skills	MSCEIT	Gc and/or Gk	Multiple acquired procedural and declarative skills	Adaptive within context for learning: May be irrelevant or counterproductive in other contexts	Learning, socialization, and training of specific skills and knowledge

worth persisting with, and some recent research (notably Tett et al., 2005) suggests that dimensions whose correlations with the FFM do not exceed 0.3 or so may be isolated.

The proverb of the sages who attributed the different parts of the elephant to different objects is rather overworked in psychology. The moral, of course, is that seemingly different entities may in fact belong to the same creature. In the case of EI, the proverb may not be so apt. Although researchers tend to assume the existence of the elephant, perhaps in this case they are indeed describing different animals: some rather familiar, some new and interesting, and some entirely mythical.

Key Issues II: Assessment of Emotional Intelligence

As we mentioned in our introductory chapter, one of the more controversial issues surrounding EI research is the thorny problem of assessment, and in particular, how to interpret the available evidence supporting (or otherwise) validity arguments. It is perhaps refreshing to see that this concern is not merely one that chapter authors assigned the task of addressing assessment tackled in isolation. Instead, with rare exception, all of the contributors to this volume have taken up the issue of assessment, pointing to its prevalence in EI research, for better or for worse.

Indeed, the "little problem" of assessment conceivably represents the Achilles heel of establishing a science of EI. Without a clear agenda for changing the status quo in measuring EI, it is plausible that like many psychological constructs that have enjoyed popular appeal but been difficult (or impossible) to operationalize, it will eventually wither and die from scientific discourse (see our earlier views on this in Matthews et al., 2002), or degenerate to a popular fad (see Murphy & Sideman, 2006). Significantly, though, not one of the contributors saw this concern with establishing reliable, fair, and valid assessments of EI as a fruitless exercise, though many new perspectives were offered, and many new challenges set. Given the breadth of expertise evident—recall our experts are variously luminaries in the fields of emotions, cognitive, clinical, educational, differential, social and industrial-organizational psychology, neuroscience, and artificial intelligence—this optimism augurs well for future innovation in the field and, over time, attendant scientific advances.

We introduced the standards for educational and psychological testing (i.e., AERA/ APA/NCME Test Standards, 1999) in our introductory chapter. It is worth noting how many of the contributors similarly used these in buttressing their various arguments, no matter what perspective they had on EI assessment per se. Where there is disagreement, though, is in much of the details, and especially how the available empirical data should be interpreted. For example, validity evidence on self-reports of EI might be construed as promising, if its overlap with personality is ignored. Similarly, in the absence of a definitive theory, it is uncertain whether a small correlation between a measure of EI and intelligence constitutes a challenge to convergent validity or is instead compelling evidence for discriminant validity. Reflecting a desire for more theoretical sophistication, which would feed into stronger claims surrounding validity, almost all of the contributors thought there were problems in how EI assessments had thus far been tied to theory and psychological concepts; this clearly could, should, and must be improved.

What Are the Strengths and Weaknesses of Current Measures of EI?

With one or two exceptions, the contributors seemed to converge on the following points of consensus concerning the strengths of current approaches to EI assessment:

Rightful Concern for Establishing Validity Evidence

The contributors agree that a major strength of the current research agenda on EI is a preoccupation with obtaining construct validity evidence. Many authors did, however, lament that research needs to be conducted with more careful hypotheses specified in advance, rigorous experimental designs, high-level methods, and with a broader selection of instruments that are not based on self-report methods.

The Reliability of EI Measures Is Acceptable

There was surprising consensus on the fact that measures of EI had acceptable reliability coefficients and that early problems associated with reliability (especially for performance-based assessment of EI) had largely been rectified (Burns et al.; Rivers et al.; Schulze, Wilhelm, & Kyllonen). Notably, however, as we mentioned in the introduction, there is still meager information on the test-retest reliability of many measures. This appears a shortcoming worth addressing as more studies are conducted with validated assessments.

Performance-Based Approaches to Assessing EI Are Superior to Self-Report Measures

With rare exceptions (most notably the chapter by Petrides et al. in the theoretical section), another strength echoed by the contributors was the use of ability based (or maximal) approaches to assess EI in preference to those focusing on self-report (or typical) measures. The overwhelming consensus was that this represented an original approach, whereas the overlap between many self-report measures of EI and personality left little room for theoretical, empirical, or practical advances. This perspective appears controversial given the prevalence of self-report measures in the literature, and we will return to it frequently in the ensuing passages.

Equally, however, many of the commentators saw weaknesses with current assessments of EI, and especially the following:

Current Approaches to Scoring EI Tests Are Open to Criticism

The nature of scoring an EI test, particularly the absence of rubrics permitting justifiably correct (or incorrect) solutions, is oft times seen as contentious (Herzmann,

Danthiir, Wilhelm, Sommer, & Schacht; O'Sullivan; Schulze et al.). Because this was an issue that we had the authors consider separately, we will return to it shortly. In fairness, and somewhat ironically, it should be noted that this criticism pertains almost exclusively to objective approaches; self-report paradigms use methods that are tried and true for scoring an individual's response on Likert-type rating scales.

Construct Validity Evidence for Many EI Measures Is Equivocal

Currently, construct validity evidence is simply not as compelling as many of the contributors would have liked. This is a frustrating feature of the field, which has been with us for nearly a decade now (e.g., Davies, Stankov, & Roberts, 1998; Matthews et al., 2002; Roberts, Schulze, Zeidner, & Matthews, 2005). Indeed, for some of the contributors, the often uttered excuse—this is a young science; give it some time and resources, and we will acquire meaningful validity data—is growing wearisome (Schulze et al.). Part of the problem may well rest with the emergence of the two totally different approaches to EI assessment—the validation strategies for each are notably different, and they fail to converge on guidelines and principles when arguably they should do so. For example, in the case of performance-based EI, demonstrating meaningful correlations with other ability measures is deemed an important piece of convergent validity evidence (e.g., Mayer et al., 2004; Rivers et al.). Many proponents working with self-report EI assessments argue the obverse; that near zero correlations with intelligence are desired, because this is evidence of discriminant validity (e.g., Sala, 2002).

What EI Predicts Over and Above Other Psychological Variables Is Uncertain

Evidence demonstrating meaningful relations with important criteria is largely mixed. Some commentators believe there is a growing body of evidence to this end (e.g., Petrides et al.; Rivers et al.); others are less sanguine, particularly when looking for incremental validity over and above cognitive ability and personality (e.g., Schulze et al.). The meta-analyses conducted by Van Rooy and Viswesvaran (2004; see also Van Rooy, Viswesvaran, & Pluta, 2005), mentioned earlier, add further fuel to this controversy. There appear very weak criterion validities for self-report measures of EI and only marginally better results for performance-based assessments.

The Outcomes EI Should Predict Are Uncertain

Related to the preceding point, many of the contributors also urged clearer specification of the exact criteria by which to evaluate the construct validity of an EI assessment. Both Schulze et al. and O'Sullivan, for example, point to a paucity of studies addressing relations between EI and emotions measures (see, however, Roberts et al., 2006). We note the problem may be especially prevalent when one examines issues pertaining to predictive validity for meaningful outcomes. Would one really expect EI to outpredict intelligence if grade point average (GPA) is the criterion, where currently in America, under No Child Left Behind legislation, premiums are placed on reading and math performance? And yet there is a raft of studies, with generally equivocal outcomes, in which GPA is the criterion of interest (see also Barchard, 2003). Instead, meaningful relations between noncognitive criteria such as drug and alcohol use, relationship quality, social support, the ability to cope with stress, psychological well-being, and so forth (many reviewed in Rivers et al.) seem far more logically compelling. Indeed, if the criterion were more meaningfully specified in advance (and tied to psychologically informative theories of human behavior), we wonder what the meta-analyses reported by Van Rooy et al. (2004, 2005) would have uncovered.

The Field Has Been Saturated With a Variety of Questionable Self-Report Measures

Although not always said so bluntly, many of the commentators also lamented that there had been too much reliance placed on self-report measures and that the sheer plethora of these was not necessarily a healthy sign for the science. Indeed, as we will argue later, with suitable caveats, many commentators were suspicious that any form of ability could be measured using this approach. Reasons for focusing on this assessment device appear generally based on pragmatic considerations rather than a solid, theoretical rationale. Notably, self-reports can be administered in a short time frame, require less advanced knowledge of psychometrics and nuanced conceptual issues, can be scored by an individual with minimal training, and seemingly as a combination of each of these factors, can lead to a publication, dissertation, or conference paper in a fast turnaround period (certainly much faster than one can do with objective measures of EI).

There Are Too Few Comprehensive Measures of Performance-Based EI

Many of the contributors pointed out the lack of options with respect to performance-based assessment. Although Rivers et al. at times rightly point to the MSCEIT as being the only comprehensive measure of various first-order factors of EI, other commentators argue for the need for viable alternatives, or point to constructs that appear pivotal but that the MSCEIT tends to ignore (see especially Ortony, Revelle, & Zinbarg). As in business, competition in science often breeds innovation; there is clearly a need for alternative, comprehensive performance-based assessments.

What Is the Optimal Approach to the Assessment of EI?

There can be little doubt that with two possible exceptions (Jordan, Ashkanasy, & Ascough; Petrides et al.), the contributors to this volume are not especially sanguine about the future prospects of research that uses self-report assessments of EI. Opinions range from this being a rather innocuous, perhaps even facile, exercise (e.g., O'Sullivan) to a belief that this is dangerous and inhibitory to scientific progress (e.g., Herzmann et al.; Schulze et al.). Usage of the term "trait EI" to describe this domain clearly rankled several of the commentators, who point out the redundancy of the nomenclature (and the attendant need to differentiate it from "ability emotional ability," as O'Sullivan puts it). The attack on the self-report approach is not one steeped merely in conceptual nuances; the vast majority of contributors base their arguments against it on logical grounds, historical precedent, hard data, and/or best scientific practices. Notably too, many charged with addressing theoretical issues (e.g., Burns et al.), break from this focus to point to major problems in the self-report assessment that they examined. And in one instance, a group that has developed a self-report instrument virtually apologizes for its existence (Rivers et al.).

Indeed, if expert consensus provides something approaching truth (as several EI researchers would have it), then self-report approaches should no longer be considered viable approaches to the assessment of EI. Elsewhere, we have suggested that it may be time to call for a moratorium on developing still further idiosyncratic self-assessments of EI (Matthews, Emo, Roberts, & Zeidner, 2006). Indeed, a purview of a random selection of self-report EI measures suggests poorly written items that might not stand tests from content experts, fairness review, or more in depth linguistic analyses (i.e., many of the items permit double meanings). Of course, the existence of many poor questionnaires should not condemn those that have been developed systematically (see Petrides et al.). Nevertheless, there seems to be a ground swell of opinion in this book that the future of EI research rests in finding assessment vehicles that are more objective and less open to faking, coaching, and self-deception biases.

The arguments against self-report EI are compelling and may, its few advocates aside, be summarized as follows:

Self-Report Measures of EI Are Often Atheoretical

There is a limited support for using self-report assessment as a basis for generating sophisticated theoretical models of EI. Indeed, even the staunchest advocates of this approach to EI in this volume—Petrides et al.—would seemingly have the assessment that they champion be considered part of the personality sphere. So be it. The suggestion should be followed, and future efforts directed toward including so-called trait EI inside differential models of personality. Because it is unclear what advantage retaining the term *EI* has in this case, we would encourage a change of nomenclature; for whatever is measured using self-report techniques, it does not subscribe to a form of intelligence. This change in focus would not denigrate those who use self-reports, though they would be required to shift at least some portion of their theoretical and practical approach to slightly different issues. For example, a major question that would arise is how best to locate each facet of EI within already existing models of the Big Five, such as that espoused by Costa and MacCrae (1992), Tupes and Christal (1992), and others (see, e.g., Schulze & Roberts, 2006). We will return to this topic shortly.

Self-Report Measures of EI Are Questionable Predictors, Independent of Personality

There is limited predictive validity evidence for self-report assessments when personality variables are taken into account. Though reiterated in virtually all of the contributors, this is evident, firsthand, in the empirical study that is presented by Burns et al. It is not sufficient to include broad assessment of Big Five factors as a control variable in many instances, because we know from personality research that facets can sometimes provide more meaningful validity coefficients. In the absence of a systematic program of research using facet level personality and facet level EI measures, and comparing this with external criteria, the source of a validity coefficient remains open to question.

Self-Reports of EI Have Limited Application in Many Practical Settings

There are limited practical applications that flow naturally from self-report assessment; though this shortcoming can be circumvented if one combines this technique with other approaches such as peer reports, structured interviews, and the like (see Vachon & Bagby). The most general difficulty is establishing that a change in self-report scores—perhaps induced by a training manipulation—actually reflects a meaningful change in emotional functioning. Changes in self-reports might simply reflect demand characteristics or the result of focusing the respondent's attention on their own emotions. The problem of faking self-reports merits special concern.

Self-Report Measures of EI May Be Faked, Coached, or Otherwise Distorted

Faking represents an important threat to validity in self-report assessment, and appears worthy of considerably greater attention than given in the past for these forms of assessment. We know largely from industrial-organizational studies that instructions to fake influence scale means (Viswesvaran & Ones, 1999), correlational structure (Ellingson, Sackett, & Hough, 1999; Holden 1995; Topping & O'Gormon, 1997), and scale validities (Holden & Evoy, 2005). In general, instructions to fake result in a boost in scale means (of the order of half a standard deviation), a reduction in the dimensionality of scale scores, and a reduction in validities against various outcomes.

Respondents may provide socially desirable responses, extreme responses, or engage in acquiescence. These may implicate different detection and remediation methods, which are seldom implemented in EI research. For many uses of EI tests, socially desirable responding may be the most important type of faking. An important distinction in socially desirable responding is between self-deceptive enhancement and impression management (e.g., Messick, 1991; Paulhus, 1984; Sackheim & Gur, 1978). There may be other independent dimensions as well, such as faking for sociability (e.g., altruism, warmth), personal effectiveness (e.g., self-discipline, competence, achievement striving), open disclosure (e.g., straightforwardness), and bold innovation (e.g., excitement seeking; Holden & Evoy, 2005). It is noteworthy that many of the contributors pointed to these various sources of validity threat to self-report measures of EI. Curiously, aside from the implementation of scales alleged to detect distortion (the actual veracity of which have never really been tested), these types of issues have been given scant attention by proponents of the self-report approach to measuring emotional intelligence.

In sum, we believe, perhaps contentiously, but in the spirit of the apparent consensus reached by the present contributors, that it is perhaps time to advocate new directions for research that focuses on self-report assessment of EI. In particular, we advocate the following:

Recommendation 1: Replace the term "trait EI." Researchers should find a new term for trait EI, and study this construct as a domain of personality, rather than as an emerging new psychological construct. As is, it is a construct that is simply confusing and has seemingly resulted in obfuscation and blind alleys within a young science seeking to develop reliable, valid, and fair assessments.

Recommendation 2: Place self-report EI inside taxonomic models of personality. In the event of this recommendation being followed, we contend there may be important advances in models of personality that might ensue. For example, one of the major strengths of the Big Five personality model is its basis in natural language and lexical analyses that have been able to uncover the factors across cultures (see, e.g., Matthews, Deary, & Whiteman, 2003; Saucier & Ostendorf, 1999). There is a need to investigate whether "trait EI" is similarly embedded in language, although it is questionable how distinctive it is from existing affective traits, notably neuroticism–emotional stability). Saucier (e.g., 2000) has recently found evidence for social attitudes tied to analyses of the so-called "–isms," and perhaps a similar approach is necessary to locate whatever is measured by self-reports of EI—what we might now refer to as the construct formerly known as trait EI (CFKTEI)—and its place in personality models. It is equally important to document what facets of CFKTEI go with what superorder constructs of the Big Five, in the event the evidence for them being an independent construct is not obtained.

Recommendation 3: Always include personality measures when researching self-report EI. Granted that both of these recommendations might be conceived of as being entirely too radical, we suggest something that should be more palatable for even those who remain optimistic about the future of trait EI approaches. Minimally, the overlap between trait EI and personality demands that any published research with self-report assessments of EI also include a measure of personality in the design to rule out rival hypotheses. In particular, the hypothesis that the source of the correlation between some criterion (whether it be stress, adaptability, job and academic performance, or satisfaction with life, to name a few) and the self-assessment of EI is not the result of personality factors. The best work in this area (e.g., Petrides et al.; Tett et al., 2005) already follows this recommendation, but too many studies fail to do so. Publishers, editors, and academics supervising graduate students would do a service to the science by rigorously controlling for overlap between trait EI and established personality constructs; though we expect at the same time a reduction in the number of studies that would be published on "trait EI."

Recommendation 4: Systematically investigate and document the influence of faking on self-report EI. To ascertain the impact of faking and other response biases on self-report indices, it is necessary to obtain far more information on the threat this poses to validity than currently is the case. We envisage here a number of studies designed to ascertain the degree, scope, and consequences of faking on "trait EI" approaches. These studies would need to take several forms. For example, one investigation might ask participants to "fake good" and to "fake bad" in the various self-report EI measures available, and examine mean performance, structural properties, validity indices, and so forth. Such approaches are already well-developed in other personality and applied research (e.g., Heggestad, Morrison, Reeve, & McCloy, 2006). Another might attempt to gauge the effects of faking using psychometric approaches, such as mixture models (Zickar, Gibby, & Robie, 2004). Still other studies might explore whether faking and acquiescence scales, sometimes used in this approach (e.g., Bar-On, 1997), have anything at all in common with those with a scientifically reputable track record.

Recommendation 5: Hold a moratorium on further self-report assessments purportedly assessing EI. A moratorium on the development of still further self-report assessments of EI is needed, at least until we understand what it adds to existing models of personality and individual differences. The sheer number of these measures is rather alarming (see, e.g., Perez, Petrides, & Furnham, 2005, for a review), and continues to grow apace (e.g., Tett et al., 2005). Very few of these instruments have been developed according to best practices in scale construction, and very few (if any) extend beyond what are ostensibly operational definitions of a construct that requires clearer theoretical demarcation (Matthews et al., 2002; Roberts et al., 2005).

All of the above is not to suggest that the contributors to this edited volume were especially sanguine about the current state of the art with performance-based assessments. Clearly, Ortony et al., O'Sullivan, Schulze et al., and Herzmann et al. point to some considerable problems with current operational definitions of EI (based on performance measure, which qualifier we will drop in the remainder of this passage following our previous comments on self-reports). Consider thus, some of the issues raised by the contributors concerning the most oft discussed measure, the MSCEIT (and to a lesser extent its predecessor, the MEIS):

Construct Validity Evidence Is Scant

As mentioned by virtually all of the commentators, there are a large number of studies exploring relations between the MSCEIT (or MEIS) and cognitive abilities (e.g., Brackett & Mayer, 2003; Ciarrochi, Chan, & Caputi, 2000; Lopes, Straus, & Salovey, 2003; Roberts, Zeidner, & Matthews, 2001; Schulte et al., 2004; to cite but a few). In general, these provide convergent validity evidence as the correlations between EI and psychometric g, crystallized intelligence, or a verbal primary mental ability are moderate. There are similarly a large number of studies showing low to moderate correlations with the Big Five personality factors, testifying to divergent validity evidence (which has proven difficult for proponents of trait EI approaches to demonstrate, as noted above). Finally, there are a large, and growing, number of studies showing meaningful correlations with important criteria, such as social support, friendship quality, and ability to cope with stress (Rivers et al.).

Arguably, however, construct validity evidence is scant. Indeed, this is explicated at length by a number of the commentators. Thus, we have no validity data showing mean differences on the MSCEIT for experts (these might take the form of truth wizards or clinicians, depending on the commentator's perspective) and novices (Ortony et al.; O'Sullivan; Vachon & Bagby; cf. Oatley, 2004). Nor do we have a systematic body of research showing relations between the MSCEIT and classic emotions measures (O'Sullivan; Schulze et al.; see however, Roberts et al., 2006). Various claims have been made about the life span trajectory of EI, but again there have been a paucity of studies exploring different age groups (see, however, Burns et al.). The direction and the extent of ethnic, cultural, and gender differences seem to be tackled in a largely ad hoc, and piecemeal, fashion.

Indeed, a staunch critic might lament that even relations between the MSCEIT, cognitive ability, personality, and external criteria are not sufficiently well-known. Thus, no studies were mentioned by any of the commentators that explored relations between spatial measures and the MSCEIT subscales that are based on pictorial materials. Indeed, taking Carroll's (1993) three-stratum model, there are a remarkable number of first and second stratum constructs that have yet to be explored in relation to EI, several of which may be relevant (i.e., all of the primary mental abilities underlying crystallized abilities, broad second-order constructs tied to memory, and so forth). There is a hint, too, that the relation between agreeableness and the MSCEIT may be psychologically meaningful; both consensus scoring and this Big Five factor construct have something to do with social conformity. However, the source of this correlation is poorly understood, certainly at the facet level. Moving on to criteria, some potentially important outcomes constituting construct validity evidence include persistence, retention (in the school and workplace), happiness, and psychological well-being. However, the psychological processes mediating these relations are either yet to be explored, or else have been given only cursory treatment. Moreover, few, if any, studies make a compelling theoretical argument as to why a relation with a specific outcome is expected of the MSCEIT, making what constitutes (or does not constitute) construct validity evidence equivocal.

There Is an Array of Social and Emotional
Measures That Could (and Should) Be Explored
as Viable Alternatives (or Complements) to the
MSCEIT

There was great agreement among the commentators, as we have alluded to previously, for the need for objective indices other than the MSCEIT. Various candidate measures from the emotions literature reviewed by the commentators include the Levels of Emotional Awareness Scale (Lane, Quinlan, Schwartz, Walker, & Zeitlin, 1990), EARS (Mayer & Geher, 1996), JACBART (Matsumoto et al., 2000), Vocal-I (Scherer), DANVA-2 (Nowicki, 2004), and PONS (Rosenthal, Hall, DiMatteo, Rogers, & Archer, 1979). This list is by no means exhaustive, and it bears mentioning that various emotions paradigms used with children and adolescents that were covered by Izard et al. could also be extended upward to assess adult participants. Similarly, O'Sullivan comments briefly on the fact that several social intelligence measures might be modified, especially in light of new technologies, to fit into an extended EI model. Indeed, it is largely through technological and methodological sophisticated techniques that Herzmann et al. are able to make a case for exploring measures of face processing as a still further assessment of emotional intelligence. In arguably the most innovative take on this problem, Ortony et al. implore researchers to consider the development of EI measures assessing more fluid capacities.

Although the vast majority of suggested measures have undoubted merits, some cautionary notes are requisite. First, not all of the paradigms mentioned by the commentators were developed as individual differences measures; it may be necessary to devote some resources to ensure these are reliable and valid for the purpose of assessment. Second, because it is likely that the reliability of these experimental measures will be marginal, they may require important modifications, and hence "new" validity studies. Finally, there may be certain design features of these tasks that researchers will need to take into account should validity evidence on them be acquired. For example, in the JACBART, items are presented very briefly to participants; if looking for construct validity evidence for such a measure, it might be judicious to include measures of cognitive speed along with it, so that the source of the correlation is well understood (cf. Austin, 2005).

Finding a Defensible Rubric for Scoring EI Tests Is a Nontrivial Undertaking

There remains the issue of scoring the MSCEIT, which we turn to later in this chapter. Suffice to say, this may represent the biggest challenge yet to a defensible assessment of EI using more ability based approaches. However, in posing the questions in the way that we did, there do appear some candidate measures from pure emotions research that hold the potential of getting around some of the limitations evident in the MSCEIT.

Summing up the views of the contributors to this volume, we propose the following recommendations for advancing a science of performance-based assessment:

Recommendation 1: A concerted effort is needed to develop and validate additional objective EI assessments. Whereas for self-reports, we called for a moratorium on the development of still further instruments of a "unique" kind, with respect to more objective indicators of EI there is clearly a need for more expansive assessments. The MSCEIT appears a novel assessment suite, and yet there are a range of classic emotion measures, information-processing, developmental, situational judgment, and experimental paradigms that might be considered viable alternatives. Indeed, our review of conceptualizations concluded that we may be able to operationalize diverse performance-based "EI" constructs, which may prove to be only weakly related, if at all. We will return to this topic later in this chapter.

Recommendation 2: Expand the construct space of EI assessments. In particular, there would appear a need for the development of assessments of what Ortony et al. refer to as the more fluid abilities of EI. One promising idea that they advocate is the use of portfolio assessment methods, an idea that Vachon and Bagby similarly champion for clinical applications, especially assessment of alexithymia. It should not go unnoticed, too, that a range of classic, fluid measures of cognitive abilities, have much in common with traditional measures of cognitive processes such as working memory and speed of information processing (see, e.g., Roberts, Markham, Zeidner, & Matthews, 2005).

Recommendation 3: Use state-of-the-art approaches to develop objective EI assessments. It would be expedient for EI researchers to use the most contemporary models to develop and validate their tests. One such approach is evidence-centered design (ECD), discussed quite extensively by Schulze et al. (see Figure 8.1). The framework may be used to guide test development, construction, and implementation. We believe that principled application of this approach holds the potential to move the field of EI assessment forward, possibly into operational settings. In any event, minimally, such a design approach requires the researcher to more carefully stipulate hypotheses and claims well in advance of data collection.

Recommendation 4: Develop a taxonomy of objective EI measures. The field needs development of a taxonomic model, similar to those constructed for ability measures by Carroll (1993), Cattell and Horn (1978), Ekstrom, French, and Harman (1976), and others. Currently, the four-branch approach is the closest approximation to this frame of reference, but the diversity of the measures reviewed by all of the contributors to this volume suggests that there is scope for many more first-order factors (i.e., primary mental abilities) of EI. For example, where might information-processing measures fit into a stratum model of EI (Carroll, 1995, places them as meaningful, independent constructs in his three-level model of cognitive abilities)? Could there be an emotional processing speed factor of the kind investigated by Austin (2005) in addition to the four branches? As mentioned in Recommendation 2, if we take Ortony et al.'s suggestions on board, we should be able to develop fluid indicators of EI. In addition, there are the concepts of emotional creativity (Averill), lie detection (O'Sullivan), and elements of face processing (Herzmann et al.) that stand out in the current volume, which might also be subsumed in an overarching taxonomy of emotional abilities. A pivotal aspect of developing such an overarching taxonomic model would be how it relates to social (Kang, Day, & Meara, 2005; Weis & Süß, 2005) and practical (Sternberg & Grigorenko, 2000) intelligence constructs, and its overall relations with the major frameworks of cognitive ability constructs.

Can Self-Reports and Questionnaires Ever Provide
Assessments of Intelligence and Competence?

Somewhat paradoxically perhaps, given many of the concerns raised with questionnaire assessments, the contributors, by and large, are somewhat less committed on this point. Indeed, more than a handful believe that there are closely related constructs that are most often measured using the self-report, including alexithymia (Vachon & Bagby), emotional creativity (Averill), metamood (Rivers et al.), and emotional engagement (Schulze et al.). Historical precedent again appears apposite. Constructs such as typical intellectual engagement (Goff & Ackerman, 1992) and metacognition (Schraw & Dennison, 1994) are thought to be key ingredients in relatively complex models of intelligence and cognitive competencies (e.g., Ackerman, 1996; Sternberg, 1990), and are often assessed using self-reports and questionnaires. It is simply both premature and likely antiscientific to dismiss a methodology—self-reported assessment—until all the evidence is in and the theoretical models of EI are more fully developed. Nevertheless, self-report is likely more promising for measuring relevant personality, motivational, and self-regulative constructs that influence the behavioral expression of EI than for abilities per se. Thus, the contribution of self-estimates of EI may depend on advances in the development and validation of objective indicators of emotional intelligence, something that currently appears more imagined than real.

What Are the Most Prevalent Scoring Procedures for EI
Measures, and Are They Valid for Ability Measures?

The commentators broached the first part of this question with a good deal of caution, generally describing in precise detail the three prevalent scoring techniques—consensus, expert, and target—without necessarily advocating one above the other. There was general agreement that application of advanced psychometric models might be useful to address this problem, although the exact details surrounding the types of techniques that might prove especially useful were sketchy. By contrast, a good many of the commentators attempted to tackle the second part of this question (i.e. the issue of how valid these approaches are) head on. However, we do not believe that there is, as yet, a clear answer to this question.

Gleaning the various commentaries offered up on this issue, there appear three major issues that led to this impasse. The first is that holding EI up to the high standards demanded of a form of ability virtually requires the establishment of veridical scoring standards, answers varying along a continuum from right to wrong. Second, in the absence of the development of such a scoring system, one can never rule out rival hypotheses depending on the scoring rubric adopted. Thus, in consensus scoring, it remains unclear whether the construct being measured is nothing other than the degree of a person's conformity to social norms. By contrast, in expert scoring, expertise is difficult to determine, and it is doubtful that academic psychologists are the best exemplars. Who has objectively verifiable expertise in handling emotional encounters, stressful situations, or perceiving when a person is happy or sad? Similarly, in target scoring, how can it be determined that the target has meaningful, declarative knowledge of his or her implicit behaviors? Finally, many other viable candidates for the assessment of EI have yet to be explored. Several of these paradigms rely on alternatives to consensus, expert, or target scoring (e.g., response latency), and may eventually supplant existing strategies for scoring.

What Are the Prospects for Assessment of EI Using Psychophysiological, Developmental, and Neurological Measures?

As with conventional personality and ability constructs, explication of the biological basis of EI is likely to play a critical role. Indeed, two theoretical chapters, one by Rolls dealing with neuroscience, the other on emotional development by Izard et al., support the potential of these respective approaches to provide alternative assessments of EI. O'Sullivan adds to this sentiment with a review of several fMRI studies that appear suggestive, noting that these certainly appear important means of validating psychometric assessments of emotional intelligence. Indeed, brain-imaging studies of EI are beginning to emerge (e.g., Jausovec, Jausovec, & Gerlic, 2001).

However, caution is needed for several reasons. First, given that all tests for EI are correlated with ability and/or personality factors that are known to correlate with brain functioning—and the small Ns typical of fMRI research—it may be challenging to contrast high and low EI individuals free of ability and personality confounding. Second, correlations between EI and activation of brain systems may not be easy to interpret. The natural assumption might be that EI would relate to higher activity of brain areas linked to emotion. However, in intelligence research, there are reports of both positive and negative correlations between brain activation and intelligence (see Neubauer, Grabner, Freudenthaler, Beckman, & Guthke, 2004). Negative correlations suggest an "efficiency" hypothesis, in other words, that more intelligent individuals can effect information processing with less expenditure of energy (i.e., glucose metabolism). In the case of EI, do we expect that more able individuals will process emotion more efficiently (lower activation) or that they are more likely to engage emotion centers during task performance (higher activation)? The more general point is that simply establishing activation correlates of EI may not be very informative; it is important also to demonstrate the functional significance of individual differences in activation.

Some of the more narrowly defined components of EI may be especially amenable to the use of psychophysiological and neurological measures. Indeed, one group of contributors—Herzmann et al.—spent virtually an entire chapter addressing this issue in the special case of face processing. We may wonder whether a focus on face processing per se takes us too far from EI as a distinctive and novel construct. Seemingly feeling this pressure, we note that the links between EI and face processing are sometimes tenuous in the Herzmann et al. account. It may not be wise to succumb to the temptation to define EI in terms only of those components that are readily "biologized." In the absence of empirical data, we refrain currently from being too critical. Instead, we would encourage these contributors to provide the necessary theoretical and empirical linkages in a systematic body of work.

Though applied in focus, Picard's account also shows the promise of various psychophysiological apparatus. In particular, she reports promising correlates of teacher's ratings of student affect from measures of chair pressure patterns (assessed with a device that records how postures shift during learning), upper facial features (captured using a sophisticated video camera and analyzed with a proprietary algorithm), and a skin-conductivity sensing glove that communicates wirelessly with the computer (see also Picard et al., 2004). Such technologies may serve to regulate interactions between both humans and machines.

What Are the Prospects for Assessment of EI Using Information-Processing Tasks?

The near universal response to this question was that the various contributors envisaged this as a particularly useful methodology, especially for constructs lower in a hypothesized hierarchical model of emotional intelligence, in other words, emotion perception. Three paradigms were mentioned on several occasions: the emotional inspection time task (e.g., Austin & Saklofske, 2005), the Emotional Stroop (McKenna & Sharma, 1995), and the Implicit Association Test (Greenwald, McGhee, & Schwartz, 1998). (O'Sullivan perhaps rightly includes measures of emotion perception like the JACBART in this list because they are often speeded; we choose to treat them separately because accuracy remains the dependent variable of interest). The advantages that this group of information-processing measures shares over extant measures of EI include:

  a. Response times may be measured on a ratio scale; unlike the problematic consensus scoring, it is measurement in the strictest sense of the term.
  b. Experimental manipulations (leading to indices of complexity/difficulty) are possible.
  c. Information-processing measures, such as the Hick, Stroop, and Posner paradigms, are part of established models of human cognitive abilities (e.g., Roberts & Stankov, 1999); it is likely that information-processing measures would similarly be important in EI models.
  d. Speed, power, and level are all part of full-blown models of cognitive abilities (Carroll, 1993), and there are likely important parameters in the emerging domain of emotional intelligence.
  e. Information-processing tasks have proven useful in developing more elaborate theoretical models of human cognitive abilities (e.g., Jensen, 1998; Roberts & Pallier, 2001), and perhaps they can serve a similar purpose in the realm of emotional intelligence.

Nevertheless, there are certain problems with information-processing measures that are worth mentioning in the current context:

  a. No operational test uses speed of information processing indices in isolation; cognitive tests (e.g., Wechsler, Woodcock-Johnson) include assessment of these parameters, but as an adjunct rather than replacement for other forms of cognitive abilities.

b. Face and content validity need to be considered when making operational tests; in general, chronometric information-processing measures are less face valid for the assessment of many constructs than are those based on accuracy.

c. The data that are obtained from information-processing measures are often unwieldy; participants can have very long reaction times that require data cleaning and manipulation to deal with outlying scores.

d. An issue oft noted for cognitive speed measures is the so-called speed-accuracy trade-off problem. Some participants will "cash-in" speed for accuracy, whereas others will concentrate on accuracy at the expense of speed. Because profiles on these two dimensions will vary, it is uncertain how to equate them. This problem is arguably minor for theoretical modeling, but can be difficult to circumvent (and certainly justify) if a test is used to make real-life decisions.

e. Even in the case of cognitive intelligence, it cannot be assumed that faster is always better; slower encoding, on occasion, constitutes a marker of higher intelligence (Sternberg, 1985). It seems plausible that sometimes slow, deliberative processing may be more "emotionally intelligent" than a snap decision. In addition, countering the prevailing trend to link EI to happiness, it seems that negative moods often elicit more careful, systematic processing, whereas happiness may bias more casual styles of processing.

f. Finally, in the case of tests like the Emotional Stroop, which have generally been used with clinical populations, the jury is still out on whether such procedures will provide meaningful individual differences in normal adults (see Roberts et al., 2006). In this instance, it is worrying that alternate measures of attentional bias fail to correlate with one another (Dalgleish et al., 2003), calling into question the reliability of the construct.

What Are the Prospects for New Techniques, Such as the Situational Judgment Test (SJT) Methodology and Applications of Advanced Psychometrics, Leading to Improved Assessment?

Largely, the contributors gave this double-barreled question limited scope, though there was a general consensus for the need for both new techniques and advanced psychometric models. With respect to the former, the staunchest advocates of new techniques are arguably Ortony et al., who suggest there is an entire cadre of paradigms that need to be implemented in order to assess fluid emotional abilities. O'Sullivan, Rivers et al., and Schulze et al. are particularly sanguine about the prospects of the SJT methodology, especially if multimedia applications and information technologies can be implemented. Finally, Schulze et al. provide a compelling unification of psychometrics, arguing that evidence-centered design may ultimately provide a framework for specifying particularly elaborate psychometric models by which to assess both new techniques (situational judgment tests) and "old" (MSCEIT). Suffice to say for now, however, that the jury is still out on whether new techniques or advanced psychometric models will advance understanding of EI. Plausibly, though, this unknown will be well-known in the next 3 to 5 years.

Assessment: Concluding Remarks

The state of the art in assessment of EI displays uncertainties that, in part, mirror those of conceptualizations of EI. Just as there are multiple strategies for defining EI, so, too, there are radically different strategies for assessing EI. As with conceptualization, we may wonder whether different measurement techniques will ultimately converge on a common, global EI construct, or whether we will arrive at a loose-knit family of constructs that do not support a general EI factor.

It is also difficult to recommend any single technique for measurement. Those methods that have been most widely explored have been found wanting. Various innovations have been suggested but thus far await systematic test development and validation. We agree with the majority of our contributors that self-reports have little to offer as direct measures of ability, although they may add to understanding of personality and related constructs. Although the MSCEIT has it merits, our view is that its utility is limited by scoring controversies, by lack of construct validity evidence, and by uncertainty over its psychological underpinnings. A general recommendation is that the domain of emotional abilities and competencies requires more systematic exploration; it is hard to predict how whatever construct is measured by the MSCEIT might find its way into a comprehensive dimensional model of emotional abilities. It is apparent, too, that building a comprehensive model requires more use of alternate technique, including SJTs, implicit assessments, and information-processing tasks, although development of psychometrically sound tests on the basis of these techniques is nontrivial in each instance.

Key Issues III: Applications of Emotional Intelligence

What Theoretical Advances Are Necessary to Support Practical Applications?

Overall, experts in the field appear to be well aware of shortcomings and problems in current conceptualizations of EI and are convinced of the importance of developing a well-defined theoretical framework as a precondition for applications of EI in the field. Several more specific issues are highlighted in the passages that follow.

Need for Greater Theoretical Clarity

In the clinical domain in particular, the theoretical foundations of EI appear to be in flux, with the universe of discourse sometimes limited to intrapersonal facets (recognition of one's own emotion), other times encompassing interpersonal facets (e.g., empathy and social skills), and yet other times encompassing clinical outcome variables (e.g., adaptive coping; Vachon & Bagby). Theoretical uncertainties also limit application. In the clinical context, a theoretically driven conceptualization of the EI construct should contribute to discriminating distinct emotional pathological processes in clinical diagnosis. Identification of a patient's specific difficulties in perceiving, regulating, or expressing emotion would have immediate implications for treatment. In fact, it is difficult to decide which of the competing and partially overlapping constructs related to emotion dysfunction (e.g., EI, alexithymia, psychological mindedness, ego strength) are to be preferred in clinical diagnosis and intervention. Although accepting that EI has future promise, Vachon and Bagby advise clinicians to steer clear of EI and work with more theory-based, well-researched, and focused constructs in clinical settings (e.g., alexithymia).

Similar concerns are expressed by the other authors dealing with applications. For example, according to Picard, in the technology domain, the array of current theories of emotion does not provide adequate models for representing affective states that arise in interaction with computers (e.g., boredom, frustration). Jordan, Ashkanasy, Hartel, and Hooper (2002) are the most sanguine regarding theory, seeing the Mayer-Salovey model of EI as providing a reference framework for organizational studies.

Resolving the Issue of Domain-Specificity

A common concern of practitioners is that theory does not easily map onto applied concerns. Several contributors called for theory that directly informs understanding of applied domains. The issue is partly one of selecting the most relevant facets of general models of EI for specific applications, and partly one of identifying new facets that feature in applied contexts (e.g., alexithymia in the clinical realm). Thus, according to Picard, we need to develop domain-specific taxonomies of emotions in human-computer interactions and gather systematic observations of human-computer interactions to develop a systematic taxonomy of emotions in situ. Furthermore, there is a paucity of theory that is domain specific, and new advances are needed. Picard proposes three key components of interest: machine identification of user emotions, machine expression of emotions, and machine management of user emotions (e.g., helping the user relax and calm down).

Applications in education center on five core social and emotional learning (SEL) skills identified by the Collaborative for Academic, Social, and Emotional Learning (CASEL): self-awareness, social awareness, self-management, relationship skills, and problem solving/decision making (Zins, Weissberg, Wang, & Walberg, 2004). In this case, the domains correspond to general features of EI. These competencies can easily be mapped onto the emotional competencies suggested by Boyatzis and colleagues in their writings (e.g., Boyatzis & Sala, 2004). One might wonder whether there are additional domains and competencies that have special relevance to education, such as emotional development and maturity (see Izard et al.; Zeidner et al., 2003), and learning from emotional encounters. Jordan et al. see the general theory provided by Mayer and Salovey as being highly relevant to organizational settings. However, they also discuss several arenas for EI that may require more domain-specific theory, including transformational leadership, working relationships and teamwork, and conflict resolution and negotiation.

Our view is that the practical value of EI has been blighted from the outset by overbroad definitions of the construct, coupled with excessive claims; although, as Jordan et al. point out, the "expansive definition" of the construct adds to its allure in the business world. However, if EI has in fact been oversold, the key to reviving its fortunes is identifying specific domains in which it can be shown to be more relevant to real-life outcomes than conventional personality and ability factors. The contributors make some valuable suggestions as to what these domains might be, but more evidence is needed that EI can play a unique role.

Need for Valid Assessments in Applied Settings

In applied settings, the development of domain-relevant measures of EI is of immediate urgency, particularly in view of the numerous professionals in applied domains struggling to choose the most valid and useful EI measure among those available. Arguably, EI assessments for applied settings should use measures gauging specific domain-relevant parameters and be of higher fidelity and narrower bandwidth than is currently the case. Experts in the applied domain seem to agree that there is an urgent need for developing validated measures of EI for applied settings that meet accepted psychometric criteria. Furthermore, consistent with what the contributors to assessment agreed, consensus is emerging that ability-based measures are presently the most promising category of EI measures to target for further development.

Among practical concerns in the clinical domain suggested by Vachon and Bagby are the following: matching clients with appropriate therapeutic interventions, monitoring clients throughout the therapeutic process, and establishing relationships between emotional competencies, on one hand, and psychopathology and treatment effectiveness, on the other hand. Accordingly, measures used for clinical purposes should be designed to allow sensitive and differential diagnosis. Optimally, EI measures for the clinical domain should allow the matching of interventions to clients with specific emotional problems.

In the occupational context, Jordan et al. show a clear preference for ability-based measures, along with self-report measures based on the Mayer-Salovey model. They are aware of shortcomings plaguing mixed models, in that they confound personality and motivational constructs. They suggest that the inconsistency in research results using EI measures in the organizational domain may be dependent, in part, on the type of measure used. By contrast, Zins, Payton, Weissberg, and O'Brien, offer little specific commentary on assessment in educational contexts. Our view is that the five "key SEL competencies" identified by these authors are plausible. However, further progress requires considerably more attention to how they can be measured as valid constructs in the educational context (see also Zeidner, Roberts, & Matthews, 2002).

Picard is not sanguine about current ability-based measures, arguing that they assess semantic rather than procedural knowledge of emotions (cf. Brody, 2004). In contrast to the other domains discussed, in which paper-and-pencil measures for assessing emotions and EI are the rule, the emotional states of users in the computer-client interface have been typically assessed via three basic somatic measures: (1) physiological sensors, (2) facial recognition (via video camera), and (3) speech recognition (via voice-recognition software). Each of these measures has a number of inherent problems that can cause serious measurement error and introduce construct-irrelevant variance into the measures. For example, computer facial recognition may be affected by facial movements of the participants, and both physiological responses and speech may be sensitive to environmental disturbances and personality factors.

The area of information technology also highlights the use of computer-assisted administration of EI measures (e.g., MEIS), although, as Picard has noted, the potential of computers for constructing emotion-laden scenarios and gauging client's behaviors has not been fully exploited. Picard also argues that current ability-based measures assess knowledge about emotional skills and test what people cognitively infer about emotion-laden situations rather than how people behave in situations that demand EI. Thus, it appears requisite to explore interactive experiences (e.g., social games) that could put EI to the test through behaviors in virtual environments, not merely abstract cognitive reasoning. For example, the computer can present situations that provoke frustration and examine person's reactions and the effects it has on the person's ability to perform under stress. Picard reports working on an assessment companion of EI, which would assess how people behave in situations that demand high EI. However, the technical challenge of such efforts resembles those noted previously for SJTs and information-processing measures, which should not be underestimated.

What Are the Cultural, Social, and Economic Factors That May Constrain or Facilitate Applications Based on EI?

There appears to be a general consensus on the important role culture and social environment can play when applying EI in practical settings. Nevertheless, there is little relevant research, and our contributors had few specific recommendations to make. In the clinical setting, given that basic emotions are universally expressed and recognized, this implies partial independence from cultural, social, and economic factors (Vachon & Bagby). Even so, as Scherer discusses, the display rules that govern socially appropriate expression of basic emotions are powerfully shaped by culture. Clinicians working in a multicultural milieu face the challenge of deciding whether seemingly inappropriate emotion is a function of the client's cultural background or of some genuine abnormality. The importance of culture also supports the value of taking an ecological perspective. Maladaption may be a function of mismatch between the person's emotional acculturation and prevalent social-emotional norms, rather than abnormality per se.

In education, Zins et al. suggests that it is best if the SEL program being implemented is congruent with the values and beliefs of the school students and setting. Furthermore, it is essential to adopt programs to meet organizational contexts and local conditions and needs, which of course are culturally dependent. In the area of information technology, Picard stresses that the specific modality (face, voice, posture) through which emotions may be expressed may vary with culture, and this needs to be considered in any future applications. Furthermore, future research on recognizing emotions from physiological sensors needs to be informed by cultural, social, and ethical guidelines, as well as by scientific inquiry, particularly because the work is invasive. In fact, in computing with emotions, there are certain levels of feelings best to keep from revealing to others, and this may vary with cultural and social settings. Finally, with respect to organizational applications, the clearest domain that culture operates is within large, multinational companies. Here individuals need to be aware of cultural differences; business negotiations may easily fail to due to lack of awareness of cultural norms for emotional expression.

Is There Any Practical Advantage to Focusing on EI, Rather Than on Specific Contextualized Skills?

As we noted in our introductory chapter, it is unclear that training for EI has any "added value" over and above training specific skills. For example, instead of training EI, we might focus on enhancing mood regulation (clinical), interpersonal negotiation (organizational), communication and study skills (educational), and use of computer applications (technology).

The key evidence would be that training EI or its components has global benefits that transfer across a range of applications. For example, O'Sullivan describes the METT tool for training recognition of fleeting microexpressions, a specific skill that may be especially relevant to detection of deceit. But would METT training enhance adaptive recognition of emotions in intimate relationships, at work, and during stressful encounters? Similarly, if an individual is trained in assertiveness techniques for the workplace, does this skill generalize to all interpersonal settings in which assertiveness is adaptive? In large part, such questions are unanswered, and current intervention studies are not designed to test them. However, the question is important because, if skills for EI generalize, then generic training in EI may produce far-reaching benefits, without the need to train each contextualized skill in isolation.

Perhaps reflecting the lack of evidence on this topic, the contributors offered few definitive statements. Notwithstanding, Vachon and Bagby suggest that, provided the client has sufficient EI initially, training in EI may be effective in that it enhances a whole range of cognitive therapies that depend on insight. However, they also caution that such an approach depends on EI being shown to be distinct from other relevant constructs. In reviewing conceptualization and measurement, we argued that "EI" may refer to several unrelated constructs. It follows that a better conceptual scheme for EI would facilitate effective training. Training skills for recognizing emotion may well provide benefits in multiple life domains, but we should not expect training to generalize to facets of EI that may not be related functionally and depend on different elements of processing. A further caution is that many skills linked to emotional competence may be implicit and procedural, rather than explicit and verbally represented (cf. Picard). Available evidence suggests that implicit skills are often rather tightly bound to specific tasks or contexts, and fail to generalize. In such instances, there is little alternative offered to the practitioner other than training the specific skill required.

In Which Real-World Domains Will EI Be Most and Least Useful?

There appears to be a good deal of consensus among experts regarding the merits of the EI construct in practical settings. However, the strength of the evidence in support of present applications and the expected utility of applying the construct appear to vary by the specific real-life domain under consideration. In the passages that follow, we evaluate each of the four focal areas of EI applications. We will assess the current state of the art in each respective field, followed by remarks on future challenges.

Organizational Settings

Current EI applications in the workplace largely revolve around the improved prediction of organizational behaviors using tests of EI and enhancing the predictive validity of assessment batteries. In their review of the burgeoning literature focusing on EI in organizations, Jordan et al. evaluate EI as being a valuable potential personal resource for organizational contexts, particularly when assessed as a type of ability. EI appears to be related to organizational performance and outcomes in tasks in which there is a clear emotional skill required for successful performance, such as in client contact service occupations (sales, customer relations, allied health, school teaching, etc.). Jordon et al.'s review shows that EI has the potential for enhancing both task performance and augmenting personal relationships in organizational settings, although the empirical data reported in research studies is far from consistent.

Obtaining applied benefits from EI requires attention to a long-standing issue in organizational psychology: the "criterion problem" of valid assessment of work performance and other job-related behaviors (Guion, 1998). It is agreed that it is not only overt job proficiency that is important for the organization, but also other classes of behavior that contribute meaningfully to the organization's goals and mission. These include willingness to support others, to apply extra effort and volunteer for assignments, and to maintain personal discipline, integrity, and honesty. These behaviors are captured by terms including *organizational citizenship* and *contextual performance* (Motowidlo, 2000). It seems plausible that we can analyze overt job descriptions for the relevance of EI. Jordan et al. (this volume) discuss how EI may relate to performance particularly in those instances in which the job requires an emotional skill such as performing emotional labor or implementing transformational leadership. Similarly, Schmit (2006) suggests four features of jobs that may enhance the relevance of EI:

1. The job involves emotionally charged situations and emotional labor; for example, social workers face long-term interaction with emotionally demanding clients.
2. Performance depends on expression of positive emotion, as in sales, recruitment, and marketing.

3. The job requires creative problem solving (assuming this to be facilitated by emotion).
4. The organization is required to confront change; EI helps employees to manage the stress of changes in business strategy and working practices.

The Van Rooy and Viswesvaran (2004) meta-analysis suggests that the performance of tests of EI as predictors of overt job performance is modest. Similarly, Jordan et al. comment on the lack of evidence supporting the idea that individuals with high EI will have better career paths. Presumably, Jordan et al. would expect higher validity coefficients if studies focused more effectively on jobs for which EI is central. It may, in fact, be more productive to investigate EI as a predictor of contextual performance; Jordan et al. provide some promising research findings along these lines. Notably, this is one area in which it is especially important to focus on the distinctiveness between EI and personality. It is known that conscientiousness promotes integrity and effort, agreeableness relates to teamwork, and that emotional stability supports tolerance of stress (e.g., Matthews, Roberts, & Zeidner, 2003; Ones & Viswesvaran, 2001; Tokar, Fischer, & Subich, 1998). Harking back to an issue that we have often raised, many of the studies cited by Jordan et al. fail to control appropriately for confounding of measures of EI with personality and ability. More generally, the key point is that there are multiple aspects of job behavior that may require careful matching to the multiplicity of constructs falling under the EI umbrella.

Our view is that future research must address various methodological challenges in order to support the utility of EI in organizational psychology. Much published research has employed student groups in simulation contexts. Additional research needs to be based on field studies, use occupational groups and leaders in true-to-life work settings, and to employ valid occupational or organizational outcome criteria. Furthermore, current research is based on a broad range of samples and differing measures of EI (ability-based and self-report) and outcomes. Systematic psychometric research needs to be conducted in different organizational settings to assess the predictive validity of both ability-based and self-report EI measures. Jordan et al.'s differentiation of "streams" of research is a useful step toward a more systematic approach.

In addition, future research needs to clarify the mediating variables through which EI impacts on outcomes variables, as well as systematically test for potential moderator variables, such as the type of work performed. Moreover, few, if any, studies have systematically assessed the differential construct and predictive validity (bias) of current EI measures for varying ethnic, gender, and age groups. Finally, additional research is needed to determine to what extent EI predicts individual- and team-level performance equally, has similar effects on workers and leaders, and predicts outcomes when work activities are strongly infused with emotion.

Education

EI skills and competencies, as cultivated and trained in social and emotional learning programs (Zins et al.), are firmly believed to be able to help students become more socially, emotionally, and academically competent, and grow to become more responsible and productive members of society. As noted in our introductory chapter, there is persuasive evidence for the efficacy of SEL programs from meta-analyses (Greenberg, Weissberg, O'Brien, & Zins, 2003). As Zins et al. discuss, such programs may help to prevent substance abuse, violence and bullying, and risky sexual practices, and they may help directly support the child's learning in the classroom. However, interventions of this kind predate the notion of EI (Zeidner et al., 2002); it is not clear that repackaging interventions as training EI makes any difference to their success (although it may help in securing legitimacy, support, and governmental funding). Zins et al. argue that SEL interventions may be enhanced through explicit focus on five key emotional competencies. Clearly, identification of specific competencies that support learning and academic engagement may indeed support the goals of educators.

Further research is clearly required to better understand how to teach students to be emotionally intelligent and productive members of society. We need to know more about how educators make decisions to adapt and assimilate evidence-based programs; what constitutes positive adaptations that enhance program outcomes; which elements are essential to success; and what ecological conditions are needed for training to be beneficial. The work on SEL described by Zins et al. has made significant progress in these directions. However, as in the case of organizational studies, there is a need for greater methodological rigor and a stronger focus on the psychological mechanisms that mediate the impact of successful interventions.

Clinical Psychology

Although EI—emotion regulation in particular—may have potential for psychiatric diagnosis and treatment (Vachon & Bagby), the current state of research appears somewhat less supportive of EI applications than in other domains targeted in this volume. Various mental disorders are related to expressions of negative affect. Yet, the diversity of these disorders is seen by our experts as mitigating against any clear, or unambiguous, relationship between low EI and mental disorders or psychopathology. Vachon and Bagby point out the major divide between the vast clinical potential of EI and the unfortunate shortcomings in current conceptualization, knowledge, diagnosis, and treatment. On one hand, EI has the potential of having a major impact in the clinical area, particularly given the many psychopathological syndromes that relate to emotional pathology. On the other hand, EI cannot presently be applied effectively to clinical settings because a number of developments prerequisite to using EI in clinical settings have yet to be adequately met. These include the following: (a) the existence of a sound clinical literature on EI and psychopathology; (b) a theoretically driven conceptualization of the EI construct; and (c) psychometrically sound, valid, and clinically relevant measures of EI. Vachon and Bagby advise clinicians to steer clear of EI and work with more theory-based, well-researched, and focused constructs in clinical settings (e.g., alexithymia) rather than broader and all-encompassing constructs, such as EI.

Because EI fails to emerge as a clear diagnostic category in the clinical literature, employing categorization based on emotional pathology may obscure the fact that many disorders (involving dysfunctional emotions that are conceptually or clinically related to low EI) have distinct etiologies and require different treatments (cf. Matthews et al., 2002). Thus, presently there appears minimal research supporting a systematic relationship between low EI and distinct clinical syndromes. Nor is there currently any solid empirical basis for the assumption that treating EI may be therapeutically effective (Vachon & Bagby).

Given the importance of disturbances of affect regulation in clinical psychology, Vachon and Bagby signal that work on EI may add new insights into this element of mental disorders. It may be especially worth pursuing those meta-emotional or metacognitive processes that have been implicated in a range of anxiety and mood disorders (Wells, 2000; Wells & Matthews, 1994). According to Wells (2000), pathology may derive from dysfunctional beliefs about the importance of one's own negative emotions and cognitions, and maladaptive strategies for seeking to control unpleasant mental states, such as preservative "worry about worry." Perhaps work on EI will lead to greater understanding of these harmful processes, though research to date provides little basis for strong conclusions regarding the utility of EI in the clinical domain.

Applications of EI pose both challenges as well as unique affordances for improving the quality of human life in the information age, but, thus far, it is difficult to understand how EI is related to psychopathology and how EI can be applied clinically. As concluded by Vachon and Bagby, until the required research is conducted, EI will remain an "ineffective and specious conceptualization of emotional pathology." These authors point out the need to gather large-scale epidemiological data on EI in clinical populations, particularly because most of the research has not been based on clinical samples. In addition, the nomological nexus of EI in the clinical domain, including personality and temperament variables, needs to be mapped out and its developmental antecedents and pathways examined. Another challenge is to evaluate whether understanding of abnormalities in EI will lead to genuinely novel treatments for emotional disorders, or whether clinicians should pursue the more modest goal of tailoring treatment to the level of EI of their clients.

Information Technology

EI is assessed as having considerable potential in this area (Picard), particularly given the strong likelihood that human emotions impact on the human-computer interface. A working assumption in this context is that humans have a tendency to behave toward a computer as though it were human. Given that human-computer interaction is natural and often social, it tends to also be emotional at times. A further assumption is that to the extent that EI is useful and important in human-human interactions, it is also likely to be useful in human-computer interaction and effect the smooth and efficient functioning of the user. A further assumption is that computing with emotions is not primarily designed to make computers more emotionally intelligent, but to improve human-computer interfaces and to help people boost their own abilities at managing emotions, both in self and others.

EI is seen as having considerable merit for information technology, particularly in programming emotionally sensitive agents, who will be able to sense and interpret human emotions more reliably via different input channels (facial, voice, postural); respond empathically to human feedback (particularly negative emotions of the user that are likely to escalate); and demonstrate skills that can be used to help people develop and assess abilities that contribute to EI. Ball (2002) has discussed how Bayesian networks can be used to represent probabilistic causal interactions between emotions and the processes that support human-machine interaction. For example, an artificial "travel agent" might be programmed both to recognize the human user's emotions (conveying urgency or uncertainty, for example), and to output emotional behaviors such as expressing sympathy if a ticket is expensive.

Artificial systems that can intelligently sense the affective content and intent of natural human language can be of special use in the intelligent management of emotion, such as managing the health of workers who are exposed to affective situations (e.g., hospital, ambulance, or police "call centers"). Imbuing computers with empathic and caring behaviors has special significance for mental health professionals. Computers now have the potential of handling the emotions of people with whom they are interacting, reacting to the user's distress by active listening, empathy, and sympathy. Use of physiological sensors (i.e., heart rate, skin temperature and conductance, muscle tension) has good prospects for health and sport settings. Also, relational agents can have important applications in areas such as health maintenance and regulation, in which long-term compliance can be improved by ongoing interaction with a computer character programmed to develop long-term social emotional relationships with people. Furthermore, machines that have the potential to show emotions will also need the intelligence to know when not to show it.

Some additional potential applications are also worth mentioning. Stern (2002) discusses how the entertainment industry has for many years capitalized on people's tendency to read emotions into inanimate artifacts. Better understanding of this process allows the design of more compelling computer-generated imagery in films and "virtual pets" that elicit emotional responses from the human user. Indeed, toys may eventually become sophisticated enough to contribute to developing the child's EI.

Another focus for application may be adaptive automation (Kaber, Wright, Prinzel, & Clamann, 2005). Human factors research recognizes that simply automating tasks may alienate the human operator who is relegated from being a skilled, autonomous agent to a passive monitor of the automated system. Adaptive automation seeks to preserve the human's active engagement with the task, but aims to automate task functions when needed to prevent operator overload or to perform key safety-critical functions. Emotionally intelligent interfaces may be able to detect when an operator is becoming overloaded, fatigued, or distracted by stress, and implement adaptive automation accordingly (see Matthews, Emo, Funke, Zeidner, & Roberts, 2003). Most generally, artificially intelligent systems may need emotions for the same sorts of reasons that the human mind does, in other words, to manage conflicting priorities within a complex modular system and to bias action tendencies appropriately. Several authors (e.g., Cañamero & Gaussier, 2005; Hudlicka, 2002) have argued that simulating emotions may be essential for solving design problems that arise in building complex artificial systems. Thus, although, as Picard discusses, current focus is on the human user's interface with the machine, future applications may increasingly need to build EI into the machines themselves.

However, a number of problems need to be resolved before a computer can accurately recognize and perceive human emotions through various input channels. For one, a machine needs to learn how to accurately and reliably recognize and discriminate relevant emotions (e.g., anxiety from sadness or anger). Future research also needs to be able to integrate emotional information from multichannel systems (face, voice, posture) using a wide array of sensors (mouse, chair, cameras, etc.). In addition, computers will need to tackle the challenge of individual differences, with the temperament of some users more expressive and active and others much less so. Although the results of physiology-based recognition remain promising, there are a considerable number of technical problems to overcome, including knowledge of specific physiological signatures, portability of equipment, invasiveness, and ethical problems. Finally, the issue of privacy is salient in computer identification of emotions. To solve this problem, computers will need to be designed to differentiate private emotions that should not be processed from emotions that are relevant to human-computer interface.

There is also a paucity of theory that is specific to the area of information technology, and new advances need to be made before we can make useful instantiations of EI. Picard provides some guidelines for the type of research needed including observation of humans interacting with machines, model building, and testing. Also, future computer applications need to be evaluated under differing emotional contexts, including comparisons of routine work versus stressful long-term conditions of personal significance to the user, and technology enthusiasts and experts versus "computer phobics" and novices.

Can EI Be Taught and, If So, How?

Our experts concur that EI can be taught in differing real-life contexts, although they do underscore different components or facets of EI as targets for focal interventions. In addition, the contributors often suggested that we need a better understanding concerning what core intervention components are essential to success and to identify and eliminate nonessential aspects so that the interventions are easier to deliver in the real world.

In the clinical domain, the identification and regulation of emotion in self appear to be particularly important to train, given the dysregulation of emotion in most clinical syndromes. Vachon and Bagby comment that EI can be trained if the client has a minimal amount of intelligence on which to base the training. Clients with low EI may lack the required EI to benefit from various forms of treatment requiring psychological insight. Rather than improve EI competencies, therapy may be designed to help low EI individuals adjust or cope with the applied situation more effectively. At present, we simply do not know what components are more responsive to training or what the threshold level of EI is required for training. Overall, at present, we are pretty much in the dark regarding the following key facets of clinical training: therapeutic goals; specific EI components most responsive to training; the most effective therapy to use for low EI clients; and the minimal level of EI client needs to benefit from therapy. There is also a need for developing standards for program implementation as well as employing cost-benefit analysis for assessing the return for costs associated with delivering EI programs.

In the educational domain, Zins et al. review research showing that effective programs provide substantial measurable benefits in dollar returns in student attitudes (self-efficacy, commitment, motivation), behaviors (prosocial behaviors, decreased interpersonal violence, study habits, participation), achievements, and class performance. As Zins et al. underscore, evaluations of SEL programs consistently show that these programs achieve their goals of improving peer relations, helping students make good decisions, promoting healthy student development, reducing risks for dysfunctional behavior, and improving student achievement and attachment to school, particularly when they are well designed and executed. Aside from the SEL skills, safe and nurturing environments are essential to combine with the skills taught, along with opportunities for application.

In the workplace, Jordan et al. surveyed studies showing that EI, assessed as an individual difference variable, can contribute to positive organizational and interpersonal outcomes. Jordan et al. cite only two studies suggesting that (a) training in EI competencies can lead to increased levels of EI as well as organizational citizenship behavior (Murray, Jordan, & Ashkanasy, 2004) and that (b) low EI teams can be trained to reach same level of outcomes as high EI teams (Jordan et al., 2002).

Computers can be taught to adapt and learn how to behave in a more emotionally intelligent way. In fact, a basic assumption of computing with emotions is that artificial agents can be trained to become more "emotionally sensitive," including the identification and regulation of the user's emotions. Thus, machines are capable of sensing a variety of emotions, learning to be empathic to user's emotions, and providing feedback on (i.e., regulating) user's emotional reactions. Training the machine's emotional self-awareness and self-regulation, involving some degree of consciousness or self-awareness, is not within the purview or capability of current programs.

It is noted that the major goal of computing with emotions is not to enable artificial agents to experience emotions, make them more emotionally intelligent, or give them some sense of consciousness or self-reflection, but rather to make people more emotionally capable when using machines and enhancing human-computer interaction. Thus, by programming emotionally savvy computers, who could detect user's emotional states, and when appropriate, respond to them, researchers could enable better technologies for the future. Intelligent dialogue systems can be used to train and improve understanding and processing of strong or traumatic emotions relating to personally significant events experienced by individuals. These systems, as described by Picard, are capable of helping people compose stories about personally meaningful events, thus disclosing often repressed or blocked emotional experiences; reinforce reflection on emotions; reason about the emotion of themselves and others in their life; and reinforce reflection on these emotions.

Thus, intervention studies—especially in the educational and organizational fields—provide some grounds for optimism about EI. The results of the SEL programs reviewed by Zins et al. are especially impressive, and are supported by a much greater body of evidence than training programs in other fields (see Greenberg et al., 2003). However, the question that arises is, what exactly is being trained? Is it really some generic EI, or more specific skills and competencies? We are persuaded by Zins et al. that SEL programs provide real benefits, but the nature of psychological change, and the persistence and transfer of training, remain to be determined.

Applications: Concluding Comments

In order to develop efficacious assessments and interventions of EI in applied settings, the following preconditions are required:

1. Derivation of a context-specific and relevant theoretical framework;
2. Clear definitional framework for the universe of discourse surrounding EI;
3. Identification of key facets and components relevant to different applied settings;
4. Development of sound context-relevant assessment, scoring, and analytic procedures;
5. Development of sound training techniques tailored to specific contexts;
6. Adaption of EI applications congenial to the affordances and constraints of the specific occupational, cultural, and social context; and
7. Consideration of developmental age, social background, and cultural norms and values of the target users.

These suggestions reflect the close associations of theory, assessment, and applications. Currently, it could be argued that both theory and measurement of EI has not especially "helped the cause" of successfully advancing applications of EI so that they become valuable tools in the practitioners' arsenal. Alternatively, history teaches us that advances in science are often made because of an applied issue that society deems as important. Psychological well-being and happiness are emerging as key variables in economic, educational, and organizational models (e.g., Kyllonen, Roberts, & Stankov, in press; Layard, 2005). It is entirely plausible that given this impetus, applications of EI may, in the future, come to fully inform theory and assessment.

Finally, we might note that we chose for this edited volume distinguished contributors from the four applied domains we have discussed in this concluding chapter. It bears mentioning that EI has also been applied in the disciplines of health, human factors, philosophy, and gerontology, with a number of specialist professional journals, among them nursing, engineering, dentistry, medicine, and the legal profession, also carrying peer-review articles on the topic (see, e.g., Matthews et al., 2002). In future discussion of applications, it might be expedient to broaden the conversation and attempt a synthesis of the varying perspectives that these special interest groups might have on the construct.

Concluding Comments

In conclusion, it seems indisputable, to the point of banality, to observe that EI is still a new field of research, and that much remains to be done to define the construct in terms of psychological theory, to develop valid measurement instruments, and to demonstrate practical utility. We will also spare the reader any boilerplate remarks about the importance of pursing future research with greater methodological rigor: This is clearly a must. However, it may be useful to briefly reiterate the main points of agreement and dissension emerging from the chapters of this book.

Conceptualization

Both theory- and data-driven approaches suggest the concept of EI to be scientifically plausible. However, there would appear a need to derive more unified, full-blown theories of emotional intelligence, models that would embrace developmental, neurobiological, genetic, and behavioral components. Paramount to theory development is resolving the adaptive function of EI, and the place of constructs in relation to other individual differences taxonomies, especially personality, intelligence, and emotions. In the case of "trait" EI, this may actually be embedded almost entirely in existing structural models of personality; ability EI offers more scope as being a unique psychological construct. Regardless, the original optimism and hope for developing a science of EI—to somehow correct the human condition and provide conditions for a more utopian society (e.g., Goleman, 1995)—seems in the distant horizon. Indeed, it may take many years of systematic, rigorous studies and theoretical refinement before our knowledge is suitably advanced to support evidence-based empirical claims.

Assessment

Since its theoretical inception, there have been some real inroads into providing construct validity evidence for a range of EI measures. Nevertheless, as indicated in the test standards, this process should be construed as ongoing. There also appears a real need to develop a systematic taxonomy wherein a wide array of performance-based emotions measures might be placed; in turn, this would feed into more fully developed theories of individual differences in emotional functioning (if not EI). We also contend that there is a need for a moratorium on developing self-report measures of EI, at least until such time as the relation of such measures has been shown to be independent from personality, or else, to be practically meaningful. Advanced psychometric models and innovative new measurement techniques are also sorely needed in order to advance this subdiscipline.

Applications

Applications of EI in the school, workplace, and at home offer much promise, although whether all such programs designed to foster this ability may rightfully be called an EI intervention remains open to question. Applications of EI in everyday life clearly rely on advances being made in the underlying theoretical models of EI, and assessment instruments. The importance of EI in clinical applications (one or two clinical symptoms aside) remains to be demonstrated in a compelling fashion. By contrast, the emerging area of affective computing not only provides several instances of EI being successfully used in resolving issues associated with human-machine interaction, but promises to perhaps inform future models of human emotional functioning (much as AI provided insight into cognitive function, with its attendant influence on cognitive assessment).

Having said all of this in a reasonably measured tone, it is perhaps worth closing with a provocative series of statements. It is likely that if it is proven to be more than a fad, pseudoscience, or myth, the concepts, assessments, and applications of EI will look very different in future instantiations from what we currently have. But whatever the future holds for the science of EI, it is our contention that the concept has proven a valuable "soup stone" in contemporary science and practice. Consideration of theory and assessment of EI has proven beneficial to the study of emotions per se and has raised consciousness of the importance of emotional components in diverse domains of human endeavor. Above all, whether there is any scientific "stock" in EI per se, it certainly has been instrumental in having emotions researchers think more carefully about individual differences, intelligence researcher to think more about the role of affect, and for applied scholars to think more about the roles of emotions, intelligence, and their interaction within wider society.

References

Ackerman, P. L. (1996). A theory of adult intellectual development: Process, personality, interests, and knowledge. *Intelligence, 22,* 227–257.
American Educational Research Association, American Psychological Association, and National Council on Measurement in Education (1999). *Standards for educational and psychological testing.* Washington, DC: American Educational Research Association.
Austin, E. J. (2005). Emotional intelligence and emotional information processing. *Personality and Individual Differences, 39,* 403–414.
Austin, E. J., & Saklofske, D. H. (2005). Far too many intelligences? On the communalities and differences between social, practical, and emotional intelligences. In R. Schulze & R. D. Roberts (Eds.), *International handbook of emotional intelligence* (pp. 107–128). Cambridge, MA: Hogrefe & Huber.
Austin, E. J., Saklofske, D. H., & Egan, V. (2005). Personality, well-being and health correlates of trait emotional intelligence. *Personality and Individual Differences, 38,* 547–558.
Ball, E. (2002). A Bayesian heart: Computer recognition and simulation of emotion. In R. Trappl, P. Petta, & S. Payr (Eds.), *Emotions in humans and artifacts,* (pp. 303–332). Cambridge, MA: MIT Press.

Barchard, K. (2003). Does emotional intelligence assist in the prediction of academic success? *Educational and Psychological Measurement, 63,* 840–858.

Barchard, K. A., & Hakstian, R. A. (2004). The nature and measurement of emotional intelligence abilities: Basic dimensions and their relationships with other cognitive abilities and personality variables. *Educational and Psychological Measurement, 64,* 437–462.

Bar-On, R. (1997). *The Emotional Intelligence Inventory (EQ-i): Technical manual.* Toronto, Canada: Multi-Health Systems.

Bar-On, R. (2000). Emotional and social intelligence: Insights from the Emotional Quotient Inventory. In R. Bar-On & J. D. A. Parker (Eds.), *The handbook of emotional intelligence* (pp. 363–388). San Francisco: Jossey-Bass.

Baumeister, R. F., Campbell, J. D., Krueger, J., & Vohs, K. D. (2003). Does high self-esteem cause better performance, interpersonal success, happiness, or healthier lifestyles? *Psychological Science in the Public Interest, 4,* 1–44.

Bonanno, G. (2004). Loss, trauma, and human resilience: Have we underestimated the human capacity to thrive after extremely aversive events? *American Psychologist, 59,* 20–28.

Boone, R. T., & Buck, R. (2004). Emotion receiving ability. In G. Geher (Ed.), *Measuring emotional intelligence: Common ground and controversy* (pp. 73–89). Hauppauge, NY: Nova.

Boyatzis, R. E., & Sala, F. (2004). Assessing emotional intelligence competencies. In G. Geher (Ed.), *Measuring emotional intelligence: Common ground and controversy* (pp. 147–180). Hauppauge, NY: Nova.

Brackett, M. A., & Mayer, J. D. (2003). Convergent, discriminate, and incremental validity of competing measures of emotional intelligence. *Personality and Social Psychology Bulletin, 29,* 1147–1158.

Brody, N. (2004). What cognitive intelligence is and what emotional intelligence is not. *Psychological Inquiry, 15,* 234–238.

Cañamero, L., & Gaussier, P. (2005). Emotion understanding: Robots as tools and models. In J. Nadel & D. Muir (Eds.), *Emotional development: Recent research advances* (pp. 235–258). New York: Oxford University Press.

Carroll, J. B. (1993). *Human cognitive abilities: A survey of factor-analytic studies.* New York: Cambridge University Press.

Carroll, J. B. (1995). On methodology in the study of cognitive abilities. *Multivariate Behavioral Research, 30,* 429–452.

Cattell, R. B., & Horn, J. L. (1978). A check on the theory of fluid and crystallized intelligence with description of new test designs. *Journal of Educational Measurement, 15,* 139–164.

Cheng, C., & Cheung, M. W. L. (2005). Cognitive processes underlying coping flexibility: Differentiation and integration. *Journal of Personality, 73,* 859–886.

Ciarrochi, J. V., Chan, A. Y. C., & Caputi, P. (2000). A critical evaluation of the emotional intelligence construct. *Personality and Individual Differences, 28,* 539–561.

Costa, P., & McCrae, R. (1992). Four ways five factors are basic. *Personality and Individual Differences, 13,* 653–665.

Dalgleish, T., Taghavi, R., Neshat-Doost, H., Moradi, A., Canterbury, R., & Yule, W. (2003). Patterns of processing bias for emotional information across clinical disorders: An investigation of attention, memory and prospective cognition in children and adolescents with depression, generalized anxiety and posttraumatic stress disorder (PTSD). *Journal of Clinical Child and Adolescent Psychology, 32,* 10–21.

Davies, M., Stankov, L., & Roberts, R. D. (1998). Emotional intelligence: In search of an elusive construct. *Journal of Personality and Social Psychology, 75*, 989–1015.

Day, A. (2004). The measurement of emotional intelligence: The good, the bad and the ugly. In G. Geher (Ed.), *Measuring emotional intelligence: Common ground and controversy* (pp. 245–270). New York: Nova Science.

Dickman, S. J. (1990). Functional and dysfunctional impulsivity. *Journal of Personality and Social Psychology, 58*, 95–102.

Eisenberg, N., Sadovsky, A., Spinrad, T. L., Fabes, R. A., Losoya, S. H., Valiente, C., et al. (2005). The relations of problem behavior status to children's negative, effortful control and impulsivity: Concurrent relations and prediction of change. *Developmental Psychology, 41*, 193–211.

Ekstrom, R. B., French, J. W., & Harman, H. H. (1976). *Kit of factor-referenced cognitive tests.* Princeton, NJ: Educational Testing Service.

Ellingson, J. E., Sackett, P. R., & Hough, L. M. (1999). Social desirability corrections in personality measurement: Issues of applicant comparison and construct validity. *Journal of Applied Psychology, 84*, 155–166.

Eysenck, H. J. (1997). Personality and experimental psychology: The unification of psychology and the possibility of a paradigm. *Journal of Personality and Social Psychology, 73*, 1224–1237.

Fellner, A. N., Matthews, G., Warm, J. S., Zeidner, M., & Roberts, R. D. (2006). Learning to discriminate terrorists: The effects of emotional intelligence and emotive cues. In *Proceedings of the Human Factors and Ergonomics Society 50th Annual Meeting* (pp. 1249–1253). Santa Monica, CA: Human Factors and Ergonomics Society.

Goff, M., & Ackerman, P. L. (1992). Personality-intelligence relations: Assessment of typical intellectual engagement. *Journal of Educational Psychology, 84*, 537–552.

Gohm, C. L., & Clore, G. L. (2002). Four latent traits of emotional experience and their involvement in well-being, coping, and attributional style. *Cognition & Emotion, 16*, 495–518.

Goleman, D. (1995). *Emotional intelligence.* New York: Bantam Books.

Greenberg, M. T., Weissberg, R. P., O'Brien, M. U., & Zins, J. E. (2003). Enhancing school based prevention and youth development through coordinated social, emotional, and academic learning. *American Psychologist, 58*, 466–474.

Greenwald, A. G., McGhee, D. E., & Schwartz, L. K. (1998). Measuring individual differences in implicit cognition: The Implicit Association Test. *Journal of Personality and Social Psychology, 74*, 1464–1480.

Gross, J. J., & John, O. P. (2003). Individual differences in two emotion regulation processes: Implications for affect, relationships, and well-being. *Journal of Personality and Social Psychology, 85*, 348–362.

Guion, R. M. (1998). Some virtues of dissatisfaction in the science and practice of personnel selection. *Human Resource Management Review, 8*, 351–365.

Heggestad, E. D., Morrison M., Reeve, C. L., & McCloy, R. A. (2006). Forced-choice assessments of personality for selection: Evaluating issues of normative assessment and faking resistance. *Journal of Applied Psychology, 91*, 9–24.

Holden, R. R. (1995). Response latency detection of fakers on personnel tests. *Canadian Journal of Behavioural Science, 27*, 343–355.

Holden, R. R., & Evoy, R. A. (2005). Personality inventory faking: A four-dimensional simulation of dissimulation. *Personality and Individual Differences, 39*, 1307–1318.

Horn, J. L., & Hofer, S. M. (1992). Major abilities and development in the adult period. In R. Sternberg & C. Berg (Eds.), *Intellectual development* (pp. 44–99). New York: Cambridge University Press.

Hudlicka, E. (2002). This time with feeling: Integrated model of trait and state effects on cognition and behavior. *Applied Artificial Intelligence, 16,* 611–641.

Izard C. E., Fine S., Schultz, D., Mostow, A., Ackerman, B., & Youngstrom, E. (2001). Emotion knowledge as a predictor of social behavior and academic competence in children at risk. *Psychological Science, 12,* 18–23.

Jausovec, N., Jausovec, K., & Gerlic, I. (2001). Differences in event-related and induced EEG patterns in the theta and alpha frequency bands related to human emotional intelligence. *Neuroscience Letters, 311,* 93–96.

Jensen, A. R. (1998). *The g factor: The science of mental ability.* Westport, CT: Praeger.

Jordan, P. J., Ashkanasy, N. M., Hartel, C. E. J., & Hooper, G. S. (2002). Workgroup emotional intelligence: Scale development and relationship to team process effectiveness and goal focus. *Human Resource Management Review, 12,* 195–214.

Judge, T. A., Erez, A., Bono, J. E., & Thoresen, C. J. (2002). Do the traits self-esteem, neuroticism, locus of control, and generalized self-efficacy indicate a common core construct? *Journal of Personality and Social Psychology, 83,* 693–710.

Kaber, D. B., Wright, M. C., Prinzel, L. P., & Clamann, M. P. (2005). Adaptive automation of human-machine system information processing functions. *Human Factors, 47,* 730–741.

Kafetsios, K. (2004). Attachment and emotional intelligence abilities across the life course. *Personality and Individual Differences, 37,* 129–145.

Kanfer, R., & Heggestad, E. (1999). Individual differences in motivation: Traits and self-regulatory skills. In P. Ackerman, P. C. Kyllonen, & R. D. Roberts (Eds.), *Learning and individual differences: Process, trait, and content determinants* (pp. 293–313). Washington, DC: American Psychological Association.

Kang, S., Day, J. D., & Meara, N. M. (2005). Social intelligence and emotional intelligence: Starting a conversation about their similarities and differences. In R. Schulze & R. D. Roberts (Eds.), *Emotional intelligence: An international handbook* (pp. 91–105). Cambridge, MA: Hogrefe & Huber.

Kyllonen, P. C., Roberts, R. D., & Stankov, L. (Eds.). (2006). *Extending intelligence: Enhancement and new constructs.* Mahwah, NJ: Erlbaum.

Lane, R. D., Quinlan, D. M., Schwartz, G. E., Walker, P. A., & Zeitlin, S. B. (1990). The levels of emotional awareness scale: A cognitive-developmental measure of emotion. *Journal of Personality Assessment, 55,* 124–134.

Layard, R. (2005). *Happiness: Lessons from a new science.* New York: Penguin Press.

Lazarus, R. S. (1999). *Stress and emotions: A new synthesis.* New York: Springer.

Leventhal, H., & Scherer, K. (1987). The relationship of emotion to cognition: A functional approach to a semantic controversy. *Cognition and Emotion, 1,* 3–28.

Lopes, P. N., Straus, R., & Salovey, P. (2003). Emotional intelligence, personality, and the perceived quality of social relationships. *Personality and Individual Differences, 35,* 641–658.

MacCann, C., Matthews, G., Zeidner, M., & Roberts, R. D. (2004). The assessment of emotional intelligence: On frameworks, fissures, and the future. In G. Geher (Ed.), *Measuring emotional intelligence: Common ground and controversy* (pp. 21–52). Hauppauge, NY: Nova Science.

Matsumoto, D., LeRoux, J., Wilson-Cohn, C., Raroque, J., Kooken, K., Ekman, P., et al. (2000). A new test to measure emotion recognition ability: Matsumoto and Ekman's Japanese and Caucasian Brief Affect Recognition Test (JACBART). *Journal of Nonverbal Behavior, 24*, 179–209.

Matthews, G. (2004). Neuroticism from the top down: Psychophysiology and negative emotionality. In R. M. Stelmack (Ed.), *On the psychology of personality: Essays in honor of Marvin Zuckerman* (pp. 249–266). New York: Elsevier Science.

Matthews, G. (in press). Reinforcement sensitivity theory: A critique from cognitive science. In P. J. Corr (Ed.), *The reinforcement sensitivity theory of personality.* Cambridge, UK: Cambridge University Press.

Matthews, G., Deary, I. J., & Whiteman, M. C. (2003). *Personality traits* (2nd ed.). Cambridge, UK: Cambridge University Press.

Matthews, G., Emo, A., Funke, G., Zeidner, M., & Roberts, R. D. (2003).Emotional intelligence: Implications for human factors. *Proceedings of the Human Factors and Ergonomics Society 47th Annual Meeting* (pp. 1053–1057). Santa Monica, CA: Human Factors and Ergonomics Society.

Matthews, G., Emo, A., Roberts, R. D., & Zeidner, M. (2006). What is this thing called emotional intelligence? In K. R. Murphy (Ed.), *A critique of emotional intelligence: What are the problems and how can they be fixed?* (pp. 3–36). Mahwah, NJ: Erlbaum.

Matthews, G., & Funke, G. J. (2006).Worry and information-processing. In G. C. L. Davey & A. Wells (Eds.), *Worry and psychological disorders: Theory, assessment and treatment* (pp. 51–68). Chichester, UK: Wiley.

Matthews, G., Roberts, R. D., & Zeidner, M. (2003). Development of emotional intelligence: A skeptical—but not dismissive—perspective. *Human Development, 46*, 109–114.

Matthews G., Roberts, R. D., & Zeidner, M. (2004). Seven myths about emotional intelligence. *Psychological Inquiry, 15*, 179–196.

Matthews, G., & Zeidner, M. (2000). Emotional intelligence, adaptation to stressful encounters and health encounters. In R. Bar-On & D. A. Parker (Eds.), *Handbook of emotional intelligence* (pp. 459–490). San Francisco: Jossey-Bass.

Matthews, G., & Zeidner, M. (2004). Traits, states, and the trilogy of mind: An adaptive perspective on intellectual functioning. In D. Y. Dai & R. J. Sternberg (Eds.), *Motivation, emotion, and cognition: Integrative perspectives on intellectual functioning and development. The educational psychology series* (p. 143–174). Mahwah, NJ: Erlbaum.

Matthews, G., Zeidner, M., & Roberts, R. D. (2002). *Emotional intelligence: Science and myth.* Cambridge, MA: MIT Press.

Matthews, G., Zeidner, M., & Roberts, R. D. (2005). Emotional intelligence: An elusive ability. In O. Wilhelm & R. W. Engle (Eds.), *Handbook of understanding and measuring intelligence* (pp. 79–99). Thousand Oaks, CA: Sage.

Matthews, G., Zeidner, M., & Roberts, R. D. (2006). Personality, affect, and emotional development. In P. A. Alexander & P. H. Winne (Eds.), *Handbook in educational psychology* (2nd ed., pp. 163–186). Mahwah, NJ: Erlbaum.

Mayer, J. D., Caruso, D. R., & Salovey, P. (1999). Emotional intelligence meets traditional standards for an intelligence. *Intelligence, 27*, 267–298.

Mayer, J. D., & Geher, G. (1996). Emotional intelligence and the identification of emotion. *Intelligence, 22*, 89–114.

Mayer, J. D., Salovey, P., & Caruso, D. R. (2004). Emotional intelligence: Theory, findings, and implications. *Psychological Inquiry, 15*, 197–215.

Mayer, J. D., Salovey, P., Caruso, D. R., & Sitarenios, G. (2001). Emotional intelligence as a standard intelligence. *Emotion, 1*, 232–242.

McKenna, F. P., & Sharma, D. (1995). Intrusive cognitions: An investigation of the emotional Stroop task. *Journal of Experimental Psychology: Learning, Memory, and Cognition, 21*, 1595–1607.

McNaughton, N., & Corr, P. J. (2004). A two-dimensional neuropsychology of defense: Fear/anxiety and defensive distance. *Neuroscience and Biobehavioral Reviews, 28*, 285–305.

Messick, S. (1991). Psychology and methodology of response styles. In R. E. Snow & D. E. Wiley (Eds.), *Improving inquiry in social science: A volume in honor of Lee J. Cronbach* (pp. 161–200). Hillsdale, NJ: Erlbaum.

Motowidlo, S. J. (2000). Some basic issues related to contextual performance and organizational citizenship behavior in human resource management. *Human Resource Management Review, 10*, 115–126.

Murphy, K. R. (Ed.). (2006). *Critique of emotional intelligence: What are the problems and how can they be fixed?* Hillsdale, NJ: Erlbaum.

Murphy, K. R., & Sideman, L. (2006). The fadification of emotional intelligence. In K. R. Murphy (Ed.), *A critique of emotional intelligence: What are the problems and how can they be fixed?* (pp. 283–299). Mahwah, NJ: Erlbaum.

Murray, J. P., Jordan, P. J., & Ashkanasy, N. M. (2004). *Emotional intelligence, work skills, and training.* Paper presented at the Academy of Management Meetings, New Orleans, LA.

Neubauer, A. C., Grabner, R. H., Freudenthaler, H. H.., Beckman, J. F., & Guthke, J. (2004). Intelligence and individual differences in becoming neurally efficient. *Acta Psychologica, 116*, 55–74.

Norem, J. K. (2001). Defensive pessimism, optimism, and pessimism. In E. C. Chang (Ed.), *Optimism and pessimism* (pp. 77–100). Washington, DC: American Psychological Association.

Nowicki, S. (2004). *A manual for the Diagnostic Analysis of Nonverbal Accuracy tests (DANVA).* Unpublished manuscript, Emory University, Atlanta, GA.

Oatley, K. (2004). Emotional intelligence and the intelligence of emotions. *Psychological Inquiry, 15*, 216–238.

Oatley, K., & Johnson-Laird, P. N. (1996). The communicative theory of emotions: Empirical tests, mental models, and implications for social interaction. In L. L. Martin & A. Tesser (Eds.), *Striving and feeling: Interactions among goals, affect, and self-regulation* (pp. 363–393). Mahwah, NJ: Erlbaum.

Ones, D. S., & Viswesvaran, C. (2001). Integrity tests and other criterion-focused occupational personality scales (COPS) used in personnel selection. *International Journal of Selection and Assessment, 9*, 31–39.

Paulhus, D. L. (1984). Two-component models of socially desirable responding. *Journal of Personality and Social Psychology, 46*, 598–609.

Perez, J. C., Petrides, K. V., & Furnham, A. (2005). Measuring trait emotional intelligence. In R. Schulze & R. D. Roberts (Eds.), *Emotional intelligence: An international handbook* (pp. 181–201). Ashland, OH: Hogrefe & Huber.

Petrides, K. V., & Furnham, A. (2003). Trait emotional intelligence: Behavioural validation in two studies of emotion recognition and reactivity to mood induction. *European Journal of Personality, 17*, 39–57.

Picard, R. W., Papert, S., Bender, W., Blumberg, B., Breazel, C., Cavollo, D., et al. (2004). Affective learning: A manifesto. *BT Technology Journal, 22*, 253–269.

Roberts, R. D., Markham, P. M., Zeidner, M., & Matthews, G. (2005). Assessing intelligence: Past, present, and future. In O. Wilhelm & R. W. Engle (Eds.), *Understanding and measuring intelligence* (pp. 333–360). Thousand Oaks, CA: Sage.

Roberts, R. D., & Pallier, G. (2001). Individual differences in performance on elementary 1 tasks (ECTs): Lawful vs. problematic parameters. *Journal of General Psychology, 128,* 279–314.

Roberts, R. D., Schulze, R., O'Brien, K., MacCann, C., Reid, J., & Maul, A. (2006). Exploring the validity of the Mayer-Salovey-Caruso Emotional Intelligence Test (MSCEIT) with established emotions measures. *Emotion, 6,* 663–669.

Roberts, R. D., Schulze, R., Zeidner, M., & Matthews, G. (2005). Understanding, measuring, and applying emotional intelligence: What have we learned? What have we missed? In R. Schulze & R. D. Roberts (Eds.), *International handbook of emotional intelligence* (pp. 311–341). Cambridge, MA: Hogrefe & Huber.

Roberts, R. D., & Stankov, L. (1999). Individual differences in speed of mental processing and human cognitive abilities: Towards a taxonomic model. *Learning and Individual Differences, 11,* 1–120.

Roberts, R. D., Zeidner, M., & Matthews, G. (2001). Does emotional intelligence meet traditional standards for an "intelligence"? Some new data and conclusions. *Emotion, 1,* 196–231.

Rolls, E. T. (2005). What are emotions, why do we have emotions, and what is their computational basis in the brain? In J. M. Fellous & M. A. Arbib (Eds.), *Who needs emotions? The brain meets the robot. Series in affective science* (pp. 117–146). New York: Oxford University Press.

Rosenthal, R., Hall, J. A., DiMatteo, M. R., Rogers, P. L., & Archer, D. (1979). *Sensitivity to nonverbal communication: The PONS test.* Baltimore, MD: Johns Hopkins University Press.

Sackheim, H. A., & Gur, R. C. (1978). Self-deception, self-confrontation, and consciousness. In G. E. Schwartz & D. Shapiro (Eds.), *Consciousness and self-regulation: Advances in research* (Vol. 2, pp. 117–129). New York: Plenum Press.

Saklofske, D. H., Austin, E. J., & Minski, P. S. (2003). Factor structure and validity of a trait emotional intelligence measure. *Personality and Individual Differences, 34,* 707–721.

Sala, F. (2002). *Emotional Competence Inventory (ECI): Technical manual.* Boston: Hay/Mcber Group.

Saucier, G. (2000). Isms and the structure of social attitudes. *Journal of Personality and Social Psychology, 78,* 366–385.

Saucier, G., & Ostendorf, F. (1999). Hierarchical subcomponents of the Big Five personality factors: A cross-language replication. *Journal of Personality and Social Psychology, 76*(4), 613–627.

Scherer, K. R. (2001). Appraisal considered as a process of multilevel sequential checking. In K. R. Scherer, A. Schorr, & T. Johnstone (Eds.), *Appraisal processes in emotion: Theory, methods, research* (pp. 92–120). New York: Oxford University Press.

Schmit, M. J. (2006). EI in the business world. In K. R. Murphy (Ed.), *A critique of emotional intelligence* (pp. 211–234). Mahwah, NJ: Erlbaum.

Schraw, G., & Dennison, R. S. (1994). Assessing metacognitive awareness. *Contemporary Educational Psychology, 19,* 460–475.

Schulte, M. J., Ree, M. J., & Carretta, T. R. (2004). Emotional intelligence: Not much more than g and personality. *Personality and Individual Differences, 37,* 1059–1068.

Schulze, R., & Roberts, R. D. (2006). Assessing the Big Five: Development and validation of the Openness Conscientiousness Extraversion Agreeableness Neuroticism Index Condensed (OCEANIC). *Zeitschrift für Psychologie, 214*, 133–149.

Schutte, N. S., Malouff, J. M., Hall, L. E., Haggerty, D. J., Cooper, J. T., Golden, C. J., et al. (1998). Development and validation of a measure of emotional intelligence. *Personality and Individual Differences, 25*, 167–177.

Stern, A. (2002). Virtual babyz: Believable agents with narrative intelligence. In M. Mateas & P. Sengers (Eds.), *Narrative intelligence*. Amsterdam: John Benjamins.

Sternberg, R. J. (1985). *Beyond IQ: A triarchic theory of human intelligence.* New York: Cambridge University Press.

Sternberg, R. J. (1990). *Metaphors of mind: Conceptions of the nature of intelligence.* New York: Cambridge University Press.

Sternberg, R. J., & Grigorenko, E. L. (2000). *Teaching for successful intelligence: To increase student learning and achievement.* Arlington Heights, IL: Skylight Professional Development.

Sternberg, R. J., & O'Hara, L. A. (2000). Intelligence and creativity. In R. J. Sternberg (Ed.), *Handbook of intelligence* (pp. 611–630). New York: Cambridge University Press.

Terracciano, A., McCrae, R. R., Brant, L., & Costa, P. T. Jr. (2005). Hierarchical linear modeling analyses of the NEO-PI-R scales in the Baltimore Longitudinal Study of Aging. *Psychology and Aging, 20*, 493–506.

Tett, R. P., Fox, K. E., & Wang, A. (2005). Development and validation of a self-report measure of emotional intelligence as a multidimensional trait domain. *Personality and Social Psychology Bulletin, 31*, 859–888.

Tokar, D. M., Fischer, A. R., & Subich, L. M. (1998). Personality and vocational behavior: A selective review of the literature, 1993–1997. *Journal of Vocational Behavior, 53*, 115–153.

Tupes, E. C., & Christal, R. E. (1992). Recurrent personality factors based on trait ratings. *Journal of Personality, 60*, 225–251.

Topping, G. D., & O'Gorman, J. G. (1997). Effects of faking set on validity of the NEO-FFI. *Personality and Individual Differences, 23*, 117–124.

Van Rooy, D. L., & Viswesvaran, C. (2004). Emotional intelligence: A meta-analytic investigation of predictive validity and nomological net. *Journal of Vocational Behavior, 65*, 71–95.

Van Rooy, D. L., Viswesvaran, C., & Pluta, P. (2005). An evaluation of construct validity: What is this thing called emotional intelligence? *Human Performance, 18*, 445–462.

Viswesvaran, C., & Ones, D. S. (1999). Meta-analyses of fakability estimates: Implications for personality measurement. *Educational and Psychological Measurement, 59*, 197–121.

Weis, S., & Süß, H.-M. (2005). Social intelligence: A review and critical discussion of measurement concepts. In R. Schulze & R. D. Roberts (Eds.), *International handbook of emotional intelligence* (pp. 203–230). Cambridge, MA: Hogrefe & Huber.

Wells, A. (2000). *Emotional disorders and metacognition.* Chichester, UK: Wiley.

Wells, A., & Matthews, G. (1994). *Attention and emotion: A clinical perspective.* Hillsdale, NJ: Erlbaum.

Zeidner, M., Matthews, G., & Roberts, R. D. (2006). Emotional intelligence, adaptation, and coping. In J. Ciarrochi, J. Forgas, & J. D. Mayer (Eds.), *Emotional intelligence in everyday life: A scientific inquiry* (2nd ed., pp. 82–97). Philadelphia: Psychology Press.

Zeidner, M., Matthews, G., Roberts, R. D., & MacCann, C. (2003). Development of emotional intelligence: Towards a multi-level investment model. *Human Development, 46*, 69–96.

Zeidner, M., Roberts, R. D., & Matthews, G. (2002). Can emotional intelligence be schooled? A critical review. *Educational Psychologist, 37*, 215–231.

Zeidner, M., & Saklofske, D. S. (1995). Adaptive and maladaptive coping. In M. Zeidner & N. S. Endler (Eds.), *Handbook of coping* (pp. 505–531). New York: Wiley.

Zickar, M. J., Gibby, R. E., & Robie, C. (2004). Uncovering faking samples in applicant, incumbent, and experimental data sets: An application of mixed-model item response theory. *Organizational Research Methods, 7*, 168–190.

Zins, J. E., Weissberg, R. P., Wang, M. C., & Walberg, H. J. (2004). *Building academic success on social and emotional learning: What does the research say?* New York: Teachers College Press.

Zuckerman, M. (2005). *Psychobiology of personality* (2nd ed.). New York: Cambridge University Press.

Name Index

Barchard, K. A., 7, 212, 222, 235, 238, 244, 264, 279, 426, 440
Barling, J., 364
Bar-On, R., 5–7, 16, 18, 19, 23, 50, 101, 102, 153, 167, 171, 200, 201, 203, 205, 207, 210, 211, 218, 232, 238, 249, 259, 264, 301n.2, 340, 346, 359, 363, 365, 380, 382, 430, 444
Barratt, L., 78
Barrett, L. F., 29
Barrick, M. R., 209
Bartlett, M. Y., 271
Barton, R., 119
Bastian, Veneta A., 173–175, 186, 189, 420
Batchelder, W. H., 213, 220
Bates, J., 7, 8
Batson, C. D., 139
Battistich, V., 383
Baudouin, J. Y., 307
Baumeister, R. F., 12, 112, 265, 433
Bay, M., 388
Baylis, G. C., 88
Bear, G. G., 129, 378
Beardsall, L., 131
Beardslee, W. R., 136
Beauducel, A., 215, 219
Beck, J. E., 134
Becker, B. E., 377, 379
Becker, T., 406
Beckman, J. F., 449
Beers, M., 239, 360; 367
Behrman, M., 320
Beid, S., 328
Beitel, M., 341, 344
Bellmer, C., 264
Beltz, C. M., 22
Bem, D., 11
Bennett, M. I., 349
Bentin, S., 319, 320
Benton, A. L., 321
Benvenuto, M., 29
Berenbaum, H., 218, 311
Berk, L., 158
Berlin, H., 89, 92
Bernieri, F. J., 117
Bernstein, L. J., 328
Berntson, G. G., 27
Best, K. M., 135
Bickmore, T., 408, 410–412, 414
Biehl, M., 117

Bierman, D., 272
Binet, Alfred, 25
Bird, C. M., 93
Blackburn, E. K., 137
Blair, R. J. R., 296
Blanchette, I., 273
Bloch, S., 339
Block, J. H., 135
Blum, R. W., 380
Böhm, S. G., 327
Bonanno, G., 57, 433
Bonner, L., 322
Bono, J. E., 425
Booj, L., 272
Boone, R. T., 247, 425
Borger, S. C., 351
Boring, E. G., 180
Borman, W. C., 366
Borsboom, D., 258, 275, 280n.1
Bosco, J. S., 239
Boswell, J., 58
Bothwell, R. K., 323
Botvin, G. J., 386
Bourne, D. R., 172, 212, 234, 266, 311
Bowman, D. B., 19
Boyatzis, R. E., 249, 356, 363, 453
Bozic, V., 327
Brackett, Marc A., 5, 7, 16, 20, 61, 151, 173, 174, 188, 202, 210–211, 232, 235–240, 243, 244, 249, 250,261–262, 358, 421, 426, 430, 435, 444
Bradley, M. M., 300, 407
Brant, L., 428
Bratlavsky, E., 265
Braungart-Rieker, J. M., 134, 135
Brave, S., 410, 414
Braverman, E. P., 28, 312
Breen, N., 315
Brennan, R. L., 24
Brigham, J. C., 323
Brody, L. R., 244, 420, 421, 427, 430, 454
Brody, N., 8, 12, 14, 153, 154, 172, 180
Brosschot, J. F., 272
Brotheridge, D., 360
Brown, A. S., 154, 220, 247
Brown, J., 131
Brown, J. L., 385
Browning, A. S., 88
Brownless, V., 173
Bruce, V., 307, 308, 314–316, 322, 323, 327

Hornak, J., 88, 91, 92
Hornung, K., 129
Horvath, A., 411
Horvath, J. A., 266
Hough, L. M., 442
Hsee, C. K., 343
Huang, S. H. S., 18, 172, 210
Huang, T. S., 404
Hubbard, J. A., 137
Hudlicka, E., 462
Hulse, S. H., 341
Humphrey, R. H., 365
Hunt, T., 117, 220, 273
Hunter, J. E., 169
Husain, M., 93
Hutchinson, K., 410

Ickes, W., 258, 276
Imboden, J. B., 341
Inoue, K., 88
Ishai, A., 320
Ishizuka, M., 405, 408, 410
Ivanov, Y., 402
Ivcevic, Z., 61
Iverson, S. D., 89
Izard, Carol E., 8, 27, 127–134, 138–140,
          142, 158, 244, 260, 289, 389,
          390, 420–421, 423, 424, 427–428,
          430–432, 434, 435, 446, 449, 453

Jaeger, M. E., 274
Jäger, A. O., 215
James, L. R., 26, 273
Janovics, J., 240
Jarvis, W. B. G., 210
Jausovec, K., 237, 449
Jausovec, N., 237, 449
Jehn, K., 369
Jenkins, J. M., 81, 87
Jenkins, R., 322
Jensen, A. R., 25, 157, 169, 450
Jentzsch, I., 315, 328
Joassin, F., 216
Johanson, J., 324
John, O. P., 112, 115, 116, 421
Johnson, C. A., 12, 173, 239
Johnson, D. W., 383, 385
Johnson, K., 249
Johnson, R. T., 383, 385
Johnson, Samuel, 58, 60

Johnson-Laird, P. N., 9, 424
Johnstone, T., 104
Jones, D. C., 131
Jones, G. V., 272
Jones, K., 170
Jordan, Peter J., 36, 357–359, 361, 365–370,
          440, 453, 454, 457, 458, 463
Jousmaki, V., 320
Judge, S. J., 90
Judge, T. A., 425

Kaber, D. B., 461
Kacelnik, A., 84
Kadis, J., 240
Kafetsios, K., 239, 428
Kagan, J., 158
Kaiser, R. B., 298
Kaiser, S., 109
Kanfer, R., 421
Kang, S., 169, 246, 248, 447
Kanwisher, N., 316, 320
Kaplan, H. B., 268
Kapoor, Ashish, 402–404
Karasu, T. B., 341
Karbon, M., 139
Kasparov, Gary, 396
Katz, L., 135
Katzko, M., 19, 154, 211
Kaufmann, J. M., 328
Keating, D. P., 170
Kelloway, E. K., 173, 364
Kelly, S. W., 351
Keltner, D., 240
Kenny, D. A., 258, 265–266
Kerlinger, F. N., 33
Kerns, J. G., 218, 311
Kihlstrom, J. F., 21, 215
Kilpatrick, L., 269
Kimchi, R., 320
Kindt, M., 272
King, Kristen A., 8, 128, 130, 131, 133,
          244, 420
Kirby, S. L., 360
Kirsner, K., 104
Kirson, D., 248
Kischka, U., 89
Klein, D. J., 27
Klein, Jonathan, 36, 400, 402, 408, 414
Kline, R. B., 177
Klohen, E. C., 135

Subject Index

emotional intelligence (EI) (*continued*)
  improving, 350, 392
  intrapersonal component, 151
  as multifaceted, 5–6
  nature of, 143–144
  shortcomings of popular models of, 357
emotional intelligence (EI) constructs, 291–292
  overlaps with other constructs, 6
  relate meaningfully to external criteria, 6–7
  and related constructs, 306, 339–340
  types of, 435–437
emotional intelligence (EI) theory/theories,
    230–232
  theoretical vs. empirical evaluation, 201
emotional knowledge (EK), 101, 128–129,
    176, 427. *See also* beliefs about
    emotions
  development, 129–131
  and longitudinal behavioral and academic
    outcomes, 132–133
  measurement, 131–132
emotional labor, 65
emotional processing, 10, 432
emotional quotient (EQ), 172
Emotional Quotient Inventory (EQ-i), 18, 19,
    94, 171, 210–212
  Ei-EQ-i, 340, 343–345
emotional reactions, pathological/
    abnormal, 108
emotional regulation (ER), 9, 87, 133–134,
    421–422. *See also* affect regulation;
    alexithymia; coping strategies;
    temperament
  defined, 133, 134
  development of, 134–136
  and longitudinal behavioral and academic
    outcomes, 132, 137–138
  measurement of, 136–137
  neurobiology and, 92–93
  reflective regulation of emotions, 176, 246
  regulation competence, 111–116, 121
emotional sharing, 5
emotional states, 58
Emotional Stroop test (EST), 218, 272
emotional syndromes, 57, 59
emotional task analysis, 31
emotional utilization (EU), 127–128,
    137–139, 427
  development, 139–140
  measurement, 140–141

and social and behavioral outcomes,
    141–142
emotional-information processing factor, 5.
    See also information processing
    measures
emotionality, positive vs. negative, 135, 136
emotion(s), 127. *See also specific topics*
  associated with different reinforcement
    contingencies, 73–77, 80, 81, 97n.1
  "basic," 293
  componential approach to, 57
  components, 289–290
  defined, 72, 73
  EI and existing theories of, 13, 54–59, 144,
    153–154
  functions, 78–82
  historical perspective on, 49
  knowledge about. *See* beliefs about
    emotions; emotional knowledge
  meanings, 57–58
  modal, 104
  nature of, 288–291
  rules of, 57
  theories of, 57, 73–78, 88
  types of, 49
    appropriate vs. inappropriate, 108, 111,
      298–299
    "natural" vs. "unnatural," 56
  using/generating, 231, 233–234
empathic accuracy paradigm, 276
empathy, 139, 140, 410. *See also* computers
  measures of, 140–141
employment. *See* occupational settings
environment. *See also* adaptation
  dynamic interaction between person and,
    433–434
episodes, 58
episodic memory, 81–82
EQ-i. *See* Emotional Quotient Inventory
essentialism, 56–57
ethical behavior, 11. *See also* moral behavior
event-related potentials (ERPs), 313, 317,
    324, 329
evidence-centered design (ECD),
    203–206, 447
evolutionary psychology, 78–83
exceptionality and EI, 7
existential beliefs about emotions, 57
expectation, 84. *See also* reinforcement
experience of emotions, 289, 291, 296